I C A O
A History of the International
Civil Aviation Organization

ICAO

A History of the International Civil Aviation Organization

DAVID MACKENZIE

UNIVERSITY OF TORONTO PRESS
Toronto   Buffalo   London

ISBN 978-1-4426-4010-8

Printed on acid-free, 100% post-consumer recycled
paper with vegetable-based inks.

Library and Archives Canada Cataloguing in Publication

MacKenzie, David, 1953–
ICAO: a history of the International Civil Aviation Organization / David MacKenzie.

Includes bibliographical references and index.
ISBN 978-1-4426-4010-8

1. International Civil Aviation Organization – History. 2. Aeronautics –
Safety regulations. 3. Aeronautics – Security measures. I. Title.

TL500.5.M35 2010   387.706'01   C2009-905008-0

All interior photographs are reproduced courtesy of the International
Civil Aviation Organization

University of Toronto Press acknowledges the financial assistance to its publishing program of the Canada Council for the Arts and the Ontario Arts Council.

 Canada Council   Conseil des Arts   ONTARIO ARTS COUNCIL
for the Arts   du Canada   CONSEIL DES ARTS DE L'ONTARIO

University of Toronto Press acknowledges the financial support for its publishing activities of the Government of Canada through the Book Publishing
Industry Development Program (BPIDP)

This book has been published with the help of a grant from the Canadian
Federation for the Humanities and Social Sciences, through the Aid to Scholarly
Publications Programme, using funds provided by the Social Sciences
and Humanities Research Council of Canada.

For Beth

Contents

Illustrations follow page 144

Preface

Hundreds of millions of people participate in air travel each year and, despite the proliferation of airlines, air routes, and tourist destinations, it is by far the safest way to travel. At the same time, most travellers fly unaware of the countless technical, legal, political, and economic arrangements that are required to make any air trip possible, let alone to ensure a safe arrival at a specified time in an airport on the other side of the world. The International Civil Aviation Organization (ICAO) is not the only organization involved with aviation safety, but it is the largest and most important one, and its technical standards, legal regulations, and operating procedures have made a significant contribution to the development of international civil aviation.

ICAO is a specialized agency in the United Nations system, similar to the World Health Organization, UNESCO, and the International Maritime Organization, and its aims and objectives are set out in the Convention on International Civil Aviation, or the Chicago Convention (see Appendix). Article 44 states that ICAO's objectives are to 'develop the principles and techniques of international air navigation and to foster the planning and development of international air transport.' In reaching its goals, ICAO is to be involved in the 'development of airways, airports, and air navigational facilities,' in encouraging aircraft design, preventing 'economic waste caused by unreasonable competition,' avoiding discrimination between members, safety promotion, and insuring the 'safe and orderly growth of international civil aviation throughout the world.' Overall, ICAO is to 'promote generally the development of all aspects of international civil aeronautics.' At the heart of ICAO's mission is the goal of international standardization of civil aviation. Article thirty-seven of the Convention states that 'each contracting State undertakes to collaborate in securing the highest practicable degree of uniformity in regulations, standards, procedures, and organization in relation to aircraft, personnel, airways and auxiliary services in all matters in which such uniformity will facilitate and improve air navigation.' ICAO's constitution and structure are similar (but different in significant ways) to the United Nations.

This book is a history of ICAO from its origins in 1944. ICAO emerged from the Chicago International Civil Aviation Conference in November 1944 and continues to operate today, from its headquarters in Montreal, Quebec. It was born at the end of the Second World War, in an era of rapid political change, social upheaval, and technological innovation. The war demonstrated the importance of both civil and military aviation and the need for international cooperation in its development, and ICAO was created in this environment and emerged from both this fear and hope for the future. A Provisional ICAO operated from July 1945 to April 1947, when the permanent ICAO came into being.

ICAO was created and largely controlled by a small group of powerful states – the victors of the Second World War – but in the following decades it evolved into a truly diverse and global international organization. It was founded on the basic principle of the absolute sovereignty of each nation over its airspace and its purpose was to help re-establish the regulatory system for international commercial aviation and to deal with security concerns such as the militarization of civil aviation. From these origins ICAO evolved into an important and successful international organization and although the problems, tensions, and fault lines have shifted, the basic principle of sovereignty remains. ICAO is an expression of the sovereign state and it reflects the will of its membership.

The safety of air travel is well known, if often taken for granted by the travelling public, but ICAO and its role in this process are relatively unknown outside the aerospace industry, parts of the business world, and the legal profession. Commercial aviation is a field of study that attracts great attention, and each year sees dozens of new books on various aspects of the subject: histories of airlines, airplanes, and their pilots, and about great moments and achievements in the history of civil and military flight. But in general there are relatively few scholarly works on the history of international commercial aviation, and as of yet there is no full length scholarly history of ICAO. There is only one complete scholarly study of the organization – Jacob Schenkman's *International Civil Aviation Organization* (1955) – which covers only ICAO's first decade and is long out of date. Most of the other books on ICAO are legal and technical examinations, aimed at a very select audience and, while many of these studies are thorough, they offer little in the way of ICAO's history or the international context within which it operated. There are also several studies that touch on different aspects of ICAO's operations, but there is as yet no single authoritative history of this important international organization.

In addition, with the rise of air hijacking, international aviation terrorism, and military attacks on civil aviation, ICAO has assumed a leading role in the struggle against international air terrorism and sabotage. These issues, along with environmental issues, globalization, and other technical and legal problems, had not been considered in Chicago in 1944, and in responding to them ICAO has demonstrated the ability of an international organization to evolve in the international system. Again, very little has been written about the history of ICAO's role in these fields, outside the legal and technical studies.

I undertook this project because of the critical need to fill this large gap in the literature and to write a full *history* of ICAO that traces the evolution of the organization and analyses its role and function in the international community today. It is the first and only study that is based not only on the organization's documents but also on extensive research in government archival sources. The book is both thematic and chronological, examining the major activities of ICAO and the people that made it work over a period of more than sixty years. ICAO provided the stage on which international aviation disputes (between east and west, developed and developing, powerful and weak, English and French, etc.) were played out and its history as a specialized agency in the United Nations system sheds some light on the workings of an important international institution.

It is impossible to do a project of this nature without receiving the assistance of many people along the way. I would like to thank all of them for their help. There are also a few individuals that I would like to single out. I was lucky to have, at different times, three research assistants: Tammy McNamee in Montreal, Dr Christine Hamelin in Ottawa, and Hema Sharma in Toronto. The three never met each other but the work they did came together at the end and helped to make this a better book, and I thank them again. I would also like to thank Mrs Ghislaine Giroux and Ms Diane-R. Bertrand, at the ICAO Archives in Montreal, who, over several years and many visits, helped make my research so much easier. I am equally grateful to Mrs Josie Bello-Colasurdo, Sue-Ann Rapattoni, and Gordana Milinic at ICAO for their help in finding the photographs for this book. Also at ICAO I would like to thank, for different reasons, Dr Ruwantissa

Abeyratne, Mr Denis Chagnon, and Dr Assad Kotaite for their help, advice, and willingness to help me understand how ICAO works.

Len Husband, my editor at the University of Toronto Press, has been a great help and supporter of this project from the very start, and his experience and knowledge of the publishing world have made the transformation of this manuscript into a book a smooth and even enjoyable process. I am very grateful for his help. I would also like to thank Frances Mundy at UTP, and Harold Otto for copyediting the manuscript.

The Convention on International Civil Aviation is reproduced as the Appendix, with the permission of the International Civil Aviation Organization. Sections of Chapter 2 have appeared as an article, and I would like to thank the editor of *Diplomacy and Statecraft* for permission to reprint that material here. The research for the project was made possible at the very start thanks to a Standard Research Grant from the Social Sciences and Humanities Research Council of Canada. I also would like to thank the Gerald R. Ford Foundation for a Research Travel Grant for research in the Ford Library. At Ryerson University I was fortunate to receive further funding through a Faculty of Arts SRC Fund Research Grant, and I would like to thank the university and Dean of Arts Dr Carla Cassidy for their support. This book has been published with the help of a grant from the Canadian Federation for the Humanities and Social Sciences, through the aid to Scholarly Publications Program, using funds provided by the Social Sciences and Humanities Research Council of Canada.

Finally, I must thank my wife Terry and daughters Claire and Elizabeth, who supported me throughout what was a lengthy process. Especially Beth, who has waited a long time for this.

Abbreviations

AACC	Airport Associations Co-ordinating Council
ACC	Air Coordinating Committee
ACI	Airports Council International
ACT	Australian Archives
AFCAC	African Civil Aviation Commission
ANC	Air Navigation Commission
ATC	Air Transport Committee
BOAC	British Overseas Airways Corporation
CAB	Civil Aeronautics Board
CAEP	Committee on Aviation Environmental Protection
CAPS	Civil Aviation Purchasing Service
CATC	Commonwealth Air Transport Council
CFPF	Central Foreign Policy Files
CITEJA	Comité International Technique d'Experts Juridiques Aériens
CNR	Canadian National Railways Company
CNS/ATM	Communications, navigation, surveillance and air traffic management systems
CVR	Cockpit voice recorder
DCER	*Documents on Canadian External Relations*
DOFAT	Department of Foreign Affairs and Trade, Australia
DOS	Department of State
DFDR	Digital flight data recorder
ECAC	European Civil Aviation Conference
ECOSOC	United Nations Economic and Social Council
EU	European Union
FAA	Federal Aviation Agency

FFMA	French Foreign Ministry Archives, Paris
FRUS	*Foreign Relations of the United States*
GASP	Global Aviation Safety Plan
GATS	General Agreement on Trade in Services
GATT	General Agreement on Tariffs and Trade
GERFA	Group of Experts on Future Regulatory Arrangements
GNSS	Global navigational satellite system
IATA	International Air Transport Association
ICAN	International Commission for Air Navigation
ICAO	International Civil Aviation Organization
ICJ	International Court of Justice
IFALPA	International Federation of Airline Pilots' Associations
ILO	International Labour Organization
ILS	Instrument landing system
INS	Inertial navigation system
LAC	Library and Archives Canada, Ottawa
LACAC	Latin American Civil Aviation Commission
LORAN	Long Range Radio Aid to Navigation
MCA	Minister of Civil Aviation
NACCA	National Association of Claimants' Counsel of America
NAI	National Archives of Ireland, Dublin
NAOS	North Atlantic Ocean Weather Stations
NARA	National Archives and Records Administration, Washington
NATO	North Atlantic Treaty Organization
NOTAM	Notice to Airmen
NUOI	Nations Unies et organizations internationals Papers
PANS	Procedures for Air Navigation Services
PICAO	Provisional International Civil Aviation Organization
PLO	Palestine Liberation Organization
PRO	Public Record Office, Kew
RNSA	Records of the National Security Agency
ROEA	Records of the Office of European Affairs
SAP	Strategic Action Plan
SARP	Standards and Recommended Practices
SCADTA	Sociedad Colombo-Alemana de Transporte Aéreos
SDR	Special Drawing Rights
SEAM	Single European Aviation Market
SNF	Subject Numeric File
SUPPS	Regional Supplementary Procedures

UAR	United Arab Republic
UN	United Nations
UNDP	United Nations Development Programme
UNOC	Operation des Nations Unies au Congo
USAP	Universal Security Audit Programme
USOAP	Universal Safety Oversight Audit Programme
USSR	Union of Soviet Socialist Republics
WATC	World Wide Air Transport Conference
WC	War Cabinet
WHCF	White House Central Files
WTO	World Trade Organization

PART ONE

1

The Puritan and the Peer

Systems of land transport operate within the boundaries of single countries; when land transport becomes international it is subject to easy control at frontiers. Ships ply across sea frontiers, and control can be exercised without difficulty at foreign ports. But the airplane flies over national boundaries and from one country into the heart of another. Thus the development of the skyways of the world has created a new international problem, that of the freedom of the air.[1]

'I feel that aviation will have a greater influence on American foreign interests and American foreign policy than any other non-political consideration,' wrote Adolf Berle, the assistant secretary in the State Department, in a letter to Cordell Hull, the American secretary of state in September 1942. 'It may well be determinative in certain territorial matters which have to do with American defense, as well as with transportation matters affecting American commerce, in a degree comparable to that which sea power has had on our interests and policy.'[2] Intense, arrogant, and intellectually gifted, Berle was a former university professor and long-time Roosevelt supporter who had come to the State Department as assistant secretary of state in 1938; he had confidence in American power and a disdain for the British Empire. His disdain was not total; according to his biographer, Berle admired many Britons personally and respected their collective accomplishments, but he had no love for the British Empire and no desire to fight a war to maintain it. Remembered by one Brit as 'a curious little fellow with lots of brain but no personality,'[3] Berle had a way of grating on the nerves of those he worked for and with; 'he was short and strong-willed, an intellectual autocrat who vented his impatience with lesser minds in sarcastic outbursts,' wrote two historians.[4] His biographer lists those in Washington who hated Berle and he seems to have had more enemies than friends in the State Department and the White House.[5] As *Time* magazine put it, his last name 'rhymes with surly.'[6] For the British who twisted the 'e' into an 'a,' it came out 'barely.' But it was from Berle and the many others of like mind in Washington that came the burst of creative energy and intellectual force that produced so many of the postwar international organizations, including the International Civil Aviation Organization.

Berle had been given responsibility for American aviation affairs in 1942 and for the next two years he pursued American interests in the air with vigour and determination. He brought his American liberal and anti-monopoly views to the task; his goal was 'prosperity' under a *Pax Americana* and he believed in the use of American money and credit for the reconstruction of the world, so long as it helped break down the old colonial empires and 'spheres of influence.'[7] Berle personified 'New Deal internationalism, that ambivalent mixture of idealism and imperialism,' according to one Canadian diplomat. He was 'an anti-imperialist imperialist, *genus Americanus,* not to be confused with the nationalists whose single dedication to the assertion of United States military and economic interest was easier to cope with.'[8] More immediately, with respect to commercial aviation, Berle's efforts were two-pronged: one, to expand American commercial aviation interests abroad, and two, to secure in the hands of the White House and State Department responsibility for the direction of American international aviation policy.

Before the war American international civil aviation was symbolized by Pan American Airways, which had been developed by its dynamic president Juan Trippe from a single service in 1927 into the dominant international carrier. Under Trippe's direction and with the help of friends and supporters in Congress, in the 1930s Pan Am expanded through Latin America, to Europe via the Azores and Portugal, and across the Pacific. And, while wartime developments either destroyed or forced most European international carriers to drastically cut their services, Pan Am continued to expand thanks, in part, to War Department contracts to construct bases in Latin America and the West Indies and to establish an air route to Africa via South America. By 1939 Pan Am was the largest international airline in the world and its route system totalled more than 60,000 miles; two years later it surpassed 98,000 – more than all of the European services combined.[9] Looking to the postwar period, Pan Am sought to entrench its position – despite being privately owned – as America's 'chosen instrument' in international aviation.

Trippe and his airline were not without opponents at home. The domestic U.S. airlines looked to the potentially lucrative international market and cried foul over Pan Am's de facto monopoly and increasingly demanded that they be permitted to compete for international routes after the war. The first step was taken as airlines such as United, TWA, and American took on international military services to aid the war effort. By 1943 most domestic carriers had launched their own lobbying campaigns to secure access to the international market.[10] These airlines found an ally in the Civil Aeronautics Board, established in 1940 to regulate American civil air transport. The CAB advocated 'regulated competition' on international routes and, in 1940, granted permission to American Export Airlines to operate a transatlantic service.[11] Pan Am used its influence in Congress to block the service, but by 1943 the CAB chair, Welch Pogue, was publicly urging the opening of the international skies to more than one American airline.[12]

The war demonstrated that aviation – both military and commercial – would have a dramatic impact on whatever kind of world emerged afterwards. International aviation raised disturbing security questions for all states, while at the same time offered improved communications, speed and safety, greater market access and business opportunities, as well as enhanced national prestige.[13] Technological improvements during the war had helped produce better airplanes and improved navigational aids and, at the same time, the allied states established air routes around the world, built great aircraft manufacturing industries, and trained thousands of pilots, and air and ground crews. Despite the curbing of commercial aviation during the war, it did not take great imagination to see the military air routes, pilots, airplanes, and factories being converted to civilian use the moment peace returned.

The need for international cooperation in aviation was recognized by all. The technical demands of air travel – the provision of meteorological and air traffic control services, the construction and maintenance of suitable airports, the need for standardized training among pilots and ground crews, the establishment of a body of air law, the setting of levels of airworthiness and safety, and so on – all had to be negotiated on an international basis if air transport were to operate smoothly. Fortunately, most air powers shared common views on the need to overcome the obstacles of weather and geography; as the American Fiorello LaGaurdia later put it at the Chicago conference: 'Everybody is against bad weather.'[14]

Problems arose when talk shifted from the technical issues of making flying safer and easier to the commercial aspects, or the 'three R's' of aviation: routes, rights, and rates. Questions of national sovereignty over airspace, the right of innocent transit, traffic privileges and aircraft capacity, and the number of frequencies on any particular service, came to dominate the debate. Before the war international aviation agreements, thanks to technological limitations as much as global rivalries, tended to be narrow in scope with strict divisions over frequencies, capacity and route selection. With a technologically inspired postwar boom in international travel looming, however, hopes turned to finding a multilateral solution that would enhance international security and prevent a return to the cumbersome pre-war system.

By the end of 1943 the commercial issues had been largely distilled into a handful of air 'freedoms,' which nations could exchange or barter with each other. The first two freedoms were transit rights: the right of innocent passage over a foreign territory and the right to land for non-traffic purposes. Freedoms three and four were commercial privileges: the right to carry passengers into a foreign state, and the right to pick up passengers in a foreign state and return them to the country of origin of the aircraft. The fifth freedom was also a commercial privilege and it became the most hotly debated: the right to pick up passengers in a foreign state and carry them to a third country.[15] The sixth freedom, or cabotage – the right to carry passengers between two stops within a single foreign country – found few supporters and was rarely seriously considered.[16] Establishing a multilateral arrangement embodying these freedoms that would suit all states was an enormous challenge, especially for the two leading air powers, the United States and Great Britain.

It was an enormously complex issue and Adolf Berle was right in the middle of it. Berle was a member of a small interdepartmental committee (including Welch Pogue of the CAB), brought together to study various policy alternatives confronting the United States. In its April 1943 report to Secretary of State Hull, Berle's committee pronounced in favour of competition in the international airways based on a liberal exchange of entry rights. There were differences of opinion within the committee, but it was generally agreed that 'the best interests of the United States are served by the widest generalization of air navigation rights. This is the historic American position.' And, while the committee recognized the need for widespread negotiations with other nations, one competitor was singled out for particular attention: 'The heart of a general navigation agreement, would have to rest on agreement between the United States and the British Empire and Commonwealth of Nations; it may fairly be assumed that once this agreement is reached, practically all countries in the world (with the possible exception of Russia) would accede.'[17]

Berle's views largely reflected those held by President Roosevelt. At a November 1943 meeting with Berle, Roosevelt went on record opposing monopolies and government subsidies for the airlines. He was flexible when it came to proposals to divide the global airmap into various operating 'zones,' but he was clear in his own mind when he added, with reference to Pan Am, that the 'scope of international aviation was too great to be trusted to any one company or pool.' With respect to traffic rights, he urged 'a very free exchange,' and as for any international aviation organization, its primary function should be to look after technical matters. Much of what the president said dealt with generalities and he was not specific on how many of these goals were to be achieved, but Roosevelt had a solid grasp of the issues, and clearly there was still a good deal of room for negotiation and manoeuvre. There would have to be private informal discussions with the British, the Soviets, and others over the following months, Roosevelt concluded, and then a general United Nations conference to which all states would be invited.[18]

Despite the divergence of views between Roosevelt and some members of Berle's committee on such issues as government ownership, the allocation of landing rights, and a chosen instrument policy, there was a growing consensus on some issues in American opinion. The United States was and would continue to be the greatest air power in the world, and any future international arrangements or organizations should recognize this fact. The message was the same in American magazines, newspapers, and Congress: the technological advantage had shifted in favour of the United States; the United States had the airplanes, the factories, pilots, and crews, and it would likely provide the greatest number of passengers in the foreseeable future; any barriers to the expansion of American aviation should therefore be avoided.[19] 'Several times when Englishmen have asked me what I think the United States wants in the post-war air,' the American civil air attaché in London wrote in 1944, 'I reply, "to fly airplanes." That is what they are afraid of.'[20] The air – like the high seas – should be open to all nations and the fewer international regulations and restrictions the better. Regardless of internal squabbles, to outsiders the Americans appeared aggressive in their flaunting of the virtues of American air power and determined to open the skyways of the world to 'free competition,' which many Europeans read as 'American domination.'

When Americans looked for competitors or potential rivals in the air they usually found only one: the British Empire and Commonwealth.[21]

Geographically, Britain had the advantage of easy access to Europe, which in the future would give it a competitive edge over the United States in services to the continental capitals. More important, the United Kingdom controlled a vast collection of colonies and territories around the world on which it could grant – or refuse – transit and landing rights. Many of these imperial possessions – in the North Atlantic, the West Indies, and the Pacific – had discovered a new-found importance during the war as air bases, and, at least until longer-range aircraft came on the scene, it was believed that they held the key to global aviation expansion. Equally, as leader of the Commonwealth, Britain might be able to line up the Dominions – the loose group of independent nations that had maintained their ties to the monarchy, including Australia, New Zealand, Canada, and South Africa – into a solid negotiating bloc that could impede and obstruct the expansion of American aviation interests and confine the United States to the Western hemisphere.[22] The United States had built many of those air bases on British territories, the United States had provided the British with hundreds of aircraft and would be asked to give more, the United States helped fund the British war effort through huge loans and the lend-lease program; now it appeared, in some American circles, that the British could still dominate the postwar air simply by doing nothing. But the Americans were determined to play their part. 'Whoever controls the main strategic postwar air bases, together with the technical facilities to keep them manned, will unquestionably be the world's strongest power,' proclaimed one author in *Fortune*. 'We have no commercial bases except in the Pacific and the Caribbean; our problem, therefore, is not to restore the *status quo ante* but to break out ... Shall we withdraw? Or shall we insist upon our right as a great power to fly anywhere? And whose air is it, anyway?'[23]

The situation appeared quite different in London. British commercial aviation policy was in a state of flux for most of the war, as concern quite naturally focused on more pressing matters and British civil aviation was almost totally mobilized for the war effort. A major concern for the British government was Britain's relative economic weakness in aircraft supply vis-à- vis the United States. The Americans had established themselves as leaders in large long-range aircraft design and manufacturing in the 1930s, and the gap between the two countries grew wider during the war. In addition, Britain became increasingly dependent on American lend-lease aid – receiving several hundred U.S. transport aircraft for military use by mid-1943 – and this reliance on American benevolence inevitably placed restrictions on British freedom of action. Recognizing the seriousness of the situation, a committee was created in 1942 under Lord Brabazon to examine Britain's aviation problems and to make recommendations on the types of civil aircraft that should be used and produced in Britain in the future.[24] The Brabazon Committee's 1943 report contained numerous important recommendations, but it could offer little immediate help for current problems.

At roughly the same time, in June 1942 an Anglo-American understanding was reached in which the British government agreed to concentrate its aircraft production on fighter aircraft and bombers while American industry manufactured long-range transports, which were then flown overseas.[25] And also in 1942 the British and Americans agreed, in what became known as the Halifax Agreement (for Britain's ambassador in the United States, Lord Halifax), that neither state would negotiate air arrangements that excluded traffic and landing rights for the other.[26] The postwar implications of these arrangements were not lost on British observers, and neither were the potential future difficulties of removing the Americans from the bases they constructed on British territories. Even the usually friendly Canadians were playing hard ball with the British by threatening to scuttle the 1944 negotiations for a huge loan to the United Kingdom unless London agreed to grant the Canadians a ninety-nine-year lease to the important airbase at Goose Bay, Labrador.[27] Such concerns were forced to take a back seat so long as the war continued, but general economic problems, the dependence on American lend-lease aid, and the dilemma of aircraft supply had a profound influence on the development of British air transport policy during the war.

A good deal of serious attention was given to the problems of postwar commercial aviation in the British press, Parliament, the Foreign Office, and several interdepartmental committees that were established to study air transport. One historian notes that at least ten such committees had been established by the middle of 1943, and this same topic had been the subject of sixteen parliamentary debates by the beginning of 1945. American superiority and potential domination of civil aviation – especially during the early postwar years – became a prime concern for British policy makers. Likewise, the security component of aviation was central to British thinking, as were the pre-war concerns over stiff international competition based on large government subsidies, and feelings were strong that in the future an international organization should be established to regulate and control international air transport. A number of possible alternatives to the 'Americanization' of international aviation were postulated, ranging from the erection of a closed imperial system, to a regional division of air routes (with Britain pre-eminent in Europe), to some kind of international control of all international air services.[28]

Prime Minister Churchill took a direct interest in the development of international commercial aviation, dating back to his days two decades earlier as air minister.[29] Given the scope of his other pressing wartime duties, that he found so much time to study, debate and pursue British interests in postwar commercial aviation is a good indication of the seriousness with which the British government approached the whole issue. To direct his government's aviation policy he chose his old friend and confidant Lord Beaverbrook. Beaverbrook was a dynamic businessman turned newspaper magnate turned politician; an 'Empire man' and 'great character' who worked hard and loathed bureaucracy. Remembered as 'quite an enigma,' he was a man of action and decision, who could be difficult to work for but got results in the end.[30] Beaverbrook had served as minister of aircraft production earlier in the war and played an important role in the creation of the Atlantic ferry route. Returning to the cabinet in 1943 as lord privy seal, he assumed the chair of the important Committee on Post-war Civil Air Transport and became the general overseer of Britain's commercial air policy.

Like Churchill, Beaverbrook outwardly trumpeted strong Anglo-American cooperation in the air while at the same time working steadfastly to further British interests. Beaverbrook was less concerned with the exchange of theoretical air 'freedoms' than he was in ensuring that Britain secure its share of the aviation pie. A staunch defender of imperial interests, he immediately advocated a British policy founded on the control of all internal and colonial routes and the division of traffic on Commonwealth services with the Dominions and India. As for European aviation, Beaverbrook noted in a 1943 memo to Churchill: 'Our geographical position and our vital commercial interests entitle us to expect that Britain can become and should become a dominating factor in the air transport system of the Continent.'[31]

Informal discussions were held between Berle and Beaverbrook with mixed results early in 1944,[32] but as the war situation improved it became increasingly important that some real progress be made. The Normandy invasion not only raised the possibility of Allied victory but it also signalled the potential revival of European commercial aviation. By the end of the summer Beaverbrook was openly pushing for a small aviation conference of friendly nations to be held in London, but he was outflanked by the Americans who sensed widespread support for their views in Latin

America, Canada, and elsewhere. Early in September, Roosevelt gave the go-ahead to stage an international aviation conference beginning 1 November, and the State Department issued the invitations and proposed agenda to draft an international aviation convention, lay the groundwork for the creation of an interim international aviation organization, and make the necessary arrangements for the rapid postwar resumption of commercial air services. Contrary to Beaverbrook's wishes, the aviation conference would be held in Chicago – not London – and it would include all non-enemy nations, not merely those with views sympathetic to the British government.[33]

Berle might have looked forward to dealing with Beaverbrook – he liked him and knew him as a man of action and decision. Indeed there was even a kind of friendship; in July 1944, for example, Berle and Beaverbrook met in the eastern Canadian province of New Brunswick for a 'rather fantastic weekend' of discussion and socializing. Between the fishing, sightseeing, caviar, and whiskey there was plenty of time to talk about civil aviation with Beaverbrook and C.D. Howe, the Canadian minister of munitions and supply. It 'was designed to be all party, though we had a little business to transact,' was how Berle described it. It was an unusual gathering: Howe, the Canadian, was born in Massachusetts; Beaverbrook who spoke for Britain, was born in New Brunswick, Canada. Also present was Dick Law, whose father, former British prime minister Bonar Law, was also born in New Brunswick. 'The whole thing from beginning to end was dominated by the abounding bounce, gaiety and endless vitality of Beaverbrook, who seems to have cooked all this up mostly for the fun of it,' Berle wrote.[34] Before the year was out Beaverbrook would send Berle a first edition copy of Cardinal Newman's occasional hymns. Berle was touched, and wrote a warm letter of thanks to Beaverbrook, noting that, contrary to what it said in the 'British intelligence dossier,' he was not Catholic.[35]

But it was not Beaverbrook that Berle would face at the International Civil Aviation Conference in Chicago. Early in October responsibility for British civil aviation matters was shifted from Beaverbrook to Lord Swinton, newly appointed as Britain's first minister of civil aviation. Swinton was a logical choice for the role as minister of civil aviation, although some questioned whether he was the best suited to lead the British delegation to the aviation conference at that time. He had served in several important government posts over his long career, including president of the Board of Trade and, more importantly, as air minister in the late 1930s. As air minister he had responsibility for civil aviation. At the time of his recall to London, however, he was serving as resident minister for West Africa, and he had scarce time to prepare for the conference. Arriving in London from Africa on 20 October he had barely a week before flying to North America at the head of the British delegation to Chicago.

The contrast between Swinton and Berle was striking, and perhaps hinted at the trouble that lay ahead. Swinton came from an old Yorkshire family and through his wife inherited the enormous Swinton estate of some 20,000 acres, and he spent his life (first as Philip Lloyd-Graeme then as Philip Cunliffe-Lister) among the British political and upper classes. The title Lord Swinton came in 1935. He was tall and handsome, with clear blue eyes and a strong lower jaw 'which a prize-fighter would regard as a stroke of genius.' He was known for his ribald sense of humour, but this side of his personality was not fully on display at Chicago. No one doubted his intellect: 'His mind seems to rejoice in the smoothness and decision with which it works,' one British journalist wrote, 'in the unerring deductions it makes from the facts it has so thoroughly accumulated, and in the lucidity of the language with which he can state an unanswerable argument or conclude an appeal to the intelligence of reasonable men.'[36] Others were less kind; 'He is, of course, apt to be a little caustic,'[37] one colleague wrote of Swinton; another wrote that his 'somewhat excitable manner of speech is apt to irritate people.'[38] Others used the words arrogant, rude, and anti-American to describe him, but he had a clear mind and could be counted on to stand firm on British principles and resist American pressure at Chicago. Together, Swinton and Berle were, in the words of two aviation historians, 'the supercilious peer and the cerebral Puritan.'[39]

The two men clashed almost from the start in Chicago and things went from bad to worse. As the leaders of the two largest delegations at the conference and the world's two most important aviation nations the confrontation between nations was personalized and only added to the antipathy. It became, according to Swinton's biographer, 'something of a gladiatorial contest between Swinton and Berle,'[40] and the personality clash threatened to wreck the whole conference. Berle found Swinton insufferable; he 'is ill prepared, not having been in civil aviation very long, and he also tends to be arrogant and inflexible, not having quite appreciated the difference between the atmosphere of the coast of the Gulf of Guinea and that of the shores of Lake Michigan.'[41] Swinton was equally critical, telling his wife that Berle 'is the most disagreeable person with whom I have ever negotiated.'[42] A few years later, in his memoirs, Swinton made reference to Berle only in passing, almost as if he wasn't there at Chicago at all.[43]

By the time the conference ended the recriminations had started to fly. 'In temperament the heads of the U.K. and U.S. delegations were completely incompatible,' wrote one Canadian observer. 'Mutual lack of trust was increased by belief on each side in the lack of ability in negotiation and the uncooperativeness of the other. Tempers ran high and at times there was virtually a complete refusal to meet or even to authorize an intermediary to act.'[44] Swinton and the British accused the Americans of intercepting their private messages and tapping their telephones, and Berle later admitted to reading some of the British cables.[45] There were suggestions that having Swinton take over from Beaverbrook in October doomed the conference before it began, according to one British observer, as Beaverbrook 'would not let anyone who was chairman for the British in Chicago make a success of the conference.' Swinton was chosen 'because there would be no glory in it and they looked around and found Lord Swinton who was, in reality, (and I quote), "a SH-T."'[46]

Yet at the end of the day there was agreement on some very basic ideas and principles at Chicago. And on one issue almost everyone agreed: there was a fundamental need for a permanent international organization to oversee the healthy development of international air travel. The size and shape of the organization was still to be decided; who would be in it; the powers it would have and the role it would play in postwar aviation would be hotly debated for many years. All that lay in the future, and the future of the International Civil Aviation Organization began in Chicago in November 1944.

The need for international organization in commercial aviation has existed as long as there has been aviation. Even before the Wright brothers' first flight in Kitty Hawk, North Carolina, in 1903 consideration was being given to the laws that should govern air flight.[47] And the moment Frenchman Louis Bleriot crossed the English Channel in an airplane in August 1909 a new international problem was created and questions were raised about international law, air sovereignty, rights and responsibilities. Who could fly where? What rights does any nation have over its airspace? How far up do these rights go? Other questions too: What about commercial rights? Could one nation prevent another from commercial flying into or across its territory? Were these rights to be negotiated bilaterally or through a larger multilateral agreement or organization? It was a good question that that American journalist asked: 'Whose air is it, anyway?'

At first there were some supporters of the idea of international 'freedom of the air'; that the air was international like the high seas, giving all nations the right to fly wherever they pleased, restricted only by reasonable national security concerns. The French and German governments argued in favour of this concept at the international aviation conference held in Paris in 1910. The conference was called primarily for technical reasons – to set standards for air navigation, personnel, aircraft registration, and other safety issues – but inevitably the more commercial issues surfaced. On one side stood the French and Germans; on the other, Great Britain and its insistence on state sovereignty over its airspace.[48]

It was a deadlock that remained unsettled during the conference; but it was a debate that was made moot by the First World War. Aviation expanded dramatically during the war, as factories produced more aircraft, more airports were constructed, and crews and pilots recruited and trained. The viability of aircraft was proven; it was clear that there was a future for aviation. At the same time, the military use of aircraft was demonstrated with tragic force during the war, and by 1918 defence and security concerns were paramount in the minds of most observers, especially those in Europe. The concern over the destructive potential of aviation outweighed any possible commercial considerations. The dream of complete 'freedom in the air' evaporated in the airspace above the Western Front.

The concept of state sovereignty over its airspace was confirmed during the aviation discussions that occurred as part of the Paris Peace Conference at the end of the war. An invitation was extended from the French government to all participating states to participate in the Aeronautical Commission. This commission was created with two major goals: first, to produce a convention for international commercial aviation to which all participating nations could subscribe in their efforts to regulate postwar international commercial aviation, and second, to create an international body to oversee the smooth growth and development of international aviation. The commission made two important achievements by the fall of 1919: the International Air Navigation Convention (the Paris Convention) and the International Commission for Air Navigation. Thirty-eight states participated in the discussions, twenty-six signed the document, and by the middle of 1922 it was ratified by enough states for it to come into force.

The Paris Convention begins with the stipulation that 'every power has complete and exclusive sovereignty over the air space above its territory.' Limited transit rights of innocent passage are granted to other nations, but no scheduled services were permitted to fly into one nation's air space without that nation's explicit approval. In addition to the convention's forty-three articles there are eight annexes that focus on technical matters such as air worthiness, licensing of pilots and crew, meteorological information, safeguards for lighting and signals, in an effort to enhance safety and to standardize international air travel.[49]

The International Commission for Air Navigation – the first major international aviation organization – was a direct ancestor of the International Civil Aviation Organization, and its creation was an explicit recognition of the need for international cooperation in aviation. It was established as a permanent body with its headquarters and secretariat in Paris, and its mandate was to oversee, implement, and modify the Paris Convention. Other functions included settling disputes between members, and the collection and dissemination of information and statistics concerning aviation. Officially ICAN was not under the direction of the League of Nations, but its fate rose and fell with that of the League. The International Commission for Air Navigation was also the child of the nations that signed the Paris Convention, and membership in the organization was not stable in the interwar years. Only those nations that signed the convention were members; Germany and other enemy nations were excluded at first. After 1923 ex-belligerents could join, but only with the support of a large majority of ICAN members.[50] Moreover, neither the Soviet Union nor the United States ratified the Covenant of the League of Nations, the Paris Convention, or became a member of ICAN or the League itself.

The Paris Convention was intended to enhance the development of international civil aviation but there were problems that emerged right at the start. Under the convention, ICAN members were not to permit non-members to fly across their airspace except in special circumstances. This stipulation may have been included to hinder the rise of civil aviation in Germany,[51] but it created difficulties, especially for those states adjacent to important non-members like Germany and the Soviet Union. Germany became a leader in European civil aviation in the 1920s and its neighbours in central Europe and Scandinavia faced a difficult choice between maintaining bilateral air services with Germany and adhering to the convention. The possibility of a Europe divided between members and non-members of ICAN appeared and led to a souring of aviation relations, although ICAN took steps to deal with these problems in the 1920s. A second problem emerged within the International Commission for Air Navigation itself. The Paris Convention gave extra voting power to the Great Powers (including, at first, the United States) to such a degree that if they voted together in the commission their votes outnumbered all the other members combined. Many smaller powers complained, and this article was removed in 1926.[52] An additional problem emerged in the form of a rival organization in 1926 as Spain, Portugal, and the Spanish and Portuguese states of the Western Hemisphere signed the Ibero-American Air Convention. There were plans for a permanent organization situated in Madrid, but this convention was never ratified by enough states to come into force.[53]

In 1929 the French government convened a large international aviation conference to amend the Paris Convention, but without much success. There was little desire to loosen each state's complete sovereignty over its airspace, with Britain being one of the few voices raised in favour of greater transit rights. And no subsequent efforts were made to amend this aspect of the convention as the international situation deteriorated through the 1930s. By the time the Second World War broke out, there were thirty-two members in the International Commission for Air Navigation, but not Germany, the Soviet Union, or, of course, the United States. Members included nations such as Australia, New Zealand, Iraq, Thailand, and several South American countries (Paraguay, e.g., joined in 1940), but ICAN remained largely a European aviation organization.[54]

The United States participated in the 1929 Paris Conference, but it never adhered to the Paris Convention or joined the International Commission for Air Navigation. In the interwar period the lack of adherence did not seriously hinder the expansion of American aviation, because until the late1930s there were no regularly scheduled air services linking North America and Europe. Such was not the case with respect to Central and South America, however, and it was here that American aviation expansion was focused. In February 1928 the Pan American Convention on Commercial Aviation was signed in Havana by twenty-two nations including, in addition to the United States, most Central American and Caribbean nations, except El Salvador, Cuba, Chile, and Ecuador. The Havana Convention was similar in many respects to the Paris Convention, although it was different regarding some technical requirements and concerning the rights of one nation to bar another's aircraft based on airworthiness considerations; it contained no technical annexes. It was also more flexible with respect to innocent passage and regularly scheduled air services, but in both the Havana and Paris conventions all commercial privileges remained the domain of bilateral negotiation.[55] Together, the Havana and Paris conventions comprised the international foundation for the development of international civil aviation between the two world wars.

For most Western nations, commercial aviation between the wars took on an importance beyond the realm of economics. The line between military and commercial aviation was not always clear, and for states like Germany that faced restrictions on military aviation, it was important to have a national airline and an aviation industry. Germany was not alone; most Western nations established aviation industries and airlines – either state-controlled or privately owned but heavily state-subsidized – for defence and strategic reasons and to provide jobs for pilots and support personnel. 'The growing importance of aircraft as an instrument of war, and the deep impression which flying makes on man's imagination everywhere, have been probably more important than its commercial merits in moulding the growth of the new means of transport,' wrote Oliver James Lissitzyn in his classic *International Air Transport and National Policy*. 'Every nation with a claim to a prominent position in the world community has deemed it necessary to take an active part in its development by generous governmental encouragement and assistance in almost every imaginable form.'[56] More than that, the development of international aviation became tangled up in the less tangible but equally important area of national prestige. A strong airline and aviation industry brought with it international prestige as well as commercial advantage. 'The possession of well-developed air transport, especially in international traffic,' Lissitzyn continued, 'is a factor enhancing the prestige of a nation at home, in its colonies and abroad. The very existence of such air transport seems to indicate that the nation is progressive, efficient and highly civilized, and that it is contributing its share to the progress of mankind. The prestige thus conferred has economic and military value.'[57]

The Dutch were the first with the creation of KLM in 1919, but the Belgians and Germans were not far behind with the creation, respectively, of Sabena in 1923 and Deutsche Luft Hansa in 1926 (becoming Lufthansa in 1934). The Soviets established Dobrolet in 1923, which eventually merged with a few smaller Soviet airlines into Aeroflot in 1932. There were several small airlines in France, where a national network of scheduled air services was established in the 1920s, and in 1933 these airlines were amalgamated into Air France. European routes were established immediately, crisscrossing the continent and connecting the capitals.

Colonial routes were established at almost the same time, and the value of aviation in managing colonial affairs was not lost on the imperial powers. 'I hate the word "prestige,"' Lieutenant Colonel Moore-Brabazon told the British House of Commons in July 1939, 'but I like to bring it in, for the reason that every English aircraft which travels from one side of

the world to the other is a little bit of England. England will be judged by
that little bit by those for whom that is the only thing they know of
England.'[58] By the mid-1930s, Sabena had established a trunk route to
the Belgian colony in the Congo; KLM flew through Cairo and Calcutta
all the way to Bangkok; Air France established services to Morocco,
Indochina, via Athens, Beirut, Karachi, and several other locations, and
to French West Africa with branches spreading throughout Africa. In
1937 Air France Transatlantique was established for the transatlantic service. Germany, excluded from military aviation, built an extensive commercial European network, including a regular Berlin-Moscow air service
that began in 1922 and ran almost without interruption until the day of
the German invasion in June 1941, and Germans participated in the creation of several airlines in South America, including SCADTA, the Sociedad
Colombo-Alemana de Transporte Aéreos, based in Colombia.[59]

In Britain, Imperial Airways was established in 1924 and at first was left
to 'fly by itself,' but within a decade it operated routes across Africa, to
India and Australia. In 1935, Britain formed a joint operating company
with Ireland, Canada, and Newfoundland to operate a transatlantic service. From this global connection came the Empire Air Mail Scheme to
link all of the British Empire in one postal network.[60] In addition to the
empire and European services, in 1935–36 Imperial Airways negotiated
an Anglo-American agreement for services to the United States. The
early transatlantic routes consisted of a series of intermediate refuelling
stops, depending on the specific route, at Bermuda, the Azores, Iceland,
Ireland, or Newfoundland. The lack of suitable long-range aircraft limited the operation of the transatlantic service to a few scheduled flights
late in the summer of 1939. That same year, after a long period of internal reorganization, Imperial Airways was united with the fledgling British
Airways to form a single airline company: British Overseas Airway
Corporation. BOAC began its operations in 1940, but, with the outbreak
of war, all available aircraft were requisitioned for the war effort,
European services were reduced and then dropped altogether, and
transatlantic flights were limited to military services.[61]

The more flying there was, the greater the need for international cooperation. All scheduled air services were negotiated bilaterally and a very
complex global network of internal, colonial, and international services
evolved. It was more a patchwork quilt, as each state protected its domestic market and guarded its colonial possessions. Competition increased
along with state subsidies; territorial sovereignty was protected jealously
and used to advantage; rivalries intensified, both between airlines and

between the states they represented.[62] Plus, all this took place in an environment of rapid technological change in aircraft design and performance that made it next to impossible to know what was coming next.[63] And, of course, there was no way to separate military from civil aviation; what one nation claimed as a peaceful aircraft industry, the building of airports, training of pilots, the establishing of air routes, provision of meteorological services, and so on, another state could regard suspiciously as thinly disguised military preparations. What was best for the passenger or for the smooth movement of airmail was often lost in the larger considerations of competitive advantage, national prestige, and security. As the international scene deteriorated in the 1930s security concerns trumped economic factors; and, as security concerns increased, so too did the desire for international regulation of international aviation.

International aviation, security concerns, and the need for some kind of regulation or collaboration and international organization were all jumbled together in international discourse in the years before the outbreak of the Second World War. For some it was absurd to talk about regulation for civil aviation because it posed a threat to international security. Other forms of peaceful transport were allowed to develop without restriction: highways and automobiles were crossing international borders in increasing numbers and no one seemed to see it as a serious problem; merchant fleets were allowed to sail the seas and few regarded them as a peacetime security threat. Why was aviation different? To others, though, aviation *was* different and the link between commerce and security could never be broken. Civilian airplanes could easily be converted to military purposes and the same was true for aircraft industries, airports, pilots, and crew. Without some kind of international regulation, cutthroat competition, runaway government subsides, and international rivalries in the air could lead to the destabilization of international relations and potentially the peace of the world. From this vantage point it was easy to make the link between military disarmament and the regulation of international commercial aviation.

In 1932 the League of Nations convened the General Disarmament Conference of the Great Powers in Geneva to thrash out an agreement on military disarmament generally and air power in particular. The United States participated, although not a member of the League. The focus of the conference was on military issues, naturally, but civil aviation became directly involved because it was inexorably linked with military aviation. The logic went like this: if the Great Powers reduced or eliminated military aviation then those nations with large civilian fleets and air industries would have the advantage over the others, because civil aviation, as British Prime Minister Ramsay MacDonald put it, 'in the twinkling of an eye, on the receipt of a telephone message, could be transformed into a fighting force.'[64] In other words, controlling military aviation but not civil aviation would transfer the arms race, the competition, and the rivalries, however disguised, to civil aviation. Civil aviation in that way became the key to the conference. 'It was a joker in the disarmament pack,' one historian wrote, 'which, depending on how it was played, could help disarmament to succeed or fail, not only in the air but across the board.'[65]

The Disarmament Conference lasted into early 1933 before finally giving up in failure. In the meantime, Hitler came to power in Germany, the Japanese incursion in Manchuria continued, and both nations announced their intention to withdraw from the League of Nations. But one idea proposed at the conference – the 'internationalization' of civil aviation – lived on for many years. 'Internationalization' was a word that meant different things to different people, ranging from the international regulation of specific trunk routes to the complete ownership and operation of all international air services by an international aviation authority. Others came somewhere in between looking for internationalization on a regional or imperial basis. Still others looked for an international version of the American Civil Aeronautics Board to regulate but not operate or own international air services. Some Americans saw internationalization as 'Europeanization';[66] some Europeans saw internationalization as a way to prevent 'Americanization.'

The French government proposed various kinds of internationalization in the 1930s, although the degree of internationalization varied over the years and rarely involved sweeping international control.[67] In Australia there was immediate and strong support for the complete internationalization of international civil aviation.[68] In Canada one government official even came up with a name for the new international aviation organization that would control civil aviation: 'World Airways.'[69] In Britain several interdepartmental committees were established during the war that examined the issue and repeatedly argued in favour of some degree of international control. One wartime report, by the Committee on Reconstruction Problems, found that 'pre-war civil air transportation was a manifestation of exaggerated nationalism,' and that in Europe 'it engendered mistrust and reflected international jealousies; that it laid heavy burdens upon taxpayers for the satisfaction of national prestige and for the creation of a war potential.' To prevent these same kinds of problems from re-emerging after the war, the committee recommended internationalization with 'a single world authority embracing all States.' The 'ideal air transport organization' the report continued, would be 'a single body in which all nations would merge their national efforts for the fulfilment of their several and joint needs.'[70] A subsequent report went even further, arguing that 'as far as civil aviation is concerned, the choice before the world lies between Americanisation and internation- alisation. If this is correct, it is difficult to doubt that it is under the latter system that British interests will best be served.'[71] Even in the United States important national figures such as Republican Governor of Minnesota Harold Stassen and Vice President Henry Wallace came out in favour of some degree of internationalization of postwar aviation. Wallace called for a 'United Nations investment corporation' that, in addition to preventing global unemployment, would operate 'a network of globe-girdling airways,' which would be 'operated by the air arm of the United Nations peace force.'[72]

Aviation was, after all, still a fairly recent development. Its effect on the imagination was strong, and visionary proposals like internationalization had appeal. It was a time when flying was still something of a novelty and contained an element of danger. President Roosevelt made his first ocean flight and couldn't help but be impressed, if not enthusiastic. 'Amazing,' he noted, 'Wednesday in Liberia, Thursday in Brazil. And I don't like flying, not one bit. The more I do of it, the less I like it.' Vice President Wallace was equally thrilled, and flew to China wearing two wrist-watches: 'one to tell the time where he was, the other to tell the time back home.' Prime Minister Churchill had similar feelings, writing after flying to the United States in 1942: 'These airplane journeys had to be taken as a matter of course during the war. Nonetheless I always re- garded them as dangerous excursions.'[73] The diaries and memoirs of this generation of politicians and bureaucrats are filled with vivid descrip- tions of airports and the adventures of air travel.[74] For many people, in- ternationalization made sense.

There was widespread sympathy in government, official, and public circles for the idea of internationalization, but support for concrete ac- tion waned as it became apparent that such visionary schemes were im- practical. Few nations were willing to give complete control over civil aviation to an international organization; civil aviation was much too im- portant in tying together empires and colonial possessions; internation- alization would damage domestic aviation industries and too many jobs depended on that. In the United States especially, where the airlines were privately owned, plans for complete internationalization were shot down as the impossible schemes of dreamers.[75] Given the Americans' competitive advantage in civil aviation in the later stages of the Second World War, there was little chance that Washington would surrender the regulation – let alone the ownership – of international routes to an international authority. There was talk of an 'American Century' and commercial aviation would be a part of it. In Congress, Representative Clare Booth Luce dismissed the talk of internationalization as 'Globaloney.' But what was American policy? 'We want to fly everywhere,' she stated. 'Period.'[76] Other continental nations, like Canada, where the fears of enemy bombing were low, soon agreed. In Britain, the Foreign Office and Air Ministry realized that internationalization was clearly unacceptable to the Americans, and, without American support, talk of the complete internationalization of civil aviation was just that – talk. Prime Minister Churchill was equally cool to these proposals, writing after reading two wartime studies favouring internationalization: 'If by this is meant a kind of Volapuk Esperanto cosmopolitan organization managed and staffed by committees of all peoples great and small, with pilots of every country from Peru to China (especially China) flying every kind of machine in every direction, many people will feel that this is at present an unattainable idea.'[77] Despite Churchill's dismissal of internationalization as impractical, Britain would continue to support internationalism in international air transport; but that internationalism would be directed more to the regulation – not the operation – of international aviation.

In all these proposals for internationalization there was a common thread, in that they all envisioned the creation of a new international air organization. During the war a few individuals suggested fashioning a new multilateral agreement from the vestiges of the Paris Convention[78] but, when it came to discussing the international authority, most voices were raised in support of a completely new organization. The Havana group was clearly regional and it had no permanent organization upon which to build; the same was true for the Ibero-American Convention, which had never come into force. The International Commission for Air Navigation was also largely European in scope, and it never really got over its image as an organization of the victors of the First World War. It was also fading during the war in the same way as the League of Nations; the last meeting before the war was held in Copenhagen in 1939, and when Paris fell in the spring of 1940 the headquarters of ICAN was closed.

The International Commission for Air Navigation was also suspect from an American point of view – because it was linked to the League of

Nations, dominated by Europeans, and doomed by the war. 'Some day, we may be faced with an entirely different situation,' Oliver Lissitzyn wrote in 1941, before the United States entered the war. 'The Old World may be controlled by a few powerful military states such as Germany and Japan with whom we may have to wage economic and military warfare on a world-wide scale. If Germany should choose to adhere to the Convention of 1919, she could easily pack the Commission with representatives of her victims that had become her puppets. And freedom of the air would merely enable the new masters of the Old World to extend their air services – which would be based on pooled resources far greater than the United States could command – to every part of the New World, including Canada, Mexico, the Caribbean and the United States itself.'[79] With such possibilities in the future, it was better to have a wholly new organization.

The war also was a time of great internationalism among the Allied nations, especially after the tide of the war had turned. The world seemed ripe for new international institutions: so much of the world lay in ruins, so many governments had toppled, so much needed to be rebuilt, and new people and new ideas were required. The time was right to rebuild the world from the ground up, and for many Americans and British, as well as French, Canadians, Australians, and many others, there was no desire to go back to the old ways and the old institutions. What was needed was an organization not mired in the failures of the past and burdened with the memories of the collapse of international diplomacy in the 1930s, but a new one built on the promise of the future. In the same way that the new United Nations Organization distanced itself from the League of Nations, those who came together to create the International Civil Aviation Organization would look ahead to the future, not the past. The Puritan and the Peer, along with their delegations and the delegations from more than fifty other countries, arrived in Chicago with the optimism that they could solve the existing problems in the air, avoid the mistakes of the past, and lead international civil aviation into the new world. For civil aviation the sky really was the limit.

2

Chicago: The Ambitious Dream

Gentlemen, the world will be disappointed if we dodge or duck or detour or evade the principles and the fundamentals ... Our distinguished Chairman, in the language of diplomacy, referred to the complete picture as an 'ambitious dream.' Let us make that a definite mandate.[1]

The International Civil Aviation Organization was born at the International Aviation Conference that took place in Chicago in November and December 1944. It is almost impossible to find anyone – in government among politicians and bureaucrats, the press, or in non-governmental organizations and groups that took an interest in international affairs – who argued that the world would be better off without such an organization. It just made sense to have an organization like ICAO. The experience of the 1930s and the early war years demonstrated the need for such a body, first, to establish common standards for the safe operation of civil aviation and second, to regulate in some shape or form the economic or commercial side of aviation. So long as there remained a perceived direct connection between military and civil aviation, the calls for an international aviation organization to oversee, regulate, or control civil aviation would continue. What this organization would look like, what powers it would have, who would be members, where it would be located – all these questions, and a hundred more, were still left to be answered.

The Chicago conference is widely regarded as a successful wartime conference, primarily because it produced ICAO, a new international air convention, and other aviation agreements. It was convened in a spirit of internationalism that was not dissimilar to other international conferences held during the latter stages of the war, such as those at Bretton

Woods and San Francisco. Indeed, because civil aviation was universally singled out for its postwar potential, it received extensive forethought and discussion from planners on both sides of the Atlantic. Here, it was widely believed, was one field of activity that required a truly internationalist approach. Equally, as President Roosevelt warned, if the United States and Great Britain could not cooperate between themselves on aviation affairs, how could they expect to work with the Soviets and others towards an equitable peace settlement? The failure of internationalism at Chicago, therefore, might well have far-reaching repercussions in other areas of international cooperation.

The invitations to the Chicago conference were issued on 11 September. Included on the list were all the Allied nations, referred to as the 'United Nations' – those states that were 'associated with the United Nations in this war' – and the neutral states. Missing from the list were the enemy states, including, among others, Germany, Austria, Italy, and Japan. There were fifty-five invitations in all, including those sent to the Danish and Thai ministers in Washington. The invitation set out broad objectives for the conference, listed under three general categories: (1) the 'establishment of provisional world route arrangements,' (2) the creation of an Interim Council, and (3) 'agreement upon the principles to be followed in setting up a permanent international aeronautical body, and a multilateral aviation convention dealing with the fields of air transport, air navigation and aviation technical subjects.'

All of the governments with the exception of Saudi Arabia accepted the invitation to Chicago. The Soviet Union accepted at first and sent a delegation to North America, but at the last moment dropped out and refused to attend. In their press release the Soviets pointed to the participation of Switzerland, Portugal, and Spain – 'countries which for many years have conducted a pro-Fascist policy hostile to the Soviet Union' – as an explanation for backing out.[2] There were questions about the sincerity of the Soviet withdrawal; Edward Stettinius, the acting secretary of state, informed Berle that 'the British Ambassador at Moscow believes that the true reason why the Soviets withdrew from the Aviation Conference was that they did not wish to become involved in what promised to be a serious disagreement between the U.S. and British delegations.'[3] Berle disagreed, and added his own view that the Soviets 'may merely have decided that they did not want to move out in civil aviation anyway because they were not yet prepared to play a decisive role in it.[4] It is tempting to speculate on the impact that the Soviets might have had on the development of the International Civil Aviation Organization had they become full participants at the very start and participated in the Cold War polarization discussed in Chapter 10. That the Soviets stayed out until 1970, however, suggests that their motives were deeper than merely wishing to avoid an Anglo-American disagreement at Chicago. It likely had more to do with the Soviet Union's view of the world and its place in it, and perhaps reflected the long-held Soviet view of international organizations as part of the capitalist world's quest for international dominance.[5] In any event, it was an important decision in that the Soviet Union remained on the outside of ICAO and took no part in its creation.

Several countries sent strong teams to Chicago. The American delegation was the largest; it was headed by Berle and included, among others, Welch Pogue and Edward Warner, the chair and vice-chair, respectively, of the Civil Aeronautics Board, Senators Josiah Bailey and Owen Brewster, and Fiorello LaGuardia, the co-chair of the Permanent Joint Board on Defense (Canada-United States). Stokeley Morgan, who headed the Aviation Division in the U.S. State Department acted as secretary general of the delegation. In addition, the American delegation included more than thirty technical experts, advisers, assistants, and secretaries, as well as representatives from Pan American Airways and American Airlines. It was an impressive team and ensured that the United States would play a role in the conference equal to its anticipated role in postwar civil aviation.

The second largest delegation was the British one, with eight delegates and almost thirty advisers and officials. Lord Swinton was in the chair and other delegates included Sir Arthur Street, the permanent under secretary in the Air Ministry who had recently participated in Commonwealth aviation discussions in Montreal, W.C.G. Cribbett, the assistant under secretary in the Air Ministry, and William Hildred, the director of civil aviation in the Air Ministry. On the advisory level the British sent a cross section of military and civil aviation experts, representatives from various imperial possessions, and a handful of departmental officials, including N.J.A. Cheetham of the Foreign Office and P.H. Gore-Booth from the British embassy in Washington.

No other state sent delegations of comparable size to those of Great Britain or the United States, but several countries, like France, China, and Canada, were represented by over fifteen delegates and advisers. The French delegation was surprisingly strong given that the liberation of France had occurred only a few months earlier, and it is an indication of the seriousness with which the French approached postwar civil aviation.[6] Max Hymans, the director of air transport, was in the chair, and he was accompanied by more than a dozen advisers and interpreters. The Canadians were led by Minister of Reconstruction C.D. Howe, who had been directing Canada's civil aviation policy since 1935. He was supported by H.J. Symington, the president of Trans-Canada Air Lines, and by a handful of advisers, including J.R. Baldwin of the Privy Council Office and Escott Reid from the Canadian embassy in Washington. The contribution of individuals like Baldwin and Reid, along with Morgan and Warner from the United States and Cribbett and Hildred from Britain, can be seen in the wording of the many drafts and final texts of the convention and agreements that emerged from the Chicago conference.

The rest of the delegations, for the most part, comprised only a handful of delegates and/or advisers. Several states were represented by their ministers or ambassadors in Washington; Haiti, Paraguay, Nicaragua, and the Dominican Republic sent only one representative each. Nevertheless, many individuals from the smaller delegations made significant contributions at Chicago. John Martin, the co-delegate for South Africa, for example, became an important figure as chair of the key committee overseeing the multilateral convention and international aeronautical body, and Frederick Tymms participated as a member of the Indian delegation and made a major contribution to the final text of the Chicago Convention.

Chicago became one of the largest international conferences to that time. In the end there were 955 individuals involved in the conference, including 185 delegates, 156 advisers, and 306 members of the conference secretariat. What is interesting is not that many of the delegations were small, but, rather, that so many nations devoted so much time and effort to attend and participate in the conference, given the great distances, the difficulties and dangers of reaching Chicago in wartime, and the wartime situation in many of the participing countries.[7]

Home for these hundreds of delegates, officials and secretaries for the next six weeks was Chicago's Stevens Hotel (later the Chicago Hilton Hotel), on the shores of Lake Michigan. The hotel's stationery claimed it to be the 'World's largest hotel' but the reviews were mixed and complaints were heard of crowding and slow service. One delegate complained that the hotel itself was a problem and adversely affected the outcome of the conference. The 'physical conditions under which it was held,' he wrote at the time, 'a mammoth second-rate hotel whose lobby was like the lobby of the Grand Central Station in New York, a hotel in which it was necessary to waste an hour a day waiting for elevators and probably half an hour a day waiting to complete telephone calls.'[8] Another wrote that the 'atmosphere of the Stevens Hotel was not good.

The hotel itself was crowded and noisy, while its food was not the best. Rooms were small and tempers easily become frayed. While it was true that delegates could get out into the city for diversion, it was also true that the atmosphere was far from restful and fresh air was at a premium.'[9] Nevertheless, many of the delegates who arrived in Chicago from countries much closer to the war must have marvelled at the tranquillity, peacefulness, and even the ordinariness of the city in the autumn of 1944. Sunday was a day off for most delegates and it gave them a chance to wander the streets and parks of Chicago. One British participant later remembered his fascination with the city, but what struck him most was the lack of devastation in a city that had been untouched by the war.[10]

The conference opened on 1 November. At the first plenary session, Berle, who was elected president for the whole conference, welcomed the delegates and read a short statement from President Roosevelt. Looking back on Roosevelt's words is a good reminder of the wartime context of the Chicago conference and how it was firmly believed that international aviation could help to win the peace. 'The progress of the armies, navies, and air forces of the United Nations,' Roosevelt declared, 'has already opened great areas to peaceful intercourse which has been closed for more than four black years. We can soberly hope that all Europe will be reclaimed for civilization before many months have passed. Steadily the great areas of the Pacific are likewise being freed from Japanese occupation. In due time, the Continent of Asia will be opened again to friendly intercourse with the world. The rebuilding of peace means reopening the lines of communication and peaceful relationship. Air transport will be the first available means by which we can start to heal the wounds of war, and put the world once more on a peacetime basis.' Roosevelt continued on a slightly more political level and put in a plea for open skies, cloaking the rhetoric of the freedom of the air with the maintainance of peace: 'some centuries ago, an attempt was made to build great empires based on domination of great sea areas. The lords of these areas tried to close these seas to some, and to offer access to others, and thereby enrich themselves and extend their power. This led directly to a number of wars both in the Eastern and Western Hemispheres. We do not need to make that mistake again. I hope you will not dally with the thought of creating great blocs of closed air, thereby tracing in the sky the conditions of future wars. I know you will see to it that the air which God gave to everyone shall not become the means of domination over anyone.'[11]

Following the reading of Roosevelt's message, Berle added his own words of welcome and several other delegates rose to make brief speeches. The tone was sober yet full of promise as each delegate underlined their dedication to achieving success in the conference, spoke to the increasing need for international collaboration as aviation was shrinking the distances between the peoples of the world, and warned of the dangers to international security of failure at Chicago. These feelings were expressed most succinctly by Viscount Alain du Parc, the chair of the Belgian delegation, as he echoed Roosevelt's sentiments: 'Aviation has played a major part in winning the war. It must play a major part in winning the peace.'[12]

Once the formalities were out of the way a handful of committees were formed, including an Executive Committee of all delegation heads, and a more influential Steering Committee, which Berle also chaired. In addition, four major committees were established, reflecting the kind of work that was to be done at the conference: Committee I, Multilateral Aviation Convention and International Aeronautical Body; Committee II, Technical Standards and Procedures; Committee III, Provisional Air Routes; and Committee IV, Interim Council. Each of these committees had their own subcommittees. Committee I, for example, had three subcommittees: (1) International Organization, (2) Air Navigation Principles, and (3) Air Transportation Principles. Committee II on Technical Standards had the most, with ten subcommittees. Participation in these committees was broad, and hardly confined to the major air powers. France, the United States, Cuba, Czechoslovakia, Australia, Belgium, Canada, India, New Zealand, Turkey, and South Africa had representatives on all the four committees and their various subcommittees. Similarly, the different committees were chaired by representatives from Belgium, Brazil, Peru, Australia, China, Poland, Mexico, and the Netherlands. South Africa, Norway, and Great Britain chaired two committees; Canada and the United States chaired three each.[13]

Fairly quickly a routine emerged in the two largest delegations. The British delegation, for example, met first thing in the morning and then moved into the conference committee meetings. Late in the afternoon was a time for private, individual meetings, and a larger meeting of Commonwealth delegations usually was held after dinner. 'The Commonwealth meetings,' wrote one participant in his diary, 'are long and verbose affairs, and all, except the Indians, have had a few drinks by then. Everyone helps himself liberally from the whiskey laid out (by myself) on a side table. Although I take no active part in the discussions, I usually attend, as it is fascinating to watch the Commonwealth in action – agreement and disagreement. His Lordship (Swinton) is not always very tactful; he has usually dined fully and well, tête-à-tête, with a member of the delegation who is rewarded with an immense Havana.'[14]

It was part of British policy to maintain as much imperial solidarity as possible, but, inevitably, there were divisions in such a large group. For the most part, the Australians, New Zealanders, Newfoundlanders, South Africans, and Indians could be counted on to support Britain, but there were problems with the Irish and the Canadians. The British were angered that the Irish, who remained neutral in the war, were even invited to the conference by the United States and London refused to have the Irish delegation attend Commonwealth meetings, even if by shunning them the Irish 'might be driven into the arms of the United States Government.'[15] Before the conference was over the Irish were negotiating the exchange of reciprocal air rights with the American delegation. The Canadians, unhappy with the treatment of the Irish, threatened to call their own Commonwealth meeting *with* the Irish, until Lord Swinton agreed to meet the Irish leader – but only if he asked for an interview.[16] The Canadians were of more concern because they came to play an important role in the conference and there were fears in the British delegation that they were falling too much under the influence of the United States.[17] 'Canadian proposals as I see it would give United States all they are asking for,' Swinton argued in a telegram before the start of the conference.[18] A few days later he added: 'It is most important that we should bring the Canadian Government into line with our essential policy or failing that to avoid any open breach of the Empire front'[19] For their part, the Canadians winced at any talk of an 'Empire front,' and strove for the middle ground between the British and the Americans. It was known that Swinton was 'pretty angry' at the Canadians, and they began to suspect that the others were meeting behind their backs.[20]

On the American side it was a somewhat similar routine of delegation meetings, committee meetings, and, in the evenings, informal meetings with individuals from various delegations as matters arose. Berle was remembered as being less formal than Swinton; he, LaGuardia, and the other American representatives would venture forth to meet other delegates for drinks in their rooms. It gave everyone the opportunity to unwind and to speak more informally about the pressing issues of the day, and it was quite a contrast with Swinton who was remembered by one participant as 'a bit stuffy' and as a man who would wait to meet people in his room rather than seek them out in theirs.[21] In addition, the American delegation began semi-formal negotiations with a handful of other delegations, including Sweden and Iceland, with a view to signing air agreements to begin civil flying as soon as the war ended.

Throughout the conference Berle received a constant stream of delegates concerning various matters of importance to the other states attending the conference. Representatives of the Latin American and Middle Eastern states appeared, concerned about the weighting of votes in the new international organization where they feared their influence would be diminished. On another day, Air Vice Marshal Karel Janousek, the chair of the Czechoslovak delegation, called on Berle to indicate 'his strenuous desire to have an American line fly into Prague, which, as he conceded, is more likely to be the center of air traffic than is Berlin after the war.' Janousek went on to ask for eighteen American DC-3s.[22] On one day alone (15 November), Berle received Jose Correa, the leader of the Ecuadorian delegation, who lobbied informally that Peru not be on the council of the new international air authority – should Peru be a member of the council, he informed Berle, then Ecuador 'would decline to go along with the convention.' Later the Bolivian delegation appeared arguing that 'Mediterranean states' (those surrounded by land) 'should have special rights of flight over their neighbor states, else they might be blockaded in the air.' Finally, Max Hymans, the chair of the French delegation, called to request consultation 'before the British, Canadians, and Americans finally agreed and presented a draft to the convention.' Berle promised each of the delegates that he would do what he could for them, and in the latter case at least, he promised more consultation, adding: 'I think the French probably have other things in mind than mere *amour propre* and will try to intrigue the situation; but we will have to deal with that as best we can.'[23]

Berle also faced some dissension within his own delegation. Senator Owen Brewster, who was a member of the Senate Committee on Commerce and supported the interests of Pan American Airways, was often at odds with Berle over the direction of American policy. Called by Berle at one point the 'stooge for Pan American,'[24] Brewster began leaking information from the American delegation meetings, information that found its way into the pages of the *Chicago Tribune* much to Berle's chagrin. Berle confronted Brewster, without much satisfaction. 'I think it is the first time in the constitutional history of the country,' he complained in his diary, 'that a member of an American Delegation, seeking to torpedo his own Delegation at the behest of a private interest, this time Pan American, has attempted to embarrass the Delegation by a press campaign and a Senate investigation at the same time.'[25]

As the work on all the committees began, Swinton and Berle met privately to discuss the differences between their governments. Neither was

completely free to make a deal; Berle had to handle the opposition of
Brewster and Pan Am, and he faced a constant struggle against those
who claimed that he was prepared to give away too much to the British.
For his part, Swinton was more firmly in control of his delegation, but he
was charged only with implementing British policy, not formulating it.
The decision-making power remained in London, in the small cabinet
Ministerial Committee chaired by Lord Beaverbrook, and all amendments,
new proposals, and responses were to be channelled through this committee.[26] And, of course, Berle and Swinton did not get along. In public there
was little hint of personal or professional animosity; as LaGuardia put it
at one stage, 'every time Lord Swinton gets up I think he is agreeing with
Mr Berle.'[27] But beneath the thin veneer of civility there lurked a mutual
suspicion of each other's personal and national ambitions.

Swinton and Berle met for lunch before the conference officially
opened, and things began badly. Berle later wrote that Swinton explained
the British position 'with great frankness and bluntness' noting that the
United Kingdom was there to establish the principles of an aviation convention with 'an equitable division of traffic,' but were not willing to discuss specific routes. What did he mean by 'equitable'? Berle asked. Swinton
answered that the British 'wanted an arrangement by which each country
had the right to carry the traffic which embarked within it – or an amount
of the traffic measured by that.' Berle balked immediately, claiming that
the British were reverting to an older position that already had been rejected. It would mean, Berle said, 'diverting part of American traffic out
and in to British lines.' 'Why was that not fair?' Swinton asked. Berle responded 'that this really came down to a request by Britain to us to assign
part of American traffic to support British aviation, and I thought it was as
impossible now as when it was broached last spring. Swinton then dropped
the subject.'[28] It was not the best way to get things started.

The conference played out in a series of plenary sessions, in the numerous committees, and in the more informal negotiations that went on
behind the scenes. In the committees, an enormous amount of work was
accomplished, especially on technical issues and where there was broad
agreement on the creation of an international organization. But with
respect to the more purely economic issues of international air transport, and especially regarding those dealing with routes and the exchange of rights, the negotiations were carried on in private discussions,
and as the conference progressed the major decisions increasingly were
made by the two major air powers. And when the Americans and the
British could not agree, the whole conference ground to a halt.

'There were fifty-two nations at Chicago, and there were about fifty different ideas' was how one British aviation expert later remembered the
divergence of opinion at the Chicago conference.[29] It also underlined
the difficulties in finding common ground among so many different nations when matters of diplomacy, security, technology, economics, and
national prestige collided. The countries represented at the conference
all had their own views, their own security needs, and their own national
interests and capabilities. Those who had the airplanes – the United
States and, to a lesser degree, Canada – wanted to start flying them right
away and this meant getting entry rights to other nations. Those who
needed aircraft, like the British and just about everyone else, were not so
sure, and often advocated a gradual reintroduction of commercial air
services and a sharing of frequencies and capacity. But every state, in
devising its aviation policy, had to factor in its industrial capacity and the
needs of its domestic airlines and aircraft industry. During the war especially, the Americans received a steady stream of requests for aircraft, and
this industrial advantage enabled the United States to negotiate from a
position of strength.

Other countries, especially those with large empires from the pre–
Second World War era like France, were concerned about re-establishing
themselves and holding on to their territories. One way to do so was to
reserve colonial services for the mother country. For example, the French
government believed strongly in regarding colonial services essentially as
internal ones. As one Foreign Ministry memorandum put it: 'Il faut tout
d'abord faire ressortir que les possessions françaises d'Afrique forment
un bloc compact qui n'est séparé de la métropole que la Méditerranée; il
est essential que l'ensemble des territories constitutés par la métropole et
le bloc africain soit considéré comme un tout et que les lignes aériennes
qui les parcourent soinent considérées, de la France au Congo, comme
des lignes intérieures assurant un service de cabotage.'[30]

Geography also dictated policy. Some nations, like Ireland and Turkey,
were located where others would have to fly over to get somewhere else,
and this geographical reality would be used to advantage. In Ireland's
case it meant withholding transit rights until forced stops at Shannon
Airport could be negotiated. This worked, until the adoption of long-
range jet aircraft made it easy to fly around Ireland and not stop at all.
Others, like Australia and New Zealand, felt themselves remote and located in a part of the world to which some airlines might want to fly, but
over which few would need to fly to get somewhere else. As a result, the
Australians and New Zealanders were less worried about granting transit

rights to other nations and more worried about security and being by-passed and overlooked on international services. Some states with colonies wanted to preserve colonial services as 'internal,' others without colonies cried foul and opposed such restrictive measures. There were small countries, like the Netherlands, with an effective state airline and a strong desire to compete in the international air; there were big countries, like China, less concerned about the exchange of transit rights than in acquiring desperately needed American aircraft. Still others, like the absent Soviet Union, viewed international aviation in their own unique way through a thick lens of national security and suspicion. The Soviet idea of an international air service was to have all in-bound aircraft land at Cairo where everything would be switched to Soviet airplanes. Finding common ground in these conditions was a very tall order.

Looking towards an international organization, views were equally diverse. It is possible to argue that virtually all states believed that the new organization should handle technical issues, set standards, collect statistics, distribute information, and so on, although even here there were debates over the extent of the authority's powers and whether or not it should be able to force a state to comply with its recommendations. When it came to the economic questions, however, the divisions were wide and pronounced, with a major fault line appearing between those states that wanted an organization with strong powers to regulate and even operate international air services and those looking for an organization with powers limited to technical issues that left the economic questions to the individual states and airlines. The Europeans, for the most part, supported the former; the Dutch, the Belgians, the French, and others supported investing the authority with the powers to determine commercial entry rights; the Belgians favoured the creation of regional groupings within the authority, each with its own executive commission. Similarly, the Indians – like the Australians and New Zealanders – drew a direct connection between international air services and national security, and supported the creation of a strong organization with broad powers. The Canadians also wanted a strong authority with regulatory powers, but, fearing American domination of their cross-border air services, wanted services between contiguous countries exempted and left to bilateral negotiation. The Chinese and most Latin American states, on the other hand, looked for a more technical organization, leaving economic questions the responsibility of state governments. Still others were flexible when it came to the international authority, but came to Chicago with their own agendas. The

Irish, for example, arrived determined to maintain their independence from the United Kingdom and to further the development of Shannon Airport – any bilateral agreements entered into would have to be approved afterwards.[31]

There were four full proposals for an international aviation convention and organization tabled at the start of the conference, one each from the United States, the United Kingdom, and Canada, and a joint plan submitted by the Australians and New Zealanders. Individually these proposals varied in opinion from support for largely unregulated competition to complete internationalization of international air services, with the international authority ranging in shape from an information collection agency to a powerful inter-governmental regulatory body. As a group, these plans formed the basis of discussion for the whole conference.

The joint Australia-New Zealand proposal was made in the form of a resolution presented to the conference on 8 November. It was based on an agreement made earlier that year in Canberra, and reconfirmed by the two governments in October.[32] Believing that the 'fullest measure of co-operation should be secured in the development of air transport services,' the Australians and New Zealanders advocated the almost complete internationalization of international air services and the creation of an international air authority 'which would be responsible for the operation of air services on prescribed international trunk routes and which would own the aircraft and ancillary equipment employed on these routes.'[33] It was a bold plan, but one doomed to failure. The Australians knew well before the conference that these kinds of proposals were completely unacceptable to the United States, as well as China, the Soviet Union, and even the British, and their resolution was quickly torpedoed. The Brazilians moved an amendment, which was adopted, calling the resolution premature, and this move effectively ended any discussion of internationalization. The Australians took some solace in that they were supported by the French (who would, however, only support *talking* about internationalization) and there were promises of future discussion of their proposals. Even Berle spoke warmly about the Australia-New Zealand proposals as they disappeared from sight.[34]

The U.S. proposals were more clearly spelled out in a draft Convention on Air Navigation published shortly before the conference opened. The American proposals envisioned a much more open system for postwar aviation, although it was not exactly the complete 'freedom of the air' often used to describe the American position. The proposed air convention enshrined the concept of state sovereignty over domestic air space and granted member nations the right of innocent passage. Commercial air services and the rights to discharge and take on passengers in foreign states were to be negotiated bilaterally (rather than being invested in a future aviation authority), with no nation giving another state exclusive operating rights. The international authority – called the International Aviation Assembly – would be largely limited to administrative functions with limited powers to collect information and statistics, to study technical procedures, make recommendations and promote standardization, disseminate technical information, to study and amend the international convention, and to arbitrate disputes between contracting states. It was the antithesis of internationalization, with the authority as a kind of 'central agency,' having no power to regulate commercial services, to own or operate airlines or aircraft, or to fix rates, determine frequency of service, or limit capacity. The Americans were adamant on this issue, many arguing that any enforcement powers given to an international organization would infringe upon the sovereignty of the United States and could be challenged as unconstitutional. Overall, Berle wrote, 'an international body at this stage of the game would have neither the machinery nor the prestige to enforce orders.'[35]

The air authority proposed by the Americans would consist of an assembly of the contracting states (the United Nations and their associates) where the rule one state – one vote would apply. In addition, there would be an executive council of the leading air nations with fifteen members: two each from the United States, the Soviet Union, and the British Commonwealth; one representative from China, France, and Brazil; and the remaining six to be selected by the ICAO Assembly on a regional basis, with three from Europe, two from the Western hemisphere, and one representing Asia and Africa. Until a further conference was held to create this organization, an interim council would be established, set up on the same regional basis as the executive council.[36]

This proposal for the make-up of the executive council of the air authority sparked a minor uproar, with the opposition to the American plan coming from an unlikely source – the Latin American states. On most issues the Central and South American countries were strong supporters of the American position. Regarding the powers of the international authority, for example, the Latin American states opposed giving it any regulatory powers that might 'infringe upon their sovereign rights,' preferring instead the American plan for a purely administrative body, 'whose sole function shall be purely of a technical consultative and advisory nature.' At the same time, however, the Latin American states refused to accept the American offer of only two of fifteen seats on the council (plus one for Brazil) reserved for all of Latin America. At a press conference on 6 November, the chair of the Mexican delegation, Pedro A. Chapa, announced the creation of a Latin American bloc, what he called a 'Union' of Latin American countries. Sharing common problems, it was agreed that all nations in the group would 'consult each other on all points,' arriving at a common policy. Chapa was elected chair of the bloc, Hahnemann Guimaraes of Brazil the vice-chair, and Luis Machado of Cuba the secretary.[37]

By joining together, this Latin American bloc could wield considerable influence over the shape of the new international organization, especially on the composition of the executive council. Within a few days, Berle was referring to it as the 'so-called Latin American revolt.' But the Latin American bloc was not the only voice against an executive dominated by a few large powers, many smaller nations agreed as well. Berle believed it was 'the backwash of a certain resentment against the four Power arrangements contemplated by Dumbarton Oaks,' the previous year's conference where the Great Powers agreed to the establishment of the United Nations and a Security Council dominated by themselves. It is not impossible that memories of the experience in the International Commission for Air Navigation also played a role. The solution, in the short term, was to put off a final decision; on 10 November the concerned subcommittees recommended that the selection of the permanent council be left for decision by the Interim Council, and that council would be elected by the conference delegates. It was a victory for the Latin American bloc in that it was agreed that each participating state would have one vote for the Interim Council rather than the American proposal of selecting council members on a weighted basis. But the question of the make-up of the permanent council remained. Berle wrote: 'I haven't a cat's idea as to the answer as yet.'[38]

Regardless of the make-up of the council, the Americans insisted that there should be relatively unregulated competition in postwar international aviation, with the international authority playing the role of a kind of referee. 'The rules of the air should be so clear,' Berle wrote, 'that an international authority does not exercise power, but rather keeps track of the observance of these rules. The power to enforce the rules should always be the power of the countries involved; but they must consult when problems arise.'[39] It was a policy that was sure to clash with the views of many others, including the British, who had not been inactive during the weeks before the conference.

Following the appointment of Swinton as minister of civil aviation, the
British government released a White Paper with a formal statement of its
proposals for international air transport. It had been first drafted during
1943 Commonwealth conversations and was revised over the course of
1944. It was time for a 'radical change,' the British announced, to establish the machinery for the smooth and effective operation of commercial
air transport, and to prevent the irrational blocking of transit rights, the
cutthroat competition, the heavy subsidization of national airlines, and
the 'international jealousies and mistrust' that had characterized the
pre-war period. A number of general principles followed: the maintenance of a 'broad equilibrium between the world's air transport capacity,' the elimination of 'wasteful competition' on global air routes, and
provision for the 'equitable participation by the various countries.' More
concretely, the British document called for the creation of a powerful
international organization to oversee the growth and regulation of international air services. They called for the exchange of the first four
freedoms among participating nations, but with the power to determine
frequencies and set rates to be given to the international organization –
proposals that the Americans had consistently opposed for more than
two years.[40]

The British government approved the White Paper as the basis for the
British position at Chicago on 12 October,[41] but Swinton and others realized that the White Paper – and its proposals for rate, frequency, and
capacity controls – would be unacceptable to the Americans. It was therefore agreed in cabinet that if Swinton could not persuade the Americans
of the benefits of strict regulation and controls, then he should fall back
to a position supporting a multilateral agreement covering those matters
on which there was some Anglo-American consensus – better to have a
weak international agreement with the Americans than no agreement at
all. In addition, Swinton was given the authority to concede the right of
innocent passage (providing the other participants agreed as well), but
he was to refrain from undertaking any bilateral negotiations with the
Americans while in Chicago.[42]

Clearly as the conference began the hard work of writing a new convention and creating a new international organization, the gap between
the American and British positions on the commercial questions – fifth
freedom rights, frequencies, capacity, and regulatory powers for the new
international organization – remained very wide. In other circles as well,
Anglo-American aviation relations were deteriorating, with both sides
accusing the other of bad faith. There was anger on the American side

over the British White Paper, which appeared to Berle as overly rigid; he also complained that it did not take into account his earlier discussions with Beaverbrook.[43] Others pointed to the Commonwealth talks that were held in Montreal just prior to the start of the Chicago conference, 'clothed in secrecy,' and warned of the formation of a Commonwealth bloc at Chicago.[44] British suspicions were aroused by the Americans who, in their eagerness to resume civil flying, commenced bilateral negotiations with several countries. In addition, only days before the conference opened Roosevelt gave permission to the U.S. military transport systems to carry civil passengers when space permitted. 'This cynical edict,' one British official protested, suggested 'that the Americans foresee a clash at Chicago; and are shaping their course accordingly with a view to going all out for world-wide air transportation, irrespective of the wishes and rights of other countries.'[45] To make matters worse, as the delegates from around the world made their way to Chicago an angry Anglo-American dispute flared up over the commercial use of Clipperton Island, a French possession strategically located on the trans-Pacific route.[46]

The Canadian proposals were similar in many respects to those of Britain and the United States, although they are often seen as an attempted compromise between the two major powers. The Canadian plan called for a strong international authority to regulate international services, the exchange of the first four freedoms, and the division of flight frequencies based on 'traffic embarked,' which pleased the British. It also included two points that appealed to the Americans: first, it called for a 'transitional period' after the war when all nations would be able to establish air services as they saw fit, and, second, it included what became known as an 'escalator clause,' which permitted an airline that consistently operated a scheduled service above a specified capacity to unilaterally increase its frequency of service.[47] The goal was admirable, to remove 'existing barriers in the way of the development of international air transport,' while at the same time 'guarding against the dangers of chaotic and ruinous conditions on international air routes which would lead to high subsidies and serious friction between the peace-loving nations.' But it was a very slippery concept, a semi-contradictory idea of 'regulated competition,' where everyone would get a slice of the pie, but the best airlines would earn the largest slices.

The American, British, and Canadian draft conventions were tabled in Committee I on 3 November and distributed to its three subcommittees for detailed consideration. Only the Canadian and American plans contained full draft multilateral conventions so these two documents became the basis for discussion, the Canadian draft in subcommittees I and III, the American proposals in subcommittee II.[48] At the same time, work progressed in the technical committees and subcommittees. These sub-committees were designated to examine the following subjects: (1) com-munications procedures, airways systems; (2) rules of the air, air traffic control practices; (3) standards governing the licensing of operating and mechanical personnel, log books; (4) airworthiness of aircraft; (5) regis-tration and identification of aircraft; (6) collection and dissemination of meteorological information; (7) aeronautical maps and charts; (8) cus-toms procedures, manifests; (9) accident investigation, including search and salvage; and (10) publications and forms.

The goal was to achieve the greatest amount of standardization in in-ternational air travel in an effort to make air travel as easy and safe as possible. The technical committee delegates were helped by being able to refer to the Paris and Havana conventions. Moreover, matters of na-tional prestige and general economic questions were not considerations for the technical subcommittees, making broad agreement that much easier to attain. There was also an understanding that no final decisions were to be made at the conference. All the technical standards would need to be examined and accepted by the member governments of the future organization, and the recommendations made by the subcommit-tees would therefore be considered tentative, to be examined further and agreed to later, once the organization and council had begun oper-ating.[49] The technical reports still needed to be approved by the confer-ence, but the technical standards and procedures would be finalized later, after the conference was over. As a result, by 18 November the ten technical subcommittees submitted their reports for final drafting, with only a few issues remaining to be decided.

This progress on the technical issues in the various committees and subcommittees in turn served only to highlight the Anglo-American im-passe on the commercial issues. On economic issues at least, the two sides remained far apart. Some faith was put in the Canadian draft interna-tional convention, which seemed to offer a compromise between the British and American positions, although neither major power was com-pletely satisfied with it. Berle sensed that the British were prepared to com-promise by apparently abandoning the White Paper and moving to the Canadian position. 'We are nearing the climax,' he wrote Edward Stettinius in Washington.[50] But Berle was perhaps unaware that the Canadian draft had been discussed and modified during the Commonwealth talks held in Montreal two weeks earlier, and the British had given tacit agreement to it (with reservations on the transitional period and escalator clause).[51] In addition, Commonwealth members met daily at Chicago, and by 9 November Swinton was reporting that he could 'safely support' the Canadian document.[52] Knowing that the White Paper would be rejected by the United States, Swinton had wisely prepared a 'compromise' position in advance of private talks with Berle.

Berle had a few unexpected plans of his own. The British and their supporters wanted to discuss investing the new organization with regulatory powers; the American draft proposals envisioned an international authority with advisory powers only. Between the two there was little room for manoeuvre. From an American viewpoint, there was little reason even to discuss granting such powers, except that the Americans also supported the idea of producing a standard form of basic principles that could be used by everyone in the negotiation of bilateral air agreements. These principles would be embodied in a standard agreement rather than under the purview of the international authority. There was still something to talk about here, and the American delegation met and put together their ideas on 11 November. 'Our obvious next step is to get in touch with the British and Canadians and fight it out,' Berle concluded. 'There is at least reasonable probability that anything these three countries agree on will go through the Conference.'[53]

Meetings of the committees discussing the multilateral convention were suspended, and on 12 November the first of a series of private meetings was held between Berle, Swinton, C.D. Howe of the Canadian delegation, and a few senior advisers. Berle took both the British and Canadians by surprise when he introduced a new document that neither had seen before; a document that Swinton labelled the 'most extreme statement of policy hitherto made by the United States.'[54] The American document included the unrestricted grant of fifth freedom rights and the removal of any frequency controls, two proposals that the British had consistently resisted. One of the Canadian delegates reported that 'the presentation of this paper ... precipitated a first-class crisis.' 'Within half an hour,' he continued, 'it became clear that we were headed in the direction of a full-dress debate between the United Kingdom and the United States on the general principle of whether there should be international control of frequencies.'[55]

With tempers beginning to flare, a brief adjournment was called to allow both sides to cool down. Following further negotiations a potential compromise was tabled, when Berle offered to accept the 'traffic embarked' principle for frequency control in return for the British agreement to the fifth freedom. Briefly, service frequency would be based on the amount of home traffic, which essentially meant that it would be divided fairly equally between two states. But there was an inherent contradiction. 'The latest American proposal seems not unattractive,' one Foreign Office official wrote: 'it would entitle an American plane flying from New York to Madrid to pick up passengers at Lisbon for Madrid. But presumably all available frequencies for the Madrid-Lisbon route would already have been allocated to Spain and Portugal under the 'traffic embarked' principle. American planes on the route would either have to have additional frequencies over and above those which had already been allocated to Spain and Portugal as being adequate for the traffic offering, which would lead to inflation of frequencies, or frequencies for American planes would have to be deducted from those allocated to Spain and Portugal, which would conflict with the 'traffic embarked' principle.'[56]

Nevertheless, there were strong reasons to accept the offer. The 'traffic embarked' proposal gave a good deal of protection to British aviation interests, especially in the early postwar period when the American advantage would be the greatest. Moreover, it meant that an agreement would be reached and an international organization created with, presumably, real powers to allocate the frequency levels – another of the British goals. Besides, opposition to the fifth freedom was not a popular stand in Chicago, and, as the same official noted, the 'advantages from the point of view of the consumer of a universal grant of the fifth freedom are obviously considerable and our public grounds for resisting it are, as Lord Swinton, points out, very weak.'[57]

After considerable discussion the Ministerial Committee in London informed Swinton that it had agreed to accept the American offer. In return for frequency determination the British were prepared to grant the fifth freedom based on a number of qualifications: there would have to be a trial period and opportunity to withdraw after three years; fifth freedom services would not be allowed to draw off local traffic; the possibility of a rate differential between local and fifth freedom traffic would have to be examined; and everything was dependant on the establishment of an international authority 'with power' to determine frequencies.[58]

For a brief time it appeared that an agreement might be reached; then things began to fall apart. The sticking point was the escalator clause. The 15 November telegram that was sent to Swinton contained the words 'we cannot agree to an escalator clause'; a few days later it was discovered that a ciphering error in the Communications Department had dropped the word 'cannot' from the telegram Swinton received. 'I am afraid that

Lord Swinton has been put in a most embarrassing position,' one official noted;[59] indeed, Swinton had been arguing the merits of the escalator clause for four days. 'Escalator clause was approved in your telegram No. 25,' Swinton wrote from Chicago. 'It has been in every draft agreement. It would be impossible to withdraw it now without putting British Delegation in a very false position.'[60]

In his negotiations with Berle, Swinton had accepted the escalator clause in principle, but only in the context of the Canadian draft, where it was applied to third and fourth freedom traffic (meaning that increases in service frequency were to be based on the number of passengers at the terminal points in the service). Acceptance of the fifth freedom followed, but when the Americans returned with a new draft it included the application of the escalator clause to fifth freedom traffic as well. On a New York to Paris service that travelled via London, for instance, an American airline would have fifth freedom rights to pick up passengers in London and carry them to Paris. The escalator clause as Swinton applied it would be based only on the traffic embarked from New York; the Americans demanded that it apply to the fifth freedom traffic as well. The fear, of course, was that the Americans would be able to increase frequencies on the London-Paris segment of the route and, ultimately, dominate it. To the Americans, however, escalation at intermediate points was essential for any major trunk route, such as a service that crossed Europe or went through Latin America to Argentina. Swinton balked immediately: 'Americans have to-day put forward proposals which are wholly unacceptable,' he complained to London, 'and in so doing have made meaningless the concessions to our point of view which they had tentatively agreed.'[61]

The application of the escalator clause struck at the very heart of the differences between Britain and the United States on commercial air privileges, and the whole discussion ground to a halt. Berle was under great pressure not to back down, and insisted that the Americans had always understood that the escalator clause would apply to fifth freedom traffic. Berle may have known of the ciphering error, but he blamed Swinton for the new impasse.[62] The result was stalemate: Swinton refused to budge, while Berle announced that there was no more he could do and threatened to turn the whole affair over to the general conference. The conference was beginning to lose focus. 'Small countries getting restive at being kept in the dark,' one Canadian adviser wrote in his diary. 'There is an air of gloom since it is known the U.K. & U.S. cannot agree on fundamentals.'[63]

Anglo-American stalemate on commercial privileges threatened to overshadow all the progress made on determining the role and functions of the interim international organization, on drawing up acceptable international standards, and on the wide number of agreements covering a vast array of technical matters. The differences between the two leading delegations were publicly aired in committee, and both Berle and Swinton appeared resigned to failure. On 20 November, a joint American-British-Canadian draft international air convention was submitted to the conference. This draft convention was an effort in compromise and set out the role and duties of the 'International Air Administration,' which would largely be confined to administrative work, information gathering, and technical activities. This draft proposed a new kind of executive council, the 'board of directors,' and it went some way in addressing the concerns of the Latin American bloc and other small nations in that it was to comprise a president, representatives of the seven most important air nations, and seven others selected by the assembly. The draft revealed a substantial amount of agreement between the Americans, British, and Canadians, but there were gaping holes in the draft convention: articles dealing with the key economic issues – the air 'freedoms,' frequencies, and capacity – were left blank, listed as 'still under consideration.'[64]

An impasse had been reached on what to do next. It was the moment of highest tension in the conference; delegates and press jammed the conference room, with each speaker's words punctuated by 'enthusiastic demonstrations by the audience.' On one side the Americans, Canadians, Australians, New Zealanders, and others wanted to press on and see things through to a final agreement. Swinton, who had earlier been given permission to settle for what he could get with a promise to talk about things later, was willing to sign what had been agreed to so far and then come back for the rest at some future date. In this view he had the support of the Chinese delegation. Swinton noted that he was 'sorry we set our aim as wide, high and broad as the air itself.' He continued: 'If we cannot achieve the whole (complete agreement on an international body) let us not minimize what we have accomplished.' Why not, he concluded, leave the unfinished business to the new Interim Council for future debate? Others followed Swinton, but it was LaGuardia who made the most passionate appeal – speaking for 'the man on the street' – to keep going for a complete agreement. 'The world will be disappointed if we dodge fundamentals,' he said. 'I cannot agree with Lord Swinton, that we may achieve more limited objectives and then call it a day. To fail to establish fundamentals and to eliminate the irritations that have troubled the world would not be accomplishing our objectives.'[65]

Adjournment was postponed – thanks, in part, to such passionate appeals – and it was agreed that the Americans and British would make one last effort to attain what Berle had called an 'ambitious dream' – a multilateral solution to the commercial problems of international civil aviation. But agreement was equally elusive during the second round of Swinton-Berle discussions, and by this time the issue had been taken out of the hands of the Chicago delegates, to be played out at the highest level, directly between President Roosevelt and Prime Minister Churchill. On 21 November Roosevelt sent the first in a series of notes to Churchill outlining the American position at Chicago and underlining the seriousness of the impasse. Churchill responded with detailed messages explaining why the British could not concede the American demands. Within a few days Roosevelt's request had become a veiled threat:

> I am afraid you do not fully appreciate the importance of reaching a satisfactory agreement. Our people have gone as far to meet yours as I can let them go. If the Conference should end either in no agreement or in an agreement which the American people would regard as preventing the development and use of the great air routes, the repercussions would seriously affect many other things.
>
> We are doing our best to meet your Lend-Lease needs. We will face Congress on that subject in a few weeks and it will not be in a generous mood if it and the people feel that the United Kingdom has not agreed to a generally beneficial air agreement. They will wonder about the chances of our two countries, let alone any others, working together to keep the peace if we cannot even get together on an aviation agreement.
>
> I hope you will review the situation once more and see if we cannot get together.[66]

Roosevelt hoped to use the leverage provided by American lend-lease aid to sway Churchill on the aviation issue and it was a wise card to play, given Britain's uncomfortable economic situation. But Churchill was unmoved by Roosevelt's request and, despite the president's threat, saw no reason to change his mind. He fully understood the implications for Britain of a reduction or termination of lend-lease aid, but he was determined to call Roosevelt's bluff. Churchill responded that he hoped that failure at Chicago would not produce 'the prospect of our suffering less generous treatment on Lend-Lease,' but 'even if I thought that we were to be so penalized, I would not feel myself able to agree to a decision contrary to the merits, as we see them, on this matter.'[67] It would be better, he added, to let the whole conference adjourn for a while, to allow both sides time to reassess their positions.

Roosevelt and Churchill exchanged additional telegrams over the following days in which they repeated their respective government's position. But neither leader was willing to make significant concessions to the other, and the fundamental divisions exposed at Chicago remained. Swinton, in the meantime, adopted Churchill's suggestion in committee, arguing that all the agreements reached so far should be signed, but negotiations on the commercial questions should be left over for future discussions. Berle was equally pessimistic, having learned on 27 November that, with the resignation of Cordell Hull and the appointment of Edward Stettinius as secretary of state, he was expected to resign his own post, effective the moment the conference adjourned. Stettinius was the brother-in-law of Pan Am's Juan Trippe, and it has been alleged that he influenced Roosevelt in his decision to replace Berle.[68] Swinton and Berle agreed on one last matter: all the outstanding issues between them – fifth freedom rights, frequency control, the escalator clause, and so on – would be handed over to the new international aviation organization for it to find a solution.[69]

An impasse had been reached, and from that moment the focus of the conference shifted away from the disagreements over economic issues to those areas where there was significant agreement. The technical documents, the draft international convention (minus the commercial clauses), the agreements on the interim council and the permanent organization were quickly brought forward for official endorsement. There were, however, a few outstanding issues that needed settlement.

None of the agreements included the grant of transit rights, so the United States (without prior consultation) proposed the signing of a separate document embodying the five freedoms. No nation would be forced to accept it, but the American plan was to attach this new document as a protocol to the international air convention. Many others found this proposal objectionable. The Latin American bloc gave it only lukewarm endorsement, while others, like the British, Canadians, and several European states, opposed it. The problem was not just that they had concerns about granting of fifth freedom rights, it was in having the new agreement as a protocol attached to the convention, an arrangement that suggested a connection between the two. Ultimately it was agreed that the American proposal would constitute a wholly separate five freedoms agreement.[70]

In a similar fashion, late in November the French government suggested the inclusion of the first two freedoms in the convention,[71] a proposal that was officially tabled in the plenary session by the delegate from
the Netherlands. The motion was seconded by Syria, and, as Berle wrote,
'at this point confusion broke loose.' After a brief moment of procedural
wrangling, Berle relegated the whole question to a closed subcommittee
meeting. Behind closed doors it was agreed that there would be another
transit agreement that, like the five freedoms agreement, would be
opened for signature to all members as a separate agreement independent of the international convention. The British went along; Swinton
had been given approval to concede transit rights before the conference
began. Max Hymans of the French delegation called it a 'very great
achievement' and, compared to the five freedoms agreement, he was
right. Berle was equally satisfied; the transit rights gave the United States
access to Europe (the British 'naked lack of assent can no longer bar us
from the European Continent,' was how he put it), and he was optimistic
for the future. 'If we did not get everything we dreamed of,' he concluded, 'we have made substantial progress.'[72]

Another question that remained was: where was the headquarters of
the new organization to be located? American and British opinion would
carry great weight in any decision, but here, as in so many other areas,
their opinions were divided – this time on continental lines. Swinton reported to London that he believed that Washington and London cancelled each other out and that another location would be needed. He
also felt that the designated committee might go for the American continent, in particular Canada. Canada was a fairly neutral choice, and the
Canadians had earned serous consideration through their tireless work
during the conference in Chicago. But Swinton preferred Europe. 'Our
feeling here,' he wrote, 'is that Paris might be best choice provided we
could induce the French not to insist on running the organisation in the
French language.'[73] The Ministerial Committee in London responded
with selections from both continents. 'We have considered various possible alternatives. We strongly favour Bermuda as first choice, and Paris,
despite possible language difficulties, as second choice.' Interestingly,
despite the continuing desire for Commonwealth unity, the British were
not keen on a Canadian site; 'For your personal information,' Swinton
was informed, 'we are unwilling to press Canada in view of United States
influence in Ottawa.'[74]

In the Executive Committee meeting of 20 November, Berle proposed
Canada as the location for the new organization; the French delegation

responded with a request to consider Paris. The other delegations split, largely along geographic lines, with Canada and the Latin American bloc on one side and the Europeans on the other. At first the final decision on the permanent headquarters was postponed until early December, but even here it was impossible to settle the issue. There were two votes, for the interim and permanent headquarters. On the first Canada won comfortably; on the second the committee was split right down the middle. Fifty votes were cast, twenty-five each for France and Canada; the delegate for Paraguay had left the room and the delegate for Luxembourg had left for Washington. When the delegate for Paraguay returned he voted for Canada, tipping the scale 26–25 in Canada's favour. According to one Canadian source, just as the committee president was about to pronounce Canada the winner, the Dutch delegate rose and requested that, given the absence of Luxembourg, the final decision on the permanent headquarters be left over to be decided by Interim Council of the new organization. The French and Canadians discussed the matter and agreed. 'The French delegation were extremely grateful and many countries congratulated Canada on the fairness of her stand,' the Canadian reported. 'In any event, Canada did not want its selection to be the result of an American bloc which it in principle was strongly opposing.'[75]

The selection of Montreal – Canada's largest and most cosmopolitan city and an important air centre – was made on 5 December. Montreal made sense, at least as interim headquarters, given the difficulties that the war situation would create for a European location such as Paris. As Berle put it at the end of the conference, 'as the inconvenience of transport in wartime dies away, the possibilities of a permanent seat in Europe can be more clearly seen.'[76] Swinton accepted the decision, arguing that, because the Interim Council would have very limited powers, 'I suggest that the political dangers of Canada to which I am very much alive, have less force.' The British were in a somewhat difficult position, in any event; they preferred Paris or even Brussels over Montreal, but could not do so 'in open opposition to Canada.'[77] But it was an issue that would be returned to in the near future.

One other issue dealt with language – what language would be recognized in the conference documents and used in the new organization? The conference was run in English and there was never any question, given the dominance of the United States and Great Britain, that English would be used in the organization. Language was important, and the French delegation, especially, made strong appeals for French to be recognized as an official language. French was, after all, a historic language of diplomacy and international affairs. It also was symbolic of the French position at Chicago and in aviation affairs generally. Berle was a little dismissive, referring to the French delegation 'making noises about being a great power,'[78] but the French had reason for concern that the English-speaking powers were making all the important decisions. During the conference the French delegates played a significant role, although Hymans earlier complained to Paris of the 'autocratic nature of the host power,' with the Americans appointing everyone and controlling everything.[79] Still, France had been a leading air nation before the war and there was every reason to expect that it would resume its position of influence after the war was over, and the French were determined to have that role recognized officially – in the use of the French language.

France was not the only state concerned, however; language was important to other nations as well.[80] As one Canadian put it, with a touch of Anglo-condescension: 'The French have proposed that the text of the convention be published in English and French, both texts being equally authentic. The Spanish American republics have proposed that, if more than one language is to be used, Spanish should be one of the languages used. The Brazilians and the Lebanese have made identic[al] proposals for Portuguese and Arabic respectively, the Lebanese pointing out that Arabic is spoken by 100,000,000 people. The Yugoslav Delegation have proposed that three languages should be used, one Anglo-Saxon, one Romand and one Slavonic, the latter being spoken by 250,000,000 people; the Slavonic language should be Russian. So far no similar proposal has been made by the Chinese Delegation.'[81] Despite the pleas, on 1 December the Executive Committee decided that there would be only three official languages – English, French, and Spanish.[82]

All that was left to do was to elect the members of the Interim Council, and then everyone could sign the documents and go home. The aviation organization had been given a new name, announced on 28 November: the International Civil Aviation Organization. The Interim ICAO Council was to consist of twenty-one nations, to be elected by the members but also representing three different categories: major air operators, eight seats; contributors of air facilities, five seats; and geographical representatives, eight seats (in the permanent organization, this ratio was changed to eight-seven-six). What the delegates had to do was elect the members of the Interim Council that would operate until ICAO officially came into being. There were three secret ballots, beginning with the seven states of chief importance (the eighth seat in the first group was reserved for the Soviet Union), followed by the pro-viders of facilities and the regional representatives.

The announcement of the election, in Berle's words, 'precipitated a tide of electioneering and political deals which would have done credit to a municipal election.'[83] The Latin American bloc claimed that they represented one-third of the delegations at the conference and there-fore deserved one-third of the seats on the council; others were not so sure. The Europeans believed that they were important aviation nations and therefore deserved an important number of seats. The British antici-pated being selected, but also thought that parts of the Commonwealth, India in particular, should be represented too. Other states also relished a seat and deals were made to exchange votes. One Canadian reported a rumour of an agreement to exchange support between the Latin American bloc and Belgium; he also recorded a meeting with a member of the Brazilian delegation who was worried about the negative reaction if too many Latin American states were elected. The two also noted, in passing, that they would vote for each other, too, but later the Brazilian returned, regretting that Brazil 'had been forced to agree to vote for Mexico in place of Canada in the first category.'[84] The leaders of the major delegations also were approached for support. Early on Berle re-corded a meeting with Ragnar Kumlin, the chair of the Swedish delega-tion, who wanted to know if Sweden or any other of the neutral states could be on the council. Berle said some nice words about Sweden but was not very forthcoming. Indeed, Berle added, 'I told him that I thought, all things considered, that the neutrals were lucky to be here at all.'[85] Berle also angered the British by reportedly telling an Indian delegate that he would not support India 'as it would be only a second vote for the United Kingdom.'[86]

When the voting was over, five European states were elected, India was overlooked completely, and seven of the twenty-one seats went to Latin American states, causing a good deal of consternation among other members. 'It still seems a little ridiculous that Chile *and* Peru *and* Colombia should have been elected,' one British adviser complained. 'I should have thought that European countries had far more experience in running their own international services. Before the war there were plenty of lines running in South America, but very few not owned and operated by foreigners.'[87] The following day, 7 December, Wilhelm Munthe de Morganstierne, the Norwegian ambassador to the United States and chair of his delegation, offered to relinquish Norway's seat on the council in favour of India. It was a generous offer only to be outdone by the Cubans, who offered their seat to India in place of Norway, reducing the Latin American representation to six seats.[88] That made everyone happy, but the wrangling over the election to the council was a regrettable finish to the conference.

Several agreements were signed on 7 December, the final day of the conference: the Convention on International Civil Aviation; a Final Act, which consisted of a standard form for future air agreements and a series of technical annexes; and, an Interim Agreement on International Civil Aviation, which outlined the size, shape and powers of the new Provisional International Civil Aviation Organization. In addition, there were the two transit agreements symbolizing the divisions that emerged during the conference. The first, the International Air Services Transit Agreement, granted the first two freedoms to all signing parties; the second, the International Air Transport Agreement, granted the five freedoms. While all states (except Liberia) signed the Final Act and most accepted the convention and Interim Agreement, only twenty-six and sixteen respectively signed the two-freedoms and five-freedoms agreements.[89] Support for the five freedoms came from the United States, a handful of Latin American states, Sweden, and a few others.

The documents were signed, the Interim Council was elected, and ICAO was created, although suspended in limbo until the convention was ratified by a sufficient number of states. The delegates met for one last time. Berle had the last words. 'We met in the seventeenth century in the air,' he said with a touch of Wilsonian optimism. 'We close in the twentieth century in the air. We met in an era of diplomatic intrigue and private and monopolistic privilege. We close in an era of open covenants and equal opportunity and status.'[90] The conference was over.

ICAO was conceived at the Chicago conference, and its blueprint is the Convention on International Civil Aviation (see Appendix). The aims and objectives of the new organization are set out broadly to 'develop the principles and techniques of international air navigation and to foster the planning and development of international air transport,' in order to ensure the 'safe and orderly growth' of international commercial aviation. The convention lists additional responsibilities and goals: to ensure 'safe, regular, efficient and economical air transport;' to promote flight safety and prevent 'economic waste caused by unreasonable competition;' to 'avoid discrimination' and protect the rights of members and ensure that they have a 'fair opportunity to operate international airlines;' to aid in the development of airports and air navigation facilities; and, in general, to promote 'the development of all aspects of international civil aeronautics.'

The Chicago Convention also sets out basic principles for the 'safe and orderly' development of international air services. There are many parallels to the Paris Convention; the convention begins with the assertion that 'every State has complete and exclusive sovereignty over the airspace above its territory.' It applies only to civil aircraft and gives the right of innocent passage across each member's territory to aircraft traveling for non-traffic purposes. But all commercial services would have to be negotiated. Regulations and rules of conduct are listed both for the states operating air services and for those member nations into which they fly, including such items as the use of air navigation facilities, registration of aircraft, prevention of the spread of disease, the right to search aircraft, customs and immigration procedures, licenses and airworthiness certificates, and so on.

The process of standardization begins with the Chicago Convention's first thirty-six articles, which set out the broad principles of air navigation that all contracting states agree to follow. These principles include the basic sovereignty, territorial, and transit rights that enable nations to control their own airspace, plus basic rules of the air dealing with a broad range of subjects such as airport charges, registration, disease control, right of search, customs and immigration procedures, accident investigation, licensing and certificates of airworthiness, and cargo restrictions. In addition, each member undertakes to 'provide in its territory, airports, radio services, meteorological services and other air navigation facilities to facilitate international air navigation, in accordance with the standards and practices recommended or established from time to time, pursuant to the Convention.' Furthermore, members agree to 'adopt and put into operation the appropriate standard systems of communications procedure, codes, markings, signals, lighting and other operational practices and rules,' and, finally, to 'collaborate in international measures to secure the publication of aeronautical maps and charts in accordance with standards which may be recommended or established from time to time, pursuant to this Convention' (Article 28).

In addition, all members agree to work to secure the 'highest practicable degree of uniformity in regulations, standards, procedures, and organization in relation to aircraft, personnel, airways and auxiliary services in all matters in which such uniformity will facilitate and improve air navigation.' To achieve this goal, ICAO is to prepare 'International Standards and Recommended Practices' dealing with different aspects of air navigation in an effort to promote standardization, safety, and efficiency in international air travel. The standards are essentially those requirements considered *necessary* for air navigation, the recommended practices are those believed to be *desirable* for air navigation. The ICAO Council was given the key responsibility to amend and/or adopt the Standards and Recommended Practices which were to be attached to the convention as annexes; the Final Act contains draft annexes dealing with the following: '(a) Communications systems and air navigation aids, including ground marking; (b) Characteristics of airports and landing areas; (c) Rules of the air and air traffic control practices; (d) Licensing of operating and mechanical personnel; (e) Airworthiness of aircraft; (f) Registration and identification of aircraft; (g) Collection and exchange of meteorological information; (h) Log Books; (i) Aeronautical maps and charts; (j) Customs and immigration procedures; (k) Aircraft in distress and investigation of accidents; and such other matters concerned with the safety, regularity, and efficiency of air navigation as may from time to time appear appropriate' (Article 37).[91]

The new organization would in many ways resemble the International Commission for Air Navigation and other international bodies of that era. It was to consist of an assembly of all contracting states and a smaller council that would administer the whole organization. The assembly is the legislative body, and it was to be convened annually by the council, and elect its own president. Each member was given one vote, a majority of members would constitute a quorum, and decisions were to be made by a majority of votes. Broadly speaking, the new assembly would oversee and modify the Chicago Convention, and it was given broad powers to accept or refer matters of importance to the council and 'deal with any matter within the sphere of action of the Organization not specifically assigned to the Council.' One of the key responsibilities of the assembly would be to elect the states represented on the council.

At its regular conference gatherings, or assemblies, several important committees were to be established by the membership, including a Credentials Committee, a Coordinating Committee to oversee the work of the various committees and commissions, and an Executive Committee. The Executive Committee includes the presidents of the council and assembly and delegates from all the contracting states, and it serves as a kind of steering committee. It considers the amendments and important matters to be referred to the assembly, prepares the lists of nominees for various positions for election by the assembly, and gives advice to the president of the assembly. In the 1950s and 1960s the Executive Committee often became the focus of sometimes acrimonious political debate on resolutions to be put to the assembly and on membership issues.[92]

The council was to consist of twenty-one states; the members would be elected by the assembly for three year terms or, more specifically, until the election of a new council. The members represent their nations and act more in terms of national interest than from a purely international perspective. As in the assembly, council decisions require a majority vote. The council was responsible for electing, also on a three-year term, its president who would be responsible for calling meetings of the council, and to select a secretary general (likened to a chief executive officer for the organization) and other personnel as necessary. The respective duties of these two key individuals were not absolutely clear at first, and much discussion ensued in an effort to clarify their relationship to each other and to ICAO.[93]

The council is ultimately responsible to the assembly, to which it reports, but it has evolved as the central institution in ICAO's framework. It decides for itself how often it will hold its sessions, and within a few years the council essentially became a permanent body meeting in continuous session, with each council member appointing a permanent representative and establishing an office at the headquarters in Montreal. In 1950 and 1952 resolutions were passed that obliged council members to provide permanent representatives to the council. The president of the council is elected from names supplied by the various members and does not need to be a current member of the council. The position of president (and secretary general) is a purely 'international' one and the president is to represent no individual nation; thus, if the person elected president is already a council representative then that nation appoints another representative to fill the vacancy. In addition, the council elects three council representatives as vice-presidents, although these individuals maintain their existing positions as state representatives and council members.[94]

The council's basic functions are to oversee the workings of ICAO, to approve and amend the Standards and Recommended Practices, to report to the assembly on its activities and any other duties or matters given to it by the assembly, to conduct research, disseminate information, study and investigate anything dealing with international aviation, and to 'request, collect, examine and publish information relating to the advancement of air navigation.' All ICAO members agree to submit to the council statistical information about their airlines, financial statements, traffic reports, and aviation agreements.

The ICAO Council also helps to settle disputes between contracting states, and is to report infractions of the Chicago Convention to the assembly and to the states involved. If those states involved in a dispute cannot agree on an acceptable negotiated solution, then, on application by one of the concerned states, the matter is to be left up to the council to decide. If one of the concerned parties still finds this arrangement unacceptable, that state can agree to a small arbitration tribunal or appeal for a final decision to the Permanent Court of International Justice. If at that stage one of the parties fails to conform to the final decision, the council can suspend that state's voting power, or, in the case of an airline, ask all other members to refuse permission to that state's airlines to fly through their airspace. The council also has the authority to approach states and make recommendations if it feels that the airports and/or air navigation facilities in that state are not adequate for safe and efficient air services. Arrangements can also be made for ICAO to agree to pick up the cost of providing the necessary facilities, and the council was given the right, with the consent of the member state, to administer and maintain airports and facilities and charge the member 'reasonable charges' for the services. But the council was given no power to force any member to do anything it doesn't want to do.

Two additional important duties of the council are to elect the Air Transport Committee and to select an Air Navigation Commission. The role of the Air Transport Committee is not clearly spelled out in the Chicago Convention. It is responsible to the council, its members 'shall be chosen from among the representatives of the members of the Council,' and its duties were to be determined by the council (Article 54). The Interim Council established a short-lived Air Transport Committee that was open to all members, but in 1948 the council established the permanent Air Transport Committee with twelve members selected from council representatives. Ultimately, among its other duties, the Air Transport Committee was given responsibility to sort out the economic questions left over from Chicago.

Conversely, the Air Navigation Commission's duties are clearly set out in the convention. The Air Navigation Commission represents the technical wing of the organization and was given the key responsibility for recommending to the ICAO Council new annexes and modifications to existing ones. It comprises twelve individuals selected from a list of names of qualified aviation experts recommended by member states. It establishes and directs the workings of the many technical sub-commissions and advises the council 'concerning the collection and communication to the contracting States of all information which it considers necessary and useful for the advancement of air navigation' (Article 57). With respect to technical matters, the Air Navigation Commission became one of the central bodies in the whole organization. Within a few years the council would find it necessary to appoint additional committees, including a Finance Committee, to handle administrative financial matters and, perhaps most importantly, the Legal Committee.

Who was to pay for all this activity? Each member-state was made responsible for paying for its own delegation to the annual ICAO Assembly, and for its representatives on the council and any of its committees or commissions. The other costs of the organization would be divided among the members 'on the basis which it shall from time to time determine.' The basic criteria for payment levels, beyond a basic minimum and maximum, were to be a mixture of the extent of each member's participation in international civil aviation and the ability of that member to pay. Any member that failed to pay its share could have its voting power suspended by the assembly. Beyond that, the council was to administer ICAO's finances, and it was given the power to decide the salaries of the president, secretary general, and all other personnel. The council would present an annual budget to the assembly; the assembly amends the budget if necessary and votes on it.

This new convention was to supercede the Paris and Havana conventions, but it did not prevent ICAO from making arrangements with other international organizations. Moreover, members of ICAO were granted the right to join other aviation organizations, subject to the International Convention and providing that they register the new agreements with the council. The convention was to come into force one month after it had been ratified by twenty-six states. In the meantime, the Provisional International Civil Aviation Organization (created by the Interim Agreement on International Civil Aviation) was to begin operations and last until the permanent convention came into force. The Interim Agreement was to come into force when 'accepted' by twenty-six states, and for the participants at the Chicago conference there was confidence that this would happen in the very near future. There were still many issues to be decided: finding a permanent location for the headquarters; admission of new members, especially ex-enemy states; relations with the United Nations; the final preparation and approval of the Standards and Recommended Practices; and, of course, all the commercial questions. But, at that moment, they were all in the future.

The delegates returned to their homes in December and soon began an examination of what had happened at Chicago.[95] The gap between the two leading air powers seemed small, and there was widespread optimism that this gap could be bridged in a relatively short period of time. Likewise, it was argued that more effort and a willingness to compromise during the final days of the conference might have saved the day. If only they had had more time, some argued, or a chance to get away from the pressures of the Stevens Hotel, if only for a few days, things might have turned out differently. A good deal of finger-pointing ensued and the responsibility for failure was distributed liberally to every major participant from Berle, Swinton, and Beaverbrook to Churchill and Roosevelt. Less attention was paid to the fact that the British and Americans remained divided on several key issues which went to the heart of their proposals for the post war air.

The United States hoped to open up the rules of international air traffic enough to permit the expansion of American aviation around the world; American airlines needed entry rights, access to airports, and the right to pick up and discharge sufficient passengers and cargo to make international services commercially viable. Fearing international regulations and restrictions, the American negotiators worked for and achieved an international organization with advisory powers only. They were willing to compromise on limited frequency control in exchange for the escalator clause and fifth freedom rights because they were convinced that American aviation strength and efficiency would be rewarded with a substantial share of future international routes and services. Failing on the fifth freedom and escalator clause, however, they concluded that it would be better to try to negotiate for them independently rather than accept less at Chicago.

The British were more defensive, recognizing their own present weakness in aviation terms and the likelihood of a continued reliance on American generosity in the postwar era. At Chicago the British team sought protection in a strong international organization with powers to regulate international aviation. It was clear to Swinton and others in advance of the conference that the Americans would not be amenable to the White Paper, so a fall-back position was prepared which Swinton largely achieved: a weaker international organization with the United States as a member, the exchange of the first two freedoms and no bilateral negotiations with the Americans. There was movement towards the fifth freedom, but only under strict conditions and providing it was exchanged for a degree of frequency control. But to concede the escalator clause on fifth freedom traffic would, at least in British eyes, unacceptably limit that control. British actions at Chicago, therefore, were hardly mindlessly obstructive; on the contrary, obstructionism was only one tactic used to prevent the signing of an agreement that would have greatly favoured the United States. Like the Americans, rather than compromise further at Chicago, the British believed they could negotiate better deals bilaterally, in situations where they could insist on an equal division of traffic and frequencies.

The development of international commercial aviation and the Anglo-American impasse at Chicago foreshadowed future difficulties between allies in the shaping of other postwar international institutions. And, perhaps more than any other single issue, Anglo-American aviation diplomacy reflected the relative shift of power and influence between Britain and the United States, a trend begun years before 1939 but accelerated by the war. The Chicago conference was hardly responsible for the great disparity in air strength or for the differences in Anglo-American perspectives, but, as one of the first and largest of wartime international gatherings, it did provide the stage on which these differences were played out.

There was a moment when the wartime internationalist spirit might have triumphed in a multilateral aviation convention with traffic privileges to which all air states could subscribe, but spirit alone could not mask the glaring divisions between one internationalism which pressed for the regulation of aviation and another which called for reduction of many barriers and the opening of the skies to more competition. Chicago showed why a multilateral convention – containing all five freedoms – was unlikely ever to be achieved. Fifth freedom rights threatened local air services between states, and few governments were willing to jeopardize these services or shed their regional perspectives in search of a truly international understanding. While there was widespread support for the ambitious dream of a multilateral air convention for commercial traffic rights, it was, after all, only a dream.

The failure to agree on commercial issues was the greatest disappointment to emerge from what was in many other ways a very successful conference. An enormous amount of energy had been invested in negotiating an agreement for the regulation of international air travel, but little progress was made. Nevertheless, the failure itself had a profound impact on ICAO and meant that the new organization would not have regulatory powers over the unfolding of post war international civil aviation. Had such powers been given to the organization it is likely that some nations would not have joined. The International Civil Aviation Organization was very much the creation of its member states, and finding a solution to these commercial problems remained an objective of the new organization. The ultimate goal of negotiating a multilateral agreement was reaffirmed regularly by the organization and, however elusive and unlikely it was to be realized, considerable time and effort were devoted to this goal over the next sixty years.

But no one who was at Chicago would underestimate what *had* been accomplished. 'Nothing could be more important,' Welch Pogue wrote many years later. 'Without ICAO, or its equivalent, worldwide airline operations between nations would be in chaos.'[96] The new organization was given very broad objectives, especially, but not exclusively, in the technical field, and its responsibilities – and moral authority – would grow through the years. And, equally important, at least in the short term, it was given the responsibility of finding a way around the Anglo-American impasse and to resolve all the economic questions left over from the Chicago conference. It was a tall order; PICAO's first agenda was full even before Adolf Berle lowered the gavel, bringing the Chicago conference to a close. It would be Berle's last act in international civil aviation; for ICAO it was just the beginning.

3

PICAO: 'An International Conference Always at Work'

Let us go forward to set up an Interim Administration, consolidate our achievements, and the Administration, if we set it up will in effect, as the President implied, be an international conference always at work.[1]

After Chicago, with so many diplomats, advisers, and technical experts – all familiar with the problems of aviation – present in North America, it not surprising that discussions, meetings, and negotiations continued in different ways after the conference was finished. The United States had opposed creating an international organization with regulatory powers and preferred that these things be settled bilaterally. Such bilateral negotiations began during the Chicago conference and continued in the weeks that followed: fifth freedom rights were bargained for with Spain, Sweden, Denmark, and Iceland, and, in February 1945, a more exclusive arrangement was made with Canada that did not include fifth freedom rights and preserved a monopoly system through a strict allocation of routes. An air agreement was also signed with Ireland, which included mandatory stops at Shannon airport. In the Middle East, the United States began negotiations with several countries and gave the Egyptians the American-built Payne Field near Cairo, in exchange for American access to Cairo itself.[2]

The British meanwhile were equally busy. Before returning home from Chicago, the British delegation flew to Montreal for more Commonwealth aviation conversations, and the result was the creation of the Commonwealth Air Transport Council, a permanent advisory group that was to try to align the aviation policies of the various members of the Commonwealth. A permanent secretariat was established and the CATC continued to operate for decades, but the original hopes that it would lead to the creation of a joint Commonwealth aviation policy were never realized.[3] It did, however, provide the machinery through which the British government began negotiating for the organization of imperial trunk air routes to Australia via India, and to South Africa via Cairo. At the same time, air talks were held with the French and other sympathetic European states in an effort to fashion a united front to resist American pressure.[4]

Despite the creation of ICAO and the level of agreement on technical issues that the Chicago conference had produced, many of the prewar commercial aviation problems reemerged in the months following the conference. The United States still had the airplanes and economic muscle, while Great Britain held fast to its widespread bases and colonial possessions, and an element of rivalry between the two nations reappeared. The British were concerned that the American negotiation of bilateral agreements would effectively bypass and isolate Great Britain, and they felt this increased pressure to reach an accommodation with the Americans. The Americans were concerned that the British were using their influence against the United States in Europe and the Middle East, making it harder for the United States to negotiate bilateral agreements.[5] The July 1945 election in Britain saw the defeat of the Churchill government, but the new Labour government did not unveil a significantly different air policy, at least with respect to international civil aviation, other than an unsuccessful attempt to resurrect the idea of internationalization (see Chapter 5). And, informal Anglo-American discussions in August that year did not result in much progress being made.[6]

The problems that had caused the stalemate at Chicago did not go away and, with the revival of international commercial aviation at the end of the war, a clash between the United States and Great Britain was almost inevitable. The two allies approached the end of the war with differing viewpoints: the Americans advocated the negotiation of bilateral agreements that would open the airways of the world to American airlines; the British, on the other hand, called for a multilateral solution, a regulated international system with controls on routes and frequencies and safeguards to protect the weaker nations. Given the great disparity between American and British strength in civil aviation (in 1945 the United States controlled an estimated 72 per cent of the world's air commerce and the United Kingdom 12 per cent,[7] thanks in part to the growth of BOAC's total route mileage to almost 70,000 miles by the end of the year), it is not surprising that American calls for increased competition in the air after the war were met with considerable trepidation in British circles. The British government was determined to receive its fair share of international air traffic, and it was feared that if the Americans were allowed to compete with less regulation it would be next to impossible for Britain ever to catch up. At the heart of the debate was the grant of fifth freedom rights; as one observer wrote in 1947: 'everybody's fifth freedom is someone else's third and fourth freedoms.'[8] To grant fifth freedom rights was in effect to give a foreign operator the right to compete with direct international services. The problem, of course, was how to negotiate this right without endangering domestic airlines.

With the end of the war the United States, Great Britain, and other states returned to negotiating bilateral agreements for the operation of international air services. The process of change from military to civilian control over aviation began in Europe and North America, as national airlines were revived and a number of military air services were transformed into commercial ones. In the United Kingdom, the transition to peacetime aviation was a gradual one and it necessitated, at least in the initial stages, limitations on the rights afforded to foreign operators in British airspace and at British airports.[9] For their part, the Americans argued that the British were blocking the spread of American aviation by refusing to negotiate for the commercial use of American-leased bases, and by using their influence in foreign and imperial capitals to thwart American negotiating efforts. The State Department accused the British of obstruction; London protested, of course. 'It has been part of our policy,' one memo in the Prime Minister's Office explained, 'to secure the maximum support in Europe and the Middle East for the principles to which we adhere. Many countries have voluntarily sought our advice and we have tendered it to others. Naturally, in advising these countries we advocate the British and not the American wide open door policy. This is a natural corollary of the failure to agree at Chicago and American resentment is clearly illogical.'[10]

In any event, the end of the war meant the revival of commercial air services in Europe and in other parts of the world; it also led to the expansion of existing air services. Many new airports had been built for military purposes, and military transport aircraft were converted for civilian use. The European state-owned airlines were resuscitated, at least among the victorious allies; for the former enemies things moved a little slower. Italy was permitted to resume commercial flying soon after the war ended; in West Germany a new company with an old name – Lufthansa – began commercial services only in 1955. In the United States, Pan American Airways' monopoly over international services was broken. The Civil Aeronautics Board gave international routes to American Export Airlines and TWA after the war, while Braniff Airways received routes to Latin America, and TWA and Northwest Airlines were given rights to the Pacific. Following the negotiation of bilateral agreements, American companies began Atlantic services through most of the major cities in Europe; in return, services to the United States were established by BOAC, Air France, and SAS in 1946, and by Sabena in 1947 and Swissair in 1949.[11]

Hopes ran high that a multilateral aviation agreement would be quickly negotiated but this was not the case, and the negotiation of bilateral agreements continued. This lack of a multilateral agreement, especially one that included the setting of airline rates, and the more general deadlock over commercial questions at the Chicago conference, was the backdrop for the creation of IATA, the International Air Transport Association. There was already an International Air Traffic Association, formed in August 1919, with its headquarters in The Hague and a membership of some thirty members in 1939. But it was decided that, like ICAO, a new airline organization was needed to replace the original one. Like ICAN, the original Air Traffic Association was dormant during the war, but it survived until it was replaced by IATA. Its last meeting was held in London on 17 September 1945.[12]

Taking advantage of the presence of so many airline executives at the Chicago conference, a meeting of representatives of thirty-four airlines was held right at the end of the conference, on 6 December 1944. The meeting was chaired by Herbert Symington, who switched hats from that of a member of the Canadian delegation to that of president of Trans-Canada Airlines. A committee was established, chaired by John C. Cooper, the vice-president of Pan Am, to draft articles of association to be considered by the airline representatives. These articles were confirmed at Havana in April 1945, and IATA was born. It was created as a voluntary association, open to any airline company that operated international commercial air services, providing that the company's country of registry was a member of ICAO. Its goals were: '(1) To promote safe, regular and economical air transport for the benefit of the peoples of the world; to foster air commerce and to study the problems connected therewith; (2) To provide the means for collaboration among the air transport enterprises engaged directly or indirectly in international air transport services; (3) To cooperate with ICAO and other international organizations.' And, regardless of the calls for open competition in the air, IATA became the key organization in the establishment – free from political pressure – of airline rates.[13]

It was recognized that there would be a need for constant liaison and collaboration with ICAO, so it was agreed to establish the headquarters of IATA near that of ICAO. Consequently, once the Articles of Association were approved by the Canadian government, the first Annual General Meeting of IATA was held in Montreal in October 1945. With over forty members and more than a dozen associate members in attendance at the first meeting, Herbert Symington became IATA's first president, John Cooper the chair, and William Hildred the secretary general. With both IATA and the future ICAO being situated in Montreal, one journalist was prompted to declare Montreal 'the air capital of the world.'[14]

There was lots of work to do before the opening of the First Interim Assembly of PICAO. A suitable location needed to be found, one with enough space to handle all of the expected delegates and advisers; rules and regulations needed to be established; agendas had to be approved, dates scheduled, and the size and shape of the secretariat needed to be discussed. The Interim ICAO Council would have to meet first, so it could produce a budget, but there was a question whether it should then issue the invitations for the Interim Assembly or the members should be advised in advance to be prepared to come on short notice. Or could the Interim Council and Interim Assembly meet together, at the same time? It was not even completely clear what the roles of the president and secretary general would be. And membership on the Interim Council – would this be a full or part-time position?

The Interim Agreement became effective on 6 June 1945, and the date for the first meeting of the Interim Council was set for August, by which time forty-four nations had accepted the agreement.[15] A few weeks in advance of the first meeting, the Canadian government established a small Preparatory Committee to make the necessary arrangements. Chaired by Wing Commander P.A. Cumyn, an official in the Canadian cabinet secretariat, this small committee prepared the first agenda for the Interim Council and oversaw the preparation of the rules and regulations for staffing and administering the new organization.[16] Moreover, informal discussions in Montreal and Washington began as early as January 1945, primarily, but not exclusively, between American, British, and Canadian officials.

The Canadians were also particularly keen on reopening the economic issues; one official explained that, because of the role they had played at Chicago in trying to bring together the Americans and British, they had a heightened desire to finish the job as soon as possible. It was also important not to lose momentum. As Herbert Symington wrote to Sir Arthur Street, the permanent under-secretary in the Air Ministry and also a Chicago alumnus, 'you will probably think that I am a hog for punishment, but I feel that a permanent convention with control should be set up soon or it may not be set up at all, and that we ought to be big enough to do it and that if we don't, we may seriously regret it.'[17] But the Americans were less than forthcoming; both Warner and Pogue vetoed any action at that time, especially before the United States had ratified the convention. 'If the Convention, as it now stands,' Pogue wrote to Symington, 'is to be extensively modified and changed, particularly in the field where there has been so much controversy, the ultimate ratification by our Senate will not only be long delayed but might even be endangered. This is a risk which I do not think we should take.'[18] The economic questions would not go away, but, in the meantime, they would be left to the Interim Council to sort out.

Almost immediately questions arose about who might be qualified to serve as president and secretary general or in the chairs of the key committees. Officially, these were decisions for the Interim Council of ICAO to make, but there were unofficial discussions months in advance. There seems to have been a desire to establish a kind of geographical balance, a mixture of Europeans and Americans in the key positions. One Canadian had an American and Briton in mind for the two top positions, and recommended that a Scandinavian be picked for another key post. At an April meeting in Washington, American and Canadian officials discussed the issues and: 'generally agreed that some attempt should be made before the first meeting of the Council to reach agreement among a few of the more important countries with regard to the senior appointments. It was felt that this agreement could not go beyond the six or seven most senior posts; and that if appointees of sufficiently high caliber were available roughly three of these should go to European nations and three to nations from the Western Hemisphere. It was felt that the President might come from the United States and the Secretary-General from the U.K. or vice-versa.'[19]

Edward Warner, the vice-chair of the U.S. Civil Aeronautics Board, was clearly the front runner. A native of Pittsburgh, Pennsylvania and a graduate of Harvard University, he had a long distinguished career in aviation as a professor of aeronautical engineering at the Massachusetts Institute of Technology, writer, editor, and civil servant, serving as Assistant Secretary of the Navy for Aeronautics. He also had been a principal player at the Chicago conference. He was later remembered by

IATA's Sir William Hildred as a 'large, loose-built man with the face of a scholar, kindly, intelligent, [and] compassionate.'[20] On different occasions both Welch Pogue of the CAB and Stokeley Morgan of the State Department informally told Canadian officials that Warner would be their choice for either president or secretary general. The Canadians were agreeable; one Canadian official later described Warner as 'a thoroughly efficient, indeed a brilliant, administrator.'[21] Within a few weeks the British indicated that they too would welcome Warner as president.

For secretary general the British recommended Albert Roper, the secretary-general of ICAN.[22] A Paris-born lawyer and veteran of the First World War, Roper became secretary-general of ICAN in 1922 and kept the position until the official termination of ICAN in 1947. Roper made sense; as the author of *La Convention Du 13 Octobre 1919* (1930), he literally wrote the book on ICAN. He had the experience and brought a certain continuity from ICAN to ICAO, and he was European. Even better, from an Anglo-American perspective, he was French.[23]

As for a British representative, the British government preferred to have a Briton in the chair of one of the important committees, such as the Air Navigation Commission.[24] Ultimately Sir Frederick Tymms was appointed as Britain's permanent representative on the council and chair of the Air Navigation Commission. Tymms had led a varied and full career in aviation as a member of the Indian civil service and had been a member of the Indian delegation at Chicago. He returned to Britain after Indian independence and was enticed out of retirement to represent Britain on the ICAO Council. The epitome of a British civil servant, he was later remembered for the 'calm authority with which he presided, fully briefed on every point however abstruse, defusing overheated debate, distilling sound common sense in outlining clear paths forward through the most complex of issues – imparting throughout "the pure milk of Tymmsian wisdom and good humour."'[25] Tymms, Warner, and Roper, along with a few others, brought their wartime experiences, dedication to international aviation, and the promise of the Chicago conference to the new organization and went on – as members of the founding generation – to develop and shape ICAO in its formative years.

The Interim Council held its first meeting in Montreal on 15 August, 1945, and more than one participant noted that this first meeting occurred the day after the surrender of the Japanese forces in the Pacific. It was an auspicious moment for the launching of the first *postwar* international aviation organization. With representatives from the twenty elected states the Interim Council met almost continuously, in four long sessions, until the first Interim Assembly meetings the following year. Several floors were rented in the Dominion Square Building in downtown Montreal, with the participating delegations taking additional rooms in nearby hotels. It was a modest beginning, with the largest room containing tables pushed together in a square with a small folded name-card on the table for each participating state. For most open meetings there was also a place for IATA at one end of the table. There were problems with the arrangements; as one American observer wrote: 'Quarters are somewhat cramped and no more than adequate at best. The large conference room is located between a noisy hall and a room from which the sounds of typewriting activity are a noticeable distraction, and people keep going back and forth from this room through the conference room to the hall. Furniture is sparse and simple. Even the offices of Mr Warner, the President of the Council, and other top officials are small and contain unupholstered furniture.'[26]

As expected, in the first order of business Edward Warner was elected president of the Interim Council and Albert Roper was appointed secretary general, and over the following months the Interim Council more clearly delineated the division of responsibilities between the president and secretary general. The latter was to act as chief executive and administrative officer for the organization, with responsibility to provide secretariat services for the assemblies, the council, the regional meetings, and the various committees, as well as the appointment of staff. The council president's duties included conducting external affairs with states and other international organizations, to act as the agent of the council when the latter was in recess, and to conduct special liaison missions, especially in dealing with the United Nations.[27]

Numerous committees and subcommittees were established to look after everything from credentials, personnel, and public information to budgets and finance. Preliminary budgets for 1945–46 and 1946–47 were prepared and revised, and each member state was informed of its proportionate share of the operating costs. Additional committees were established as well, for particular matters. For example, in February 1946 the Committee on Joint Support of Air Navigation Services was created when the government of Greece requested financial assistance to help rebuild its damaged airports and facilities. The Interim Assembly ultimately agreed that it should provide funds for conferences, investigations, and discussions of these kinds of issues, but not for capital expenditures for airport construction in Athens or anywhere else.[28]

In addition to the Interim Council were the Air Transport and Air Navigation Committees, whose roles were set out in the Interim Agreement. The Air Transport Committee was responsible for examining the economic issues left over from the Chicago conference and some legal issues dealing with air law and the settlement of disputes. The major task of the Air Navigation Committee was to coordinate and supervise the activities of the technical subcommittees or working groups, which were renamed ICAO divisions by the Interim Council on 30 November 1945.[29] The Air Navigation Committee was chaired by the Australian A.R. McComb, with Lieutenant Colonel J. Verhaegan of Belgium serving as vice chair, but the divisions were comprised of aviation experts recommended by the various member states (rather than state-appointed delegates) and their goal was to examine the draft technical annexes from the Chicago conference and the responses from the participating states, and to continue work on the production of technical annexes setting out the standards and procedures to be followed by all ICAO members.

The focus of these various technical divisions included aerodromes, air routes and ground aids, airworthiness, meteorology, rules of the air, communications and radio aids to air navigation, search and rescue, accident investigation, operating standards, aeronautical maps, and personnel licensing. In addition, the Special Radio Technical Division was created (convening for the first time in September 1946) to consider 'the problems of coordination among member States of technical research and development which may lead to improvements in air navigation radio facilities and related Standards, Practices and Procedures.'[30] Considerable agreement on technical standards had been reached at the Chicago conference, but the final approval of the annexes was postponed to give more time for the member governments to study and make further recommendations.[31]

These committees and the technical divisions met numerous times in the months leading up to the first meeting of the Interim Assembly, and much work was accomplished. All members of the organization were welcome to participate in the work of the divisions, but the greatest contributions came from those countries with well-developed aviation industries. It is no surprise that the official comments on the draft annexes produced at the Chicago conference came primarily from the United States, the United Kingdom, Canada, Australia, and Sweden, although responses to several drafts also came from France, South Africa, India, Spain, Norway, Switzerland, and the Netherlands.

Much of the work was focused on reconciling the different safety and technical standards then in use by the different members and trying to find not only the best and safest methods to use globally, but also methods that would be acceptable to the members. In some cases it was necessary to agree on basic terminology – did the American word 'airways' have the same meaning as 'air routes,' which was used in more countries? Even with the agreement on the words 'air routes' there was a need further to classify air routes into different classes of navigation depending on how they were organized (established for visual flying or non-visual flying, etc.). Similarly it was agreed to replace the words 'landing fields,' which had been used in the Chicago draft annexes, with the more generic 'aerodromes,' a term that was then further subdivided into 'land airports,' 'water airports,' and 'airfields.' The need for agreement on methods of classification and definitions served to highlight the basic function of the organization to provide the framework for discussion and negotiation and to collect information and statistics from its members.[32]

With the safety of international aviation being the primary objective of the organization it is not surprising that much attention was focused on establishing the rules of the air with a view to facilitating the movement of air traffic while at the same time maximizing air safety. Here the organization benefited from its predecessor, in that the rules laid down by ICAN in 1919 were already largely accepted and used by most nations. Agreement in principle was reached easily, and the ICAN rules were amended and ultimately adopted by the Rules of the Air Division and Interim Council to be published as 'Recommendations' and accepted and implemented by the member states. These rules included general flight rules, both visual and instrument flight rules, and listed the lights and signals that were to be used to facilitate air navigation.

Important work was completed by other divisions too. The RAC Division, responsible for air traffic control procedures, took the existing ICAN procedures, the relevant draft annex from the Chicago conference, plus comments from the governments of the United States, Australia, Canada, and India to produce new procedures for adoption by the Interim Council. Its goal was generally to devise procedures that would prevent air collisions but also to factor in airport congestion and different atmospheric conditions that might affect aircraft safety. It agreed that air traffic control should be a 'state service' and devised a new text establishing standards for visual and instrument flight control and standards for flight information service. These recommendations were adopted and published for the use of members early in 1946. The Airworthiness Division, which was charged with revising Annex G of the Chicago Convention, met in March and April 1946 and, using ICAN's similar codes as a starting point, produced new safety standards for the design and construction of aircraft. If approved, these new standards were to be applied to passenger aircraft manufactured after 1951 and used on regularly scheduled air services.[33]

Agreement was not reached in several divisions, however. In the PEL Division, which was given responsibility for establishing standards for the licensing of operating and mechanical personnel (including airline pilots, air traffic controllers, and flight engineers), there were divisions over important questions. The British, for example, rejected the method for determining the amount of flying experience that was necessary for licensing an airline pilot. Similarly, the American representatives opposed the proposed length of time between required medical examinations for pilots. Consequently, these issues and several others were left over for further discussion and study.

Nevertheless, by the time the first meeting of the Interim ICAO Assembly opened in May 1946, nine of the eleven technical divisions reporting to the Air Navigation Committee had produced recommendations that had been approved by the Interim Council and were to be published and sent out for the comments of the various member states.[34] These were still only recommendations however, and the Interim Assembly subsequently resolved that it was premature to accept these recommendations as legally binding at that time and to leave them for further study. It was left for the permanent council and organization to finalize the Standards and Recommended Practices (see Chapter 4).

One decision of the Interim Council that would have far reaching ramifications was the decision to hold Regional Air Navigation Meetings, even though a regional dimension for ICAO was not called for specifically in the Chicago Convention. PICAO turned out pretty much as expected, wrote Edward Warner in 1946, but 'those who worked at Chicago failed to anticipate some of the needs that have manifested themselves in practice ... It was inevitable,' he continued, 'that there would have been such omissions in agreements prepared under such pressure and with the world still at war; and fortunately they have done no harm, for the documents contain language broad enough to cover almost any action that the nations may agree would raise the standards of safety and regularity in air navigation.' In this category Warner included the 'indispensable role of the regional meeting.'[35]

Navigational requirements for the successful operation of air services differed from one region to another – trans-Pacific services spanning great distances to connect only a few nations were quite different from

European operations that connected many contiguous nations. 'As the operational and technical problems inherent in different parts of the world varied considerably,' ICAO *Journal* explained, 'it was logical that planning and implementation of the required ground services should be carried out on a regional basis.'[36] It was also believed to be important to maintain air navigation standards in all parts of the world, and to do so required international collaboration, but in many cases the use of facilities and the problems in maintaining them in different parts of the world affected only a few nations. Why not have the countries in a particular region – including those who would be expected to provide the facilities and those who would be affected by the lack of them – gather together to come to a mutual agreement on the technical problems behind the operation of air services? Consequently, the Interim Council divided the world into ten regions and called for meetings to be held in each of them. (In 1952 the number of regions was reduced to eight, with the merger of the North and South Pacific regions into one and the same for the South Atlantic and South American regions.) But there was some division over whether these regional gatherings might usurp some of the functions of the central organization.[37]

The North Atlantic area was a good example. The first regional meeting was the North Atlantic Air Route Service Conference, hosted by the Irish government in Dublin in March 1946. It was called to examine what was needed to support civil air travel in the North Atlantic area and to discuss 'the arrangements which should be made through the Provisional Organization for the future maintenance of any needed Secretariat of a regional character.'[38] It was particularly important at that moment because, with the end of the war, many existing military air facilities would be suspended.[39] Most North Atlantic states attended, as did several observers. The conference compiled a *North Atlantic Route Service Manual* to help implement the Standards and Recommended Practices across the North Atlantic. The conference recommendations were approved by the Interim Council in April 1946.[40] A second meeting – for the European and Mediterranean region – was held later in Paris, and it also produced a route manual and many recommendations for the institution of air navigation facilities.[41] By early 1947 additional regional meetings were held in the Caribbean, the Middle East, and the South Pacific.[42]

A logical development from the staging of regional meetings was the establishment of permanent regional offices in key locations around the world, an idea first recommended by the Air Navigation Committee. Ultimately, each region was to have its own regional office to compile and edit regional manuals, to act as a clearing house for correspondence and information, and to organize and serve as a secretariat for the regional meetings.[43] Not surprisingly, Paris was chosen as the site of a regional office, taking over the vacant premises of ICAN. Another office was soon opened in Cairo. Additional regional offices – in Melbourne and Lima, for example – were created in subsequent years, and they have come to play a central role in the smooth functioning of ICAO.

It was also important to maintain liaison with other international or-ganizations, at least those with which ICAO would be closely involved. For example, close relations were maintained with ICAN, made all the easier thanks to the presence of Albert Roper in positions of influence in both organizations, until ICAN permanently dissolved once the new con-vention came into force. Similarly, representatives from IATA attended the second session of the Interim Council, and the close collaboration between the two aviation bodies continued from that point. Indeed, for more than ten years following the creation of IATA and ICAO, it was common for the two leaders – William Hildred and Edward Warner – to meet for lunch every Friday the two men were in Montreal.[44] There were other groups, too, that sent observers to various PICAO activities,[45] but the most important outside organization was the United Nations. No relationship existed with the United Nations, but a negotiating commit-tee was set up to make the arrangements through the U.N.'s Economic and Social Council to have ICAO brought into a 'relationship' with the United Nations.[46]

Louis Hyde, an American official, travelled to Montreal during the last session of the Interim Council and he made some interesting observa-tions about its first few months of activity. 'The general impression,' he reported, was 'of a fast-growing agency in a new field moving ahead with energy and determination in an atmosphere of excellent morale.' Hyde also noted, perhaps unintentionally, how the Interim Council of ICAO was largely dominated by the English-speaking nations. In most meet-ings, he noted, 'the bulk of the discussion seemed to be carried on by the U.S., U.K., Canadians, and to a lesser extent the Dutch and French rep-resentatives.'[47] For example, of the ten technical working groups or div-isions reporting to the Air Navigation Committee established before the first meeting of the Interim Assembly (the eleventh division was estab-lished later), nine of them were chaired by representatives from English-speaking countries. The lone exception was H.L. Hof of the Netherlands, who chaired the Committee on Communications and Radio Aids to Air Navigation.[48] Things were not helped by the exclusive use of English, but

Hyde did not seem to mind. It was the 'only language used in meetings,' he wrote. 'A few of the non-English speaking delegates seem to experience a certain amount of strain in understanding the discussion of particular points, but the meetings gained greatly in avoiding the cumbersome translating procedure characteristic of United Nations meetings.' Interestingly, Hyde also noted (and he was not the only one to do so) that the 'absence of U.S.S.R. representatives was conspicuous.'[49]

In any event, by the time the first meeting of the PICAO Assembly officially opened on 21 May 1946, much work had already been completed by the Preparatory Committee, the Interim Council, at the regional meetings, in the Air Transport and Air Navigation Committees, and in forging new relationships with several other international organizations. Moreover, a new quarterly magazine – the *PICAO Journal* – was established to 'record the activities, studies, and projects of the Provisional International Civil Aviation Organization' and its successor.[50]

The Assembly of the Provisional International Civil Aviation Organization held its first meeting on 21 May 1946, in Montreal's Windsor Hotel. It was a good, old hotel and, while it met PICAO's immediate needs, it was generally recognized as unsuitable as a permanent home for an organization such as ICAO. Forty-four member nations sent delegates (only Greece and Poland did not attend, although the latter was represented by an observer), a further ten states sent observers, and more than half a dozen organizations were represented. Each state was permitted five delegates and five alternates, along with as many advisors as it wished, but few nations sent that many representatives, and many sent only one. Australia, Canada, China, France, and the United Kingdom sent more than a dozen representatives each, and the United States surpassed them all with sixty five representatives, including officials from the largest airlines. 'It was a well-coached team, to all appearances free from dissension,' one observer wrote of the American delegation. 'It had plays to meet every situation. If they included "power plays" and if a few overstepped the boundaries of the field, practically all gained ground. The delegation had specialists for every situation and substitutes for every specialist.'[51] These numbers serve as a reminder of the importance attached to PICAO by the United States and a small group of nations that had played important roles at Chicago, and ensured that these states, especially the United States, would dominate much of the decision-making in the new interim organization.

Speeches were the first order of business as the delegates were welcomed by various Canadian officials and then by each other (and, while most of the delegates spoke in English, translation services were provided in French for all the debates[52]). The Canadians were especially welcoming; not surprisingly, given their desire to have Montreal selected as the site of the permanent headquarters. The city's mayor, Camillien Houde, made reference to the uneven quality of the accommodations and even apologized for the bad weather, stating that 'I hope that our hospitality will be such that you will not think for one moment of going elsewhere!'[53] The delegations were entertained – everyone at receptions; the delegates and alternates at private dinners – and there was even a boat tour down the St Lawrence River.

The Interim Assembly elected Louis de Brouckère, head of the Belgian delegation, as its president. An elder statesman (he enjoyed his seventy-sixth birthday during the conference), de Brouckère was a tall man, 'with a full white beard and a bald head, either of which would have made him the center of attention.' He had spent much of his life in the world of aviation and he brought all his skills and experience to bear on the issues at hand. It was widely agreed that he was an excellent choice for president of the PICAO Assembly.[54] De Brouckère chaired the Executive Committee and steered the assembly through a very busy eighteen days of work.

The goal of the assembly was to make the preparations for the coming into force of the International Convention and to pave the way for a smooth transition to the permanent organization. Like the Interim Council, the structures of the Interim Assembly of PICAO, the secretariat, and the various committees and commissions were fashioned along the same lines as those envisioned for the permanent organizations and set out in the International Convention. Maintaining a kind of continuity between the provisional and permanent organization was an end in itself.

There were five plenary sessions and several committees established, but most of the work of the assembly was undertaken by the five commissions created to examine specific issues: General Policy, Air Navigation, Air Transport, Legal Questions, and Administration and Finance. Each of these commissions was furthered divided into various subcommittees. The assembly also had the opportunity to consider the Interim Council's report on its activities, its preliminary budget, and the Air Transport Committee's report, all of which were presented to the assembly by Interim Council President Edward Warner at the second plenary meeting. Finally, there were the reports from the technical divisions to consider. It was a busy few weeks, and several important decisions were made.

One of the first issues raised at the first meeting of the Interim Assembly was the question of admitting new members. Membership in ICAO was open only to members of the 'United Nations,' their associates in the war effort, and the neutral states. Thus, Argentina, which had remained neutral during the war and had not participated at Chicago, was permitted to join in time for the first meeting of the Interim Assembly. Ex-enemy states could be admitted with a vote of four-fifths of the assembly, plus the express approval of any nation that had been invaded or attacked by the state seeking admission to ICAO. All of this, though, was to be 'subject to approval of any general international organization set up by the nations of the world to preserve peace.' Shortly before the first meeting of the Interim Assembly, the Italian government expressed its interest in sending an observer to attend. There was some debate over the question, with the United States supporting observer status for Italy. The argument was that Italy had been permitted to resume civil flying and therefore was in a different position from the other ex-enemy states. In the event, the Interim Assembly authorized the council to invite Italy to send an observer to future assembly meetings.[55] Other requests would soon follow.

Of more immediate importance was an issue that concerned not those states which wished to attend the assembly but, rather, the one nation that had been invited and had a seat reserved for it but had so far declined: the Soviet Union. The Soviets had backed away from Chicago, but anticipating future participation, the conference had agreed to reserve a seat for the USSR in the Interim Council. The twenty-first seat remained empty, and the Soviets had made no effort to attend the first meetings of the Interim Council or Interim Assembly. This fact raised the obvious question: what do you do with the seat left for the Soviets if they refused to sit in it – leave it open in case they changed their mind, or fill it with another PICAO member that had made a significant contribution in commercial aviation? Opposed to filling the seat were the Australians, Canadians, and most European states; in favour stood the United States, Ireland, and most of the Latin American delegations. The Australians advocated leaving the seat open until the next meeting of the assembly 'in hope that universal membership of P.I.C.A.O. might be achieved by the inclusion of the only major nation (Russia) not yet a member of the Organisation.'[56] The United States rejected this option. Relations with the Soviet Union had already begun to sour in the developing Cold War, and the Americans saw no need to wait for the Soviets. 'Many states not members of the Council have contributed much to the success of the organization during the past year,' William Burden told the first plenary session, 'and the presence of any of them will aid greatly in the work of the Council during the coming year.'[57] There was considerable debate, both in subcommittee where a proposal to fill the vacancy was defeated, and in the full assembly, where a final vote was taken in favour of electing a new member in place of the Soviet Union.[58]

Once the decision was made to fill the vacant seat, the selection of a candidate was relatively easy to make. Ireland was nominated by the Chinese delegation and had the clear support of the United States and many other states, especially given Dublin's impressive contribution to the Atlantic Regional Meeting earlier that year. The only other contenders were South Africa and Argentina. One delegate was less than encouraging, noting that Argentina 'joined PICAO just in time to nominate herself for membership in the Council but not in time to participate in any other activity.'[59] In the end South Africa received one vote and Argentina six, and Ireland won easily with thirty-two votes.[60]

With respect to relations with the United Nations it was generally assumed that some kind of a relationship would be negotiated, but when this arrangement would come into force was uncertain. The American delegation was in no hurry; Burden even went so far as to recommend that 'discussion on this matter be deferred as premature.'[61] Ultimately it was agreed to authorize the council to become involved in discussions on this matter if asked, and then to report back to the next assembly meeting.

One of the legacies of Chicago was that the selection of a permanent headquarters was left over to be made by the Interim Assembly. At Chicago there was a basic division between the states that supported Canada (or at least somewhere in the Americas) and those that preferred a European location. It was agreed to let the issue rest until the meetings of the Interim Assembly; presumably by then Europe would have begun its recovery from the war and could make a stronger case for its candidacy. Nevertheless, when the debate about ICAO's headquarters resumed in Montreal it was clear that the divisions remained. But, as is often the case in international diplomacy, the public debate focused on a surrogate issue – whether to make a final decision at that time or defer it until later. Canada had the votes to win; those who preferred Europe over Canada hoped to delay the vote until such time as their prospects appeared brighter.

It was an important debate but it hinged on a somewhat arcane point. Article 45 of the Chicago Convention states that the permanent seat of ICAO would be decided at the final meeting of PICAO's Interim

Assembly: the question was whether or not this first meeting of the assembly would also be its last? Some who wanted to vote now said yes, pointing to the need to get the permanent organization working as soon as possible; others who wished to delay the decision argued that it might be necessary to keep the Interim Assembly in existence until the permanent organization was operating, and maybe even a little bit longer. The issue was relegated to a subcommittee of Commission 1 and it was there and in subsequent subcommittees that the real debate occurred. In the end, a British and French motion that the final decision be postponed for an additional three years was defeated and the commission recommendation that a vote be held now was accepted 20–0, with Britain, France, and six others abstaining.[62]

The official secret vote was held at the plenary session on 6 June. The main contenders were Canada (Montreal) and France (Paris), although the Swiss offered Geneva as a possibility and the Chinese suggested a location in China, although even the Chinese representative saw it as a bit of a long shot.[63] Montreal was nominated by Chile and Peru, but the strong support of the United States was the key. William Burden explained his government's views that Montreal was already established as the headquarters and was doing the job well, and, without compelling reason, why fix what wasn't broken? Besides, Canada with its links to both the Western Hemisphere and Europe, could act as a bridge between the two. In addition, he noted, it was desirable 'to have the Organization located in a country which is not one of the largest but which has achieved great things in aviation. Canada would certainly qualify in this respect.'[64]

The Belgians and the French spoke in favor of Paris, a city that had strong arguments in its favor. Paris was, after all, the home of ICAN, and the city had the facilities and the experience to host ICAO. Things had worked well in Paris in the past and they could do so again in the future. In addition, Max Hymans, the head of the French delegation, argued that Europe was the 'true center of gravity of the world network of airways,' and it was more central than Canada in that the average travel distances for members would be lower and it would save time and reduce costs to have Paris as headquarters. Finally, there was the future to think about, selecting Paris would help Europe recover from the war – 'she must rediscover a sense of responsibility in world affairs,' Hymans explained.[65]

One Canadian observer described the atmosphere: 'the USA playing it like a hard hitting team, the Latin Americans thoroughly enjoying the intrigue and the UK trying to support both sides at once.'[66] But it is unlikely that any views were changed. Most European states backed Paris; the United States and Canada wanted Montreal. The Mexican delegation briefly flirted with the idea of throwing Mexico City into the competition, which might have split the votes of the Western Hemisphere, but could not rally enough support from the other Latin American states. As a result, Latin American support came in behind Montreal. That left the British Commonwealth. A.S. Drakeford, the Australian, strongly backed Montreal, while Sir Frederick Tymms, who still spoke for India, warned of the 'extreme cold of a Canadian winter,' and threw India's support behind Europe.[67]

The British government had earlier opposed the selection of Montreal, but there was less certainty about the alternatives. The Foreign Office favoured a European location – Geneva, Paris, or Brussels[68] – especially over the possibility of shifting the headquarters to an American site. One brief for U.K. representatives noted that: 'it would be contrary to U.K. interests for the Headquarters of PICAO to be located in the U.S.A., which would only tend to increase still further the preponderating influence which America already yields.' Thanks in part to the personal intervention of Canadian Prime Minister Mackenzie King, and 'after mature consideration,' the British government agreed to support Montreal.[69] The endorsement from Britain sealed the issue: on the vote Canada won a clear majority of twenty-seven votes to France's nine, with six for Switzerland and one for China.[70]

With the selection of a permanent location for its headquarters the work of the Interim Assembly was largely complete. When the delegates left Montreal to return home there were few who left feeling that the Interim Assembly had been a failure – it marked 'a further valuable milestone along the path of international collaboration in Civil Aviation,' was how one Australian described it.[71] It had been a remarkably busy eighteen days and several key decisions had been made – about the permanent location, the regional meetings, on new members and the vacant council seat and, of course, further progress had been made on the revision of the technical annexes.

In the end the assembly passed fifty-three resolutions dealing with topics ranging from financial arrangements to the invitation to Italy and other ex-enemy states to send observers to future meetings, to the holding of regional meetings, on the development of a multilateral agreement, on air mail, on the recording of air agreements and the submission to ICAO of aviation statistics, to the creation of a Public Information

Group within the secretariat to publicize the work of ICAO. Several of the resolutions simply called for more discussion and study of important but difficult issues before any final decisions were made, for example, on the multilateral agreement (discussed in Chapter 5) or on a standard system of measurements. In other cases the assembly merely agreed to postpone any decision at all; for example, it was agreed to leave several pressing legal issues to the permanent organization and the official creation of ICAO's Legal Committee (see Chapter 4). There were even resolutions thanking everyone from the secretariat and Interim Council president to the city of Montreal.[72]

Budget estimates for the first two years were submitted and approved, with the operating expenses for the Interim Organization estimated at $1,081,251 for 1945–46 and almost Can$2 million for 1946–47. The scale of each member's annual payment was agreed as well, with the cost of the organization divided into three hundred units of approximately Can$3,972 each and distributed among the various members (the Canadian dollar was used until 1962 when, following its devaluation, the council decided to base ICAO's finances on the U.S. dollar). Not surprisingly, the United States was responsible for the biggest payment at forty-five units; the British were second with thirty; France, China, and Canada were responsible for fifteen each, and the other members were accorded smaller amounts on a declining scale, based on the state's ability to pay and its role in commercial aviation.[73]

Preparations for the first meeting of the permanent organization were also well underway. The Interim Council encouraged all members to ratify the Chicago Convention as soon as possible, and it also agreed, in an effort to ensure a smooth transition, that the major positions in PICAO would continue to function until they were replaced by similar ones in the permanent organization. In the meantime, the Interim Council began work on the preparation of an agenda for the First ICAO Assembly and continued its ongoing efforts to attract personnel, training staff in Montreal, preparing budgets, and establishing the requirements of the organization. It also continued to meet regularly, assessing the reports of the Air Navigation and Transport committees and the regional meetings, approving the publication of various documents, such as the 1947 *Manual of Visual Signals*, and approving the preparation of a glossary of terms used in air transport operations.[74]

With the ending of the first meeting of the Interim Assembly the evolution of PICAO into a permanent organization was nearly complete. Over the next few months work in the Interim Council continued in

Montreal and among the various member states. There were still major hurdles to overcome – Berle's 'ambitious dream' of a multilateral solution to the economic problems in international aviation being the major one. That was an idea that was still alive, but only just. In many other areas, however, the future of ICAO was certain. 'The First Assembly at Montreal,' one Australian delegate concluded on an upbeat note, 'achieved a further very real measure of progress and allows us to see vistas of close cooperation in ever widening spheres of Civil Aviation.'[75]

4

The First Assembly – and After

It is a good start.[1]

'The appointed hour having arrived, I call the first Assembly of the International Civil Aviation Organization to order.' With these words Edward Warner, president of the Interim Council, opened the first session of the First ICAO Assembly on 6 May 1947. The International Civil Aviation Organization was officially born a month earlier, on 4 April, thirty days after the Chicago Convention had been ratified by the required twenty-six states. The membership of the organization had increased to fifty (although not all had yet ratified the convention) as Guatemala, Iran, Siam, and Transjordan were accepted as new members, and thirty-six were represented with delegations at the First Assembly; another eleven states sent observers, along with seven international organizations. Warner had reason to be optimistic for the future: 'That this organization has passed so quickly through the interim period of its life, and that the ratification of the Convention has been accomplished so nearly in accord with the schedule made a year ago, is one among many evidences of the universal recognition of the need for the work that ICAO is to do. This recognition will spur us all on to further effort.'[2]

The organization's offices remained in Montreal's Dominion Square Building and, in March 1947, it took over the twelfth floor of the nearby Sun Life Building. This new location now housed the offices of the president and council members and the secretary general and their staffs. The Canadian government announced its intention to build a new building to house both ICAO and the International Air Transport Association,[3] but the organization would have to make do with the existing arrangements for the foreseeable future. As was the case in 1946, the meetings of the First ICAO Assembly were to be held in the nearby Windsor Hotel.

The Interim Council had been busy in preparing the agenda, distributing information, organizing for the first assembly, and coordinating the work of the permanent committees and technical divisions. The agenda contained some fifty items and was distributed to the members well in advance. 'Each item called for action of some kind by the Assembly,' one American reported, 'either in the form of reviewing and approving or disapproving the many-sided activities of the Provisional Organization or in the form of guiding recommendations for the new Council to take into account during the coming fiscal year. The PICAO secretariat, working under the guidance of the Interim Council, had prepared 1,000 pages of detailed documentation covering each agenda item or sub-item.'[4]

Furthermore, the Interim Council had created – by resolution on 10 September 1946 – a new permanent committee: the Committee on International Convention on Civil Aviation. This new body was charged with the 'further development' of the convention – to consider amendments suggested by the council, the assembly, or individual members. It began work in February 1947 with representation from fourteen member nations and chaired by an American, Paul T. David.[5] The creation of this committee reflected the view that the convention was still to be completed, and that changes to the convention might be an issue of ongoing importance to the International Civil Aviation Organization. Within a few months, however, the new committee was seen to be unnecessary, and it was abolished in October 1948.[6]

By the spring of 1947 the organization had taken on the look of an established institution. Total personnel in the secretariat now numbered 341 (193 permanent and 148 emergency), and a Staff Association had been formed. With nationals from more than a dozen nations, there had been problems finding accommodation for all the staff and their families; they were also facing problems regarding taxation, immunities and privileges, and in various other areas not uncommon in diplomatic life. The establishment had expanded significantly; it now had a library to house and index ICAO documents and to collect aviation books, a separate Language Section had been created to deal with the enormous volume of translation services, an auditor had been hired for the staff of the secretary general, the Air Navigation Bureau had been expanded significantly, and a new section had been added to the Air Transport Bureau. Names of sections were changed, rules were devised and sometimes amended, new duties assigned or transferred from one section to another. The organization was growing and evolving into a permanent structure.

With a population a little over one million people in 1947, Montreal was Canada's largest and most cosmopolitan city. Set on an island where the St Lawrence meets the Ottawa River, the city had a long history as a strategic outpost and economic centre. From the Anglo-French wars of the seventeenth and eighteenth centuries to the Atlantic Ferry route of the Second World War, Montreal's strategic location had attracted natives, immigrants and settlers, traders and trappers, business people, soldiers, and conquerors. A predominantly French-speaking city with a large English-speaking minority and containing many diverse ethnic communities – 'the second French city in the world' with a 'population representing, as we do, two cultures – French and English,' was how Mayor Camillien Houde described it – it was also a vibrant city, known across North America for its entertainment, artistic, cultural, and social life. 'It is the end of the Old World and the beginning of the New,' the mayor continued. It was also, as one author noted, 'a wide-open town, uniquely sinful in strait-laced Canada.'[7] At the end of the Second World War Montreal remained Canada's leading city and its financial capital.

When the delegates arrived in Montreal those who came via the city's airport in Dorval (now the Pierre Elliott Trudeau International Airport) may well have smiled a little at its dilapidated condition. Work would soon begin on general improvements and a new terminal building, but in 1947 the airport remained much the same as it had been during the war when it had been used for Ferry Command operations.[8] The city itself was at the beginning of a major building boom that, through the next decade, would see it expand to the east and west. The International Civil Aviation Organization was not the only institution that was growing rapidly, and building sites and construction activity became part of the fabric of Montreal life in the postwar era.

It was also one of the coldest springs in years; in fact, the opening day of the First ICAO Assembly was the coldest 8 May on record for Montreal, with the high reaching only 41.8° F. – far below the normal for that time of year. But at first it seemed as though the delegations would have relatively little time to enjoy the sites and sounds of Montreal. With plenary sessions and meetings during the day and receptions at night – usually hosted by one delegation and open to the others and local notables – the agenda was full. One reporter for a Montreal newspaper sat looking at all his invitations to the receptions put on by the various delegations and was overheard saying 'If invitations were news releases, we'd have an awful lot to write about!'[9]

It was a historic conference, and most states sent full delegations to attend, although the size of each delegation varied considerably. There were new faces from new member nations, and many familiar faces, including W.C.G. Cribbett, deputy secretary in the Ministry of Civil Aviation, at the head of the British delegation, and Max Hymans and Henri Bouché representing France. Hymans was a lawyer, engineer, and veteran of the First World War who had fought hard in the pursuit of French interests at the Chicago conference. Bouché had less experience than Hymans, but he would serve as a French representative at the International Civil Aviation Organization for most of the next two decades. In ICAO's early years, Bouché was a major influence in and a staunch defender of the organization and in addition to defending the interests of France he served as spokesperson, at different times, for the interests of all French-speaking nations, of smaller nations generally, and for all of Europe. He was described by one British official (in a letter to Sir Frederick Tymms) as 'indeed an interesting study. I have been trying to get inside his mind. Sometimes he drives me to despair, but other times he comes out with an illuminating truth. I agree with you that it does not do to despise him. He is so knowledgeable in the past history of ICAO that he has to be treated with the greatest respect. He is, of course, a most delightful person outside the Council and the A.T.C. (Air Transport Committee).'[10]

The American delegation that arrived in Montreal for the First ICAO Assembly contained forty-three official members and almost another thirty observers and 'semi-official' representatives. At its head was Garrison Norton, the assistant secretary of state and current chair of the Air Coordinating Committee, and included were Major General Laurence S. Kuter, the U.S. representative on the ICAO Council, Rear Admiral Paul A. Smith, Paul T. David, and William Burden and Welch Pogue, both of whom had long experience in international aviation and knew ICAO well. It was easily the largest delegation at the assembly, a fact not lost on other members: 'A delegation of this size is not only hard to control but also is susceptible of the interpretation that the United States attempts to run the show through sheer force of man-power,' Norton later reported. 'Adverse comments on the size of the Delegation were heard from representatives of the United Kingdom, France, the Netherlands and some of the smaller countries.'[11]

Speeches were the first order of business, with words of welcome coming from Montreal's mayor and C.D. Howe, the minister of reconstruction in the Canadian government. Howe, a veteran of Chicago and wartime negotiations with Berle and Beaverbrook, declared the assembly 'a landmark in the history of aviation.' He continued by linking the growth of the International Civil Aviation Organization with the expansion of international aviation itself: 'Since we met here last year, civil aviation has witnessed another period of expansion in its activities. Countries that had suffered from the effects of war have recovered to a point where they can enter the field of civil aviation. More and better airplanes have become available and more air personnel have been trained. It is estimated that the world's civil air lines carried some forty per cent more passengers in 1946 than in the previous year and nine times the number of passengers in any pre-war year. The prospects for the future are limitless, and the need for an international civil aviation organization is more than ever apparent.'[12]

The next matter was to elect the president of the assembly and to establish and select the chairs for the following six commissions of the assembly: (1) Constitutional and General Policy Questions, (2) Technical Questions, (3) Economic Questions, (4) Legal Questions, (5) Administrative and Financial Questions, and (6) Financial and Technical Aid through ICAO. The dominance of the English-speaking members over the commissions and, more generally, the whole organization, continued. The Australian A.S. Drakeford, who had represented Australia at the PICAO Assembly, was elected president, by acclamation, and four of the six commission chairs were selected from English-speaking countries (the United States, the United Kingdom, Ireland, and Canada). The two exceptions were France (Commission I) and Peru (Commission V). When the Peruvian resigned (over the Spanish issue, discussed below), he was replaced by the delegate from the Netherlands.

What also became clear at the First ICAO Assembly was the substantial (some would have said dominant) role of the United States on the actions and evolution of the organization. There was little surprise at this state of affairs, but concerns had been expressed privately and occasionally publicly (e.g., in the debate over the location of the headquarters in Montreal, where some members believed that American influence would prevail). The United States was the dominant global power in commercial aviation and the only superpower in the organization, and these two factors alone guaranteed a significant American influence in the organization. In addition, the United States paid the greatest share of ICAO's costs, sent the largest delegations to the annual assemblies, and English was the dominant language in the proceedings. Finally, the United States also placed great importance on its aviation policy and its role in the International Civil Aviation Organization. As Civil Aeronautics Board Chair James Landis succinctly explained to the House of Representatives Committee on Interstate and Foreign Commerce soon after the war: 'without our rightful position in air commerce, it is inconceivable that we can maintain the prestige we now hold in world affairs.'[13]

The United States also ensured a dominant role at ICAO meetings by being well prepared. The White House and State Department continued to direct American commercial aviation policy, especially in the crucial early postwar years, usually with the assistant secretary of state – transportation and communications overseeing the American role in ICAO. The State Department appointed and supervised representation at ICAO meetings. At the heart of policy formation was the Air Coordinating Committee which was established in 1945 and began operating in 1946. The ACC was an interdepartmental agency with members, usually at the assistant or undersecretary level, from those departments involved with aviation (including the departments of State, Commerce, Navy, War, the Post Office, and the CAB). Its role was to study and consider aviation issues and to make recommendations to the president, and within its structure was an ICAO Panel which focused specifically on the organization.[14] Close liaison between the ACC, the State Department, and the ICAO representatives produced an effective coordination of American policy and the prosecution of this policy in the council and assembly.

For the French there was always concern about the dominance of the 'Anglo-Saxons' and, however inaccurate this description, there was a degree of truth in the sense that English-speaking countries – especially the United States and the United Kingdom – largely dominated the organization, and English was the common language of its operations. Council meetings were conducted almost exclusively in English, with some translation available, and all official documents were prepared in English only and then were sent for translation. The backlog of documents waiting to be translated grew rapidly, and in March 1947 the Interim Council agreed to stop the translation of council minutes and supporting documents.[15] In June, the first council of the permanent organization agreed to continue the practice of English-only documents but agreed to provide 'simultaneous translation' into French and Spanish in the council meetings, and it also agreed to translate all the documents for the upcoming multilateral conference in Geneva (see Chapter 5).[16] For the French representatives, especially Hymans and Bouché, this linguistic situation was objectionable, and they worked tirelessly on the behalf of the 'others' or the 'Old World' in ICAO in the face of what they perceived as American ascendancy. At the same time, they strove to defend French aviation interests and to enhance the role of France and ensure a place of importance for the French language in the organization. Language was a problem that never went away.

Even within the English-speaking group there were concerns, in the early years at least, that the United States was seeking to control ICAO and make it follow an American lead, and the concern was that it would have an impact not only on administrative issues but also in the policy and technical fields. The British were particularly sensitive on this point. For example, at one point in the First ICAO Assembly there were suspicions that the United States delegation was conspiring to gain control of the secretariat through the creation of a new senior position of deputy secretary general. It was suggested that this new position would be filled by a representative known to be friendly to the United States and would be used to influence and even undermine Albert Roper, the secretary general. And, along with an American council president and several other Americans in positions of influence, the fear was that the whole organization would fall under the domination of the United States. Even before arriving in Montreal, Sir Frederick Tymms, the new British council member, was informed of these machinations. Tymms was told of all these backroom dealings and American pressure tactics – even allegations that the Americans were trying to block his own appointment to the council – and how they were lowering the morale of the whole organization.[17] It is difficult to know how much, if any, truth there was in these accusations, and there is little evidence of American plotting or trying to block the appointment of Tymms, but they are an indication of the level of concern among some delegations about undue American influence in ICAO.

In addition, there were occasions when the British representatives identified themselves more as Europeans than as English-speaking cousins of the Americans. In these situations France became a natural ally in ICAO, especially vis-à-vis the United States, and these occasions, in the field of aviation security, for example, increased in number over the years as Britain turned towards closer relations with the rest of Europe. In the debate over the appointment of a deputy secretary general, for example, the British left it to Henri Bouché to oppose the Americans and scuttle any talk of a new position. Bouché 'has been a magnificent and staunch defender of what is right and just,' wrote one British observer, 'and has been the outstanding personage of the Council.'[18] In the end, no new position was created.

An early example of American influence came with the election of the new council. American policy was to re-elect all those nations that had been effective on the Interim Council. Believing that some of the representation from Latin America had been poor, Norton discussed the problem with the Latin American delegations and received their approval to reduce Latin American presence on the council from six to five. The problem arose over which nation to drop, and when it came down to choosing between Chile and Venezuela the Americans chose to support the former. According to the American report, the Venezuelans were predictably upset and one delegate even briefly threatened to pull his country out of the International Civil Aviation Organization. The United States did not publicly campaign for any nation but in the end, 'owing to extensive behind-the-scenes negotiations, the exact slate voted for by the United States was elected to the council.'[19]

In the first category Belgium, Brazil, Canada, France, Mexico, the Netherlands, the United Kingdom, and the United States were elected. Argentina, Australia, China, Egypt, India, Ireland, Portugal were elected in the second round, and in the third it was Chile, Czechoslovakia, Iraq, Peru, Sweden, and Turkey. The council membership was much the same as in the Interim Council with a few exceptions: Sweden had replaced Norway, El Salvador and Colombia were dropped and replaced by only one Latin American state – Argentina – and the Portuguese took the remaining seat.

One of the first tasks of the new organization – and subsequently one of the most difficult – was to formalize its relationship with the United Nations. The Interim Assembly had set things in motion earlier that spring, and on 19 September 1946 the Interim Council appointed a negotiating team, led by Sir James Cotton of the United Kingdom, to make an arrangement to bring the International Civil Aviation Organization into a relationship with the United Nations.[20] It was an idea that was embedded in the convention: Article 64 anticipated such an action even before the United Nations actually existed; the convention noted that 'by vote of the Assembly,' ICAO could 'enter into appropriate arrangements with any general organisation set up by the nations of the world to preserve peace.' Within a few weeks negotiations were begun with the U.N. Economic and Social Council at Lake Success, New York, and by 30 September a draft agreement was ready. To become effective, this draft agreement needed approval from the Interim Council and ICAO Assembly and the U.N. Economic and Social Council and the General Assembly. There was little that was controversial about the draft agreement; the U.N. Charter specifically made provision for such arrangements with specialized agencies, and the one negotiated with ICAO followed a standard form.[21] By the end of October both organizations had given their approval to go ahead with formal ratification.

The one hitch in the whole arrangement had to do with Spanish membership in ICAO. Spain was a member of the International Civil Aviation Organization; it had been represented at the Chicago conference and had signed the Chicago Convention, but it was denied membership in the United Nations because of the continuing existence of the fascist government of Francisco Franco. In December 1946 the U.N. General Assembly pronounced that 'the Franco Government of Spain be debarred from membership in international agencies established by or brought into relationship with the United Nations' until 'a new and acceptable government is formed in Spain.'[22] As a result, the International Civil Aviation Organization could not become affiliated with the United Nations unless it ejected Spain from the organization.

The ejection of Spain and the draft U.N. agreement was at the top of the agenda for the assembly. It was agreed that because Spain had ratified the convention and was a full member of ICAO that it would be necessary to amend the convention to remove Spain from the organization.[23] The wisdom of such a move and the wording of the amendment became the focus of debate for the first week of the assembly session.

In the vanguard of the movement to expel Spain was the United States, and its role in the affair provides another good demonstration of the power of the United States and its ability to influence and manipulate the organization on an issue in which it felt strongly. At first there were minor divisions in the United States concerning the appropriate actions to take with respect to Spanish membership. The U.S. confidential report on the assembly meetings noted that there was opposition to the expulsion from some individuals in the Civil Aeronautics Board, the Navy, and in the private airlines. Their concern was that Spanish airspace was important for both commercial and strategic reasons and that ICAO 'as a technical organization should not concern itself with such a highly political matter.' The American administration and its delegation to the ICAO Assembly, however, were adamant in their position that Spain be ejected, with Garrison Norton, the delegation chair, noting in his report that 'our support of the U.N. was more important by far than continued participation by the Franco Government in the technical activities of ICAO.'[24]

The Americans arrived in Montreal determined to orchestrate subsequent events. Prior to the first meeting Norton met with the heads of the

French and British delegations (Max Hymans and W.C.G. Cribbett, respectively) to discuss the issue and to ensure that they were on side with
the United States. The Spanish delegation was also called in on arrival
for an explanation of the American views 'on a formal, firm, yet friendly
basis.' The day before the first session the United States delegation lobbied to change the order of opening addresses so the American representative could speak first and make it clear where the United States
stood on the matter so that everyone else could be 'put on notice that we
intended to press strongly for the early adoption of the affiliation agreement with the U.N. and, as a part of that action, to press for the adoption
of an amendment to the Convention which would debar Franco-Spain.'[25]
It was easy to manage; at the first assembly session Edward Warner announced that because the delegates had spoken in alphabetical order at
the Interim Assembly, this year the order would be reversed, with the
United States going first.[26] It is not completely clear, but apparently the
Venezuelan delegate had no wish to speak.

The American pressure appeared to have had some effect; just before
the opening of the Session, the Irish government was involved in the
negotiation of a bilateral agreement containing fifth-freedom rights with
Spain and had informed Madrid that Ireland would support Spain's continued membership in ICAO,[27] but once the session began Ireland was
seen as one of the strongest supporters of the expulsion of Spain.[28]
Moreover, when it came time to vote the Americans ran things a little like
a political convention. 'In order to keep informed on the line-up of the
Delegations,' Norton wrote, 'I appointed a "Floor Manager" who maintained a running tally on the attitudes and physical locations of the other
National Delegations. In addition, liaison officers were appointed to
each doubtful Delegation whose duty it was to explain in detail the
United States position and to insure the presence of those Delegations
during the crucial vote on the floor of the Assembly. So successful were
these efforts that even the Peruvian Delegation, which had abstained
from voting in Commission I, cast an affirmative vote for the United
States position on the Assembly floor.'[29]

Nevertheless, a two-thirds vote in the assembly was needed in order to
amend the Chicago Convention to oust the Spanish delegation, and
there was considerable and acrimonious debate on the Spanish issue,[30]
with opposition to the expulsion coming from Argentina and Portugal,
with the United States, United Kingdom, France, South Africa, Ireland,
and Switzerland strongly in favour. (The opposition of the Portuguese
might have been tempered somewhat; earlier the American embassy in

Paris reported to the State Department that the French government had offered to support Portugal in its bid for a council seat but only if the Portuguese acquiesced in the expulsion of Spain.)[31] The end result was a 'tedious and controversial discussion' that ultimately lasted a week and distracted the assembly from other more important business.[32] At one point the National Film Board of Canada reportedly began screening general interest films for delegates with nothing else to do. More fallout occurred when the Peruvian delegation supported the resolution to oust Spain, contrary to the wishes of the Peruvian government to abstain from the vote. Consequently the Peruvian delegation submitted its resignation from the conference.[33]

The focus for American criticism on the Spanish question fell on the Argentines and, secondarily, the Australian Arthur Drakeford, the president of the assembly. The Americans condemned what they considered 'Argentine procrastination and specious argument to delay final action' and accused the Argentines of 'obstructionism' and blamed Drakeford for letting it happen. Thanks to the Argentines, Norton concluded, the 'substantive work of the Assembly practically ceased during this period. At one point a constitutional crisis arose so serious that it appeared that ICAO would be rendered incapable of continuing its effective substantive work.'[34] For their part, the Argentines explained their ultimate abstention on the vote excluding Spain as a matter of principle and it 'was to be regarded as a vote against the exclusion of countries from ICAO on political grounds.'[35]

In the end the assembly passed two resolutions. The first approved the agreement to enter into a relationship with the United Nations; the second amended Article 93 of the Chicago Convention to bring the International Civil Aviation Organization in line with the United Nations on membership issues. The wording was unequivocal: 'A State whose government the General Assembly of the United Nations has recommended be debarred from membership in international agencies established by or brought into relationship with the United Nations shall automatically cease to be a member of the International Civil Aviation Organization.'[36]

The passage of the resolution to amend the convention did not end the affair, but it did lead to the removal of the Spanish delegation, at least temporarily. Under the terms of the convention, all amendments must be approved by two-thirds of ICAO member states, and this process is a lengthy one – the amendment to Article 93 did not come into force until 20 March 1961. In an effort to remove Spain immediately the assembly began to debate a resolution to force Spain out, but it was never passed, as the Spanish delegation withdrew on its own, registering its surprise at how political influences had impinged on a supposedly technical organization and noting that 'we could hardly accept the role of an unwelcome guest.'[37] Ironically, in 1950 the United Nations removed its opposition to Spanish membership in the specialized agencies, years before the amendment to Article 93 was ratified. It thus became easy to welcome Spain back into ICAO in 1950; it could be argued that Spain had never officially been outside the organization.[38]

Being 'brought into relationship' with the United Nations meant that ICAO now became one of the U.N.'s 'specialized agencies.' This relationship included the sharing of information, increased contacts between the two organizations, including the sending of observers to each other's meetings, and representatives from ICAO would be invited to any U.N. gathering that discussed civil aviation matters. It was also meant to lead to cooperation on budgetary and financial arrangements and to prevent the overlap of 'facilities and services' provided by ICAO and all the other organizations in the U.N. system. With respect to personnel matters it was hoped that agreements like these would lead to an international civil service in an effort to 'develop common personnel standards, methods and arrangements designed to avoid competition in recruitment of personnel, and to facilitate interchange of personnel in order to obtain the maximum benefit from their services.'[39] It also brought ICAO where it belonged: in a larger community of international organizations.[40]

The debate over Spanish membership in the First ICAO Assembly had been a lengthy one and unsatisfying for all states concerned. It also turned out to be something of a chimera – airlines still had to fly over Spanish airspace and arrangements needed to be made for such activity regardless of Spanish standing in ICAO; within four years Spain was back in ICAO again, and looking for a seat on the council. Nevertheless, a political dimension had been added to the organization, and now membership in the International Civil Aviation Organization was to be aligned with that of the United Nations. It also opened ICAO to future political problems inherited from the United Nations.

The expulsion of Spain and the formal agreement with the United Nations took far more time than most members had anticipated, dominating the first week of the assembly and deflecting attention away from other important matters. In other ways, however, political maneuvering and posturing had little impact on ICAO's technical side, where things were moving ahead at a rapid pace. Meeting at the First Assembly provided a good opportunity to acknowledge and approve the work that was going on, and it gave the members the opportunity to keep the others informed of progress that had been made implementing the many technical recommendations. It also provided a more direct opportunity for the dissemination of information. For example, early in the assembly, a refitted Royal Canadian Air Force Liberator, known as the *Ice Wagon*, was flown to Montreal for a demonstration for ICAO delegates. This aircraft was operated by the National Research Council of Canada. It had been converted into a flying laboratory to examine the problem of aircraft icing and to test new equipment to deal with it. One newspaper report commented on the considerable interest in the *Ice Wagon* shown by the ICAO delegates and noted that the ICAO members 'swarmed over the aircraft.'[41]

In Commission II on Technical Questions, the reports of the technical divisions were considered; where there was agreement resolutions were proposed; in other cases more study was recommended. An enormous amount of research and study had been undertaken since the Interim Assembly. For example, a survey had been undertaken of national laws on accident investigation with a view to preparing an accident prevention manual, and plans were under way for an investigation of runway limitations, runway lighting, and the impact of air density on aircraft landing and take-off. Considerable work had also gone into the more mundane elements of ensuring the clarity, translation, and distribution of the technical documents. All the draft annexes had been reviewed, amended, and, hopefully, clarified.[42]

Some of the decisions were easy to make and the resolutions passed smoothly. Others took a little more time. Everyone wanted to facilitate the smooth operation and development of international commercial aviation, but in doing so the impact of the technical decisions and their implementation could often mean a great deal of expense and the overturning of long-held practices and customs. For example, one of the most hotly contested issues was the desire to standardize units of measurement for international aviation. The fault line ran between those who supported the European metric system and those who favoured the Anglo-American system of feet and pounds. There were strong forces in the international community behind the metric system, but the American government had decided to oppose changing over to it.[43] The debate on standardizing units of measurement occurred on the second to last day of the assembly and dragged on for more than three hours – so long that when a reporter asked a delegate leaving in the middle of the debate if the session would finish by Wednesday, his reply was: 'In what year?'[44] The final resolution passed eighteen to seventeen, and the resulting system contained a mixture of both metric and English units of measurement.

If there was any complaint about the work of the commissions it was that they were trying to do too much, too quickly – a concern expressed for the whole assembly, not just the technical commissions. 'The general policy of the United Kingdom delegation in all these [six] Commissions was to press for the limitation of the activities of I.C.A.O. to essential functions and to check a manifest tendency to inflate the organization and to assume added responsibilities' was how the British report explained it.[45] The agenda was 'overcrowded' another delegation complained, and the assembly 'seemed to be trying to cover more subjects than it could adequately deal with.'[46] For some participants the solution was to focus on what needed to be done and then to do those things thoroughly. 'In the technical field considerable progress has already been made in the standardization of equipment types and aids to navigation,' Cribbett, the chair of the British delegation explained, 'but there are still many unresolved problems to be settled. In all these discussions I would urge that the paramount need is to give the highest priority to measures designed to secure the greatest measure of safety of air travel in the present.' It was important to keep the long term goals of the organization in mind, he continued, but 'the first essential, which should remain in the forefront of consideration, is the equipment of the world's air routes *now* so that the highest measure of attainable safety with equipment at present available, can be achieved as speedily as possible.'[47]

By the end of the assembly more than a dozen resolutions on technical questions were passed, dealing with issues ranging from studies on limitation of runway requirements to standardization of units of measurement, on search and rescue, on technical definitions, representation at divisional meetings, and on reporting of inadequacies in air navigation facilities. In addition, all these technical matters dealing with safety, standardization, the provision of facilities, the collection and distribution of information, and so on, were part of a process that continued uninterrupted by the assembly meetings.

One of the most significant developments of the First Assembly was the creation of the Legal Committee. Earlier, at the Interim Assembly, it was agreed to establish a Permanent Committee on International Air Law that would ultimately absorb the International Technical Committee of Experts on Air Law, known by its French acronym CITEJA (Comité International Technique d'Experts Juridiques Aériens), which was created in Paris in 1925. CITEJA's mandate was to 'develop a code of private international air law through the preparation of draft international conventions for final adoption at periodic international conferences on private air law.'[48] CITEJA had been suspended during the war and was in the process of reviving its operations, and there was some question about its future relations with ICAO and the sense that in some way its activities should be coordinated with the Provisional ICAO and ultimately the International Civil Aviation Organization. CITEJA was thus 'invited to place at the disposal of the said Committee its records and archives and any secretarial staff suitable for employment by the Organization.'[49]

On 23 May 1947 ICAO's permanent Legal Committee came into being. It was a committee of the assembly, but it operated largely under the direction of the council, and its duties were straightforward: 'to study any legal matters referred to it' by the council.[50] It was comprised of legal experts appointed by the member states (and they served as representatives of their states) and all members had a right to be represented on the committee. The committee was normally to meet annually, and its members, in turn, elected a chair and three vice-chairs for each session. This new Legal Committee took over the responsibilities of CITEJA, which held its last meeting in Montreal during the First ICAO Assembly, and in doing so assumed responsibility for revising the various draft conventions on international air law under its consideration.[51]

The First Assembly considered three draft conventions on air law – on Recording of Rights *in rem* in Aircraft (formerly Recordation of Title to Aircraft and Aircraft Mortgages), on Assistance and Salvage of Aircraft, and on the revision of the 1929 Warsaw Convention – but made no final decision on any of them. The Warsaw Convention (which dealt with liability of air carriers) was a particularly difficult matter that had been discussed in PICAO and CITEJA for years, and it was agreed to postpone for further study any action at this time (see Chapter 9). A similar fate awaited the other two conventions.[52]

The draft Convention on the Recording of Rights *in rem* in Aircraft was of particular importance to the American delegation, and there was growing impatience with the other delegations and accusations of foot-dragging. It was felt that to achieve an understanding on the rights of mortgage holders on aircraft was important for American aircraft manufacturers and banks that might be hesitant to hold mortgages on aircraft destined for export. What kind of protection would these banks or aircraft manufacturers have when aircraft were exported and registered by another state? The Americans put the problems down to the difficulties arising from the basic differences between the various legal systems, but there were also suspicions that politics were involved. 'There is also at least a good chance,' the American delegation reported, 'that the feeling, on the part of several states who had dominated CITEJA, against incorporating the functions of the old private air law outfit into the new ICAO showed themselves in tactics of delay and procrastination.'[53] It was agreed to hold over any decision and for the Legal Committee to discuss further the matter later that year.

The Legal Committee held its first full session in Brussels in September 1947, where it agreed to a draft convention on the recognition of rights in aircraft. At the Second ICAO Assembly in 1948, the Convention on the International Recognition of Rights in Aircraft was opened for signature. Rather than try to align the different legal systems among the different members, this convention focused simply on the *recognition* of the rights of one nation by another.[54] By 1978 thirty-nine states had ratified or adhered to this convention.[55]

Since 1947 the Legal Committee has considered questions of both private and public international air law. Its constitution has been amended slightly since 1947, and its annual sessions rarely coincide with the meetings of the ICAO Assembly, but its work has been widely acknowledged and accepted by members since its creation. The Legal Committee, along with the Air Transport Committee and Air Navigation Commission, became one of the central permanent committees of ICAO.

The creation of the Legal Committee underscored another trend in ICAO in the early years: rapid growth. By the time of the First Assembly, ICAO's involvement in international aviation was rising steadily in the technical, economic, and legal spheres. With a growing permanent staff and increasing membership, and with regional offices and a steady stream of meetings, tours, and conferences, the cost of the organization was growing rapidly. How to pay for it all was a constant question facing the organization, especially in the early postwar years when many member states faced major reconstruction costs. To add to these costs the expense of airport development, meeting the standards established by ICAO, and even paying ICAO contributions created for many members a heavy financial burden, one that was often compounded by serious currency problems. 'I hope that the cost factor will be fully considered,' wrote W.C.G. Cribbett of the British delegation. 'We are becoming increasingly conscious of the heavy expense falling upon the national exchequers in providing a modern airport organization to the requisite standards.'[56]

One way to limit costs was to ensure that the International Civil Aviation Organization did not take on too much too quickly. Another possibility was to reduce the cost of the annual assemblies, which were expensive for smaller nations and especially for the delegations that had to travel the farthest to attend. The solution might be either to make each meeting more productive or to reduce the number of assemblies. 'It would seem,' the Canadian delegation report noted, 'that if large meetings in the order of the First ICAO Assembly are to be held annually in the future, it would be wise to consider ways and means of making them more fruitful. The solution may be to hold such large meetings at three or four years intervals only and convene small meetings in the off years, which would be confined to dealing with administrative matters and urgent items.'[57] This was an idea that would return in the future.

The British were not alone in being concerned about rising costs, and many of these concerns were aired in Commission V during its debate on the budget. The budget submitted by the Interim Council – which proposed a budget of $3,190,855 for the 1947–48 fiscal year – was pared down considerably, with cuts in salaries, office budgets, and money set aside for entertainment. In the end the assembly approved $2,600,000 for 1947–48, a much reduced amount but still more than a third higher than the 1946–47 budget. But a statement about holding costs down had been made. 'The reduction was not only justified in itself,' the British reported, 'but will probably have a salutary effect on the Secretariat General in producing future estimates for Assembly consideration.'[58]

The question remained, of course: who would pay for the increased cost of the organization? These decisions had always been based on fairly straightforward criteria: the ability to pay, the importance of each member in the world of commercial aviation, and recognition of the wartime damage suffered by some members. There really was only one answer: most states could afford slight increases but in the early years it was the United States that could carry the heaviest burden. The Americans had no wish to pay more than they had to, but, alternatively, having smaller nations withdraw from the organization because they could not meet their contributions ran against American interests. It was American policy to keep their payments to international organizations below 25 per cent of total budgets and down to the 20 per cent level if at all possible, but this lower level was never reached in ICAO. In the event, the United States volunteered to raise its payment from forty-five to fifty-seven units. The United Kingdom remained next highest at thirty; the Chinese, Canadians, and French rested at fifteen. For some there were reductions. For example, South Africa went from eight to six units; Czechoslovakia was reduced from four to three, and Denmark dropped from five units to four. Conversely, the United States was now paying more than ever, and its share of ICAO's whole budget often reached 30 per cent.

ICAO's First Assembly was a significant moment in international civil aviation, with the inauguration of a permanent organization to set the standards and to oversee the safe operation of international aviation. From that point onward, the International Civil Aviation Organization would play a central role in the unfolding development of international aviation. The moment was also a testament to the value and success of PICAO in that so much preparatory work had been accomplished that the organization was already operating smoothly by the time the delegates arrived in Montreal in May 1947.

The British were understated in their estimation of the whole affair: 'Although the first meeting of the Assembly of I.C.A.O. has not achieved spectacular results, it has been successful in bringing many difficult and important problems nearer to solution.'[59] The lengthy debate over Spanish membership had got things off to a slow start, and there was criticism at the intrusion of politics into the functioning of the organization. There had also been problems with the translation services and the slow distribution of documents. Nevertheless, there were important achievements: the meeting of delegations at the assembly had given a public face to the new organization and a relationship was established with the United Nations; the first ICAO Council was elected and a budget negotiated; and the ICAO Assembly passed numerous resolutions putting into effect the work of the Interim Council and the permanent committees in the technical, legal, and administrative spheres. No longer a theoretical or anticipated institution, the First Assembly added an element of permanence to the organization.[60] Moreover, the First Assembly was only a beginning, and work continued long after all the delegates returned home. The secretariat was well established and functioning, and an ICAO Service Code was produced, setting out the employment rules and regulations. Liaison with the United Nations and other international organizations had been established, and considerable progress was being made in the technical field.[61] Equally important, the new council was up and running, and it remained in almost continuous session following the First Assembly.

The First ICAO Assembly was one more step in the process of the standardization of international civil aviation which had begun with the International Commission for Air Navigation in 1919. The goal of the

International Civil Aviation Organization was to ensure and enhance the safety of air travel through the standardization of international regulations and rules and procedures. ICAO collected and studied the existing standards (from ICAN, the other aviation organizations, and from individual states); these standards were thoroughly studied and revised at the Chicago conference, and the draft annexes produced at that conference were further re-examined during the Provisional ICAO years by the various bodies of the organization. All the recommendations were considered by the organization as a whole, at the First ICAO Assembly and in committee, and all the contracting states were invited to discuss and comment on them. The next crucial step was to take all this work and for the council officially to adopt the recommendations and procedures as International Standards and Recommended Practices and then, ultimately, have them implemented by the contracting states. These objectives were the prime function of the council in its first years of existence.

On 28 May 1947 the council held its first meeting, and Edward Warner was elected president and Albert Roper was confirmed as secretary general of the organization – the positions both had held in the interim organization. Many familiar faces were there, including Tymms, Bouché, van Hasselt from the Netherlands, the Canadian C.S. Booth, Ali Fuad Bey from Iraq, and the American Major General L.S. Kuter. At the third council session, on 13 January 1948, the new representative from Argentina, Walter Binaghi, took his first step in what would be a lifetime attachment to the International Civil Aviation Organization.[62] The selection of Warner and Roper took only minutes, and there were no speeches as the council immediately got down to business discussing rules and procedures, the distribution of documents, the languages to be used, the granting of permission to outside observers to attend meetings, arranging for the entrance of new members, dealing with the Canadian government, especially over finding a new home for ICAO, establishing the terms of reference, duties, and responsibilities of the Air Transport Committee, Air Navigation Commission, and the other committees, and, of course, reviewing, amending, and discussing – line by line – the proposed annexes.[63]

The process for adoption of the Standards and Recommended Practices is relatively straightforward: the council approves them with a two-thirds majority; they are then submitted to the contracting states and each one comes into force 'within three months after its submission to the contracting States or at the end of such longer period of time as the Council may prescribe, unless in the meantime a majority of the contracting

States register their disapproval with the Council.' In addition, the council also approves Procedures for Air Navigation Services, which are 'procedures regarded as not yet having attained a sufficient degree of maturity for adoption as International Standards and Recommended Practices ... or [are] susceptible to frequent amendment,' and Regional Supplementary Procedures which contain operating procedures that apply only to certain regions.[64]

As discussed in Chapter 2, the council adopts Standards and Recommended Practices and they are then attached to the Chicago Convention as annexes. The SARPs and annexes are not absolutely binding on any member and any state can notify non-compliance to the ICAO Council; the only exception concerns the rules of the air over the high seas, where, according to Article 12 of the Chicago Convention, 'the rules in force shall be those established under this Convention.'[65] Constant reminders of the non-binding nature of much of ICAO's activities can be seen in its resolutions, where the words 'must' and 'ordered' are rare but members are 'urged,' 'reminded,' 'invited,' 'encouraged,' and 'asked' to take action.[66] It was hoped that a general desire for international standardization would encourage all members to adopt the SARPs. As council president Edward Warner explained in 1946, 'PICAO lacks those powers which offhand consideration might suppose it most likely to possess. It has no direct legislative power, or power of regulation. It adopts recommendations on technical matters. There is every reason to expect that the recommendations will be generally accepted and put into effect; and in fact the member states undertake to apply them "as rapidly as possible"; but they are still recommendations.' International pressure rather than legal obligation will help to ensure compliance, he continued:

> It will still lie open to the member States, at least in theory, to hold to their own ideas where those differ from the standards internationally adopted. Their only obligation will be to file a report with the international organization in any instance in which they fail to bring their own practices into accord with those internationally agreed upon. Each State is to be a free agent. Its neighbor's protection will be that any notice of failure to comply would be broadcast to the world, and pilots entering the territory of the non-complying State would be put on notice that a special hazard existed there – whether the hazard of sub-standard meteorological service, of non-standard radio aids to navigation, or of eccentricities in the rules of the air. Travelers by air would weigh such hazards precisely as they weigh the natural hazards of abnormally difficult terrain, passage over wide bodies of

water, or exceptional liability to dangerous weather, in deciding whether a flight is justified and what route it should take.[67]

The council approves the Standards and Recommended Practices and therefore is the key player in the whole process, but the vehicle for ICAO's technical operations is the Air Navigation Commission, which was mandated by the Chicago Convention to replace the PICAO-created Air Navigation Committee. The new, smaller, commission was not established in 1947 with the creation of ICAO, however, and the delay in setting it up was largely the responsibility of the American representatives, who had been instructed by the State Department to delay its implementation. The American argument was that PICAO's Air Navigation Committee was still doing a good job and that changing things 'would disrupt the Organization at a time when it was beginning to function more efficiently, and would place into effect an unworkable administrative system.'[68] In addition, the existing committee was a committee of the council and under the direct control of its members, whereas the new ANC would be more independent. The American delaying tactics were met with serious opposition from the British and the French and, moreover, there was some discomfort on the American side with the State Department instructions, especially since the instructions seemed to contravene directly the Chicago Convention.

It was not until the Second ICAO Assembly in Geneva in 1948 that a solution was reached. Wanting to avoid a public confrontation, Russell Adams, the leader of the American delegation in Geneva, gave a small dinner party for Hymans, Bouché, Tymms, and a few others, at which a compromise was worked out. Adams agreed to drop U.S. opposition to the creation of the ANC and in return accepted a resolution in which it was underlined that the council would continue to have 'supervision and control over all aspects of the work of the [Air Navigation] Commission.'[69] This agreement dropped all the barriers to the establishment of the ANC, and the permanent commission came into operation on 1 February 1949.

Articles 56 and 57 of the Chicago Convention call for a commission of twelve aviation professionals appointed by the council from nominations submitted by the contracting states. The convention requests qualified individuals (with 'suitable qualifications and experience in the science and practice of aeronautics'), but does not list those qualifications specifically. The tradition of the council has been to seek out people with a breadth of aviation knowledge rather than specialists in a particular area. As one historian explained, 'the Commission is not a panel of specialists but a body of people who can understand the conclusions arrived at by specialists, approaching such conclusions with constructive criticism.'[70] The ANC's responsibilities are to study and recommend to the council amendments or modifications to the annexes and to 'advise the Council concerning the collection and communication to the contracting States of all information which it considers necessary and useful for the advancement of air navigation.' The ANC works through its divisions or sub-commissions and a series of meetings and groups all of which report to the main commission.

Despite its broad powers, the ANC is very much under the control of the council in that it can only recommend – not dictate – changes, which must be approved by the council. Also, its chair is appointed by the council, and it can be assigned new duties by the council (under Article 55b). The convention is also unclear whether or not the members of the ANC are to be national representatives (i.e., speaking for the state from which they come), although, as mentioned above, the Americans were adamant that the members of the ANC be national representatives and very much under the supervision of the council, and the commissioners' salaries were to be paid by their respective states and not by the International Civil Aviation Organization. For most member states, however, a degree of flexibility and an open mind were seen as necessary qualifications for appointments to the ANC and its technical divisions and panels. One early press release asked members 'to avoid giving their representatives at the ICAO Technical Division Meetings such rigid instructions as would prevent agreement being reached and recommendations being made in the general interest of international civil aviation.'[71]

There was also considerable constitutional debate on two other issues. First, there was a question over who could be appointed to the Air Navigation Commission – just citizens of members of the council or representatives from all contracting states? At first the council tried to reserve the ANC to nationals of the council-member states, but ultimately it complied with the convention and opened up membership on the ANC to all ICAO contracting states. Second, in 1949 there were only nine nominees for the ANC (partly the result of looking at first only to council members for representatives), and there was a question whether or not it was possible to form the commission without the twelve members specifically called for in the convention. It was agreed that it was, and for many years the ANC operated without a full complement of members.[72]

Decisions on technical standards or efforts to propose and amend the annexes are not made in haste. Ideas and proposals are discussed in a variety of meetings of expert panels (for specific technical issues), regional meetings (for technical problems specific to a geographic region) and Air Navigation Conferences (for discussion of several inter-related technical issues), among and between delegations, in conjunction with other international organizations (especially the International Air Transport Association), at the assemblies, and in the permanent bodies of the organization. The proposals then go to the ANC and ultimately are recommended to the council, where they are approved or rejected. Once approved, the council informs the members, and the Standards and Recommended Practices become binding on all members (those who cannot or do not wish to comply can file a 'difference'). The International Civil Aviation Organization cannot force members to accept anything or do anything that they do not want to do, and therefore a consensus is sought for all amendments to the annexes and new SARPs. This consensus building is admirable and usually successful; it also makes the implementation of some decisions very time consuming.[73]

Between 1948 and 1953 fifteen annexes were officially adopted by the council and the organization, and all members were encouraged to begin the process of applying the new standards and procedures at home. The following is a list of the first fifteen annexes:

Annex 1. *Personnel licensing.* Dealing with licensing of operating and maintenance personnel, it was first adopted by the Council on April 14, 1948. It provides the general rules concerning licenses, licenses and ratings for pilots, licenses for flight crew members other than licenses for pilots, licenses and ratings for personnel other than flight crew members, medical requirements, physical features, etc.

Annex 2. *Rules of the air.* Dealing with the rules of world-wide application and those relating to visual flight and to instrument flight, it was first adopted by the Council on April 15, 1948.

Annex 3. *Meteorological codes.* Dealing with aeronautical codes used for the exchange of meteorological information between ground stations and air-ground communications purposes, it was first adopted by the ICAO Council on April 16, 1948.

Annex 4. *Aeronautical charts.* Dealing with the standardization of practices in the operation of charts for use in international aviation, it was first adopted by the ICAO Council on April 16, 1948.

Annex 5. *Dimensional units to be used in air-ground communications.* Dealing with reduction in the variety of dimensional systems to be recognized for user in international aviation, it was first adopted by the ICAO Council on April 16, 1948.

Annex 6. *Operation of aircraft, international commercial air services*: Dealing with specifications which will ensure in similar operations throughout the world a level of safety which will be above a prescribed minimum, it was first adopted by the ICAO Council on December 10, 1948.

Annex 7. *Aircraft nationality and registration marks*: Dealing with the requirements for registration and identification of aircraft, it was first adopted by the Council on February 8, 1949.

Annex 8. *Airworthiness of aircraft*: Dealing with the certification and inspection of aircraft according to uniform procedures, it was first adopted by the Council on March 1, 1949.

Annex 9. *Facilitation of international air transport*: This annex deals with matters that are the responsibility of the Air Transport Committee.

Annex 10. *Aeronautical telecommunications*: Dealing with the standardization of communications systems and radio air navigation aids, it was first adopted by the Council on May 30, 1949.

Annex 11. *Air traffic services*: Dealing with the establishment and operation of air traffic control service, flight information service and alerting service, it was first adopted by the Council on May 18, 1950.

Annex 12. *Search and rescue*: Dealing with the organization to be established by states for the integration of facilities and services necessary for search and rescue, it was first adopted by the Council on May 25, 1950.

Annex 13. *Aircraft accident inquiry*: Dealing with the promotion of uniformity in the notification, investigation and reporting of aircraft accidents, it was adopted by the Council on April 11, 1951.

Annex 14. *Aerodromes*: Dealing with the physical and associated characteristics to be possessed by and the equipment to be provided at aerodromes used or intended to be used for the operation of aircraft engaged in international air navigation, it was first adopted by the Council on May 29, 1951.

Annex 15. *Aeronautical information services*: Dealing with uniform methods of collection and dissemination of aeronautical information in the interest of safety, regularity and efficiency of international air navigation, it was first adopted by the Council on May 15, 1953.[74]

All of the above fell under purview of the Air Navigation Commission with the exception of number nine: *facilitation of international air transport*. Facilitation is best described as 'the simplification of the formalities involved in moving an aircraft and its contents across international boundaries,'[75] and because it had more to do with air transport than navigation – and dealt with passengers, their luggage, customs, and so on – it fell under the supervision of the Air Transport Committee. The

Facilitation Division began its work immediately and made significant progress towards the standardization of visa requirements, health declarations, and other paper work in the clearance of aircraft and disembarkation of passengers in international airports. By 1952 Edward Warner could boast that 'I believe that the total lapse of time from the instant when an aeroplane stops taxi-ing at the end of an international flight to the moment when the passengers are free to leave the airport with their luggage is now at least a third shorter, on the average, than the corresponding lapse for the same type of flight five years ago.'[76]

Adopting the annexes was a landmark achievement in the history of the International Civil Aviation Organization, but it was really only the first step in another long process that included the implementation and application of the Standards and Recommended Practices by the members. In addition, there was a constant need to revise and amend the existing annexes, first through the issue of supplements and, second, the production of new editions of existing annexes. Moreover, as economic, political, and technological conditions changed there was a need, on a few occasions, for the research, study, negotiation, and preparation of new SARPs and annexes. All over the world, safety standards rose; the introduction of new kinds of aircraft placed new demands on members to provide up-to-date facilities and air traffic control services, runways, meteorological information, customs regulations, and search and rescue procedures. The existing standards had to adapt to changing technology, new equipment, new problems, and the lessons learned from previous experience. In the early years the members were likely to complain about the slow adoption process;[77] ironically, the pace of change – adoption, revision, amendment – to the Standards and Recommended Practices increased so rapidly that some governments soon complained that they could not keep up with the speed and number of amendments and changes initiated by ICAO.[78]

The technical division meetings, the regional meetings, conferences, and the preparation of manuals, and the review, study, and amendment of the technical annexes carried on without stop from one assembly session to the next. The transfer to the permanent organization did not significantly affect ICAO's technical dimension: the regional offices were up and running, conferences were being held, documents were being distributed, aviation statistics were being collected, and the *ICAO Journal* was being published. Throughout there was a constant process of updating, reviewing, and sharing of information. The American government, said

Garrison Norton, had 'at times been left breathless by the pace of Council meetings, Committee meetings, Division meetings, Regional meetings and special meetings. Aviation is not a business on which matters can be left to wait forever, nor one in which the problems disappear if simply left unattended.'[79]

What the First Assembly, like the Interim Assembly, failed to agree on was the establishment of a multilateral agreement to cover all the economic problems left over from the Chicago conference – the so-called missing chapters. The problems of routes, rights, rates, and freedoms continued to elude consensus. The Bolivian delegate hinted at the problems near the end of the First ICAO Assembly when he 'expressed the hope that the States of chief importance in air transport would come to the next Assembly with a greater degree of unanimity of view than they had sometimes displayed at the present gathering.'[80] That was a tall order and, given past history, there was some question whether any kind of unity on the economic questions could ever be achieved. It was the last stumbling block for the new organization to overcome, and in seeking solutions to these economic questions the participants would help determine the kind of organization that the International Civil Aviation Organization ultimately would become.

5

Remembering the 'Forgotten Man': ICAO's Quest for Multilateralism

The 'Forgotten Man' should always be present, that is to say, the individual traveler, who should have the right to go anywhere with the widest possible choice as to the aeroplane in which he wishes to travel. The 'Forgotten Man' cannot possibly be delivered as an easy prey to anarchy, and should not be submerged in exaggerated protectionist or nationalistic policies.'[1]

One of the central questions for the International Civil Aviation Organization in its early years was what to do about all the economic issues that had remained unresolved from the Chicago conference. Unable to achieve agreement on these 'missing chapters,' as they were called, the conference delegates at Chicago turned them over to the new organization to sort out. The Five Freedoms Agreement produced at Chicago had been signed by so few governments that it was almost officially dead. This agreement contained little by way of provisions for rate, frequency, or capacity controls, and it was clearly unacceptable to a majority of air-minded nations, including the United States, which renounced the agreement soon after the war was over.[2] As a result, at the top of both the provisional and permanent organization's agenda was the thankless task of drafting an acceptable multilateral convention.

One of the first acts of the Interim Council in the summer of 1945 was to establish the Air Transport Committee and to hand to it the pressing multilateral problems. Dr F.H. Copes van Hasselt of the Netherlands delegation was selected to chair the committee, the Canadian Anson McKim was appointed vice-chair, and there were also representatives from the United States, the United Kingdom, France, New Zealand (in place of Switzerland), and Iraq. The committee soon divided into three subcommittees – on transport, economic, and legal issues – and from October 1945 through April 1946 held more than thirty-five meetings, at which a proposed multilateral agreement was prepared for submission to the first meeting of the Interim Assembly. The problem of national differences on aviation issues was clear and, in the words of the committee chair, in an effort to bypass them at the start, it was agreed 'that the members of the group working on this project should not express primarily the views of their respective Governments but should strive to seek objectively the best solution possible. Only by this means was it felt that the best solution – and hence the solution which would have the best chance of general acceptance – could be reached.'[3]

The Air Transport Committee produced a draft multilateral agreement by April 1946. It was an ambitious document, linking the development of international commercial aviation to the future peace of the world:

> it is the belief of this Committee that international air transportation, properly developed, can be an extremely important influence for peace, but that, if developed in a spirit of international jealously and selfishness, its contribution to peace may be negative. The general motivating purpose of the draft Multilateral Agreement is to foster and encourage the widest possible distribution of the benefits of air transport for the general good of mankind at the cheapest rates consistent with sound economic principles, and to stimulate international air travel as a means of promoting friendly understanding and good will among peoples, insuring as well the many indirect benefits of international air transport to the common welfare of all nations of the world. In this way, we think international air transport can best realize its potentialities as an influence for peace.[4]

The way to achieve these lofty goals was through the exchange of the five freedoms. In this draft multilateral agreement all members would grant and receive these freedoms and would be able to establish international air services with their own airlines, freely across the globe, providing their air services constituted 'reasonably direct lines.' In an effort to protect local traffic that might be siphoned off, this exchange of fifth freedom rights would be based on 'the general principles of orderly development of international air transport,' and with non-specific restrictions on capacity based on the 'traffic requirements between the country of origin and the countries of destination.' It also included a rate differential of up to 10 per cent that states could place on fifth freedom traffic picked up on international services above that charged to local services.

There was no escalator clause in this agreement, or any mathematical formulae for determining frequencies, rates, or capacity.[5]

Much of the concern – then and later – over the granting of fifth freedom rights revolved around what was known as 'change of gauge' or the right of a foreign air line to change aircraft at intermediate stops along a trunk route. As one British cabinet memo explained it at the time, with the right to change of gauge, 'a United States operator running a service, say from New York to Paris, would be able to bring a load of passengers to this country in a transoceanic aircraft and thereafter carry on those who wished to proceed to Paris or elsewhere in one or more smaller aircraft. The fear expressed at the cabinet was that this would enable the American operator to run an unlimited number of smaller aircraft from this country to Paris or elsewhere in competition with our air lines, and thus virtually establish an advanced base here.'[6] The British were not alone in their concerns, and the change of gauge permitted in the draft agreement was restricted to prevent the addition of extra frequencies 'at the point of change.'[7]

To oversee the smooth operation of these rules and regulations, the draft agreement called for the creation of an 'International Civil Air Transport Board' to be set up within ICAO. Composed of five to seven individuals, this board would 'interpret and administer the provisions of this Agreement,' with the board members speaking not as representatives of their state's government but as individuals. Only states (rather than airlines or individuals) could appeal to the board if any one member country believed that another nation was abusing the terms of the agreement. The board was to be given significant discretion to decide disputes between members and real power to punish offenders. Punishment of offenders could include suspension from the International Civil Aviation Organization, although the members were given the option of a last minute appeal to the ICAO Council.[8]

It was a difficult undertaking, to say the least, even to imagine that a new committee of Provisional ICAO officials would be able to satisfy all the various interests and participants and, especially, to overcome the differences between the major air powers, the United States and the United Kingdom. In addition, despite the best efforts at objectivity, the proposals of the Air Transport Committee would still need to be approved by the various member nations. And perhaps most importantly, this new committee could not work in isolation and ignore any outside developments in commercial aviation and, more generally, in postwar Anglo-American relations. What happened in the outside world inevitably had an impact on the effectiveness of PICAO, and in 1945–46 America's determination and Britain's economic weakness influenced the future course of multilateralism in international commercial aviation and its place in the International Civil Aviation Organization.

By the time of the first meeting of the Interim Council in the summer of 1945 Anglo-American problems in the air had been overshadowed by more pressing economic issues. The abrupt termination of lend-lease aid only a few weeks following the end of the war in the Pacific precipitated a major financial crisis in Britain. Faced with staggering domestic economic problems caused by the war, the Labour government introduced an austerity program at home and turned to North America for huge loans. Estimates put the amount of foreign aid needed in the neighbourhood of $3.75 billion. Late in the summer, a team of British officials, led by Lord Keynes, was dispatched to Washington to undertake the financial talks, and soon after there were suggestions that the U.S. government might seek 'to take advantage of the financial talks to negotiate, under pressure, an (aviation) Agreement favourable to them.' Lord Winster, the British minister of civil aviation in the new Labour government, was invited to visit Washington to settle the outstanding aviation problems, but he, along with Ernest Bevin, the foreign secretary, 'agreed with Lord Keynes' recommendation that negotiations on this topic should, in time and space, be kept as far apart as possible from the financial talks.'[9]

Nevertheless, in mid-November Prime Minister Clement Attlee was in Washington to discuss the control of atomic energy with President Harry Truman, and at one stage during his visit he discussed civil aviation matters with Truman and James F. Byrnes, the secretary of state. The Americans pressed Attlee to agree to participate in an Anglo-American aviation conference in the near future and again linked civil aviation to the loan negotiations, which were then reaching a critical stage. 'Mr Byrnes stressed the point that the Aviation Lobby was very strong,' Attlee recorded. 'He was afraid that when finance matters came up the Aviation Lobby would induce a number of Senators [and] Representatives to vote against the proposals with a view to bringing pressure to bear on the Civil Aviation problem.'[10] Lord Halifax, the British ambassador in Washington, received comparable signals. He reported to the Foreign Office that he had met with Dean Acheson, the undersecretary of state, and the American had told him 'that the civil aviation question constitutes one of our greatest dangers in the forthcoming congressional discussions on the loan. Mr Acheson asked whether it would not be possible to get one or two fair minded people on both sides to come over to Bermuda or to the Azores and explore the ground.' Others on Halifax's staff had 'been similarly warned by other friendly officials.'[11] Linking the settlement of aviation problems with the far more crucial loan negotiations forced the hand of the British government and it agreed to participate in the proposed aviation talks, to be held in Bermuda early in 1946.[12]

The civil aviation conference in Bermuda opened on the morning of 15 January 1946. The British delegation was chaired by Sir Henry Self, who had been the director of the British Purchasing Commission during the war; the American team was led by George Baker, the director of the Office of Transport and Communications Policy in the State Department. Over the next ten days a tentative bilateral agreement was hammered out, and Baker informed Washington that a 'meeting of minds' had been reached with the British delegation. 'Agreements involve British giving way completely from Chicago position on control of frequencies and capacity and our giving way completely on rate control. On Fifth Freedom, the British have also given way.' The Americans also conceded the right of consultation if the British believed they were being treated unfairly, but such consultation would happen only after the fact and would not detract from the real benefits of the agreement. 'Since our delegation, including all the CAB [Civil Aeronautics Board] members, all believe rate control desirable, anyway,' Baker concluded, 'we believe this arrangement constitutes a real victory.'[13]

The American government signalled its approval to sign the agreements, but the British government still had to agree. The loan agreement, meanwhile, had been finalized in December 1945 and was inching its way through Congress. Public opinion was not fully behind the deal, and the aviation companies were lobbying hard to slow up its progress. Moreover, there were strong interests in Congress opposed to the loan. As one Congressman exclaimed, a loan to the British government would serve only to 'promote too damned much Socialism at home and too much damned Imperialism abroad.'[14] But the still uncertain future of the loan agreement gave the Americans some leverage on the aviation issue. On 31 January, Byrnes wired Ambassador Winant in London that 'the signature of this [Bermuda] Agreement as soon as possible would not only be desirable as a fair and reasonable settlement of the long standing civil aviation controversy, but would contribute materially toward a favourable reception in Congress to the loan agreement.' For these reasons, Winant was instructed to talk with Bevin and Attlee and press the American case.[15]

At almost the same time in Washington, Lord Halifax was summoned to a meeting with Dean Acheson. The American explained that the government had approved the tentative agreement and 'expressed the very strong hope that His Majesty's Government would find it possible to authorize Sir H. Self to accept the agreement also. They emphasized the powerful effect which a successful outcome to the Conference would have on Congress in connexion with consideration of loan agreements.' Halifax had received a copy of the agreement just that evening and had 'no doubt' that certain aspects raised 'a number of difficult technical questions.' Nevertheless, he concluded, 'on broad grounds of policy, I have no hesitation in urging you to accept settlement of this inflammatory question, which is recommended by our negotiators at Bermuda. Moreover, I would also recommend that we should act as quickly as possible and strike so that full impact of success of negotiations should come while the iron is hot.'[16]

The American pressure began to have its desired effect. On 4 February the Bermuda negotiations came up for discussion in cabinet, and the focus of the debate was not on aviation but, rather, on the loan agreement. Lord Winster explained his reasons for not liking the Bermuda agreement, but added that 'if the Cabinet felt that the signing of the agreement was of vital importance from the point of view of our general relations with the United States and the consideration of the loan agreement by Congress, he was willing that our Delegation should be authorized to sign.' Hugh Dalton, the Chancellor of the Exchequer, spoke next and reiterated that Britain was 'not likely to secure anything better' through continued negotiations. He also recommended acceptance of the agreement.[17] The other ministers present were of a like mind. Bevin agreed that the agreement was 'not entirely satisfactory and would be difficult to defend in Parliament.' But, he continued, 'in view of the weakness of our position, due to the delays in the production of suitable British civil aircraft, there seemed to be no alternative but to accept this draft.' Prime Minister Attlee revealed that he had been approached by Ambassador Winant and urged to accept the terms of the Bermuda agreement. 'It was thus clear,' he surmised, 'from the point of view of the loan debate in Congress, it was desirable that we should meet the desires of the American Government.'[18]

The Bermuda Air Transport Agreement was signed on 11 February 1946. The agreement set out what became known as 'Bermuda Principles.' Fifth freedom rights were central to the deal and could not be removed from it, but they were to be utilized under rather broad principles and only on designated routes and at agreed airports set out in an annex attached to the bilateral agreement.[19] Routes across any other states on the service could be changed without mutual consent. On the issue of rates, it was agreed to allow the International Air Transport Association to establish fares that would then be subject to government approval. On the crucial question of capacity and frequencies, the two states were free to set their own levels, again within general limitations. The key clause stipulated that the two states would retain as their primary objective the provision of capacity 'adequate to the traffic demands ... [and] in accordance with the general principles of orderly development.'[20] There was a general vagueness in capacity limitations that enabled both sides to put a positive spin on the deal and permitted those who liked the agreement to call it flexible and those who were critics to charge that it was unworkable. If either the Americans or the British believed that the other was not acting in the spirit of the agreement and a mutual understanding could not be reached between them, then the issue could be given to the Provisional ICAO for an impartial judgement. Clearly such a request would only be made after the disputed activity was in effect, and PICAO would have no power to enforce any of its decisions. The British government had won the right of consultation with the international authority, but, equally, the United States could ignore any PICAO decision it did not like.[21]

This agreement negotiated at Bermuda has often been depicted as a compromise,[22] but on the key points – fifth freedom rights, limited regulation of frequencies or capacity, change of gauge, limited powers for the international authority – the United States got its way. In contrast, the British achieved the right to have rates set by the International Air Transport Association, but that was something the Americans were willing to accept in any event, and they won the right to appeal to PICAO if the Americans acted unfairly over questions of capacity and frequencies. The latter was a questionable victory at best; as one American author later wrote: 'in theory there could be 'ex post facto consultations,' but since the facts always changed for next year, the understanding and practice were that capacity would be essentially unregulated.'[23] Moreover, the looming Anglo-American loan negotiations cast a long shadow over Bermuda, and forced the British government at all times to weigh its interests in aviation against the possible negative effects a collapse in the talks could have on the loan.[24]

These negotiations at Bermuda ran parallel with the deliberations of the Air Transport Committee, and the Anglo-American agreement came into effect immediately, before the Air Transport Committee had completed its draft multilateral agreement. The signing of the Bermuda

Agreement was followed by the American negotiation of more than twenty-five similar agreements with other states, and transatlantic permits were issued to Pan Am, TWA, and American Overseas Airlines. By the time of the first meeting of the Interim Assembly, meanwhile, BOAC, Air France, and KLM had inaugurated air services to New York. What followed was an explosion in transatlantic aviation, with over 120,000 passengers flying the Atlantic in 1946, with more than half – 66,500 – in Pan American airplanes.[25] As a result, while the ATC was searching for a multilateral solution to the commercial problems in international aviation, the Americans and, to a lesser degree, the British had moved back to bilateralism, with the 'Bermuda principles' as their standard.

The agreement negotiated at Bermuda early in 1946 broke the Anglo-American impasse over commercial privileges in international air transport, and the Americans began pushing for the principles of that agreement to serve as a template for American and most other bilateral civil aviation agreements. A few weeks after the end of the Interim Assembly, Dean Acheson wrote to the British ambassador asking the British government 'to join with us in publicly espousing the principles of the Bermuda agreement in toto as a model for bilateral air negotiations between all countries.'[26] By September 1946 the two countries issued a statement declaring that 'both parties believe that in negotiating any new bilateral agreements with other countries, they should follow the basic principles agreed at Bermuda.'[27] The British never fully complied with Bermuda principles in their dealings with other nations but, nevertheless, when the American and British delegations arrived in Montreal for the opening of the Interim Assembly in the spring of 1946, outside events had already overshadowed some of the efforts of PICAO on this central issue.

At the second plenary meeting of the Interim Assembly, Edward Warner presented the Air Transport Committee's proposed multilateral agreement to the assembly. It was not a complete surprise to many there because the document had been circulated confidentially in the weeks prior to the meetings, but it was up to the assembly to decide what to do with it. The Australian delegate called it 'the most important subject discussed during the Assembly';[28] one American observer noted that the assembly's decisions on the problems of commercial rights 'would affect every government on the globe and would have influence directly and indirectly on the well-being of the civilized world.'[29] Yet what had happened earlier at Bermuda was in the air in a number of ways. For one, the wording of the ATC draft agreement on the exchange of fifth free-dom rights was similar to that 'in certain bilateral agreements recently entered into between the United States and certain other countries, notably the United Kingdom and France.' Even more important, the reluctance of the United States to move away from Bermuda and to em-brace a multilateral agreement with more rigid controls was apparent. Even in his remarks introducing the agreement to the Interim Assembly Warner added that although he had helped write the document, 'it should be regarded not as *the* basis for an international agreement but merely as *a* basis for agreement. Many Governments, no doubt, will have reservations as to the terms of the Agreement (I know that my own Government has such reservations).'[30]

Many of the assembled nations had had an opportunity to read the draft agreement in advance, but few members had responded to it and none of the responses that were received were incorporated into the final draft. Consequently, much more discussion of the draft agreement was required. To meet this need, a new commission, or subcommittee, was established, chaired by Irish delegate John Leydon, to discuss, amend, and improve the draft agreement. Many meetings were held, written submissions were presented from nineteen nations, there was much debate over change of gauge, capacity, rate protection, and over specific wording, but the whole effort achieved only limited success.[31] Clearly the United States and a few others were moving in another direction. The American delegation was adamant that no decision be made at this assembly.

While still officially in support of negotiating a multilateral agreement, the American position was to delay any final decision on the matter and to let the bilateral agreements work for some time so the various partici-pants could gauge how effective they were. Then, once the system was working smoothly, perhaps a multilateral agreement could be reached. The Bermuda Agreement was not necessarily the ultimate solution, William Burden, the head of the American delegation, informed the commission, but the 'operation' of Bermuda and other bilaterals should be allowed to proceed so all states can learn from them what works and what doesn't. Once the members had the experience then a multilateral could be negotiated. 'Such a structure has a better chance of survival than an elaborate edifice constructed in the vacuum of more or less pure theory,' Burden argued. 'We will not again urge adoption of a multilat-eral agreement on the basis of a *hope* that it will receive universal accept-ance but *only* after experience can demonstrate a reasonable possibility of acceptance by all of the nations of the world.'[32]

The work of the Air Transport Committee floundered on the shores of Bermuda. Neither the United States nor the United Kingdom wished to pursue this multilateral agreement at this stage, and all the discussions wound down into an inconclusive ending. There was still some hope; both large powers remained open to at least further discussing the subject, and it was here that the Interim Assembly made its final recommendations. The members of the first meeting of the Interim Assembly passed two resolutions on the issue; the first introduced by France, the second reflecting the position of the United States. First, the assembly agreed that 'a multilateral agreement on commercial rights in international civil air transport constitutes the only solution compatible with the character of the International Civil Aviation Organization created at Chicago.' Second, it was resolved that discussions continue. All members were to be canvassed for their opinions and the ATC was to continue discussions with a view to produce another draft agreement ('which will take into account such national points of view') to be discussed at the *next* assembly.[33]

The chair of the American delegation was optimistic, calling the proposals a 'cautious program' that would 'safeguard against the adoption of a multilateral agreement that in a limited period of time will fall into disrepute because of its own shortcomings.'[34] Others were less confident in the American position. One Canadian delegate essentially blamed the Bermuda Agreement, writing that the British government had 'recently concluded with the United States a bilateral agreement granting the Five Freedoms and has thus abandoned the position [it] had so strongly supported at Chicago. The United States–United Kingdom alignment was perhaps too formidable for those countries, chiefly in Europe, which one would have thought had much to gain from a multilateral convention.'[35] The French delegation looked for a silver lining; because the British and Americans has settled their differences at Bermuda there was less antagonism between those two delegations at the First Assembly, and 'les Américains ne cherchent plus à dominer la Conférence comme à Chicago.'[36] There was no going forward, and there the matter rested.

The resolutions of the Interim Assembly on the question of the multilateral were clear in their language, but ambiguous in their meaning and certainly in their implementation. The resolutions reaffirmed the organization's belief that a multilateral solution was the best way to go ahead, but the means to achieve that multilateral solution were left open. Moreover, there was no indication of how to bridge the great divide between nations on the economic issues. All they had agreed to do was to keep talking. Over the following months there were numerous discussions, reports, conferences, and disputes spiced with equal measures of hope, despair, optimism, and defeatism.

The Interim Assembly agreed to turn the economic issues back to the Air Transport Committee and left to it to arrive at an agreement on a multilateral agreement. All members were invited to submit their views on the questions and these views were to be taken into consideration by the ATC. In October 1946 the ATC formed a smaller subcommittee to draft a new agreement, and over the next three months the ATC subcommittee held twenty-three meetings (and permitted the attendance of many non-committee members). By the end of January 1947 a draft multilateral agreement was ready for submission to the whole committee. The ATC debated the draft agreement over the following weeks and on 28 February approved the document for submission to the First Session of the ICAO Assembly later that spring.

It all seemed to be going according to plan, except that this new document did little to settle the outstanding issues. The fundamental divide now as in the past concerned the granting of fifth freedom rights and whether these rights along with route selection should be written into the agreement or left for bilateral negotiation. The draft agreement, approved by the majority of the subcommittee (opposed by the United States and the United Kingdom), was similar in many ways to the draft agreement presented to the Interim Assembly (although there was no stipulation for rate differentials between local and through services and no transport council to settle disputes), and it offered what the committee called a 'complete set of rules' for the operation of international civil aviation. Included in the agreement were fifth freedom rights with few general limitations beyond bearing in mind local traffic and maintaining 'sound operating practices,' but the main sticking point in the draft agreement was that the fifth freedom was a general right and not tied to specific routes (each member had the right to designate airports, however).

A second problem arose over capacity limitations. The wording of the draft agreement was simple in its text but somewhat confusing in its implementation. Capacity was to be related to: 'Traffic requirements between the country whose nationality the airline possesses and the countries of destination of the traffic,' and 'Traffic requirements of the area through which the airline passes after taking account of other air transport services established by airlines of the States concerned.' Did this mean that capacity and frequencies would be based on the original number of passengers or on fifth freedom traffic picked up along the way? And would the number of passengers be telescoped down at successive stops along the way? It was also agreed that selection of routes would not be left out of the agreement, as a 'so-called multilateral agreement which left room for substantial items, such as routes, to be settled by bilateral negotiation would in fact be nothing more than a revised form of standard bilateral agreement ... [and] it would not represent compliance with the duty laid upon the Air Transport Committee by the Resolutions passed by the First Interim Assembly.'[37]

During this whole process in the ATC, the United States was actually preparing its own multilateral agreement – an agreement based on American policies. By early November 1946 a draft agreement had been endorsed by the ICAO Panel in the U.S. Air Coordinating Committee and by the Civil Aeronautics Board. This American draft followed the basic principles set out in the Bermuda Agreement signed earlier that year, with its broad grant of freedoms ('in accordance with the general principles of orderly development of international air transport'), limited control of frequencies and capacity, and the right to change of gauge. There would be no transport board with teeth to ensure compliance, only the right to submit disputes to the ICAO Council. The fifth freedom was part of the agreement, but 'such grant to take effect with respect to any other contracting state after separate arrangements have been made between them concerning routes to be flown between their respective territories.'[38] In other words, it was a different sort of multilateralism, with the contracting states agreeing in the multilateral agreement to grant the fifth freedom, but the specific services, the routes, the airline, and the airports to be negotiated bilaterally.

There is often the sense – then and now – that the United States was opposed to the whole idea of a multilateral agreement,[39] but this was not completely accurate. In the first place, a multilateral agreement would help the United States get access to countries with which the American government had been unable to secure landing rights or negotiate a bilateral agreement. As members of the International Civil Aviation Organization, all contracting states would have to play by the same rules set out in the multilateral agreement. It might even open up the Soviet Union, because under the multilateral all members would be expected to denounce existing agreements and to negotiate new ones consistent with the multilateral. The Soviet Union would have little choice – if it wanted to have international air services – but to conform to the standards of the multilateral. 'The multilateral appears to be the strongest weapon which can be brought to bear against Soviet intransigence,' was how one U.S. document described it.

Second, there was an argument that achieving a multilateral agreement was necessary in order to preserve the gains already negotiated by the United States, and that the lack of such an agreement might lead other nations to negotiate more restrictive bilaterals than the United States had at Bermuda. 'As long as there is no universal agreement on the principles which should govern the operation of international air services,' the same document added, 'the U.S. will continue to have difficulty in obtaining operating rights on non-restrictive terms. Moreover, it will become increasingly difficult to keep the gains already achieved. The existence of restrictive bilateral agreements constitutes a bad example which is a constant threat to the principles advocated by the U.S.'[40] The way to prevent this kind of patchwork quilt system from developing was to have a multilateral agreement that played to American strength and locked in the policy goals of the United States.

Third, there was a constant fear in American aviation circles of a kind of 'regionalization' of international aviation, with different blocs forming to reserve the traffic within specific areas. The Soviet Union was a good example – the Soviets had remained aloof from the International Civil Aviation Organization and as relations between the two superpowers deteriorated into the Cold War, the likelihood of American airlines being able to penetrate the Soviet bloc diminished. Other countries and regions (such as France and Europe) might do the same. Regionalism, one American noted, 'offers a real threat to the advancement of our international air transportation. A successful multilateral treaty alone will check this movement.'[41]

The goal, however, was to include in the agreement only those elements that would serve American interests and reflect American power. There were the essentials such as capacity and frequencies with only limited restrictions and the fifth freedom, which it was believed was absolutely necessary for the successful operation of American through air services. Beyond that, however, the American proposals were relatively restrictive in terms of competition and still rooted in the bilateral system. For example, there was little desire to include in any agreement sweeping rights to establish routes. Such a grant would open up the lucrative, high-traffic American market to any number of foreign services, especially to smaller countries with strong and competitive airlines but with little to offer in terms of traffic.[42] For the United States it was essential, therefore, to remove any discussion of routes from the multilateral agreement and to leave these decisions for bilateral negotiation.[43] For many other nations, however, if all decisions about route selection, airport designation, and airlines were removed and left for bilateral negotiation then what remained could hardly be considered a 'multilateral' agreement.

The one thing that made all the other governments in the world different from the American government was that the others had to negotiate air agreements *with* the United States and they had to come to terms with the enormous power of the United States in the world of commercial aviation. In this context, for many countries to grant the fifth freedom in a multilateral agreement without including strong limitations on its use was difficult to accept; to include it in a multilateral agreement and then leave route selection to bilateral negotiation along the lines suggested by the United States was completely unacceptable. This arrangement would give the Americans what they wanted – guaranteed fifth freedom rights – before negotiations began and leave route selection to tough bargaining, where the United States could use its power and influence to get what it wanted.[44] Why give away the one right that gave a small power some leverage – the fifth freedom – and then have to bargain with the United States for entry rights into the United States? One on one in bilateral negotiations with the United States, most small powers were at a disadvantage. From the American perspective, leaving many issues for bilateral negotiation – or even maintaining the whole bilateral system – had distinct advantages.

For its part, the French government was concerned not only about the possible competition from the United States and Great Britain but also from small European nations – like the Netherlands and the Scandinavian countries – that offered relatively little in traffic but had strong national airlines. Reluctant to give these states fifth freedom rights to French traffic, Paris was looking for a different arrangement on regional services.[45] The Australians, meanwhile, were asking for joint operating companies for trunk routes; the Irish and Portuguese were talking about forced stops in their territories for international services that flew overhead. The British were trying to reconcile their specific aviation requirements with their commitment to the United States and the Bermuda Agreement. Rather than preparing their own separate draft agreement, the British agreed with the Americans to 'try to shape the PICAO draft to conform with U.K. and U.S. views.' The British position would be to adhere as closely as possible to Bermuda – not because of its clarity but because of its vagueness. George Cribbett received directions from Lord Winster, that the 'vagueness' of Bermuda 'cloaked two different and conflicting philosophies and too great precision in wording would bring this conflict into the open. Our aim should be to have only so much precision as would enable an impartial tribunal to build up a system of definition by means of case law.'[46]

For the United States, having a multilateral agreement meant that it must include the fifth freedom but leave route selection for bilateral negotiations. For others there were geographical and economic factors that made them less enthusiastic for the American plan. For still others, inclusion of the fifth freedom required inclusion of route selection in the agreement to make it work; but if route selection was to be off the table, then the option to withhold the fifth freedom or remove it from the agreement altogether must be included. For just about everybody, a multilateral agreement without either the fifth freedom or route selection included would really be no multilateral at all. Given these circumstances, and with the positions hardening on both sides, there was growing pessimism that there was any chance of agreeing on a multilateral agreement during the First Assembly.[47]

It was not the ideal way to start the new round of negotiations on the multilateral agreement, which began at the First ICAO Assembly in May 1947. Discussion of the Air Transport Committee's draft multilateral agreement (and the American draft agreement) was given to Commission III of the First Assembly, chaired again by John Leydon of Ireland and consisting of members from twenty-nine states and with dozens more advisers and observers (the American team alone numbered eighteen). Ten meetings were held, and the discussion was dominated largely by the United States, Great Britain, France, the Netherlands, and Canada. Written statements were submitted, the benefits and drawbacks of Bermuda were rehashed. The old issues were covered once more and the old divisions resurfaced. The final commission document ran over two hundred pages. At the end of the day all they could agree on was to meet again – this time in Rio de Janeiro – and to keep on talking. In Rio there would be no distractions; the conference would focus exclusively on completing the multilateral agreement. A resolution to this effect was passed and incorporated into the commission's final report.[48]

One interesting sidelight during these meetings was the resurrection of the idea of the internationalization of commercial aviation. It was an idea that the Australians and New Zealanders had supported from before the Chicago conference, and they had never strayed from their goal. The idea had received pleasant comments at Chicago from the French and others, before disappearing from sight. What brought it back to the agenda was the British Labour government, which came out in favour of

internationalization, at least as a long-term goal. The British were particularly interested in establishing Commonwealth trunk lines to connect Britain and the various Dominions and former colonies, undertakings
that were permissible under the Chicago Convention. A joint operating
company to operate an Atlantic service had been created in 1935 with
the Irish, Canadians, and Newfoundlanders (it had dissolved by 1943),
and in the early postwar era a new company – British Commonwealth
Pacific Airlines – was created with Australia and New Zealand for the
Pacific service.[49] British support was enough to get people talking about
internationalization again, first at the Interim Assembly in 1946 and then
again at the First Assembly in 1947.[50]

The British were successful in having a resolution passed in Commission
III that would have had ICAO look seriously at the creation of an international air company and make this a focus of study for the Air Transport
Committee. The idea met stiff American resistance – not only because
they opposed the idea but also because it would divert the energy of the
ATC away from its prime concern of preparing a multilateral agreement.
One member of the American delegation even urged withdrawal from
the commission. Garrison Norton, the chair of the delegation, later admitted to be being caught 'flat-footed' during the vote on the resolution
and blamed the Chilean delegate for coming in late and voting 'the
wrong way.' Quick work by the Americans led to a second vote in favour
of reconsidering the first resolution. 'The differences were resolved,'
Norton reported, 'only after I whispered to Mr Cribbett that the action
of his country on the resolution was undoing all our efforts to fight the
Chosen Instrument Bill now before the Congress, a bill which would pit
the United States Treasury against the treasuries of all other countries in
the field of international commercial aviation, including that of the
United Kingdom.'[51] The linkage with other financial issues seemed to
work. In the end the matter was not turned over to the Air Transport
Committee; instead a resolution was passed asking ICAO members only
for submissions on the matter, which would then be distributed to the
other governments.[52]

With the end of the First ICAO Assembly those nations still interested
in the multilateral ideal pulled back and reassessed their positions. There
was surprising optimism, given the lack of success after more than two
years of debate and negotiation. Some believed that the length and in-
tensity of the debate about Spanish membership at the First Assembly
(see Chapter 4) had distracted attention away from the multilateral
agreement and that, with more time, a successful outcome might have

been achieved. There were some recriminations, too, about individuals and how things might have worked out differently.[53] In Washington, there was a degree of confidence that an agreement could be reached and that the United States could count on the support for Bermuda principles from Great Britain, Holland, China, South Africa, Brazil, and the Scandinavian countries. The main antagonists remained the French, the Canadians, the Indians, and the Australians.[54]

Informal discussions took place over the summer and new proposals were produced in preparation for the conference scheduled for Rio de Janeiro in October, but little progress was made. The British and Americans discussed strategy on several informal occasions and early in September brought in the French to see if there was any chance of a convergence of views. After three days of talks in London, Cribbett could only conclude that 'the short result is that the three countries are convinced that a comprehensive Multilateral Agreement, leaving nothing to supplementary bilateral Agreements, is not attainable at this stage.'[55] The Canadian government came up with a compromise (to leave fifth freedom rights to bilateral negotiation along with route selection),[56] but neither the Americans nor British gave any indication of support for this proposal. The Australians, meanwhile, moved ahead under the banner of internationalization, even though they acknowledged that it stood no chance at the fall conference.[57]

The Brazilian government withdrew its invitation to hold the multilateral conference in Rio and the venue was changed at the last minute to Geneva, Switzerland. 'Instead of the sunny month of October in Rio,' one journalist noted, 'final choice fell upon the misty month of November in Geneva.'[58] The conference opened on 4 November 1947 in Geneva's Palais des Nations and lasted until 27 November. The American delegation again was the largest and included a wide variety of representatives and advisers, with Garrison Norton in the chair. ('The strength of the U.S. delegation would seem to indicate that this will be an important conference,' noted one Canadian with an optimistic spin.[59]) Thirty ICAO member nations participated and three more sent observers, and there were various representatives from other governments and organizations. Professor Eduard Amstutz, the chair of the Swiss delegation, was nominated to chair the conference. A drafting committee was established, along with a working group comprising the United States, Great Britain, France, and Canada, to examine the capacity issue. It was agreed that the ATC draft agreement would not be the basis for the discussion but only as a guide for the participants.[60]

There were problems from the start, and even wonder and uncertainty over how the participants could ever agree to anything. Oswald Ryan of the Civil Aeronautics Board and vice chair of the American delegation reported home his views on the situation: 'India thinks in different terms from the United States; so does Egypt; Portugal and Ireland favor restrictions but for still different reasons (the desire to force all countries to stop in Lisbon and Shannon on their international journey); and the meeting of minds becomes difficult.'[61] Furthermore, the method of breaking into small committees to focus on particular issues – like the precise wording for a specific article or clause – made sense, but so many of these issues were contingent on the wording of the other articles. For example, how capacity and fifth freedom rights were worded in any draft article depended on whether or not route selection would be included in the final agreement; in other cases more general wording was acceptable but only if the dispute/arbitration method was clear – and vice versa.

To make matters worse, the ICAO Council did not provide simultaneous translation, so discussions were occasionally slowed to a crawl as there was a delay after each speech while it was translated. As in the past, English was the working language of the conference, and translation usually meant from English into French and Spanish, which placed the real burden on the non-English speaking delegates. There were also foul-ups: at one point the English word 'expansion' apparently was translated into 'exploitation.' At another, British delegate George Cribbett's words, 'Your proposal, sir, would be passing the buck,' reportedly came out as 'the delegate from the Argentine is passing the wet baby.' These issues of translation and cultural difference were factors at all meetings of the International Civil Aviation Organization, as the meaning of one phrase – even simple ones like 'free and equal opportunity' – might have a totally different meaning and nuance in another language or culture.[62] At Geneva such delays and misunderstandings only added to the confusion.

Despite the best intentions, little headway was made. A host of problems were revisited and many views were exchanged, with nations shifting in their support from issue to issue, and on no two questions were the divisions hard and fast. But there was a major (and not unexpected) divide between the participating states. One group, led by the United States and Great Britain, looked for a broad grant of fifth freedom rights in the multilateral agreement along the lines of the Bermuda Agreement, with the reservation of route selection to bilateral negotiations. It was argued that because the language of Bermuda had been used so many times already in existing bilateral agreements it therefore had 'the advantage of having been tested in actual practice, and that it is flexible enough to meet changing conditions.' Those opposed included many smaller aviation states, which refused to give away fifth freedom rights without strong controls. For these nations Bermuda principles gave too much power to the stronger states, and the language was 'so vague as to be meaningless and that the experience alleged to have been gained with this language can be discounted since traffic conditions have been abnormally good.'[63] One Canadian complained that the American and British positions 'offered little more than a form of bilateralism thinly disguised by a veneer of vague multilateral principles.'[64] There was a third group, comprising mainly the Netherlands and the Scandinavian countries, that argued for as much freedom of the air as possible, but these views were largely sidelined in the unfolding dynamics of the conference.

The American and British delegations made it clear at the start of the conference that they would not accept any multilateral agreement that included automatic route selection.[65] With route selection reserved to bilateral agreements, these two delegations then began looking for areas of agreement that could be included in a multilateral agreement. It was relatively easier to keep things *out* of the agreement, however, than it was to get everyone to agree on what was wanted *in* the agreement. At Geneva this worked to the disadvantage of the United States and Great Britain, the two nations that wanted Bermuda-style wording on the fifth freedom and capacity, because those opposed could block the insertion of such specific language. Moreover, once route selection was off the table, the resistance to a broad inclusion of fifth freedom rights increased. The conference began to lose focus and approached stalemate. One journalist reported on the growing malaise: 'The negotiations have been dragging along for three weeks and are heading towards an impasse. The first words which strike my ear upon entering the room are spoken by the Spanish interpreter: "Mañana – Tomorrow." He pronounced them softly, rather sleepily. "Mañana": one is unfortunately tempted to complete the saying: "Mañana por la mañana," which is Spanish for "Let's put it off until tomorrow," thus internationally significant of something which will never come to be.'[66]

The impasse was broken on 23 November, when the Mexican delegation, supported by Portugal, Egypt, Greece, Italy, and India, introduced the following resolution: 'Nothing in the present Agreement shall prevent a Contracting State from entering into a Route Agreement which will only grant to another Contracting State the privileges of taking on and putting down international air traffic originating in or destined for the territory of the other party to the Route Agreement and not the privilege for the carriage of international air traffic both originating in and destined for points on the agreed routes in the territories of States other than the parties to the Route Agreement.' This resolution effectively took the fifth freedom out of any multilateral agreement – a development unacceptable to the United States and Great Britain. The resolution was allowed to go to a vote immediately and it passed thirteen to nine, with five abstentions (two other delegates were absent). The United States, along with Great Britain and France, opposed the resolution, and before an adjournment was called their delegates announced that the vote 'held grave consequences for them insofar as their future participation in the work of the Commission was concerned.'[67] The final conference report explained the situation with a degree of understatement: 'It was this conflict of views that led to statements by certain Delegations than [*sic*] an agreement acceptable to them was no longer attainable.'[68]

The Mexican resolution was the deal-breaker, and once it passed the delegations essentially acknowledged the failure of the conference and began preparations to return home. The conference continued until the early morning hours of 27 November, but little progress was made. In the end it was agreed to produce a document that would be distributed to the members of the International Civil Aviation Organization for their information, but would not be open to signature – for there was nothing to sign. It would contain an annotated record of the proceedings and a summary of the discussions.[69] It was also a testament to the failure of the conference to agree on any of the fundamentals.

'If multilateralism had expired at this conference,' one participant reported at the conclusion of the Geneva conference, 'the fragrant aroma of the wreaths, which many delegations would have littered on its grave, could not have brought it back to life. Fortunately multilateralism did not die. Many useful discussions on rates, capacity, arbitration, and route principles have been recorded, and the crux of the problem is now readily apparent to most nations.'[70] A few others were equally optimistic with this assessment – that everyone would brush off the dust of Geneva, relax, and then get back to work preparing for another attempt at fashioning a multilateral agreement. Even the American government maintained its official support for the idea of a multilateral – the 'desirable ultimate goal.'[71]

Nevertheless, a chapter in ICAO's history had been closed. There was no multilateral document – draft, working, or final – and there were no plans to meet again. The idea or dream of a multilateral agreement lived on and was resurrected occasionally into the next decade, but the collective will to continue in the face of such profound divisions appeared to have weakened.[72] Soon even the request of the assembly for member nations to study the issue and submit their views was garnering little interest. By 1950 the Air Transport Committee was reporting that, despite some continuing interest in drafting a multilateral agreement, there was not much point in continuing.[73] The Economic Commission of the Fourth ICAO Assembly summarized American opinion with these words: the United States 'finds no evidence to indicate that further discussion at this time would produce satisfactory results. Recommend Council report to Assembly that discussion be deferred until situation more promising.'[74] In 1953, at the Seventh ICAO Assembly, a resolution (A7-15) announced that even though multilateralism remained one of the goals of the International Civil Aviation Organization, there was 'no present prospect of achieving a universal multilateral agreement.'

What had begun at Chicago, and even earlier, died at Geneva. Enormous effort had been put into drafting a multilateral air transport agreement, but after years of work the members of ICAO had little to show for it. It began as a division between the United States and Great Britain, personified by the different personalities of Lord Swinton and Adolf Berle and their inability to settle their aviation differences at Chicago. The Bermuda Agreement of early 1946 made these two nations uneasy allies but they were unable to bridge the gap between themselves as major air nations and the smaller states that feared 'Bermuda principles' and regulated competition in the air. That division remained long after the memory of Geneva had faded.

The failure of multilateralism was an important development that helped determine ICAO's future course. It meant that the International Civil Aviation Organization would develop primarily as a technical organization with a central role in establishing international standards and practices, collecting statistics, and overseeing all the non-economic aspects of international commercial aviation. Its future affairs would never escape international politics and its actions and policies would always have political overtones, but there would be no political and economic regulation of international air transport by ICAO and there would be no more dreams of an international airline or an ICAO with CAB-like powers to determine routes and rights. Without powers beyond a technical nature, '*ICAO's wings are clipped*,' was how one journalist described it.[75] From now on all those things would unfold bilaterally. In the world of international diplomacy there is always tomorrow – another day to fight the good fight – but for the International Civil Aviation Organization and its dream of a multilateral air transport agreement it did not seem likely that this tomorrow would ever come.

PART TWO

6

Headquarter Headaches

Canada has been proud to be host to ICAO throughout the years of its growth and accomplishment. [Its] increase in number reflects not simply the widespread application of aviation but the importance attached to it by virtually every country in the world, whether newly independent or older. International civil aviation has expanded to service the demands made upon it by the wider community of nations. ICAO has expanded to provide that service.[1]

One of the first tasks for the International Civil Aviation Organization was to settle into a permanent location and to iron out all the problems that remained on the questions of immunities and privileges. In May 1947 the Canadian government unveiled plans for the construction of a new aviation building to house ICAO, the International Air Transport Association, and several air companies, including Trans-Canada Air Lines. The building was to be built by the Canadian National Railways Company on the site adjacent to its main downtown railway station, and the new building was to be leased to the Canadian government, which in turn would lease space to ICAO. This arrangement was accepted by the ICAO Council in 1948,[2] although there was considerable debate in subsequent years over how much the rent should be. The lease was to be on a non-profit basis, and an agreement was reached with the Canadian government in which it made up the difference between what ICAO considered a fair price and what the railway company believed to be the going rate. Such arrangements were not very different from those made with other international organizations in other countries.

Excavation of the site began in 1947 on a three-building complex on the corner of University Avenue and Dorchester Boulevard (now boulevard

René Lévesque) including a new hotel – the Queen Elizabeth – an office building for the CNR, and a new home for the International Civil Aviation Organization. The ten-story International Aviation Building opened on 1 June 1950, with ICAO occupying the top six floors, with the council chamber on the tenth floor.[3] For the first time all the meeting rooms, the secretariat, and most of the offices of the council members were contained under one roof.[4] The original lease was for twenty years, but it was possible for ICAO to break it if it chose to leave Montreal for another location. That might have settled things, but this was only the beginning of ICAO's location problems.

In addition to having a secure location, the Council of the International Civil Aviation Organization was desirous of a 'headquarters agreement' similar to the kind established with the United Nations and several other specialized agencies that would cover the various privileges and immunities to be granted to ICAO personnel.[5] The lack of such privileges and immunities had been an issue among the council members from the very beginning. On one hand these kinds of concerns seemed minor. In 1945 the British member of the Interim Council complained about problems buying alcohol. 'There is one privilege I consider they should be allowed,' he wrote to the head of the Canadian Preparatory Committee, 'and that is to be able to get wines and spirits without having to stand in queue at the spirits shops. I am not aware that any well-known character in Canada stands in a queue at the spirit shops and I think it is somewhat unfair to expect representatives of other governments on the Interim Council to do this.'[6] Getting an exemption on liquor taxes was mentioned, at least on one occasion, as 'the most attractive and urgent prize desired by Council Members.'[7] Another sore point was the need to purchase licence plates for cars used by ICAO members – the request to the Quebec provincial government for free plates was rejected.[8] On the other hand, the need for immunities and privileges dealing with immigration requirements, a whole range of taxes, judicial responsibility for the organization, and so on, were necessary for the organization to operate effectively and to help keep the rising costs to a minimum.

There had already been problems; in 1947 one Italian delegate travelling on an Italian passport was held as an 'enemy alien' at the border crossing into Canada from the United States.[9] In addition, early in the 1950s the Canadian Department of Citizenship and Immigration introduced an 'Immigration Manifest Card' for completion by all visitors coming into Canada (other than from the United States) in an effort to enhance medical inspections (to prevent, e.g., the introduction of smallpox into Canada). The card was inconvenient to fill out and led to considerable delays entering the country. To add insult to injury, these cards asked new arrivals for their religion, racial origin, mother tongue, and the vague but offensive question: 'has any member of your family been physically defective?' Complaints were received regularly about these cards, including from council president Warner and IATA's William Hildred. On one occasion in 1952, Warner entered Canada from overseas and was forced to fill out the card, and his response was a long letter of complaint to the Canadian government on how its policies were making life difficult for ICAO representatives and, in general, for any foreign nationals who had to travel to Canada regularly. The Canadians found Warner a little 'overly sensitive and somewhat unco-operative,' and were reluctant to change the process.[10] Indeed, Canadian immigration policies did not change significantly until the 1960s; nevertheless, incidents such as these caused aggravation and inconvenience for the representatives and were embarrassing for the host government.[11]

A Headquarters Agreement was signed on 14 April 1951 by Edward Warner for ICAO and Lester B. Pearson, the Canadian secretary of state for external affairs. It was similar in nature to the privileges and immunities agreement signed by the United Nations and it set out the various exemptions and immunities to be granted to the organization and its representatives. The agreement granted the organization 'juridical personality,' allowing it to acquire property, let contracts, and institute legal proceedings, and it gave ICAO 'the same immunity from suit and every form of judicial process as is enjoyed by foreign governments.' ICAO's property and its assets were to be immune from search and expropriation, exempt from all direct taxes, customs duties, and excise taxes. Immigration restrictions were removed from all ICAO representatives and their families, and they were to be immune from arrest and detention, and exempted from federal income and other taxation.

The purpose of these diplomatic and legal immunities was 'to safeguard the independent exercise of their functions in connection with Organization.'[12] Nevertheless, unforeseen issues arose occasionally that appeared to impinge on the smooth operation of the organization. For example, early in the 1950s the United States embarked on a loyalty screening of its nationals working for the United Nations and its specialized agencies, including ICAO. Screening American employees in the United Nations headquarters – on American soil – was one thing, but could the American government do the same in a foreign territory? In

1953 the ICAO secretary general was asked by U.S. authorities to distribute loyalty questionnaires to the sixteen American nationals in the employ of the International Civil Aviation Organization, and this led to
considerable concern that ICAO was being used to carry out American
domestic policies.[13] Likewise, the Canadian government was unhappy
with the prospect of ICAO employees being fingerprinted in the ICAO
headquarters, and, as Sir Frederick Tymms noted at the time, there were
no provisions in the ICAO Service Code for any actions like these.[14] In
the event, it was agreed that the American employees of ICAO would go
to the American Consulate in Montreal to be fingerprinted, and there
were few subsequent complaints.

Another potential source of trouble with the Headquarters Agreement
was that Canadian citizens were not exempted from paying Canadian
income tax. All employees paid a kind of income tax or 'staff assessment'
to ICAO but Canadian citizens would be required to pay income tax as
well. It was a problem faced by other international organizations, and
ultimately the Canadian government permitted Canadian citizens to deduct the amount of their staff assessments from their federal income tax.
As the former was always slightly higher than the latter it meant that
Canadian employees effectively paid no federal tax.[15]

The Headquarters Agreement was signed between the International
Civil Aviation Organization and the government of Canada, but it did
not cover all aspects of the relationship between ICAO and the municipal government of Montreal and, more importantly, the government of
the province of Quebec. In the Canadian federal system, municipal governments were responsible to the provinces, and the provincial governments controlled a wide range of legal and taxation powers. For example,
the Headquarters Agreement did not include exemption from the provincial sales tax or the provincial income tax. As a result, negotiations
were undertaken to come to an agreement with the government of
Quebec. There were also complaints that even the subsidized rent paid
by ICAO for its office space was substantially greater than that paid by
other international organizations.[16]

These two issues – high rental costs and difficulties with the provincial
government – along with a growing unease over the apparent high cost
of living in Montreal combined with political motives in the early 1950s
to launch a movement within ICAO to transfer the headquarters out of
Montreal. ICAO was paid for by its members; several countries were having difficulties paying their annual assessments, and any way that could
be found to cut costs would have its appeal. Furthermore, Canada was a

dollar country and the value of its currency had recently risen, putting additional economic strain on some members. Throw into the mix the desire of some members to see the headquarters move to another location for political reasons, or to see it in their own country, and you have the makings of a major dispute. 'It was not the scenic beauty of Montreal nor the hard currency of wealthy Canada which decided in favour of Montreal,' one journalist reported. It had been the best choice at a time when America was strong and Europe was weak, but 'it became apparent that Montreal was not the ideal place for these important bodies (ICAO and IATA) after all. The Russians refused to play, Europeans, South Americans, Africans, air transport people from the Middle and Far East found the trip to Montreal tedious and costly ... and the Canadian dollar too sound.'[17]

The first shot in what became a long campaign to move the headquarters from Montreal came at the Fourth ICAO Assembly in Montreal in June 1950. Article 45 of the Chicago Convention states that the seat of the organization would be chosen at the final meeting of Provisional International Civil Aviation Organization and that it 'may be temporarily transferred elsewhere by decision of the Council,' but it makes no provision, however, for the permanent removal of the headquarters. It became the goal of those members who wished to see the headquarters moved to amend the Chicago Convention in such a way as to permit its permanent transfer.[18] A draft resolution to that effect was introduced jointly by the delegations of Argentina, Cuba, Mexico, and Venezuela calling for an amendment of the convention enabling any future Assembly of ICAO to select another headquarter city 'by a two-thirds majority vote of the total number of contracting States represented at the Assembly and qualified to vote at the time the vote is taken.' The opposition to the idea came mostly from the United States and other English-speaking countries,[19] but there was considerable support for the proposal among other members. In the end the amendment received a majority of votes, but it failed to get the necessary two-thirds vote to pass, with eighteen in favour, twelve against, and seven abstentions.[20]

Rumblings of discontent continued through 1951, but it was not until 1952 that the headquarters issue resurfaced. Shortly prior to the opening of the Sixth ICAO Assembly the Canadian government announced an increased subsidy on the rent, but it was not enough to prevent what J.A. Irwin, the Canadian representative, called 'a full-scaled attack on Montreal.'[21] As is often the case in matters such as this, the specific issue at hand was not a call to move the headquarters, only to study the possibility of such a move. A motion was introduced by the Portuguese delegate at a meeting of the Executive Committee asking that the ICAO Council 'be directed to make a thorough study of the relative merits and benefits to the Organization and contracting States of the present and other possible sites for the headquarters of ICAO and to present its conclusions and recommendations to the Seventh Session of the Assembly, having particularly in mind the need to maintain the highest standard of efficiency and at the same time effect a substantial reduction in the budget of the Organization and in the expenses of contracting States generally.'[22]

The Canadian government was incensed at what it saw as a thinly veiled attempt to move the headquarters to another location. 'Although the motion called for only a "study,"' the Department of External Affairs in Ottawa informed its High Commissioner in London and various other embassies, 'it was evident, from the active lobbying on the part of its supporters, that they considered this an important first step in advance of their seeking a final decision at next year's Assembly session ... Judging from the activities of some of these supporters, the conclusion could easily be drawn that their main interest in the business of the entire recent session of the Assembly was to promote dissatisfaction with the arrangements in Montreal and to assure the undertaking of a "study" which would keep the issue alive during the year.'[23] In the view of the Canadians it was the Portuguese and the Mexicans in the vanguard of the 'anti-Montreal faction,' as they called it (it was believed that both states would be willing to offer new headquarter sites in their countries), and they could count on the support of most of the members from Latin America and Western Europe.

Opposed to the move were the Americans, the British, the Canadians, and the other Commonwealth nations. The American delegate strongly stressed his government's opposition, calling the 'interjection' of this issue 'untimely and unfortunate,' and he continued by reviewing all the reasons that had led to the selection of Montreal in 1946. In his view those reasons were valid still and therefore there was no need to study the question any further.[24] The French representative reported that the American intervention only made things worse: 'la réaction de la délégation des Etats-Unis a été brutale et il en est résulté une tension dont toute la session s'est ressentie.'[25] The French supported the Portuguese motion, but a French official later explained his government's actions as the result of a little bitterness ('un peu d'amertume') over the Canadians' failure to support the French candidate in the appointment of a new secretary general, but this argument was somewhat disingenuous given the tone of the French report on the original debate. The French government was concerned over the 'preponderant influence' of the United States in civil aviation, and it is possible that French support for moving ICAO's headquarters, presumably to Europe, arose in this context of reducing American influence in aviation affairs.[26]

The Canadians attempted to counter the 'anti-Montreal faction' essentially by going over the heads of the ICAO delegates and appealing directly to the member governments. It was believed in Ottawa that some of the opposition to Montreal came from the personal feelings of a few ICAO representatives and did not necessarily represent or reflect the official policy of their governments. 'A good many of the delegates who voted in favour of the Portuguese motion are Council members living permanently in Montreal,' noted the Department of External Affairs, 'and we are inclined to believe that some of the them at least cast their vote mainly on grounds of personal preference and we doubt that they accurately reflected the views of their Governments. These delegates find life expensive in Montreal, and, anyway, would prefer to live in Western Europe.' In response, discussions were held with American officials and the two countries agreed to make direct approaches to the various governments that had supported the Portuguese motion 'in order to persuade them not to support any further move which might lead to the removal of ICAO from Montreal.' According to the Canadian document, the Canadians were to make representations to Belgium, Denmark, France, the Netherlands, Norway, Sweden, and India while asking the British government to take similar action with respect to the three Scandinavian countries, and the Americans agreed to approach several European members and instruct their representative at the United Nations to speak with his Latin American counterparts, 'stressing the procedural point that the possibility of moving the headquarters has been fully considered by the ICAO Assembly and that, therefore, the matter should not be reopened again by the Council.'[27]

The question of ICAO's headquarters was not raised at the 1953 assembly. The previous year's offer of the Canadian government to increase its contribution to ICAO's rent to $200,000 per year was well received and likely helped reduce much of the interest in moving the headquarters.[28] It is also impossible to know for sure, but it was suggested by the British Foreign Office that what it called the 'diplomatic activity' of the Canadians and Americans may also have helped dampen the enthusiasm of some governments.[29] Nevertheless, there remained considerable support among many members for the proposal to move the headquarters and this support lurked just under the surface, ready to rise up again when conditions improved.[30]

The 'anti-Montreal faction' revived in 1954, thanks largely to the actions of the host government in Quebec. Since signing the Headquarters Agreement, ICAO's efforts to meet with representatives of the Quebec government and to negotiate a solution to the outstanding problems had met with little success, and the problems over sales taxes and other privileges and immunities remained unsolved. Then, in February, the provincial government introduced legislation for a new provincial income tax law and Maurice Duplessis, the provincial premier, announced that the representatives and staff at ICAO would not be exempt from this new tax. ICAO's internal study of the legislation suggested that the legislation actually would exempt all ICAO salaries from provincial taxation, except those incomes earned by Canadian citizens, but, as C. Ljungberg explained in a letter to Canadian Secretary of State for External Affairs Lester Pearson, it would be 'most disturbing if it be the case that Canadian nationals on the staff of ICAO are left unprotected in the Quebec Bill. Discrimination between our employees in regard to their net emoluments would be most unfortunate. The same is the case with regard to the possibility that ICAO may be expected to deduct, on behalf of the Province, income tax from the salaries paid to its staff members and also, possibly, to file returns or submit its archives and premises to inspection and entry by officials of the Provincial Income Tax Department.'[31] In any event, the provocative words of the premier and the apparent unwillingness of the Quebec government to discuss the issues of privileges and immunities prompted the ICAO Council to reopen the whole issue of the headquarters location. As one Canadian cabinet memorandum described it, 'the majority of the I.C.A.O. Council took this [action of the Quebec Government] as evidence of something akin to hostility on the part of the Quebec Government towards the Organization, and the old issue of removing the Headquarters from Montreal was at once revived.'[32]

The whole affair was debated in the council sessions early in April 1954, and there was little doubt that action of some kind would be taken. One suggestion was to move the headquarters to another location within Canada. After all, Canada – not Montreal – was selected as the home for ICAO, and it was argued that a move within Canada would eliminate the problems with the Quebec government and presumably require no amendment to the Chicago Convention. Even the Canadian government considered moving the headquarters *within* Canada but, at a 14 April 1954 cabinet meeting, decided against such a move.[33]

There was also considerable support for amending the convention along the lines envisioned in 1952, enabling a headquarters move if enough members desired it. For example, Colonel Martinez Merino, the Spanish representative, argued to the effect that 'recent developments made the amendment of Article 45 a matter of urgency, to get the Organization out of the intolerable position of a tenant trying to establish a *modus vivendi* with an unfriendly landlord who knew that he could not move.' Merino claimed to be opposed to moving the headquarters (indeed, it is hard to find any member who was openly calling for a move, although it was known that several were willing to accommodate the organization in their countries), but in his view, amending the convention would be a kind of tactic to use in ICAO's struggle with the Quebec government. Not everyone agreed. For the Australians, who had opposed all efforts to move the headquarters, this new call for amending the convention was little more than 'a continuation of the move begun at the 1950 Assembly.' Similarly, it was pointed out that amending the convention might create a constitutional issue because Article 94 states that new amendments shall 'come into force in respect of States which have ratified such amendment.' What if some states declined to ratify the amendment – would there be two conventions? Or would the majority force the issue and oust from ICAO any member that refused to ratify the amendment (also a possibility under Article 94)?[34]

On 7 April, after several meetings, the ICAO Council agreed to recommend to the assembly an amendment to Article 45 of the Chicago Convention. The text of the amendment gave the assembly the power to move the headquarters following an affirmative vote of 'not less than half the total number of Contracting States.' The vote on the proposal was not even close – it passed with thirteen in favour and only two opposed. The United States, Great Britain, France, and Canada abstained.[35]

The action of the council set the stage for a major debate in the Eighth Session of the ICAO Assembly that opened in Montreal on 1 June 1954. There were few doubts that a proposed amendment of some kind would pass, but there was considerable and occasionally acrimonious debate in any event, especially over the number of states that would need to support a move of the headquarters for it to come into effect. Should a majority of the membership be sufficient? Or two-thirds of those actually present at an assembly? Should any decision made at an assembly need to be subsequently accepted by the membership, and if so, how many affirmative votes would it take? These matters were thrashed out first in the Executive Committee and then in the plenary session of the assembly.[36]

The Canadians abstained from the debate, but followed it with great interest. On one side were the Americans, Australians, and a few others who were opposed to what the Australians called the 'Shift Headquarters Movement' and to any amendment to the Chicago Convention to enable such a move. On the other side were some European and Middle Eastern nations and most Latin American states, which argued in favour of an amendment. The Brazilians, for example, proposed a motion that would enable a headquarters move with only a two-thirds affirmative vote in an assembly representing one-half of the total number of contracting states.[37] Between the two sides were the British, French, Irish, Dutch, and others who tried to find a compromise position.[38] A modified amendment, suggested by the Lebanese delegate, that would ensure that at least half the contracting states would need to support the move was brought to a vote but failed to get the necessary votes to pass. After more debate an agreement was reached that gave the assembly the right to decide how many votes would be necessary to initiate a move but that the number would always have to be at least equal to three-fifths of the contracting states. Those supporting the move 'thereby accepted in principle the very Amendment they had opposed 3 days earlier,' the Australian delegate later noted, but this formula was accepted by virtually everyone with the exception of the United States. The Americans cast the only negative vote, while the Chinese abstained. Even the Australians went along; 'I believe,' the Australian delegate continued, 'that the three-fifths affirmative vote of the total number of Contracting States will be difficult to get and therefore provides an ample safeguard.'[39]

The amendment to Article 45 of the Chicago Convention (which permitted a temporary move of location) added to the last sentence the words: 'and otherwise than temporarily by decision of the Assembly, such decision to be taken by the number of votes specified by the Assembly. The number of votes so specified will not be less than three-fifths of the total number of Contracting States.' In an effort to ensure that a proposal to move the headquarters would not be introduced at the last minute (as many members believed the amendment to Article 45 had been), a second resolution was passed stating that no future discussion of the transfer of the headquarters would be permitted without notification and the distribution of relevant documentation at least 120 days in advance of any ICAO Assembly meeting.[40]

The amendment of the convention was a victory for the so-called Shift Headquarters Movement but only a minor one. The amendment still needed to be accepted by two-thirds of the membership to come into effect (it came into force in 1958), and even when it did everyone knew that it would be very difficult to get the direct support of 60 per cent of the total membership in order to initiate a move. Knowing that it would be next to impossible for any disgruntled member to rally that much support, it became possible for most members to support the amendment, even if they opposed moving the headquarters. This group included the Canadians. As C.S. Booth, the Canadian representative to ICAO wrote, the result was 'much more satisfactory than had been hoped for. Looking to the future, and having regard to the fact that quite a number of contracting States do not attend Sessions of the Assembly, it would seem that even under the most adverse circumstances, the possibility of there ever being a sufficient majority to approve a move is extremely remote.'[41]

For those who supported the amendment as a bargaining tactic in ICAO's ongoing relations with the Quebec government, the amendment appeared equally ineffective. The intransigence of the Quebec government in dealing with the issues of taxation and immunities and privileges continued and, in some ways, worsened. In May 1955 a controversy erupted over the demand of the Quebec government that ICAO pay succession duties on an insurance policy paid to the wife of an ICAO employee who had died in a 1947 aircraft accident. When ICAO refused to pay, the Quebec government threatened legal action.[42] At the same time, the Canadian government appeared inactive in helping to resolve the outstanding difficulties – even a Canadian cabinet document admitted that the 'Canadian Government has been reluctant to act as a go-between for ICAO as regards its problems with the Quebec Government. In fact it has made no real serious effort to intercede with the Quebec Government on ICAO's behalf in relation to the over-all picture.'[43]

The frustration began to show. During the Ninth Session of the ICAO Assembly held in Montreal in May–June 1955 a Venezuelan delegate introduced a motion calling on (a) the Canadian government to intervene in ICAO's dispute with the Quebec government, and (b) on ICAO to initiate a study of the costs of operating ICAO from a headquarters in another city. In a move that can be seen as indicative of the degree of frustration felt by many members, the British delegation, which had always supported the Canadians in their desire to maintain the headquarters in Montreal, broadened the motion with lengthy resolving clauses that set out some of the details of the ongoing dispute.[44]

On the morning of the final plenary session, just prior to the vote on the resolution, Edward Warner, the council president, announced that the Canadian minister of transport had intervened to arrange a meeting between Premier Duplessis and a delegation of ICAO officials in an effort to settle the outstanding difficulties. The announcement was welcomed and reopened debate on the resolution. Had not the threat of the resolution achieved its goal, some members asked? The Americans and French believed it could be withdrawn – even the British, who had proposed it in the first place, agreed that it now was unnecessary. But the majority refused and the resolution was passed with only minor changes. The resolution noted 'with regret' that the Quebec government essentially had failed to live up to the promise it made at the first session of PICAO to 'extend its full co-operation' to ICAO, and invited the council '(a) to communicate with the Federal Government of Canada and to request that it continue its intercession with a view to securing a solution of the problems pending with the Province of Quebec and (b) to carry out a study in order to determine the cost of maintaining ICAO in those cities which might be most suitable as possible headquarters for the Organization.'[45]

The meeting with the premier took place in Quebec City on 16 June, but it produced few concrete results, other than a promise to keep on talking and an announcement that the Quebec government had decided not to proceed with legal proceedings in the case discussed above involving succession duties on payments to the widow of an ICAO employee.[46] Nevertheless, in the year between the 1955 and 1956 ICAO Assembly sessions the Canadian government took steps to resolve most of the outstanding issues. For one thing the Canadian government took a hard look at the value of having an international organization like ICAO in Montreal and concluded that even with additional subsidies and tax breaks the benefits of ICAO's presence in Canada far outweighed the costs in terms of foreign spending in Canada, savings for Canadians in terms of travel costs, providing employment for almost three hundred Canadians, and international recognition and prestige that Canada received.[47] And once it was agreed that having ICAO in Canada was a good thing, the government became more determined to find a way to keep it there.

The Department of External Affairs recommended three courses of action to stifle any future agitation to move the headquarters. First, the department recommended, as in 1952, diplomatic efforts over the heads of the ICAO delegates directly with their home governments. By approaching the various foreign offices rather than the individuals or even the departments responsible for civil aviation it was believed that 'other factors might be taken into account such as Canada's record in international affairs.' (The thinking here, again, was based on the feeling that the opposition of many members to the Montreal location was personal rather than the stated policy of the member nations.) Approach the governments concerned, convince them that the problems with Montreal were trivial, and you might have instructions sent to the delegations to ease their enthusiasm for relocating the headquarters. Second, DEA suggested more concrete action: if the problem over taxation with the Quebec government could not be settled it might be best for the federal government to step in and reimburse ICAO an amount equal to that deducted for provincial income taxes from the salaries of Canadian citizens. It would be a convoluted arrangement on paper, but it would remove the financial issue from the table. Third, it was argued that the only long-term solution to the whole issue of the headquarters location was for ICAO to have its own building, and DEA recommended that the government consider the idea of extending the International Civil Aviation Organization an interest-free loan to enable the organization to construct its own building. This made sense in a number of ways and would even save the Canadian government money – what would be lost each year in interest payments would be more than compensated by eliminating the $200,000 annual rent subsidy that Ottawa was providing ICAO.[48]

The Canadian government moved to implement these recommendations before the opening of the Tenth ICAO Assembly in Caracas in June 1956. In May, Ottawa sent a memorandum to its embassies instructing the heads of missions to approach the various governments to explain the views of the Canadian government and to ask for their 'continued support of Montreal as the headquarters site.'[49] In addition, the Canadian government announced that it would reimburse ICAO the income tax that it paid the Quebec government on behalf of its Canadian employees and that it was seriously considering granting an interest-free loan to ICAO for it to construct its own building. Moreover, the Quebec government announced at the same time that it was willing to meet ICAO's requests on the matter of immunities and privileges.[50] This new policy of the Canadian government was explained by the Canadian delegate to the Executive Committee in Caracas on 6 July 1956.[51]

These actions combined largely to end the dispute over the headquarters location. At the Tenth Assembly, the assembly adopted a resolution which expressed ICAO's 'deep appreciation to the Federal and Provincial Authorities of Canada for their generous efforts and arrangements regarding the extension of facilities, privileges, and immunities to the Organization, representatives of States, and the personnel of the Organization.'[52] As the Australian delegate in Caracas described it, this resolution 'very effectively kills the "shift headquarters movement" for the foreseeable future.'[53]

It would be many years before the International Civil Aviation Organization got its own headquarters building, and the settlement of the outstanding issues with the Quebec and Canadian governments did little to resolve ICAO's chronic space problems. For the rest of the decade and through the 1960s the steady expansion of the organization led to repeated requests first, for more space in the International Aviation Building, and second, for a new building altogether. By the early 1960s ICAO had taken over virtually the whole building above the ground floor, and there were expectations that even the ground floor would be needed by the end of the decade.[54]

In 1968, as the expiration of the twenty-year lease on the International Aviation Building approached (15 July 1969), the ICAO Council began to study the organization's accommodation needs. It was believed that the existing premises were no longer sufficient: there was no room to grow even though membership continued to rise, and the meeting rooms were inadequate. Conversely, there were benefits to be had in 'a clearly identifiable ICAO building.'[55] Discussions with the Canadian government along these lines were undertaken and an arrangement was made for the construction of a new aviation building in the heart of downtown Montreal, on Sherbrooke Street, across from McGill University, and only a few blocks north of the old location. This new building – on International Aviation Square – opened on 3 October 1975, with ICAO occupying fifteen of the new building's twenty-seven floors along with an adjacent conference complex. The new location was now home for more than six hundred staff and personnel and representatives of ICAO's 132 member nations.[56] This new building would be ICAO's home for the next two decades.

The American Delegation to the 1944 Chicago Conference. Left to right: A.M. Burden, Assistant Secretary of Commerce for Air; L. Welch Pogue, Civil Aeronautics Board; Alfred L. Bulwinkle; Senator Josiah W. Bailey; Adolph A. Berle, Jr, Assistant Secretary of State, Chairman; Senator Owen Brewster; Edward Warner; Rep. Charles A. Wolverton; Fiorella H. LaGuardia. 'I think it is the first time in the constitutional history of the country,' Berle wrote in his diary, 'that a member of an American Delegation, seeking to torpedo his own Delegation at the behest of a private interest, has attempted to embarrass the Delegation by a press campaign and a Senate investigation at the same time.'

Max Hymans, lawyer, engineer, and veteran of the First World War, fought hard in the pursuit of French interests as the Head of the French Delegation at the Chicago Conference. (ARLESS 130)

One of the earliest meetings of the PICAO Interim Council, in the Council Chamber in the Sun Life Building, Montreal, 1946. Around the table from the left: Major Alf Heum, Norway; Mr B.M. Gupta, India; Dr Kuis Alvarado, Peru; Sir James Cotton, UK; Major General Laurence S. Kuter, US; Mr Hikmet Anter, Turkey; Dr F.H. Copes van Hasselt, Netherlands; Mr Luis L. Duplan, Mexico; Ali Fuad Bey, Iraq; Mr Henri Bouché, France; Mr Shehab-El-Din, Egypt; Dr M.T. Obregon, Colombia; Captain L. Tacchi, Chile; Dr T.F. Reis, Brazil; Mr A.R. McComb, Australia; Mr T.J. O'Driscoll, Ireland; Dr Josef Kalenda, Czechoslovakia; Dr Albert Roper, Secretary General; Dr Edward Warner, President of the Interim Council; Lt. Colonel Jean Verhaegen, Belgium; Mr Anson C. McKim, Canada; and Mr T.Y. Yang, China.

Henri Bouché, the French representative, makes a point at the first session of the Interim Council in 1946. Seated next to him is H. Roushdy representing Egypt. A major influence in ICAO, Bouché was a staunch defender of the Organization, France, and of all French-speaking nations. 'Sometimes he drives me to despair; but other times he comes out with an illuminating truth,' wrote one British official. 'He is, of course, a most delightful person.'

The Hon. C.D. Howe, Head of the Canadian Delegation, voting during balloting which chose Canada (Montreal) as the permanent site for ICAO. (ARLESS 164)

ICAO's first permanent headquarters, the International Aviation Building, 1080 University Street, Montreal, Quebec, opened on 15 July 1949. For the first time all the meeting rooms, the Secretariat, and most of the offices of the Council members were contained under one roof.

Edward Warner, the first President of the ICAO Council (1947-57), with Albert
Roper, the Secretary General (1947-51), seated. These two men oversaw the
transition of ICAO from a good idea and provisional arrangement into a
permanent organization and specialized agency of the United Nations.

Sir Frederick Tymms, one of the key architects of the Chicago Convention, was with ICAO from the beginning, first as the Indian delegate at the Chicago Conference and then as British Council member (1950–53).

ICAO delegates at the Twelfth Assembly session in San Diego, California (1959) inspect a mockup of a Convair 880 Jet.

Three leaders of ICAO in the 1950s. Left to right: Ronald M. Macdonnell, Secretary General (1959-64); Walter Binaghi, President of the Council (1957-76); and Carl Ljungberg, Secretary General (1952-59), at the San Diego Assembly (Post Assembly Session). Binaghi personified the evolution of ICAO into a more diverse organization, and he was representative of a new generation of leaders. By the 1960s, most of those who had created ICAO were gone or soon to leave.

The members of the ICAO Council and visiting dignitaries at the inauguration of the new ICAO headquarters building on Sherbrooke Street in Montreal, 3 October 1975. At centre, in the lighter-shaded jacket, is the Right Honourable Pierre Elliott Trudeau, the Prime Minister of Canada. To his left is Walter Binaghi, President of the ICAO Council. At the far right of the front row is Assad Kotaite, ICAO Secretary General and, fourth from the right, wearing glasses, is Jean Drapeau, the mayor of Montreal.

ICAO Council President Dr Assad Kotaite (right) shakes hands with IATA
Director General Giovanni Bisignani, after signing a Memorandum of
Cooperation on 17 March 2006, by which each Organization agreed to provide
the other with safety information from their respective oversight audit programs. They are joined by ICAO Secretary General Dr Taïeb Chérif (right)
and Günther Matschnigg, IATA Senior Vice President, Safety, Operations and
Infrastructure.

7

Growing Pains

Even though it had failed to achieve a multilateral agreement by the end of the 1940s, the International Civil Aviation Organization was still forced to deal with its own success. The original organization was the creation of a small number of nations; nations that, by and large, shared a similar culture, language, and degree of wealth. All that changed in the 1950s and 1960s, and the rapid pace of change led to some growing pains in the organization's operations and procedures. The original design was sound and the basic policies, goals, and objectives remained unchanged, but over its first two decades ICAO evolved into a quite different organization in terms of its size, structure, and administration.

The story of ICAO in its first two decades was one of steady growth. In the early years the membership grew, as expected, as the participants at the Chicago conference ratified the Convention on International Aviation (the Chicago Convention). Furthermore, after the First ICAO Assembly, all non-contracting states that were eligible for membership were contacted by the Council of the ICAO and invited to send observers to various meetings of the Legal Committee, the technical divisions, and the different regional groups.[1] Not surprisingly, however, the greatest increase in ICAO's membership came from welcoming new states, many of which were created during the postwar decolonization of the old European empires. Former colonies did not automatically receive ICAO membership, but virtually all were admitted once they had adhered to the Chicago Convention and requested membership in the organization. Occasionally, new states were created in the partition or dissolution of existing states, and the same rules applied – each new state had to request admission and adhere to the convention. One example was the partition of British India and the creation of independent India and

Pakistan in 1947. Pakistan was required to apply for membership on its own, despite the fact that colonial India was already a member of ICAO. Pakistan joined near the end of 1947, Ceylon and Burma followed in the summer of 1948. This pattern was reversed somewhat in the case of two other members – Egypt and Syria – when they formed the United Arab Republic in 1958. The new country assumed the seat on the ICAO Council held by Egypt, but when Syria withdrew from the United Arab Republic in 1961 it reassumed its old membership.[2]

By 1949 the membership of the International Civil Aviation Organization was up to fifty-six with the entrance of Israel, Lebanon, and Cuba. Cuba had tried to join earlier but had made a reservation of Article 5 of the convention (i.e., Cuba was unwilling to grant automatic transit rights to other members), but this reservation was not accepted by all members. As a result Cuba stayed out until 1949 when it ratified the convention without reservation. A similar situation developed with Yugoslavia and Panama, both of which attached reservations to their memberships that were not accepted by the other members (Panama had, in fact, attended the Chicago conference). Both remained outside ICAO until 1960 when they ratified the convention without reservation.[3]

The International Civil Aviation Organization expanded with the addition of a few Eastern bloc nations including Romania (1965), Bulgaria (1967), and Hungary (1969), but the greatest growth in the late 1950s and through the 1960s came from the developing world, especially among African nations. Ghana joined in 1957, but the real wave of African membership occurred in the early 1960s with Nigeria, Senegal, Mali, Cameroon, and the Ivory Coast joining in 1960, Niger, the Central African Republic, Dahomey, Sierra Leone, and the Republic of Congo (Brazzaville) in 1961, and Gabon, Chad, Tanzania, and the People's Republic of Congo in 1962. Others followed, including Algeria (1963), Kenya, Malawi, Rwanda, Somalia, and Zambia (1964), Togo (1965), Uganda (1967), and Burundi (1968). There were other new members: Cyprus (1961), Malta (1965), Guyana (1967), and many more from Asia (Malaysia, 1958; Nepal, 1960; Singapore, 1966), the Middle East (Kuwait, 1960; Saudi Arabia, 1962; Yemen, 1964), and the Caribbean (Trinidad and Tobago and Jamaica, 1963; Barbados, 1967). By 1969 there were 117 members, the majority from the developing world, or the 'less developed countries' as they were often referred to by other ICAO members. By this time the so-called less developed countries wielded a significant influence in ICAO and they increasingly challenged the dominance of the older Anglo/European members.

It was agreed at the end of the First Session of the ICAO Assembly in 1947 that the second session, in 1948, would be held in Geneva, and it became a kind of a pattern to hold every third session at some location other than Montreal. Very early on it became apparent to most members that a full assembly every year was unnecessary and expensive, especially for the secretariat and council, which had to make extensive preparations for such a large gathering. It was also a heavy financial burden for many members to prepare and send a delegation to Montreal every year. Consequently, support rose for limiting the number of full assemblies to once every three years, to coincide with the election of the new council, and by limiting the other assemblies to administrative or financial matters. In 1948, at the Geneva session, it was agreed that 1949 would be a limited assembly; at the full session in 1950 the assembly agreed to hold a full Assembly of the ICAO once every three years, with 'limited' sessions to be held in the intervening years.[4] The 'limited' sessions were held in Montreal; the full sessions every third year were staged at different locations.

As interest rose in limiting the size of the sessions and/or reducing the number of assemblies from annually to once every three years, staging a session of the full assembly in a member's state became an even more attractive prize. By the end of the 1950 session the council was actively encouraging that every third session be held away from Montreal, with the assembly voting nearly $100,000 to defray expenses.[5] Not surprisingly, there was considerable competition for the right to hold these sessions and the jockeying for support began months before the different sessions began.[6] After Montreal in 1950, full assemblies were held in Brighton (1953), Caracas (1956), San Diego (1959), Rome (1962), Buenos Aires (1968), Vienna (1971), and Rome (1973); one extraordinary session was held in New York City (1973). There the tradition ended, and since 1973 all sessions have been held at the headquarters in Montreal, largely because the organization had grown so large that few members could effectively stage a full assembly session.

The holding of limited sessions in 1951 and 1952 was deemed a success in 1953. Money was saved both by ICAO and the member states, with no noticeable drop in the ability of the organization to fulfil its obligations. 'It is important to note,' recorded one Executive Committee Working Paper, 'that no essential business of the Organization was seriously impaired, delayed, or left undone because the agenda of the 1951 and 1952 sessions were limited, in the main, to budgetary and administrative questions. There would not in fact have been enough business to

justify full-fledged meetings of the Assembly in those two years.'[7] Even
the concern that limited sessions prevented the coming together of aviation officials from around the world to meet, discuss, and exchange information – one of ICAO's prime goals – seemed unjustified. Although
the assembly met only in limited fashion, there were constant meetings
of the many committees, air navigational conferences, and the regional
offices and groups. And, of course, the council continued to meet regularly throughout the whole period. 'The Council acts as a corporate body
and as a steward of the interests of all contracting States; it constitutes in
effect an "interim committee" of the Assembly between sessions of the
plenary body.' Because the council meets so regularly, it 'should make it
unnecessary for the plenary body to meet with the same frequency as in
organizations whose governing body does not exercise almost continuous control over its activities.'[8]

At the 1954 session the assembly passed a proposal to amend the
Chicago Convention permitting ICAO to hold its sessions triennially
rather than annually as required under Article 48.[9] The motion passed
easily but would not come into effect until ratified by the necessary number of states. At that time, forty-two ratifications were required. There
was little hope of securing this number of ratifications immediately, so it
was agreed to hold another session in 1955. By 1956, however, the required number of ratifications had almost been received, and 1957 became the first year in which there was no assembly session. Starting in
1959 triennial sessions became the norm, although there were additional 'extraordinary' sessions staged to discuss important specific issues.[10]

Running parallel to this movement to stagger the holding of full assemblies was a major push to increase the size of the council. With an
expanding membership and more geographic diversity within ICAO it
made sense to many members to expand the council to make it more
representative of the organization's changing membership. The movement gained considerable support and, at the Twelfth ICAO Assembly in
San Diego in 1959, in response to 'intense interest' within the assembly,
a resolution passed calling on the council to study the idea of enlarging
the council (and if so, then by how much) and then bring its conclusions
to the next full session in 1962.[11] A preliminary study was produced by
the council and the response from the membership was overwhelmingly
in favour of increasing the council membership.

Rather than waiting until 1962, an extraordinary session of the assembly was called for Montreal in 1961. Under Article 48 of the Chicago
Convention, an extraordinary session can be called by the council or at

the request of ten contracting states. At a January 1961 meeting of European aviation personnel at The Hague it was agreed to request the extraordinary session, with the specific request coming from the British government, which strongly supported the enlargement of the council. Having a session in 1961 rather than waiting until the full session in 1962 would preclude the necessity of debating the question of increasing the size of the council at the same time that a new council was being elected. Furthermore, by making the decision in 1961 it would be possible to have the necessary ratifications in place *before* the 1962 session, which would permit the election of a larger council at that time.

It was the first extraordinary session in ICAO's history; its sole purpose was to discuss the expansion of the council. This goal would be achieved through an amendment to Article 50 of the convention, which stated that the council would have twenty-one members. All they had to do was agree to change the number twenty-one to whatever larger number they agreed upon. More than fifty members attended (most were represented by their council representatives or by one or two of their diplomats posted in North America), and the session lasted only a few days, from 19 to 21 June. The assembly agenda contained one item, and many of the normal activities were dispensed with; for example, no Administrative Commission was established and the usual election of four vice-presidents was suspended.

Most of the discussions occurred in the Executive Committee. There was broad support for increasing the size of the council, with the United States being one of the very few members opposed to the idea. The American memo outlining the U.S. position noted the 'the experience of the United States on the ICAO Council had been that there were probably not even twenty-one States from different parts of the world which were able to send and backstop fully qualified aviation personnel to serve on the Council at Montreal. Consequently, the United States preferred to see the membership on the ICAO Council strengthened rather than increased.' The memo, produced by the Interagency Group on International Aviation, continued by noting that the larger the council the 'more unwieldy and less efficient the Council may be expected to become.' And, there were always political motives: 'The experience of the United States on the Council has already demonstrated that many Council representatives whose political interests outweigh their aviation interests can be expected to play politics and swing a vote in one direction or another depending on the personal whim.'[12] But the Americans realized they were in a small minority, and their official position was to go with the flow: if everyone wanted a larger council the United States would support it, but try to keep the size of the increase as small as possible.[13] The French delegation hinted at more political motives, suggesting that the Americans feared a diminution – however slight – of American influence in a larger council.[14]

The pros and cons of enlarging the council were discussed fully in the Executive Committee. Although there were very few voices that spoke in opposition, there was some debate on how big the council should be: twenty-five? twenty-seven? twenty-nine? Or one-third of the membership determined at each triennial session? The greatest support coalesced around twenty-seven. Ultimately this number was chosen without opposition.[15]

Much more concern was expressed about what a larger council would mean, and different motives for supporting the motion were revealed. For many members it was straightforward: the International Civil Aviation Organization had grown significantly in membership and the council should reflect this growth and, because the assembly now met only every three years, membership on the council became an even more important matter for many states. For others, a larger council meant a broader geographical membership that could provide the machinery through which the voices of some smaller members could be heard. The question was asked, however, if these smaller members could afford the cost – especially the expense of maintaining a full-time office at headquarters in Montreal?

Some of the biggest support came from the new African members, and several of the African delegates specifically expressed their hope that an enlarged council would make room for their countries. The observer from the Congo (Brazzaville), for example, was not the only one to make a specific request that 'States that had recently gained their independence would be given preference in the filling of the six additional seats, in the interests of equitable geographic representation and, in particular, of adequate African representation.'[16] The British, conversely, also supported expanding council membership, but out of a desire to maintain *European* membership on the council.[17] Still others, like the Americans, who had no specific regional interests to defend on the council and were virtually guaranteed a seat at the table, were focused on limiting the size of the increase of the council.

At the end of the day the assembly unanimously agreed to enlarge the council to twenty-seven, and it passed a resolution to that effect to amend the Chicago Convention.[18] Moreover, in an effort to move things ahead rapidly, a resolution was introduced, sponsored by Italy and Venezuela, calling on all members to ratify the amendment as quickly as possible.[19] The goal was to have all the required ratifications in hand before the next session – scheduled for 1962 – so that the new larger council could be elected at that time. To help matters even more (and ensuring the greatest amount of time for ratification), the Italian government agreed to stage the 1962 assembly in the late summer of 1962 rather than in the late spring, as had been the custom since 1947. As a result, there was pressure on governments to ratify the amendment immediately, and in some cases there was concern about the negative reaction if any state was seen to be dragging its feet.[20] As the Australian delegate noted after the assembly, it was imperative to ratify the amendment as soon as possible, because 'speed of ratification will be taken as an indication of the co-operative and international spirit of the State concerned.' More important, it could have a bearing on subsequent council elections: 'I have no hesitation in stating,' he added, 'that the next election to Council will be substantially influenced first of all by whether the candidate has ratified the Protocol or not, and secondly by the speed with which this ratification took place.'[21]

With sufficient ratifications in hand, the election of the new – larger – council occurred at the Fourteenth Session of the ICAO Assembly, held in Rome in August and September 1962. What needed to be settled before the vote actually took place was the question of how the new seats were to be divided. Council members are selected under three categories: the first group includes states of prime importance in international aviation; the second, states that are important providers of air facilities; and third, states representing the major geographical areas. The ratio established for the original twenty-one was eight-seven-six. The question now was in what categories should the new seats fall? In answering that question, the usual divisions appeared. On the one hand, the United States supported a ratio of ten-nine-eight.[22] The Europeans met in Ireland a few months before the session opened and also agreed on a ten-nine-eight distribution (with several new seats being filled by European states).[23] Such a breakdown would mean dividing the new seats equally in the three categories, two-two-two, and would give a boost to the major aviation states and those that provided air facilities, and give the smaller states only two new seats. On the other hand, the smaller states insisted that more of the new seats go to category three, geographical representation. In the Executive Committee discussions, the representative from Nigeria proposed that the breakdown be one-one-four, meaning that two-thirds of the new seats would go to the third category and give much more voice to the smaller states that could not be elected under the other two categories. In the end the committee compromised on an Ethiopian proposal to divide the seats one-two-three, which meant that each category would now contain nine seats.[24] It was a small victory for the smaller states.

In the process of enlarging the council a few other issues appeared. The increase in ICAO membership and in the size of the council sparked a discussion about the need for membership rotation; the Scandinavians had been rotating their council seat for years, and the Latin American states had done so too, at least informally. Now the Japanese, Australians, and others began discussing it as well.[25] Others complained about the *way* the council vote was handled, in that those nations that had tried unsuccessfully to be elected in categories one and two were automatically considered for category three. This arrangement seemed unfair, especially for the smaller nations that felt under-represented and whose only hope of council membership was in category three. 'It must be galling for Nicaragua,' one British official in the Ministry of Transport and Civil Aviation noted dryly after the 1956 elections in Caracas, 'to see some of the scanty category C seats filled by Venezuela (failed A and B) and still more by Ireland (failed B, in which category she has a good claim) seeing that both Western Europe and the North Atlantic (Ireland's two regions) are fully represented already. That does not necessarily mean, however, that we should wish so to rearrange the procedure as to increase Nicaragua's chances at the expense of Ireland.'[26] Nevertheless, there were calls to change the procedure and make those unsuccessful nations at least have to be re-nominated before seeking election in the third category.[27]

There were even complaints about the whole process and how easy it was to call an extraordinary session of the organization – only ten members could band together and force the holding of a session. In other words, a minority of the council could force the majority to hold an extraordinary session against its will. The British government, without acknowledging the irony that it was the United Kingdom that had initiated the 1961 extraordinary session, was one of the first to warn of its dangers. In the brief to the British delegation to the 1962 session, note was made of the 'anxieties as to awkward consequences which might ensue from an Extraordinary Assembly called on inadequate grounds, diverted from the agenda for which it was called to consideration of some quite other topic, and even stampeded into an ill-considered amendment of the Convention.'[28] The Americans felt the same, and at the 1962 Assembly in Rome, the United States delegation introduced a resolution to amend the Chicago Convention to make it harder to call an extraordinary session of the ICAO Assembly. The Americans asked first for one-third of contracting states, then lowered the threshold to one-quarter, and then finally to one-fifth. This last number was accepted and Resolution A14-5 was passed.[29]

However anyone looked at it, politics was emerging as a driving force behind council membership. Nations strove for membership for reasons of prestige; membership became a way for smaller nations to be heard, regardless of their contribution to international aviation; a seat on the council could provide a platform to further the interests of a particular state, a region, a group, a political agenda, or a language. The French delegation believed that the African nations had made a very good impression at the assembly,[30] but others worried about the implications of bloc voting and the use of the council and assembly sessions to further political agendas. As the Australian delegate at the 1961 session concluded, 'I should like to reiterate that the political nature of debates in the Assembly is growing and that it is obvious that in the future politics will play an even greater part in Council elections.'[31] He was right; through the 1950s and 1960s national interest and political motives increasingly became factors in council elections and the operations of the council and, indeed, of the whole organization.

A larger council had relatively little impact on the election process itself and the political manoeuvring that accompanied each triennial council election. Despite the rhetoric of being above politics, every three years votes were sought, bargained, and promised as members jockeyed for one of the few available seats. It is a little surprising, given that the council membership changed relatively little from year to year. Countries like the United States, the United Kingdom, France, Canada, Australia, the Netherlands, one Scandinavian country, Mexico, Brazil, Argentina, and India were elected just about every time. In Rome in 1962, for example, for the first election of the enlarged council, only nine states stood for election for the nine seats in the first category. The 1959 session in San Diego was a little unusual; as one observer reported, 'San Diego witnessed something that has not been seen for years: lively competition ... amounting almost to a battle,' with smaller states vying for more representation on the council.[32] In most years, however, only a few members were defeated; in 1953 all twenty-one candidates were elected. This fact does not preclude the possibility that some members declined to be nominated knowing that their chances of success were small. And, as membership expanded, new contenders appeared, such as Italy, West Germany, Japan, Israel, and several states in the Middle East and Africa. These members had supported council expansion as a way to make room for themselves.

Decisions to support another state for council membership were not always made on qualifications or contributions to international aviation. For example, when approached by Italy for its support for a seat on the council in 1950, one Canadian official noted Italy's 'substantial contributions to civil aviation,' but then added that there were 'strong political reasons for supporting Italy: our partnership in the North Atlantic Pact, the desirability of encouraging Italians to look to the west for encouragement, and the fact that our negotiations over war damage and Italian assets are not going very well.'[33] Such considerations were not unique to the Canadians, and the archival records provide many similar examples.[34] In 1950 one delegate reported that a representative from a South American state made a considerable splash in his efforts to garner support for council membership: 'at a recent reception,' the delegate reported, 'which started at 7:30 p.m. and continued until 3 a.m. for those who did not have sense enough to go home, the only drink available for a large part of the time was a very expensive champagne.'[35] Other times a political statement could be made by withholding a vote; in the 1962 and 1965 elections, for example, the United States, despite being by far the largest and most important aviation state, received the fewest votes of the nine candidates in the first category.

Even more common was the informal division of seats along regional lines, with different groups getting together in advance to decide which members of that group would stand for election to the council. The Latin America bloc had been operating along these lines since the Chicago conference, and by the 1960s so were the Middle Eastern states and the newer members from Africa. Likewise, the Europeans began to organize separately, going a further step in 1954 by creating the European Civil Aviation Conference following a meeting of European aviation officials in Strasbourg. The ECAC began its regular meetings in 1955. The goal of the ECAC was to review, discuss, and coordinate European aviation policies. There would be no secretariat and a very close liaison would be maintained with ICAO; indeed, in 1956 the ICAO Assembly passed a resolution to 'direct the Council to provide ... the secretariat and other services requested by ECAC to the extent necessary for its proper functioning.'[36] Within a few years ECAC had negotiated several

European agreements, including, in 1959, an agreement on a set of standard clauses for its members to use in their bilateral air agreements.[37]

By agreeing on council nominations in advance each region could prevent the splitting of votes between candidates from the same region and also ensure the greatest number of votes for their own candidates. 'The Latin-Arab bloc voted in unison,' one delegate complained after the 1953 election in Brighton, and there was 'no reason to believe that the majority will be any more kindly disposed toward the "Anglo-Saxons" at Caracas [in 1956] and in fact the situation could be worsened.'[38] There were also a few anomalies. Czechoslovakia, although a European nation, was not welcomed in the European region for political reasons; it was not until 1965 that the first communist state was elected to the council.[39] Another example was South Africa which, by the 1960s, thanks to its racist apartheid policy, could not count on any support from its fellow African nations. In fact, the African members launched a sustained campaign to oust South Africa from the organization. Similarly, not only could Israel not count on support from its Middle Eastern neighbours, it could expect open hostility against its election to the council. In 1962, for example, the British Foreign Office was approached by Lebanese and Libyan officials in their opposition to Israel's candidacy.[40]

In addition to regional divisions there was an even deeper split within the International Civil Aviation Organization along linguistic lines, and this division spread throughout all operations of the organization. The major cleavage developed between English on one side and, on the other, French and Spanish, the other two official languages. English had the advantage right from the start; the Chicago conference was conducted almost entirely in English; in the Provisional ICAO and then in the permanent organization most of the major offices and committees were chaired by English-speaking people or others who spoke English. English also was the common language of the secretariat and staff. Moreover, the English-speaking members dominated international civil aviation, and there were many people who believed that English was *the* language of international aviation. For these people, things were unfolding as they should – in English. It is hard to find an English-speaking representative who was concerned about the dominance of the English language. On the contrary, most were happy and relieved not to have worry about translating or following another language.

In addition to those who spoke English were the members whose mother tongue was not one of ICAO's official languages. For the most part these delegations chose English as their official language, although there were exceptions; an American delegate complained in 1959 that one Czechoslovak representative insisted on speaking Spanish even though 'it later developed that he spoke better English than Spanish.'[41] Nevertheless, from the Scandinavians, the Chinese, Indians, and others, there were complaints that it was unfair that they were being made to pay for the cost of translation of the proceedings of the organization into languages other than their own. Some members of this group even began to advocate that English be declared the sole official language, leaving it up to each non-English-speaking member to do the translation on their own. Why should they pay to translate the English into other languages that they did not use? Little came of these ideas (and the 1950 Assembly refused to separate the cost of translation from the general budget),[42] but they do give an indication of the growing level of frustration over language in the International Civil Aviation Organization.

The French, of course, saw things differently, and they were especially concerned about their language, making a concerted effort to increase its usage in the organization. It was a difficult task. After each ICAO Assembly the French delegation reported on the use of French; in 1952 twenty-six delegations always spoke English, four Spanish, and only three spoke French (France, Belgium, and Switzerland). The Italians, it was noted, spoke French when they voted with the French and English when they voted with the Americans.[43] At the larger session at Brighton in 1953 the French delegation reported that things had improved a little: thirty-four spoke English, fourteen Spanish, and eight French. The Brazilians and Portuguese however, spoke English.[44]

At the head of the effort to promote the use of French was Henri Bouché, who represented France on the ICAO Council for most of its first two decades. Bouché was tireless in his promotion of the French language, to the point that he began to antagonize his English-speaking colleagues. His methods were straightforward: he encouraged the use of French in the assembly, council, and committees; he complained when French was overlooked and demanded that French be used whenever and wherever it could; he sought out allies with similar views – the French usually could count on the support of the other French-speaking and Spanish-speaking states, which included the Latin American bloc of members from Central and South America; and he worked to secure the election of French-speaking candidates to the important committees and positions and, of course, French-speaking nations to the council. In the process, he risked being seen by the more self-confident – if not pa-tronizing – English-speakers as something of an irritating nuisance. One early American report described Bouché as an 'effective debater,' but also 'touchy, but friendly.'[45] A Canadian report echoed these views, reporting that Bouché could 'be so dam[n]' plausible,' and he could 'often sway a meeting.'[46]

In his reports to Paris, Bouché complained of bad translations into French – and of no translations, as it was common practice to print all of ICAO's working papers and documents in English only. When translations did arrive they needed to be scrutinized very carefully, and inevitably serious mistakes were discovered. What do you do when mistakes are discovered? In the final meeting of the Executive Committee at the Second ICAO Assembly in Geneva in 1948, Bouché protested the continuation of the meeting because he had only received the translations of the resolutions that morning at 9 a.m. and they contained 'grave errors.' The British delegate reported that Bouché 'emphatically refused to accept a vote on any subject until the French text had been in the hands of delegates for at least 24 hours, and then only if the translations were found acceptable.' The meeting was postponed, but it is hard not to read a degree of irritation at the actions of Bouché among those who supported one official language for ICAO.[47]

In 1951 the language issue spilled over into the election of a new secretary general to replace Albert Roper on his retirement. Of the potential candidates, two stood out: Carl Ljungberg of Sweden and Jacques Lucius of France. The Paris-born Lucius was educated in the law and political science and had been a military pilot and academic, but he did not have Ljungberg's civil aviation experience; the latter had been director-general of civil aviation in Sweden and had participated in the International Civil Aviation Orgnization from the beginning, including acting as the chair of two commissions at earlier assemblies. But of ICAO's three official languages, Ljungberg spoke only English (and he was earlier identified in at least one letter as a supporter of English as the single official language for ICAO).[48] In the council deliberations, Lucius was backed by the French and Spanish-speaking members; the others supported Ljungberg. The council divided, with Ljungberg receiving the majority of votes but not quite the two-thirds necessary to win.

With the council deadlocked, Rear Admiral Paul Smith, the American council representative, met with his Canadian counterpart, Brigadier C.S. Booth, to talk things over. Booth's memorandum on the conversation illustrates some of the language concerns within what some people were calling the 'Anglo-Saxon bloc.' Booth reported that while the Americans 'are anxious to see the vacancy filled, they would not be at all happy, on political grounds, to have a Frenchman. They object particularly to Lucius because he is essentially a political scientist, with all that that implies in a Frenchman, and while he has some knowledge of aviation, he is completely unknown in international aviation.' The American expressed 'fears that Lucius would get into "politics," and particularly in view of his close association with Bouché who has, upon occasion, demonstrated antagonism towards Warner, particularly on external relations matters.' The Canadian continued with his own views:

> A further possible danger, if we have Lucius, is in regard to languages. English is the working language of the Council and its Committees so far as documentation is concerned and, in fact, has become to a considerable degree the universal language in international civil aviation. The French and Spanish are quite understandably resentful of this and lose no opportunity to press for the use of their own languages. While everyone agrees with the necessity for providing interpretation services and French and Spanish texts on all proper occasions, any undue extension in this field could have very serious financial consequences, as language staffs and interpretation services are extremely expensive. If Lucius is elected, he will know who elected him and will find it extremely difficult to resist their demands for bigger and better language services. This also applies in regard to employment of French and Spanish speaking secretariat. Certainly, we need a more balanced representation in the Secretariat but this must not be achieved at the expense of efficiency which, under present conditions, is the only way it could be achieved.[49]

At one point in April, according to the report of the Canadian representative, Edward Warner, the council president, offered to resign his place and turn over the presidency to the Argentine (and Spanish-speaking) Walter Binaghi, which would offset the selection of Ljungberg as secretary general. 'The purpose of this proposal was to satisfy the obvious demands of the Spanish-French group for one of their own in either of the top two posts in the Organization.' Warner's offer was rejected.[50] The deadlock lasted through the summer and into the fall. Roper, who had hoped to retire by his sixtieth birthday in April 1951,[51] was asked to stay on in his position until the end of the year, and on 15 November the council finally announced Ljungberg's appointment as secretary general. He took up the position early in 1952 and served until 1959.[52] The majority had won the day, but the linguistic divisions remained.

A somewhat similar situation occurred in 1958–59 in finding a replacement for Ljungberg when his term came to an end. There were two prime candidates for the post: General Claude Tessyier of France and Ronald Macdonnell of Canada. Tessyier had served as a pilot in the Second World War and then on ICAO's Air Navigation Commission from the beginning to 1954; Macdonnell was a senior member of the Canadian Department of External Affairs and had been a participant at the Chicago conference. He left aviation for a series of diplomatic posts, although he had been part of the Canadian team at the 1956 ICAO Assembly. Macdonnell was seen as the better administrator, Tessyier as more of a technician. Tessyier had the support of France and the other French-speaking countries and, oddly, Australia. Macdonnell was strongly backed by the United States and United Kingdom and had, in the words of Henri Bouché, the vote 'du groupe anglo-saxon.'[53] He also had the support of the Italians, and not supporting the French candidate was 'a political decision of some delicacy,' according to the Italian chargé d'affaires who, in return, expected Canadian support for Italy's election to the council.[54] Clearly, the Canadian had the votes to win and, in the event, Bouché graciously conceded and personally nominated Macdonnell, making the choice unanimous. Macdonnell took over as secretary general on 1 August 1959 and remained in the post until 1964.[55]

An even more important election took place a year earlier, although the divisions it sparked were more regional than linguistic. In 1957 an end of an era occurred with the retirement of Edward Warner as president of the council. Warner was one of the framers of the Chicago Convention and he, more than anyone else, had helped to shape ICAO into the organization it had become. He had been re-elected president in 1953, but not long afterwards expressed his desire to retire. 'It will be a big change,' he wrote his friend and long-time ICAO colleague Sir Frederick Tymms, 'and there is much that I shall miss, but I haven't for a moment doubted that my decision to leave was the right one.'[56] An award was to be named in his honour, and a plaque commemorating his service to the organization placed in the council chamber. There would be numerous other awards and honours. He left big shoes to fill.

Informal discussions began years before Warner's official retirement and lists were drawn up, qualifications of individuals were debated, national interests were considered. Should the new president be an American, or would that be unacceptable to too many members? If not an American then from which nation should the new president come? And politics was never far behind; from which bloc should the new president come? In February 1954, Sir George Cribbett met with a Canadian official and told him that he opposed a French-speaking president, and he made particular reference to Henri Bouché. He was equally cool to a Spanish-speaking president, although he did make an exception for Walter Binaghi of Argentina, whom Cribbett thought would make an excellent choice. Cribbett wanted an English-speaker, however, and his first choice was Sir Frederick Tymms, the British representative on the council.[57] Cribbett was prescient, for these two men became the main contenders to succeed Warner as council president.

Sir Frederick Tymms was with the International Civil Aviation Organization from the beginning, when he was an Indian delegate to the Chicago conference, and he could claim to be one of the major authors of the Chicago Convention. After the war he returned to the British civil service and, in 1947, was appointed British representative on the council and chair of the important Air Transport Committee. He was a distinguished 'aviation-man' and a tremendous administrator who knew the convention, ICAO, and the world of international aviation inside-out. He retired in 1954, but was persuaded to throw his hat in the ring for the council presidency.[58] His rival, Walter Binaghi, was a much younger man, an engineer and civil servant who had been a council member and member of the Air Navigation Commission since 1947 and was appointed its chair in 1949. Well respected and equally well qualified, he had been elected president of the 1954 ICAO Assembly.[59]

Tymms was a bit of a late entry into the race and was the underdog from the very start, but by the end of 1956 the British government was actively seeking support from all the other council members. 'Tymms' strongest qualification,' the Foreign Office said in a telegram to the British Ambassador in Mexico City, 'is his long experience in aviation administration and as Chairman of the I.C.A.O. Air Transport Committee he has been primarily concerned with this side of I.C.A.O.'s work which Mexico strongly supports.' Binaghi, on the other hand, was 'primarily an air navigation man. In our view, I.C.A.O. needs first and foremost administrative quality.'[60]

Not everyone was convinced. There were concerns over some of Tymms' drawbacks – that he was already beyond retirement age and, even though he was in good physical shape, he would be a one-term president and the whole matter of choosing a president would be raised again in three years. There were other concerns as well, not with Tymms specifically, but because he was a representative of the United Kingdom. Politics was never far from the surface, and the decision about a new president was being made in the aftermath of the Suez Crisis, which had dealt such a heavy blow to the prestige and moral leadership of both Britain and France: 'There is also some question,' an official in the Canadian Department of External Affairs wrote,

> in view of the strained relations between the United Kingdom and much of the Arab world, of how successful any United Kingdom President would be in working with the Arab (Egyptian and Lebanese) Council Representatives. There has in the past been a tendency for Latin American Representatives to seek to exploit any real or imagined grievances on the part of the Arabs and attempt to establish an Arab-Latin (and to some extent Continental European) bloc opposed to alleged Anglo-Saxon domination of ICAO and international civil aviation generally. We have done our best to discourage such tendencies and have had some success: it is difficult to believe, however, that in present circumstances the choice of a United Kingdom President could contribute to harmony and co-operation on Council.[61]

An early election would likely produce a victory for Binaghi, and the British and the French knew it. The French backed Tymms, arguing that the Englishman was far more experienced than Binaghi; in a sense, they turned Binaghi's youth against him as an indication of inexperience. It seemed a little strange that France, which had championed the rights of the French and Spanish-speakers in ICAO, should now turn to back an English-speaking person for president, but they did so because they saw – and referred to – Binaghi as 'the American nominee.' The French 'felt that Benagi [*sic*] would be far too subject to U.S. influence' and, with his victory, the International Civil Aviation Organization 'was in danger of being dominated by the United States.'[62]

After a meeting in Paris on 21 December 1956, between the British civil air attaché and representatives from the French Foreign Ministry, it was agreed that Tymms did not have the votes to win. Again concerns were raised about the aftermath of the Suez Crisis and how the 'Anglo-French action in Egypt' would 'not work in favour of a French or British candidate.' The best that they could do would be to work for a postponement of the election and to continue to support Tymms' candidacy behind the scenes 'in the hope of later choosing a more favourable time for holding the elections.'[63] It wasn't much of a strategy, and it ultimately failed.

The United States backed Binaghi. At a mid-February 1957 meeting with the French ICAO representative and a member of the French embassy in Washington, American officials from the State Department's

Aviation Branch outlined their position. Neither nation had a candidate in the race, but this small detail did little to prevent long uncomfortable silences in the meeting as the two sides disagreed on their choice of candidates. The Americans explained their support for Binaghi, pointing to his broad experience, his youth (late thirties, compared with Tymms, who was in his late sixties), and his technical abilities. Also, it was pointed out that the Americans had already publicly backed Binaghi – it was unlikely they would change their mind now.[64] In their report on this meeting and the election generally, the French concluded that, with the support of the Latin American and Middle Eastern members and the influence of the United States on other council members, Binaghi's election was 'une quasi-certitude.'[65] They were right.

In the mid-February vote the ICAO Council overwhelmingly selected Binaghi, by a margin of seventeen votes to four for Tymms. It was a secret ballot, but the French representative believed that the four for Tymms came from the United Kingdom, France, Belgium, and India.[66] It was a clear victory for Binaghi. 'Had I known that the result was likely to be so decisively in Binaghi's favour,' John Riddoch, the new British council representative wrote Tymms, 'I might have withdrawn your name before the secret ballot took place.'[67] Binaghi took office on 18 April 1957, the date of Warner's official retirement, becoming ICAO's second council president. It was a position he held until 1976.

Binaghi's defeat of Tymms and his selection as council president was significant and reflected some of the changes taking place in the International Civil Aviation Organization. Coming from Argentina – a country that had not even been present at the Chicago conference – Binaghi personified the evolution of ICAO into a more diverse organization, and he was representative of a new generation of leaders. By the end of the 1950s, those who had created and built ICAO were all gone or soon to leave – Warner, Tymms, Cribbett, Roper, Hymans, and a host of other Americans, Britons, Canadians, Australians, and French (Henri Bouché was, perhaps, the exception that proved the rule). In addition, the rise to prominence of people such as Binaghi and Macdonnell – with administrative strengths more than purely aviation backgrounds – also hinted at future developments when the ranks of ICAO increasingly would be filled by civil servants and government officials rather than the aviation professionals of the early years.[68]

A new dimension was added to the language controversy with the expansion of ICAO's membership in the late 1950s and early 1960s to include many more French-speaking nations, primarily former French colonies in Africa. The French government preserved a degree of influence in many of these states through a network of treaties, associations, and exchanges, all channelled through a ministry in the French government.[69] These new members therefore maintained close relations with France and, as ICAO members, served as important components in the French-speaking bloc. 'During the debates the support given to the French delegation by the ten or eleven French African States was noticeable,' complained one British observer in 1962. 'During the course of the Assembly the French delegation (M. Bouché and Mr Hagenau in particular) wasted much time by long and unnecessary interventions, and by conducting a propaganda campaign on behalf of the French language.'[70] But the impact was clear; after the 1965 assembly Bouché could report that the use of French had increased with forty-seven delegations speaking English, seventeen Spanish, and twenty-nine using French.[71]

These new states tended not to speak English as a mother tongue and they also tended to be smaller, less developed states; few were prominent actors in international civil aviation. As a result, the language debate gradually divided along the fault line of wealth, with the powerful states in the English camp and the less developed members on the Spanish and French side. 'Language controversies,' recorded a British Foreign Office official after a conversation with R.S.S. Dickinson, the British council representative, 'are in part a symptom of a line-up between the major contributors, which are mostly English speaking, and the much more numerous States (about two-thirds of the total membership of ICAO) which are assessed for contribution at or near the minimum percentage. These, the "have nots," generally desire to see ICAO doing more work and spending a great deal more money; this is contrary to our interests. It so happens that the "have not" States are, in great majority, users of French or Spanish rather than English.' And from the British perspective, the French were exploiting this division for their own benefit. Bouché 'is a very able debater,' the official continued, 'and enjoys the role of leader of the French and Spanish Group. The policy of France, under its present President, is to promote in every possible way the use of the French language, as a boost to France's national prestige. This policy, which Mr Bouché has to carry out in ICAO, is very congenial to him.'[72]

By the mid-1960s the linguistic divisions became noticeable in the ICAO Council. Thanks to the larger council and an expanded membership, the language balance began slipping away from English – a development that greatly concerned the powerful 'Anglo-bloc.' 'On paper,' one British official wrote in 1964, 'the English speakers [in the council] have a majority of one over the French speakers; but whereas many of the English speakers are using English as their chosen foreign language, the French-speaking and Spanish-speaking contingents contain a much larger proportion of persons speaking their native languages ... Our position is therefore not as strong as might be wished, and it would be a great advantage if the elections next year produced a Council with a more favourable language balance.' Dickinson of the United Kingdom suggested that 'we should put the language criterion ahead of other considerations that have influenced us in previous elections and should deliberately seek to replace French-speaking states by English-speaking states where this is at all possible.'[73]

It was not clear how this new balance was to be achieved. One suggestion[74] was to oppose actively the re-election of Belgium to the council, but such a policy would be judged a success only if another European state was elected in Belgium's place, and it would inevitably create serious difficulties within the European region, especially between the United Kingdom, France, and Belgium. What *was* clear, however, was that it was now harder for the more powerful members like the United Kingdom and the United States to influence council elections. English remained a dominant force in the International Civil Aviation Organization despite all these developments, but the nature of the organization was changing, and all members would have to adapt to these new circumstances. Language was a problem that would not go away.

One place where these divisions over language and between the rich and poor members of ICAO were expressed was in the continuing debate over the financing of the organization. A not uncommon problem in ICAO's membership in the 1950s and 1960s years was the failure or inability of many smaller states to fulfil their financial contributions to support the organization. How do you deal with members that could not or would not pay their share? Article 62 of the Chicago Convention gives the assembly the right to suspend the voting power (in the council and assembly) of any member that fails to make its payments to the organization. The situation was later clarified by the assembly when it announced that 'two years is a reasonable period in which to permit a State to discharge its financial obligations and that this period is in conformity with the practices of other International Organizations.'[75] And any member that made payment in full would have its suspension lifted immediately.

In the great majority of cases it was the result of economic troubles at home – especially in the first decade after the Second World War – that made it difficult for many members to meet their specific financial obligations. Therefore, in most cases suspension was not seriously considered until other arrangements were made to either adjust the amount of the payment or to extend the time in which payment could be made. For example, in 1951 Nicaragua had its assessments reduced retroactively and then divided into monthly instalments to be paid over 1952.[76] If the member still seemed unwilling to at least try to pay its share then suspension was discussed and, beginning at the First ICAO Assembly, the members began taking action against the members that had not paid. At the Second Assembly, in 1948, for example, Bolivia, El Salvador, Nicaragua, Paraguay, Poland, and Jordan had their voting rights suspended because they had fallen behind in their payments; the following year most of the same states were again suspended. In 1952, at the Sixth Assembly, it was the turn of Bolivia, Czechoslovakia, El Salvador, Guatemala, Jordan, and Poland to be suspended. That same year, Guatemala denounced the Chicago Convention for financial reasons but soon withdrew its denunciation when new arrangements were worked out.[77]

At the Sixth Assembly in 1952, a major debate erupted in the Executive Committee over the suspension of members who did not live up to their financial obligations. There was a rough division between the larger nations that paid most of the bills and the smaller states that were more likely to find themselves in financial difficulties, but the lines were not always clear. There was also a third group comprised of members from both sides that wished to amend the convention to permit the expulsion of any member that flagrantly failed to make its payments. For many smaller states the answer to non-payment was not the suspension of voting rights but the renegotiation of assessments and other arrangements to make it possible for members to meet their obligations. For the larger states it made good sense to suspend countries that had not paid, but there was a general unease with the idea of reducing the payments of members, unless the circumstances warranted change. The Americans, for example, had 'always supported reasonable arrangements for time payments of arrears,' but they also 'opposed anything in the nature of a writing-off of debts to the Organization.' Distinction had to be made, the Portuguese delegate on the Executive Committee noted at the same meeting, between 'States in arrears against their will and because of circumstances; and States which were obviously disinterested in the Organization.' Negotiation and some satisfactory arrangement was necessary for the former; punishment for the latter. Those states that 'patently did not intend to pay their contributions' did a disservice to ICAO as their assessments were made each year and their failure to pay put a serious strain on the capital funds of the organization. For the Portuguese delegate, these states should be expelled. Several states agreed, including the delegates from the Netherlands, India, and Canada. Others disagreed, and asked about the bilateral agreements the expelled member had signed and their other obligations as members, such as transit rights, the provision of facilities, or as members of regional groups. 'Expulsion was a measure to be considered only in the gravest circumstances,' the American delegate warned. 'It raised large questions of responsibilities under the Convention which had to do with rights reciprocally exchanged, in addition to the simple matter of payment of dues.' Would it not be better, several states asked, to keep these states in – even as non-paying members – than to lose them altogether?[78]

The debate over suspensions of non-paying members continued for years. Rarely did members have their voting rights suspended, providing their governments made an honest effort to make its payments. Those who could not pay could bring their case to the Executive Committee and have new arrangements made. In rare cases, members that defaulted and made no effort to deal with their responsibilities had their voting rights suspended. Most states made the necessary arrangements to pay their arrears and were welcomed back with full voting rights. None was expelled.

In some cases, however, politics came into it. Poland attended the Chicago conference and was one of the first states to ratify the convention, but the government that undertook these steps was the wartime Polish government-in-exile, situated in London. Following the liberation of Poland a new – different – government was established in Warsaw, and this new government did not recognize the actions of the previous government in signing the convention. The new government claimed it was not bound by the actions of the previous government and refused to pay its assessments to ICAO. Poland sent an observer to the First Assembly and the following year tried to adhere to the convention.[79] The United States refused, arguing that Poland already was a member, and the assembly suspended Poland's voting power for non-payment of its arrears under Article 62. In response, Poland severed its remaining connection to ICAO and sent no observers to meetings. Only in 1957 was a compromise worked out enabling Poland to pay a reduced amount of arrears but, in return, Poland acknowledged that the previous Polish government had indeed ratified the Chicago Convention.[80]

On one side there were the smaller states that experienced difficulties keeping up with their payments; on the other were those larger nations that paid the greatest share of ICAO's expenses, and they were just as likely to be unhappy with the existing state of affairs. Who should pay for the operation of ICAO and how much has been a much debated question throughout the organization's history. As ICAO expanded and salaries and costs grew, and as the headquarters expanded under pressure from the rapidly growing membership, the pressure increased on the various members to pay more. At the same time, most nations, while they judged what the other members were paying to be fair and reasonable, believed that their assessments were too high and needed to be adjusted downward. It was an endless debate that revived with each assembly over the annual budget discussions.

The decision about how much each member was to pay was made based on a number of factors such as the size of the member's economy, its role in international aviation, and, in particular, its 'capacity to pay.' New members were assessed accordingly and complained, while older members tried to have their assessments reduced, but the basic structure remained and the relative contribution or ranking of each member remained fairly stable. At the very top was the United States, and the Americans hovered in the 30 per cent range throughout the 1950s and 1960s. Next in line was the United Kingdom, followed far behind by the French, Canadians, Australians, and several other European states. The great majority of the new states, especially the less developed countries, were assessed at a comparatively low rate. The states that had borne most of the cost of the International Civil Aviation Organization in the 1940s still did so in the 1960s, increasingly with the help of a few new members such as the Japanese, West Germans, and, finally, the Soviets.

The United States was consistently unhappy with its economic burden, which was far greater than any other member – not only in ICAO but also in most other international organizations – and there were efforts throughout these decades to first limit and then reduce the American contribution. The argument went that with the arrival of so many new members the cost of the organization could be spread out more evenly among the larger membership. Some members disagreed and claimed that the smaller powers would be unable to meet greater financial responsibilities. Others, like the Canadians and Australians, argued that on a per capita basis they contributed more than did the United States and, therefore, if anything, the Americans should pay more.[81] The Americans, meanwhile, increasingly believed that they were shouldering an unfair economic burden and sought to reduce their contributions within *all* the international organizations.

At the Eleventh ICAO Assembly in 1958, for example, the United States introduced a proposal to reduce gradually the upper limit of its

contribution and to establish a new maximum of 30 per cent. This reduction to the United States would mean an increase would be passed on to
several new members. The proposed reduction of the maximum payment was similar to that initiated by the United Nations, but the proposal
met with considerable resistance and sparked a heated debate in ICAO.
The Americans anticipated some trouble; before the session opened,
seventy requests for support were distributed to members – only four
positive replies returned.[82] At the assembly, several amendments were
introduced in the Administrative Commission; some members called for
delay; others suggested adding a per capita ceiling to the American proposal. In the end the Americans prevailed and the resolution establishing a 30 per cent upper ceiling was passed, but not without some bad
feelings. 'Whether the United States cause was right or wrong,' the
Australian delegate later noted, 'it must be said that very many delegations felt that the United States was adopting a most insensitive
"bulldozer"-like approach to the whole matter and the United States
Delegation would certainly have lost a lot of sympathy and good will if
not support on that account.'[83]

Nobody wanted to pay more and the only alternative was to reduce the
costs of the organization and its tendency to inflate its activities. As a result, one of the offshoots of the budget and assessment debates was a
constant desire to economize and cut costs wherever possible. The easiest targets of the cost-cutters were the assembly and council, and reducing expenses was a prime motive of those members who tried to limit
the frequency of assemblies. Again the fault lines of language and wealth
appeared, with the wealthier and usually English-speaking members supporting cost reductions on one side, and with the smaller non–English-
speaking states – including the less developed countries – on the other.
This division spread into areas such as the high cost of translation services from English into French and Spanish.

For example, throughout the long debates over expanding the ICAO
Council and limiting the frequency of assemblies there was a concerted
effort to streamline and reduce the sessions of the council. Again the motive was one of cost-savings. One proposal was to shorten the council sessions and to hold them and the meetings of the various council committees
sequentially rather than concurrently. 'The aim is to save time,' one
Canadian official wrote, 'by permitting Council representatives who are
members of Committees to give their undivided attention to Committee
work during stipulated periods, and by permitting Council to deal with the
completed productions of Committees together and at one time.'[84]

The effort to shorten the council sessions dragged on for years, with the United States, the United Kingdom, South Africa, and other Commonwealth nations, on one side, and the French, Dutch, Belgians, and most Latin American states, on the other. At the 1955 ICAO Assembly in Montreal the United States delegation introduced a motion in the Executive Committee to that effect, and it led to some acrimonious debate. When Arnold Irwin, the Canadian delegate, suggested that the American proposal was improper and not in good taste tempers began to flare, so much so that it made headlines in the local press.[85] 'We wish to shorten the sessions of Council,' reported one Foreign Office official attending the assembly, 'so as to arrange for our permanent representative at Montreal to be recalled to London and to go out to Council sessions for fairly short periods of about six weeks, which would fall twice a year.' Unfortunately, the official continued, 'there are delegates with strong vested interests in the Council who do not wish to see any such drastic curtailment of the Council's functions.'[86] The British also supported the idea of amalgamating the positions of secretary general and council president into one director-general for the whole organization.[87] Little progress was made on these issues; the only point of agreement between the two sides was to keep on talking. Budget problems remained, as did the cost-cutters, and debates over who paid and how much resurfaced continually over the following decades.

Despite the efforts of those who wished to place limits on its sessions, the ICAO Council emerged from its first two decades more powerful than before. The ICAO Assembly contained many more members but met less frequently; by the end of the 1960s the council was larger and more diversified and was more than ever the decision-making focal point of the organization. Nevertheless, the council had changed too. Thanks to the influx of new members and the expansion to twenty-seven seats, the ability of the larger more powerful aviation states to dominate its proceedings had been somewhat reduced. There also now were significant fault lines in the council along regional, financial, and linguistic lines. There had always been divisions in ICAO, but increasingly the deliberations of the council and assembly reflected the political considerations and national interest of the contracting states. ICAO was becoming a much more political organization.

A kind of equilibrium was achieved by the mid-1960s, and there were hopes that it would last for many years and that ICAO would be spared the divisive debates about language or over the size of its council and the functioning of its assembly. By the beginning of the 1970s however, with the entrance of the Soviet Union and other changes in the world of international civil aviation, these issues would reappear on the ICAO agenda. Nevertheless, by the end of the 1960s ICAO had become a more open, multilingual, and diverse international organization; it was no longer a small club of the wealthy, largely English-speaking, victors of the Second World War. The world had changed. So had ICAO, and in the future it would have more languages, not fewer.

8

Maintaining Standards

International air transport is constantly changing. Problems arise every day. It is our rôle to try to solve them before they become acute. In so doing we must always keep in mind that it is preferable to have a good solution on time than a better solution too late.[1]

'It must be admitted that the standardization of equipment and procedures has progressed considerably where international air routes are concerned,' wrote Max Hymans, the secretary general of civil aviation for the French government and the president of the Second Assembly of the International Civil Aviation Organization, in 1948. It was also true that 'all governments have accepted the majority of the recommendations made by ICAO, signifying the latter's incontestable authority in this respect.'[2] Most member governments had made considerable progress in meeting ICAO's standards and recommended practices for their air services and facilities, but it was a slow and difficult process.

All could agree on the need for standardization, but implementing these standards was both expensive and time-consuming. Accepting a new standard might mean having to replace expensive equipment and adopting new ways of doing things, and these adjustments could be difficult and even dangerous, especially during a transition period. Hymans and others of like mind advocated caution in ICAO's decision making on technical issues because 'new methods invariably upset certain old habits and frequently call for the replacement of equipment or the utilization of new equipment. These problems are rendered all the more delicate, as the systems at present in competition for a certain number of navigational and airway control operations are often far from being perfected or have not yet completely proved their practical utility.'[3]

The development of international civil aviation in the postwar era was characterized by rapid growth and technological change. New airlines appeared and old airlines were revived at the end of the war. In the United States, Pan American's international monopoly was broken; by the end of the 1940s several private airlines were operating internationally and American air services connected all corners of the globe. By 1952 all ICAO members were connected to the outside world with at least one international air service. That same year there were twenty daily regular scheduled flights connecting London and Paris; there were fifteen between London and Dublin; three European services connected with Montreal and ICAO headquarters; both Air France and KLM inaugurated services to Mexico City; Air France also established services to Venezuela and Tokyo; the Qantas service from Australia to London cut the journey from seven days to four, and a service directly connected Australia and South Africa. In Asia, new airlines appeared in South Korea and Taiwan; in 1946 Air India was nationalized as a state airline; Pakistan followed suit with the creation of Pakistan International Airlines in 1951. Similarly, in the Middle East airlines such as Middle East Airlines (Lebanon) and Libyan Arab Airlines began operations, while in Israel El Al Airlines was created in 1948 and soon developed into one of the largest airlines in the region, with services stretching to Europe and North America. In Latin America, several states began to nationalize formerly foreign-owned airlines. State airlines were created in Brazil, Paraguay, Peru, Cuba and elsewhere, and began operations to North America, Europe, and Africa. In Africa, as the old colonial regimes crumbled, new airlines appeared in the newly independent countries, more often than not with the help of their former colonial powers, especially France and Britain. For example, in 1961 eleven former French colonies grouped together – with French help – to form Air Afrique. Air Afrique, along with other companies like Air Ethiopia and South African Airways created an African network of services and began expansion to Europe, Asia, and other parts of the world.[4]

In all aviation categories the numbers were way up: passengers carried, cargo and mail carried, number of passengers per aircraft. In 1952 the airlines of the world combined to fly a staggering 39.5 billion passenger-kilometres – the equivalent, according to the ICAO Council, of transporting the total population of greater New York City from Montreal to Western Europe. Flying was safer and cheaper; aircraft were faster and bigger and performed better. New technology – with the introduction of jet engines, jumbo aircraft, charter-class travel, and even supersonic aircraft – changed the way people looked at the world and, especially, air travel. By the 1950s travel by air became common and no longer the preserve of the wealthy or well-connected few. Equally, the emergence of the Cold War, rapid decolonization, and the great economic divisions between nations all had an impact on the way aviation evolved. Politics continued to play a role as hundreds of bilateral agreements were signed, and some nations still felt blocked from some routes and entry points due to political machinations. The tensions of the Cold War were the obvious example, as international air services between East and West usually necessitated a change of aircraft and an intermediate stopover in Vienna, Prague, or Helsinki.[5]

In adjusting to these new realities and complexities of postwar life, the need for technical standardization in international civil aviation became even more important. It is possible for this technical side of ICAO to be overshadowed by the organization's more public face, especially when international politics were involved. Yet, like the typical iceberg, most of ICAO's activities took place below the surface and away from the public spotlight; but it was these essential technical operations that truly defined ICAO as an international organization.

Once the process of adopting an annex was completed a second process began – getting the acceptance of the standards by the contracting states. All ICAO members had considerable time to analyse, discuss, and comment before the standards were adopted. Any concerns or problems could be fully aired long before the standard came into effect, and considerable effort went into trying to find common ground that was acceptable to all members. Much has been written about the legislative process of the International Civil Aviation Organization and the legal aspects of the annexes, especially on the wording and meaning of the Chicago Convention and the powers of enforcement – if any – it confers on the council and the organization as a whole. What is clear, however, is that the members were encouraged to adopt the annexes as soon as possible, and that most standards were eventually accepted – at least in principle – by virtually all the members, even though they were under no legal obligation to do so.

It was a slow process, but looking back over the technical achievements in the first few years of ICAO Edward Warner was impressed with the progress: 'Of the aspects of aeronautics that are within the province of governments, either in governments' role of providing necessary public services or in their regulatory one, and that seem presently amenable to world-wide standardization and liable to benefit by it, fully three-quarters have already been covered by ICAO Standards, Recommended Practices, Specifications, or Procedures. The proportion so covered ought to exceed ninety per cent by the end of 1951.' Warner continued with a broad survey:

> Aircraft over most of the surface of the earth are already flown in accordance with ICAO's Rules of the Air. Their personnel are beginning to be licensed to ICAO's standards. Their pilots are briefed before flight by the use of NOTAMs (Notices to Airmen) prepared and transmitted in accordance with an ICAO-shaped pattern. The meteorological forecasts given them are drawn to an ICAO specification. After the flight begins, communication between the aircraft and the ground is conducted in ICAO-adopted codes and in ICAO-specified phraseology. The pilot makes his instrument approach, if an instrument approach be necessary, on an ILS [instrument landing system] of which the characteristics have now been standardized by ICAO to assure the closest possible uniformity of approach path and of character of instrumental indication at aerodromes throughout the world. The charts of the country over which he flies, and the larger-scale chart that shows the surroundings of the airport at which he is to land and the standard method of approaching it, have their size, color scheme and the meaning of their symbols determined by an ICAO standard.[6]

The speed of applying the standards and procedures, however, varied greatly from country to country. Although there were few notifications of disapproval of the annexes, it was not uncommon for some members to fail to implement all or part of a standard. It was also common for members to fail to notify the organization.[7] The greatest discrepancies in implementation were found between the developed and developing nations, with those members with broad and sophisticated civil aviation administrations embracing and implementing the annexes and amendments immediately, and those smaller members who had fewer resources or reasons to implement a myriad of regulations and technical standards. It was a costly affair in some instances to extend runways, to supply air traffic control services where none existed before, to amend or pass legislation conforming to ICAO standards, and to provide all the other facilities and services required to operate international air services. Some nations had relatively little aviation legislation of any kind and introducing ICAO standards or keeping up with the constant flow of amendments was just too expensive; others had the extra burden of translating the standards from one of ICAO's official languages.[8]

In 1956 a Special Implementation Panel was established to investigate the problems members faced in implementing ICAO's Standards and Recommended Practices. The panel suggested a broad array of changes to smooth the implementation process including better training, enhanced technical and financial assistance from outside sources, and more cooperation between ICAO and its member nations. But the task was formidable, especially given the expansion of membership in the late 1950s and early 1960s and the great jump in membership from the developing world. In 1965 it was reported that 50 per cent of the members were more than three years behind in maintaining ICAO's current operating instructions and only 25 per cent of members were up to date.[9]

Adding to these problems of implementation, especially for many of ICAO's smaller members, was the constant need to keep up with changing technology. The advent of jet aircraft perhaps best illustrates this dilemma. Widespread commercial jet service was introduced in 1958 by the United States and the United Kingdom (an earlier British jet – the Comet 2 – had been taken out of service in 1954 after two serious accidents). It was a remarkable achievement and welcomed by all; the new jet aircraft significantly cut travel time, offered more capacity to the airlines, and were embraced by the paying customer. By the end of the decade the global airlines had hundreds of orders in for jets, and the days of the piston engine and the propeller were numbered. But the new aircraft also put more demands on air navigational facilities such as air traffic control and on the length and strength of airways; other problems such as the damage to aircraft caused by bird strikes, were exacerbated by the new jets.[10] As one former senior ICAO official later wrote, 'the advent of the jet age brought about a change of all ICAO regional plans and practically all the annexes and related documents since these were tailored for a far different flight profile of speed, altitude and passenger seating.'[11]

In 1958, at the Eleventh Session of the ICAO Assembly, another Special Implementation Panel was established to examine the impact of jet operations. The panel members travelled, studied, and discussed all aspects of the problem to come up with ways to smooth the implementation of the changes that were required. For those nations that lacked the sophisticated air navigational facilities of the major powers, however, the extra burden was especially onerous, and they fell even further behind. In the Executive Committee at the Twelfth Assembly in San Diego in 1959 a few members, 'chiefly from delegations of smaller States,' raised the issue, 'emphasizing that they were not against progress in aviation but wished it to be achieved in a more orderly and economical fashion than it had been in the very recent past, and express[ed] their reliance upon ICAO for adequate warning of future technological and traffic developments and for guidance in preparing for them.'[12] But there was little the smaller powers could do to slow the process of technological change.

The problems facing the smaller states in adapting to new technology only became larger in the 1960s with the introduction of the jumbo jet. The new larger and heavier aircraft meant more passengers and a greater strain on runways, navigational facilities, airports, and, in general, the facilitation of air travel. In addition, the arrival of supersonic aircraft loomed on the horizon, and was discussed at the 1959 assembly. In 1960 an ICAO panel on supersonic aircraft was created, and the matter was discussed again in Rome in 1962. Concerns were raised about the economic impact these new aircraft might have on airports and on members' aviation industries, and over the social and environmental consequences, especially the problem of noise.[13] Council President Walter Binaghi warned of the difficulties many members had keeping up with each new wave of aircraft, but he could offer few solutions other than asking for more time to enable the members to make the necessary improvements.[14]

For many of those involved, however, stopping the advent of supersonic air travel appeared next to impossible. By the early 1960s the British and the French had combined in a supersonic program and were forecasting the first commercial flight of the Concorde for the early 1970s.[15] In the United States, the Federal Aviation Agency was calling for the development of an American supersonic jet as part of what was being called the 'Race to the Supersonic Transport.'[16] The Kennedy administration's Supersonic Transport Advisory Group noted in its 1962 report that 'supersonic travel over the world's commercial air routes is inevitable,' and the development by the United States of a supersonic aircraft was 'vital to the national interest.'[17] Appearing before the Aviation Subcommittee of the Senate Committee on Commerce to report on the Supersonic Transport Development Program, FAA Administrator N.E. Halaby said: 'when viewed in the light of aviation's history, the development of a supersonic transport is consistent with the primary mission of commercial aviation to provide safe and fast transportation, and is, in fact, an inevitable step forward. If for any reason the United States should not produce a sound commercial supersonic transport, we will have defaulted the leadership in commercial aviation to the British and French or to the Russians.'[18]

The development of supersonic aircraft became part of a larger discussion concerning noise pollution. With more aircraft in service, with larger, more powerful jet engines, longer runways, busier airports, and the thought of sonic booms crashing down from the sky like thunder, noise pollution became a global issue in the 1960s. The International Civil Aviation Organization was the logical venue to discuss joint efforts to deal with it, and noise quickly fell under ICAO consideration. 'It has been said that ICAO should regard the aircraft noise problem as now assuming an importance akin to that of safety, regularity and economic operation,' said one Australian delegate at a 1968 Plenary Committee meeting. 'The problem of the impact of noise on their daily lives is so serious at many of the world's airports that neighbouring communities are beginning to doubt the economic and social advantages of aviation.'[19] A resolution passed in 1962 (A14-7) called for study of the noise problem, but little progress was made; even agreeing to what was too loud and how to measure a sonic boom was difficult.[20]

In the months following the 1968 assembly in Buenos Aires, work began in earnest on what would ultimately become a new annex to the Chicago Convention. Resolution A16-3 called on the council to convene a Special Meeting on Aircraft Noise in the Vicinity of Aerodromes, which was held in Montreal in November–December 1969, and the report of these meetings was passed on to the Air Navigation Commission. In response to Resolution A16-4, the ANC also created a small 'Sonic boom' panel, which held its first meetings in October.[21] A draft annex was distributed to ICAO members in 1970, and their comments were considered and revised by the ANC. The new Annex 16 – *Aircraft Noise* – was approved by the ICAO Council on 2 April 1971 and became effective on 2 August. This new annex was only the second one not directly focused on aviation safety (the other is Annex 9, Facilitation), and it was the first annex introduced since 1953.

Annex 16 deals with different aspects of aircraft noise in the vicinity of airports – how to measure it, how to control it, and how to reduce it. Noise certification standards are produced for each different kind of aircraft, and each state is required to assess its new aircraft for compliance before granting them certification. One of the recommendations of the 1969 special meeting in Montreal was to create a Committee on Aircraft Noise, which could produce noise certification requirements and oversee the development and revision of the annex, especially as it applied to the production of new kinds of jet aircraft. Consequently, revisions to Annex 16 began immediately, and a third edition was published in 1978. The main problem that arose, as in other technical issues, was in the implementation of the standards, especially when it came to cost. As the delegate from Tunisia explained during the 1974 ICAO Assembly, 'something must be done' about aircraft noise pollution, but the 'solution would undoubtedly be expensive and in some countries the main question was how to distribute the cost among the airlines, airport operators and States. For many of the countries of the "third world," however, the solution of environmental problems had to take second place to mere survival, and while certainly not opposing further work on them, he doubted whether those countries in the near future would be able to participate very actively in that work.'[22] Nevertheless, noise levels began to fall as older aircraft were phased out and new aircraft meeting ICAO standards were introduced.

The issue remained on ICAO's agenda, as the specifications became more stringent and as ICAO standards were applied to more and more aircraft (and the subsequent noise level at most airports was greatly reduced).[23] The Committee on Aircraft Noise met regularly to study and update Annex 16 and its procedures; it dealt with aircraft ranging from propeller-driven airplanes and helicopters to supersonic aircraft.[24] This was a continuous process, although the basic fault line between the developed and developing world remained unchanged. In 1981, however, the name of Annex 16 was changed from *Aircraft Noise* to *Environmental Protection*, reflecting the broadening of ICAO's interest in this subject to include newer environmental concerns and issues such as aircraft engine emissions.[25]

Changing technology also had an impact on the larger powers, and on occasion political implications protruded into technical decisions. For example, in its efforts to achieve international standardization there was a considered need for a single ground-based radio navigational aid to be utilized by all members. A decision was made by the PICAO Interim Council in 1946 on one specific system (the one used in the United States) that was to be the standard system, at least until 1966. By the late 1950s, however, the British government and a few other members became strong supporters of a rival radio navigational system, and a long and sometimes bitter contest followed between the proponents of the two systems – 'a running Anglo-American fight which grew almost unprecedentedly sharp for ICAO,' was how one journalist described it.[26] There were economic factors of importance beyond the technical, in that choosing one system over another had an impact on industry, research, and employment in different member states. Ultimately the council stayed with the original American system, a decision that 'set in train a series of global purchasing and implementation schedules that virtually ruled out any further considerations of alternative systems in the foreseeable future.'[27] Such situations were relatively rare, but they were reminders of the council's considerable influence and how its decisions could have economic ramifications beyond specific technical matters.

In an effort to help the members in the difficult task of implementation, the International Civil Aviation Organization introduced a variety of programs to promote the standardization of air navigation; from the printing of technical publications and manuals (such as the *Communications Codes and Abbreviations*, the *Manual of Aircraft Accident Investigation*, and the *ICAO Aeronautical Chart Catalogue*) to the production of training films, to the implementation of aviation training and assistance programs. One early program brought trainees from member states to Montreal to learn about how the organization worked.[28] Moreover, ICAO introduced a broad research program to study technical issues and then collect, analyse, and publish its research findings and statistics, including the many bilateral air agreements entered into by member governments. In 1949, for example, ICAO initiated what the council called 'the most comprehensive survey ever undertaken of the ground facilities that governments operate and the services that they provide in aid of international civil aviation.'[29] Several dozen serious problems were uncovered around the world; the most common deficiencies were insufficient meteorological facilities and airways that were too short and therefore inadequate for take-offs for four-engined aircraft.[30]

Mention must also be made of the regional offices and the contribution made by the wide variety of groups, conferences, and meetings in the different regions. Although never very large in size and under the supervision of the headquarters in Montreal, the regional offices played an important technical role in ICAO in helping members in each region implement the organization's standards and procedures and acting as a kind of information liaison between local governments and the headquarters. Each office was staffed by administrative personnel and specialists in a wide variety of technical areas. They also conducted research on the existing state of local navigational facilities, held seminars and workshops to discuss regional issues, provided secretariat services for various groups within the region, and produced regional plans to facilitate improvements.[31] In this way, the regional offices and the regional plans became the main vehicle for the achievement of regional standardization in civil aviation. 'The field offices have become steadily more important,' the council reported in 1949, 'as the growing body of Standards and Recommended Practices and of general recommendations has increased both the importance and the complexity of the problems of national implementation. The role of the field offices as continuous points of contact through which personal liaison may be maintained between ICAO personnel and civil aviation officials of the various States and to which governments may conveniently turn for explanations of developments in Montreal and of the status of ICAO also becomes more important as it comes to be better appreciated. The field office personnel have been able in numerous cases to assist in implementation either through advice to individual States or through helping in the coordination of the action of neighbouring States.' The only drawback was that 'such action has been severely limited by the smallness of the field office staffs.'[32]

In addition, the International Civil Aviation Organization worked to achieve standardization in civil aviation through a systematic policy of coordination with other international organizations, including both governmental and non-governmental organizations and the other specialized agencies of the United Nations. They exchanged information, sent observers to each others' meetings and assemblies, and coordinated activities in the field. The closest relationship, not surprisingly, was with the International Air Transport Association. Meetings were regular and frequent, and IATA representatives were present for most meetings of both the Air Navigation Commission and the Air Transport Committee. Representatives from IFALPA, the International Federation of Airline Pilots' Associations, were also invited to various ICAO meetings. For example, in February–March 1965 a large Special North Atlantic Meeting was convened to discuss ways of handling the growing traffic on the North Atlantic route, which was approaching 'virtual saturation.' The meeting was held under the auspices of ICAO, but representatives from IATA and IFALPA played a major role, and the work of this meeting was coordinated with the work done by the other organizations at their meetings.[33]

Relations were close with other organizations as well, and not only with groups that dealt specifically with aviation. Several organizations devoted to the study of international law, for example, regularly cooperated with the ICAO Legal Committee. Another example was the collaboration with the World Health Organization to prevent the spread of disease through air travel. ICAO also undertook a study of air mail with the Universal Postal Union, and, in 1949, ICAO acted as co-sponsor of an Inter-American Radio Conference in Washington with the International

Telecommunications Union.[34] The web of relations only grew over the years, thanks to the increasing interconnection of the international community and the rising importance of international civil aviation.

Other difficulties arose in implementing the annexes to the Chicago Convention, especially in two general areas. The first was in those parts of the world where no state provided and maintained the necessary facilities. The oceans were the obvious example, but some nations also believed that the burden placed on them to provide air navigation facilities in more remote areas was far greater than any benefit they derived from using those facilities. The second problem arose with those countries that could not provide the necessary air navigation facilities. Noncompliance usually did not mean that a member opposed the standard; more likely, it indicated that the member lacked either the financial resources or the technical personnel to apply them. As Edward Warner wrote in 1948, aids to air navigation had to be established everywhere, even in remote regions and in countries that could not afford them. They 'must be placed in states whose nationals operate airlines to every part of the world; and in states that do not as yet operate with their own resources and their own personnel even within their own territory. They must even be located on occasion upon the high seas, or in some of those bits of land of which the nationality has not yet been conclusively established. They are needed in the wealthiest areas of the world; but also in the poorest; and obviously, but ironically and painfully, it happens that the installations which are most difficult to make and most costly to maintain, because of remoteness or of climatic and geographical conditions, are very commonly located in the territories of the governmental authorities which would be least able to bear even moderate expenses for such purpose.'[35] The lack of air navigational facilities in large parts of the world and the inability of some members to implement the standards would hinder the development of international aviation not only for the smaller countries that could not provide the facilities but also among the major powers, which would be unable to safely operate air services to various parts of the world. It was in everyone's interest to find a way to solve these problems of implementation.

The authors of the Chicago Convention addressed these concerns by giving the ICAO Council powers to aid and provide assistance to members unable to fulfil their obligations and, if necessary, to bring together nations of like mind to provide the necessary services in remote areas or territories beyond members' jurisdiction. If the council decides that 'the airports or other air navigation facilities, including radio and meteorological services, of a contracting State are not reasonably adequate for the safe, regular, efficient and economical operation of international air services, present or contemplated, the Council shall consult with the State directly concerned, and other States affected, with a view to finding means by which the situation may be remedied, and may make recommendations for that purpose' (Article 69). No member is required to accept the recommendations of the council, but if the member does agree an arrangement can be worked out with the council with either the state in question paying for it or, in some circumstances, the organization. In addition, and again with the approval of the state concerned, the council can 'provide, man, maintain and administer any or all of the airports and other air navigation facilities' in that state (Article 71), and provide 'technical assistance in the supervision and operation of the airports and other facilities, and for the payment, from the revenues derived from the operation of the airports and other facilities' (Article 74). The First Assembly in 1947 created the Committee on Joint Support of Air Navigation Services and set out terms for the provision of financial and technical assistance.[36]

ICAO's first venture into joint financing was the establishment of the North Atlantic Ocean Weather Stations. One of the most important results of the 1946 North Atlantic Air Route Service Conference in Dublin (see Chapter 3) was the agreement to maintain thirteen weather ships in the North Atlantic 'for meteorological observations, communications, air traffic control and search and rescue.'[37] These weather ships had been established across the North Atlantic during the war to aid air navigation. The Interim Council approved the idea, and in 1947 the participating North Atlantic nations met and formally agreed to share the cost in maintaining the weather ships.[38] For almost forty years NAOS made a significant contribution to the safe and orderly development of North Atlantic commercial aviation.

The number of ocean stations was reduced from thirteen to ten in an agreement signed in 1949, but the stations continued to perform their vital functions of providing meteorological information and communications services, in addition to search and rescue operations, in the North Atlantic. Problems arose in the 1950s over the cost of maintaining the ships, as more and more countries inaugurated North Atlantic services and, therefore, benefited from the weather stations. Payment to maintain the stations was based on the value derived from their use, and the United States was the major contributor. There were other 'non-aeronautical' benefits, such as meteorological information, taken into consideration as well. It was not always an equitable division, and the more other nations began using the services, the more the original participants encouraged the others to contribute financially, although no one state could be forced to pay.

The United States in particular was unhappy with the arrangement and at one point in 1953 threatened to walk away from the agreement altogether. There was concern over the expense of the stations; the Eisenhower administration was looking for any ways it could to cut costs, and the North Atlantic Ocean Weather Stations became an easy target. Nevertheless, the Americans derived military benefits from the stations, and, although they did not use this as a reason for staying in the agreement, it was a factor in their decision to maintain the stations.[39] Consequently, in 1954 the United States agreed to continue in the agreement with a reduction to nine ships and with several new members, including Italy and Switzerland, agreeing to share in the expenses.[40]

Other joint support arrangements were made with Iceland and Denmark. In April 1947 six ICAO members agreed to finance a LORAN (Long Range Radio Aid to Navigation) Station at Vik, Iceland, and an official agreement between Iceland and ICAO was signed in September 1948. The next year an agreement was reached with Denmark to provide joint support for air navigational facilities for Greenland and the Faroe Islands. Both these agreements were between ICAO and the two members (the nations that used the services made a financial contribution). In 1956 two new agreements were signed in which the participants were more directly involved; this new arrangement was more similar to the NAOS agreements and left ICAO playing only a general administrative role.[41]

Not all of the joint financing arrangements were successful. In 1954, for example, a plan to establish an Upper Air Station at Tegucigalpa, Honduras failed when the nations expected to pay for it backed away from the scheme.[42] Without the financial support from those who would benefit, the plan collapsed. Indeed, ICAO subsequently became involved in very few other joint support plans.

An equally important component of the work of the International Civil Aviation Organization was its technical assistance program, which emerged in the late 1940s and grew considerably through the 1950s and 1960s. Civil aviation could play a limited but significant role in the economic development of new nations, but it could not develop in a vacuum and had to be a part of a larger development policy.[43] In this way it made sense to cooperate with other organizations, especially the United Nations, to enhance coordination and prevent duplication in the provision of technical assistance in the developing world.

The Chicago Convention does not specifically call for a broad venture in technical assistance for ICAO members in the developing world, but the council explained its rationale for embarking on such a program in its Annual Report for 1949:

> Heretofore the efforts of ICAO have been directed primarily towards the standardization of international air navigation through the preparation of International Standards, Recommended Practices and Procedures, and Regional Procedures. Although many difficulties have been encountered, and agreement has still to be reached on many questions of importance, the foundation has now been laid. The States most advanced in technology may be expected to put the Standards and Procedures into effect without serious difficulty or delay; others may not fare as well. Lack of trained personnel, lack of experience and knowledge, and the difficulties of translating the written word into concrete action will hinder under-developed countries in carrying out many of ICAO's recommendations, however willing they may be to do so. Without outside help, their handicaps may seriously delay the attainment of the Organization's objectives, the realization of which will benefit all countries, advanced and under-developed alike. Technical assistance by ICAO could, at least in some cases, supply the needed help.[44]

The major powers in ICAO supported providing technical assistance to the members that needed it. For example, the council received offers of assistance aid almost immediately after the announcement of the program from Argentina, Australia, Belgium, Canada, Denmark, France, the Netherlands, Sweden, the United Kingdom, and the United States.[45] It was in the interest of these nations and others to have the proper facilities and navigational aids in place everywhere in the world, especially in the key regions that lay on the major international air routes. It was, after all, the airlines of the major powers that might benefit the most from these facilities.

The United States in particular had a lot to gain from the provision of air navigational facilities, but it was also the United States that would be expected to contribute the most in the provision of those facilities. The United States had the most experts and the know-how and the financial resources to pull the whole thing off. Indeed, it was questioned in some American bureaucratic circles whether or not the United States might be better off providing technical assistance on its own, regardless of the ICAO policy. ICAO had no equipment or experts to call on, and it would rely, in any event, on contributors like the United States to support its technical assistance projects.

Nevertheless, the United States became a staunch supporter of ICAO's technical assistance program. As the influential U.S. Air Coordinating Committee explained as part of a 1954 review of American aviation policy, the 'basic reasons behind United States support of multilateral technical assistance programs are political and psychological, as well as practical.' There were financial savings by being part of a program where the expenses are shared with others, and the 'motivations of our own bilateral programs are less subject to misunderstanding by other countries if at the same time we are supporting vigorously and contributing to the multilateral programs of the U.N. agencies. Occasionally, underdeveloped countries find it easier to accept assistance from an international agency than from a single government, no matter how friendly. In civil aviation, experts from other countries – which the U.N. agencies can recruit – are frequently better qualified than United States experts would be, in language and understanding of local culture, for specific jobs in underdeveloped countries.'[46] Overall, another ACC statement explained, with the 'position of the United States as a major operator of civil air services on the majority of the major world air routes, and with due regard to the military potential of well equipped and operated civil airways, it is in the national interest of the United States to support all practicable policies and steps directed toward the establishment of a world-wide system of aids to air navigation which is planned, provided and operated so as to promote the safe, regular and efficient operation of aircraft.'[47]

By the early 1960s American support for technical aviation assistance became even more explicit and tied to larger American foreign policy objectives, in particular the 'strengthening of the free world and winning its cold-war struggle – by the imaginative use of civil aviation assistance.'[48] A 1963 classified report on international air transport policy prepared for the Kennedy administration argued that helping developing states in the field of civil aviation 'can be of immense benefit in promoting political cohesion and internal security, the benefits of which in this cold war era need hardly be detailed. A civil aviation capability, properly designed, could serve the security interests of the non-Communist world in three important aspects: (1) it could enhance the effective authority and stability of local regimes; (2) it could be a major instrument for determining and combating internal coups and rebellions; (3) it could facilitate the local deployment of U.S. forces in the event of an external attack by an unfriendly third country, where the U.S. was forced to intervene to assist the victim in the attack.' More specifically, by helping a developing nation you could try to influence its civil aviation policies in a way complementary to American interests: 'it can try to direct the aviation efforts of these countries away from international long-haul operations, which are generally a drain on the country's treasury and energies and a complicating factor in the rest of the world's air transport system.'[49]

With the support of the United States and the other major powers, ICAO's efforts in technical assistance were much more likely to be successful. Most of ICAO's activities were conducted under the auspices of the United Nations and were coordinated by the U.N.'s Economic and Social Council. Under the U.N. Charter, ECOSOC was given the power to coordinate the activities of the specialized agencies in an effort to prevent the overlapping and duplication of assistance activities. Begun in 1950, it became known as the United Nations Expanded Programme of Technical Assistance, and in 1958 an additional Special Fund was created for larger specific projects. ICAO and the five other participating organizations (the United Nations, the World Health Organization, the Food and Agriculture Organization, the International Labour Organization, and the United Nations Educational, Scientific, and Cultural Organization) were required to submit their annual reports and future plans each year to ECOSOC. ICAO representatives also participated in U.N. meetings dealing with matters of interest to international civil aviation; U.N. representatives regularly attended sessions of ICAO; and information and studies were exchanged between organizations, and so on. In addition, the United Nations established several technical commissions in which ICAO had direct and immediate interest, including the Transport and Communications Commission to help coordinate activities in these areas. For example, in 1948 the commission supported the International Conference on Safety of Life at Sea in London, at which representatives from ICAO and other interested specialized agencies participated. As a result, ICAO's role in technical assistance was very much a part of a larger international effort.[50]

Given the requirements of the developing world there was no shortage of need for technical and development assistance in civil aviation. The process to acquire assistance began with the request of a member government and it involved ECOSOC and its Technical Assistance Board (which had an ICAO representative) and the ICAO Council. It was up to the council to decide on the parameters of the assistance program and the agreement was made with the cooperation and approval of the member government. The council granted the president the authority to decide what projects could be undertaken, and the president made the decision based on the recommendations of the secretary general. A Technical Assistance Fund was created under the secretary general, who in turn made the payments and supervised the administrative side of things. The secretary general was aided by an advisory board of senior ICAO officials who helped in the selection of technical experts. The whole arrangement was coordinated with the help of ECOSOC, and, in some instances, the United Nations itself sponsored an assistance project of some kind in which ICAO participated. Unlike ICAO's Joint Support Program, which was specific and immediate and was funded by the states most likely to benefit from the services, ICAO's technical assistance was part of a larger and more gradual development program financed by contributions to a fund controlled by the United Nations through its Technical Assistance Programme. At a June 1950 Technical Assistance Conference in Lake Success the participants pledged a little over $20 million annually for the U.N. assistance fund. Of this money, ICAO was promised 1 per cent ($200,000); when the number of requests for assistance far surpassed the available funds, the United Nations earmarked an additional $300,000, bringing the total allotted to ICAO to $500,000.[51] By the early 1960s that amount had more than tripled.

There were limitations on what and how much ICAO could do – financial restrictions, the nature of the problem, and so on – but the program was relatively broad. ICAO was willing to 'act as general adviser in the field of civil aviation to a government that requests such assistance.' In addition, the goal would be to 'to help States to help themselves.' In other words, no assistance program would be undertaken unless it was affordable and of limited duration: 'no project should create a permanent need for the experts initially sent to aid the country, and no permanent "operating" responsibilities could be accepted by ICAO as part of the Technical Assistance Programme.' Within those parameters, the type of assistance projects that ICAO would consider included:

a) Training abroad of the assisted country in such matters as:
   i: Administration and regulation of civil aviation;
   ii. Air Transport organization and administration;
   iii. Aerodrome and air route administration and control;
   iv. Flying, aircraft engineering, navigation, radio, aeronautical meteorology and other technical professions.

b) Technical missions to the assisted country to advise on and supervise
   the setting up of national and local organizations, e.g.:
   i.   the establishment of the administrative and regulatory machine;
   ii. the establishment of local training schools for any of the technical
        professions important to civil aviation;
   iii. the setting up of air transport or other operating organizations;
   iv. the establishment of air routes and the planning of aerodromes and
        ancillary navigation services.
c) The provision of expert technical personnel, on a short or long-term
   basis, to perform special services in the national organizations and enterprises set up in pursuance of sub-paragraph (b), until such time as
   national personnel are trained and fully ready to take over.[52]

In the first year more than a dozen requests for technical assistance
were submitted to ICAO. Following on-the-spot investigations, five requests were approved for 1951: for Colombia, Indonesia, Iran, Nicaragua,
and Thailand. By early 1951 the number jumped to nineteen approved
projects, including Afghanistan, Egypt, El Salvador, Ethiopia, Finland,
Greece, Iceland, Iraq, Israel, Italy, Jordan, Lebanon, Pakistan, and the
Philippines. The requests ranged considerably in size, but most asked for
the dispatch of aviation experts to the member state or requested a
fellowship for one of its nationals to travel and learn abroad. Experts
were sent to investigate problems and help establish civil aviation departments, policies, and planning, to train local personnel, and, more generally, to advise member governments on aviation issues. Fellowships were
granted to several member governments to send individuals to other
countries for flight training and to study such issues as airport management and maintenance, control tower operations, and aeronautical meteorology. The policy was judged a success, with more than forty experts
appointed and an equal number of fellowships granted by 1952. There
were, however, problems in finding a sufficient number of qualified experts who could be seconded to other governments.[53] Still, by 1961 there
were over one hundred experts providing aid, recruited from twenty-
eight different countries.

Within its first ten years, hundreds of individuals received fellowships
and were trained as technicians, mechanics, and in other fields, and dozens of governments and civil aviation establishments received aid, advice, and organizational help from trained experts. Each year the ICAO
Council's Annual Report catalogued all the assistance projects in which
the organization was involved, and each year this section in the report

got longer. There was never enough time or money to do everything, however. As E.R. Marlin, the director of ICAO's Technical Assistance Bureau wrote in 1959, 'the demand for this technical assistance still vastly exceeds the supply. The total of the funds contributed in each of the last few years to the United Nations Programme has remained almost stationary, and aviation in each assisted country has to compete for a share of these funds with agricultural, medical and other interests in whose fields there are many weighty problems awaiting a solution.'[54]

The most dangerous technical assistance project occurred in the Congo in the early 1960s. The crisis in the former Belgian colony was a very complex problem and the product of a multi-layered mixture of European decolonization, local rivalries, and international power politics. The Europeans had been planning their exit for some time, but rioting in the capital of Leopoldville in January 1960 hastened the Belgian departure, and Congo achieved its official independence on 30 June. A new national government was created, but politics on the local level intertwined with ethnic and tribal rivalries as different factions struggled for supremacy and control. Unprepared, divided, and facing a secessionist movement in the southern province of Katanga (backed by Belgian financial interests), the whole country threatened to descend into civil war, as violence erupted and anarchy spread across the Congo. Included among the rioters and looters were members of the Armée National Congolese, and their threats against the Belgians sparked the evacuation of most Belgian nationals, including most of those who operated the civil air transport system.

Calls for aid and support went out from the different factions to the major powers, including the Soviet Union and the United States, and Cold War rivalries began to influence the international response. The Congo contained vast mineral wealth, including rich deposits of uranium, which made it a place of interest for both the Soviet Union and the United States, and American policy in the crisis – beyond finding a peaceful solution and establishing a stable government – became one of excluding the infiltration of Soviet influence in the region either directly or through the establishment of a Soviet-friendly government in the Congo. In an effort to prevent the crisis from escalating into a global struggle between the superpowers, a U.N. peacekeeping force – the Operation des Nations Unies au Congo (UNOC) – was assembled to intervene in the situation. Believing that the Soviets would use its Security Council veto to prevent any U.N. *military* force for the Congo, on 13 July U.N. Secretary-General Dag Hammarskjöld called for a U.N. force that would provide 'technical assistance for security matters.'[55]

On 23 July 1960 the U.N. secretary-general asked ICAO to dispatch a team of technical advisers to maintain the airports of the Congo and keep them open to international traffic. The council responded immediately, sending an official to the Congo to report on the situation, and within a few days the recruitment of the ICAO team began. French personnel from the neighouring Congo (Brazzaville) filled in to keep the airport at Leopoldville open until the ICAO team could arrive. It was an alarming situation in the country, as the violence increased and the infrastructure of the state began to crumble. Things got worse with the evacuation of the Belgian technicians who maintained the ground services, and there were relatively few Congolese personnel to replace them. At the same time, the arrival of the U.N. force made it all the more important to keep the airports open and operating.[56]

By the end of the year ICAO had thirty-one personnel in the Congo (from Canada, France, Greece, Spain, Sweden, Tunisia, the United Arab Republic, the United Kingdom, the United States, and West Germany). Their main duties were to provide the essential services to keep the airports operating at Leopoldville and seven other locations, to train Congolese nationals so they could one day replace the ICAO personnel and, finally, to advise the Congolese government on civil aviation issues. The last duty was difficult in the early months of the mission because the central authorities in the Congo were unhappy with the presence of outside – and largely Western – personnel in their country. Things did not improve in 1961 as civil war broke out and attacks against Westerners increased in scope and number, including the murder of eleven Irish U.N. soldiers and thirteen members of the Italian Air Force. The violence even claimed the life of Dag Hammarskjöld, who died in a plane crash on 17 September 1961 while on a peace mission. In the meantime, the central government essentially collapsed, leaving the whole U.N. mission in a quandary as to which faction, if any, it should support. In the face of this danger, the ICAO mission – now representing sixteen ICAO states – increased to seventy personnel by the end of the 1961, and in addition to maintaining the ground services and air traffic control services at Congo's airports, it established an aviation training school. The 'circumstances in which the operational services were provided were almost always difficult and sometimes hazardous,' the Annual Report for 1961 announced with a degree of understatement. 'During the last few months of the year, technical emergencies were occurring almost daily because of the general deterioration of the extensive aeronautical infrastructure that had been installed before the Congo gained its independence.' The major problems came as a result of frequent power failures and the lack of spare parts and equipment.[57]

The situation in the Congo stabilized somewhat in 1962, in part because of the negotiation of a peace plan and the installation of a more pro-Western government following the murder of deposed Prime Minister Patrice Lumumba a year earlier. Relations between the government authorities and the ICAO mission improved and the number of ICAO personnel rose to almost one hundred. The ICAO team continued to maintain aviation services at all the country's airports as well as performing its other duties, but as the year progressed the numbers began to decrease. Unrest and violence flared up in different parts of the country over the following months and years, but the ICAO mission remained. There was even hope for the future as hundreds of Congolese trainees – both government and non-government personnel – attended courses in the training school and acquired the necessary skills as radio operators, air traffic controllers, and airport managers.[58]

The other technical assistance projects of the 1960s were much less dangerous but they were no less important. As the International Civil Aviation Organization expanded, with the arrival of dozens of new members from the developing world, the need – and the requests – for technical assistance increased. In 1962 the Executive Committee at the Fourteenth ICAO Assembly in Rome noted that the 'consensus of opinion was that the technical assistance activities of the Organization – to which great importance was attached by all delegates who spoke – needed to be expanded considerably, particularly with the emergence of new States that had become members of the Organization and whose need for assistance was pressing.'[59] By 1965, for example, there were thirty-one requests for assistance from Africa alone.[60] There was never enough money to go around, and the decision to focus the assistance on basic training, especially in the provision of ground services, came under criticism from some members who believed that ICAO's technical assistance should reflect the growing sophistication and specialization of civil aviation.[61]

An even more serious note of discord appeared at the Sixteenth ICAO Assembly in Buenos Aires in 1968, when a Tunisian motion passed creating a fellowship fund in the regular ICAO budget. Up until this time all of ICAO's technical assistance had operated through its connection with the United Nations. Opposition to this motion came from many members, but the fault line was clearly between rich and poor, as the major contributors to the organization did not want to have to pay for this new fund out of the ICAO budget. The American delegation fought against the proposal vigorously and tried to rally the opposition, but to 'no avail since the developed countries were easily outvoted by the combined Afro-Latin American blocs.' The funding was proposed for three years, but the Americans were worried about the long-term implications. Donald Agger, the chair of the American delegation, wrote in his confidential report on the assembly 'that the ICAO Assembly was willing to take action to establish a technical assistance fund in the regular ICAO budget, when such action is completely contrary to the current policy set by the United Nations General Assembly for the specialized agencies, portends the power of the developing country bloc in ICAO.'[62]

It should also be mentioned that as the years passed, more and more of ICAO's technical assistance work was conducted via the regional offices, which were more on the spot and could have a better idea of the needs of each particular region. Similarly, in the implementation of the various regional plans, local needs could be assessed and be followed up with technical assistance projects. In 1970, the ICAO Council reported that the services of the regional offices were used 'for the co-ordination of the requests originated by States, for assistance in the implementation of new projects, for provision of advice to experts on implementation matters and on ICAO policies in general, for evaluation of reports on T[echnical] A[ssistance] missions and projects, and for the maintenance of close relations with UNDP [United Nations Development Programme] Representatives, ICAO/TA missions and ICAO-assisted civil training centres.'[63] Specific activities were reported from Bangkok for the Far East and Pacific Region, Mexico City for the North American and Caribbean Office, and Lima for the South American Office.

In the end, and despite all the problems, the numbers were impressive. By 1968 ICAO granted technical assistance to a total of eighty states in the developing world – providing scholarships and fellowships, short investigative missions, and, in forty-one of those nations, providing resident missions to study and report, to advise governments, and to establish aviation training schools, centres, and institutes. The cost for 1968 was $2,703,178.[64] The assistance varied from country to country, and all the projects were listed each year in the ICAO Council's Annual Report. For example, in 1972 the organization provided Nigeria a variety of flying instructors, instructors in radio and aircraft maintenance, a senior aircraft engineer, and a project manager. In addition, 366 individuals had successfully completed courses at the Nigerian Civil Aviation Training Centre in Zaria and more than thirty Nigerian pilots had completed training there. In Egypt, ICAO supplied a training adviser, airport lighting instructor, and an aerodrome services expert. Almost five hundred students attended the Civil Aviation Training Institute, with a majority of them coming from outside Egypt. In Nicaragua, however, ICAO's technical assistance comprised one fire and rescue expert who spent two months there to study and advise on fire and rescue requirements at Nicaragua's airports.[65] By the end of the 1970s, ICAO employed 453 experts from forty-six countries working on approximately 450 projects in one hundred countries.[66]

The standardization of international civil aviation is an admirable goal, and few states that operated international air services opposed the attempt to achieve it, however unreachable it was. Even the countries that remained outside ICAO, such as the Soviet Union until 1970, were affected by ICAO's Standards and Procedures whenever they signed bilateral agreements with or wanted to fly over the territory of an ICAO member. In addition, the standardization of international civil aviation – in the provision of air traffic control services, meteorological services, in the facilitation of air travel, and so on – inevitably influenced *all* aviation, including domestic and purely local air services. In its simplest form, ICAO's technical efforts made flying so much easier, faster, and safer for millions of passengers around the world. All of this work went on behind the scene, without the knowledge of the passengers, except perhaps when they noticed that they could now fly safely to places where they could not before, or when they arrived in half the time and made it through customs and immigration more smoothly than ever before.

The implementation of the standards and procedures, the annexes, the technical assistance, the joint support programs, and all the work of the regional offices, the Air Navigation Commission and its divisions, the air navigation conferences and experts' meetings, the council and assembly, all the research, reporting, consultation and negotiation, and the publication of statistics, reports, and manuals together comprised ICAO's most significant achievement. There were setbacks and difficulties: the process of preparing and amending the annexes could be glacial; for a variety of reasons many members did not implement the standards as quickly as hoped and some failed to implement them at all; there was never enough money to undertake all the worthy projects; and there were political divisions everywhere. But the results were clear, if not obvious, every time a person went to an airport and boarded an airplane for an international flight.

The success or failure of all this work relied on the willingness of the member-states to implement voluntarily the standards and procedures. Much has been written comparing the International Civil Aviation Organization to the earlier International Commission for Air Navigation. In contrast to ICAN, an organization in which an amendment to its convention could be done by a three-fourths vote of its members and the decisions were binding on all members, ICAO, with a few exceptions, could only recommend, advise, and urge its members to accept and implement the annexes. But rather than hinder its effectiveness, this voluntarism and the non-binding nature of ICAO's standards has turned out to be ICAO's secret of success – the 'real genius' of ICAO's system, according to one author. 'The complex and sophisticated aviation code, consisting of ICAO SARPs, PANS, SUPPS, and Regional Air Navigation Plans that the Organization has been able to develop over the years with almost no opposition from the Contracting States, would not be in existence today without this built-in flexibility.'[67]

The United States and several other countries opposed the delegation of strong legislative powers to any international organization, and they likely would have done the same with respect to ICAO. There was a reason that ICAN failed to get a very broad membership. If ICAO had tried to force its members to implement what it considered binding obligations, then many nations might not have sought membership in ICAO at all, especially those which knew that, for economic, political, or constitutional reasons, it would be impossible to implement them. Existing members would also be less charitable: 'knowing that it would be bound to implement them, each state would scrutinize these amendments with great care and primarily in terms of its ability to comply with them. This in turn would have generated strong pressure to settle for less stringent technical requirements in order to obtain the passage of the amendment which, for that very reason, would have little practical significance.'[68] By setting very high standards as a goal, but allowing members to get there at their own pace, and by helping some members along the way, the International Civil Aviation Organization took great strides towards achieving the standardization of international civil aviation and, along the way, became one of the most successful postwar international organizations.

9

Problem Solving in ICAO: The Unfinished Symphony

The 1929 Warsaw System did not remain static and underwent, under the aegis of ICAO, a series of amendments or attempted amendments – a true unfinished symphony of half-hearted governmental efforts to improve the Convention.[1]

The International Civil Aviation Organization bends to the will of its membership. It has the ability to influence, cajole, and, on the odd occasion, threaten, but it cannot force any member to act against its national interest. Within that reality, however, the organization has considerable ability and a degree of independence to pursue its goals. It has the authority to settle disputes between members, at least in some circumstances, and, through its Legal Committee, it has been in the vanguard of the establishment of international air law. Both fields, in their own separate ways, deal with solving problems facing the orderly development of international civil aviation.

Chapter 18 of the Chicago Convention (Articles 84–88) sets out the aims and goals of the organization in the matter of disputes. The powers of the ICAO Council, at least on the surface, are very broad in that Article 84 notes that 'if any disagreement between two or more contracting States relating to the interpretation of this Convention and its annexes cannot be settled by negotiation, it shall, on the application of any State concerned in the disagreement, be decided by the Council.' In addition, there was the possibility of an appeal of a council decision to either an arbitral tribunal (chosen by concerned states and/or by the council president) or, ultimately, to the Permanent Court of International Justice. The decisions of the Permanent Court or arbitral tribunal are binding and final. Failure to comply with the decisions can lead to serious penalties; if an airline rejects the decision each member might be asked to refuse to allow that airline to fly through its airspace (Article 87), and if a state fails to comply with the decision then that state could have its voting power suspended in the council and the ICAO Assembly (Article 88).

The International Civil Aviation Organization has the authority to settle disputes arising from other sources as well. In both the International Air Services Air Transit Agreement and the International Air Transport Agreement, which were drawn up during the Chicago conference, there is a clause stipulating that if the two sides in a dispute over the interpretation of the agreement cannot negotiate a settlement then Chapter 18 of the Chicago Convention would apply. The same kind of arrangement could be found in many of the bilateral air agreements signed between ICAO members in which unresolved disputes could be appealed to ICAO. In the Anglo-American Bermuda Agreement, for example, if the two sides could not agree on the interpretation of parts of the agreement they could appeal to ICAO for an impartial judgment.[2] Moreover, in some multilateral arrangements, such as the North Atlantic Ocean Weather Stations and the joint support arrangements with Iceland and Denmark, disputes over the interpretation of the agreement could be handed over to ICAO if a settlement could not be reached between the participants. A similar arrangement was included in the multilateral agreement negotiated by the European Civil Aviation Conference in 1956.[3]

Council members were placed in a somewhat unusual position in that they were on occasion asked to act in judicial manner, even though they were appointed to the council as representatives of their nations and were expected to act in their nation's interests. Article 84 states that 'no member of the Council shall vote in the consideration by the Council of any dispute to which it is a party,' but was it possible for them to act impartially in all other disputes? Also, as legal expert Bin Cheng points out, ICAO Council members are aviation specialists or civil servants – not lawyers or judges – and they might not be best suited for serving on a judicial tribunal.[4] To answer some of these questions the council established a working group in 1952, and over the next five years it produced ICAO's *Rules for the Settlement of Differences* in 1957.[5]

The dispute settlement mechanism has rarely been used in ICAO's history, but by the time its rules were in place the council had already become involved in a number of disputes between members. Five years after the partition of British India, on 21 April 1952, India complained that Pakistan unfairly established a prohibited zone along its border with

Afghanistan, making it impossible for Indian airlines to fly directly between Delhi and Kabul, and making it necessary to fly around Pakistan and through Iran to get to the Afghan capital. The detour turned what was a 642-mile voyage into one of almost nineteen hundred miles. Moreover, the Afghans lacked aviation fuel, which made it necessary for Indian airplanes to carry sufficient quantities on board to make the return flight and, in the process, reduced the cargo load that the airplane could carry.[6] In their invocation of Article 84, the Indians were supported by the government of Afghanistan. Pakistan countered that the prohibited zone had existed before partition and was necessary for security reasons, although it was reported that Pakistan had given transit rights through the prohibited area to an Iranian airline.[7] India claimed that it was being discriminated against and that Pakistan was breaking the terms of the Chicago Convention and denying India its rights.

Both sides agreed to let ICAO investigate the issue, and a working group was established to investigate in June 1952. Council representatives from Belgium, Brazil, and Canada were appointed and they conferred with India's and Pakistan's high commissioners to Canada.[8] The two sides were encouraged to negotiate, and a meeting of civil aviation officials was held in Karachi in December 1952. In January 1953 a settlement was announced. Pakistan agreed to open two corridors, each twenty miles wide, to enable a more direct route across the prohibited area (although still not a direct connection between Delhi and Kabul) and to provide a certain amount of aviation fuel to Afghanistan for Indian airlines to make the return voyage.[9] It was more an accommodation than a decision, and although it wasn't a perfect solution, both sides accepted it. Everyone was happy, it seemed, and for some it set a precedent for the future: 'What can be done in civil aviation can be done elsewhere,' pronounced Council President Warner, 'What has been done by two nations in the present case can be done by others in the future. Every international disagreement that is settled makes the next one easier to settle by providing a good example. The cornerstone of healthy international life is international trust, and nothing stimulates mutual trust like success in overcoming difficulties through common effort. It will be as gratifying to men of goodwill everywhere, as it is to us here in ICAO, that India and Pakistan have had such a success.'[10]

A similar dispute occurred five years later when, in 1958, Jordan complained to the council that the United Arab Republic refused transit and landing rights to its aircraft flying over UAR airspace. Jordan responded by closing its airspace to the aircraft of the UAR. Both nations appealed to the council, but neither invoked Chapter 18 of the convention. As in the case of India and Pakistan, the council acted as a mediator and tried to keep the two sides talking. A temporary agreement was reached in which the two sides agreed to reopen their airspace; ultimately this modus vivendi became permanent and the dispute evaporated.[11]

Legal scholar Thomas Buergenthal points out that the council is not a court of law and that it sees its task as 'to assist in *settling* rather than in *adjudicating* disputes. Up to the moment of final decision, the Council in fact acts more like a mediator than a court.'[12] Indeed, as Buergenthal argues, the longer the council can delay formal proceedings and keep the two sides talking, the more likely it is to achieve an amicable solution to the dispute. This helps to explain why so few cases are carried through to the end. The council's 'effectiveness may be attributed, in part at least, to the fact that the Council does possess rather extensive adjudicatory powers, which place the Council in a much stronger position to compel negotiated settlements than a body lacking this authority. Thus, when the Council "invites" the parties to enter into further negotiations, for example, it is rather difficult for them to decline such an invitation, for there is always the possibility – real or imagined – that this uncompromising stance might affect the Council's decision in the case.'[13]

In the above cases, however, the mediation efforts of the council worked largely because both sides in the disputes were willing to negotiate and neither wanted to force the matter. In other disputes this was not always the case, and in those circumstances the council was much less fortunate and successful. In addition, if the disputes over civil aviation matters were a part of a larger problem between nations and the chance of an accommodation being reached was in many ways tied to the larger problem – the more intractable or hostile the situation, the less likely that the council would be able to find an amicable solution to the aviation question. Civil aviation problems in the Middle East, especially between Israel and its neighbours, were the classic examples of this dilemma.

The Middle East was and still is a very important region in international civil aviation, as it is situated under the main air routes connecting Asia, Africa, and Europe. Flying through the region's airspace is in the interest of most ICAO members and the provision of dependable air navigational facilities is therefore important, but the instability of the region has made that difficult to achieve. Israel became an ICAO member in 1949; by the early 1950s many Arab nations had also joined, and the tensions of the Middle East manifested themselves in the halls of the International Civil Aviation Organization.

During the 1950s and beyond, Israel's neighbours discriminated against Israelis and Israeli aircraft: the Egyptians barred Israelis from the Cairo regional office; there was no communication between Cairo and Lod Airport in Tel Aviv, even though Israel was in the Cairo Flight Information Region, and no flight information was passed on to any airline flying into or out of Israel.[14] In an effort to provide some stability for civil aircraft in the region, in 1951 the council called on the Middle Eastern states to establish an Eastern Mediterranean Flight Information Centre 'to provide complete and non-discriminatory service to the aircraft of all other contracting states.' It would not solve any of the larger problems in the region but at least it would make it a little safer to fly there. Finding an acceptable location to establish this centre was difficult and, in 1952, the ICAO Council selected Nicosia, Cyprus, which was still a British colony (until it achieved independence in 1960). The British government quickly announced that it could not pay for the centre, and the council turned to those nations that would benefit from the proposed centre and asked them to create a joint support project to fund it. Very few of the nations involved were willing to commit their support, and the project collapsed.[15]

The Israelis complained to the council about the discrimination against their aircraft that clearly contravened the Chicago Convention, but found little more than sympathy from some and hostility from others. At one meeting of the Executive Committee, during the Tenth Session of the ICAO Assembly in Caracas, an Egyptian delegate reminded the committee members that such actions were 'part of a boycott instituted in the interests of self-preservation and based on the existence of a technical state of war between Israel and its neighbours.'[16] In this case there was little that the council could do. In its annual report for 1956, for example, the ICAO Council reported that the Israelis 'sought the help of the Assembly in regard to the situation in the Middle East, maintaining that certain measures being taken by the Arab States with respect to aircraft en route to or from Israel were infractions of the Convention that should have been reported by the Council under Article 54(j).' The council's response was a testament to its inability to handle the situation: 'After a brief discussion, the Rules of Procedure were invoked to stop debate, on the ground that although the situation had technical aspects, it was part of a larger political problem outside the purview of ICAO.'[17]

Efforts at mediation worked only when – and to the extent which – the parties involved permitted it to. Such was the case with respect to the British colony of Gibraltar. Gibraltar, the small rocky peninsula on the southern coast of Spain became a British colony in 1713, but in the mid-twentieth century Spain renewed its claims to the territory. Spain took its case to the United Nations and hoped to pressure the British into ceding Gibraltar to Spain. The British responded by granting the small population of Gibraltar control over their internal affairs, and proposed a referendum for the people of the peninsula to choose their future course of action. The Spanish were opposed, and in the months leading up to the referendum the Spanish government declared a prohibited air zone in the vicinity of Gibraltar. The British claimed that they could only operate the Gibraltar airport properly and safely by using the airspace in the new prohibited zone and therefore must negotiate a bilateral agreement with Madrid. Relations between the two governments soured, and in May and again in September 1967, the British government appealed to the ICAO Council invoking Chapter 18 of the Chicago Convention.[18]

The council began the formal process leading to arbitration, and encouraged the two sides to negotiate, but in the 10 September 1967 referendum, the people of Gibraltar overwhelmingly voted to maintain their tie with the United Kingdom. The Spanish and many members of the United Nations were unhappy with the result and in 1969 Spain closed its border with Gibraltar (preventing thousands of Spaniards from getting to their jobs on the peninsula). That same year – before the council had really even become involved in the dispute – the two sides asked the council to drop the whole question indefinitely.[19] The focus for debate over the fate of Gibraltar then fell into the hands of the United Nations; the border with Spain did not reopen until 1985.

Similar results were experienced elsewhere, and in circumstances much more violent. Relations between India and Pakistan had been bad for many years, especially over the state of Kashmir. Bilateral relations deteriorated further in 1971 when an Indian aircraft was hijacked to Lahore Airport in Pakistan and destroyed by the Kashmir Liberation Front. India demanded compensation and the extradition of the hijackers and, in retaliation, in February closed its airspace to Pakistani aircraft. On 10 March 1971, Pakistan complained to the ICAO Council that India had contravened the rules of the Chicago Convention (and Pakistan's rights under the International Air Services Transit Agreement and an Indian-Pakistani bilateral agreement) by refusing transit rights over its territory. The council responded to the crisis as it had to other disputes and encouraged the two sides to negotiate a settlement, giving the two governments eight weeks to respond. In June, the government of India protested and argued that the agreements between India and Pakistan had been broken and therefore the council had no jurisdiction to examine the complaint; the council disagreed and following several meetings in late July, argued that under Article 84 it did have the jurisdiction. Without waiting for the council to decide the issue, the Indian government appealed to the International Court of Justice essentially to decide whether or not the council had the jurisdiction to consider and rule on the matter. The council, citing Article 86 of the Chicago Convention (which states that when a ruling is under appeal with the court 'decisions of the Council shall ... be suspended until the appeal is decided') resolved 'to defer further consideration of the matter until later.'[20]

At roughly the same time, trouble erupted in East Pakistan between the government and military forces and a rebel group that favoured breaking ties with West Pakistan. The rebels of East Pakistan declared independence on 26 March 1971, and fierce fighting followed as the government forces of West Pakistan ruthlessly suppressed the rebellion. The Indian government was sympathetic to the rebels and accepted thousands of refugees from the territory. In December the Pakistani air force bombed airfields in India and India responded by invading East Pakistan. A short war ensued in which India defeated the Pakistani military within a few days, and the new state of Bangladesh was proclaimed and a new government took office in January 1972. The council was helpless in the situation, weakly noting only that 'early in December, cables from India and Pakistan placed before the Council indicated that, due to the emergency which had arisen, they might not find it possible to comply with any or all provisions of the Convention and Transit Agreement.' The council simply asked the two governments to inform ICAO when the emergency was over.[21]

On 18 August 1972, the International Court of Justice rejected India's appeal and decided that the ICAO Council did, in fact, have the jurisdiction to consider Pakistan's March 1971 complaint.[22] Nevertheless, the council put off further discussion of the issue indefinitely on the request of the two governments involved. In December of that year Bangladesh adhered to the Chicago Convention and became a member of the International Civil Aviation Organization; two years later Bangladesh joined the United Nations and was recognized by the government of Pakistan. Relations between India and Pakistan – including aviation relations – normalized although tensions remained, especially with India's detonation of a nuclear bomb in March of 1974.

The ICAO Council has significant ability to arbitrate and adjudicate disputes between its members, at least on paper. In some cases this power was effective and led to amicable settlements of relatively minor problems. The council has shown itself very cautious in using this power, however, preferring to encourage a negotiated settlement in all cases rather than forcing a decision on either party. The secret has been to keep the two sides talking and, in most cases, let them make their own arrangements to work things out. ICAO does not use coercion in technical matters, and the same philosophy is applied to dispute settlement. It has had limited success when the parties concerned are willing to let ICAO help, but when the parties are not willing the council has a more disappointing track record. In matters in which the dispute over civil aviation is only one small part of a larger quarrel, the council can do little. ICAO can mediate aviation disagreements between members, but it obviously cannot solve major confrontations.

Another sort of problem solving that became increasingly important for ICAO as international civil aviation expanded, developed, and became more sophisticated was in the field of international air law. The standardization of air law became as important to the smooth operation of international civil aviation as the provision of standardized navigational aids and air traffic control services, and the negotiation, codification, and implementation of international air law was equally difficult and time consuming for ICAO members.

The focus of ICAO's legal activities was the Legal Committee, created by the assembly in 1947 and the successor to CITEJA (Comité International Technique d'Experts Juridiques Aériens), which ceased to exist the same year. The following year, the Legal Studies Section was removed from the Air Transport Bureau and established as the Legal Bureau, under the direction of the secretary general.[23] The Legal Committee inherited CITEJA's work-in-progress, and one of its first accomplishments was the Convention on International Recognition of Rights in Aircraft. This convention was adopted by the ICAO Assembly and opened for signature at its Second Session in Geneva in June 1948 (see Chapter 4).

The Legal Committee is open to membership from all the contracting states, and the members of the committee are legal experts and representatives of their home governments, not international civil servants. Decisions of the Legal Committee are taken by a majority vote, although, as is the case in most other areas of ICAO, considerable emphasis is placed on consensus building. It would be very difficult to impose significant changes on the legal systems of the minority nations that opposed a decision, especially if that minority included some of the world's more powerful aviation states. The committee meets fairly regularly, although it has not met in every year since its creation; it also establishes subcommittees to examine specific legal issues and problems.[24]

A new constitution for the Legal Committee was written and embodied in a resolution during the Seventh Session of the Assembly in Brighton in June 1953, bringing the committee more directly under the control of the council. This 'proper relationship,' in the view of the British delegation, 'will enable Council to limit the activities of the Committee to the study of subjects having an importance commensurate with the expense of the studies to the ICAO.'[25] The new duties of the Legal Committee were to include:

a) to advise the Council on matters relating to the interpretation and amendment of the Convention on International Civil Aviation, referred to it by the Council;

b) to study and make recommendations on such other matters relating to public international air law as may be referred to it by the Council or the Assembly;

c) by direction of the Assembly or the Council, or on the initiative of the Committee and subject to the prior approval of the Council, to study problems relating to private air law affecting international civil aviation, to prepare drafts of international air law conventions and to submit reports and recommendations thereon;

d) to make recommendations to the Council as to the representation at sessions of the Committee of non-Contracting States and other international organizations; as to the coordination of the work of the Committee with that of other representative bodies of the Organization and of the Secretariat and also as to such other matters as will be conducive to the effective work of the Organization.[26]

The Legal Committee studies and debates the legal issues and prepares a draft convention, which it submits to the ICAO Council. The council deliberates on it and, if it chooses, distributes it to the membership. The members have the opportunity to comment on it and, if it seems acceptable, the draft convention is presented to a special diplomatic conference. If accepted by the conference, the convention is adopted and opened for signature by the members. Finally, the convention must be ratified by a specified number of governments to come into force. This is a very long and difficult process, not that dissimilar to the process for establishing and implementing the ICAO's Standards and

Recommended Practices, and moves only as quickly as the members wish it to. As a result, several key matters in international air law remained on the work program of the Legal Committee for many years.

In Mexico City in January 1951 the Legal Committee completed a draft convention to replace the 1933 Rome Convention (Unification of Certain Rules Relating to Damage Caused by Aircraft to Third Parties on the Surface) and the 1938 Brussels Protocol (the Insurance Protocol of Brussels), both produced by CITEJA. The ICAO Convention (Convention on Damage Caused by Foreign Aircraft to Third Parties on the Surface) was discussed at the First Diplomatic Conference on Private International Air Law, held in Rome, from 9 September to 6 October 1952. The goal of the ICAO Convention was to establish limits for the damage to people and property on the ground as the result of an aircraft accident. The damage caused in an accident could be enormous, and it was believed that without some limits to the liability of the aircraft that the price of insurance would be so high that it would be impossible to operate an air service. Setting a limit to the aircraft's liability would help keep insurance rates down and enable the operators to acquire insurance. The new Rome Convention maintains the absolute liability of the operator for damage caused in an accident, but it also sets a ceiling limiting the amount of liability, including for the death and injury of third parties. This amount of liability was calculated based on the weight of the aircraft involved in the accident; the ceiling remained no matter how much damage occurred.[27] In the view of many states the ceiling was set far too low and did not nearly compensate third parties who suffered from an aircraft accident. As a result, only twenty-eight states became a party to the Rome Convention before 1978, when it was amended in Montreal.[28]

Even less success was attained with the draft Convention on Aerial Collisions, in which the Legal Committee picked up on work begun by CITEJA in 1930–36. As the name suggests, this convention dealt with liability for damage caused in air collisions. The Rome Convention applied only to aircraft in flight, but this new one was to include damage done by the collision of two or more aircraft in the air and on the ground if they were moving under their own power. The Legal Committee established a subcommittee to start work on a draft convention in 1953, and it began work in 1954. There were difficulties right from the start; as the Australians pointed out at the tenth session of the ICAO Assembly in Caracas in 1956, the air collisions convention was so closely related to the Rome Convention that it made little sense to work on the former until the latter was accepted by more members. They also reported that the Americans suggested dropping it from the work program altogether.[29] At the fifteenth session of the Legal Committee in 1964, the American team proposed amalgamating the air collision convention together with the Rome Convention and a draft of the Convention on the Liability of Air Traffic Control Agencies into a single convention, but this proposal was rejected.[30] The subject of air collisions was discussed on several more occasions in the 1960s, but no draft convention was prepared, and by mid-decade the discussions ceased. It was, one legal expert wrote, 'a good example of a subject that developed its own momentum within the closed circuit of the Legal Committee.'[31]

The Legal Committee became involved in the drafting of several other conventions on international air law. Some of the other subjects examined by the committee included the legal aspects of the nationality and registration of aircraft, problems arising from charter aircraft, insurance issues, aircraft noise, and the transport of goods. By 1980 the Legal Committee had drafted more than a dozen international instruments.[32] Increasingly, however, in the 1960s and 1970s more and more attention of the Legal Committee was focused on security issues and jurisdiction over air offences and on preventing acts of sabotage and the unlawful seizure of aircraft and punishing those who committed such unlawful acts. These legal developments, which are examined in Chapter 11, produced a more rapid response from ICAO and stood in contrast to the slower developments in other areas, and demonstrated that success in the development of international air law was very much a function of the desire of the member-states to get things done.

By far the most controversial aspect of the work of the Legal Committee, outside the issues dealing with aviation security, involved the Warsaw Convention and its various amendments and protocols that comprised the 'Warsaw System.' The Warsaw Convention, officially known as the Convention for the Unification of Certain Rules Relating to the Liability of the Carrier in International Carriage by Air, was signed in Warsaw in 1929. In a world with increasing diversity and great differences in legal systems, languages, and customs, the Warsaw Convention created a uniform system of documentation and law regarding the rights of passengers and air carriers involved in international civil aviation. It also established an upper limit for the liability of air carriers in case of accident and damage to passengers, cargo, luggage, and so on in international flight to U.S.$8,300, unless the damage was caused by 'willful misconduct'– in that case there was no limit. The Warsaw Convention came into force in 1933, the United States ratified it in 1934, and more than one hundred nations subsequently became a party to it.

The Warsaw Convention inherited by ICAO in the 1940s already seemed out of date to many members. Questions of interpretation were raised from different quarters: did the convention cover mental injuries? What exactly was an international flight and did the convention apply to a flight to a non-contracting state? Did it apply to aircraft on the ground? Did it apply to the operator of the aircraft or to the owner? Others argued that certain of the articles in the convention were 'obscure' and that its provisions 'have created substantial practical difficulties and dangers for air carriers and their insurers.'[33] On the positive side, it was argued that set liability limits made it possible for many airlines to operate and that without such limits the cost of insurance would be prohibitive and insurance unobtainable for many operators. Plus, by having set limits on liability it helped many people avoid lengthy and very costly legal proceedings. On the negative side, some members began arguing that the established limits were set far too low and needed to be increased, and that, given the great improvement in the safety of air travel, raising or removing the limits would not place an undue extra insurance burden on operators.

As early as 1946 the PICAO Interim Council recognized that a revision of the Warsaw Convention might be necessary,[34] and revision of the convention was discussed by the Legal Committee in Brussels in September 1947, in Geneva in May and June 1948, in Lisbon in September–October 1948, in Montreal in June 1949, and in Madrid in September 1951. A subcommittee of the Legal Committee was established in 1951 to write a new draft convention; it was discussed at the ninth session of the Legal Committee in Rio de Janeiro in August–September 1953, where it was agreed to amend the Warsaw Convention to bring it up to date rather than create a wholly new convention to replace it.[35] The first revision occurred in 1955 with The Hague Protocol, which among other things raised the limit of liability to U.S.$16,000.[36] In 1961 the new Convention for the Unification of Certain Rules Relating to International Carriage by Air Performed by a Person Other Than the Contracting Carrier – better known as the Guadalajara Convention – became part of the Warsaw System. This convention dealt with liability protection for operators other than the contracting carrier, for example in cases of rented or chartered aircraft. Relatively few members accepted the Guadalajara Convention at first because of the low limit set on liability.[37]

Many nations ratified the Hague Protocol, however, and it came into effect in August 1963. It did, however, run into serious trouble in the

United States, even though the Americans were strong advocates of hold-ing the conference in the first place, and they signed the protocol in June 1956. The Eisenhower administration sent the protocol to the Senate for ratification in 1959, but no action was taken on it before the election of 1960. After 1960 the new Kennedy administration re-evaluated American international aviation policy and, although it at first ap-peared willing to resubmit the protocol to the Senate, opposition – both public and private – rose significantly. The major sticking point was the $16,000 liability limit, an amount already far below what was be-ing awarded in many American domestic cases. The critics had a point; in 1959, for example, the average compensation for a death under the Warsaw System was U.S.$7,654; under a non-Warsaw case in the United States the average compensation for a fatality was U.S.$79,857.[38]

As one British air law specialist explained, there was a 'large number of "plaintiffs'" lawyers in the United States who receive a percentage fee and are therefore bitterly opposed to limitations of liability as being totally immoral.'[39] The American legal profession saw it differently, of course; one group, the National Association of Claimants' Counsel of America, was quick to point out that the Hague Protocol found its great-est number of supporters among the Communist states and their allies. In its brief to the American government's interagency committee set up to examine these issues, the NACCA wrote that there was 'no longer any reason or justification for shackling widows, cripples, orphans and other victims of air disasters to foreign moral, economic and legal standards, for the benefit of foreign air carriers which collect their handsome fares in U.S. dollars.'[40]

In 1964–65 the Johnson administration expressed a willingness to ratify the Hague Protocol and submitted it to the Senate with the provision that the domestic American airlines agree voluntarily to raise their liability lim-its to the $100,000 range. The airlines were less than enthusiastic, and the Senate refused to act on the protocol 'unless limits can in some way be substantially increased.'[41] As one Senator explained to a State Department official, the Warsaw Convention was 'no damn good to us.'[42] As a result, the State Department recommended to President Johnson that he denounce the Warsaw Convention while at the same time supporting the staging of a diplomatic conference to discuss the whole question of liability limits.[43] On 18 October President Johnson announced the United States' intention to withdraw from the Warsaw Convention, effective 15 November 1965. The American withdrawal would come into effect in six months (15 May 1966), and the State Department indicated that Washington would remove its notification of withdrawal if, before that date, an alternative agreement addressing the American concerns was worked out.[44] That gave everyone a few months to negotiate a new agreement.

If any other member failed to ratify the Hague Protocol or denounced the Warsaw Convention it might not matter, but without the United States the whole system could collapse. For one thing, it was reported that at least two other nations – West Germany and Canada – were under pressure to drop out if the United States did.[45] Even more important, denouncing the Warsaw Convention would mean that in U.S. courts there would be no limits to the liability of airlines after an air accident, and this would apply not only to American airlines but also to all airlines that flew into or out of American territory.[46] In other words, an American withdrawal from the Warsaw Convention would affect virtually all of the world's major airlines and they therefore had good reason to be concerned and to take the necessary steps to keep the United States in the Warsaw System.

The ICAO Council quickly called for a diplomatic conference on the Warsaw Convention, to be held in Montreal during the first two weeks of February, 1966. Almost sixty member states sent representatives to the conference and two non-members (Hungary and the Soviet Union) and seven international organizations sent observers. The discussions were wide ranging, as a number of delegations brought proposals with them and new ones were hammered out in committee, all in an effort to satisfy the United States and to keep it in the Warsaw System. But the divisions remained. Many member nations liked the Warsaw System because of the liability limitations – outside the United States, most airlines were government-owned, and it was in the interest of these governments to limit their liability and to keep costs down.[47] In the United States, many of the private airlines supported the Hague Protocol, but strong factions in the Senate and legal profession argued for no limitations at all. The White House and State Department wanted liability limitations, but the American proposal at Montreal was to set the limit at U.S.$100,000, which many others believed to be too high.

The reaction to the American proposal was, according to the American delegation, 'almost totally negative.'[48] Many members were willing to support a figure in the $50,000 range, but the opposition was strong even to that amount. It was really a case of the United States against the rest, but in the conference the major fault line ran between rich and poor, developed and developing. Andreas Lowenfeld, State Department official and chair of the American delegation, reported that 'it became

clear that states with major aviation interests and a developed airline industry were more flexible than those without. Germany and Belgium
spoke in favor of a reasonable compromise and Sweden suggested that
$100,000 was not an unreasonable amount. On the other hand, de-
veloping states, particularly the African group, supported by Poland and
Czechoslovakia, argued that if a very high limit were agreed upon, the
burden would fall on their airlines and their passengers to pay higher
insurance costs and higher fares in order to be able to cover judgments
and settlements paid primarily to United States citizens.' To make matters worse, the Nigerian delegate characterized this arrangement as akin
to 'the peasant paying for the King,' and, as Lowenfeld reported, 'this
expression set the prevailing tone and thus the marked division that developed as the conference continued.'[49]

In the end neither the king nor the peasants could find a compromise.
The American fall-back position of a U.S.$75,000 liability limit including
legal fees or U.S.$58,000 without, and an acknowledgement of absolute lia-
bility, garnered considerable support, but no consensus could be reached
and the conference ended in failure. A few delegations grasped at straws and
suggested that another diplomatic conference be called to settle the outstanding issues, but nothing happened at the conference sufficient to prevent the United States from withdrawing from the Warsaw Convention.[50]

With the end of the Montreal conference, the International Civil
Aviation Organization lost the initiative to the International Air Transport
Association. Even before the conference opened, William Hildred, a veteran of the Chicago conference and long-time director general of IATA,
began putting together an arrangement with the airlines that might work
on an interim basis. The United States government issued its minimum
requirements: liability of $75,000 including legal fees, $58,000 without,
based on absolute or strict liability, except for cases of 'willful misconduct'
(to avoid litigation in most cases and speed up settlements for the victims
by removing the need for victims to prove fault), and including the participation of all the major airlines. A deal was announced on 13 May, just two
days before the American withdrawal from the Warsaw Convention was to
take place. The new agreement was dubbed the 'Montreal Agreement' of
1966 and it met the conditions proposed by the United States, although
not all airlines signed on. Nevertheless, on 14 May 1966, the United States
formally withdrew its notice of withdrawal from the Warsaw Convention,
announcing that 'by acceptance of the plan the United States and all of
the other participating countries have assured the continuation of the
uniform system of law governing airlines, shippers and passengers and

have demonstrated again the viability of the system of international cooperation in civil aviation and in international law.'[51]

The Montreal Agreement was an interim arrangement and could be cancelled on twelve months' notice. It also wasn't lost on observers that the agreement was made outside of ICAO, indeed, outside of government altogether. Questions were also raised about the relationship of the new agreement to the Warsaw Convention – was the new agreement a revision of Warsaw or a companion? The Warsaw Convention permitted the addition of extra liability in a private capacity if governments or operators wanted it, but didn't the new arrangement work against the very basis of Warsaw – the establishment of a uniform system for all international civil aviation?[52] The Montreal Agreement was not the last word on the Warsaw System, and it was still widely believed that a more permanent solution was necessary; as two participants noted soon after the conference, 'the present way station is only an interim arrangement, to be tested, studied, revised, and eventually either abandoned or embodied in a new formal treaty.'[53]

The ICAO Council and Legal Committee returned to the issue immediately, and more meetings of the Legal Committee, subcommittees, and conferences followed. In June 1966, the council established a Panel of Experts to examine and report on the whole issue. In September 1967, the Legal Committee created a special Sub-Committee on Revising the Warsaw Convention to assess the findings of the Panel of Experts. The subcommittee met in Montreal in November 1968, but arrived at no final conclusion, other than to keep talking. The frustrations began to show; Warren Hewitt, the chair of the American delegation to the meeting, reported 'a mistaken but nevertheless deeply felt attitude' among the other members of the subcommittee 'that the United States has been toying with their good will.' The other members, he continued, 'clearly have exhausted their willingness to cope with further delay or presumed procrastination on the part of the United States.'[54] Finally, a tentative agreement was reached in 1970 at the Seventeenth Session of the Legal Committee on a proposal submitted by New Zealand – a 'package deal,' comprising the American's 'minimum position.'[55] This new deal became the basis of the Guatemala City Protocol.

A major ICAO conference on air law took place in Guatemala City in 1971, and on 8 March it produced the very long-named Protocol to Amend the Convention for the Unification of Certain Rules Relating to International Carriage by Air, signed at Guatemala City, March 8, 1971, commonly known as the Guatemala City Protocol.[56] This new protocol contained a few innovations and raised the limits of liability for injury and fatalities to U.S.$100,000, with strict or absolute liability, and it permitted members to introduce their own supplementary insurance plans if they chose to (a similar measure was included to cover baggage, both stored and carry-on). There also was a clause to permit the automatic raising of the limits in the future. In addition, a clause was added requiring thirty ratifications to bring the protocol into effect, but in this group there had to be five members whose airlines made up 40 per cent of the total travel of all members. This stipulation ensured that the protocol would never come into effect unless the United States ratified it.[57]

The American delegation signed the Guatemala City Protocol, along with twenty-one other nations, but the protocol was already a dead issue. For one thing, the $100,000 level was considerably higher than that in the Hague Protocol, but by the end of the 1960s the Civil Aeronautics Board had determined that the average award for a fatality in the United States for aircraft accidents not covered by the Warsaw Convention was already over $200,000.[58] Furthermore, efforts to get the domestic American airlines to agree to an insurance supplement to raise the level of liability in the United States failed. Moreover, a new wrinkle was added to the American opposition in that all these previous agreements were based on the value of gold, and as the value of gold began to fluctuate dramatically in the early 1970s, the United States wanted to base the liability limits on another form of currency. As a result, the Guatemala City Protocol was never sent to the Senate for ratification.[59]

A final attempt to amend the Warsaw System to balance the needs of the United States with those of most other members occurred in Montreal in September 1975, at a conference, somewhat ironically, called to discuss cargo and air mail rather than personal injury. On 25 September, the final day of the conference, four new protocols were opened for signature. Because of the problems with using gold as a standard, the liability amounts in the new protocols were now to be measured by the 'Special Drawing Rights' of the International Monetary Fund, which was a value established by a daily averaging of the major currencies in the world. The use of the SDR was to apply to the Warsaw Convention and the Hague and Guatemala City protocols, so all three had to be amended: Montreal Protocol 1 amended the Warsaw Convention; Protocol 2 dealt with Warsaw as amended by the Hague Protocol; and Protocol 3 dealt with Warsaw and the two amendments of the Hague and Guatemala City. The Montreal Protocol 3 was very similar to Guatemala City; it set the liability limit at $100,000, with absolute liability and the inclusion of the right for any government to establish its own supplementary insurance or compensation plan. It should also be noted that by ratifying Montreal Protocol 3, each state would automatically ratify the new versions of the Warsaw Convention as amended by the Hague and Guatemala City protocols.[60] Finally, because the Guatemala City Protocol dealt only with passengers and luggage, but not cargo, the Montreal Protocol 4 set liability limits for damage to cargo.[61]

In the United States, a supplementary compensation plan was devised by an insurance company and the major airlines that flew in and out of the United States that provided an extra $200,000 compensation for a fatality or injury.[62] With this added protection, President Ford sent Montreal Protocols 3 and 4 (the United States did not sign Protocols 1 and 2) to the Senate for ratification on 14 January 1977, noting that the 'development of a comprehensive system of compensation for injured parties in aviation accidents, and modernized rules relating to baggage, ticketing procedures, and cargo documentation and damage provisions are achievements that, upon the entry into force of Montreal Protocols No. 3 and No. 4, will bring the legal regime which has developed under the 1929 Warsaw Convention into today's world.'[63]

The U.S. Senate held hearings, discussed it, passed on it, looked at it again, and, in 1983, after years of deliberation, declined to vote on it. Senatorial opposition derived from the same source – a resistance to placing any kind of limitations on liability for personal injuries in air accidents. For some Americans, especially trial lawyers, it was wrong to put any limits on the value of human life; for other observers, the objections of the Senate seemed unwarranted and even irrational, since the new arrangements would raise the liability limit to the equivalent range of the awards for accidents not covered by the Warsaw Convention. 'The attitude of the U.S. Senate towards the Warsaw system has been one of hesitation and opposition,' one critic wrote, 'irrespective of the fact that all the modernizing Protocols to the Warsaw Convention have been negotiated and adopted with the active participation of the U.S. and that many other countries have, no doubt, done their utmost to accommodate the desires of U.S. delegations. Such an attitude undermines the credibility of the U.S. in international relations.'[64]

Without the Americans on side it made little sense for other members to ratify the Montreal protocols either. Consequently, little action was taken by the membership – or ICAO – for more than twenty years, other than repeated requests from the council that members consider ratifying the protocols, especially Protocol 3. In the meantime, international airlines made their own agreements to raise their liability limits and a patchwork quilt arrangement developed.[65] The Montreal protocols never garnered overwhelming support. The first two protocols received enough ratifications to come into force only in 1996 and Protocol 4 came into force in 1998. Montreal Protocol 3 has never come into force.[66]

The reviews on the legal activities and problem-solving capabilities of the International Civil Aviation Organization are mixed. Without a doubt the organization has played an important role in the settlement of aviation disputes and in the development of international air law; the old adage, that if there were no ICAO someone would have to invent it or something similar to it, applies here. But the organization and its efforts to solve problems legal and otherwise were susceptible to political interference. Over the years, as the membership expanded and became more diversified, it became harder to get things done. By the 1970s ICAO was a global organization with a broad mixture of languages, cultures, and economic, political, and legal systems. As one legal expert wrote in 1978, 'gone are the days when a few dominant "mother countries" would attend an international meeting, sign and ratify a convention, and incorporate it into law for a group of dependent territories.'[67] Finding common ground in this mixture has grown progressively more difficult.

ICAO demonstrated on several occasions that it could solve problems and disputes between members with a minimum of fuss, using its methods of conciliation, mediation, and negotiation, and by constantly urging the two parties to settle things on their own. The process has worked remarkably well when it was called for and the world of international civil aviation was the better off because of it. The dispute settling power was used only a few times, although the point has been made that the very fact that ICAO has this power has likely encouraged members to settle their disputes on their own before turning to ICAO for a decision.[68] But ICAO can only solve those problems that the membership allows it to; without the cooperation of the disputing parties there is little that the organization can do. And in those situations involving the larger powers or broader economic, security, or national issues, especially within the context of the Cold War, the organization has had little influence. ICAO is a United Nations organization; it is not the United Nations.

Similarly, ICAO's contribution to the field of international air law has only been as successful as the membership allowed it to be. It is the nature of ICAO to seek consensus and to have its members act voluntarily.

That has been the reason for its success in the area of standardization, and the same philosophy has been applied in the legal field. 'ICAO has played a useful role in the development of conventions on international air law,' was the assessment of one legal scholar. 'Structurally and organizationally the machinery exists for the production of good conventions. But the machinery is no better than its operators and the use they wish to make of it.'[69] The results, consequently, have been very uneven. A scan of the council's annual reports reveal a maze of legal instruments, with some in force and ratified by a large majority of members, a few in force but only barely, others pending, garnering modest support, still others moribund. All of the work of ICAO and its Legal Committee means nothing if the members fail to embrace it.

ICAO also suffers from all the problems of any large organization; the Legal Committee, its subcommittees, and the Legal Bureau are overworked and the work that is done advances at a snail's pace. There is what has been described as a 'vicious circle' in the preparation of legal conventions, as draft proposals meander from committee to subcommittee, then to the membership for comment, and then to a diplomatic conference, where changes are requested, and then back to subcommittee and committee where the whole process begins again. By this time the membership of the Legal Committee has changed, or several delegations that were present at an earlier conference are absent or arrive unprepared at the next, and so on.[70] The whole process is particularly difficult for the states from the developing world, which often lack the resources to maintain a sustained presence in this long process. 'Usually the developing States do not attend the Conferences for fiscal or other reasons,' one critic has argued.

> The lack of advocates who would present arguments common to these States (not always similar to those of developed States) causes low interest in the act for those States which do not agree with principles adopted. This in turn causes reluctance in ratification and the eventual failure of an act. Quite often the delegates (sometimes not even lawyers) come to the Diplomatic Conference expecting great political battles and all of a sudden they are asked to resolve 'minor points' such as the limit of liability, particulars in an air waybill or air carrier's defences. Too often the level of some purely legal remarks, to be mild in opinion, show the lack of legal background of some speakers. For this reason, and others, a syndrome called the 'silent majority' – well known to everyone who ever attended a conference – develops. Senseless decisions are adopted and everyone wonders why they were discussed only by a few delegations.[71]

Achieving a consensus between the developed world and the developing world was one of the greatest challenges for ICAO's Legal Committee; it had to deal with differences between members in terms of legal systems, terminology, and legal concepts, and with even greater disparities in wealth and resources. But the weaker members were not the only barrier to progress. As demonstrated by the struggle over the amendment of the Warsaw System, when a key member of ICAO (or at least part of its government) is out of sync with the other members it can lead to frustration, acrimony, and stalemate. Indeed, when one of the larger member-states opts out, the negative impact on the organization and international aviation can be even more profound.

By the end of the 1970s, the world was more diversified, complex, and dangerous than it had been when ICAO was created in 1947. In the future it would get harder, not easier, to solve the problems between members and to contribute to the development of international air law. The rise of air piracy and terrorism and the growing concerns over the security of international civil aviation brought new challenges for ICAO to face. The stakes were higher, and the need for international collaboration was never more vital to the maintenance of global peace and security.

10

The Cold War Comes to ICAO

It would be a matter for regret for the entire international community if important meetings dealing with essentially technical, social and economic questions,
and depending for their success on this vital element of international cooperation, were to fail to yield solid results because of the introduction of political
considerations into the work of these bodies.[1]

Like all international organizations, ICAO has had to face questions
dealing with the admission, suspension, withdrawal, and, as in the case of
Spain, expulsion of some of its members. Likewise, more often than not,
the debates concerning these questions were clouded in a political fog,
even for a largely technical organization like ICAO. Some of the biggest
political problems faced by ICAO in its first two decades dealt with the
questions of who got in and who could be forced out; the answers to
these questions were shrouded by the Cold War and shaped by the evolution of the Organization itself.

   The goal of the International Civil Aviation Organization was clear
from the start – to get as many sovereign states into the organization as
possible – and the members have been willing to interpret the Chicago
Convention fairly liberally to achieve these ends. The Chicago Convention
(Articles 91–93) is open in its rules concerning membership; ICAO
membership is open to all those states at the Chicago conference that
ratified the convention and any other sovereign state that subsequently
ratified or adhered to the convention. The only restrictions were placed
on former enemies of the 'United Nations' in the Second World War. In
these cases a four-fifths vote of the ICAO Assembly and the approval of
any state that was invaded by the potential member nation was required.

This restriction, as it turned out, may have seemed more important at the time it was written, during the latter stages of the war, than it turned out to be, because it had little effect in keeping any state out after the war was over. Indeed, in the Cold War former enemies became new friends and allies, and for the most part they were welcomed into ICAO.

ICAO was and is, after all, primarily a technical organization and, in general, there were few good reasons to keep any nation out. There were, however, many good reasons to bring everyone in – unless a country cut itself off and refused to participate in international aviation or was prevented to do so by international ban, there would still be a need for transit rights and the use of the air space above its territories. For safety reasons alone, if a nation was to establish commercial air services it was better to have that nation inside ICAO (and maintaining its standards) than have it remain on the outside. ICAO's 'membership should be universal,' one U.S. State Department memo noted. 'This is particularly true of the ICAO International Standards and Recommended Practices, the universal adoption of which is one of the foremost objectives of the organization.'[2] One of the first resolutions of the First Assembly recognized this policy with the words: 'universal membership in the International Civil Aviation Organization is desirable to achieve its maximum usefulness in promoting safety in the air and the efficient and orderly development of air transport.'[3]

Any member can denounce the Chicago Convention and quit the organization, effective one year from the date of notification (Article 95), but the convention is almost silent on the question of expulsion. Political infighting, power struggles, national rivalries, and so on were not anticipated. Why would you want to get rid of a nation once it had become a member? The one condition for expulsion came in Article 94b: if an amendment to the convention was believed to be vital, the assembly 'in its resolution recommending adoption may provide that any State which has not ratified within a specified period after the amendment has come into force shall thereupon cease to be a member of the Organization and a party to the Convention.' It was an article rarely applied in ICAO's history; indeed, in the American view, expulsion was to be used only as a last resort. It was one thing for the United Nations to bar a nation from all the specialized agencies, it was quite another to exclude one nation from ICAO for political reasons. 'The policy of universality of membership of States should be subject to the exemption only of decisions to the contrary taken by the United Nations as the supreme body acting in the name of all its Member States on a matter affecting them all equally.'[4]

Once ICAO became a specialized agency of the United Nations an additional condition was placed on membership – an applicant state needed the approval of the United Nations. Conversely, it was not absolutely necessary to be a member of the United Nations in order to be a member of ICAO; as one U.S. State Department memo noted, 'there is no reason to believe that membership of such states in specialized agencies should have any important effect on their status as would-be members of the United Nations or on international problems other than those within the cognizance of the particular specialized agency of which they are members.'[5] Switzerland was one example of an ICAO member that did not join the United Nations until much later.

The major air powers in North America and Europe had an enormous investment in international aviation and had no desire to rip apart ICAO on issues of membership. Nations needed to be encouraged to join and to be welcomed as members, and they should be expelled rarely and only in extraordinary circumstances. The result has been that ICAO has welcomed most states that wanted to join the organization and has almost always chosen compromise and accommodation over expulsion in dealing with serious membership problems.

Another factor was that, unlike the United Nations, the Soviet Union rejected membership in ICAO for many years. The American government favoured the entrance of the Soviet Union (going back to the reserved seat on the Interim Council) and wanted to open up Soviet airspace to international aviation, but the Soviets resisted joining. Without Soviet participation the organization was spared many of the debates, tensions, and bitter divisions that manifested in the United Nations. Nevertheless, ICAO was not immune to these problems and over the years faced its share of membership questions. The Soviet Union remained outside until 1970 but several of its satellites and allies were members, and they made an impact on the organization. Furthermore, the rising membership of ICAO in the 1950s and 1960s included many new states that gradually coalesced into a group of non-aligned nations. By the 1960s this group began advocating change in the United Nations, ICAO, and in other organizations in the U.N. system.

However technical the organization, ICAO could not operate in isolation from outside events, and in the 1950s and 1960s the Cold War descended on ICAO. The division of Germany, the formation of NATO and the Warsaw Pact, the descent of the Iron Curtain across Europe, wars in Korea and Vietnam, and the emergence of revolutionary and decolonization movements across the developing world all produced reverberations felt in ICAO.

The absence of the Soviet Union from the International Civil Aviation Organization in the early postwar years may have saved ICAO from some of the early controversies, but the 1949 revolution in China brought the Cold War to ICAO. With the movement of the Nationalists to the island of Formosa (Taiwan) the question arose over who could speak for China in international organizations. It was an issue of great concern in the United Nations but it affected ICAO as well. Some members recognized the new Communist government and the People's Republic of China (including the United Kingdom, India, Pakistan and Ceylon, the Scandinavian states, the Netherlands, Switzerland, the Soviet bloc, and a few others) while most others (including the United States) supported the Nationalists and the Republic of China.[6] There was no question of admitting the Communist government to speak for China in ICAO: the Nationalist government had the direct support of the United States and the process of joining ICAO included depositing the instrument of ratification or adherence to the Chicago Convention with the American government. In May 1950 the Chinese Communist government demanded that the Nationalists be ousted from the organization and replaced by the new Chinese government, which they considered the only legitimate government of China,[7] but there was little chance that the United States would have allowed the Communists to replace the Nationalist Chinese. And, within a few months China was supporting North Korea against U.N. forces in the Korean War. Nevertheless, it could prove problematic and embarrassing if the question of Chinese representation was raised in open meetings or if the credentials of the Nationalists were challenged.

American policy regarding China was straightforward: keep the Communists out and the Nationalists in. It was believed that the best way to achieve this policy was to limit any discussion of the Chinese representation issue and deflect any efforts to have the matter come to a vote. The issue was 'most likely to be raised by the Soviet bloc states or by such states which recognize the Chinese Communist regime as India or Burma,' noted one memorandum prepared by the State Department and the Air Coordinating Committee. To prevent any of these nations from doing so it became U.S. policy to try to secure appointment of nations sympathetic to the American position on committees where the matter might be raised. Failing this, if the issue was raised the American delegations were instructed to raise procedural points to secure an adjournment or have the debate ruled out of order. It was a technique used in the United Nations and in other specialized agencies. 'By advancing a procedural position which avoids a vote on the substance we can most easily achieve our basic objectives with respect to the Chinese representation issue, i.e., the continued seating of the representatives of the Government of the Republic of China in all United Nations and specialized agency bodies and the continued exclusion of Chinese Communists.'[8]

The Chinese representation issue became a little more complicated after 1950. On 31 May 1950, in response to difficulties in maintaining payment of its annual assessments, the Nationalist government denounced the Chicago Convention and announced its decision to withdraw from the organization, effective in one year. There was a question if it was possible for the Nationalist government to pull China out of ICAO (especially for those members which recognized the Communist government and therefore believed that the Nationalists could not take such action), but the ICAO Council accepted the decision. Within three years however, the situation stabilized in Formosa/Taiwan and civil flying resumed, and the Nationalist government reconsidered its action and began the process of returning to the organization.

Once again the question arose: could the Nationalist government speak for China in ICAO? There was little chance of the Communist government filling the seat – it had not asked and the Americans would never have accepted it – but it nevertheless made many members uncomfortable, especially those that had recognized the new regime in mainland China. The British, for example, had recognized the Communist government and had never accepted that China had left ICAO, and they were less than thrilled to have the Nationalist government back in. 'It has been agreed,' one Foreign Office official noted, 'that we must continue to regard China as a member of I.C.A.O. but unfortunately it now seems that the Formosans want to come back to I.C.A.O. representing China.'[9] For the British, however, there was little desire to make an issue of it either in ICAO or in the United Nations, especially given the fact that the Americans would back the Nationalist Chinese, and the British acquiesced and followed the American lead. For its part, the U.S. State Department did not like the idea of renegotiating China's annual assessment, but claimed it was a unique situation – and not to be taken as a precedent by others – and 'for political reasons would welcome the renewed participation of the Chinese National Government in ICAO.'[10]

The Nationalist government of the Republic of China re-ratified the Chicago Convention on 2 December 1953 and rejoined ICAO in January 1954. China was assessed at a lower rate of ten units and a new payment arrangement was negotiated to spread the payment of arrears over fifteen years. There were no negative votes in the ICAO Assembly (there were seven abstentions) and there was no challenge from the People's Republic or any other government.[11]

The issue of Chinese representation in the International Civil Aviation Organization did not go away with the readmission of the Nationalist Chinese, but it took a back seat in the 1950s to the question of the admission of former enemy states. Once the Second World War ended new governments were established in the ex-enemy states, and they began the difficult task of reconstruction of their economies and societies. Part of that process was to re-enter the community of nations and, for most, this included entrance into the United Nations and, secondarily, membership in ICAO. Italy was the first ex-enemy nation to join ICAO; when no member opposed its application its membership was approved at the First ICAO Assembly. Austria applied in September 1947 and in this case there were some questions about procedure: was Austria actually an enemy nation and therefore in need of a four-fifths vote and the approval of all those nations invaded? Or, was it in fact a victim of Nazi aggression through its forced unification with Germany before the war? The ICAO Council accepted the latter – since the Allies had not recognized the *Anschluss* of Germany and Austria, it was agreed that it would not be necessary to get the approval of those nations that had been invaded by Germany in order to admit Austria. A similar kind of thinking was applied to Finland in that it was agreed to waive the need to get the assent of any victim of invasion before permitting Finland to join the organization. Both states adhered to the Chicago Convention, no objection was raised by the United Nations, and in 1948, at the Second ICAO Assembly, resolutions were passed welcoming Austria and Finland into the organization.[12]

Italy, Austria, and Finland were admitted into ICAO in the early years of the organization, as the Cold War was evolving; by the early 1950s, in the midst of the Korean War, the two sides in the Cold War struggle had hardened and become more intransigent. In addition, Austria and Finland were hardly enemies of the 'United Nations' at all in the Second World War, and Italy was a minor player and had invaded few countries compared to Germany and Japan. The entrance of West Germany and Japan into ICAO, however, could have been a long drawn out affair with bitter recriminations on both sides of the Iron Curtain, but thanks to the efficient management of the United States, the United Kingdom, and France, their entrance was implemented with little fuss and even less debate.

In the early 1950s, the still-divided Germany remained the flash point in the Cold War. For the United States and its allies, rebuilding West Germany was an important part of Western strategy; a strong Germany could help the economic well-being of all of Europe and assist in the containment of the Soviet Union. Part of that rebuilding was to increase German involvement in civil aviation. After the war the Germans were prohibited from operating civil aviation, and control was vested in the Allied High Commission's Civil Aviation Board. Some commercial flying took place over German airspace, but only by foreign operating companies. By the early 1950s, however, the Western allies began to consider the revival of West German civil aviation.[13] Agreements were made, aircraft manufacturing sprang up, and in 1953 control over civil aviation was handed back over to the West German government.Within a couple of years Lufthansa was operating again. West German membership in the International Civil Aviation Organization was a logical step, at least for the Western allies.

Similarly, the Japanese signed a peace treaty in 1951 and soon after had resumed civil flying. Relations with the West had improved markedly as Japan was turned into a staunch ally and a Western bastion in the struggle against communism in Asia. Japanese civil aviation was resumed following the peace treaty, and bilateral agreements were negotiated with the United States (leading to the inauguration of a trans-Pacific service), Canada, France, and several other nations, and conversations were underway with half a dozen more.[14] For most nations it made sense to have Japan in ICAO – there were 'no perceivable disadvantages,' was how one Canadian described it[15] – and the Japanese application was issued on 27 August 1952.

Discussions between the American, British, and French governments began as early as the Sixth ICAO Assembly in 1952 in an effort to bring Japan and Germany into the organization.[16] There was little doubt that both Japan and Germany could garner the four-fifths vote in the assembly, and both, eventually, were approved for membership by the United Nations. The concern among the leading Western nations in ICAO was the need to get the assent of all nations invaded by Japan and Germany during the Second World War. By withholding that consent a single nation could veto the entrance of either state, and it was believed that members of the Soviet bloc and its allies might take this route for reasons having as much to do with the politics of the Cold War as their wartime experience. The Soviets had no say (Article 93 was interpreted to mean that only *ICAO members* who had been invaded needed to assent to an applicant's request for membership), but there was considerable concern that Czechoslovakia or Poland – both ICAO members and states that had been invaded by Germany – would veto German membership.

Moreover, because China had been invaded by Japan, the question rose again regarding China's membership in ICAO and its need to give assent to the entrance of Japan. For the Americans it was straightforward: the Nationalist government spoke for China and it was no longer a member and if and when it rejoined ICAO it likely would give its assent to the entrance of Japan. For the British government it was more problematic; 'the Japanese question is bedeviled by the position of China,' one Foreign office official minuted. 'We still regard China as a member of I.C.A.O., while the Americans (and the majority of other member States) think she has resigned. The Americans therefore, do not fear a veto from any state "invaded or attacked" by Japan but we know quite well that if the C.P.G. [Chinese People's Government] were consulted they would object to the admission of Japan and obviously any attempt to consult them would be most undesirable at the present time.'[17]

The United States wanted Japan in ICAO and encouraged the Japanese government to seek out the attitudes of those member nations that had been invaded by Japan during the Second World War. In the American view it was important to have all those nations present at the upcoming 1953 Assembly so they could vote affirmatively on Japan's membership. Abstention would not be considered as giving assent, and those not present would need to be contacted for their assent – either written or in some future ICAO forum – approving Japan's application[18] (e.g., when Italy was accepted as a member there was no delegate from Ethiopia at the assembly so the Ethiopian government was requested to send its written assent).

On this point the British disagreed and argued that only the vote in the ICAO Assembly mattered and that if a country did not vote or failed to be represented then there was no need to seek out its written permission. According to the British, 'an abstention means "I am not enthusiastic, but if the majority wants it I will not obstruct." The proviso does not call for positive "approval" or for "an affirmative vote" but only for "assent," which would seem to cover passive acquiescence, such as is conveyed by an abstention from voting.' Furthermore, 'any State which is entitled to vote, but which does not actually cast either an affirmative or a negative vote, whether it is represented at the Assembly or not, is considered to have abstained.'[19] And for the British what happened with regard to Japan might have repercussions in dealing with the entrance of

Germany. Would later assent be needed from all those ICAO members invaded by Germany but absent from the meeting? If so, 'it leaves the battle to be fought all over again in another Assembly, when Czechoslovakia and Poland may seek to impede the admission of Germany.'[20] By embracing the view that the absence of a vote was the equivalent to 'passive acquiescence' in the decision, the British were able to rationalize and justify what was about to happen.

The way to avoid any problems was, as in the case of Chinese representation, to limit debate as much as possible. 'Since the experience of the State Department has been that the less oral and written discussion there is concerning the admission of States to international organizations, the easier their admission,' one memo suggested, it might be best to prevail on the Secretariat to 'limit the documentation' and to talk to the British and ask them not to raise any questions about their interpretation of the convention. 'Too much discussion and documentation might result in adoption by the majority of procedures which would make it more difficult for Japan or later some other ex-enemy State to become a party to the Chicago Convention.'[21]

Japan's application for membership in ICAO was approved by resolution during the Seventh ICAO Assembly in 1953. There were no opposing votes and only two abstentions (neither by states that had been invaded by Japan). It worked quite well for those supporting Japan's application. For the United States, China was not a member and therefore need not be asked for its assent; for the British, there were no Chinese representatives at the assembly to vote at all but, in London's view, no vote was a tacit admission of assent, and that ended the matter. In the end it was possible 'to get a Resolution passed in the Assembly which admitted Japan but did not raise the various difficulties and embarrassments connected with the position of China and did not set a precedent which would make it harder to get Germany admitted when she is able to apply for membership, probably next year.'[22]

A similar procedure was agreed to by the United States, the United Kingdom, and France with respect to the question of German membership. Well before the issue was discussed at the Ninth ICAO Assembly in 1955, the three governments discussed the matter and agreed on procedures, and the German application of 26 May was accompanied by letters of support from these three nations.[23] It was also agreed that only those states entitled to vote in the assembly would have the right to give their assent to West Germany's entrance; that is, the states that had been suspended for not paying their assessments would not be able to vote. In other words, it was agreed that the only way to withhold assent on West German membership was to vote against it in the assembly and, as discussed in Chapter 7, since both Czechoslovakia and Poland (the most likely states to oppose) had been suspended for non-payment of their annual assessments and therefore had lost their voting rights in ICAO (Poland had not even attended the assembly for several years), neither would be consulted on the question. 'The United Kingdom view,' one Foreign Office memo noted, 'which is that assent under Article 93 of a State invaded or attacked by Germany during the war can only be withheld by a negative vote cast in the Assembly of I.C.A.O. It follows from this, (though we do not put this forward as our main premise), that States which have no voting rights in the Assembly are not able to exercise their right of assent.'[24]

The only concern for the Western nations was the possibility that the Czechs or the Poles might pay their arrears in time to regain their voting rights for the 1955 ICAO Assembly meeting. That was unlikely in the case of Poland, as the Poles claimed not even to be members of ICAO and were unlikely to send anyone to the assembly. The Czechs, however, would be there and, as one Foreign Office report suggested, they might 'have political motives for withholding assent as a form of blackmail.' To get around the problem of the Czechs, at one point it was even suggested that an argument could be made that because Czechoslovakia was occupied *before* the war it was not technically invaded by Germany *during* the war – but this rather silly suggestion was quickly shelved.[25]

It is a telling point (and indicative of the lack of communication between groups in ICAO and the larger Cold War) that the British and, presumably, the Americans did not really know how the Czechs would react to German membership. On the one hand, they could pay their arrears and vote against German membership, and there would 'be nothing to prevent her from stymying Germany indefinitely.'[26] On the other hand, it was also possible that the Czechs, in their desire to acquire transit rights over German territory to get access to Western Europe, might not stand in the way at all. In any event, the way to avoid all these potential problems was to move quickly and, as had been the case regarding Japan, to limit the debate as much as possible. At one meeting in the State Department between American officials and a representative from the French Embassy, the French official was informed that the State Department 'would instruct the United States Representative on the ICAO Council in Montreal to attempt to suppress any ICAO notices or documentation in advance of the Assembly and suggested that the

French might want to instruct their representative on the ICAO Council, M. Henri Bouche, along similar lines.'[27]

It was a little tricky: the Western powers were looking for a resolution that made it clear what was happening regarding German membership but at the same time did not invite debate on the issue at hand.[28] It also had to settle the Anglo-Franco-American debates over the wording, with the Anglo-American divisions over whether or not absent states with voting powers needed to be contacted for assent, and with the French desires for the inclusion of a reference in the resolution that it had not been vetoed by any member. There was also discussion whether or not Libya was to be considered to have been an independent state during the war and therefore required to give its assent to German membership – they agreed that it was not. And, much to the consternation of the British, French, and Americans, while the discussions concerning German membership were proceeding, another debate arose on the suspension of nations for non-payment of their arrears. In addition to the Bolivians and Cubans, the Czechs submitted a plan to make good on their debts by having their assessments reduced retroactively and to pay the remainder over a series of years. If this was accepted, the Czechs expected to have their voting rights restored. The French, with American support, responded with a resolution denying the return of voting rights to any member until they were restored by the assembly at a future meeting. Poland and Czechoslovakia remained voteless.[29]

The resolution upon which they agreed was simple – it merely confirmed West Germany's admission into ICAO following its acceptance into the United Nations and its adherence to the Chicago Convention.[30] In addition, the resolution was introduced in the Executive Committee meeting by the American delegate and prefaced with the words: 'it is implicit in this Resolution that all of the conditions of the Convention applicable to the Assembly, its Member States and the Organization will have been satisfied when this Resolution is approved by a roll call vote of this Session of the Assembly.'[31] The Czech delegate was present and made no protest at the Executive Committee meetings where the matter was discussed, and it was approved by the assembly without a negative vote. Only Israel abstained, 'in mild but continuing protest of the Nazi atrocities to members of the Jewish race preceding and during the last war,' was how one American explained it.[32] Those who had lost their voting powers or were not members of the organization were not sought out for their opinions.

West Germany and Japan quickly became important members of the organization, but relations between East and West did not noticeably improve. Indeed, the next year, 1956, a new dispute arose between the United States and Czechoslovakia. In January the Czechs complained to the organization about American balloons carrying propaganda leaflets crossing into their territory from West Germany, and they claimed that the balloons were dangerous to air navigation and contravened the Chicago Convention and Czechoslovakia's sovereignty over its airspace. The Americans responded that the U.S. Air Force had stopped launching weather balloons from West Germany, but that another group – the Free Europe Committee – continued, but that their balloons posed no hazard to air flight. The Free Europe Committee was a group created by the U.S. government in 1949 as the National Committee for a Free Europe. It was funded through the Central Intelligence Agency, using emigrés from Communist European countries to spread propaganda into the Soviet bloc. Its usual activity was to publish statements in European languages, write articles, and broadcast radio news and information via Radio Free Europe. The committee also had a supply of several thousand Second World War surplus balloons, which it filled with leaflets and released into the prevailing easterly winds, which took the balloons into Czechoslovakia and other points in the Soviet bloc. In one campaign in 1953 it was reported that over ten million leaflets were dropped in Eastern Europe; the Czechs responded with fighters to shoot down the balloons, without much success.[33]

At the Tenth ICAO Assembly in Caracas in June 1956, the Czechs reiterated their charges, claiming that one of their aircraft had collided with a balloon and crashed. The Czech representative introduced a resolution calling on all members not to send up balloons over other members' airspace, but this resolution, facing strong American opposition, failed to get through the Executive Committee. Following another Czech complaint to the ICAO Council, Secretary General Ljungberg was appointed to investigate the facts of the case. In the meantime, the United States announced that it (and the Free Europe Committee) would launch no more balloons.

Matters were left there until 1960 when the Czechs again complained that balloons from West Germany had crossed into their airspace. Once more they demanded that ICAO pass a resolution on the matter. The Americans proposed a resolution that was at first unacceptable to the Czechs; as J.R.K. Main, the Canadian council representative, described it, the U.S. State Department 'went into a high velocity flap and came up with another proposal which, according to well founded rumors, accused the Czechs in effect of lying for propaganda purposes. But no one in

ICAO would have anything to do with it.'[34] In the end, the council responded with a resolution stating that balloons needed to be controlled for the safety of air flight and asked all members to take the appropriate measures to see that this happened.[35]

Once Romania joined in 1965, all ex-enemies were members of the International Civil Aviation Organization,[36] but the entrance of the ex-enemy states did not end the controversy over membership. Indeed, the debate continued in a variety of ways over the following decades. In the evolving Cold War, the two Chinas continued to be a sore point, as were the related questions of membership of the divided states of Germany, Korea, and Vietnam. Inevitably these different issues became linked in ICAO as in many other international organizations.

South Korea and South Vietnam had been kept out of the United Nations thanks largely to the Soviet veto, but membership in the United Nations was not a requirement for membership in ICAO. With strong American backing and without the presence of the Soviet Union, the Republic of Korea and the Republic of Vietnam became members of ICAO in 1952 and 1954 respectively. Representatives of the Czechoslovakian government usually spoke for the Eastern bloc in ICAO and they challenged the entrance of both South Korea and South Vietnam. The Republic of Korea 'cannot be regarded as a State and less so as a member of the United Nations or a State associated with them or a State which remained neutral in World War II,' the Czech ambassador to the United States wrote in 1953, and its membership would be 'illegal and contradictory to the provisions of the Convention.'[37] As for South Vietnam, the Czechs complained in 1955 that its membership in ICAO contravened the truce agreed to at the Geneva conference staged a year earlier.[38] Nevertheless, if enough members were willing to accept these nations as members – and there were – and the United States was willing to accept the deposit of the instrument of adherence to the Chicago Convention – and it was – it was nearly impossible to block the entrance into ICAO of any state.

Ousting South Korea, South Vietnam, Nationalist China, and West Germany might have been a next-to-impossible task, but their presence at meetings and assemblies through the 1950s and 1960s made them targets for attack by an increasing number of members. Soon every assembly was punctuated with protests about their continued membership and demands for representation from mainland China, North Korea, North Vietnam, and East Germany. For example, in 1956, at the Tenth

ICAO Assembly in Caracas, the Indian delegate on the Credential Committee dissociated his government from the committee's report because of the presence of the Nationalist Chinese. 'We regret to note,' he explained, 'that the seat of China in this Assembly is not occupied by the representatives of the People's Republic of China. To us there appears to be no reasonable ground for ignoring the basic facts of the situation in regard to China.'[39] He was supported by the delegates from Egypt and Indonesia, and in the vote on the report there were no 'no' votes, but nineteen abstentions. Three years later in San Diego, California, at the Twelfth ICAO Assembly, the protests, according to the confidential American report, 'were more numerous and stronger than at any previous session,' with statements of objection from India, Iraq, Poland, Indonesia, Czechoslovakia, Afghanistan, and the United Arab Republic.[40]

By the early 1960s, both private and public sources were referring to the 'usual' protests in the meetings; in 1965, one newspaper described it as 'almost as a formality – delegates stood up on behalf of their governments to be counted over the China issue.'[41] And by this time it was not unusual for a majority of the Credentials Committee to recognize the People's Republic of China. In addition, the People's Republic and North Korea adhered to the Warsaw Convention on aircraft liability and, when specific meetings were arranged to discuss this topic, there were calls to invite both these nations to participate (East Germany tried to adhere to the Warsaw Convention, but its adherence was not accepted).[42] It seemed illogical to many members to prevent them from attending an international conference set to discuss a convention to which they were parties, but logic in the Cold War took on its own unique characteristics.

Membership squabbles began to have an effect on the functioning of the organization. Before each assembly strategy meetings were held on both sides, memos were written and instructions given explaining why the one country should be recognized but the other should not. Debates became increasingly fractious and focused on political rather than technical issues; committee selection became chess matches as allies were recruited and selected for membership based on how they voted on the China question. It was particularly hard on the United States as the prime supporter of the Nationalist Chinese, South Koreans, and South Vietnamese, and the Americans bore the brunt of considerable criticism. It also required a delicate balance to argue, on the one hand, that trying to oust these countries was a political matter and best left to the United Nations to decide and, on the other, pointing to the inaction of the United Nations on these matters as justification for leaving things in

ICAO as they were. American troubles were compounded in the 1960s by the presence of Castro's Cuba. Washington could hardly challenge Cuba's right to be present, but its efforts to isolate the Communist state in the outside world were brought into ICAO as delegates were instructed to have as little as possible to do with the Cubans.[43]

The divisions seemed to be splitting the organization into two camps, and they spilled outside the meetings as well. As one American report noted in 1958, 'it was apparent during the coffee breaks and social gatherings attendant to the Assembly that few foreign delegates were particularly willing to engage in conversations with the Chinese and Korean delegates.' The American official continued with a degree of understatement: 'The United States Delegation was pleased to have the support of the Chinese Delegation at the Assembly, but a singular problem is attached to this as long as there are two Chinas.'[44] By the beginning of the 1970s the situation had become intolerable. The classified report of the American delegation to the Eighteenth ICAO Assembly in Vienna gives some sense of the state of affairs: with the submission of the interim report of the Credentials Committee a statement by the Hungarian representative was read,

on behalf of his own Delegation and other socialist states, protesting against the invitation extended to the Delegation of Taiwan to attend the Assembly and its presence there. Similar views were expressed by Pakistan, Romania, Yugoslavia, Cuba, the People's Democratic Republic of Yemen, Bulgaria, U.S.S.R., Tanzania, Congo (Brazzaville), France, Italy, Algeria and the UAR. Romania also said it did not recognize the right of the Government of Phom Penh [Cambodia] to be present at the Assembly and regretted that the German Democratic Republic, the Democratic People's Republic of Korea and the Democratic Republic of Vietnam were not participating in ICAO. China, the U.S. and Saudi Arabia supported the presence of the Government of the Republic of China. When the final report of the Credentials Committee was submitted on the final day of the Assembly, Pakistan, Romania, Kenya, Guinea, Tanzania, the People's Democratic Republic of Yemen, the UAR, Bulgaria, France, Congo (Brazzaville), Cuba, Chile and the U.S.S.R. all stated that they did not recognize the Government of the Republic of China. Romania also stated that it did not recognize the Saigon and Cambodian Governments. Tanzania said it recognized only *North* Vietnam, *North* Korea and the German *Democratic* Republic. The U.S. reiterated its earlier statement regarding China as did Saudi Arabia and the Government of the Republic of China.[45]

Adding to the confusion were the equally divisive debates between Israel and the Arab states that continued throughout this period. The Israeli government complained that its neighbours were refusing transit rights, interfering with air communications, and withholding flight information on flights into Israel. Tensions rose even higher during the 1956 Suez Crisis and during other periods of war in the Middle East. For the members of ICAO it was not an issue of expulsion or suspension, and few members wished to engage in a full-blown debate on the Middle East because the problems of that region could not be solved by ICAO. At the same time, the activities of ICAO could not be divorced from the simmering tensions of the outside world.

The most divisive of membership issues in the 1960s concerned South Africa and, to a lesser degree, Portugal, and it effectively split ICAO in two and threatened permanently to harm the organization. International condemnation was rising dramatically, especially among the African states, over South Africa's racist apartheid system and Portugal's colonial policy in Angola and Mozambique, and the issue began to polarize many international organizations. African membership rose dramatically in the United Nations as in ICAO, and these states gave their support to the 1960 U.N. Declaration on the Granting of Independence of Colonial Countries and Peoples and to the U.N. Special Committee on Decolonization, created in 1961. In this context, the major aviation states in Europe and elsewhere found themselves the target of international criticism and U.N. resolutions concerning the fate of their remaining colonies and territories.[46] In addition, by the early 1960s, the African states and others that opposed apartheid began actively to target South Africa and work towards its expulsion or suspension from international organizations such as the World Health Organization, the International Labour Organization (South Africa withdrew 11 March 1964) and the Food and Agriculture Organization (South Africa withdrew 18 December 1963). South Africa withdrew from the Commonwealth in 1961, and this meant withdrawal from the Commonwealth Air Transport Council as well.

Inevitably the situation regarding South Africa had an impact on ICAO and, more generally, on international civil aviation in the region. In November 1962 a U.N. resolution asked all nations to refuse landing and transit rights to South African aircraft (the United Nations passed a similar resolution with respect to Portugal in 21 December 1965). This resolution was unusual in that the United Nations clearly crossed into ICAO's jurisdiction and contravened Article 5 of the Chicago Convention, under which all members agreed to grant transit rights to other members. By 1964 South Africa's participation in African regional meetings was becoming increasingly unacceptable to the new African members. Moreover, the Organization of African Unity, established in 1963 to eradicate colonialism and to foster unity within Africa, at its March 1965 meeting called on the African members of ICAO to take joint action to oust the South Africans from the organization. In some quarters this kind of action was seen as an attempt by the African states to 'take over' ICAO,[47] and there were fears – and warnings – that such action would damage or even destroy the organization.

There were suspicions that the whole thing was being orchestrated by the Communist bloc in an effort to bring together an anti-Western bloc of African, Asian, and Middle Eastern states. The thinking of at least one British official was that the Middle Eastern states would support the ouster of South Africa in exchange for the support of the African nations for the expulsion of Israel,[48] but there is little evidence to back up this assertion. A U.S. State Department memo explained the American view: 'In recent years, the Africans have enlisted the support of Communists, Arabs, Asians, and others to exclude or suspend South Africa and Portugal from participation in international conferences and meetings of the specialized agencies of the U.N. They have resorted to a wide variety of devices, including constitutional amendments, declarations of exclusion, invitations to withdraw, walk-outs, and even disorderly demonstrations. The choice of tactics has varied and, as a result, it has not always been possible to predict in advance which will be employed.'[49]

For most observers, under the Chicago Convention expulsion of an ICAO member could not be done except under Article 93bis (i.e., on the request of the United Nations) and therefore any effort to oust South Africa would be unconstitutional. If the African states forced the issue the other members would have no choice but to walk out – of the meeting and perhaps even ICAO itself. 'Controversy could seriously impede work of Assembly or conceivably cause its breakdown as well as damage ICAO itself,' one Canadian reported.[50] Even if the African states realized that it would be unconstitutional, one Briton argued, it 'will not stop the Africans from trying it on. If sufficiently supported by Arabs, Asians and Communists, they might even obtain a majority prepared to disregard the Convention. This would put us in a frightful difficulty.'[51] If some illegal motion was passed, wrote R.S.S. Dickinson, the British representative on the ICAO Council, 'the responsible States would seem to have no alternative but to disassociate themselves from the illegal action by withdrawing and indicate at the time of withdrawal that they would not regard themselves as being bound by any subsequent action taken by the Assembly.'[52] If it were the Africans who chose to walk out 'and stay out,' noted an official in the British Ministry of Aviation, 'the Assembly will get on very well without them.'[53]

In advance of the 1965 ICAO Assembly there were concerns that the South African issue might lead to deadlock and even a break down of the organization. The British, for example, were worried about the constitutionality of ousting South Africa, and they gave serious consideration to withdrawing from the upcoming assembly and even the organization itself. The debate within the Foreign Office and Aviation Ministry reveal the extent of British frustration at the direction ICAO was taking – the politics and disruptions, the efforts of the smaller nations to influence the organization contrary to British policy, and the difficulties of implementing ICAO policies in the developing world. 'Let us face it,' one Aviation official complained, 'the increase in Member States is entirely due to the emergence of developing countries, many of whom joined ICAO purely for prestige reasons, probably do not pay their subscriptions and have very little to offer. I must accept that this is modern democracy, but at the same time you cannot let it run wild in a highly specialized technical industry.'[54]

The major benefit of withdrawal would be tactical; if other members could be persuaded to leave with Britain it might lead to the closing of the assembly. On the other hand, it was argued that the risks were too great, and the British had more to lose than win from such a course of action. As another aviation official explained: 'If one takes a narrow view of our "balance of payments" with ICAO, we contribute far more in ideas and in solutions to problems than we receive. This must apply to all the leading aviation nations on whom, obviously, ICAO must rely for leadership. To withdraw from ICAO because our expenditure exceeds our income in this particular account would deal a heavy blow to British prestige (as well, presumably, as to ICAO's finances) and would therefore be a political act of high importance.'[55]

At the heart of the matter was the fact that the United Kingdom, the United States, and all the other major air nations needed ICAO or something like it, and if they pulled out they would likely have to create a similar organization to do all the things that ICAO was doing so successfully to enhance the development of international civil aviation. In this new world, these nations would still want to fly all over the world, and they would insist on cooperation and as much standardization of the rules of the air as possible. Indeed, the major powers had *more* interest in keeping ICAO going than did the smaller and less developed members. 'If the Western bloc States, including Australia and New Zealand, denounced the Convention,' noted one confidential British memo, 'ICAO as at present constituted would presumably disintegrate because these States bear about 75% of the whole cost of running the Organization. In such an event they would presumably convene a conference and endeavour to set up a new organization. But the problem would remain of forging effective links between any new organization and those countries standing outside it. Interdependence is both the strength and the weakness of international civil aviation.'[56]

Despite the dire warnings, the International Civil Aviation Organization did not fall apart on the issue, but apartheid and South Africa became the focus of the Fifteenth ICAO Assembly in Montreal in June–July 1965, in the form of an attempt by the African nations to include on the agenda the question of South Africa's membership. The matter played out in the Executive Committee on two motions backed by some thirty-one African nations: (1) a proposal to include South Africa's membership in ICAO as a topic of discussion (without giving sufficient advance notice to the members) and (2) to amend Article 93 of the Convention to include the words: 'any State whose government violates the principles laid down in the Preamble to this Convention and practices a policy of apartheid and racial discrimination shall be suspended or excluded from membership in the International Civil Aviation Organization by the Assembly.'[57] The proposal to discuss the question was passed with a slight majority of the members (forty-one to thirty-four, with eight abstentions).

The debate on the amendment of the Chicago Convention was long and often passionate. For most of those members that supported South Africa's membership, or at least opposed the idea of expelling it from ICAO, it was a matter of introducing a political question into a largely technical organization. The best place to deal with it, they argued, was in the United Nations. One after another these states lined up to condemn apartheid and to underline that their support for South Africa was in no way to be interpreted as support for the apartheid system. Apartheid was an evil system and needed to be denounced, they said; it was just that ICAO was not the place to do anything about it. Others added that by spending time talking about it the delegates were reducing the time available to carry out the work of the assembly.

Such thinking was unacceptable to the African states and many other members. To these states apartheid, ICAO, and aviation were all connected. 'It was impossible to say, in good faith,' argued the delegate from Senegal, 'that apartheid did not exist in international air transport or that it did not exist at South African airports and on aircraft bound for South Africa. The moment one expressed the intention of going to the Republic of South Africa he was subjected to the practices in force there. To insist, after this, that the solution of the problem must be sought in the United Nations was to accept complacently the South African racist concept of international air transport.' Given such a situation it was imperative to act; conversely *not* to act was essentially to condone the apartheid system. 'An act of genocide was being committed in South Africa,' the delegate from Guinea explained, 'as thousands of men, women and children were herded into reservations and oppressed simply because of their colour. Their only crime was that they were fighting for freedom and the triumph of democracy.' By permitting South African membership in ICAO the future of the organization was therefore in jeopardy. 'History was being made in this room at this moment,' he continued. 'To permit South Africa to remain in ICAO was to accept the ultimate disintegration of the Organization, because that State's policy of apartheid was contrary to its aims and principles. It was difficult to believe in the sincerity of States that claimed to be friends to Africa while lending their support to a Government that aimed at exterminating Africans. For the African States apartheid was the barometer by which they judged the feelings others said they had for them.'[58]

The members opposed to the resolution can be roughly labelled the 'Western nations' and their allies, including North America, Europe, and many Latin American states. They were in a difficult position in not wanting to oust South Africa while at the same time not wanting to appear to support its policy of apartheid. Moreover, the African members insisted on open votes on all the motions and resolutions, so the Western states had nowhere to hide. On the day of the vote on the resolution to amend the Chicago Convention the Western members, in the words of one Canadian delegate, 'decided that it would be a good idea to have a quick meeting in the coffee-break of like-minded delegations to consider what common action we might take on the resolution condemning apartheid.' As a result, a meeting took place in the American delegation's office, and there it was agreed to form a kind of 'united front' and to abstain from the vote en masse.[59]

The African nations had the numbers to win the votes, but they lost on their larger mission. The vote on the resolution to amend the Chicago Convention (to oust South Africa) passed with forty in favour and only

one (South Africa) opposed. The remaining forty members abstained.
As one Canadian put it after the vote, the result 'can be considered a
rebuff to, and perhaps even a defeat for, the African resolution. At any
rate, it was a clear indication that most of the European nations and
many of the Latin American ones as well as Australia, New Zealand,
Canada and the United States did not think this political resolution had
any place in the I.C.A.O. Assembly.'[60] The Canadian was correct; in the
ICAO Assembly on 14 July the vote in favour of the proposed amendment received a majority, with forty-two votes, but it was clear that it
would never attain the two-thirds majority needed for it to come into effect (two-thirds not just of those participating and voting at the assembly
but of all contracting states – around one hundred in 1965).

The African states settled for a resolution condemning South Africa
and apartheid, introduced on 16 July at the final plenary session of the
assembly. Noting that 'the policies of apartheid and racial discrimination
are a flagrant violation of the principles enshrined in the Preamble to
the Chicago Convention,' the Assembly '(1) Strongly *condemns* the apartheid policies of South Africa; (2) *requests* all nations and peoples of the
world to exert pressure on South Africa to abandon its apartheid policies; and (3) *urges* South Africa to comply with the aims and objectives of
the Chicago Convention.' After some procedural wrangling, the new
resolution was discussed and voted on. It passed by a vote of thirty-nine
to one (South Africa), with forty nations again abstaining.[61]

The campaign against South Africa and Portugal continued in 1971,
following two U.N. resolutions calling on the International Civil Aviation
Organization essentially to isolate the two states by withholding information and documents that they received from ICAO and by limiting their
role in the organization to only those things specified under the Chicago
Convention. It led to hours of debate at the Eighteenth ICAO Assembly
in Vienna in June–July over two resolutions – one regarding South Africa,
the other regarding Portugal. The parameters of the debate were familiar, as were the main participants. In the end the resolution against South
Africa passed but the one concerned with Portugal was defeated by one
vote.[62] The close vote on Portugal sparked a minor flap when the delegate from Tanzania questioned whether an American delegate, who happened to be sitting in the Zambian chair, had in fact voted for Zambia.
The ballots were checked, and when no Zambian vote was found the
chair of the American delegation demanded and received an apology.[63]

Just how divided an organization ICAO had become was demonstrated
at the Extraordinary Session in New York in 1973. An extraordinary session

usually has a single issue – in 1973 it was called to elect three new ICAO Council members – but at the last minute three items were added to the agenda: the ouster of Portugal; demands for an investigation (and condemnation) of Israel for shooting down a Libyan civil aircraft; and an American request to reduce the maximum annual assessment below 30 per cent of the total budget. The election of the new council members was dispensed with quickly, and the rest of the session devolved into acrimonious disputes over the other issues. In all three the split was largely between the same states, although under different names depending on the issue – rich versus poor, east versus west, developed versus undeveloped.[64] At one point there were 'informal' but 'serious' suggestions that the twenty-six members that voted against ousting Portugal should leave and form a new aviation organization of their own.[65]

By 1974 Portugal had a new democratic government and was out of its old colonies in Angola and Mozambique, and pressure to expel Portugal from the International Civil Aviation Organization gradually evaporated. But pressure on South Africa increased. Anti-apartheid resolutions, the exclusion of South Africa from various meetings, and restrictions on flying to South Africa were all tactics used in the following years.[66] In 1974, South Africa's involvement in ICAO was reduced by indirect means. Thanks to the 1971 resolution, which limited South Africa's participation in meetings and access to ICAO documents, the South African government announced that it would unilaterally reduce its annual assessment payments by 30 per cent. Using this reduction in assessment payments as a pretext, a resolution was passed at the 1974 ICAO Assembly to suspend South Africa's voting power in the assembly because it had failed to make its annual payments.[67]

The suspension of South Africa's voting rights effectively completed its isolation within ICAO, but as long as the system of apartheid existed the attacks on South Africa continued. In 1986 ICAO passed a resolution asking all ICAO members to ban air links to South Africa. This resolution was repeated and superseded by a second resolution in 1989.[68] Only in 1994, once the system of apartheid was abolished and a new government was in place in South Africa, were all the resolutions suspended and the air bans lifted.[69]

One consequence of this period of rancorous debate over membership and the political attacks on different members was that it led many participants – on both sides – to question both the continuing value of ICAO and their commitment to it. Calls for the destruction of ICAO usually arose out of frustration and faded with the realization that another, similar organization would be needed to take its place. That meant reforming the existing organization, but efforts in this direction were equally unsatisfactory, at least for the major players. In 1968, for example, the United States introduced a working paper to the assembly in Buenos Aires with a plan to overhaul or 'streamline' the operations of ICAO to make it 'more effective to meet present and future problems of international civil aviation.'[70] To the Americans the goal was a more effective council with shorter sessions, a more efficient Air Navigation Commission and Air Transport Committee, and a revamped secretariat. To many of the smaller members it looked like an American effort to enhance the U.S. position in the organization. Needing 'considerable corridor work and some brinkmanship' just to garner some early support to introduce the issue in the Executive Committee, the American delegation found little sympathy for its proposals even to *study* the idea of reform. Once introduced, the committee accepted a motion (an 'obviously pre-arranged motion,' according to Donald Aggar, chair of the American delegation)[71] introduced by the Kenyan delegate to postpone any discussion of organizational change.[72]

For some British aviation officials these developments were seen as part of a power struggle within the organization. One former British council representative noted that the American efforts to change the ICAO Council would be regarded by the smaller members 'as a move on the part of the Americans to increase their influence which for some years now has been tending to decline as indeed has that of all the major States.'[73] ICAO remained a necessary and successful organization, another official wrote, but 'what we are faced with is the next stage in the continuing struggle for control of ICAO ... There is a total inevitability about this next stage. It may be triggered by the U.S. (who blundered badly in their tactics at the last Assembly); it may be triggered by any one of the blocs of States whose actions are governed by colour, language, economic advantage or regional bias. It will certainly be triggered by the adherence of the U.S.S.R. and its satellites. We must decide how to meet the challenge when it comes.' He continued with an explanation of his view of the problem: 'there are only about 20 out of the 116 Member States who have a big enough aviation problem to need an efficient ICAO and who have the resources to make a really useful contribution to ICAO. I believe that, if ICAO is to continue to serve the real needs of these States and therefore of international civil aviation, means must be found to enable them to exercise effective control. In the Assembly they are outvoted 5 to 1. In the Council they could have at least a 2 to 1 majority. Unfortunately, although these States have similar interests in the limited field of civil aviation, they have conflicting interests of race, colour, language, politics and economics.' His warning was clear, at least for the developed nations: 'I am convinced that if the advanced States do not get together and act cohesively they will be swamped by the developing States.'[74] He was less clear on how that cohesion would be achieved.

The impact of these disputes also could be seen in the divisions and the blocs that were created. There had always been a Latin American bloc in ICAO; a Communist bloc appeared in the 1950s, and a bloc of less developed countries, primarily African nations, emerged in the 1960s. The increase in membership, especially with the arrival of many new states from the developing world, was perceived as a potential threat by many of the older members, not just the 'Anglo-Saxons' but in most of the developed world and its allies. One American report described the situation in 1968: 'African participation in the ICAO Assembly has developed rapidly in the six years since a large number of these states became members. At the 1962 session, most African States simply voted with the French. At the 1965 session, the Africans took up most of the time of the Assembly in their attempt to expel South Africa but were still willing to work with the French to the extent of accepting advice on how to avoid action which would be contrary to the rules of procedure or the Chicago Convention. At the 1968 session, the Africans were not only highly familiar with the rules of procedure but successfully used them to accomplish their own ends.'[75]

The Western nations did not always consider themselves to be part of a bloc, but they acted and voted as if they were, although the lines of this bloc were always fluid and shifted from issue to issue on the basis of region and language. Sometimes the Europeans worked together against the United States (on the headquarter location issue, for example) or the less developed countries; sometimes language issues brought the British and the Americans together against the French and/or the Spanish-speaking members; and most often the Western nations – as the major aviation nations and contributors to ICAO – worked together to pursue and protect their interests in the organization. From the beginning the United States, the United Kingdom, and France, along with several other Western European states, Canada, and Australia, dominated the work of ICAO. These nations often agreed informally about committee memberships, agendas, and other decisions affecting the organization. They could secure sufficient votes to ensure that ICAO evolved as they believed it should – the way they stage managed the entrance of Japan and West

Germany was a good example of their control. It all made sense; they were, after all, responsible for most of the international aviation in the world – they had the airplanes, they provided most of the passengers, the cargo and air mail, and the facilities, and they paid for most of ICAO's operations. When they believed that their hegemony over ICAO was challenged – especially by countries that had little in the way of international aviation – they reacted like a bloc to protect their interests.

Soon the new members of the International Civil Aviation Organization began to test their strength and demand change. And when the various blocs voted together they could command a majority of the assembly on virtually any question before it. For many in the West, this was a challenge to the very fabric of ICAO. As one American representative explained in a 1971 letter sent to the White House, ICAO 'has done a lot for international civil aviation, especially in safety matters, and by and large has been a pretty professional group. Not any more. Now there is a political element in the vote on every issue, and the vote of a Togo or shortly a Qatar (population 60,000, – no aviation) equals and cancels out the vote of a United States or a United Kingdom. Now there are "lesser developed country" voting blocs.' The implication of such a situation was clear: 'With bloc voting prevailing over professional and practical aviation considerations, and with the resulting waste of time and aviation talent, ICAO is coming on some evil days … Indeed, there is a question whether ICAO has not largely fulfilled its original purpose.' Furthermore, 'if ICAO is rethinking its role, perhaps we ought to rethink the U.S. role in ICAO and see whether some other mechanisms may not advance U.S. aviation objectives more effectively.'[76] The response from the President's assistant in the White House was: 'we should just agreeably live with it rather than fight it because it is the only such organization we've got.'[77] Such words were hardly a ringing endorsement for the International Civil Aviation Organization.

The United States never intended to surrender any of its sovereignty to the organization. Over and over again, in the debates over the size of the ICAO Council, on the location of the headquarters, on technical assistance, over the future of the Warsaw system, on the membership of the Air Navigation Commission, on the negotiation of a multilateral agreement, and on membership and Cold War questions, the American government pursued American interests in ICAO. The same applied to the other large aviation nations, although there were some regional variations: the French used ICAO to enhance their national and linguistic prestige, especially in the early rebuilding years following the end of the Second World War; the British, for economic reasons, were constantly on guard to check ICAO's propensity to expand; others, like the Canadians, were more open to multilateral solutions as a way to offset their uneven bilateral arrangement with the United States, and so on.

Nevertheless, in many ways all these countries shared common goals for ICAO, and for many years it was relatively easy for the United States and its allies to shape the organization in their image and to get it to further their technical as well as strategic goals. Indeed, given that the developed nations would have been likely to maintain fairly high technical standards in their own states even without the existence of ICAO, it could be argued that the developed nations needed and used ICAO as a tool to ensure that the rest of world introduced and maintained aviation standards at much higher levels, thus enabling Western nations to fly into and across these other parts of the world. ICAO provided the necessary machinery for the developed world to encourage other states to improve their technical standards and, in this way, ICAO was an essential organization.

Conversely, the smaller members were more willing to sacrifice their ability to act independently within international organizations such as ICAO, because they had much less to lose. Membership gave them a platform; as one British historian wrote about the United Nations, it 'bestows prestige on the smaller countries as they find a place on numerous high-sounding committees and commissions.'[78] Indeed, through their membership in ICAO these nations could *enhance* their independence and sovereignty. And, if in return for their immersion into a larger group or bloc they could in some way harness the power of the United States and the other large powers, it was a good trade off. In the early years they were at the mercy of the larger powers and sat by while a few members dominated the activities of the organization; by the 1960s, however, things had changed and membership numbers alone gave these smaller members considerable power and influence – at the expense of the larger members.

By the end of the 1960s many were asking whether the International Civil Aviation Organization was to be a democracy ruled by the majority of members or whether it was to be guided – as it always had been – by the largest air powers. Was it to be a political organization reflecting the larger outside world of international rivalries and tensions and providing a stage for the unfolding of global tensions, or was it to be a technical organization focused on attaining the highest possible levels of air safety? Could it be both? Many observers believed that the answer was no, and they began to ask their own question: whether or not ICAO still had any role to play in international civil aviation.

PART THREE

11

'Closer to the Heart than the Purse': ICAO and the Problem of Security

Law is, in my view, only a 'minimum of morality' enforced by the power of a State or States. We have to strive to achieve much more than the minimum of morality, a true international morality enforced by the pressure of public opinion of the nations and peoples of the world.[1]

In September 1961 the Kennedy Administration initiated a complete re-examination and review of U.S. aviation policies to meet the challenges facing the American aviation industry and its airlines. An inter-agency committee was created, chaired by the director of the Federal Aviation Agency and comprising members from the Civil Aeronautics Board and the departments of State, Commerce, and Defense. After sixteen months of work, in January 1963, the committee submitted its confidential 'Report on the International Air Transport Policy of the United States.' The report highlighted the strategic and political aspects of aviation and made recommendations concerning route selection, capacity restrictions, cargo rates, user charges, and other issues in an effort to ensure for the United States 'a fair and equal opportunity to compete in world aviation markets.' Still, the report noted, there was more to international aviation and airlines than market forces and industrial targets: 'the fact remains that the various international air carriers of the world are enterprises of quite special, emotional concern to their home countries – be they industrial or underdeveloped. The carriers lie rather closer to the heart than the purse of these nations – they are pieces of their history, indicia of their importance as world powers, or evidences of their arrival as independent modern nations.'[2]

The Kennedy administration was not alone in its acknowledgement of the special nature of airlines and, more generally, international aviation. Airlines and their aircraft do more than carry passengers and cargo from one location to another. More than any other form of transportation, the aircraft of the major airlines constitute a kind of international manifestation of their individual nations. No matter where they fly, they represent, or at least can be seen to represent, their country of origin. For much the same reason, the aircraft of the international airlines can serve as ideal targets for criminals and terrorists. From British Airways and Air India to American Airlines and Air France, airlines such as these became targets – not because of their destination or the country within which the attack occurred, or the citizenship of the passengers on board, but because the aircraft themselves were a symbol of the airline's home country.

Hijacking and armed attacks against aircraft have always been special acts of terror in the international community, in that few other criminal acts can grab so much public attention so easily, and few other targets appear as vulnerable – even fragile – as aircraft in the public imagination. As one commentator explained, as a 'vital and vulnerable component of world commerce and communications, aviation was a natural target for terrorist attack. The terrorist campaign threatened not only the passengers and material value of the aircraft and cargoes, but also the fundamental public confidence that flying was safe.'[3] Aircraft became targets of international significance and for many years attacking an aircraft was one crime that seemed relatively easy to undertake – and to get away with.

Political gain or the spread of terror were not the only reasons for armed attacks on civil aviation. The motivation for such criminal acts ranged widely from the political to the personal, and the perpetrators spanned the spectrum from asylum seekers and political idealists to common criminals and deranged fanatics. As one legal scholar wrote, the 'intent of the hijacker is not always readily discernible, as the threat may be no more than a joke, an exhibition of an inebriate's bad temper, youthful folly, manifestation of mental imbalance, or, it may be the real thing.'[4] What to do about it was not always easily discernible, either, and agreeing to an international response sparked debate over resources and the proper tools to be used, and raised issues of political ideology and the political will to capture, extradite, try, and punish hijackers and others who threatened or committed offences against aircraft. Legal questions were raised as well, concerning jurisdiction and national sovereignty over each country's airspace and how to fashion a unified response within the context of many varied legal systems.[5]

The safety and security of international aviation has always been the goal of the International Civil Aviation Organization, although there was little discussion at the Chicago Conference of the kind of unlawful seizure and armed attacks that became common in the modern era.[6] The Chicago Convention is largely silent on the issue, and in the early years aviation safety and security were largely focused on technical innovation and the facilitation of air transport. Since the 1960s, however, aviation security has taken on a new meaning with the rise of an extremely violent global aviation terrorism that was infused with political ramifications and woven into the fabric of the major issues confronting the international community. As a result, in its efforts to protect aircraft, airlines, airports, passengers and crew, and nations from hijackings and other terrorist activity and to bring the perpetrators to justice, the security of international civil aviation has become one of the key elements of ICAO's role in the world today.

ICAO is not alone in its efforts to combat aviation terrorism. The organization is the focus of this study, but that role is shared with other national and international organizations. In the forefront is the United Nations itself and the other specialized agencies within the UN system that have worked tirelessly, and with mixed success, to foster international collaboration to combat all forms of terrorism.[7] In the field of international aviation, ICAO works side-by-side with the International Air Transport Association. In the 1960s, IATA established a Security Advisory Committee and passed a resolution to permit the active involvement of IATA, through its director general, in terrorist incidents while they were happening – a role ICAO has never embraced. IATA also sponsored a broad investigation of airports around the world wherever there was a question of poor standards, and collaborated with ICAO in its efforts to enhance airport security.

Other participants in the development of international aviation have created their own associations to protect their interests and enhance aviation security. The two most important are the organizations formed by airline pilots and airport operators. The first is the International Federation of Airline Pilots' Associations (IFALPA), organized in 1948 from a handful of pilots' associations. In its efforts to protect the interests of airline pilots, IFALPA grew into a global organization with many thousands of members. The second evolved from airport operators' associations in the United States and Europe; first as the Airports Association Co-ordinating Council and then, in 1991, as Airports Council International (ACI). Both these groups have made important contributions to the security of airports and in the prevention of hijacking.[8]

Mention should also be made of several national and regional organizations. In the United States, the FAA can make decisions and establish standards for U.S. aviation. Although the FAA has no direct power over other nations or airlines, the U.S. aviation industry and its airlines are such powerful forces in international aviation that the FAA's decisions and rules are often followed by others around the world; the desire of foreign airlines to gain access to the huge U.S. market is often sufficient inducement for them to conform to American regulations. Similarly, the European Civil Aviation Conference also represents a powerful aviation bloc (and the United States and Canada are permanent observers in the ECAC), and their decisions on security issues can have ramifications far beyond the borders of Europe. Indeed, agencies like the FAA and ECAC can, in some cases, reach conclusions, set standards, and take action more quickly and more easily than the larger and more diverse ICAO.[9] Moreover, by the late 1970s and 1980s other international groups – such as the G-7 and G-8 – also began to have input on aviation security and make decisions affecting international aviation.

The first recorded hijacking occurred in Peru in 1930 when a Pan Am mail plane was seized by revolutionaries who wanted to distribute their propaganda leaflets over Lima, but modern hijacking did not really begin until after the Second World War. There were a few acts of sabotage – usually onboard explosions – from the late 1940s through the 1950s, but these incidents were rare and relatively isolated occurrences. Hijacking appeared as well, but during the early 1950s they were largely confined to eastern Europeans escaping from behind the Iron Curtain and seeking freedom in the West. For the most part these individuals were welcomed as freedom seekers and they escaped punishment, even if, as in some cases, people were killed during their escape. For many people in the West these hijackings were justifiable and understandable, and not really even considered a crime so long as the aircraft was returned. Only with the global expansion of civil aviation and the introduction of jet aircraft in the late 1950s and early 1960s did the number of incidents begin to rise dramatically.[10]

Concerns over terrorism and, more generally, for the safety and security of aircraft and aviation predated ICAO. Piracy had long been an international crime, and although air piracy was different in nature than that on the high seas, the need for international collaboration was evident. The League of Nations made an effort in this direction with its 1937 Convention to Combat International Terrorism, but it never went into effect. In the international aviation community security issues were discussed as early as 1926 by CITEJA. A draft Convention on the Legal Status of the Aircraft Commander was submitted to PICAO in 1946 and was discussed further by the ad hoc legal committee of PICAO in 1947. In June 1950, the Legal Committee, on the prompting of E. M. Loaeza, the Mexican representative on the council, established an ad hoc subcommittee to examine the question of the 'Legal Status of Aircraft.' Loaeza had earlier raised the issue with the Air Transport Committee, and others had pointed out the need for a clarification of the legal status of both aircraft and aircraft commanders. The Legal Committee agreed to examine both topics, although neither appears to have been given the highest priority, and two rapporteurs were appointed: Loaeza for aircraft and A. Garnault of France for aircraft commanders.[11]

An official subcommittee on 'The Legal Status of Aircraft' was established in the late summer of 1953, but the whole question remained an issue of study for several more years. The work of this committee focused primarily on civil matters, but criminal issues did receive attention. Thanks to strong support from the United States, however, it was agreed in 1956, at the Tenth ICAO Assembly in Caracas, to focus the discussion in the subcommittee specifically on criminal rather than civil matters. At the same time, the subcommittee determined that it was necessary to establish an international convention on the question of offences committed on board aircraft. The reasoning was simple: aircraft were regularly flying over territory where there was no territorial sovereign or flying so quickly over several states that determining jurisdiction was next to impossible. In such cases, jurisdiction could be claimed by several states and might never be satisfactorily determined; in cases of multiple claims of jurisdiction, it might even lead to the offender being punished more than once for the same crime.[12]

The key questions for the subcommittee revolved around the issue of jurisdiction: Which nation had jurisdiction over crimes committed on board an aircraft, the state of registry of the aircraft or the state in whose airspace the crime was committed? Or should jurisdiction be determined by to the nationality of the victim and/or the criminal? Perhaps, others argued, jurisdiction should be given to the state where the flight originated or the state in which aircraft first landed. And, was it possible to have concurrent jurisdiction or was it essential to establish a priority of jurisdiction? Other questions were also raised. For example, would the convention limit the scope of offences to those committed by individuals on board the aircraft? Or would it be expanded to include those who might be involved but not actually on the aircraft? Answering these questions became the focus of debates in the subcommittee for the next half decade.

The subcommittee produced its first draft convention on the legal status of aircraft and aircraft commanders in September 1958. For the most part the draft was based on an American draft that had been used as the basis for discussion in the 1958 meetings. This document gave primary jurisdiction in most cases to the state of registry of the aircraft, not the state in whose airspace the crime was committed. The proposal met significant opposition from other committee members, but remained on the table throughout the discussions. This draft convention was revised and reconsidered by the subcommittee over the following months and was considered at the 12th session of the Legal Committee in Munich in August– September 1959. In Munich, the Legal Committee reconfirmed the need for an international convention on offences that endangered aircraft safety and, even though there was continuing division on the question of jurisdiction, the committee produced a new draft convention that was circulated to ICAO members for their consideration.[13]

While these proposals were being considered, the United States experienced a rash of domestic hijackings. Beginning in May 1961, several U.S. airliners (including aircraft from Pan American, Eastern, National, and Continental Airlines) were seized by hijackers and forced to fly to Cuba. These events reversed an earlier trend when, following the 1959 Cuban Revolution, there had been a handful of hijackings by Cuban nationals wishing to flee the new Castro regime. These individuals had been welcomed in the United States, and in some cases the hijacked aircraft were kept in the United States as partial payment of Cuban debts to American companies. When American aircraft began regularly to be seized and flown to Cuba, however, the Kennedy administration became determined to combat this new form of terrorism with special legislation. Washington responded with domestic legislation to deter these acts of 'aircraft piracy'; outlawing the carrying of concealed weapons on aircraft, and making it illegal to attack, threaten, or intimidate air pilots and crew. In some cases, airlines began to include armed guards onboard their aircraft.[14]

Several of these incidents occurred while the aircraft were engaged in international flights; most involved Cuba, with which the United States had no diplomatic relations. Without any kind of extradition arrangements it was often difficult to retrieve the hijacked passengers and crew, and these incidents only worsened an already poisoned relationship. But

Cuba was a member of ICAO, and as a result, for many in Washington it made sense to include in the new ICAO convention some provision to protect members in the case of international hijacking. The recent Convention on the High Seas, signed in Geneva in 1958, included aircraft as well as ships, but it applied only to the high seas and excluded the actions of passengers and crew, and therefore was seen as insufficient protection for the kinds of incidents that might occur with respect to aviation.[15] Consequently, in 1961 the United States proposed the inclusion of a new article in ICAO's draft convention to deal specifically with air hijacking.[16]

The American concerns were addressed at a meeting of the subcommittee in the spring of 1962 and the ICAO Council agreed to make the subcommittee's new draft convention the focus of discussion at the 14th Session of the Legal Committee held later that year in Rome. Meeting in Rome early in September 1962, the Legal Committee refined the wording for the convention, and a new draft was then distributed to the members for their consideration. The United States had been the driving force behind the convention on criminal matters, and this penultimate draft largely reflected its views. 'There are some areas where the text can be improved,' the American delegation at Rome reported, 'but in great part, the convention reflects almost exactly the position that the U.S. Delegations have advocated at the several meetings concerned with this problem.'[17]

ICAO called for a full diplomatic conference on air law to finalize the convention and to open it for signature to all the members. The conference was held in Tokyo, in August–September 1963. Fifty nations attended and another eight sent observers, along with representatives from several international organizations, including IATA, IFALPA, and the International Law Association. Participation was open to all members of the United Nations, not exclusively to ICAO members, and as a result there were delegations from a few non-ICAO members, including the Soviet Union.[18]

Politics remained largely on the sidelines, although there were a few complaints from the Soviet bloc about the presence of Nationalist China, the absence of the Peoples' Republic of China and East Germany, and concerning which nations could become signatories to the convention. South Africa did not attend the conference, but the presence of Portugal sparked some complaints, primarily from the African representatives. The Portuguese representative 'a supporté avec beaucoup de sang froid les attaques extrèmement violentes,' recorded the French delegation.[19] In addition, there was some political division on the question to what degree would the provisions of the convention apply to territories under the control of signatory states? The Soviets began to refer to this article as the 'colonial clause,' but their opposition was easily bypassed by the British, Dutch, and Americans in the Committee on Final Clauses. In any event, there were relatively few political interruptions during the conference. 'It was clear to all,' wrote the American Delegation, 'that in this particular matter the Bloc delegations were merely going through the motions of opposition without any real intention of disrupting the work of the Conference.'[20]

The outcome of this conference was the signing of the Tokyo Convention (officially the Convention on Offences and Certain Other Acts Committed on Board Aircraft) on 14 September 1963. Generally, the Tokyo Convention deals with (1) jurisdiction over crimes committed on board an aircraft, (2) the rights and responsibilities of an aircraft commander in such cases, (3) the duties of the state in which the aircraft lands after a crime has been committed, and (4) the restoration of the aircraft to its rightful owners after an air hijacking.[21] The convention deals with offences 'against penal law' and 'acts which, whether or not they are offences, may or do jeopardize the safety of the aircraft or of persons or property therein or which jeopardize good order and discipline on board.'[22]

At the heart of the Tokyo Convention is Article 3, paragraph 1: 'The State of registration of the aircraft is competent to exercise jurisdiction over offences and acts committed on board.' This provision applies even when an aircraft registered in one state is in the territorial airspace of another nation. There were a few restrictions, however. The convention applies only to aircraft in flight (defined as 'from the moment when power is applied for the purpose of take-off until the moment when the landing run ends') and aircraft used in 'military, customs or police services' are exempted. Moreover, the convention also does not require any state to take action against crimes of a 'political nature or those based on racial or religious discrimination.'

Once the aircraft doors are closed and until they are reopened for disembarkation, the commander of the aircraft (and in some cases crew members and even passengers) has the right, when there are 'reasonable grounds to believe that a person has committed or is about to commit' an offence, to use reasonable force to restrain the offender and protect and maintain the safety and security of the aircraft. In a forced landing, the aircraft will be considered to be in flight 'until competent authorities of a state take over the responsibility for the aircraft and for the persons and property on board.' The commander is also to notify the authorities and has the right to disembark anyone who has or was about to commit an offence. The convention also protects the commander, passengers, and crew from civil litigation resulting from their actions.

What constitutes a crime on board an aircraft is not specified in any great detail, and the convention does not force any member to change its laws or write new ones. It does oblige a contracting state to take custody of an individual who has been disembarked from an aircraft, and that state 'may' return the individual to his/her state of nationality or to the territory where the voyage began, but the convention does not 'create an obligation to grant extradition.' What is important is that regarding extradition, offences will be treated 'as if they had been committed not only in the place in which they have occurred but also in the territory of the State of registration of the aircraft.' With respect to the unlawful seizure of an aircraft, or hijacking, once an aircraft has landed the convention stipulates that the contracting state where the plane landed 'shall take all appropriate measures to restore control of the aircraft to its lawful commander or to preserve his control of the aircraft,' and allow the aircraft, its passengers, crew and cargo to continue their voyage 'as soon as practicable.'[23]

The Tokyo Convention was open to all members of the United Nations and its specialized agencies and was to come into force ninety days following its ratification by twelve states. From then it would apply to those states and all others that ratified it in subsequent years. It could also be denounced by any signatory on six months notice. No member was forced to relinquish any sovereignty over its airspace or revise its national legal system, and, as is the case with most of ICAO's activities, members would be advised and encouraged to ratify the Tokyo Convention, but no one would be forced to accept it.

The Tokyo Convention was ICAO's first step in what would become a major international effort to combat the spread of aviation terrorism. At the same time, questions about the convention and its effectiveness were raised; and, while some of the questions were unique to this convention, others plagued all of ICAO's subsequent efforts in this field. For one thing, the Tokyo Convention would only apply to those countries that ratified it, and while it would be unrealistic to expect ICAO to create a mandatory convention that would apply to all nations, the Tokyo Convention – and subsequent ones – was by default limited in its application. Any state that might not wish to subscribe to its conditions could choose not to ratify it. In addition, hijacking and acts of terror were easy to denounce but – as in the case of the Tokyo Convention – sometimes hard to define. Everyone concurred that terrorism and any armed attacks on international aviation were bad things, but what should or could be done about them was less clear. Agreeing to a definition of the crime of air piracy was an intractable problem and was something that the Tokyo Convention did not do. Attacks on civil aviation were perpetrated by individuals for a variety of personal, political, and other reasons; and, in some cases, one nation's terrorist was another nation's freedom fighter.

For many ICAO members, the lack of specific rules for extradition emerged as one of the serious flaws in the Tokyo Convention. Jurisdiction was given to the state of registration of the aircraft, but when the aircraft landed in another state that state could extradite the criminal if it wanted to but was under no obligation to do so. This lack of extradition enforcement sparked many calls for more stringent extradition rules in future discussions. Another serious weakness was that the Tokyo Convention applied only to aircraft in flight, as it defined it, and did not consider attacks on aircraft that were parked or, more generally, acts of sabotage on airports and other aviation facilities.[24] As Robert Boyle, the chief American negotiator at the Tokyo Conference later wrote: 'it is obvious that the Tokyo convention left major gaps in the international legal system in attempting to cope with the scope of aircraft hijacking. There were no undertakings by anyone to make aircraft hijacking a crime under international law, no undertakings to see to it the crime was one punishable by severe penalties and most important, no undertaking to either submit the case for prosecution or to extradite the offender to a State which would wish to prosecute.'[25] In other words, there were large holes in the Tokyo Convention through which countries – and terrorists – could manoeuvre.

None of these concerns really mattered if the Tokyo Convention never came into force, and only a few ICAO members ratified it quickly. Although signed by most participants at the conference, by the end of 1966 only two nations had ratified the convention; by the start of 1969 five more ratifications occurred, bringing the total to seven. Part of the reason for the slow progress was that the number of hijackings dropped significantly in 1962 and for the next five years there were relatively few incidents. In some years there were no hijackings at all in the United States. Everything changed, however, in 1967 with the Six-Day War in June and, for the first time, the appearance of hijacking in the Middle East. What started as a trickle turned into a flood with thirty-four more hijackings in 1968, eighty-seven in 1969, and a total of 364 between 1968 and 1972.[26] What had earlier been perceived largely as a problem in Cuban-American relations – something, one author wrote, 'the rest of the world thinks it can safely snicker about as a remote and isolated problem' – was no longer the case.[27]

The rash of hijackings highlighted the fact that only a few members had ratified the Tokyo Convention. Even though its flaws had been exposed it was still widely believed to be a valuable tool in the fight against terrorism. As a result, several members were prompted to ratify it, and, with the twelfth ratification – by the United States – the Tokyo Convention came into force on 4 December 1969.[28] In addition, what to do about these continuing unlawful attacks on civil aviation became an issue at the Sixteenth ICAO Assembly in Buenos Aires in September 1968. On the prompting of the United States delegation, and with 'strong statements' from the representatives from IATA and IFALPA,[29] the assembly passed an important resolution on the issue of hijacking. Resolution A16-37 called on all members to ratify the Tokyo Convention and, until they did, asked them to 'give effect to the principles' of the article in the Tokyo Convention dealing with the return of control of the hijacked aircraft to the pilot and allowing the aircraft to continue on its voyage. Equally important, the resolution called on the council to begin to study 'other measures to cope with the problem of unlawful seizure.'

The assembly at Buenos Aires was an important moment in ICAO's history. The assembly's resolutions called on the ICAO Council – and the member states – to take action in a number of areas to combat international aviation terrorism. The council responded in different ways over the following months and years, although its actions can be divided roughly into two major categories – technical and legal. The former dealt with specific plans and actions to enhance aircraft and airport security through study and investigation, the preparation of standards and manuals, the dissemination of information, and the encouragement of contracting states to raise their security levels. The latter dealt with a prolonged series of negotiations – always difficult and sometimes acrimonious – to prepare new legal documents and agreements to achieve a unified legal response to the wave of hijackings, sabotage, and other unlawful attacks on international civil aviation.

The ICAO Council took action immediately. In December, acting on the recommendation of the Buenos Aires Assembly (Resolution A16-37), the council directed the Air Transport Committee and the Air Navigation Commission to initiate their own studies of the technical aspects of the problems of aircraft and airport security.[30] The ATC was directed to study only those 'preventative measures' that might be taken *before* a flight began; the ANC was to consider safety measures that could be implemented *during* flights. Their recommendations were in many ways preliminary, with emphasis on methods to enhance detection through metal detectors and the searching of passengers and the use of warning posters to discourage would-be hijackers.[31]

The council itself also soon became a focus of activity. In the days following the Buenos Aires Assembly, a group of council members introduced a resolution to create a wholly new committee to focus exclusively on the broad issue of unlawful interference with aviation. The group included Argentina, Canada, Colombia, the Federal Republic of Germany, Japan, the Netherlands, and the United Kingdom, but the strongest support came from the United States. The plan was to have a committee that could coordinate ICAO's response to international aviation terrorism and that could, in some instances, deal with specific cases involving ICAO members. But the difficulties of reaching an agreement on such a plan became immediately apparent and the original proposals were met by stiff resistance from some council members who were concerned about the powers that this new committee would have. Not surprisingly, the divisions in the council reflected those in the outside world. Some members whose states had been victims of unlawful interference wished to take dramatic, concerted, and automatic action against terrorists, while others spoke for nations that were less likely to have been victimized but might have to bear the brunt of international sanctions or the reprisals of the terrorists and their supporters, and still others were less convinced that a hard-line approach was suitable and believed that, as a technical organization, ICAO should not become embroiled in what were essentially political affairs.

The debate in the council revolved around the responsibilities of the new committee and whether or not to link its creation to Article 52 of the Chicago Convention.[32] Article 52 allows the council to 'delegate authority with respect to any particular matter to a committee of its members.' For several members this would give the new committee too much power and independence of action. This group also hoped to limit the actions of the committee to non-political matters. The debate became quite divisive at times, as different members argued over the wording of the resolution, the duties of the new committee, and its relationship to the council. One Canadian delegate gave an interesting glimpse of the council in action when he recorded his impressions of the debate: 'It appears that there is a definite division between the co-sponsors of the

Resolution and the Delegations of Lebanon, Tunisia, Congo (Brazzaville) and Senegal, who are against the creation of a Committee with any kind of independent power. The U.S.A. has gone as far as it can in watering down the Committee's powers by limitations set out in the proposed terms of reference. In fact, Columbia [*sic*] is afraid the Committee may be *too* powerless and the whole point of the Resolution will therefore be lost. Several Delegations – France, Spain, Australia, Belgium, Denmark and Italy, want to see some progress but within rather defined limits. Their attitude is cautious support of the Resolution and the creation of the Committee provided the latter has carefully drafted terms of reference. Nigeria, Tanzania and Mexico are more forthcoming towards the Resolution than they were, and will probably vote for it in the end. India, Guatemala, and Czechoslovakia are less antagonistic than formerly and may also accept the Resolution, though it may depend on whether Article 52 is retained as a basis for the creation of the Committee. Brazil and U.A.R. have not taken part in the debate and have given no indication of their positions.'[33]

By early April a compromise of sorts was worked out (after much lobbying and 'persuasive discussions'[34]), and on 10 April 1969 the ICAO Council passed a resolution creating the new Committee on Unlawful Interference with Aircraft. Essentially, the new committee was to do for the council on security matters what the ANC does on technical issues. Established 'in accordance with Article 52 of the Convention,' the new committee was to consist of eleven members selected from council members. Its mandate was to develop 'preventive measures and procedures' to protect international civil aviation from unlawful interference, attack, seizure, and sabotage, and to assist the members in adopting these procedures. All contracting states were asked to provide a report on 'all non-political aspects of cases of unlawful interference' and after deliberation and study, the committee would recommend possible actions and procedures to the council. In the course of its work, the committee could 'invite advice and recommendations' from the members and their airlines and airport authorities and from other international organizations. There were also limits placed on the authority and range of the committee. It was to be a permanent body, but its responsibilities and continued existence were to be reviewed regularly by the council. Furthermore, the committee was to 'refrain from considering any case which may involve the Committee in matters of a political nature or of controversy between two or more States.' One final point, although not included in the resolution, it was agreed that there would be a geographical basis for the new committee, with one member from North America, one from the Middle East, three from Europe, and two each from Africa, Asia and the Far East, and Latin America, although the council president was not absolutely obliged to select the committee along these lines[35]

The new Committee on Unlawful Interference with Aircraft reflected the divisions in the council. The connection to Article 52 remained, but so too did the limitations of its power and its subordination to the council. It was to have the ability to consider individual cases, but events of a political nature were exempted, and what was considered 'political' was not clearly spelled out. The Americans, who had been far more adamant than most other members for aggressive action to combat terrorism, were concerned about the make-up of the committee. Robert Boyle, the American representative on the council, reported his views to Washington. 'As you know,' he wrote, 'we pressed the Council very hard in establishing this Committee and there remain elements in the Council who may, out of a feeling of resentment, endeavor to hamstring its activities. The easiest approach to this is for them to call any specific case of unlawful interference that occurs a "political matter" and, therefore, one on which the Committee should take no action.' Little could be done about the committee's terms of reference, however, and he suggested that the way around this kind of a problem was to support states with sympathetic opinions to the United States for membership on the committee. 'I suspect that some of the activity that has gone on in connection with the selection of members of the Committee,' Boyle concluded, 'has been motivated by a desire to have on the Committee as many as possible of those who might be persuaded that instances of unlawful interference are "political" and thus effectively prevent Committee activity.'[36]

The other major area for council activity was in the legal field. The resolution of the Buenos Aires Assembly marked the beginning of a new process to either refine the Tokyo Convention or to create a wholly new convention that would take a tougher stance against hijacking and deal with the issue of extradition, which was widely seen as the greatest weakness of the Tokyo Convention. At the end of 1968, the ICAO Council turned the matter over to the Legal Committee, which in turn created a new subcommittee to examine the issue and begin work on a new draft convention on the unlawful seizure of aircraft. The subcommittee comprised thirteen nations (Algeria, Canada, Colombia, Denmark, France, India, Israel, Japan, Nigeria, Switzerland, Tunisia, the United Kingdom, and the United States) and was chaired by Gilbert Guillaume of France.

The subcommittee met twice in 1969, in February and September, without a formal agenda other than to begin work on a new draft convention that would 'deter persons from committing acts of unlawful seizure of aircraft and, more specifically, to ensure, as far as practicable, the prosecution and punishment of these persons.' There were basic disagreements, even over whether this new convention would be a protocol to the Tokyo Convention or an entirely new convention. The major stumbling block, however, remained extradition. Most members believed that hijacking was and should be an extraditable crime, but the subcommittee was divided on the issue, basically with the United States on one side and everyone else on the other. The Americans wanted 'special provisions for extradition of hijackers'[37] written into the convention and political motives excluded as a reason to deny extradition. Virtually all the other members argued that the extradition rules should be subject to their own legal systems; in other words, extradition might be refused in some cases where it was not in accordance with a member's national laws. An example was given of a nation that might refuse extradition, 'where an offender was its own national or was seeking asylum from persecution or acted from political motives.' Conversely, they all agreed that extradition could be denied if it was 'considered that the request had been made for a political purpose.'[38]

By the time of the subcommittee's September meeting the international situation had worsened seriously. The number of hijackings rose through 1969, and on 29 August a TWA flight from Rome to Athens was hijacked by Palestinian terrorists and forced to fly to Damascus. Once they arrived in Syria the passengers were evacuated and an attempt was made to blow up the aircraft. The Syrian government held on to the damaged aircraft and two Israeli passengers for several months until an exchange could be made for some Syrian prisoners held in Israel. In the aftermath of the hijacking, the U.S. government became more committed to action; in September President Nixon spoke to the U.N. General Assembly and called for concerted action against hijacking; in December, the United Nations passed a resolution calling on its members to take 'appropriate measures' to fight aviation terrorism and to support ICAO's actions.[39] In the ICAO subcommittee, the American delegation became more determined to produce a new draft convention.

Substantial agreement was reached at the September meeting, largely because the United States agreed to 'work along the lines' of the earlier draft agreement from the February meetings. Thanks to recent events there was an urgency in the American desire to move things along and a degree of realization that the other members of the subcommittee were not likely to come over to the American position.[40] This realization was confirmed in the discussions, as the Americans found that 'most of the delegations were unable or unwilling to accept restrictions on prosecuting discretion, either in the form of mandatory prosecution or the form of excluding personal motivations from consideration.'[41] In the event, a new draft convention was submitted to the Legal Committee, but its terms were weaker than had been hoped for by the U.S. Delegation and reflected the majority opinion that each nation should have discretion in the extradition and punishment of hijackers.[42]

The United States conceded on the new convention in the face of stiff opposition, but this did not stop American efforts to achieve broader agreement on some kind of concerted action against terrorist hijackers. Before the end of the Legal subcommittee meetings, State Department officials were already confidentially raising the possibility of the major air powers taking joint action against hijacking, outside the auspices of ICAO.[43] In December, the thirteen leading aviation states from Western Europe and North America, plus Australia, Brazil, and Japan, met in Washington to look at these issues. The American position was clear: the way to defeat hijacking was through the detection of hijackers before they struck and by apprehending, extraditing, and severely punishing them after the fact. Having failed to achieve the inclusion of mandatory extradition in the new convention, the Americans turned to sanctions against those states that aided or harboured terrorists. What they had in mind was an agreement among the leading aviation states to suspend air services to and from any state that acted 'contrary to international norms in hijacking incidents.' It was a risky proposal, the Americans agreed, but 'there were also risks in allowing hijacking to spread around the world.'[44]

The Americans found few supporters for their position; indeed, the Japanese, Australians, French, Norwegians, and British all immediately spoke against the idea and made it clear that they 'were not prepared to embark on a program of sanctions.'[45] It was argued that sanctions would breach existing bilateral air agreements and would, in any event, likely produce few results other than to spark anger and retaliation from the other side. The French delegation suspected that the Nixon administration was staging the talks in a public relations effort to convince the American public that it was doing all that it could to fight terrorism.[46] While the French assessment perhaps underestimated the seriousness of the United States, the Americans had miscalculated the potential for support for sanctions. The Washington meetings achieved little, but the United States persisted in its campaign for sanctions for many years.

As was so often the case in the world of aviation diplomacy, international events overtook the slow process of negotiation, conference, and diplomatic procedure. On 21 February 1970, a Palestinian terrorist group exploded bombs on two European airlines en route to Tel Aviv. The first bomb exploded in the baggage hold of an Austrian Airlines jet but the aircraft managed an emergency landing in Frankfurt; the second destroyed Swissair 990, killing all forty-seven passengers and crew. These were not the first terrorist attacks that emerged from disputes in the Middle East, but international outrage was immediate and intense. 'The hijacking era in air transport that began only a few years ago with a comic-opera aura of unexpected excursions to Havana,' one journalist wrote a few days after the attacks, 'has now grown into an extremely ugly and dangerous cancer that undermines the safety of every airline passenger. Too many pilots, stewardae and passengers have already died at the hands of hijackers and air assassins to warrant any further delay in tackling the problem on a full-scale international basis.'[47]

One of the immediate responses to these tragic events came from the Austrian and Swiss governments in the form of a request to the ICAO Council to hold a conference on aviation security. The other European nations were in support and on 16 March, ten members of ECAC made a formal request for an extraordinary session of the assembly. The council agreed and called the members together for the Seventeenth Session (Extraordinary) of the ICAO Assembly for Montreal in June. Because the Legal Committee's draft convention, which had been under consideration for several months, dealt primarily with hijacking and not the kind of attacks and murder experienced by the Swiss and Austrians, many members believed that a second new convention was necessary. As a result, the members of ICAO found themselves in the unusual situation of working on two security air law conventions simultaneously, one for hijacking and the other for sabotage.

Ninety-one of ICAO's 119 members were present at the Montreal Conference, which lasted for two weeks from 16 to 30 June 1970, and several commentators noted that the presence of delegations from both Israel and several Arab states augured well for a successful outcome.[48] The Soviet Union also sent an observer along with thirteen international organizations (including the United Nations, IATA, IFALPA, and INTERPOL). Because of time constraints and such a large turn-out, the formal opening statements were skipped, but several members circulated working papers containing proposals that ranged from new draft conventions to amendments to the Chicago Convention. The main work of the conference, however, was undertaken by two committees: one for technical issues, the other for legal issues.[49] 'This was probably the most intensive ICAO Assembly ever held,' was the verdict of one British participant.[50]

The extraordinary session produced a series of resolutions dealing with a wide range of security matters. On the technical side, the assembly called on members to adopt a series of practical measures to enhance the security of civil aviation, especially against hijacking and acts of violence. These measures were to include, among others, the training of personnel to detect hijackers, the use of metal detectors, the use of warnings to dissuade potential hijackers, the reorganization of baggage handling and inspection, and the reorganization of airports to isolate passengers from visitors. ICAO was to study and update these measures with a view to incorporating them into existing SARPs and through the creation of a new annex for adoption by all contracting states.

The Committee on Unlawful Interference, with the help of the ANC and the ATC, began this process immediately following the extraordinary session. All the existing annexes were examined to see where they could be amended to incorporate changing security standards. By December 1972, a group of initial proposals were circulated to the members for their comments.[51] On 22 March 1974, the council officially adopted the new Standards and Recommended Practices, and they were embodied as Annex 17, with the official title: *Security – Safeguarding International Civil Aviation against Acts of Unlawful Interference.*[52]

Annex 17 calls on all members to create their own security program and to coordinate efforts between government departments, airport authorities, airlines, and pilots and crew. Members are encouraged to develop training programs and to cooperate with neighbouring states and other ICAO members. Airport security is central to the annex, of course, and it calls for the establishment of a variety of airport programs, committees, and training facilities with the aim of enhancing airport security. Most of the recommendations were practical in nature and dealt with baggage, access to the aircraft, and other procedures, and some were already widely in use, such as the recommendation that the door between the flight crew and passengers be lockable. Not surprisingly, much attention in the annex is focused on airport security, with recommendations to create 'sterile areas' to keep passengers who have passed through security checkpoints separate from other visitors. Annex 17 also contains an attachment incorporating all the security specifications found in the other annexes. Overall, it was a slim document, but the adoption of the new annex was only the start, and it was revised and updated regularly over the following years.[53]

In addition, Resolution A17-10 of the Seventeenth Session 1970 Extraordinary Assembly called on the secretary general to prepare a 'Manual on Security,' which would assist members in implementing all the security recommendations. It would cover aspects of security control, weapons and explosive detection, airport design, and so on, and would be constantly revised and updated. Largely the work of a group consisting of representatives from Brazil, France, Switzerland, the United Kingdom, and the United States, the *Security Manual for Safeguarding Civil Aviation against Acts of Unlawful Interference* was first published in November 1971, and it became a very useful document in helping members apply the standards and recommendations of Annex 17. Amended versions were released in 1974 and 1977, and a second edition was published in 1983.[54]

On the legal side, the 1970 Extraordinary Assembly passed several resolutions, calling on the members to ratify the Tokyo Convention (A17-2), to support the new convention on hijacking that would be discussed later that year (A17-3), and to report incidents of unlawful interference (A17-16). In addition, a resolution introduced in the Executive Committee by the Swiss delegation to amend the Chicago Convention to oblige members to take effective action against acts of unlawful interference was watered down into a general resolution for the council to study the matter (A17-21).[55] The most important resolution (A17-20) called on the Legal Committee to draft a new Convention on Acts of Unlawful Interference against International Civil Aviation with a view to its being adopted at a diplomatic conference the next year, 1971. There was little debate on the resolution and the final version passed without opposition. The question of sanctions was not raised; nevertheless, the American delegation concluded that the 'results of the Assembly were highly satisfactory.'[56]

The operations of the new Committee on Unlawful Interference, the Legal Committee's finalizing of the new conventions, all the work on the new annex and *Security Manual,* and the various other activities carried on through the summer and fall of 1970 in an atmosphere of intense crisis and rising urgency. In the spring, the Japanese Red Army terrorist group hijacked a Japanese Airline B-727 to Seoul and the ensuing eighty hour hostage drama played out on television sets around the world. In July, terrorists hijacked an Olympic Airways B-727 to Athens and successfully demanded the release of several jailed terrorists. There was also an attack on an El Al B-707 at Athens Airport and a grenade attack on some

El Al offices, and the Israelis responded with a controversial reprisal raid on several aircraft of Middle Eastern Airlines in Beirut. Then, over a period of two days, four aircraft were hijacked by the Popular Front for the Liberation of Palestine; three (a TWA B-707, a Swissair DC-8, and a BOAC VC-10) were flown to Dawson's Field near Amman, Jordan, the fourth (a Pan American B-747) to Cairo. Hundreds of passengers and crew were held hostage in a drama that lasted several days and the four aircraft were destroyed. It was the worst hijacking incident to that time and it sent shock waves through the international community.[57]

At the United Nations, Secretary-General U Thant proposed the creation of a tribunal to focus on hijacking and, in November, U.N. Resolution n.2645 was passed, condemning all acts of hijacking, sabotage, and unlawful interference against civil aviation.[58] IATA implemented a new anti-hijacking program and Knut Hammarskjöld, IATA's Director-General, embarked on a personal initiative with visits to Damascus, Beirut, Cairo, Amman, and elsewhere.[59] In the United States, President Nixon appealed to Congress for $28 million in funding for anti-sabotage training and for the placing of armed guards, or the sky marshals, on American airlines. He also called for more comprehensive use of metal detectors, especially at U.S. international airports, and renewed the call for international action to impose sanctions or boycotts against those states that aided or harboured terrorists or held passengers as hostages after the fact.

On 18 September, U.S. Secretary of Transportation John Volpe attended the ICAO Council meeting and appealed to its members to create a 'common front' and embrace sanctions against the states that refused to extradite or punish terrorists and hijackers.[60] Outside, in meetings and press conferences, he declared that 'the United States will act and expects other States to act, in order to quarantine promptly and effectively any State which supports or condones air piracy for international blackmail purposes.'[61] The House Foreign Affairs Committee opened hearings on how best to handle the terrorist threat; at the same time, Democratic Senator Warren G. Magnuson, chair of the Senate Commerce Committee, called for Senate hearings on the use of sanctions, and recommended taking action against Algeria, Cuba, Jordan, Lebanon, Syria, and the United Arab Republic (Egypt). 'Only through a determined U.S. attitude do we have a chance to bring these vicious terrorist acts to a halt,' Magnusson said, 'a boycott will be overwhelmingly convincing evidence that the civilized nations of the world will no longer permit this threat to its citizens throughout the world.'[62]

In this atmosphere of crisis, considerable progress was made on the new conventions. In December 1970, seventy-seven states met in The Hague for the signing of the Hague Convention, officially the Convention for the Suppression of Unlawful Seizure of Aircraft. The text had been agreed to earlier, and there was little change made at The Hague, despite some last minute discussion of proposed amendments. It was open for ratification by all nations, not just the members of the United Nations, and was to come into force thirty days following its ratification by ten states.[63]

The Hague Convention takes the Tokyo Convention and builds on it, incorporating several articles from the earlier agreement. Like Tokyo, the Hague Convention sets out rules for jurisdiction after a hijacking and it applies only to aircraft in flight, but does not apply to 'aircraft used in military, customs or police services.' Unlike Tokyo, the Hague Convention broadens the jurisdiction over the offence somewhat to include the nation where the aircraft lands and to other states in some cases, and it includes a definition of the offence, although neither the word 'hijacking' nor 'crime' is used. The offender is anyone, or an accomplice, who 'unlawfully, by force or threat thereof, or by any other form of intimidation, seizes, or exercises control of, that aircraft, or attempts to perform any such act.' All contracting states agree to report to the ICAO Council information about the offence and what action was taken to deal with the situation. In addition, the offence is deemed to be extraditable and is to be 'punishable by severe penalties,' although what those penalties should be is not mentioned. On the key question of extradition, if the state where the offender is captured fails to extradite the hijacker that state is 'obliged, without exception whatsoever and whether or not the offence was committed in its territory, to submit the case to its competent authorities for the purpose of prosecution. Those authorities shall take their decision in the same manner as in the case of any ordinary offence of a serious nature under the law of that State.' The Hague Convention came into force on 14 October 1971.

The stage was also set for the signing of the convention on sabotage. By the end of October 1970, the Legal Committee agreed to a text and in November the ICAO Council called for a full diplomatic conference. This international air law conference was held in Montreal on 8–23 September 1971, and was attended by sixty-one states and seven international organizations.[64] The Legal Committee's draft convention was reconsidered, clause by clause, and on 23 September, the Montreal Convention, officially the Convention for the Suppression of Unlawful Acts against the Safety of Civil Aviation, was opened for signature. The

Montreal Convention builds on the Hague Convention, with many paragraphs copied verbatim or with only slight amendments. For example, the clauses dealing with the definition of 'in flight,' the application of 'severe penalties,' the exemption of military, customs, and police aircraft, and the key article on the need to prosecute or extradite the offender are the same in the two conventions. Where the Montreal Convention differs is in the nature of the crime: it defines the offence as any attack, damage, or violence against aircraft, individuals, and facilities that endanger aircraft while in flight or in service (and 'in service' meant from the start of 'preflight preparation' by the ground crew to twenty-four hours after landing).[65] It was 'an effective and forceful measure,' concluded the American delegation, and together with the Tokyo and Hague conventions, they 'set out the international rules of law governing unlawful interference with aircraft.'[66] The Montreal Convention came into force in January 1973.

The weaknesses of the new conventions were quickly apparent to many observers. For one thing, both conventions called for severe penalties, but what those penalties should be is not explained. For another, the conventions apply only to aircraft 'in flight' and/or 'in service' and leave out all manner of potential targets on the ground or against airports and airline facilities. Also, although the conventions appear to commit the states to either extradite or prosecute offenders, critics were quick to point out that they only oblige states to 'submit' for the 'purpose of prosecution' and do not actually insist on prosecution. As one British official explained at the time of the Hague Convention, 'discussions in the (Legal) Committee showed that an absolute obligation either to prosecute a hijacker or to extradite him to a State which would prosecute would be unacceptable to many States. Since the Convention would be ineffective unless it was widely ratified, the Committee recognized that it would be necessary to leave some loophole.'[67] And, of course, the conventions would only apply to states that ratified them, and no ICAO member was under any obligation to do so.[68]

The signing of two international air conventions within a few months of each other did not end the attempt by the United States and a few other states to produce a further convention on sanctions. There were loopholes in the three existing conventions, especially over extradition, and even if extradition was mandatory there were no guarantees that all ICAO member states would either ratify the conventions or live up to them if they did. As a result, terrorists could still find safe havens in various parts of the world, and some states believed that, until action could be taken against those states that aided or harboured terrorists or failed to live up to their international responsibilities, unlawful acts against civil aviation would continue.

The Americans took their proposals to the ICAO Council and to the meetings of the Legal Committee being held in London in September 1970, and in both venues proposed a resolution calling for the suspension of air services to any state that held onto hostages and aircraft or failed to extradite terrorists after a hijacking. Despite the heightened sense of emergency, the United States found little increase in international support for sanctions. The Legal Committee extended its session to discuss the U.S. resolution but did not embrace it; indeed, the Americans reported that there was 'little disposition' to discuss it and, in fact, some delegations left before the session ended.[69] The American resolution fared little better with the members of the ICAO Council. Even among the Europeans there was little support. At a separate ad hoc meeting of the council members from North America and Europe, the Americans found the British sitting on the fence, the Belgians negative, the Germans 'very negative,' and the French absent, having failed even to send a representative to the meeting. This was a bad sign, given that the meeting was held in Paris.[70]

At the emergency meeting of the whole ICAO Council in Montreal the results were not much more encouraging.[71] The Americans revised their resolution, but could not get the others to embrace it beyond giving general support to the idea of concerted action. The British reaction was not untypical. Sanctions would be extremely difficult to implement, they argued, they likely would contravene existing bilateral agreements, and they would probably backfire, leading to retaliation. 'In the first place,' one confidential British report explained,

> action against the State or its airlines pre-supposes that the State concerned perpetuates, or is actively associated with or condones, the offence. Secondly, in the most likely case in the short term, i.e. one involving a Middle East country, action to be effective would need to be taken together by all the major Western aviation countries in respect of both terminating and transitting flights not only against the offender but possibly also against active supporters. An offending country might well receive support from other countries which would retaliate against those imposing sanctions. Quite apart from the general political repercussions of such an escalation, the airlines of the countries imposing sanctions could suffer major losses. If, in

the worst case, Middle East and North African countries denied us the ability to fly to, from and over their territory, BOAC and BUA [*sic*]services to East, Central and Southern Africa would at a minimum be severely disrupted, while flights to Pakistan, India and most flights to the Far East would have to be re-routed, if indeed possible, over Eastern Europe, Turkey and Iran. There would also be important defence implications. Furthermore, in circumstances where the lives of hostages were already at risk the possibility of increasing the risk might well give rise to hesitation over the imposition of sanctions.[72]

It was also argued that sanctions would damage European interests more than American ones, and this fact helped explain why the Europeans were less eager to move forward in this area. 'We suspect that the Americans have rushed into action,' one British memo noted, 'largely for presentational reasons and without really thinking through the issues involved.'[73]

The only allies the Americans had were the Canadians. Earlier at the extraordinary assembly and again in the meetings of the ICAO Council and Legal Committee in September, the Canadians introduced a proposal to modify existing bilateral air agreements to include a special anti-hijacking clause. This bilateral approach could bypass the concern about contravening existing agreements and permit the application of sanctions if one of the parties to the bilateral agreement failed to live up to its side of the bargain.[74] The Americans were supportive but preferred their own multilateral approach, arguing that any state that endangered the safety of civil aviation was already in breach of its bilateral agreements and the terms of the Chicago Convention and therefore was liable for sanctions.[75] The rest of the council was more skeptical of both plans from the North Americans, and ultimately the Council passed the two plans on to the Legal Committee for further study.[76]

The study on sanctions was undertaken by a new subcommittee of the Legal Committee consisting of members from Argentina, Brazil, Canada, Chile, Egypt, France, Israel, Jamaica, Japan, the Netherlands, Tanzania, the Soviet Union, the United Kingdom, and United States. By the time the subcommittee first met in April 1971, the Americans and Canadians had combined their efforts into one (largely based on the U.S. proposals) and co-sponsored a new draft multilateral convention to establish rules and the machinery to enforce the Hague and Montreal conventions and to take action against those states that failed to live up to their responsibilities under them.[77] Very little progress was made, however. More talks were called for, but at the Eighteenth ICAO Assembly that met in Vienna in July, the sanctions issue was removed from the Legal Committee's active list and the whole process was effectively derailed.

Efforts to revive the study of sanctions were made in the ICAO Council early in 1972, but without success. As in the past, however, international events forced the members to re-open the whole issue. Early in May, the terrorist group Black September hijacked a Belgian aircraft to Lod Airport in Tel Aviv demanding the release of hundreds of Arab prisoners in Israeli jails and threatening to kill the 100 passengers and crew on board. After two days of tense negotiations the hijackers were killed or captured by the Israelis. At the end of the month, three members of the Japanese Red Army boarded a plane in Rome – using false documents and carrying weapons and grenades in bags that were not searched – and when they landed in Tel Aviv they opened fire in Lod Airport, killing twenty-six people and wounding another seventy-six.[78] A few days later, in June, a Czechoslovakian aircraft was hijacked to West Germany; the pilot was murdered and a U.S. Western Airlines aircraft was hijacked and flown to Algeria, where the hijackers were released.

The U.N. Security Council responded with a resolution calling upon nations to 'take all appropriate measures within their jurisdiction to deter and prevent such acts and to take effective measures to deal with those who commit such acts.'[79] IFALPA called for a one day international airline pilots' strike for 19 June, and that same day the ICAO Council agreed to create a new subcommittee to look at the issue of sanctions. The word 'sanctions' was not used in the resolution, and its convoluted nature hinted at the trouble ahead. The new subcommittee was 'to work on the preparation of an international convention to establish appropriate multilateral procedures within the ICAO framework for determining whether there is a need for joint action in cases envisaged in the first Resolution adopted by the Council on 1 October, 1970, and for deciding on the nature of joint action if it is to be taken.'[80]

The American government invited the reconstituted Subcommittee to meet in Washington 4–15 September.[81] The day after the conference started the murder of eleven Israeli athletes at the Munich Olympic games occurred, and this massacre brought an unprecedented degree of international attention on the workings of the subcommittee. Before the conference was over, the subcommittee had the unusual experience of being addressed by both U.S. Secretary of Transportation John Volpe and Secretary of State William Rogers. The press coverage was intense and not always fair, with both the British and Canadians complaining of biased reporting and the British accusing the American delegation of deliberately falsifying the information it was giving to the press.[82] To make matters worse, on the eve of the conference the American government, unhappy with what it saw as French intransigence on the sanctions issue, cancelled negotiations with the French government on its request for air services to selected locations in California.[83]

In the end, no agreement was reached in Washington, but more meetings were scheduled over the following year. These difficult, complicated, and ultimately unsuccessful negotiations on sanctions have been well documented elsewhere and need not be discussed in detail here,[84] but it was beginning to look as if the process was being forced despite the lack of agreement on content. 'The Legal Sub-Committee's report, which we, as members of the ICAO Council, have now seen,' wrote one British participant, 'is not suitable for immediate consideration by a diplomatic conference. To send this incomplete draft direct to a diplomatic conference would, in our view, be a certain recipe for failure.'[85] Nevertheless, new meetings of the Legal Committee were scheduled and preparations were made for a full diplomatic conference, but at no time was any kind of consensus reached. Indeed, at the January 1973 meetings of the Legal Committee there were more proposals on the table than had been the case in Washington. The main fault line appeared between those who supported sanctions and those who either opposed them or argued that sanctions were the jurisdiction of the United Nations, not ICAO; another division emerged between those who wanted a new convention and those who advocated the revision of the Chicago Convention to include the Tokyo, Hague, and Montreal conventions. One side argued that amending the convention was too slow a process and pointed to the difficulties in securing the necessary support of two-thirds of the membership; the other side pointed to the difficulties of reaching an agreement on a separate convention and whether or not it might contravene existing bilateral agreements and the Chicago Convention itself.[86]

It is hard to find anyone who was optimistic for success. The Americans, with the support of a few others, appealed to the United Nations to take a strong stand in the aftermath of the recent terrorist attacks and submitted a draft resolution to the United Nations calling for consideration of a new international convention on terrorism. The problems facing ICAO were a reflection of similar divisions in the United Nations, where any talk of anti-terrorist action sparked angry debate about the need to study the 'root causes' of terrorism and not merely efforts to stamp it out. Many members, especially in the developing world and those still under or only recently freed from colonial rule were adamant on the right of peoples to defend themselves in their liberation struggles. And, in some cases, this might mean 'desperate acts' or what others might consider terrorism. For many U.N. members, acts of terrorism in the name of liberation or for some legitimate end were acceptable, if the cause was just.[87]

The discussion in the United Nations on this issue, therefore, quickly shifted from condemning terrorism to understanding its 'underlying causes,' and the American resolution was sidelined.[88] In its place, the General Assembly adopted a new resolution, sponsored by Algeria and Yugoslavia, that condemned 'the continuation of repressive and terrorist acts by colonial racist and alien regimes in denying peoples their legitimate right to self-determination and independence and other human and fundamental freedoms.'[89] In light of this failure to achieve any form of consensus in the U.N. General Assembly or the Legal Subcommittee, the British saw little prospect for change in the future. 'States supporting the Palestine Liberation Front and other "freedom movements",' one government brief concluded, 'will be out to scotch a convention in the form proposed and they will be supported in varying degree by France, USSR and others who argue that the imposition of sanctions is a prerogative of the Security Council. Some of the South Americans will also fight against any agreement which requires them to take action against political fugitives.'[90]

The final act was played out in Rome, at a full diplomatic conference that was held simultaneously with the Twentieth (Extraordinary) Assembly, from 28 August to 21 September 1973. A variety of proposals were tabled, including draft conventions from the Scandinavian countries and Belgium, a proposal for a protocol to the Hague and Montreal conventions from the Soviet Union, and proposed amendments to the Montreal Convention from Greece. All the proposals failed, as did a French-British-Swiss proposal to amend the Chicago Convention.[91] There was enough blame to go around, but one British official took aim at the Middle Eastern and African participants: 'A major contribution to the failure was the Israeli hijacking of a Lebanese airliner over Beirut on the eve of the Conference, which set the Arabs off on a counter attacking course at the expense of their support for our proposal. The African countries too, with an eye on guest "liberation" movements in their territories and not previously seriously exposed to major hijackings, took a narrowly parochial stand in the proceedings to our disadvantage.'[92] The delegate from Zaire was a little more charitable: 'there is not the shadow of a doubt,' he said, 'that some governments were not willing ...to make mutual concessions to reach an acceptable compromise.'[93] Whoever was to blame, the conference ended without any formal agreement, and there were no plans to meet and try again.

The failure on an ICAO-wide level led some states to look closer to home. 'The Rome failure and the failure of the United Nations to come to grips with the general problem of international terrorism,' one British official wrote, 'have led us to examine the scope for action on a narrower front.'[94] The Europeans were already working together on a common anti-terrorism program; in 1974, the ECAC created a Working Group on Security Problems, and, in 1976, the Council of Europe adopted the European Convention on the Suppression of Terrorism. This convention was aimed at terrorism in general; there were shortcomings in that it applied only to those who ratified it – and not everyone did – and there were loopholes on extradition, but it included in its scope the offences covered by the ICAO conventions.[95]

The Americans also took steps on their own, through tougher regulations for airports at home[96] and a bilateral Cuba-United States agreement that was negotiated in 1973. Thanks to the latter agreement, the number of hijackings to Cuba dropped significantly.[97] In 1974 two pieces of U.S. domestic legislation were passed: the Anti-hijacking Act and the Air Transportation Security Act, which shared responsibility for domestic security among the airlines, airport authorities, and government. Following a deadly bombing at La Guardia Airport in New York on 29 December 1975, the Ford Administration established a task force to examine airport security (the bomb at LaGuardia was left in an airport locker) and it led to more recommendations for improved security.[98]

In 1978 an even larger arrangement was made with the issuance of the Bonn Declaration on International Terrorism by the G7 governments. This agreement essentially declared what the United States and others had been working for since at least 1969: if any state was considered to be refusing to extradite or punish a hijacker or refused to return a hijacked aircraft, the members of the G7 agreed to cease all flights to that country and bar all flights and airlines from that country. It was a bold and clear statement, even though it was unsigned, difficult to enforce, and very unclear in a number of areas (for example, did it apply to third states? Did it need unanimous agreement to come into force? How were the sanctions to be terminated? Would it contravene existing bilateral agreements?)[99] Despite these drawbacks, the declaration was widely popular and considered effective, at least in the short term.[100]

Sanctions were applied only once, in 1981 when a Pakistani aircraft was hijacked to Afghanistan and the G7 governments deemed that the Afghan government failed to live up to its obligations under the Hague Convention and applied sanctions. This was not a major blow to the world of international aviation; of the seven governments only Germany, France, and the United Kingdom actually had air services to Afghanistan and cancelled them. Even then, they had to give one year's notice under the terms of their existing agreements with Afghanistan, so the sanctions did not come into effect until 1982.[101] It was also a reminder that ICAO had failed to agree on the use of sanctions, and that actions such as these would be taken independently of the international organization.

It had been an incredibly busy few years. Within half a decade ICAO had produced two new air conventions and ratified a third, which together provided a basic set of rules for dealing with hijacking and sabotage against aircraft. It had also fashioned a new annex to the Chicago Convention and the *Security Manual* with specific recommendations to enhance aviation security, and collaborated in a combined anti-terrorism effort with its allies, including IATA, the ECAC, IFALPA, and the United Nations. All these things were achieved in a period of rapid expansion of international civil aviation, and not infrequently in an atmosphere of crisis.

By the 1970s the global community had learned that the very things that made aviation so appealing, successful, and vital to modern life also made it a target for those wished to use it for their own ends. As one aviation publication explained in 1975, 'civil aviation appears to have been selected as a target for such attempts because an aircraft is relatively easy to capture, since in the event of non-compliance by the crew the risk to passengers is infinitely greater than it would be in the case, say, of a train; also aviation still retains a newsworthy glamour which ensures maximum publicity; and finally the aircraft can be directed to transport the hijacker to a safe haven where his act would ... often go unpunished.'[102] Defending aviation against such attacks was an enormous and ultimately impossible task.

'Terrorism is the symptom of a disease,' wrote one aviation specialist. 'It is the disease of the militarily weak, the politically frustrated, and the religiously fanatic,'[103] However true this statement is, ICAO had no power to deal with the underlying causes of the disease, it could only treat its outward symptoms – the unlawful acts against civil aviation. Clearly, there were limits to what ICAO could achieve: it had no police forces or weapons, and it could not force hijacked aircraft to land or arrest hijackers on the ground; it could only encourage its members to take the appropriate actions. It had the power of persuasion, which had been very effective for ICAO in many areas, but persuasion alone was not always successful in dealing with terrorists. At best, it had to hope that states would comply with its conventions, standards, and resolutions when there were no guarantees that all the members even subscribed to the security goals of the organization.

To make matters more difficult, hijackings and other unlawful acts against aviation, especially those that led to hostage taking and the destruction of the aircraft, were more often than not crimes of a political nature, and this inevitably brought an element of politics into the response of nations and organizations like ICAO. ICAO could never completely rise above politics; even with the best intentions, ICAO is the handmaiden of its member governments, and these governments saw the issues in different ways. The application of sanctions, for example, became something of a flashpoint and exposed some of the political divisions – and the complexity – of dealing with international aviation terrorism. Between the opposing pillars of support and opposition were a range of views on sanctions; views that shifted in some cases from one hijacking incident to the next.

It would be a mistake, however, to see these divisions as only between rich and poor, between the major developed powers and the lesser developed ones. The Americans and the Europeans, for example, split on the sanctions issue. In addition, many developed countries caved in to the demands of terrorists or released 'political' prisoners in exchange for hostages, and the Europeans and Americans had a long history of harbouring hijackers fleeing from behind the Iron Curtain and Cuba. But the lesser developed countries did have a harder time implementing the security standards and, in the process, faced great pressure from the Western nations to maintain them. Moreover, all the measures put in place against terrorism could only be as strong as the weakest link, and so long as some countries were willing to provide safe havens for terrorists or give in to their demands there would always be ways to thwart ICAO's – and the international community's – efforts. Terrorists may have been ruthless and murderous but many of them were also very inventive, and if one avenue was blocked they found another. With more airports, more flights and air services, and more passengers traveling all around the world, there were always more holes in the security perimeter through which terrorists could strike. It took a constant effort merely to keep up.

The question that remains after all the work was done is: did ICAO's efforts have an impact? In some ways, the answer to that question is an automatic – yes. If nothing else, the conventions, Annex 17, and other security measures made aircraft and air travel a little safer – through detection and screening, baggage reconciliation, the creation of sterile areas at airports, and so on – and ensured that most perpetrators eventually would be captured and held accountable. There was some comfort in the numbers: the frequency of hijacking after 1972 began to drop, and the number of successful hijackings dropped even faster, at least for a few years.[104] Observers were quick to point out, however, that ICAO could not claim all the credit for this improvement; the American anti-hijacking agreement with Cuba, for example, was likely directly responsible for the decrease in hijackings to Cuba after 1973.

On a different but equally important level, the rise of the security issue gave ICAO a new relevance and importance in the international community. The gloom of the 1960s – with the endless political debates over membership, language, administrative costs, and the growing divergence between the members that had large aviation administrations and wanted the organization to follow their desires and the smaller members that did not have the airlines or passengers but did have the numbers in the ICAO Assembly and Council – dissipated quickly with the advent of hijacking and sabotage. No one questioned the relevance of ICAO anymore. Because of its ability to mobilize opinion, to spark discussion, to intervene in disputes, to persuade governments, and to develop international air law, ICAO provided the machinery through which international aviation terrorism could be addressed and, it was hoped, stopped. In this way, the security issue gave ICAO new life, and it gave the larger powers an additional reason to support it.

Finally, the rise of ICAO's role in aviation security can be seen as the connecting bridge between the old International Civil Aviation Organization and the new; from the early days of postwar aviation, the advent of jet engines, and the select group of Second World War victors, to the modern world of mass travel, instant communications, and international terrorism. ICAO had emerged as a leader in the fight against international aviation terrorism, but it was only the start. The conventions needed to be accepted and ratified; Annex 17 and the revised Standards and Recommended Practices needed to be implemented by the members; and everything needed constantly to be revised, updated, and monitored. At the same time, aviation terrorism would get far worse before it got better.

12

Evolution Not Revolution: ICAO in a Changing World

The entrance of the Union of Soviet Socialist Republics was the start of a new era in the history of the International Civil Aviation Organization. In the late 1960s, the Soviet Union, which had resisted membership for more than two decades, began sending observers to meetings and giving hints that it planned to join ICAO. The Soviets officially deposited their instrument of adherence with the United States on 15 October 1970, and within days the new member began suggesting making Russian one of ICAO's official languages.[1] The Soviets immediately became active members of the organization.

The Soviet delegates, like those of all ICAO member states, had reason to worry about air security and the likelihood of being hijacked, and safety remained the prime goal of ICAO. But aviation security and the legal apparatus to combat hijacking were only one part of the larger objectives of the organization. ICAO continued to grow and in this new era faced challenges that had not been anticipated by the framers of the Chicago Convention. Old problems remained, such as dealing with the discrepancies between the developed and the developing members, while new issues emerged, including environmental concerns over noise pollution and engine emissions, and the problems of transporting dangerous goods.

The entrance of the USSR provided an immediate opportunity to re-examine ICAO's financial arrangements and, in the process, produced the first sharp exchange in the organization between the Cold War adversaries. As a major aviation state, the Soviet Union was expected to contribute significantly to the organization's financing, and, in 1971, the Soviet assessment was set at 14.37 per cent of the organization's budget.

For the United States – the state that paid the greatest amount of ICAO's budget and had always believed that it paid too much – ICAO's growing membership meant that more states should share in the burden of financing its operations. For years the maximum contribution was set at 30 per cent and the United States had been paying around that rate (sometimes slightly over) for most years, and at the 1971 ICAO Assembly in Vienna the United States requested the Administrative Commission to lower the maximum assessment from 30 per cent to 26.85 per cent.

Few other members were eager to reduce the American share, but many members were willing to reduce the *minimum* level of assessment (set at 0.13 per cent), and between the two a deal could be struck. In between the Americans and most of the small States were those states which believed that a sharp reduction in both the maximum and minimum levels would increase their financial burden, at least on a per capita basis. Ultimately a compromise of sorts was reached in the Administrative Commission to reduce the assessment levels, lowering the maximum level to 27.55 per cent and the minimum assessment to 0.10 per cent. This compromise went to the plenary session as a package but once in the plenary it was divided into two and, in a secret ballot, the new lower level was accepted but the reduction to the higher level was defeated. An outraged American delegation pulled out of any further discussions on the issue – 'the first U.S. walkout, I'm told,' wrote Secor Browne, chair of the Civil Aeronautics Board and the U.S. delegation[2] – and blamed the Soviets and their allies for the whole affair. Without American participation, a new maximum of 28.75 per cent was eventually established.[3]

In November 1972, the U.S. Congress passed a bill establishing a 25 per cent ceiling level on American contributions to United Nations organizations, and this act sparked another round of discussions in ICAO and other organizations, including the U.N. General Assembly. The American government requested the addition of annual assessments to the agenda for the 1973 Extraordinary ICAO Assembly in New York. The hope was for ICAO to reduce the maximum contribution to 25 per cent, along lines similar to what the United Nations had recently agreed to do. The whole matter bogged down in procedural matters as the Soviets tried to defer discussion and insisted on a secret ballot to decide the issue. Under normal circumstances, in order to have a secret ballot another vote – also by secret ballot – is necessary to decide the matter. The result was several ballots to determine whether or not to continue talking about the issue. The Soviets, calling the American proposal 'completely unwarranted,'[4] managed to stop the discussion the first day, and when the Americans tried to reopen it the next the Soviets asked for another deferment and then a secret ballot, which meant another secret ballot vote on whether or not to have a secret ballot on the original deferment. And so on it went, until finally – after six secret ballots – the American resolution was passed along with an overwhelmingly supported resolution to lower the minimum level to 0.06 per cent.[5] The Americans were angry over the resistance of the USSR, although they felt that the Soviets probably did themselves more harm than good, at least in the court of public opinion, and in the delegation's confidential report called the outcome 'a psychological victory as well as a substantive policy win.'[6]

The debate over assessments may have sparked the first confrontation between the superpowers, but, in other ways, an improving Cold War situation spilled over into the halls of the International Civil Aviation Organization, with the emergence of the policy of détente developed and pursued by U.S. President Richard Nixon and his national security adviser, Henry Kissinger. By the early 1970s this policy led to an easing of tensions with the Soviet Union and to an opening with the communist government of the People's Republic of China. Secret Sino-American talks were held in 1970 leading first to Kissinger's and then Nixon's visit to China in 1972 and, ultimately, to full diplomatic relations.[7] Most other nations had already recognized the government of mainland China and in November 1971 the ICAO Council followed the United Nations and recognized the government of the People's Republic 'as the only legitimate representatives of China to the International Civil Aviation Organization.'[8] This decision ended the controversy over which government spoke for China in ICAO and ended almost two decades of bickering.

The Chinese declined an invitation to the 1973 Extraordinary Session of the ICAO Assembly, but, in February 1974, the government of the People's Republic of China officially adhered to the Chicago Convention (it also recognized that the 'then' government of China had ratified the Convention in 1946). The new Chinese delegate at the 1974 assembly quickly got into the spirit of things: at the second plenary meeting, while discussing the interim report of the Credentials Committee, he noted the seat reserved for the 'Lon Nol clique' of Cambodia and stated that he 'thought it necessary to point out that this traitorous clique was the scum of the Cambodian nation, long since repudiated by the Cambodian people. Illegitimate since its inception, it had no right to represent the Cambodian people at the ICAO Assembly.'[9]

Membership in the organization grew at a steady pace through the 1970s and 1980s, with the entrance of almost forty states by 1990, including

Equatorial Guinea and the United Arab Emirates in 1972, Fiji, Oman, and Swaziland in 1973, Mozambique, Angola, Sao Tome and Principe, Seychelles, and Gambia in 1977, and many more: Monaco (1980), Vanuatu (1983), Tonga (1984), the Solomon Islands (1985), the Cook Islands (1986), San Marino (1988), and Bhutan (1989). By 1990 the total membership reached 162, but fell by one with the merging of the Yemen Arab Republic with the People's Democratic Republic of Yemen. The withdrawal of American forces from Vietnam in the early 1970s and the ending of the war in 1975 also served to relieve tensions over Vietnam's membership. The collapse of the government of South Vietnam in 1975 and its absorption into the Socialist Republic of Vietnam was followed by a period of uncertainty with respect to Vietnamese membership in ICAO, but the new government joined the United Nations in 1977 and finally adhered to the Chicago Convention on 13 March 1980.

Thus, with years of steady growth, the arrival of the Soviet Union, and the recognition of mainland China, ICAO encompassed virtually all the earth's surface. Membership continued to grow over the years, and there were some discussions over membership for new geographical alignments such as the European Union[10] (the EU accepted observer status in ICAO in 2003), but there were no more major gaps in ICAO's membership. What had begun as a group of Allied nations at the end of the Second World War had evolved into a truly global organization, and, in the future there would be fewer disputes over the entrance of new members into ICAO like those seen in the 1950s and 1960s.

There were a few exceptions. Korea remained divided and in 1977 the Democratic People's Republic of Korea joined ICAO, ensuring that some Cold War rhetoric remained in the minutes of the Assemblies and committees. Instability and tension in East Asia – between China, Vietnam, the two Koreas, Japan, and others – continued to cause difficulties over the use of airspace in the region. Moreover, there was Taiwan. The island was no longer a member of ICAO but it still lay on one of the busiest airways in East Asia (known as Amber 1) and its air traffic control system continued to operate, albeit unofficially. 'We are an integral part of the ICAO system, even though we are no longer a member of that organization,' one official in tne Taiwan Civil Aeronautics Administration was quoted, 'because there is no one to take our place.'[11]

In the Mediterranean, the dispute over Cyprus lingered for years and on occasion the war of words descended into actual fighting, but only verbal shots were fired in ICAO.[12] The ongoing quarrel between Greece and Turkey over an area of disputed airspace in the Aegean Sea and the creation, in the late 1970s, of rival flight information centres for Cyprus led to considerable confusion for international aviation in the region. ICAO could do nothing to settle the issue, although the various meetings provided a platform for both sides to vent their feelings, and the whole controversy was unfortunate, considering Cyprus's important airspace in the Mediterranean.[13]

Other problems just wouldn't go away. For example, Cuba-United States relations remained frozen and ICAO could do nothing to change things. But the ICAO Assembly sessions provided a platform for the two members, and some of the venom in the relationship spilled over into the activities of the organization. The Cuban refusal to cooperate with the United States on the question of hijacking, and their steadfast rejection of multilateral solutions, only worsened the relationship between the two countries. And ICAO was one of the few international settings where the two sides came face to face. In meeting after meeting the accusations flew. The comments of the Cuban delegate at the 1968 ICAO Assembly were not atypical: 'Cuban investigations into the spate of hijackings had revealed,' declared one Cuban delegate, that 'those responsible for the seizures were to some extent either citizens of the United States fleeing from the genocidal war in Viet Nam or coloured citizens of the United States who apparently could no longer support the law of the revolver and had decided to seek refuge in Cuba. The mere ratification of a convention dealing with the unlawful seizure of aircraft would not, of course, lead to a cessation of the practice, which had its roots in the convulsed society of the United States. Let the massacre of the coloured people of the United States cease, let the unjust war in Viet Nam cease, and undoubtedly the hijacking of United States aircraft and their diversion to Cuba would also cease.'[14]

The Middle East provided some of the most serious problems for international aviation and ICAO in the latter part of the twentieth century primarily, but not exclusively, because of the growing problem of sabotage, hijacking, and armed attacks on civil aviation. The shooting down of a Libyan civil aircraft (with the deaths of all 109 on board) by the Israelis in 1973 led to an angry dispute in the ICAO Council and at the Nineteenth (Extraordinary) Session in New York City early in 1973.[15] The Israelis tried to explain their actions in the context of a very tense warlike situation and their offers of compensation for the victims did little to mollify the situation, and the Israelis were condemned almost unanimously for their actions.[16]

A dispute also arose over the use of the airport in the divided city of Jerusalem and, in 1974, ICAO passed Resolution A21-7, acknowledging that Jerusalem was 'under the jurisdiction of Jordan in the ICAO Middle East Air Navigation Plan,' and lay in the 'occupied Arab territories,' and restricting the use of Jerusalem's airport for international aviation. At the same time, debate began on the question of giving an official invitation to the Palestine Liberation Organization to send an observer to attend ICAO meetings.[17] The United Nations opened the door on the issue in 1974 with its own Resolution 3237, granting the PLO observer status at the U.N. General Assembly and other specialized agencies, meetings and conferences. The PLO subsequently attended sessions of the FAO, the ILO, UNESCO, and the WHO, and sent observers to meetings such as the World Population Conference and the United Nations Conference on the Law of the Sea.

A resolution granting the PLO observer status in the International Civil Aviation Organization was introduced at the Twenty-Second Assembly, in Montreal, in September–October 1977. The resolution was introduced by Saudi Arabia to the plenary meeting on 3 October and was sponsored by nineteen Middle Eastern and African members, and it had broad support from other states. The Chinese delegate, for example, explained his support for the resolution because a great many states recognized the PLO as 'the sole legitimate representative of the Palestinian people.'[18] The delegates from Indonesia, Cuba, Pakistan, Yugoslavia, Bangladesh, Afghanistan, the USSR, Senegal, Angola, and India followed in support. The lone voice in opposition, not surprisingly, was the Israeli delegate who called it a 'ludicrous contradiction' to invite the PLO 'to the deliberations of ICAO, an international organization whose aim was to devote its joint efforts and thoughts to assure and enhance the safety of universal civil aviation, whereas the PLO had a bloody record and an aim of just the opposite. If civil aviation today was beset with the enormous costs for security measures, encumbering air passengers and placing a very heavy burden on governments, international organizations, airlines and the public at large, it was thanks to the threats and acts of this terror organization.' The PLO may have been invited to other groups he continued, but ICAO was different given the PLO's involvement in air hijacking and sabotage; it 'was a sad commentary of our times that an organization responsible for wholesale murder and other acts of indiscriminate terror caused to innocent civilians should be considered to be invited to this Organization whose basic purpose was the assurance of safe and economic air transport.'[19] Given that the United Nations had already approved the step, there was something of the inevitable in the vote, and the Resolution granting the PLO observer status to ICAO

Assemblies and conferences and regional meetings 'dealing with matters related to its territories' passed easily, with seventy in favour, twenty-three abstentions and only three opposed: Israel, South Africa, and the United States.[20]

The Palestine Liberation Organization was represented at the next session of the ICAO Assembly in 1980. In his first statement to an ICAO Plenary meeting, the Palestinian delegate called for the suspension of 'racist Israel' for its continued occupation of the Jerusalem Airport, contravening ICAO's (and the U.N.'s) 1974 resolution. 'Our land has been usurped by a racist Israeli Zionist entity, that seizes the land and loots the heritage and civilization. It went so far in its actions as to legalize the looting terror and occupation by promulgating a law declaring our sacred Jerusalem an eternal capital under its absolute authority, disregarding your will and the United Nations and Security Council resolutions and human rights.'[21] The Israeli delegate called to have the comments declared out of order; R.S. Nyaga, Kenya's chief delegate and the president of the assembly, asked the members to stick to the technical matters under review. There was little more that ICAO could do, but the Arab-Israeli dispute simmered under the surface for many more years. It is hard not to see this whole affair as anything but a political manifestation of outside tensions within ICAO; as aviation specialist Eugene Sochor argues, even if a case could be made for official status for the PLO in the United Nations, 'there were no technical reasons for the PLO to sit as an observer in ICAO Assembly sessions. It controlled no territory and operated no aviation facilities.'[22]

Another offshoot of Soviet membership in the International Civil Aviation Organization was an enlarged ICAO Council. The Soviets were an obvious selection for the first category of council membership; a seat had been saved for them at the very start of ICAO and few would argue that they were undeserving in the 1970s. But Soviet membership, combined with a growing membership, led to calls for a larger council to reflect the new state of affairs. As early as 1967, the European members were discussing the two – Soviet membership and a larger council – as if they were one issue. Not all were in favour of an enlarged council, although states that were, like France, saw it as a way to secure and even enhance European membership in the council.[23] As was the case in the earlier discussions in 1961, it was the United States that was the major opponent. In anticipation of Soviet membership in the ICAO Council the Americans were willing to change the distribution of the existing

Council seats from 9-9-9 to 10-9-8 and thereby accommodate Soviet membership without increasing the size of the council, but this proposal was opposed by the Europeans and almost guaranteed to fail.[24]

Increasing the size of the council had always meant different things to different members of ICAO. For the Europeans and others it was seen as a way to maintain a voice in the face of growing competition. More and more members were resorting to bloc voting and representation, with groups forming for Central America, North Africa, Scandinavia, the Caribbean, and elsewhere. For the smaller, and often newer, members a larger council meant more opportunity for them to secure a seat at the table. As they were usually excluded from categories one and two, it was especially important if the greatest enlargement went to the third category. With assemblies meeting only once every three years and the focus of the organization increasingly shifting on to the council, it made council membership all that more prestigious, even if, as one observer wrote, these states 'have little to qualify them for council membership other than their sovereignty.'[25] For the United States, the one nation more than any other that was virtually guaranteed council membership, there were other factors to be considered. For one thing, while council membership might be an end in itself for some members, there were questions whether the smaller states could fill the position with qualified individuals who could undertake the demanding tasks of council membership and financially maintain the necessary establishment in Montreal. For another, the larger the council the more difficult, even unruly, it would become, and the more likely political considerations would intrude on its deliberations. 'The United States Government believes the ICAO Council is already too large to function efficiently,' the U.S. embassy in Paris informed the French government, 'with a tendency for some of its representatives to vote on the basis of political rather than aviation considerations.'[26]

The Americans found themselves badly outnumbered. The ICAO Council discussed the matter within weeks of Soviet ratification, and in December 1970 the European Civil Aviation Conference came out in favour of an increase of three seats. Early in 1971 the council called for an extraordinary session to increase the size of the council; all that remained was to decide by how much. The Seventeenth-A (Extraordinary) ICAO Assembly took place at the headquarters of the United Nations in New York over two days, 11–12 March, 1971. Council president Walter Binaghi served as president of the assembly and many of the formalities were dispensed with, although, in recognition of the new member and the approval of Russian as an official ICAO language a few weeks earlier in February, simultaneous Russian translation was provided. Two resolutions were passed: one to increase the ICAO Council size to thirty (A17 A-1), and a second calling on all members to ratify the change as quickly as possible (A17 A-2), so the new members could be elected at the full assembly scheduled for Vienna in the summer.[27] The American delegation had few options; 'there appeared to be no other ICAO issues through which the U.S. could exert leverage and thus effectively muster support for restricting the Council to its present size,' the delegation reported. The report continued, with a bit of understatement, 'in view of the overwhelming vote in the Council to increase its membership to 30 (24-0-1 [U.S.]), the U.S. felt it would be futile and potentially damaging to U.S. interests in other ICAO matters to continue to oppose any increase.'[28]

The amendment to the Chicago Convention agreed to at the 1971 Extraordinary Session of the ICAO Assembly received sufficient ratifications to come into effect only in January 1973. In anticipation of this event, the ICAO Council called for another extraordinary session in New York City, beginning at the end of February, to elect the three new council members (there had been a proposal to elect the new members at the 1971 session in Vienna even though sufficient ratifications had not been received, but this idea was dropped as it likely would have contravened the Chicago Convention[29]). It was a short but very contentious session, in that three divisive issues (dealing with Israel, Portugal, and annual assessments) were added to the agenda. The election of the council members, however, went smoothly; the division of the new seats was split equally among the three categories, with the new seats going to the Netherlands (category 1), Pakistan (category 2), and Trinidad and Tobago (category 3).

The whole process was repeated in 1974 at the Twenty-First ICAO Assembly, in Montreal, when another three seats were added to the ICAO Council, raising the total membership to thirty-three. Much of the support for this increase came from the developing states who felt excluded from the council, and resolution A21-2 enlarging the council to thirty-three read, in part, 'in order to permit an increase in the representation of states elected in the second, and particularly the third, part of the election.' This resolution for a larger council came into force in February 1980.

With a larger membership and a larger council, it made sense, for many members at least, to have a larger Air Navigation Commission as well, and discussions to this end ran parallel with the movement to enlarge the council. The basic issues were the same: the Soviet Union would be a logical member of the ANC, and with many more members and from different parts of the world it seemed logical to increase the size of the ANC, given its central importance to ICAO's mandate. The delegate from Senegal argued that the goal was to have an efficient ANC 'whose membership would reflect not only the expertise of specialists from highly developed States in the field of civil aviation but the desires of less developed ones to make their views known.'[30] For others it was not merely the growth in numbers that mattered; as a Pakistani delegate argued at the 1971 ICAO Assembly in Vienna, 'any increase should be based not on consideration relating to the growth of the Organization's membership but on the heavier workload facing the Commission and the greater availability of experts around the world.'[31] Few members opposed the idea, with the lone exception of the United States, which had consistently argued against the expansion of either the council or its major committees. 'The Chicago Convention requires that members of the Commission have suitable qualifications and experience in science and in the practice for aeronautics,' the U.S. government earlier explained, 'The United States doubts whether more than 12 states are able to nominate and support qualified members to serve on virtually a full-time basis. The expansion of the Commission by the addition of members who would not meet these criteria would only complicate its work and tend to introduce political elements into its activities.'[32]

The expansion of the ANC was on the agenda at the Eighteenth ICAO Assembly, in Vienna, in 1971. As was the case with the council, any decision to increase its size must be done through a resolution to amend the Chicago Convention, in this case Article 56. There was no way the United States could stop the movement towards a larger ANC in the face of strong united support by a large majority of the members; the only remaining question was whether to add two or three new members. The U.S. delegation hoped to limit it to two, bringing the total membership up to fourteen, and introduced an amendment to this effect, but the American effort was defeated in the face of an Indonesian proposal raising the ANC to fifteen members. This resolution (A18-2) was passed with eighty-seven in favour, none against, and only the United States, Iraq, and Japan abstaining,[33] and came into force on 19 December 1974.

Before too long there were complaints about politics and bloc voting in the council over ANC membership[34] as new members arrived, many from states that had never served on the Air Navigation Commission before. At the same time, and for many of the same reasons, the issue of language reappeared on the agenda. From the beginning, the ANC operated in English in both its meetings and documents; indeed it was only in the 1970s that simultaneous translation was provided at meetings. For most non–English-speaking members it was a given that their candidate to the ANC would be proficient in English and, consequently, since everyone on the commission spoke English there was little need for translation and there were relatively few complaints about the process. From the start of ICAO, 'English had been considered as the specialist language,' explained one Norwegian to the Executive Committee at the Twenty-Second ICAO Assembly in 1977, 'English had an acknowledged status as the language used in civil aviation operations.'[35] That may have been so in the past, several members argued, but it was no longer the case, and at that assembly a resolution was introduced calling for the ANC's working papers to be translated into the other working languages of the organization (ANC reports to the council were already translated, but after the fact). As it stood, one Greek delegate explained, the 'present practice systematically excluded participation, in one of the most important bodies of ICAO, of experts from many parts of the world who were not familiar with the English language.'[36] Others pointed out that English no longer dominated aeronautical technology. The delegate from Madagascar expressed surprise about the level of controversy the issue had created: 'it was a question that went beyond cost considerations as it was primarily one of principle which affected the worldwide character of the Organization.'[37] The result was Resolution A22-29 calling for the translation of ANC working papers into ICAO's four working languages.

The expansion of the organization was felt on the ground level as well as in the ICAO Council and the Air Navigation Commission. Supporting these and all the other activities was an enormous and demanding challenge, and the secretariat was forced to grow rapidly, just to keep up. The secretariat staff had grown, reaching almost eight hundred employees by 1975.

The lack of space was also a problem, as the old International Aviation Building was jammed to capacity by the early 1970s. As Duane Freer, one-time director of the Air Navigation Bureau wrote, 'the once spacious and modern 1950-vintage office accommodations over Montreal's central railway station had become too cramped and restrictive for efficient operation.'[38] Moreover, the facilities in the building were inadequate for an organization of ICAO's size. The Canadian government responded to ICAO's problems and oversaw the construction of a new building at 1000 Sherbrooke Street in downtown Montreal, across from McGill University campus. Although not far distant from the old locations, it contained modern facilities and had the space that ICAO needed. The new building was built specially for ICAO and contained twenty-seven floors and an adjacent conference complex. Few other cities had the facilities to stage a gathering the size of an ICAO Assembly, and from the early 1970s all assemblies have met at the Montreal location. ICAO moved in in 1975, occupying, at first, fifteen floors.[39]

The expansion that took place in these years made ICAO a bigger – and more complex – organization. It also made more apparent the need for better coordination between the council and the other bodies and secretariat, and placed a greater burden on the council members, the members of the different committees, and all the employees. It had perhaps the greatest impact on the council president whose role as administrator, arbitrator, ambassador, conciliator, civil servant, international aviation diplomat, and part-time referee was growing with each year. And the move into the new building on Sherbrooke Street was followed closely by the election of a new council president and secretary general.

At the end of July 1976, Walter Binaghi stepped down as president of the ICAO Council after serving for almost twenty years. Binaghi had been only the second person to hold the position, taking over from Edward Warner in 1957. He had evolved from being labelled the 'American nominee,' at least according to the French in 1957, into a widely respected leader – the 'quintessential technical expert turned international diplomat and executive.'[40] Membership in the organization nearly doubled in his years as president and, in the process, Binaghi had overseen the transformation of ICAO from a small club of mainly Western-industrialized states that dominated all aspects of the organization, into a truly global and diverse international grouping. In addition to the general growth of the organization, he had led it through a very difficult period of Cold War politics, membership quarrels, and the earliest appearance of international aviation terrorism. Under his leadership ICAO had entered the jet age and the modern world. With his retirement ICAO lost a link with its past, in that he was the one remaining individual who had attended all of ICAO's assemblies since 1947 and had served as assembly president at four sessions.

If anyone could rival Walter Binaghi for his experience in ICAO it was his successor, Assad Kotaite. Born in Lebanon and educated in law in Beirut and Paris, Kotaite worked with Lebanon's Directorate of Civil Aviation through which he was first introduced to ICAO, becoming a member of the Legal Committee in 1953. Kotaite later told an interviewer

that he knew he 'had found my true vocation. For ICAO combined everything that I was searching for. Namely international affairs and the law.'[41]
Within a few years he was appointed Lebanon's council representative
and a member of the Air Transport Committee, which he chaired from
1959 to 1962 and again from 1965 to 1968. These activities gave him thorough knowledge of ICAO's legal, technical, and political dimensions. In
1970 he was appointed secretary general, a position he held until his election as council president. Three candidates were put forward, although
the actual secret council vote was between two: Kotaite and the Norwegian,
Erik Willoch, who had been nominated by the Swedish council member.
Kotaite won easily and was elected for a three-year term; he began his term
as council president in 1976.[42] He was re-elected every three years and retired only in August 2006. He became the longest-serving council president
with thirty years experience – a record unlikely ever to be broken.

Kotaite understood international aviation, he knew the organization
from the inside-out, and he brought with him a set of skills in negotiation and compromise. He also brought a breadth of knowledge of ICAO's
history. He spoke five languages, he knew what had worked in the past
– and what had not – and he had the ability to get things done. He was
well groomed for the job, and he quickly emerged as a truly international civil servant. Given that the Chicago Convention says little about the
role of the president, Kotaite put his personal stamp on the job, and his
name became synonymous with the public face of the organization during the 1980s and 1990s. He embraced his role as international aviation
diplomat and added a personal touch, later telling a journalist that telephone calls could never replace face-to-face contact: 'Les conférences
par téléphone ne remplacent pas les contacts directs,' he said, 'où l'on
peut voir les grimaces aussi bien que les sourires de son interlocuteur.'[43]
As the respected head of the organization, Kotaite was able to translate
his position and personal reputation into action as a negotiator in several aviation disputes to help settle them before they developed into
more serious confrontations.[44]

Important changes also occurred in the secretary general's position.
In 1964 the Dutch economist Bernardus Tieleman Twigt was appointed
secretary general on the retirement of Canadian Ronald Macdonnell.
Twigt had been a government official in the Netherlands before he
joined ICAO in 1949. He left ICAO in 1956 for a variety of positions in
the United Nations and returned to ICAO as secretary general in 1964,
serving in that position until 1970. Twigt brought years of experience as
an administrator especially in the areas of relief and technical assistance;

he had worked, for example, with the U.N. Congo operation in the early 1960s. His years as secretary general coincided with considerable development in ICAO's technical assistance program. He was followed as secretary general by Assad Kotaite, who served from 1970 to 1976 and the changeover in many ways signified the arrival of a new generation into positions of influence in ICAO.

In 1976, when Kotaite assumed the council presidency, Yves Lambert succeeded him as secretary general. Lambert was a well-educated Frenchman who had served the French government in several capacities as a technical expert. From 1969 to 1972 he was technical adviser to the French minister of transport, and he represented France on the ICAO Council from 1973 to 1976 and at different times chaired the Finance Committee and the Committee on Joint Support of Air Navigation Services. He became secretary general on 1 August 1976, just a few weeks after his fortieth birthday, and he served in the position for twelve years, retiring in 1988.[45] Kotaite, Lambert, and others of a younger generation, personified the entrance of ICAO in the modern age, and it was up to them to lead ICAO through some very difficult periods.

Although it was not written down, the usual practice was to limit the secretary general to a two term maximum and it was unusual for any ICAO secretary general to serve more than that. Lambert was the exception, and this led to some problems in 1988 when he ran for his fifth consecutive term. Elections for the secretary general were usually fairly straightforward, but in 1988 there was a re-appearance of the kinds of divisions and arm-twisting that had not been seen since the 1950s and 1960s. And the divisions were familiar, between the developed and developing world, or as some liked to call it, between the West and the rest. 'There's a feeling among some states,' one unidentified ICAO Council delegate told a journalist 'that it has been a rather long time for one man to serve in a position and that that position doesn't always have to be held by a westerner.'[46] Challenging Lambert were three candidates: Kenneth Rattray of Jamaica, Adyr da Silva from Brazil, and Shivinder Singh Sidhu from India. Lambert could probably expect the support of the Western nations and he did win the most votes in the first council secret ballot, but in the end it was not enough; Lambert's unprecedented attempt for a fifth term failed and Shivinder Singh Sidhu was elected secretary general.[47]

Sidhu was a civil servant who was relatively new to the International Civil Aviation Organization. Born in India in 1929, he served in the Indian civil service in a number of capacities. As Director of India's Civil

Aviation Administration (1985–87) he was part of the team sent to investigate the Air India bombing in June 1985. He came to ICAO in 1986 as
head of the Indian delegation to the Twenty-Sixth ICAO Assembly and was
elected president of the assembly. Two years later he was secretary general
of the organization. Sidhu arrived in Montreal with taking action on environmental issues such as noise pollution and the commercial problems
facing international civil aviation, especially in the developing world, as
major goals but, perhaps because of his experience in the Air India disaster, security was paramount in his mind. 'Security is our highest priority,'
he told one journalist, 'We must wage a continuous war on terrorism.'[48]

The provision of technical assistance to ICAO members remained at the
heart of the organization's ongoing activities, although the expansion and
promise of the 1950s and 1960s was muted by increasingly difficult economic times in the 1970s and 1980s. As in the past, the principal source
for funding ICAO's Technical Assistance Programme came via the U.N.
Development Programme, which was created in 1965 through the amal-
gamation of the U.N. Expanded Programme of Technical Assistance and
the U.N. Special Fund. The program was administered through ICAO's
Technical Assistance Bureau, and despite the financial hard times, it became one of the largest and busiest of ICAO's four bureaus.
    In addition to the UNDP, several other forms of funding were developed
and came to play an increasingly important role in ICAO's Technical
Assistance Programme. Reflecting the new economic realities of development, these new forms of funding put more of an emphasis on the financial input of the receiving states themselves. First, a Trust Funds system was
established to enable states to finance their own (or another state's) technical assistance activities through the UNDP and with the help of ICAO
experts and technicians. Second, a Cost Sharing Program was created,
which, as the name suggests, permitted an individual state to share the
cost of technical assistance on a civil aviation project with the UNDP. With
two funding sources, the logic ran, it enabled larger projects to be undertaken. Third, the Civil Aviation Purchasing Service, or CAPS, was established to help developing states acquire major aviation equipment, from
the preparation of specifications to the procurement, contracting, and
purchasing of the equipment. Relying on ICAO's expertise and purchasing systems was a real advantage for many smaller states that did not have
the same kind of resources or experience. All of these programs that
shared resources or relied on the members' financing were, of course,
most beneficial to the financially prosperous developing countries.[49]

Training personnel remained the primary activity in ICAO's Technical Assistance Programme, along with the creation and improvement of civil aviation training centres. Airport development and support for the strengthening of civil aviation infrastructure and civil aviation departments was also important. Studies were commissioned and supported, on economic issues in developing nations, as well as manpower and training surveys. Hundreds of fellowships were awarded to individuals, and by 1980, 110 countries received technical assistance of various kinds, and there with fifty-five large-scale projects (with budgets over U.S.$500,000).[50]

Total funding for technical assistance grew in the 1970s, levelled off in the 1980s, and, in real terms, began to drop. The total amount from all sources reached U.S.$11.9 million in 1974, rising to $25 million in 1976, $40.6 million in 1979, and peaking at $64.8 million in 1982. Through the 1980s the level of funding fluctuated but never rose above the 1982 mark, hitting $48.1 million in 1989 and $54.7 million in 1990. Taking into account the high inflation of these years, the relative value of the funding dropped as well; given the rise of the global population in need of assistance, ICAO had less money that had to be stretched farther. Years of global recession led to a significant drop in contributions to the UNDP, and throughout these years the UNDP fell well below its anticipated targets. What was also significant was that the percentage of UNDP funding was dropping; in 1979, 73 per cent of ICAO's technical assistance funding came from the UNDP; in 1982 the total had dropped to 53 per cent.[51]

There were other problems as well. Civil aviation departments in developing countries were often very small and carried relatively little influence in government circles; civil aviation itself was often considered a lower priority for governments facing other major problems. As a result, it was often difficult to allocate scarce resources to civil aviation matters or to find suitable candidates who could be spared from their regular duties to take up ICAO fellowships. On the other side, in the developed world it often took a long time for governments to nominate individual experts to fill the technical assistance positions. The situation tended to get worse in bad economic times as members were less willing to let trained personnel go.[52] But the biggest problem remained the lack of sufficient funds; there was never enough money to go around and ICAO had to compete with all the other organizations in the U.N. system. As Eugene Sochor, a former ICAO official, wrote, 'there is no escaping the plain fact that all the funds ICAO receives from the UNDP and other sources in one year would not even cover the cost of one jumbo jet. Faced with scant resources, ICAO has had to concentrate its Technical

Assistance on manpower development, leaving it to others – the World Bank, the regional development banks, bilateral funds and the countries themselves – to build the infrastructure and acquire the fleets.'[53]

At the start of the 1990s technical assistance remained a central part of ICAO's mandate, but the financial problems were very serious. Ravindra Gupta, the Indian representative on the ICAO Council in the mid-1990s, warned of the dangers of the financial constraints in the field of technical cooperation. 'With the new orientation given to UNDP, the funding of civil aviation activities has been dwindling just as new technological challenges require ICAO to give more assistance than ever before. ICAO has been experimenting with a variety of options but has yet to come up with an effective solution.' Indeed, he concluded, 'financial problems have been the bane of the entire U.N. system, and, of course, of the world as a whole.'[54]

At the heart of ICAO's technical assistance activities were the regional offices. The original division of the globe into air navigation regions had been amended slightly over the years with a reduction in the 1950s to nine regions; seven were territorial, two covered oceans (the Pacific and North Atlantic regions). Six regional offices were established in the remaining seven regions. The North American region and Caribbean regions were given one regional office, in Mexico City; others were established in Bangkok (Asia and Pacific Office), Cairo (Middle Eastern Office), Lima (South American Office), and Paris (European Office). In 1962 an office was established in Dakar for the African states, and in 1965 the Cairo Office was renamed the Middle Eastern and Eastern African Office. In 1983 a new office was established in Nairobi and it assumed responsibility for Eastern Africa, returning Cairo to its original function as the Middle Eastern Office. In the 1980s the Nairobi office became the Eastern and Southern Africa Office, and the one in Dakar was renamed the Western and Central Africa Office.[55] All the activity of the regional offices was coordinated through the Regional Affairs Office in the Montreal headquarters.

In addition to the regular assortment of activities in providing liaison with headquarters and with the members in each of the regions, the regional offices assisted members in implementing the directives of the organization, organized workshops, helped with regional planning, provided, on occasion, administrative and secretariat services for regional meetings and conferences, and maintained specialists in various aspects of aviation including air traffic services, meteorology, communications, and aircraft operations.[56] In addition to the important regional air navigation meetings, the regional offices also helped in the planning and implementation of technical assistance projects. For example, in 1990, the Eastern and Southern Africa Office in Nairobi helped with training, equipment procurement, gave 145 awards under regional programs, and undertook technical missions to several states, including Ethiopia, Mozambique, Rwanda, Uganda, and Zambia. That same year, the South American Office in Lima gave lectures, organized seminars, helped procure equipment, and provided administrative support and technical assistance to several members in the region.[57]

Throughout this era of rapid growth, the work of the organization continued without interruption. Most of this could be considered typical for ICAO: the council met almost continuously and oversaw the work of its committees – the Air Navigation Commission, Air Transport Committee, Legal Committee, the Committee on Unlawful Interference, the Committee on Joint Support of Air Navigation Services, and the Finance Committee – and conducted the business of the organization. Each new edition of the council's annual report catalogued a wide variety of activities, including revisions to the annexes, Standards and Recommended Practices, Procedures for Air Navigation Services, and so on, the collection of statistics, the updating and revision of the various manuals, the monitoring of the implementation of the SARPS, and the myriad conferences, panels, and working groups studying and discussing important issues in air transport.[58] In 1980, for example, in addition to the regular array of committees, conferences, and meetings in Montreal and at the regional offices, there were twenty-two workshops and seminars on subjects ranging from security, accident investigation, and bird hazards, to aviation medicine, instrument flight procedures design, and aeronautical information services.[59] By the early 1990s it was estimated that the ICAO Council had adopted close to eight hundred amendments to the annexes, primarily to keep in step with technological advances.[60]

There were also constant headaches in financing the organization and over the non-payment of assessments, and on occasion the problems threatened to disrupt the normal workings of the organization. In the mid-1980s, for example, the United States announced its intention to withhold part of its annual assessment (which stood at approximately U.S.$33 million or 25 per cent of the budget) unless the decision-making power on budgetary issues were weighted in favour of the greater contributors. Payment was made only when the council reaffirmed its

commitment to consensus on budgetary decisions, meaning that no decisions would be made without the approval of the United States.[61]

There were also a few issues that stood out for special attention. For
example, by the 1970s it was increasingly common for airlines to lease
some or all of their aircraft rather than purchasing them, a scenario unforeseen in the Chicago Convention. It now was not unusual to have aircraft registered by the owner in one state and in operation under lease in
another state. This state of affairs raised questions about liability and
flight safety responsibilities that had not been a significant problem in the
1940s. After months of examination and debate, at the Twenty-Third
ICAO Assembly in 1980, the assembly adopted Article 83 bis amending
the Chicago Convention allowing states to enter into agreements with
other states to transfer their responsibilities under the Chicago Convention
to the state where an aircraft was leased. The transfer was to be strictly
voluntary and it was negotiable which rights were to be transferred, but
Article 83 bis now made it possible for an operator in one state to lease
another state's aircraft and assume that state's responsibilities for the aircraft as well. The amendment is 'utterly uncontroversial,' wrote one
Federal Aviation Agency official. 'The world aviation community gives its
assent to bilateral transfers of oversight authority through Article 83 *bis*,
but States need not enter into them.'[62] Nevertheless, ratification was slow
and Article 83 bis did not come into force until 1997.

Another concern emerging by the mid 1970s arose from the growing
realization that a significant percentage of all the goods and cargo carried by air transport fell into a 'dangerous' category – explosive, flam-
mable, corrosive, toxic, radioactive, and so on – which could pose a risk
to the safety of air travel. Most states had their own domestic rules, but
there were no uniform internationally accepted procedures for the transport of dangerous goods, especially for international air transport. Other
international organizations were investigating the problem, especially
the United Nations and its Committee of Experts on the Transport of
Dangerous Goods.

Using the recommendations of this U.N. committee as a starting point
(along with the Regulations for the Safe Transport of Radioactive
Materials of the International Atomic Energy Agency), ICAO launched
its own preliminary studies, first within the secretariat. Then, in 1976, it
established under the Air Navigation Commission a Dangerous Goods
Panel comprised of government officials and aviation experts to develop
guidelines for air transport.[63] This was a coordinated effort from the start,
with the goal of establishing regulations that would ensure the safety of

air travel without impeding the smooth conduct of air transport, and at the same time allow a seamless movement of dangerous goods from one form of transport to another. As the ANC's Duane Freer explained, what was being developed reflected 'a co-ordinated, United Nations sponsored, world-wide effort, to facilitate and harmonize international regulations among the several modes or transportation. Thus, a shipment of potentially dangerous materials can be packaged and labeled for an uninterrupted international, intermodal journey by truck, train, ship and aeroplane to its destination.'[64]

The ANC approved the report of the Dangerous Goods Panel, the members of the organization were consulted, revisions were made, and on 26 June 1981 the council approved the new Annex 18, *The Safe Transport of Dangerous Goods by Air*, which was to be applied as of 1 January 1984.[65] The annex contains the basic rules for the transport of dangerous goods, and part of the standard gives regulatory force to the companion technical manual containing detailed instructions for the handling of dangerous goods. This manual – *Technical Instructions for the Safe Transport of Dangerous Goods by Air* – was adopted by the ICAO Council at the same time. The annex and manual contain detailed instructions and specifications on the labelling, packaging, handling, carrying, and processing of dangerous materials, and contains a list of more then 3,000 commodities, broken down into nine categories such as explosives, fire hazards, poisons, medicines, and so on, as well as a list of those goods that should never be carried on an aircraft under any circumstances. Together, the annex and manual made it easier for pilots and airline personnel to assess the risk of carrying dangerous cargo, made it easier to locate it, and enhanced the ability of airlines to transport dangerous goods safely with the minimum amount of disruption.[66]

The issue of noise pollution also reappeared at the top of the agenda in the 1970s with growing local activism in the vicinity of airports and with the arrival of the Anglo-French supersonic Concorde. ICAO was not alone in its growing involvement with environmental issues; within the U.N. system of specialized agencies, committees, and conferences there was a rising awareness of ecological concerns and the need for what was being called 'eco-development.' This new concern and desire for action was reflected in the creation of the U.N. Environment Programme in 1973.[67]

That same year, U.S. President Nixon had assured French President Georges Pompidou that his administration would not stand in the way of the development of the Concorde and that the Federal Aviation Administration would 'issue its proposed fleet noise rule in a form which will make it inapplicable to the Concorde.'[68] But Washington was not the only player in domestic American politics, and serious opposition to the entry of the Concorde into American airspace emerged on the Congressional, state, and local levels. The British and French launched a lobbying campaign to get the aircraft accepted; local groups in the United States and members of Congress organized and protested against it. It was a dilemma for the Ford administration. On the one hand, Secretary of State Henry Kissinger opposed rejecting the Anglo-French request because he knew how much they had invested in the project and refusing access to the United States 'could adversely affect U.S. relations with the British and French.' On the other hand, the Concorde was the 'noisiest, most polluting, least energy-efficient aircraft made. The noise impacts would be immediate and severe.'[69] The Concorde became a kind of a symbol of the problem of aviation noise pollution.

In the Ford administration's review of its international aviation policy considerable attention was given to the problem of noise. Many American aircraft did not meet the ICAO standards, but the United States and most other Western nations were far ahead of the developing states in re-equipping their fleets. Nevertheless, the opposition to noise pollution was stronger and more organized in the United States than elsewhere, which put increased pressure on Washington to act. 'We will seek an ICAO agreement on application of noise standards for existing aircraft in international operations,' the Ford policy announced, but if an agreement could not be reached, 'the United States may then find it necessary to develop U.S. national standards more stringent than those which can be developed through ICAO, in order to protect human health and environment quality.'[70] To emphasize the point, Transportation Secretary William Coleman prepared a statement for President Ford in which he stated that if ICAO could not come up with a deal within four years 'we will begin to apply U.S. standards to foreign aircraft unilaterally.'[71]

The Concorde received its approval for landing in the United States, but the discussions over noise pollution continued for years. Annex 16 classified aircraft based on a variety of noise specifications and divided most subsonic aircraft into a series of chapters with progressive deadlines for the implementation of each chapter's specifications. Chapter 1 aircraft included most non–jet-powered aircraft and were, in some ways, the easiest to phase out. Chapters 2 and 3 applied to jet aircraft: those designed before October 1977 were classified in Chapter 2; those designed after 1977 were included in Chapter 3. In the late 1980s there were still almost five thousand Chapter 2 aircraft in service, including some sixteen hundred Boeing B-727s.[72] Phasing these aircraft out by the specified deadlines would prove very difficult and expensive for many members, and refitting the existing aircraft to make them operate more quietly, although possible, was very expensive. On one side were the Western nations with newer fleets, better financing possibilities, and strong public opinion at home opposed to noise; on the other were the developing nations, often using older and noisier aircraft (in many cases bought from the Western states) without the financial resources to re-equip their fleets or refit existing aircraft with noise reduction equipment.[73] The former tended to favour stronger noise standards and for them to be applied more swiftly; the latter called for breaks, exemptions, and delay. The International Civil Aviation Organization was caught in the middle, and through the 1980s noise was discussed at every ICAO Assembly session and several resolutions on the noise issue were adopted.

In 1980, at the Twenty-Third ICAO Assembly, considerable opposition appeared to the strict application of the organization's noise standards. Many of the members from Central and South America, for example, were worried about their ability to meet the standards, especially if the Americans went ahead on their own to force foreign aircraft to meet the noise – and engine emissions – requirements by 1985. The ICAO Council agreed with this view (in June 1979) and these states spoke for probably what was a majority of ICAO-members in favouring 'an extension of the time the aircraft in question may operate, to ensure their amortization and avoid costly investments during the last part of their useful life, which would have an unfavourable effect on air transport.'[74] The result was Resolution A23-10, which asked members to delay the prohibition of foreign aircraft that failed to meet the specific noise requirements until 1988. In 1986, at the Twenty-Sixth ICAO Assembly, another resolution (A26-11) asked members 'to grant exemptions for up to two years from the date of such an imposition for existing levels of service and frequencies through mutually acceptable temporary agreements.' The resolution also asked for restraint in the application of prohibitions against foreign aircraft that failed to meet all the required certifications.[75]

No agreement could be reached at the 1989 Assembly, and the noise issue was included on the agenda of the 1990 Extraordinary Session of the ICAO Assembly, originally called to discuss an increase in the size of the council. In advance, work continued within the Air Transport Committee and its technical working group. The issue was also discussed regionally, by the European Civil Aviation Conference, the African Civil Aviation Commission, and the Latin American Civil Aviation Conference, and ICAO Council President Kotaite embarked on a personal mission to various member states all in an effort to reach a consensus that would balance the desire to meet ICAO's noise specifications while at the same time limiting any negative economic consequences or unilateral restrictions applied by individual states. The council also debated the issue and prepared for the assembly's consideration a draft resolution that extended the phase-in period for those aircraft that met the requirements of Chapter 2 but not Chapter 3 and recommended that the lifespan of an aircraft (considered to be twenty-five years) should not be unnecessarily shortened because it failed to meet the noise specifications.[76]

At the 1990 Extraordinary Assembly the ICAO Council proposal was largely accepted and a new resolution was passed unanimously. It was agreed to establish the date of 1 April 1995 to begin the phasing out of Chapter 2 aircraft over a period of seven years, meaning that they would be gone by 1 April 2002 (twenty-five years after 1977). Exemptions were made to exclude from restrictions being applied *before* 2002 against any aircraft less than twenty-five-years-old and against wide-body aircraft that had been fitted with high bypass ratio engines (this latter category included most B-747s in use at that time). Finally, it was requested that members not apply restrictions to Chapter 2 aircraft from developing countries if they could prove that they had at least put in an order to purchase or lease Chapter 3 aircraft.

Not everyone was happy, but this agreement was accepted by the council and assembly participants, among whom included representatives of the ECAC, the ACAC, the LACAC, IATA, and the Airport Associations Co-ordinating Council. It was also believed that the ICAO guidelines were consistent with those established domestically in the United States.[77] Airports would become much quieter in the future, just not as quickly as some ICAO members had wished.

The new annex on the transport of dangerous goods and the tightening of noise pollution standards reflected the maturing of ICAO as an international organization in the 1970s and 1980s. The organization had expanded over the two decades and now, at last, was truly universal in its membership – the goal dreamed of by the creators of ICAO in 1944. With this new membership came a larger council and Air Navigation Commission, a new building, and a new generation of leaders faced with problems – including security and environmental issues – not considered by the framers of the Chicago Convention. Thanks to the improving international climate of the 1970s, the organization was able to expand physically and operationally with relatively few outside distractions. All this changed in the 1980s with the revival of Cold War tensions and the rise of serious new crises in the form of deadly armed attacks on civil aviation. These attacks inevitably placed the international confrontation of the two superpowers at the very top of ICAO's agenda.

13

The Cold War Comes to ICAO – Again

The rise of détente in the 1970s accompanied by the end of the war in Vietnam helped to ease tensions within the International Civil Aviation Organization – a difference that can be noticed in the tone of the minutes of the various committees. The signing of the Camp David Accords in 1978, the second Strategic Arms Limitation (SALT-II) Treaty in 1979, and the Carter administration's increasing focus on human rights and the north-south relationship added to the improved situation. But several events – the Iran-Iraq War, the Iranian hostage crisis, turmoil and civil war in the Middle East, the 1979–80 Soviet invasion of Afghanistan followed by a wide boycott of the 1980 Moscow Olympics – made it clear that détente was dead and the old Cold War antagonism was alive and well. The SALT-II Treaty was also dead, and early in 1980, President Carter announced the Carter doctrine, essentially proclaiming a new containment policy for the Middle East.

Within a year, Ronald Reagan was president. His goal was to revive the American spirit and restore the United States to what he saw as its rightful place of leadership. He also brought a more traditional hard line view of the Soviet Union and the Cold War and he introduced the Reagan doctrine to support anti-communist forces around the world, all underpinned by a massive military build-up and a desire to negotiate from a position of strength. The Soviets labelled Reagan a war monger and refused to move ahead on arms talks, but while the Soviet Union became bogged down in Afghanistan and faced a growing challenge in Poland from the Solidarity labour movement, Soviet leadership was in a state of flux. Leonid Brezhnev died in 1983; his successor, Yuri Andropov, fell ill almost immediately and died in 1984; he was followed by Konstantin Chernenko, and on his death in 1985, Mikhail Gorbachev assumed power. We know now that it was the beginning of the end of the Cold War, but it was hard to see that end in 1983.

These outside events inevitably affected ICAO, if only in the way they encroached on the speeches and actions of the various members. Old divisions that had never really disappeared were revived; positions on both sides hardened. New fault lines appeared; for example, the introduction of Reagan's Strategic Defense Initiative – 'Star Wars' – in 1983 added a new dimension of weapons in space that could not help but reverberate in ICAO. Even if it never worked, the thought of the militarization of space under the guise of a 'defence system' challenged some of the basic tenets of ICAO and the Chicago Convention, and the SDI became something of a symbol for the Cold War and it raised issues that would have to be addressed in ICAO.

A more immediate problem for ICAO in the 1980s, however, was the destruction of civil aircraft by military forces, especially those actions perpetrated by the Soviet Union and the United States. Armed attacks on civil aircraft were not uncommon before the 1980s; one report conducted by International Federation of Airline Pilots' Association noted thirty-three incidents of attacks on civil aviation from 1947 to 1986, resulting in the deaths of 746 people.[1] Most of these attacks occurred in areas that were embroiled in civil strife, few of them were reported to ICAO, and there was little that ICAO could have done in any event. Furthermore, the circumstances and loss of life in each case were different, and the international community did not react in a consistent manner to these events. In the international arena it made a difference whose aircraft it was that was attacked and which nation did the attacking.[2] And in the 1980s it was the superpowers who were doing the shooting.

Both China and the Soviet Union had, on occasion, shot at civil airliners that strayed into their airspace. In April 1952, Soviet fighter jets shot at an Air France airplane flying from Frankfurt to Berlin. In June 1954, a British Cathay Pacific aircraft was attacked by Chinese fighters and forced to land in the sea; ten of the eighteen people on board were killed. The Chinese government apologized and paid compensation. In July 1955, Bulgarian jets shot down an El AL aircraft flying from London to Tel Aviv, killing fifty-eight passengers and crew. In this case the Bulgarians refused to accept responsibility. And, as discussed in Chapter 12, in 1973 the Israelis military shot down a Libyan civil airliner. Israel apologized and offered compensation and was condemned for its actions at an Extraordinary ICAO Assembly. In April 1978, in an incident that eerily foreshadowed later events, Korean Air Lines Flight 902 (Paris to Seoul, via Anchorage, Alaska) with ninety-seven passengers and a crew of thirteen, strayed hundreds of miles into Soviet territory where it was mistaken for an American spy plane and shot at. The pilot managed to land the plane on a frozen lake in Soviet territory. Two passengers were killed in the explosion when the plane landed, and the Soviets detained several crew members for a few weeks, but the USSR was generally not condemned for its actions.[3]

The international reaction was radically different following the downing of Korean Air Lines KE 007 on 1 September 1983. The flight originated at John F. Kennedy Airport in New York, flew to Anchorage, where it was refueled and then left for Seoul, South Korea with 269 people on board, including a U.S. Congressman. The flight route – called Romeo-20 – ran alongside Soviet airspace and had been travelled thousands of times. KE 007 began to drift off course soon after takeoff and, after several hours, it crossed into Soviet airspace over the Kamchatka Peninsula, where it was picked up on Soviet radar and tracked by Soviet fighter aircraft. The aircraft was on a course that would take it over the Sea of Japan – international airspace – and then back into Soviet airspace and directly over Vladivostok, an important Soviet military and naval base. The whole region, including the Kamchatka Peninsula and Sakhalin Island, was an important strategic area for the Soviets, as it was home to several military and naval bases and other military facilities. The Soviets were on alert and concerned over possible incursions and spy missions, and they were sensitive to the actions of their Cold War rivals. It may have been a remote – even desolate – area, but it was one of the fronts of the Cold War.

There has been much debate about exactly what happened in the air that night. Part of the confusion came from the presence of a U.S. Air Force RC-135 reconnaissance aircraft (essentially a modified Boeing 707) on a regular surveillance mission, flying along the edge of Soviet territory monitoring Soviet military bases and radar sites. There had been instances in the past where these aircraft crossed over Soviet territory, and at one point that night the RC-135 came so close to KE 007 that the two aircraft briefly merged and then separated on Soviet radar screens. Unaware that the aircraft being followed was not the RC-135, and without making radio contact with the airliner or verifying its identity, two Soviet missiles were fired at KE 007 just before it crossed out of Soviet airspace. At least one of the missiles struck the aircraft; cabin pressure was lost, and it took twelve minutes for the jet to crash in the Sea of Japan. All 269 people on board – including 105 South Koreans, sixty-two Americans, twenty-eight Japanese, twenty-three Taiwanese, sixteen Filipinos, twelve Hong Kong Chinese, eight Canadians, five Thais, two Australians, two British, and one national each from the Dominican Republic, Vietnam, Iran, Sweden, Malaysia, and India[4] – were killed.

International reaction to the attack on KE 007 was immediate and sharp. Many condemned the Soviet actions and lowered their flags to commemorate the dead. IFALPA called for temporary boycott of all flights to Moscow, and although this boycott had mixed success, several states refused landing rights to Aeroflot aircraft for weeks after the incident. The United States supported the ban but had been boycotting Aeroflot since December 1981, following the imposition of martial law in Poland.[5] There were also thousands of spontaneous personal actions across the globe, from the Sea of Japan to Australia and Europe to small-town America, all denouncing the Soviet Union and calling for dramatic action. Soviet flags were burned; Soviet liquor was boycotted or destroyed; conferences, visits, and agreements were cancelled.

In the aftermath of the crash there was much speculation about what had happened: why had the aircraft strayed so far off course and was it possible that the crew was unaware of what had happened? Was the crew on some kind of a spy mission? Did the Soviets know that it was a civilian airliner, or did they mistake it for an American spy-plane? Why had the aircraft not been warned by either the air traffic controllers or the Americans who were patrolling the area that night? And, if the flight was intentional then did the United States bear some responsibility for the crash? Within hours journalists were asking questions like these; within weeks they were writing magazine articles pointing out the inconsistencies and unknowns in the whole affair; within months they were publishing books with titles like *The Cover Up, The Hidden Story, The KAL 007 Massacre, Shootdown,* and *'The Target is Destroyed.'*[6]

There was no question where the American administration stood. On 5 September President Reagan appeared on American television and said: 'My fellow Americans, I'm coming before you tonight about the Korean airline massacre, the attack by the Soviet Union against 269 innocent men, women, and children aboard an unarmed Korean passenger plane. But despite the savagery of their crime, the universal reaction against it, and the evidence of their complicity, the Soviets still refuse to tell the truth. They have persistently refused to admit that their pilot fired on the Korean aircraft. Indeed, they've not even told their own people.' Noting that no one should surprised at the 'inhuman brutality' of the Soviets, Reagan added that 'they deny the deed, but in their conflicting and misleading protestations, the Soviets reveal that, yes, shooting down a plane – even one with hundreds of innocent men, women, children, and babies – is a part of their normal procedure if that plane is in what they claim as their airspace.' Reagan made passing reference to the MX missile, defence spending, disarmament negotiations, and an upcoming conference on human rights, and discussed the response of the United States, noting, 'We have joined with other countries to press the International Civil Aviation Organization to investigate this crime at an urgent special session of the Council.'[7]

The incident also made the Americans uneasy in other ways. If the Soviets knowingly shot down a civil airliner then all the criticism was justified; but if the aircraft drifted in Soviet space for two hours without the Soviets knowing about it; and if it took them hours to track it down; and if they shot it down not knowing it was a civil airliner, then what did this say about the state of Soviet defences or their ability to act responsibly as a nuclear power? If this kind of mistake can happen, Reagan asked, 'what kind of imagination did it take to think of a Soviet military man with his finger close to a nuclear button making an even more tragic mistake? If mistakes could be made by a fighter pilot, what about a similar miscalculation by the commander of missile launch crew?'[8]

At almost the same time, the United States called for an urgent meeting of the U.N. Security Council asking for a resolution denouncing the Soviet action and an international investigation into the whole affair. The United States turned to the United Nations in part because the American government was unlikely to take any other more aggressive or retaliatory measures against the Soviet Union. Reagan could use the crisis to help gather public support for his weapons build-up, to get his massive defence budget passed, and, more generally, as a rhetorical tool to hammer away at the Soviets in the Cold War 'war of words.'[9] All this could be achieved without retaliation. Besides, what else was to be done? Efforts could be made to prevent such a tragedy from reoccurring, but retaliatory actions might destabilize the international situation at a very difficult time and additional sanctions – such as boycotts, refusing the Soviets landing rights, restrictions against flying to the Soviet Union – would likely do more harm to the state that introduced them than the Soviet Union. At the United Nations, on the other hand, the tragedy could be used as a propaganda tool to condemn the Soviets. As one journalist wrote, the 'decision to turn to the United Nations, a forum for which the president and his top aides had little respect, was the clearest sign of the administration's ultimate policy in the crisis: to flay the Soviets publicly wherever and whenever possible.'[10]

The Soviets responded with equal outrage but different spin, putting the blame on the United States and its allies the South Koreans. It took several days for Moscow even to admit that an aircraft had been shot down (the first few Soviet news reports left the aircraft still in the air on its way to the Sea of Japan). The Soviets claimed that the aircraft was an American spy-plane that had violated Soviet airspace; in other words, it was an American provocation to which the USSR had responded, and they were within their rights to shoot it down. Even when they acknowledged that it was a civilian airliner with 269 people on board, the government position was that the identity of the aircraft was unknown at the time and the whole episode was part of a 'malicious and hostile anti-Soviet campaign.'[11] As one author nicely put it, the 'Soviets would focus solely on what the plane was doing, while the Americans would focus solely on what was done to it.'[12]

The Security Council met on five separate days between 2 and 12 September to debate a resolution condemning the Soviets and a call for a U.N. investigation of the incident. The whole affair turned into a piece of political theatre as the accusations flew. Tape recordings of the chilling conversation between the Soviet pilot and his ground controllers were played, and new information was revealed daily in the press, sparking more charges and counter-charges. The Soviets matched the Americans in accusations and vigour, and the tension in the Cold War rose to levels not seen since the 1962 Cuban Missile Crisis. It is unlikely that many positions were changed through the course of the debate. And, in the end, on 12 September the Security Council resolution – supported by seventeen states – was vetoed by the Soviets.[13] International attention turned to ICAO.

It made sense, for a number of reasons, to hand things over to ICAO. For one, ICAO provided an international body that could look at the situation, investigate, and make recommendations on how to prevent such disasters from happening again. The safety of aviation was ICAO's primary goal, and examining this incident was one concrete step that could be taken by the international community that might lead to something positive. For a second, more political reason, the Soviet Union had no veto in the ICAO Council and could not block efforts to chastise it for its actions, and ICAO could be used as an international public platform to condemn the Soviets not just for their actions but for their system, their values, and way of life. From the perspective of the United States and its allies, it was a unique Cold War opportunity. Third, ICAO was an excellent forum for debate, but it also could not force the United States, the USSR, the Japanese, the Koreans, or any other state to do anything it did not want to do. It could not requisition any information or require any testimony, and had no power to enforce its decisions. As one author wrote, ICAO was a place where the United States had considerable influence and the Soviets could be condemned, but it had no power to subpoena information and was forced to rely on what governments gave to it, making it 'an eminently controllable organization.'[14] Finally, by permitting ICAO to undertake an investigation into the affair, the main protagonists could take a positive and public action – in other words, be seen to be doing something – that would permit the international tensions to relax somewhat while the investigation continued. In this way, ICAO could act like the valve on a pressure cooker that allows the steam to escape. Turning to ICAO was a way to avoid applying additional sanctions and provided an opportunity for both sides to cool off when neither really wanted things to escalate any further. Whatever the reasons, ICAO found itself moving into a much more blatantly political area, and not since the height of the Chicago conference when President Roosevelt threatened to cut off U.S. aid to Great Britain over fifth freedom rights had ICAO found itself at the centre of such tense international rivalries and the focus for such great public attention.

The ICAO Council met in extraordinary session on 15–16 September at the request of South Korea (which was not a council member) and Canada (which was). It was an 'extraordinary' session in a number of ways, not least because investigating aircraft accidents is not something that ICAO or the council usually does. Indeed, Article 26 of the Chicago Convention states that following an accident the responsibility falls to the state in which the accident occurred to conduct the investigation, with the participation of the state of registry of the aircraft. The Soviets immediately established their own inquiry into the crash and promised to inform everyone else of their findings. Few other council members believed that the Soviets would do an adequate job, however, and the downing of KE 007 was hardly an 'accident' in the usual sense of the word. And in 1973, the Israeli attack against the Libyan aircraft had been on the agenda and debated at the Nineteenth Extraordinary Assembly of the ICAO, so having the council discuss KE 007 was not unprecedented. Moreover, public outrage and horror over the Soviet action was so strong and the attack seemed to challenge directly ICAO's basic goal of the safety of civil aviation that it seemed appropriate for the council to look at the whole issue. Indeed, Article 55(e) gives the council the right to investigate and to prepare reports on 'any situation which may appear to present avoidable obstacles to the development of international air navigation' and the downing of KE 007 seemed to be one of these 'avoidable obstacles.'[15]

The first day of the ICAO Council session was devoted to delegation statements. The second focused on two resolutions; the first was sponsored by Australia, Canada, Denmark, France, Germany, Italy, Japan, the Netherlands, the United Kingdom, and the United States, and the second was introduced by the Soviet Union. The Czech delegate tried to have the whole debate on the resolutions put off to give the delegations more time to study the draft proposals, but this motion was easily defeated. Council President Kotaite declared that the two resolutions were 'alternative proposals' and therefore if the first one was adopted then the second (from the USSR) would not be considered. In this end this is what occurred, and the Soviet resolution was never discussed.[16]

Several important decisions were made at this council session. In the first resolution, passed with overwhelming support – twenty-six in favour, two against (USSR and Czechoslovakia), and three abstentions (Algeria, China, and India) – the council deplored the destruction of KE 007, recognized that an armed attack on civil aviation was 'incompatible with the norms governing international behaviour and elementary considerations of humanity,' and stated its concern that 'the Soviet Union has not so far acknowledged the paramount importance of the safety and lives of passengers and crew when dealing with civil aircraft intercepted in or near its territorial airspace.' Given this state of affairs, the council directed the secretary general, Ives Lambert, to launch an investigation into the crash of KE 007, 'to determine the facts and technical aspects relating to the flight and destruction of the aircraft and to provide an interim report to the Council within 30 days of the adoption of this Resolution and a complete report during the 110th Session of the Council.' The same resolution directed the Air Navigation Commission to study all aspects of the Chicago Convention, the annexes, and other related documents with a view to initiating amendments to help prevent such a disaster from reoccurring. The ANC was also asked to 'examine ways to improve the coordination of communication systems between military and civil aircraft and air traffic control services and to improve procedures in cases involving the identification and interception of civil aircraft.'[17]

In a second and much more technical resolution, proposed by France, the ANC was directed to review several specific annexes, especially Annex 2, Rules of the Air, and its Attachment A, which deals with the interception of civil aircraft and contains standard procedures for the manoeuvring of the approaching intercepting aircraft.[18] The idea was to see if it was possible to amend these guidelines and, if possible, incorporate them as part of the annex itself. The goal was to improve communications between air traffic services and the military and, through better coordination and harmonized procedures, reduce the chances of reoccurrence of a similar KE 007 disaster. But this resolution was passed by only a simple majority of six in favour to four opposed. That seventeen members abstained on the vote revealed stark divisions in the council over this idea and foreshadowed the problems that lay ahead.[19]

During the discussion the French delegation also introduced a much more popular proposal that ICAO give the highest priority to devising an amendment to the Chicago Convention calling on all members to abstain from the use of armed force on civil aircraft. A second part of the proposal called for the convening of an Extraordinary Session of the ICAO Assembly, early in 1984, to discuss and adopt the proposed amendment to the convention. Only the Soviets and Czechs were opposed and the resolution was adopted by the council – twenty-six in favour, two opposed, and two abstentions (Egypt and India).[20]

These council resolutions were thoroughly debated at the Twenty-Fourth ICAO Assembly, which took place in Montreal from 20 September to 10 October. The staging of the triennial assembly just at that time was coincidental, but it furnished a further opportunity for everyone to vent their anger and frustration. A number of issues were on the agenda, but in the Executive Committee and the plenary sessions most speakers focused on KE 007. Outrage was the order of the day; in the Executive Committee only the Soviet Union, Czechoslovakia, Poland, Vietnam, Hungary and a very few others spoke against the council resolutions, and then only to say that they were premature. A few voices were raised over procedure, suggesting that ICAO was putting the cart before the horse; the delegate from Bangladesh, for example, 'was at a loss to understand how, while the Secretary General was being urged to institute an investigation, the Assembly was already condemning one contracting State. He considered that this was a prejudgment of the case and would impair the validity of the findings of the Secretary General by introducing an element of bias in the investigation.'[21]

It was, however, far too late to avoid 'an element of bias.' In the plenary sessions the condemnation of the USSR continued, with the Koreans calling the Soviet act 'despicable,' and the New Zealanders leading an ultimately unsuccessful movement to prevent the re-election of the Soviet Union to the council as a kind of punishment for its 'barbaric attack.'

That the USSR seemed 'unrepentant and not ready to rule out further resort to the use of force against the civilian aircraft of other countries' only made things worse. 'Is it too much to ask for understanding?' asked the American delegate. 'To ask for integrity? To ask for compassion? To ask for expressions of regret? I call upon the Soviet Union to join the community of nations, which has spoken with one voice, in declaring that military attack against civil aircraft is unlawful.'[22]

The Soviets remained unmoved, however, noting only that the current session occurred during 'a complex international situation.' The 'incident,' the Soviet delegate stated, 'is being exploited in some quarters to aggravate the international situation and provoke anti-Soviet hysteria. These people are deliberately evading the main fact that a criminal violation of the sovereignty of the USSR and of the rules of international flight was committed by a spy-aircraft.' The facts, he continued, 'show irrefutably that the intrusion of the South Korean aircraft into Soviet airspace was organized by the USA as a large-scale intelligence operation and that the civil aircraft was deliberately selected regardless of the possibility – and perhaps even in the calculated expectation – that human lives would be lost. Naturally enough, the whole responsibility for what occurred falls entirely upon those who organized this operation.'[23] He then repeated that the Soviet Union was already conducting its own investigation into the matter and that was all that was required. But the Soviets could not withstand the majority opinion, and the council resolutions were endorsed by the assembly.

The events of September–October 1983 set in motion three separate but related activities for ICAO. First, the organization committed itself to amending the Chicago Convention essentially to declare that the use of weapons against civil aviation was unacceptable in the international community. Amending the convention was something that had been accomplished only rarely in the past and not in such a significant way. Second, the assembly instructed the Air Navigation Commission to examine all the technical aspects of the issue and to review ICAO's documents – the convention, Standards and Recommended Practices, annexes, manuals, and so on – to see how they could be amended to improve aviation safety and prevent a reoccurrence of such a disaster. Third, the secretary general was commissioned to investigate the crash of KE 007 and to report back to the council. This was the most political of the three activities and the one guaranteed to receive the greatest public attention, given that there were still many lingering questions about what happened to KE 007. It also was likely the most difficult of the three tasks and the one most prone to failure, given the reluctance of the Soviets and, to a lesser degree, the Americans and the Japanese to cooperate. Without power to compel access to the relevant information, coming up with firm conclusions would prove to be a very difficult undertaking.

The five-member team established under Secretary General Lambert conducted fact-finding missions to the states involved to gather what they could about the details of the crash. They travelled to the Sea of Japan near the crash-site and conducted interviews with air traffic controllers and just about anyone else who was connected to the incident. In Seattle, several experts on the inertial navigation system were brought together for simulation tests of what happened aboard KE 007[24] The Soviets, however, were less than forthcoming; although they shared their own preliminary investigation report with the ICAO team, they at first resisted even hosting members of the ICAO team and denied having found the cockpit voice recorder and the digital flight data recorder that were essential for any thorough investigation. As a result, when his final report was submitted to the ICAO Council on 12 December 1983, Lambert was already warning that it was incomplete and that 'a number of elements were missing from the report.' All he could do was state that if these things became available in the future he could write another report.[25]

The report of the secretary general's team – the Lambert Report, as it was called – was inconclusive on why KE 007 had strayed off course but found no indication that the crew was aware of the deviation or that the deviation was in any way premeditated. It argued that the misdirection of the aircraft was likely the result of one of two possible scenarios, both of which involved pilot error. As the report stated, with words not likely to instill public confidence in air travel, 'each of those postulations assumed a considerable degree of lack of alertness and attentiveness on the part of the entire flight crew but not to a degree that was unknown in international civil aviation.'[26] The Soviets were singled out not so much for evil intent but, rather, for ineptitude and laxity: the fighter pilot had not known that KE 007 was a civil airliner and mistook it for an American spy-plane, the report concluded, but the Soviets had not made a thorough attempt to identify it.[27]

The Lambert Report was a confidential document, but it was quickly leaked to the press and became the source of much speculation and criticism, especially from those who suspected that the American government was covering up its complicity in the affair. It also was used by some of the victims' families in their civil litigation against Korean Air Lines and the United States government.[28] The investigation team was limited in the information it received and it admitted that, because of time pressures, they essentially accepted at face value much of what they did have. The result was a flawed report that had enough gaps in it for any critic, doubter, or conspiracy theorist to drive through. It seemed to stretch credulity that the crew could be unaware that the aircraft was off course for such a long time, and the report merely dismissed the idea – which seemed plausible at least to several critics – that the crew had purposely flown a more direct route, over Soviet territory, to save fuel.[29] Another critic observed that the ICAO report 'in effect declined to consider any explanation which might involve military intelligence, and directed its efforts to the simulation of plausible navigation errors on the part of the crew. Although the exploration of navigation error is an essential element in reviewing the KAL tragedy, the argument used by the ICAO report in refusing to appraise the electronic intelligence aspects is extremely weak.'[30] Another author slammed the report for its bias because the ICAO team refused to look at all possible explanations for the crash; the report, accordingly, was 'full of sloppiness, carelessness and inconsistencies.'[31]

The first thing the council did with the Lambert Report was to pass it to the ANC for a review of its technical aspects.[32] Any hope that the ANC would be able to provide a more definitive explanation of the crash quickly evaporated. The ANC report arrived in February 1984; it was just as non-committal as the Lambert Report and was unable to verify the secretary general's conclusions. 'The Air Navigation Commission is unable to establish the exact cause for the significant deviation from track,' the report announced. 'The magnitude of the diversion cannot be explained, particularly as the aircraft was equipped with navigation equipment which should have enabled the crew to adhere to its track.' In addition, the report continued, 'the commission found it difficult to validate and endorse the conclusions connected with the scenarios postulated in the Secretary General's report because any one of them contained some points which could not be explained satisfactorily.'[33] Clearly, many questions remained unanswered.

The council reconsidered the Lambert Report at the end of February and early March 1984. Resolutions were proposed, familiar divisions appeared, and, in the end, the council agreed to send copies of the Lambert and ANC reports to the members. The council also passed a resolution that was very critical of the Soviet Union. Recognizing that the ICAO investigation was unable to determine why the aircraft was so far off course, the council nevertheless condemned 'the use of armed force' against

KE 007 and 'deeply' deplored the 'Soviet failure to cooperate in the search and rescue efforts of other involved States and the Soviet failure to cooperate with the ICAO investigation of the incident.'[34] It was the strongest official condemnation of the Soviet Union yet made by ICAO and a rare occurrence in the history of the organization.

The reports were inconclusive, but in some ways they were of secondary importance in all this debate; *why* the aircraft was off course was of interest to many observers, but the *fact* that it was shot down and the Soviets seemed to be trying to justify their actions was enough to convince most members of the need to respond in a serious manner. There had always been a political dimension in the whole affair, and the possibility that ICAO, and especially the council, could be used as a blunt instrument against the Soviet Union, and in this respect the investigations into the crash – undertaken with limited information and impossible time constraints – gave a kind of official legitimacy for what was about to happen in any event. It is not too much to suggest that at that moment the council spoke for more than just its members and expressed a broader sentiment, or that international public opinion needed to hear those words. In addition, the United States and others got their way – their pound of Soviet flesh – in the council. For their part, the Soviets were condemned in the court of public opinion, but suffered from no additional sanctions or other serious consequences.

For those who believed that the truth about the crash of KE 007 was waiting to be discovered there still were enough questions, suspicions, possibilities, theories – and aviation experts ready to explain almost any scenario – to keep them busy for a long time. It would be ten years, in fact, before any more definitive answers could be made. In the meantime, ICAO had the more pressing tasks of studying its documents for ways to improve them and to amend the Chicago Convention in an effort to prevent future armed attacks against civil aviation. But, as one legal scholar has pointed out, that the council had denounced the Soviet Union 'in no uncertain way' set the stage and perhaps made it easier in the following weeks to achieve consensus on amending the Chicago Convention.[35]

Two draft resolutions for amending the convention were received by the council; one from the United States and the second a joint proposal from France and Austria. Additional drafts were subsequently introduced by others, including one from the Soviet Union, and these draft proposals became the focus of the Extraordinary Assembly in Montreal, from 24 April to 10 May 1984 (also on the agenda was the approval of the Arabic text of the ICAO Assembly's Standing Rules of Procedure). One hundred and seven delegations participated, and Assad Kotaite was elected president of the assembly. The Executive Committee established a working group, chaired by N. Elaraby, the chief delegate from Egypt, to produce the final wording for the amendment.[36]

The assembly opened more than seven months after the KE 007 incident, and the passage of time was reflected in the tone of the statements by the various delegations. Much of the shock and anger had faded, although considerable determination remained. 'The eight months that have elapsed since 1 September 1983 have been a period for reflection,' stated the delegate from Australia during the first plenary meeting,[37] and others seemed to agree. The chief delegate from Nepal captured the moment nicely: 'Whilst the painful memory of KAL Flight 007 is still in our minds, we are gathered here in this distinct forum of ICAO with the crucial task of evolving procedures which, we hope, most assuredly will prevent the repetition of such disasters. In spite of the greatest sophistication and still advancing technology in aviation ... the fact that one can never be too complacent becomes more painfully real than ever. It is still the human mind behind all those machines which has the moral obligation, conscience, skill and rationality to avert any incident from turning into a catastrophe.'[38]

There was considerable debate about the primary goal of amending the convention to prohibit armed attacks on civil aircraft, and there were problems over the wording of the amendment. Questions were raised about restricting the amendment to civil aircraft. Some members believed that it was essential to do so, and in fact, that ICAO could not legally do otherwise; others supported a wider interpretation because it was possible for some aircraft to be used primarily, but not exclusively, for commercial purposes – and would this then open a loophole? Likewise, would the amendment apply to aircraft only when they violated the territory of another nation, or would it apply to all civil aircraft no matter where they were? And, would it apply only to contracting states or should it be applied to all civil aircraft? In addition, some of the less developed states worried that the amendment might put restrictions on their sovereignty, especially on their right to protect themselves if, for example, rebel groups used civil aircraft to attack their governments.[39]

These and other questions were debated for several days, and at one point it looked to Council President Kotaite as if no consensus was possible. He later recalled his concerns that if the meetings broke down without an agreement it might tarnish ICAO's image and weaken its authority and ability to appeal to the nations of the world to refrain from the use of force against aircraft. Thus, it became important to get an agreement of some kind. 'I sat at my desk here for a half an hour and then decided to meet with delegates from the Western bloc,' he later told a journalist. He met with other delegations separately as well, including the Soviets and a group representing Asian, African, Middle Eastern, and South American members. By the end of the day he had received word that the wording of an agreement was agreed to by all the delegations.[40] The final text was approved – by acclamation on 10 May 1984 – by the ICAO Assembly as Resolution A25-1.

The new Article 3 bis followed the short original Article 3 (which states that the Chicago Convention applies only to civil aircraft, that no one should fly over another state without permission and that, in making their aircraft regulations, the contracting states 'will have due regard for the safety of navigation of civil aircraft.') and contains a much longer text of four paragraphs. The first sets out the basic principle and the subsequent paragraphs set limits or qualify the first. It was, one aviation specialist noted, a bit of a compromise between the American and Soviet positions, containing both a ban on the use of weapons against civil aircraft and a reaffirmation of the complete sovereignty of all states over their airspace.[41] In the new article, all contracting states 'recognize that every State must refrain from resorting to the use of weapons against civil aircraft in flight and that, in case of interception, the lives of persons on board and the safety of aircraft must not be endangered.' That was a fairly clear statement; the second paragraph notes that all states have the right 'to require the landing at some designated airport' of an unauthorized aircraft and may 'resort to any appropriate means consistent with relevant rules of international law.' In addition, each contracting state agrees to comply with an order given under the previous stipulation and to amend its laws to make compliance mandatory (and to punish those who break these laws). Finally, each contracting state agrees to 'take appropriate measures to prohibit the deliberate use of any civil aircraft ... for any purpose inconsistent with the aims of this Convention.'

It was a landmark achievement for ICAO, even though Article 3 bis was more a declaration of principle than any new legal instrument. It already was assumed to be illegal in most cases to attack civil aircraft; it has also been pointed out that Attachment A of Annex 2 already stated that 'intercepting aircraft should refrain from the use of weapons in all cases of interception of civil aircraft.'[42] What the assembly did with Article 3 bis was to remind everyone in a forceful and unambiguous way that attacks of this nature were unacceptable and beyond any normal standard of behaviour. In other words, what the Soviets had done to KE 007, despite their protestations and justifications, had gone beyond acceptable international norms. Putting it in the convention also gave the basic principle more authority.

There were some remaining questions, of course. The use of the word 'refrain' in the first paragraph as opposed to 'abstain,' which had been used in the original French draft, raised a few eyebrows, as the changing of a few letters in one word could have made a significant difference in meaning. Furthermore, as legal scholar Bin Cheng notes, the word 'force' was removed from an earlier draft and replaced with the word 'weapons'; he asks if this meant that it was permissible in some cases to use force but not weapons against civil aircraft? He also argues that Article 3 bis goes farther than perhaps originally intended in that it could be seen to apply not only to foreign aircraft but also to each member's domestic aircraft. And if this is the case, he asks, what happens if criminals use a helicopter to break their accomplices out of prison – would it then be legal to use weapons on the convicts but illegal to use weapons against the helicopter? What about people transporting illegal drugs or smuggling weapons or other contraband?[43] Today he might have cited the example of using weapons against terrorists using a civil airliner to crash into buildings – would that, too, contravene Article 3 bis?

The adoption of the new amendment was really the first step in a process of study, revision, and integration of all the new ideas about dealing with the interception of civil aircraft. Throughout the whole process, the ANC was working behind the scenes reviewing the annexes and making recommendations to the council on how they could be updated and improved. Within months, changes had been approved for Annexes 2, 6, 10, and 11.[44] Some of the changes were small, such as Amendment 26 to Annex 2, which introduced some changes to the Spanish text and brought it into closer alignment with the other languages.[45] Other changes were more significant: in June 1984, for example, ICAO published the first edition of the *Manual Concerning Interception of Civil Aircraft*, which brought into a single document all of ICAO's procedures and recommendations on this issue in effort to help their application by the contracting states.[46] There were also a few developments outside the auspices of ICAO; for example, in July 1985 the United States, the Soviet Union, and Japan signed an agreement to help improve air traffic control services in the North Pacific Ocean.[47]

One significant change to ICAO's annexes – and the most interesting, given that it inadvertently brought the two superpowers into an uncomfortable alliance – was Amendment 27 to Annex 2.[48] This process was put in motion by the September 1983 council resolution on the French proposal to upgrade Annex 2. The goal of the amendment was to take the procedures set out in Attachment A of Annex 2 and incorporate them as standards in the body of the annex. Annex 2 deals with Rules of the Air and the attachment sets out guidelines for identifying and intercepting civil aircraft. The ANC established a working group and sought legal advice from the Legal Bureau but there were problems right from the start. The main issue was the legality of adopting a standard that by definition also would apply to military aircraft (because it would set out the procedures for a military aircraft to intercept a civil aircraft). Military – or state – aircraft were clearly outside ICAO's jurisdiction, specifically under Article 3a of the Chicago Convention. As long as the procedures were guidelines attached to the annex, members could follow them but were not required to; as a standard, members would have to either follow these rules or file a difference with ICAO.

The division in the ICAO Council was predictable but unusual. The strongest support for the amendment came from the smaller states (several of which, it was pointed out, had no capability to intercept aircraft of any kind – civil or military) and the opposition came from the larger air powers, especially the United States and the Soviet Union. After much debate the amendment was slightly weakened but, in the end, numbers prevailed and the amendment was adopted on 10 March 1986. The four opposed to the amendment were the United States, the Soviet Union, Czechoslovakia, and Egypt. No member registered a disapproval, however, and the amendment came into force later that year. Nevertheless, the United States informed the secretary general that the United States 'does not accept any provision of Annex 2 or any other Annex, as constituting a Standard or Recommended Practice applicable to State aircraft.'[49] 'For the first time a comprehensive set of Standards was adopted relating to the interception of civil aircraft,' wrote Michael Milde of ICAO's Legal Bureau, and 'the Amendment includes a comprehensive set of "Special Recommendations" on interception of civil aircraft which have no legally binding force, but States have been invited by the Council to notify any departure from these "Special Recommendations." It is to be believed that a large degree of uniformity has been introduced for interception procedures and that the safety of international civil aviation will be enhanced.'[50]

Article 3 bis needed 102 ratifications from 152 contracting states to come into force. This took several years; only two states ratified it in 1984, twenty in 1985 and eleven more in 1986. Then the numbers began to drop off, to three in 1989, eight in 1990, three and four and 1991 and 1992, respectively, far short of the required number. In 1997 the council again asked for members to ratify it, and the amendment only came into effect in 1998.[51] But would it have made any difference to the Soviet Union in the North Pacific on 1 September 1983 had the amendments and Article 3 bis already been adopted and in force? It is hard to believe that it would have, given that ultimately, for nations to 'refrain' from these kinds of attacks the aircraft must first be identified as a civilian airliner, and in most cases the offending nation claims (often truthfully) that it could not confirm or had no way of knowing that the aircraft was civilian when it was attacked. Such was the case with the downing of an Iranian airliner by the USS *Vincennes* in the Persian Gulf in 1988.

The turmoil in the Gulf region had been causing headaches for civil aviation for many years, and the Iran-Iraq War that began in September 1980 made the region even more dangerous. Both sides in the conflict declared states of emergency and flights were rerouted, with Bahrain taking over the responsibility for most of the air traffic control services previously handled through Tehran. Civil aviation in the region continued on a contingency basis over the following years but there were repeated incidents, warnings, and emergencies as the war evolved. In 1985 Iraq essentially declared Iranian airspace a war zone and warned all civil aircraft to keep out; in protest Iran called on the ICAO Council to discuss the Iraqi demands. For two days in April 1985 the council debated the issue and urged the two sides to maintain the safety of civil aviation in the region. And although no permanent solution was agreed to, thanks to the efforts of Council President Kotaite, the Iraqi government ultimately 'gave formal assurances that international traffic would not be affected.'[52]

Throughout this period the United States maintained military and naval forces in the region, and relations with Iran especially had been very strained dating back to the Iranian revolution and the Iranian hostage crisis of 1979. In May 1987 the American frigate, the USS *Stark*, was struck by a missile from an Iraqi warplane, killing thirty-seven American sailors. Subsequently, the Americans changed their rules of engagement, giving ship commanders the right to fire on the enemy without having to wait to be attacked first, and the United States began warning all aircraft in that region to stick to prescribed flight plans or they might be at risk of attack. Stationed in a war zone where they had been attacked before, the U.S. naval forces in the Gulf were on edge and nervous, and many journalists describe what happened next as an accident waiting to happen.[53]

On the morning of 3 July 1988, an Iran Air Airbus A300, Flight 655, took off from Bandar Abbas in Iran flying to Dubai in the United Arab Emirates; a thirty-minute flight of about 150 miles across the Strait of Hormuz in the Persian Gulf. The aircraft was picked up on the radar of the American cruiser the USS *Vincennes*, with Captain Will C. Rogers in command, while this ship was in Iranian territorial waters and in pursuit of Iranian gunboats. The Americans mistook the civilian aircraft for an Iranian F-14 fighter, and as it approached the U.S. ship fired two missiles destroying the aircraft in mid-air. All 290 people were killed, including the crew of sixteen and 274 passengers from Iran (238), India (10), Pakistan (6), the United Arab Emirates (13), Italy (1), and Yugoslavia (6).

The Americans were quick to call it an accident, stating that the airliner had not taken the proper precautions and had violated all the necessary requirements for safe air flight in that area. Claims were made that the Iranian aircraft had not been flying at the proper altitude and that it was several miles off course and not in the correct corridor. The American government also claimed that the aircraft was flying directly towards the *Vincennes* and that it failed to identify itself properly or respond to repeated warnings. The crew of the ship believed the aircraft to be an Iranian F-14 jet on a hostile mission, and therefore it was shot down. President Reagan called it a 'terrible human tragedy,' but an 'understandable accident' and stated that it would not change United States policy in the Persian Gulf. He also expressed his regret over the incident and shortly thereafter offered compensation for the families of the victims.[54] The *New York Times* asked readers to put themselves in the shoes of the ship's captain: 'Iranian F-14's had recently been seen in the region; U.S. forces had been warned to expect attacks around July 4; and Captain Rogers already had a battle on his hands. Baring surprising findings, it is hard to fault his decision to attack the suspect plane.' Indeed, the *Times* continued, the blame might lie with Iran and the Iranian pilot for flying in that area, in that way, and at that time.[55]

The obvious comparisons to KE 007 were immediately raised and denied by the United States and, for slightly different reasons, the Soviet Union. It was a war zone, the Americans pointed out, there had been warnings made and the aircraft seemed to have not responded as it should; the whole incident was a tragedy but, they reminded everyone, the United States, unlike the Soviet Union, does not shoot down civilian aircraft and therefore there must have been extenuating circumstances that led to this tragic accident. A spokesperson for the Soviet foreign ministry also said that comparisons with 1983 were false; KE 007 was a spy plane and had violated Soviet territory, he said, while the Iranian aircraft was flying from its own territory into international airspace. And, of course, KE 007 flew at night, while the Americans had shot down a civilian airliner in broad daylight. The Soviets blamed 'trigger-happy' American servicemen for the incident and called on the United States to remove all of its forces from the Persian Gulf. But it was also quickly apparent that the Soviets were unlikely to take additional actions; upcoming visits of Soviet officials to the United States were not cancelled, no economic sanctions or boycotts were announced, and overall the Soviets gave a fairly subdued response.[56]

The Iranians were understandably outraged and sceptical of the American military's version of events. An Airbus A300 is twice as wide and almost three times as long as an F-14, so how was it possible to mistake the two and why did U.S. radar not notice that it was a civilian aircraft? Flight 655 was also a regularly scheduled flight; it had left a little late but that was not unusual, and the Iranians denied that it had deviated from its proper flight path or that it was descending toward the American ship as the Americans contended. The Iranians clearly saw parallels with KE 007 and they demanded an extraordinary meeting of the ICAO Council and the U.N. Security Council, much the same as had happened following the downing of KE007. Here the Iranians would get their chance to condemn the United States as the Soviets had been condemned a few years earlier.[57]

Council President Assad Kotaite expressed his shock at the incident and, after contacting the members of the council, called for an extraordinary meeting for 13 July, which, as it turned out, was in advance of the meetings of the U.N. Security Council on the same topic. As it has been pointed out, this schedule denied the ICAO Council any opportunity merely to follow the lead of the senior organization.[58] The Americans, although they had launched their own military investigation into the tragedy, agreed to participate in the council session, and the Iranians, although not members of the council, agreed as well and sent half a dozen observers to Montreal.

The two-day meeting (13–14 July 1988) had less rancour than the similar extraordinary meeting in 1983, and from the opening minute of silence to honour the victims the tone of the meetings was more civil than in 1983. Still, the Iranians accused the United States of lying, fabricating, and denying the truth and called for an 'explicit condemnation' of the

American actions, along the lines of 1983–84. The Americans responded by reminding everyone that President Reagan had expressed his 'deep regret' over the accident and already offered compensation to the families of the victims. This compensation, the American ICAO Council member added, was offered 'on an *ex gratia*, or voluntary basis, and not on the basis of any legal liability or obligation.' After all, he concluded, the shooting down of the Iranian airliner 'was, in fact, an accident.'[59] The Soviets condemned the American action and again called for the withdrawal of the U.S. Navy from the Persian Gulf,[60] but beyond that there was a general sense that an investigation was needed before any further actions were to be taken.

In the end the council did not condemn the United States, but 're-affirmed the fundamental principle that states must refrain from resorting to the use of weapons against civil aircraft.' It also agreed to ask Secretary General S.S. Sidhu to launch an investigation into the crash and to report on the investigation's findings. The Americans called this a compromise and agreed to cooperate with the ICAO investigation; the Iranians failed to get the condemnation that they wanted, but professed satisfaction in that the affair was far from over.[61]

At the United Nations on 14 July, a similar kind of exchange occurred between Iranian Foreign Minister Ali Akbar Velayati and American Vice President George H.W. Bush. Both men remained calm, but charged the other with responsibility for the disaster. The Americans were incompetent, said the Iranian, as he repeated that the Airbus was on course and acted properly throughout its short flight; Bush said the blame rested with Iran and its senseless continuation of the Iran-Iraq War, which made such disasters more likely to happen. Had the Iranians accepted an earlier U.N. resolution calling for an immediate ceasefire in the war then the accident would never have happened. In the end the Security Council passed a resolution expressing its regret and distress over the incident, but, like the ICAO Council, it did not condemn the United States.[62]

The Americans' predicament was made all the more difficult with the results of their own investigation, which appeared in August. Although later dismissed by two American journalists as 'a pastiche of omissions, half-truths and outright deceptions,'[63] the U.S. military report blamed human error for the disaster, noting that there were no apparent equipment malfunctions and that the radar tracking system was working fine. The report also acknowledged several other facts: the aircraft was not flying off course but, rather, in its designated corridor; it was also flying slower than originally stated, and it was at an altitude of twelve thousand feet and climbing not, as earlier suggested, at nine thousand feet and descending. A crew member had checked the roster of scheduled flights but failed to note that Flight 655 was on the list, and various crew members mistakenly believed that the aircraft was an F-14 and reported false information to the captain, who ordered the missile launches.[64]

The ICAO report was submitted to the council in December. Based on the work of a team of five experts who traveled from Tehran to Washington, the secretary general's report was cautious in its findings, noting that without the digital flight data recorder or the cockpit voice recorder the report was submitted 'with the qualification that additional research may be required on the part of ICAO.'[65] Its findings were unspectacular and focused on technical issues; there were no problems on the airliner, the experts announced, but there was crew error on the American side, and the report outlined the circumstances of how it was possible for the American ship to mistake the civil airliner as a hostile fighter jet. The report concluded with a list of 'safety recommendations' to help prevent a reoccurrence of the tragedy.[66] In many ways the report confirmed the earlier American report; indeed the Czech council representative at one point criticized the report for coming to no conclusions at all despite the evidence, and for being, in part, 'copied from the report prepared and presented by the United States.'[67]

The council debated the report over three days in December, but there was little change in view from the previous summer. The Americans largely supported the report and advocated sending it to the ANC for further study, and, in response to criticism from Iran, reminded everyone that what happened in the Gulf was an accident and one for which the Iranians were partly responsible. The representatives of Canada, France, West Germany, Japan, Italy, and Sweden all stressed the need to make sure tragic accidents like this never occurred again, but none of these nations condemned the actions of the United States. The Iranians were less forgiving, and after listing numerous American infractions in Iranian airspace, denounced the Americans, stating that the United States 'contrary to its strong positions and statements made in previous cases, in practice attaches no importance to international law and order and clearly ignores internationally accepted principles.'[68]

The Iranians again demanded a strong council resolution condemning the American actions, but they had no vote in the matter and they found support only among a few council members, including the Soviets, Cubans, and Czechs. Even the Soviet suggestion to include in a resolution an explicit condemnation of the 'use of armed force which led to the destruction' of the Iranian aircraft (with no specific reference to the United States) found few supporters (only the Cubans and Czechs) and was withdrawn without a vote.[69] In the end the ICAO Council passed a lesser 'decision' rather than a full 'resolution' on the affair in which it pronounced its regret over the incident, offered its condolences to the Government of Iran and to the families of the victims, called on the ANC to examine the results of the investigations, urged members to ratify Article 3 bis, and reaffirmed the 'fundamental principle' that states not use weapons against civil aircraft. There was no condemnation of the United States; indeed the United States was not mentioned in the 'decision.'[70]

The council returned to the issue in March 1989, but the views of the members had changed little. A council resolution was introduced by the British in which the whole affair was called a 'tragic incident' and made no comment on the actions of the United States. The Iranian observer noted that this new resolution 'lacked certain elements' that had been expected, and the Soviets, with the support of Czechoslovakia, China, and Cuba, introduced an amendment to the resolution specifically condemning the United States. This amendment was easily defeated, and the original resolution passed with only minor changes, including the replacing of the words 'deeply regrets' with 'deeply deplores' what had happened 'as a tragic consequence of events and errors in identification of the aircraft.'[71]

The Americans were satisfied if not completely pleased with the outcome, but the Iranians were unhappy. It was clear that few council members wanted to condemn the United States and, lacking strong support within the council, the Iranians were left with little more than their protests.[72] With the path through ICAO blocked, Iran took its case to the International Court of Justice where it received a little more satisfaction in its efforts to have the ICAO Council resolution declared 'erroneous.'[73] In early 1996 the Clinton administration settled a case brought by the Iranian government by paying U.S.$61.8 million to the families of the Iranian victims on the flight; in 2003 the ICJ 'concluded that the U.S Navy's actions on the Persian Gulf at the time had been unlawful.'

The treatment of the United States in the affair differed in tone and substance from that accorded the Soviet Union after the downing of KE 007. Where the Soviets had suffered universal censure, a few economic sanctions, and ICAO's condemnation, the United States came through chastened and apologetic perhaps, but otherwise without suffering any serious repercussions. The reaction of ICAO and the international community was different for several reasons. For one thing, ICAO had already done just about everything that it could do in the months following the KE 007 disaster; the new article, the amendments, the examination of procedures, and so on; there was less to be done the second time, other than to remind the members to ratify Article 3 bis. A new updated edition of the *Manual Concerning Interception of Civil Aircraft* was published in 1990. Second, the United States quickly acknowledged and apologized for what it had done, which removed much of the sting, compared to the Soviets who offered no apology or compensation and continued to justify the shooting down of KE 007 because it intruded into Soviet airspace. It was a much harder position to defend and made the Soviet Union more of a pariah in international public opinion. Third, the Soviets chose not to pursue the Iranian Airbus incident, perhaps because they did not want to jeopardize their improving relations with the United States. With less desire to castigate the United States publicly, there was less political theatre, and the Iranians found themselves more isolated in their efforts than had the South Koreans in 1983– 84. Finally, and perhaps most importantly, it made a difference that the guilty party was the United States rather than the Soviet Union. The Americans were very powerful in ICAO, with many allies and friends in the council – allies and friends who might shake their heads over the American action in the Persian Gulf but were not inclined to side with Iran, the USSR, and *their* allies in an anti-American campaign. The Americans could rely a majority to condemn the Soviet Union; they could also rely on a majority to prevent their own condemnation.

The only good that one can see coming out of this tragedy was that it may have hastened Iran's acceptance of a ceasefire in the war with Iraq; in the words of Eugene Sochor, the 'destruction of its airliner provided a face-saving excuse for seeking a political solution to the war.'[74] Conversely, it has been widely suggested, if not completely proven, that there was a link between the Iranian Airbus disaster and the bombing of the Pan American aircraft over Lockerbie, Scotland a few weeks later. It is alleged that the Lockerbie bombing was connected to or ordered by Iran in retaliation for the destruction of its airliner.[75]

Moreover, the attacks on civil aircraft did not end, although subsequent disasters did not produce the scale of confrontation as seen in the KE 007 and Iranian Airbus incidents. In November 1988, for example, the Pakistani Air Force shot down an Afghan aircraft, killing everyone on board, when it mistakenly intruded into Pakistani airspace. ICAO received no report on this incident and took no action.[76] On 24 February

1996, a Cuban jet shot down two small American Cessna aircraft in international waters, killing four people. This incident sparked another in a long series of diplomatic disputes over aviation between the two nations dating back to the hijacking incidents of the 1960s and the 1976 destruction of a Cuban passenger aircraft.[77]

The American aircraft were operated by a Miami-based, anti-Castro Cuban-American group known as 'Brothers to the Rescue,' an organization that had reportedly flown hundreds of flights in the waters around Cuba before 1996 searching for Cubans in boats and rafts fleeing the Castro regime. The Cuban authorities claimed that this group regularly violated Cuban airspace and were part of an ongoing harassment by Cuban exiles based in Miami, and that the American government stood by, giving tacit support for these illegal activities.[78] Washington took the matter to the U.N. Security Council and, in a 27 February statement, the Security Council 'strongly deplored' the incident and called on the ICAO Council to investigate the matter.[79] Cuban-American relations once again played out in the halls of ICAO, this time against an uneasy backdrop of anti-Cuban activity in Washington, with the U.S. Congress debating legislation that would penalize all third countries trading with Cuba.

The ICAO Council discussed the issue several times at the end of February and early March. Both the Cubans and Americans made reference to Article 3 bis, calling on states to refrain from attacking civil aircraft, although neither had yet ratified it. Frederico Pena, the American transportation secretary, arrived in Montreal and described the events as 'murder in the skies' because the attack had occurred in international waters against unarmed civilian aircraft, and he demanded compensation for the families of the victims and that ICAO take strong action against the Cubans. Cuba was not a council member, but sent a team of sixteen observers to the 6 March council meeting, headed by Ricardo Alarcon de Quesada, the Cuban minister of foreign affairs. De Quesada accused the Americans of numerous violations of Cuban airspace and sovereignty, and argued that what happened was not an isolated incident. In addition, he disputed the 'civilian nature' of the flights in question because the Brothers to the Rescue group never carried passengers, mail, or cargo and therefore was not a civilian airline but, rather, operated 'para-military aircraft.' Council President Kotaite noted that, nevertheless, the U.S. aircraft were registered as civilian aircraft in the United States, and the council ordered an ICAO investigation into the whole affair. In its resolution the council also 'strongly deplored' Cuba's actions, which upset the Cubans for its apparent acceptance that the aircraft were 'civilian' and because they wanted an investigation into *all* the violations of Cuban airspace by Brothers to the Rescue, not just this one incident.[80]

The ICAO investigation, headed by Secretary General Philippe Rochat, who had assumed the position in 1991, reported in June 1996, and concluded that the Cubans had not given the American aircraft proper warning and shot them down in international waters. Cuba denounced the report's conclusions, charging that the Americans had influenced the investigation; Ricardo Alarcon de Quesada depicted the ICAO report as full of 'U.S. lies and fabrications.'[81] The final council resolution, on 27 June, however, was more favourable to the Cubans; although it deplored what had happened, it did not specifically condemn the Cubans for their actions. Moreover, the resolution reminded all ICAO members (including the United States) that governments must take the appropriate action to prevent civilian aircraft from taking actions that contravened the Chicago Convention (such as flying over the territory of another member to drop leaflets or rescue fleeing individuals). Largely the work of President Kotaite, the resolution was a good example of how the council dealt with heated political issues in a principled yet balanced way, especially when there was nothing that ICAO could do about the poisoned relationship between Havana and Washington.[82]

The American government turned to the U.N. Security Council in an effort to have sanctions applied against Cuba but had equally little success, as the Security Council did little more than 'note' the ICAO resolution. This lack of action and support for the United States, one U.N. source suggested, was the consequence of international unease over recent American threats to punish those nations that continued to trade with Cuba.[83] Another suggests that the muted international response likely reflected the members' sense that Brothers to the Rescue had been provoking the Cubans for many years,[84] making the Cuban action more understandable if not excusable. In the end no one was happy, and the affair did little to improve Cuba-US relations.

What would be the final act in ICAO's Cold War began in December 1990 when Eduard Shevardnadze, just as he was resigning his position as Soviet foreign minister, apologized to South Korea for shooting down KE 007. The Soviets also published interviews with the pilot and announced that they had searched for evidence of espionage equipment but had found none.[85] More information – various transcripts, KGB reports, and so on – was revealed in subsequent months, and, in January 1993 the Russian government turned over to ICAO the cockpit voice recorder and the digital flight data recorder that it had for ten years denied having. At almost the same time, the governments of the Russian Federation, the United States, Japan, and South Korea asked ICAO to complete its investigation into the crash.[86] The ICAO Council agreed.

A new team of four ICAO staff members and two consultants was assembled under the direction of Secretary General Rochat. Over the next months they studied the CVR and DFDR tapes in Paris and traveled to the other countries involved, including the Russian Federation. The tapes were examined closely to ensure that they had not been tampered with, items of wreckage were examined for clues, meetings were held with the manufacturer of the INS that KE 007 used, and transcripts of the cockpit conversations were produced. An interim report was given to the council in March; in May the team's findings were reviewed by members of the observer states; and in June the final report was submitted to the council.[87]

The report confirmed many of the conclusions of the original 1983 investigation. No equipment malfunction was discovered, the aircraft was properly certified and maintained, and the crew was fit and qualified. The problem was human error – on both sides. The crew activated an autopilot soon after take-off from Alaska and set a heading of about 245 degrees, which was maintained until the attack occurred. The report concluded that the 'maintenance of a constant magnetic heading and the resulting track deviation was due to the crew's failure to note that the autopilot had either been left in the heading mode or had been switched to INS when the aircraft was beyond range (7.5 NM [nautical miles]) for the INS to capture the desired track.' The report concluded that the 'flight crew did not implement the proper navigation procedures to ensure the aircraft remained on its assigned track throughout the flight,' and the 'failure to detect the aircraft's deviation from its assigned track for over five hours indicated a lack of situational awareness and flight deck co-ordination on the part of the crew.' As for the Soviets, they mistook KE 007 for the American RC-135 aircraft that was in the vicinity and were worried that it might cross into international airspace. The pilot fired before 'exhaustive efforts' were made to identify the aircraft, 'although apparently some doubt remained regarding its identity.' In conclusion, the 'USSR military aircraft did not comply with the ICAO standards and recommended practices for interception of civil aircraft before attacking KE 007.'[88]

The council released the report to the public, although it did not endorse its conclusions. Instead, it passed a resolution on 14 June 1993 calling on those members that had not yet ratified Article 3 bis to do so, and urged states 'to take all necessary measures to safeguard the safety of air navigation of civil aircraft, in compliance with the relevant rules, Standards and Recommended Practices enshrined in the Chicago Convention and its Annexes.' The council also declared the investigation complete.[89]

In many ways this resolution was a reflection of the changing times; with the Cold War over and a new government in the former Soviet Union, old enemies turned into new friends. Most the venom had vanished from the rhetoric as the old animosities evolved into warmer relations. There was not much point in pursuing the matter further, even if outside ICAO there were many members of the victims' families who continued to suffer great loss, and others who still had questions about KE 007 and found the ICAO report incomplete and unsatisfactory.[90] But the investigation and report effectively closed the book on the KE 007 incident, at least as far as ICAO was concerned, and can be seen as a symbolic ending of ICAO's Cold War too.

In the process, however, what also had vanished was any pretense that ICAO was simply a technical organization outside the realm of international politics. The rise of international terrorism, armed attacks and sabotage, and the interception of civil aircraft brought the outside world into the halls of ICAO and there was no way to escape it. ICAO provided an ideal international stage where antagonists could face each other and international aviation disputes could unfold through political debates, investigative teams and reports, and public condemnations. ICAO also had a large group of talented individuals – from aviation specialists and technicians to leaders such as Assad Kotaite and others – who provided the skills, knowledge, and diplomacy necessary for ICAO to function successfully in the international arena while also maintaining focus on its prime goal of enhancing aviation safety. The modern era had transformed ICAO and brought it an unprecedented degree of public attention in the latter part of the twentieth century. The Cold War may have faded away, but this transformation for ICAO was permanent.

14

The Politics of Aviation Security

In dealing with international terrorism, we must – and do – constantly evaluate the nature of the threat, which changes markedly over time. As we take steps to reduce our vulnerability to terrorist attack, terrorists continue to try to find new 'weak links' in the security chain which they can exploit. There are no quick fixes in this business.'[1]

Regardless of the crises sparked by armed attacks against civil aviation and the changes in location, personnel, and status, the safety and security of international civil aviation remained the primary function of the International Civil Aviation Organization. The 1960s and 1970s witnessed a flurry of activity, including the Tokyo, Hague, and Montreal conventions, the development of a new Annex 17 and *Security Manual*, the creation of the Committee on Unlawful Interference, and a host of other committees, conferences, and resolutions, as ICAO acted in conjunction with the United Nations, individual states, and regional groups such as the G7 (later G8).[2] In some ways it appeared that the efforts were successful in that the number of hijackings decreased through the late 1970s and into the 1980s (although the number of fatalities continued to rise). For many observers the key now was to ensure that ICAO members implemented and complied with the standards and ratified the conventions.[3] In the 1980s and 1990s, however, that goal seemed to become increasingly difficult to achieve and the organization found itself responding and reacting to outside events.

In the 1980s the international community and, in particular, the United Nations responded to the challenge of international terrorism in a somewhat uneven way. The United Nations played a central role directing a broad range of international activities, and it fostered and promoted international cooperation in the war against international terrorism. International concern over the possibility of terrorists acquiring and using chemical, nuclear, or other weapons of mass destruction was also on the rise, and the United Nations and its specialized agencies took a number of steps to control these new threats. International conventions and protocols were negotiated that dealt with many different issues such as the protection of nuclear material (1980), the taking of hostages (1979), the protection of fixed ocean platforms (1988), and the suppression of unlawful acts against maritime navigation (1988). At the same time, however, the United Nations often found itself relegated to the sidelines in the more direct state counter-terrorist activities, as nations, especially the United States, took action outside the United Nations. Moreover, eradicating terrorism was always difficult if not ultimately impossible, and the United Nations lacked the financial and material means to make a major contribution on the ground compared to many of its members. The United Nations also remained divided over how best to respond to international terrorism, or even how to define it, leading one observer to refer to the United Nations as a 'reluctant belligerent' in the war on terror and to note its 'persistent ambivalence about tackling terrorism.'[4]

For the International Civil Aviation Organizaiton it was almost impossible to be ambivalent about aviation terrorism. Sabotage, hijacking, and other attacks on civil aviation were common methods of international terrorists in the 1980s, and these attacks struck at the very heart of ICAO's objectives. Such a challenge could not be ignored, however much its members would have liked it to go away. ICAO was fortunate in that aviation safety was a goal that was shared by all members and, as a result, ICAO was spared many of the debates witnessed by the U.N. General Assembly over how to define and respond to terrorism. Without the same degree of political division and animosity within the organization, and thanks to its reliance on consensus building, ICAO was well suited to negotiate international instruments to enhance aviation safety. International cooperation was a necessary step in the elimination of international aviation terrorism, and ICAO provided the machinery for that cooperation.

International efforts to combat hijacking and aviation terrorism in general continued through the 1980s and into the 1990s, but the problem only worsened, as the world experienced a series of increasingly deadly hijackings and bombings, culminating in one of the bloodiest periods in aviation history between 1985 and 1988. There also was a troubling difference in these attacks; the traditional hijackings of the 1970s had given way to devastating acts of sabotage against airports and aircraft that led to the death of hundreds of individuals. In the aftermath of several catastrophic aircraft bombings the issues of arrest, extradition, and punishment remained important but less central, and the members of ICAO increasingly shifted their focus to matters of prevention and detection. This shift was important because it brought ICAO into a more direct involvement in the fight against terrorism, broadening its role from the development of international conventions and security standards into overseeing and ensuring their acceptance and implementation in the international community.

The 1980s were a dreadful decade for aviation security, with a series of catastrophic attacks and bombings, and ICAO and the rest of the international community needed constantly to renew their response. As usual there was a variety of motives behind the series of attacks and bombings, but the deadliest ones arose from the actions of Middle Eastern and Sikh terrorists and their supporters. In early June 1985 a bomb exploded in the Frankfurt airport, killing three, and a TWA aircraft was hijacked on a flight from Athens to Rome. On 23 June, an Air India B-747 en route from Montreal to New Delhi, via London, was blown up off the coast of Ireland killing 329, mostly Canadian citizens, in what was then the worst act of aviation terrorism in history. On the same day, another bomb exploded in the luggage removed from a Canadian Pacific Airlines flight at Tokyo's Narita Airport. Two luggage handlers were killed, but had the bomb detonated a short while before the flight landed or after, when the luggage was to be transferred to an Air India aircraft, it might have led to the death of hundreds more. In September, a bomb exploded at Kimpo Airport in Seoul, killing five airport workers. On 23 November 1985, Palestinian terrorists hijacked an Egyptair aircraft en route from Athens to Cairo, and the subsequent attack on the hijacked aircraft by Egyptian forces ended with the death of fifty-seven passengers. On 25 November, gunfire erupted on an Iraq Air flight between Baghdad and Amman leading to the crash landing of the aircraft and the death of sixty-five people. Then, on 27 December 1985, terrorists from the same Palestinian organization involved in the Egyptair attack attacked the El Al check-ins at the international airports in Rome and Vienna, killing nineteen people.[5]

In December 1985, the United Nations – both the General Assembly and the Security Council – passed resolutions condemning the recent violence, called on ICAO to continue its efforts to combat aviation terrorism, and asked all states that had not yet done so to ratify the three air conventions.[6] In the summer of 1986, at the Tokyo economic summit of the G8, the leaders reaffirmed their commitment to the 1978 Bonn Declaration to apply sanctions against states that refused to extradite hijackers (see Chapter 11).[7] The International Air Transport Association, the International Federation of Airline Pilots' Association, and other aviation organizations responded in their own ways to upgrade airport and airline security levels.[8] Individual states also introduced their own measures to combat terrorism at home. In the United States, for example, President Reagan established a Task Force on Combating Terrorism under the direction of Vice President Bush and pursued several measures to protect American airports and airlines. One year earlier the Anti-Terrorist Assistance Program was created to train American and foreign students in airport security and police management.[9]

ICAO responded in its traditional legal and technical ways: through the revision of its annexes and manuals and the establishment of international air law through the negotiation of protocols and conventions. On 14 June 1985 the ICAO Council passed a resolution calling on all members to ratify the security conventions and to 'take more effective preventive measures.' That same month in the council, the Canadians introduced the idea of 'model clause' to be inserted into bilateral air agreements that would commit the parties to ICAO's security arrangements. It was an idea that the Canadians had unsuccessfully introduced in the early 1970s, but by 1985 times had changed. Indeed, it was now not uncommon to include some security elements in bilateral agreements; for example, the Anglo-American Bermuda II Agreement (see Chapter 15) contained several specific security clauses that others were beginning to copy. As a result, the reception of the Canadian idea was much more positive and the council agreed to pursue the matter. By June 1986, a model clause was approved and the council urged all members to insert the clause in their bilateral agreements.[10] The clause essentially asked the parties to act in conformity with the annexes and the Tokyo, Hague, and Montreal conventions and to do what they could to inspect and protect each others' passengers and aircraft while in their territory. The traditional opposition of many members to sanctions in case of non-compliance remained, and the model clause contained no reference to sanctions. The model clause, or variations of it, began to appear in bilateral agreements and was widely accepted in subsequent years. In 1989, the council formulated a broader 'model agreement' for bilateral negotiations that contained similar security provisions.[11]

In the wake of the Air India bombing, several ministers of transport and aviation, including U.S. Secretary of Transportation Elizabeth Dole, and Admiral Donald Engen, the U.S. Federal Aviation Agency administrator, attended the 27 June 1985 ICAO Council meeting to discuss ICAO's response to the new spate of terrorist activities. The tone of the visitors was sombre, but they were united in their calls for action from ICAO, primarily to review its procedures, annexes, and manuals, and for the contracting states to ratify the existing conventions, to improve airport security, and to increase the screening of baggage. Secretary Dole emphasized that President Reagan was determined to act unilaterally to enhance American security precautions at home (more air marshals in the sky, more training, total baggage reconciliation, etc.), and that the American government was considering the suspension of air services from foreign states that failed either to implement adequate airport security or to ratify ICAO's security conventions. She also called on ICAO to 'make stronger aviation security procedures a standard to be observed exactingly throughout the world,' again through better training and the review of existing security procedures. In addition, she called on ICAO to focus much greater attention on how its standards and procedures were being applied by the contracting states. Dole recommended the direct inspection and certification of security at international airports. 'We must send international terrorists and their supporters a clear message that we will never appease them,' she concluded. 'We must, in short, prevail, or else our children will inherit a world of infernal barbarism.'[12]

The proposal for ICAO inspections of airport security was a little unusual because it was a call for an oversight role that ICAO did not usually perform. The council would ultimately embrace the idea, but only after further terrorist acts. In the meantime, it endorsed a 'Plan of Action' that called on the secretary general to review ICAO's Standards and Recommended Practices and procedures with a view to enhanced security and training.[13] In addition, the council created an Aviation Security Panel consisting of aviation security experts to report to the Committee on Unlawful Interference. This AVSEC Panel was given the job of revising Annex 17 in an effort to tighten security standards. A number of amendments to Annex 17 were introduced, the most important dealing with the rules for baggage reconciliation. The problem of unaccompanied luggage on board aircraft was considered a major risk factor; efforts had been made in the past in ICAO and among individual members to manage the issue, but progress was slow. Everyone agreed that unaccompanied luggage posed a risk, but there was considerable division on how best to deal with the problem (complete prohibition, rescreening, etc.) and even whether to make baggage reconciliation a standard or keep it as a recommendation. After months of debate, the fourth edition of Annex 17 (October 1989) required operators to remove all unaccompanied luggage unless it was subjected to other, additional security measures.[14]

Another revision to the annex required states to provide navigational aids and air traffic services to hijacked aircraft and to permit them to land in their territory if considered necessary in the situation. Rodney Willis, a former director of security for IATA and a member of the AVSEC Panel, later wrote of IATA's long desire – and ICAO's resistance – to having hijacked aircraft recognized as 'aircraft in distress,' which would oblige states to permit them to land. It was widely agreed that the best and safest place for a hijacked aircraft was on the ground, but some states saw it as an infringement on members' sovereignty and others were less enthusiastic about the possibility of being involved in a hijacking incident. This revision, in the fourth edition of Annex 17, did not contain the words 'aircraft in distress' but, according to Willis, that was its intent.[15]

Another particular concern was the increasing number of deadly attacks at airports. The focus of the Tokyo, Hague, and Montreal conventions was aircraft rather than airports, which was not surprising given that they dealt with questions of jurisdiction and extradition that were not really an issue with respect to airports. There was no question that airports were under the jurisdiction of the states where they were located and that local laws applied, and there was even some question whether an airport attack fell within the purview of *international* aviation. Following the December 1985 attacks at the Rome and Vienna airports, however, much of this concern evaporated, and there were growing calls for ICAO to take action either through a new convention or by broadening the existing ones to include attacks against airports, at least those that served international civil aviation. At the Twenty-Sixty ICAO Assembly in the early fall of 1986, the Canadian delegation submitted a paper to the Executive Committee (on behalf of its own government and the governments of Austria, the Netherlands, New Zealand, and Italy) calling for action on this matter. The result was Resolution A26-4, which turned over to the Legal Committee the responsibility for preparing a draft of a new legal instrument to deal with violence at airports.[16]

The ICAO Council endorsed the proposal and set in motion the usual process of discussion and study through a subcommittee to the Legal Committee to the council and the member states and back again. In this case however, things unfolded rapidly. The Legal Committee met in

Montreal in April–May 1987 and drafted what it decided was best suited as a protocol to the 1971 Montreal Convention.[17] After weeks of further consultation, in February 1988 a full international air law conference was staged in Montreal where the new instrument was signed, the Protocol for the Suppression of Unlawful Acts of Violence at Airports Serving International Civil Aviation. The new protocol was supplementary to the Montreal Convention [18]

The new protocol amended the Montreal Convention by expanding the scope of the criminal offence to include 'an act of violence against a person at an airport serving international civil aviation which causes or is likely to cause serious injury or death.' In addition, an offender was anyone who 'destroys or seriously damages the facilities of an airport serving international civil aviation or aircraft not in service located thereon or disrupts the services of the airport.'[19] The crimes included in the protocol were already offences in the member states, but now the extradition rules of the Montreal Convention came into play. And, because it was attached to the Montreal Convention, states could not ratify the protocol unless they also ratified the Montreal Convention. Nevertheless, the protocol was widely accepted and came into force on 6 August 1989.

The Montreal Protocol filled a gap in aviation security but did little to assuage the growing concern over the use of explosives to destroy aircraft in flight. The 1985 Air India disaster and the bombing at the Tokyo airport renewed concern over the safety of baggage and the need to reconcile all passengers with their luggage. In April 1986 hundreds of travelers at Heathrow in London narrowly escaped death when a bomb was discovered concealed in the luggage of an innocent passenger; in May a bomb intended for an Air India aircraft was discovered at New York's JFK Airport. In November 1987, a South Korean airliner was blown up en route from Abu Dhabi to Seoul, with 115 people on board, and the Koreans accused the North Koreans of complicity in the attack. The next year, on 21 December 1988, Pan Am Flight 103 was destroyed over Lockerbie, Scotland, killing all 259 passengers and crew on board and eleven more people on the ground. The bomb was concealed in a portable radio/cassette player and had been transferred from another aircraft after its arrival from Frankfurt. It was hidden in unaccompanied luggage and exploded in the baggage hold of the Pan Am aircraft.

The Lockerbie tragedy sparked outrage around the world, seriously damaged U.S.-Libyan relations, and set in motion a series of investigations and legal activity in the United States and Great Britain. In August, President Bush established the President's Commission on Aviation

Security and Terrorism to review U.S. aviation security policy; it ultimately produced a very critical report and made a series of recommendations, including possible military strikes against 'terrorist enclaves in the nations that harbor them'[20] One recent source argues that President Bush resisted establishing the commission and only acquiesced under pressure from the victims' families because he feared exposure of 'secret intelligence records that would have revealed US complicity with Iran since 1980.'[21] But most of the fingers were pointed at Libya, and the next decade saw a series of U.N. sanctions introduced against Libya as part of a long struggle to bring the perpetrators to justice. This struggle involved at different times the ICAO Council, the U.N. Security Council, and the International Court of Justice and revealed the continuing difficulties involved in the extradition of suspected terrorists, even among ICAO members.[22]

The international frustration over the failure to prevent horrible terrorist acts like Lockerbie spilled over into the halls of ICAO. It was pointed out that the crises of the late 1980s revealed that many of ICAO's standards were not being applied at the same level around the world, and that many members had fallen behind or found them too expensive to implement. Other critics warned of the dangers of complacency and the tendency of members – in periods of relative calm – to relax security vigilance.[23] What good was it to devise conventions if members failed to ratify them or, like Libya, failed to respect them? What good was it to revise the annexes and to publish new editions of the manuals if the members failed to implement the standards and recommendations? This was especially important with respect to Annex 17 because many members were understandably reluctant to publicize their failure to implement the standards, fearing that this information would only give more ammunition to potential terrorists if they knew which states had complied with which parts of the standards and which had not.

In January 1989 the American and British governments requested a special session of the council to discuss what could be done to heighten aviation security standards. The session was scheduled for 15–16 February and was held at the ministerial level, which guaranteed the presence of greater media coverage if somewhat less aviation expertise. A few days in advance, the British and American governments announced their proposals for the meeting of the ICAO Council, and both governments called for a complete review of baggage screening procedures and for an exploration of means for detecting plastic explosives. Paul Bremer, President Bush's ambassador-at-large for counterterrorism, told a Congressional Committee that American priorities included: '(a) detection of sabotage devices, especially explosives; (b) comprehensive screening of checked baggage; (c) comprehensive screening of passengers and hand baggage; (d) controlling access to aircraft by ground personnel, and (e) establishing a new ICAO service available to members at their request to assess security at individual airports, and to recommend improvements as necessary.'[24]

The two-day council session opened on 15 February 1989, with ministers from more than a dozen states in attendance. Draft resolutions were introduced and various plans were discussed, with the most forceful coming from the American and British representatives, while those from less-developed states tended to be more cautious, raising concerns about the financial burdens of increased security actions.[25] A compromise of sorts was reached with an agreement on a U.K.-U.S. eight-point plan of action. These new points included taking action to improve baggage screening at check-in and during transfers; 100 per cent reliable baggage reconciliation; improved screening for cargo and mail; better control of access to aircraft, ramps, and other sensitive locations at airports, action to ensure security regarding the transport of electronic items; and action to find a way to make it possible to detect plastic explosives.[26]

The ICAO Council had already taken some steps on its own. A few weeks earlier, in response to a report from the Committee on Unlawful Interference, the council initiated an investigation into ways of detecting plastic explosives. The one used in the Lockerbie tragedy, and suspected in others, was Semtex, manufactured in Czechoslovakia. Plastic explosives were virtually undetectable by conventional means such as X-ray machines or trained dogs, and one proposal was to introduce a chemical additive into the production of these explosives that would enable their detection at airport screenings. It needed much study and investigation, but, as in the case of the Montreal Protocol signed the previous year, when the members of ICAO were motivated things could move very quickly. There was a bit of a difference this time in that ICAO's previous activities in this regard were exclusively focused on aviation matters whereas this new general convention on plastic explosives would apply to the broader international community. There was some question whether ICAO was the proper vehicle to develop such a legal instrument, but any doubts about the legitimacy of ICAO's actions vanished in June when the U.N. Security Council passed Resolution 635 encouraging ICAO to 'intensify its work' in this direction.[27]

There were both legal and technical problems that needed to be addressed. In January, the council established the Ad Hoc Group of Specialists on the Detection of Explosives to examine the technical dimensions of the problem. The group faced several complex technical questions because there were many different possible detection agents and few standards to follow. As one participant in the group later wrote, there was 'no unique method of testing which is optimal for all explosive detector systems; no universal definition of a suitcase or its contents; no universal sampling method; and no "standard" explosive device – the list keeps growing.'[28] Finding the best – and most cost effective – method and one that could be translated into clear legal language was extremely tricky. After weeks of work the group submitted a report and the council decided to move ahead. At ICAO's Twenty-Seventh Assembly in September– October, in response to a joint British-Czechoslovakian proposal, a resolution was passed calling on the Legal Committee to draft a new international convention on the marking of plastic explosives.

The resolution initiated the usual process of air law development from the selection of a rapporteur to the subcommittee (including observers from the United Nations, IATA, IFALPA, the International Maritime Organization, and the International Criminal Police Organization[29]) to the Legal Committee to Air Law conference. The council called an international air law conference for February 1991 to settle on a final text, and on 1 March 1991 the Convention on the Marking of Plastic Explosives for the Purpose of Detection was signed. U.N Secretary General Javier Pérez de Cuéllar, who attended part of the conference, called it a 'substantial development of international law relating to the combat against internationalism terrorism.'[30] Others agreed, and the convention came into force in 1998 after receiving the necessary ratifications, including the five required from producer states.

Support for a new convention was almost universal, but some differences in opinion appeared, for example, between the states that were major manufacturers of plastic explosives and maintained stockpiles of them for military and industrial use and the states that neither manufactured nor stockpiled them. The latter tended to favour more dramatic action, often calling for the immediate destruction of existing stockpiles and, in some cases, for widening the convention to include other forms of explosives. The former were less enthusiastic; they supported limiting the convention to plastic explosives and suggested strict controls on existing supplies and a more gradual elimination of existing stockpiles.

An even more pronounced division appeared, as in the past, between the developed and the developing nations. All these actions to combat terrorism were welcome but expensive, several members noted. As the

Ethiopian delegate explained, 'the cost of contending with increasingly sophisticated terrorist acts was very high, and the richer nations of the industrialized world should be prepared to offer greater financial and technical assistance to less fortunate States that needed help in order to implement agreed aviation security standards.' Moreover, he continued, 'unrelenting efforts were necessary to root out the sources of terrorism, including massive educational projects to sensitize the public to the total immorality of such acts.' The Cubans, who had yet to ratify the Tokyo, Hague, or Montreal conventions, supported the initiative but were pessimistic that it would solve the problem; the Cuban delegate stated that 'such crimes would go on and people would continue to die if technology for marking of explosives became a business that was out of reach for the poorest States.'[31]

The Convention on the Marking of Plastic Explosives for the Purpose of Detection consisted of two parts, the final text and an attached Technical Annex. The text was explicit: all parties agreed to prohibit the manufacturing and transport of unmarked plastic explosives (with an exception for military or police functions). In addition, the necessary steps were to be taken to destroy or mark all existing stockpiles not used for military or police functions within three years; all stockpiles were to be destroyed or marked within fifteen years. The Technical Annex contained the definitions of explosives and the various acceptable detection agents that could be added to the manufacture of plastic explosives. In recognition that explosives technology was always changing, the convention called for the establishment of an International Explosives Technical Commission to evaluate technical changes and to make recommendations to the ICAO Council to amend the Technical Annex. Including the definitions in an annex rather than in the official text made it easier to amend the convention; in this case the council had the power to make the amendments to the annex unless five or more members gave written notification of their opposition within ninety days. Finally, the Convention on the Marking of Plastic Explosives for the Purpose of Detection referred only vaguely to technical assistance, noting that the council would take 'appropriate measures' to provide help, including 'the provision of technical assistance and measures for the exchange of information relating to technical developments in the marking and detection of explosives.'[32]

Another legal instrument that filled a gap in international air law was a valuable tool against air terrorism, but it could not solve the problem of the implementation of ICAO's security standards by its members. The

International Civil Aviation Organization could not force its members to ratify the conventions or to implement its standards; it could urge and encourage – even plead – but it had only limited ability to force any member to do something which it chose not to do. 'States and only States can take the appropriate actions to safeguard aviation security,' Council President Kotaite noted. 'The Organization itself does not possess any implementation powers.'[33] Any kind of action that ICAO took regarding the implementation of standards would run the risk of contravening the basic principle of the Chicago Convention – each member's sovereignty over its airspace.

There was, however, a large – and growing – gap between the states that maintained ICAO's security standards and those that either did not or were falling behind in their implementation. The costs involved in upgrading airport security to full compliance with ICAO standards were great. Providing personnel and the cost of training and skills mainten-ance was just the beginning; the advent of new expensive screening ma-chines created an impossible financial burden for many states. For example, in 1989 the delegates at the Twenty-Seventh ICAO Assembly were invited to a demonstration of a new *thermal neutron analysis* system for detecting explosives: the system worked well, but the price tag for each unit was $750,000.[34] At the same time, funding through technical assistance continued to fall and, even with the support of individual members, there was never enough money.

At the February 1989 ICAO Council meeting, following the Lockerbie disaster, the Anglo-American resolution that was adopted called for the enhancement of ICAO's role in security, taking it beyond the develop-ment of air law and standards into an oversight position to ensure the implementation of security standards. The Americans had recommended such an action in 1985 and, together with the British, reintroduced the idea in 1989 and found a more receptive audience. 'Our efforts to pro-vide security to civil aviation have fallen behind the ruthlessness, callous-ness and ingenuity of those who mistakenly and malevolently believe that by murdering innocent air travelers that may further their cause,' explained the British representative. 'I believe we must now apply our-selves with resourcefulness and determination to a systematic improve-ment of security standards in every international airport where terrorists may operate. I believe that Annex 17 is an admirable document, but I suggest that in several important matters it does not go far enough.' The time was right, he concluded, for a much greater and more direct role for ICAO in the training of personnel and 'for the Organization to play a more active part in helping States to ensure the implementation of those Standards and Recommended Practices which it has laid down in Annex 17.'[35]

With the acceptance of this Anglo-American resolution the council – and ICAO as a whole – began a new course of direct involvement in the implementation of its security procedures. At its July 1989 meetings, the council called on members to increase their financial and technical assistance for the members to improve their aviation security programs. By the following year a new program had emerged, the awkwardly named 'Mechanism for financial, technical and material assistance to States with regard to aviation security and other assistance programmes.' The goal was to help members implement and maintain the security standards and procedures found in Annex 17, by giving advice and assistance to members, by helping members establish their own aviation security program, by supporting regional workshops and seminars, by creating a comprehensive training program for use by the members, and by conducting confidential surveys and evaluations of members to assess the implementation of the ICAO standards. The program was to be financed by contributions from members, in conjunction with the United Nations Development Programme and other international aviation organizations, at least at first, and through the loan of experts to help undertake the assessments and participate in the training programs (in 1989, the UNDP earmarked about $45 million of a total budget of $800 million for personnel training, equipment, etc. for airports). It was also to be strictly voluntary, with no member being obliged to participate.[36]

The program was launched immediately, with financial contributions from Australia, Belgium, Canada, Finland, France, Germany, India, Italy, Japan, Netherlands, the Soviet Union, Saudi Arabia, Spain, Switzerland, Turkey, the United Kingdom, and the United States, and aviation experts were provided by, among others, the member states, IATA, ACI, and ICAO's Aviation Security Branch. By the end of 1990 more than sixty requests for assistance had been received, and AVSEC had undertaken evaluations at sixteen airports. Many training fellowships were also awarded, and two-week seminars were staged in Buenos Aires and Nairobi. By 1994 over a hundred states had requested assistance and the provision of training aids, security equipment, workshops, and training courses. ICAO had provided security seminars and technical assistance in the past, but not to this extent in aviation security. Security development workshops were held in Cairo, Mexico City,

Montevideo, and elsewhere, and, in addition, regional and subregional AVSEC aviation security training facilities were established at Quito, Nairobi, and Penang. By 1997 seven more training facilities had been set up in Amman, Brussels, Casablanca, Dakar, Kyiv, Moscow, and Port-of-Spain. The Aviation Security Branch also produced a series of standardized training packages containing training course material necessary to address security problems at international airports.[37]

The most notable and far-reaching element of the program was the voluntary and confidential evaluations of members' aviation security policies undertaken by ICAO personnel. ICAO was moving into an area that had previously been left to the members themselves – overseeing the implementation of its standards and procedures. There was some concern that such actions might lead to duplication of work undertaken by the members, but as I.G. Gilchrist of ICAO's Aviation Security Branch wrote, 'it rapidly became apparent that the depth and scope of the ICAO evaluations went beyond any inspection, assessment or evaluation that had gone before. In addition, they focused not just on the visible symptoms of possible problems as seen at international airports, but delved into the root causes of the problems by examining the nature and capability of States to organize and coordinate a successful aviation security policy.'[38]

It was a slow process, and the evaluations more often than not revealed that many members had not maintained the ICAO standards. 'Unhappily,' one security expert wrote, '*effective* security exists in only a minority of countries around the world. It is frequently missing even from those states which comprise ICAO's governing council.'[39] In 1994 it was reported that very few members had established a national civil aviation security program;[40] in 1999, after 110 evaluations, it was reported that not one state had fully complied with Annex 17.[41] Overseeing the implementation of its security standards was a new endeavour for ICAO, but it quickly became apparent that it would not be a temporary or short-term one. Over the next decade, ICAO's oversight role would evolve as one of its prime functions in the field of international aviation security.

The new conventions and protocols and all the work undertaken in conjunction with other organizations and states seemed to be having some effect, as the number of acts of unlawful interference – attempted and actual – declined throughout the decade. In the ten years from 1991 to 2000 there were only three reported acts of sabotage and the number of people killed dropped significantly, especially when compared to the late 1980s. In 1985, 1988, and 1989 the number of people killed through unlawful interference was, respectively, 473, 300, and 278; in 1991 the number dropped to zero; in the years 1997 and 1999 only four people were killed in each year. There were a few exceptions, of course (134 were killed in 1996), but by the end of the 1990s it looked as if aviation terrorism was on the wane.[42]

At the same time, however, the 1990s witnessed a general increase in terrorist acts outside the world of international civil aviation, from the 1993 bombing at the World Trade Center in New York and the poison gas attack in the Tokyo subway in 1995, to the variety of terrorist attacks on U.S. military bases and embassies in the Middle East and Africa later in the decade, culminating in the attack on the USS *Cole* off the coast of Yemen in 2000.[43] Clearly terrorism remained a serious problem for the international community, and its escalation forced the United Nations and its specialized agencies to respond.

In 1994, during the U.N.'s fiftieth anniversary celebrations, the General Assembly issued its Declaration on Measures to Eliminate International Terrorism in an effort to reaffirm its commitment to fighting terrorism. Three years later, at the end of 1997, the U.N. General Assembly adopted the International Convention for the Suppression of Terrorist Bombings and opened it for signature at the start of 1998. This new convention addressed the issue of terrorist bombings in public places and extended and complemented the existing international legal arrangements. In words similar to the ICAO conventions, the new U.N. convention set out state responsibilities regarding extradition, prosecution, and jurisdiction for any terrorist captured following the bombing of a public place. The new convention was at once broader and narrower in focus than the ICAO conventions in that it on the one hand applied not only to aircraft and airports but to all public places, while on the other it was focused exclusively on the illegal use of explosive devices rather than on the use of other weapons – like guns and knives – that were included in the ICAO conventions.[44]

Perhaps the most striking divergence between them was the inclusion of a far more political clause – not found in the ICAO conventions – stating that states are to enact legislation, if necessary, to 'ensure' that the acts covered by the convention 'where they are intended or calculated to provoke a state of terror in the general public or in a group of persons or particular persons, are under no circumstances justifiable by considerations of a political, philosophical, ideological, racial, ethnic, religious or other similar nature and are punished by penalties consistent with their grave nature.' This clause reflected the emergence of a broader consensus on the criminal nature of international terrorism, but the U.N. convention remained un-ratified at the end of the twentieth century. In addition, the appearance of an international consensus on definitions was only a small step towards the elimination of international terrorism, and one that was unlikely to stop terrorists determined to use violence in the pursuit of their own causes. And, for international aviation, looking ahead at the start of the new century, there was no time for complacency.

15

Back to the Future:
The Return of Multilateralism

Throughout the modern era the postwar system of bilateral agreements remained the cornerstone of international commercial aviation even though, in many ways, the international economic environment had changed significantly. The decline and disappearance of the old colonial empires removed all questions concerning the negotiation of landing rights in colonial possessions. In the place of these empires emerged many new states and new national airlines and more international traffic (and airline capacity). In addition, the link between military and civil aviation had never completely disappeared, but by the 1970s it was less direct and immediate than it had been in the pre-war era and through the 1940s and 1950s. Also, the advance of technology, with the introduction of jet engines and aircraft with longer operating ranges, had reduced the need for intermediate stops on most international routes; with the rise of longer more-direct flights came a corresponding drop in the need for the negotiation of fifth freedom rights for international air carriers.

The desire for reciprocity in bilateral agreements, however, remained strong. Among the new states in the developing world the airlines were largely state-owned, and their fleets tended to be older than in the developed world; these countries also tended to lack aviation facilities and trained personnel at home and they remained dependent on the developed states for economic aid, technology, and other assistance.[1] The one thing they all maintained was their sovereignty, and their willingness to grant foreigners what they considered unfair access to their markets remained as low as it had always been.

Equally constant was the fact that no matter how eager international airlines were to acquire new traffic rights through bilateral agreements, the power to grant these rights remained in the hands of national governments. 'Traffic rights,' wrote one aviation analyst, 'essential as they may be to airlines, do not "belong" to them: they *"belong" primarily to States.*'[2] The involvement of states ensured a couple of things: one, that matters of prestige, sovereignty, politics, and other national interests would continue to influence international civil aviation, and two, that ICAO inevitably would be drawn into the issue because it was the international expression of the states' involvement in commercial aviation.

The negotiation of a multilateral aviation agreement under the auspices of the International Civil Aviation Organization had never been achieved, but a multilateral regulatory system of sorts had evolved, based on the rules laid down by ICAO and the Chicago Convention, the fare setting mechanism of the International Air Transport Association, and the existence of hundreds of bilateral air agreements. It was a complex and sometimes uncomfortable arrangement, and it had been criticized at various times by its participants, especially the United States (in the 1960s, e.g., several attacks were launched at IATA as a kind of un-American cartel[3]). By the 1970s the old regulatory system was showing signs of age, and the problems that dealt with the economic issues of international air transport returned to ICAO's agenda. What were called, in the 1940s, the 'missing chapters' of the Chicago Convention reappeared under the guise of deregulation and 'open skies' in the 1970s, 1980s, and 1990s and brought ICAO back into the heart of the debate over liberalization and the negotiation of a multilateral agreement for international civil aviation.

In many ways the development of international civil aviation in the 1970s and 1980s was encouraging: the safety of air travel was improving with every year and the numbers proved that, despite lingering concerns in the public mind about flying, air travel was the safest form of transportation in the world. Once the Soviet Union became a member of ICAO, two members dominated air traffic, with the United States and USSR being responsible for 52 per cent of the total volume of air traffic produced by ICAO members in 1977 (the number is explained by the large amount of domestic traffic in these two countries). Looking at international air traffic, the numbers were a little different, with the United States being responsible for 17 per cent of the total international traffic volume and the United Kingdom second, with 9 per cent. And the trend was moving away from the West to the developing world. From 1970 to 1977 the North American share of international traffic fell from 31.3 per cent to 20.8 per cent, whereas the Asia and Pacific region jumped from 11.2 per cent to almost 20 per cent, and in the Middle East, its share rose from 3.4 per cent to 5.7 per cent. In 1980, for the first time the number of foreigners traveling by air to and from the United States exceeded the number of American citizens doing so.[4]

While the fatality rate was dropping, the route and passenger mileage was rising steadily into the 1970s and, although it leveled off in the latter part of the decade, it rose even more dramatically in the 1980s.[5] New airlines and routes appeared; almost all states had international air services. The Chinese government, perhaps in recognition of its growing involvement in international affairs, initiated several international services in the mid-1970s to regional destinations such as Japan and elsewhere, including Pakistan and Europe. In 1977 British Airways and Air France inaugurated their supersonic Concorde services to New York (from London and Paris); a few weeks earlier, the Soviet Union introduced its supersonic TU-144 on a domestic service within the USSR. That same year, Gabon introduced a subsonic service to Paris via Rome and Geneva; Air Mauritius began a weekly Mauritius-London service. Air Jamaica introduced a Kingston-Frankfurt service; Lufthansa opened a direct service from Frankfurt to Los Angeles. The expansion in Asia and the Pacific was even greater, with multiple services connecting the major cities, and the region saw the growth of several airlines, including China Airways in Taiwan and Singapore Airlines.[6]

In other areas the numbers were less encouraging. The new air services and airlines meant more sovereign states and businesses wanting a piece of the aviation pie, and the result was more international competition for scheduled and charter flights. The rapid escalation of fuel prices beginning in 1973 sent shock waves through the industrialized world, and the ramifications for international aviation were profound. The energy crisis affected all aspects of business and produced rising operating costs for airlines. At the same time, many airlines had invested heavily in expensive jumbo jets and other new equipment. The big new aircraft combined with the general slump in the world's economy to create an excess of capacity in the world's airlines.

It was the beginning of an era of retrenchment in the aviation world, with the curtailment of many air services and the restructuring of the industry. In 1980, for example, Aer Lingus gave up its Dublin to Chicago service; Avianca suspended its service from Bogotá to London and Zurich; and SAS dropped its Copenhagen-Montreal service. Earlier, in the United States, several airlines became involved in route exchanges to reduce competition. In 1973, TWA gave up its route to East Africa; in return Pan Am suspended its service to Dublin, eliminating the competition from both these routes. In 1975, further arrangements were made, with TWA removing itself from Asia while Pan Am gave up many of its European destinations.[7] In 1974, for the first time in many years, the number of passengers on the North Atlantic scheduled air services fell.[8] In 1975, one aviation expert observed, there were enough empty seats on the North Atlantic route to fill 15,000 Boeing 747 round trips.[9]

By 1977 Council President Kotaite was speaking of the 'very serious problems' facing the airline industry.[10] In the view of IATA's Director General Knut Hammarskjöld, it was a crisis built from a number of factors, including oil shocks, over-capacity, and 'the multiplication of sovereign states.'[11] In September 1976 he elaborated, in a speech to the U.S. National Aviation Club in Washington. 'For a number of years the world air transport system has been in a mess,' he said, 'Governments have been struggling with a thirty year old regulatory framework. The leading aviation nations have had policy disagreements between them and within themselves. The consumer has become suspicious of the airlines. There is disenchantment with the fare structure and confusion with the scheduled and charter product options. In recent years most airlines have stopped making profits; manufacturers' equipment orders are drying up. And the bankers and financing institutions have lost confidence in the industry.'[12] Whatever the cause of the crisis, however, it served to bring ICAO back into the discussion of the economic regulation of international aviation.

On 22 June 1976 the British government denounced the 1946 Bermuda Agreement, which had governed bilateral aviation relations between the United Kingdom and the United States for thirty years. The British argued that the existing arrangements were unfair and heavily weighted in favour of the United States and that the American carriers had captured too much of the market, especially on the North Atlantic route. Some estimates put revenues for American airlines at three times as much as those earned by the British.[13] As one British minister in the British Embassy in Washington, and a participant in the subsequent negotiations, wrote, the original Bermuda Agreement (or Bermuda I as it came to be called) 'was showing signs of age.' The original deal had outlived its usefulness, he continued: 'the plain fact was that the day-to-day management of our bilateral civil aviation relations on the basis of Bermuda I was proving more and more complex. The words of the original text did not really bear on many of the problems which had arisen in recent years. We needed a fresh start.'[14] It came at a time of great economic difficulty for the airlines and international civil aviation generally, and the British announcement sparked a new round of Anglo-American negotiations that were watched closely by governments and airlines around the world.

The positions staked out by the two states were in many ways similar to the ones exhibited in 1946. The United States wanted more competition in the market and fewer controls, and, in the words of their chief negotiator Alan Boyd, 'stated in the strongest terms it will not agree to a regulated market split, will not agree to a U.K. veto of U.S. airline capacity increases, and will not agree to limit the right of U.S. airlines to pick up and discharge passengers beyond London.'[15] Conversely, the British called for more managed competition, an equal share of the traffic, limits on capacity, and a reduction in fifth freedom rights, from which it was believed that they had not really benefited.[16]

After protracted negotiations that were hampered by the change of administrations in the United States, the Bermuda II Agreement was signed 23 July 1977. 'The new agreement,' President Carter announced, 'provides for continuing the basic principle of a fair and equal opportunity for the airlines of both countries to compete, and dedicates both Governments to the provision of safe, adequate, and efficient international air transportation responsive to the present and future needs of the public and to the continued development of international air commerce.'[17] But many critics, especially in the United States, charged that the agreement favoured British interests over American. The new agreement put limitations on fifth freedom rights for U.S. airlines, and the multiple designation of airlines was restricted to two markets, New York and Los Angeles to London; in the rest only one airline from each state could operate on the route. The British also received new entry rights at four American cities: Atlanta, Dallas/Fort Worth, Houston, and San Francisco. Bermuda II also called for stronger regulation of capacity; rather than the 'ex post facto' review of Bermuda I, under Bermuda II both sides were to present schedules for consultation in advance and if they could not agree their room to maneuver was more limited to a level based on their original estimates. Charter flights, which were becoming a very serious concern, were not included in the agreement and left aside for future negotiations and a separate agreement.[18] It was, wrote one aviation historian, one of the most restrictive agreements ever negotiated by the United States.[19]

Many observers wondered about the impact of Bermuda II: would it have the same influence as Bermuda I and set a kind of pattern to be followed in other bilateral negotiations? And what would happen to all the other bilateral agreements that had been modeled on the terms of Bermuda I? The American government was already having trouble in its aviation discussions with the French and the Israelis, and Japan began to make noises about including the same kind of conditions in their negotiations with Washington to replace the U.S.-Japanese bilateral agreement signed in 1952.[20]

Bermuda II turned out not to be the landmark that many thought it would be; the agreement was criticized both in the United States and abroad, and very soon the Carter administration embarked on a very different course in its aviation policy. Carter's predecessor Gerald Ford had already moved to deregulate the domestic American market, and Carter himself had campaigned on a platform of less government regulation.[21] Work on a new international aviation policy was already underway during the Bermuda II negotiations (which had been initiated by the Ford administration), and it was developed during the rest of the year and released in August 1978. Under the new policy, the United States would 'work to achieve a system of international air transportation that places its principle reliance on actual and potential competition to determine the variety, quality and price of air service. An essential means for carrying out our international air transportation policy will be to allow greater competitive opportunities for U.S. and foreign airlines and to promote new low-cost transportation options for travelers and shippers.' To achieve these goals, the American government's objectives would be to eliminate or reduce all restrictions on capacity, frequencies, route selection, and the multiple designations of air carriers, and the removal of restrictions on charter air services.[22]

In this new atmosphere the U.S. Civil Aeronautics Board issued a 'Show Cause Order' to IATA that threatened to label the international grouping a cartel and eliminate its immunity from American anti-trust legislation. The American action sparked widespread international shock and protest over what was seen as the United States unilaterally applying its anti-trust laws on an international scale. The order was ultimately withdrawn but the CAB prohibited further American participation in IATA-sponsored North Atlantic Traffic Conferences.[23] The whole affair was seen as an attack on the tariff mechanism that had governed international aviation for thirty years. If the administration in Washington wanted to get the aviation world's attention it succeeded.

The new American policy was accompanied with two pieces of legislation: the 1978 Airline Deregulation Act and, in 1979, the International Air Transportation Competition Act. The former gradually dismantled the CAB and with it the CAB's regulation of the domestic market, leaving it open to much more competition in routes, pricing, and quality of service, all in the hope that this would lead to better service and lower domestic fares. The latter act essentially tried to export these same values to the international market by setting out the American position for future bilateral agreements, which would now emphasize the greatest amount of competition in its international aviation agreements. The American policy maintained restrictions in a few areas such as airline ownership and cabotage, but embraced the removal of all foreign discrimination, traffic restrictions and regulations for international civil aviation. The plan – dubbed the 'Encirclement Strategy' – was to negotiate with smaller states and, it was hoped, divert traffic from the larger markets (especially Japan and the U.K.), drawing the larger states into what in the 1990s became known as 'open skies' agreements.[24]

It was not easy to get everyone else to agree to deregulation and 'open skies,' but the new American policy had a profound effect on international civil aviation. In the United States the announcement of deregulation was followed by a period of restructuring and consolidation that saw the disappearance of several airlines, including Eastern Airlines and Pan Am, and the formation of air alliances or partnerships, such as the alliance of Northwest Airlines and KLM in 1992. By the end of the 1980s the American market was dominated by five mega airlines (American, United, Delta, USAir, and Northwest) and reconfigured with the emergence of the 'hub-and-spoke' networks.[25] Internationally, the negotiation of 'open skies' agreements was slow. The Japanese and British, for example, were unwilling to go along, but almost two dozen more liberal bilateral agreements were reached with, among others, Belgium, Korea, the Netherlands, Singapore, and Thailand. At the same time, the United States had upset the applecart, and the old system of restrictive bilateral agreements began to look increasingly out of date. Liberalization was in the air, if not on the negotiating table, and many people began re-examining existing arrangements in the light of the challenge presented by American deregulation and to question whether the old system could be maintained. Soon critics were calling restrictive bilateral agreements obsolete and others were raising the issue – securely off the agenda since the early 1950s –of a new multilateral aviation agreement.[26]

For many nations the answer to American unilateralism was an ICAO-based multilateralism. With deregulation, skyrocketing fuel prices, rising competition from charter air services, inflation, and a global economic slump all putting pressure on the airline industry, and with the regulations governing capacity, frequencies, routes, and tariff-setting being challenged, especially by the United States, it made sense at least to start to reconsider some of the foundations of the postwar system of regulation of air traffic. To this end, ICAO staged a series of air transport conferences. Thanks to the success of the first – the 'Special Air Transport Conference' in 1977 – two more were held, in 1980 and 1985. In some ways these conferences were the antidote to unilateralism, and there was wide agreement that it remained 'useful to consider, within ICAO, economic problems related to the development of international air transport on a world-wide basis; and that the air transport system exists within an economic and regulatory environment that is in process of change.'[27] Each conference was well attended and drew considerable attention, and this interest was a testament to the global concern over the economic problems facing international civil aviation.

The agendas of the conferences were very broad and contained many subjects for which there were no immediate solutions. The problems of overcapacity and fares were examined and calls were made for more study of the ways to regulate them. Few solutions were presented, but there was broad agreement that unilateral action was not the way to proceed, especially when it came to setting fares, and that more study of the issue was necessary.[28] Much attention was also directed at ways of clarifying the differences between scheduled and non-scheduled air services. Scheduled and non-scheduled services are mentioned in articles five and six in the Chicago Convention, but they are not really defined. The rise of charter air services, not to mention the proliferation of tour operators, tourist services, varying rates for air flights, promotional packages with hotel accommodations, and so on, challenged many of basic aspects of the bilateral system established at the end of the Second World War. In 1952 the ICAO Council established that a scheduled international air service must be a series of international flights, operated on regular basis, and open to use by members of the public. By the 1970s it appeared that many charter services fell within that definition, blurring the separation between scheduled and non-scheduled services. The 1977 Special Air Transport Conference called on the council to set out guidelines and a definition distinguishing between the two types of services.[29]

There was also considerable concern expressed over the American policy of deregulation and its assault on the tariff-setting mechanisms. The American views of competition, even though they were not in favour of complete deregulation, were not shared by all members of ICAO. The United States had several very powerful privately owned airlines that might thrive in a competitive environment, but the great majority of ICAO members had state-owned airlines and, for many of the smaller nations, they might not be able to survive in a competitive free-for-all. And state airlines were not just *any* business that might go bankrupt; with the issues of national prestige, state security, and sovereignty involved, there was little support for risking the potential damage that competition might bring to them. There was also considerable fear that deregulation would lead to the domination of the air by a few airlines, and these airlines would not likely come from the smaller ICAO nations. It was clear that many members would rather have inefficient, debt-loaded state airlines than become a branch operation of an international mega-carrier.

Opposition to deregulation tended to be strongest in the states that still maintained other values – prestige, security, national interest, and so on – in their state airlines; indeed, one analyst argued that support for 'open skies' rose and fell with state ownership.[30] Another analyst has argued that the developing states turned to ICAO as a way to defend their national interests against the American actions, and that they 'sensed that the air transport cartel that allowed them to charge high fares and hence avoid large subsidies for their airlines was disappearing.'[31]

Another division in ICAO between the developed and the developing world appeared, with the United States and a few of its allies on one side and the great majority of ICAO members on the other. 'We are faced with the fact,' said A.B.M. Kamara, the minister of transport for Sierra Leone, 'that as air travel eases for the people of advanced nations, it is becoming more difficult for the people of developing nations.'[32] The African states, for example, tended to rely less on non-scheduled services, and with their concerns about protecting their national airlines, they tended to be very restrictive in their bilateral exchange of traffic rights.[33] The African Civil Aviation Commission, which was created in 1969, established a Panel of Legal Experts that met in Dakar, Senegal in May 1982. This meeting produced two standard texts for bilateral agreements – one for use between African nations, the other for negotiations with non-African nations.[34]

As a result, the United States occasionally found itself alone at the Air Transport Conferences, where even some friendly states that might privately offer theoretical support for open competition failed to come through with the votes. For example, at the Second Air Transport Conference, held in Montreal in February 1980, with 101 contracting states and observers from half a dozen international organizations in attendance, the American delegation's proposal to discuss the removal of all restrictions on capacity control was soundly defeated by a large majority. One State Department official explained to a reporter that the defeat was a leftover from the CAB's attack on fares; 'There are still quite a few government officials and airline officers who are displeased and unhappy over the IATA incident,' he said, 'but some are on the border and no longer have hard feelings as they once did. The vote may have given the opponents an opportunity to vent their spleens.'[35]

Most of the recommendations of the Special Air Transport Conferences were endorsed at the following ICAO Assembly sessions, and various resolutions were passed calling for more discussions and asking the council to take action in a number of areas. But the bulk of the work following these conferences fell to the council, the ATC and other committees, the Air Transport Bureau, and the ICAO secretariat generally. Following the 1977 conference, for example, the council established an ICAO Panel on Regulation of Air Transport Services to look a number of regulatory issues. It recommended broadening the definition of scheduled services to reclassify some charter services as scheduled services; it also devised some flexible guidelines for capacity regulation in an effort to maintain equality of treatment and to ensure that the capacity provided on any given service was sufficient for traffic requirements. In addition, in March 1978 the council approved a standard tariff clause for bilateral agreements in which the airlines would agree to a tariff arrangement after government discussions and 'using the appropriate international mechanism.'[36]

The ICAO Council maintained a constant level of research on the regulation of air transport, and also began work on two projects in response to assembly resolutions. First, it began the preparations for a manual on regulation that would contain 'descriptive material on existing national regulatory policies, practice and arrangements; on bilateral agreements, including updated information on the bilateral administrative and capacity clauses...; on multilateral and regional coordination of regulatory policy; and on conclusions reached on various regulatory subjects by ICAO and already available.'[37] The manual would provide accessible information for governments, airlines, and individuals on how international air transport services were regulated. It was published as the *ICAO Manual on the Regulation of International Air Transport*. Second, the council established a computer data base containing reference files with the basic provisions of all bilateral agreements. It was quite a task, given the existence of hundreds of bilateral agreements, and even though they were all supposed to be registered with ICAO, many were not. This data base was to be made available to members, and it was expected that the information would 'assist national administrations, especially those with limited resources in the regulatory affairs area, as well as other potential users, to obtain a broad range of summarized information on the contents of bilateral air transport agreements.'[38]

While all this work progressed the international situation only worsened. Another round of fuel price hikes badly hurt the air transport industry, and a severe global recession had a negative impact on industries associated with air transport, such as tourism. From 1990 to 1993 the American airline industry lost $10 billion; from1990 to 1992 the airlines of the European Union lost U.S.$7 billion. The numbers were impressive, even if in a negative way. In those same two years, the 221 airline members of IATA lost a combined U.S.$11.5 billion on scheduled international services – these losses totaled more than all the profits made by airlines since the Second World War.[39] What could be done about it?

In 1993 U.S. President Bill Clinton appointed a National Commission to Ensure a Strong Competitive Airline Industry; the European Union established the Committee of Wise Men to examine the state of the airline industry. The EU was already acting more like a domestic market and experiencing an era of reform leading to a broad deregulation policy within Europe (although each member maintained its bilateral and independent relations with outside states) and, ultimately, the Single European Aviation Market by 1997.[40] Both groups came out in favour of further liberalization in international air transport – the removal of government regulations and the elimination of restrictions on capacity, frequency, traffic rights, routes, and the number of airlines designated for each route.[41] 'Open skies' was back on the agenda, this time with more force. In 1992 an 'open skies'-type agreement was signed between the United States and the Netherlands, this one much more liberal and less restrictive than Bermuda II (no restrictions on capacity, frequencies and open entry into each others' markets).[42] The new agreement was accompanied by an alliance between KLM and Northwest Airlines.

Many people began talking about a new multilateral agreement, this one embodying the philosophy of 'open skies'; others saw the great difficulties and obstacles and argued that regionalism was the way to go, for the Europeans to put together the SEAM first and then to negotiate with the Americans, until the regions themselves united. Still others talked of 'plurilateralism,' where two or more states would form an agreement and then expand it even one at a time as new members were brought in, until it evolved into a multilateral agreement.[43]

The air transport world appeared to be in a state of upheaval, and it was in this atmosphere that the ICAO Council issued invitations in April 1992 to an ICAO-sponsored World-wide Air Transport Colloquium. Approximately five hundred delegates arrived in Montreal to talk about the present and future of regulation, and to question whether or not it was time to resume the quest for the multilateral agreement that had eluded ICAO members in the 1940s. It was a week-long meeting, with no working papers, resolutions, or recommendations, only presentations, panel discussions, comments, and summations.[44] With representatives from governments, airlines, and airport authorities, as well as ICAO, the colloquium was considered a huge success even though the discussions displayed 'sharply divided views' on whether ICAO should 'abandon the bilateral system' and move towards a new multilateral agreement.[45] It was an informal affair, with a free exchange of ideas on the economic regulation of international air transport, but it also confirmed for many participants the need for ICAO to take a leading role in this area and not to lose whatever momentum had been gained.

An undercurrent running beneath these discussions was the evolution of the Uruguay round of the General Agreement on Tariffs and Trade, which led to the founding of the World Trade Organization in 1995 and the signing of the General Agreement on Trade in Services. GATT had been around since the 1940s but had rarely crossed into the field of international aviation; in the early 1990s, however, it began periodic reviews of the air transport industry. And, with the new powerful organization it was not that big a stretch of the imagination to see the possibility of the WTO applying its rules to civil aviation.[46] In addition, the GATS, which also came into effect in 1995, contained an annex that applied to air transport services. This annex pertained to what were called 'soft rights,' including computer reservations systems, aircraft repair and maintenance services, and the marketing of air services, but not the 'hard rights'– route selection, fares, capacity, frequencies, and so on. Again, it was not difficult to imagine the scope of the agreement expanding into other areas. The GATS 'offers the first worldwide, potential multilateral alternative to the bilateral system of air services agreements,' wrote one analyst.[47] Others worried that in the future decisions about air transport would be made by economists and bureaucrats in the WTO rather than by aviation specialists, as in the past.[48] ICAO was the natural organization to play a leadership role in defending the interests of international aviation, and it had already declared at the 1985 Third Air Transport Conference and in 1986 Assembly Resolution A26-14 that

ICAO 'was the multilateral body in the United Nations system competent to deal with international air transport.'[49] Stating it was one thing, but it was also important for ICAO to demonstrate some leadership in the field.

Thanks to the interest in and success of the 1992 colloquium, the ICAO Council believed the conditions were right for a full, official air transport conference. In advance, the council established a small twelve member group of aviation specialists – officially the Group of Experts on Future Regulatory Arrangements, or GEFRA – to study all the issues raised at the colloquium and to prepare recommendations on possible future courses of action. Revised and rewritten by the ICAO secretariat, these recommendations were included in working papers which were to be used as background information at the proposed air transport conference – the World Wide Air Transport Conference, scheduled for 1994.

There was no plan to negotiate a new multilateral agreement – that had been tried before, without success – nor would there be any effort to amend the Chicago Convention; this time the conference would try to establish more of a direction for the future than a specific end. A multilateral agreement was not specifically a goal of the conference, indeed it was hoped that whatever possibilities were explored would be able to be applied within *either* a bilateral or multilateral framework. As one observer wrote at the time, 'the basis of the Conference will not be the structure of the future regulatory regime but rather the content of it.' The agenda comprised three sections: (1) present regulation, (2) future regulatory content, and (3) future regulatory process and structure.[50] The GERFA experts and ICAO Secretariat subdivided future regulatory content into six distinct topics: market access, safeguards, ownership and control, structural impediments, the broader regulatory environment, and 'doing business' matters.[51]

Throughout these proposals ran a strong theme of liberalization: states would open up their market access through the exchange of basic rights; ownership requirements would be a little more flexible; more carrier designations would be permitted; and a system of safeguards would be incorporated into agreements that would help prevent any abuse of the system. Joseph Chesen, the coordinator of GERFA , explained the study group's proposals:

> States would continue to exchange access to each other's markets for the air carriers they designate, but would introduce far more flexibility, much greater simplicity and considerably more freedom for air carriers to decide

which routes and cities they would serve and with what aircraft types to carry all available international traffic. Essentially, governments would no longer 'micro-manage' access to air transport markets, employing myriad control devices, but would 'macro-manage' each market as a whole. Any cities in the territory of each party to the agreement could be served with complete flexibility. Any number of designated carriers could use the rights. Carriers could switch en route to any number of aircraft of a different size, routinely determine their own capacity and freely operate services on behalf of each other, sharing carrier designation codes, buying and selling blocks of space on board, using franchising, etc. All international traffic in passengers, cargo and mail could be freely carried separately or in any combination.[52]

These agreements would be bilateral, regional, or plurilateral – but they would all lead in the direction of liberalization and, ultimately, multilateralism. As some observers pointed out, countries such as the United States, having failed in its attempt to achieve liberalization through the negotiation of bilateral agreements, turned to internationalism and the negotiation of a multilateral agreement to achieve the same ends.[53] Any success the WATC had in the direction of liberalization would be a positive result.

Scheduled exactly fifty years after the Chicago conference, the World Wide Air Transport Conference opened in Montreal on 23 November and closed 6 December 1994. Almost eight hundred delegates from 137 nations and representatives from more than two dozen international organizations arrived in Montreal ready to talk, but like the 1947 Geneva multilateral negotiations and even the Chicago conference itself, every participating state had its own ideas about the future of regulation of international air transport and finding any kind of agreement on the big issues was an almost impossible task. 'Expectations from Icao's landmark conference on international air transport regulation in November,' wrote Chris Lyle, who headed ICAO's economics and statistics branch, 'range from cynicism – based on a perception of Icao as a bureaucratic monolith – to hype. After all, the conference does coincide with the 50th anniversary of the signing of the Chicago Convention.'[54]

The conference did not have the authority to negotiate a new multilateral agreement, but even if it had there was little chance of finding enough common ground on which to construct one. For example, there was agreement on the need to maintain safety as the highest priority in air transport; there was consensus on the need to protect the environment

and to lower taxes; there were many calls for and explanations of the
benefits of liberalization; there were nods in the direction of equal opportunity, competition, open markets, and so on, but only a few nations were
ready to embrace liberalization and endanger their ability to protect their
markets and airlines.

For some participants, especially from the developing world, access to
financial resources was as important as access to foreign markets, and
their concerns were to ensure their participation in future air transport
– not liberalization. One observer wrote: 'as soon as the first theme –
market access – was tackled, speaker after speaker took issue, often con-
vincingly, with what was judged to be too liberal an approach: the
developing countries were unanimous in rejecting it, joined by major
Asia/Pacific countries seeking to retain their ascendancy and judging
that their protectionist interests would be best served by retaining the
traditional bilateral framework (Japan, China, India, and even Australia),
and by Eastern European countries newly emerged from Communism
and anxious to protect themselves (Russia in particular).'[55] The Andean
Group of States argued that a multilateral regime should be 'limited to
the sub-regional level,'[56] while a group of forty-three African states submitted a paper suggesting that future air services should be operated
based 'on the sovereignty of States, equality of opportunity and reciprocity.'[57] Even the Europeans, who were in the process of transition to
the Single European Aviation Market, were hesitant about applying it
outside Europe. As a result, 'the United States soon began to look very
isolated as defenders of hard-line liberalization.'[58]

The conference issued several recommendations, most of which were
sensible and acceptable to most states, but they only underscored the
remaining distances on the key questions. The participants reconfirmed
their faith in the Chicago Convention, and most delegates left realizing
that the bilateral system would remain in place for at least a few more
years. The conference established a general goal of the 'gradual, progressive, orderly and safeguarded change towards market access in
international air transport regulation,' but recognized that 'each State
will determine its own path and own pace of change in international air
transport regulation, on the basis of equality of opportunity and using
bilateral, sub-regional, regional and/or global avenues according to
circumstances.' The participants also concluded that 'in view of the disparities in economic and competitive situations there is no prospect in
the near future for a global multilateral agreement for the exchange of
traffic rights.' The conference also recommended that ICAO work with

the World Trade Organization and any other organization to safe-guard the 'special needs of international air transport' and 'in line with its global responsibilities, take, and be seen to take, effective action to exert a leadership role in the development of economic regulation of international civil aviation'[59] ICAO was also asked to continue studying a wide variety of topics dealing with regulatory issues – more studies than ICAO could perform, was how ICAO's Chris Lyle characterized it.[60]

The supporters of liberalization and deregulation were less enthusiastic about the outcome; one American official expressed disappointment, saying that the weak support for liberalization 'should be a cause for concern.'[61] There was always hope for more successful bilateral negotiations and for the expansion of the few regional groupings, but the WATC fell short of American expectations. Bilateral negotiations already under way were continued, and the United States reached 'open skies' agreements with Austria, Canada, the Czech Republic, Denmark, Iceland, Norway, Sweden, Switzerland and others in 1995. More followed in 1996 and 1997.[62]

Supporters of deregulation may have taken some comfort from the fact that, thanks to the WTO and the GATS, liberalization was the wave of the future, and it might prove that these organizations rather than ICAO would lead the way to deregulation.[63] But so long as the issues of 'fair competition,' sovereignty, national prestige, security, and defence were intertwined with international civil aviation, it was unlikely that ICAO would achieve any kind of multilateral agreement. 'It is nearly impossible for countries to agree on a multilateral liberalization package on air transport without the opportunities to tradeoff with other sectors of economy,' concluded one academic observer.[64] Only more broadly based organizations like the WTO could do that. Another observer, looking back from the end of the century, wrote that it was 'clear that ICAO with its large and diverse membership, is too unwieldy a forum to take the lead on liberalization issues, and that ICAO should maintain its status quo of dealing with safety and technical matters. But many other countries, in particular the African bloc, are equally insistent that no liberalization moves on a multilateral basis should take place outside ICAO.' The end result was an impasse in the global search for liberalization in air transport. 'The situation can at best be described as a stalemate and, taking into account the absence of any development in the 5 years since the ICAO Conference, it is difficult to see any global change emanating from ICAO itself.'[65]

'The liberalization of air transport is already under way in much of the world,' said Council President Kotaite, speaking to the annual meeting of IATA in Sydney, Australia, in June 2000. The numbers showed that a significant majority of ICAO members had signed on to a liberal air agreement, either bilaterally or regionally, and more were moving in that direction every day. And all this activity was taking place outside the WTO and the GATS and within the existing framework provided by ICAO and the Chicago Convention. The future looked promising, he added, and the most likely scenario 'is for an expanding patchwork of phased-in liberalization under the aviation umbrella, both through bilateral agreements and through new or geographically extended regional agreements, all of which may eventually offer opportunities for coalescence.'[66]

For the second time in its fifty years ICAO had failed to achieve a multilateral agreement to regulate the economic aspects of international civil aviation. There was less sting this time, perhaps, as there had been less expectation of success from the start. On the contrary, there was room for optimism, in that the emphasis of ICAO's efforts was shifting to the *process* of moving ahead toward liberalization rather than on the ultimate *goal* of multilateralism. And in the aftermath of the WATC, the ICAO Council launched a new study program on various regulatory topics recommended by the conference, and the 1995 ICAO Assembly reconfirmed ICAO's prime role within the U.N. system dealing with the regulatory issues of international air transport. For many observers, it appeared that things were moving in the right direction.

It all had a familiar ring to it, however, with discussions of equality and sovereignty, route exchange, capacity and frequencies, and so on. Some of the words and topics had changed – computer reservation systems, GATS, 'hard' and 'soft' rights, for example – but discussions in Montreal in 1995 were reminiscent of those held in Geneva in 1947 and even at Chicago itself. The economic climate had changed; so had ICAO. But the basic issues of sovereignty, national prestige, and economic self-interest remained virtually the same. The ghosts of Adolf Berle and Lord Swinton, had they wandered through the halls of the International Civil Aviation Organization, eavesdropping on these discussions, would have understood those words very well.

PART FOUR

16

From Development to Implementation: ICAO in the Modern World

The aviation world came through a period of profound transformation in the 1970s and 1980s and faced many new challenges in the 1990s. The end of the Cold War created a new reality in the international system and was accompanied by a severe international economic recession. The impact of the computer revolution and globalization was being felt across the aviation industry and produced a blurring of the boundaries between international civil aviation and communications, environmental protection, international security, tourism and other industries, and most other modes of transportation. The global importance of international civil aviation – and its interconnection with the rest of the world – was never clearer, but questions remained over how commercial aviation and ICAO, in particular, would adapt to the new realities. From the World Trade Organization and the General Agreement on Trade in Services to computer reservation systems, satellite navigation services, 'open skies,' deregulation, strategic alliances, downsizing, and privatization, it appeared as if constant turmoil had become the norm in international aviation.[1] The International Civil Aviation Organization could not retreat without becoming a kind of anachronistic relic in the modern world.

The issues on the table were numerous and intractable. Satellite technology was the wave of the future and ICAO needed to embrace it. Airports were becoming increasingly congested and, with heightened security measures, this was likely only to get worse. The airline business was suffering a financial crisis. The old bilateral system of aviation agreements was showing its age and just about everyone wanted change, but there was little agreement on what form that change should take. In the growing environmental movement, aircraft emissions were being singled out as a significant part of the problem. ICAO members were falling behind in their implementation of the technical and security standards, demands for technical assistance were rising, and various annex amendments, ICAO protocols, and legal conventions sat waiting to be ratified by pre-occupied governments. The calls for ICAO to take action were getting louder; at the same time the organization was facing its own serious financial problems, with some members falling behind on their assessments and others demanding that ICAO tighten its own belt. 'ICAO has historic-ally had the reputation of being among the most efficient of agencies within the United Nations system,' wrote Chris Lyle of ICAO's Air Transport Bureau, 'but it cannot afford to be complacent.'[2] In the 1990s, complacency was eschewed in favour of reform and modernization.

The end of the Cold War inevitably had an impact on ICAO's member-ship. The collapse of the Berlin Wall and the reunification of Germany, the dissolution of the Soviet Union, and the installation of democratic governments in Eastern Europe combined to eliminate virtually all mem-bership problems in ICAO and spark a rush of new members. In 1990 the German Democratic Republic ratified the Chicago Convention and be-came an ICAO member, but months later merged with the former West Germany into one state. ICAO recognized the transfer of the Soviet membership to Russia and a Russian delegate, rather than a Soviet one, now sat in the ICAO Council seat.[3] In 1991, Albania joined, along with Belize and Namibia. In 1992 they were followed by several former Soviet republics and satellites, including Lithuania, Latvia, Estonia, Armenia, Ukraine, Kazakhstan, Azerbaijan, and Uzbekistan. The breakup of Yugoslavia and Czechoslovakia created a little confusion; in the former, the Federal Republic of Yugoslavia (Serbia and Montenegro) was denied its request to assume the membership of Yugoslavia; in the latter, Czechoslovakia was no longer considered to be a member (or a party to various conventions, etc.) and the two new states needed to seek admis-sion independently. Croatia and Slovenia joined in 1992, and new mem-bers in 1993 included Bosnia and Herzegovina and the former Yugoslav Republic of Macedonia, the Czech Republic and Slovakia, along with Kyrgyzstan, Turkmenistan, Belarus, Tajikistan, and Eritrea. With the en-trance of Georgia (1994), Palau (1995), and Western Samoa (1996), the total membership reached 185.

The end of the Cold War did not mean the end of problems in inter-national civil aviation, and the post-Cold War era had its first crisis very early on, when Iraq invaded Kuwait on 2 August 1990. Kuwait International Airport was attacked and much of its infrastructure was destroyed, and

fifteen Kuwait Airways airliners were seized and brought to Iraq. Air traffic control services were disrupted, and Kuwaiti airspace was closed to all
international traffic. The United Nations responded quickly and through
a series of resolutions condemned Iraq and called for its withdrawal from
Kuwait and asked all members of the United Nations to deny landing
rights or permission to overfly its territory to any Iraqi aircraft and to
refrain from flying there until Iraqi forces had withdrawn from Kuwait.[4]
Iraq refused and the situation deteriorated over the following months as
a U.S.-led coalition of forces was assembled in the Middle East.

The implications for international civil aviation were apparent, and
for ICAO it was a clear example of being prompted into political action
because of its relationship with the United Nations.[5] An Extraordinary
Session of the ICAO Assembly was set to begin in October (the purpose
was to increase the size of the council and to discuss the problem of aircraft noise), and at the request of Kuwait, the Iraqi invasion was included
on the agenda. This decision set the stage for some acrimonious exchanges between the Kuwaiti and Iraqi delegations. The Iraqis even objected
to the presence of the 'so-called State of Kuwait' and insisted that talking
about the invasion fell outside of ICAO's jurisdiction.[6] But, it was clear
that the majority of members were in sympathy with the United Nations
resolutions, and ICAO Resolution A28-7 reflected these views: ICAO
'Condemns the violation of the sovereignty of the airspace of Kuwait and
the plunder of Kuwait International Airport by Iraqi armed forces including the seizure and removal to Iraq of 15 aircraft of Kuwait Airways
and their purported registration by Iraq.' Members were also called
upon not to recognize the annexation of Kuwait by Iraq or to supply Iraq
with any parts or equipment, and to return the Kuwaiti aircraft if any of
them landed in their territory.[7] Thanks to the international pressure and
the personal shuttle diplomacy of Council President Kotaite, the Kuwaiti
aircraft were ultimately returned.[8] The international consensus about
Iraq's invasion, which was reflected in the ICAO resolution, translated
into joint military action against Iraq in early 1991 and, after a short war,
Kuwait's independence was restored. It took some time, but Kuwait's
role in international civil aviation was resumed as well.

Another form of cooperation with the United Nations was seen in the
international campaign against the use of illegal drugs. In 1987 the United
Nations staged a large global conference on drug abuse and followed the
conference with a list of specific targets to deal with the problem (under
the categories of prevention and reduction, control of supply, suppression
of trafficking, and treatment and rehabilitation). The transport of illegal

drugs by air was recognized as a serious problem, and ICAO was inevitably drawn into the broader anti-drug campaign.[9] The Chicago Convention was sufficiently broad for most states to take legal measures to handle the transport of illegal drugs, and various resolutions were passed by the ICAO Assembly (A26-12; A27-12) encouraging the ICAO Council and member states to continue their efforts in the 'War on Drugs.'[10] ICAO participated in the U.N. conferences and undertook its own examination of its procedures in the areas of search and seizure, customs examinations, and the ways drugs could be hidden onboard aircraft by airport personnel. The investigation of the problem was broadened to include the illegal use of drugs by flight crews and air traffic controllers. At the end of the day, most studies suggested that there was little need for additional legislative action by ICAO and that drug use among air crew was not a significant problem.[11] Nevertheless, throughout the 1990s ICAO worked in conjunction with the United Nations and the other specialized agencies in an effort to control the transport and use of illegal drugs.[12]

The first post-Cold War decade was equally eventful in Montreal, where the organization was overseen by Assad Kotaite, who had settled in as a permanent fixture as council president and as the public face of the organization. The secretariat, however, got a new secretary general in 1991: Dr Phillippe Rochat. Rochat was a Swiss-born and educated lawyer who, after many years working as a journalist, served in various aviation agencies in the Swiss government and at the Geneva airport. He came to ICAO in the 1980s as the Swiss council representative and was elected secretary general in 1991, leaving the post in 1997. Early in his term he told a local reporter that among his top priorities were reform of the secretariat and the enhancement of its public image. It was time, he said, for a major clean-up ('un grand nettoyage') and a re-examination of the secretariat's internal structure and the way it did things.[13] As part of a broad renewal of the organization, Rochat initiated a 'comprehensive review' of ICAO's structure and procedures.[14]

One of the most pressing issues facing the new secretary general was the low recruitment of women into the professional ranks of the organization. There had never been many women working in ICAO above the general service level; indeed women were underrepresented throughout the whole U.N. system and especially in the aviation world, from the boardroom to the cockpit to the halls of international diplomacy. There is little evidence of anyone complaining about this anomaly at the Chicago conference or in ICAO's early years and nothing was done to rectify it, but by the 1970s and 1980s the underrepresentation of women was a noticeable issue that needed to be addressed. ICAO responded, along with the other specialized agencies in the U.N. system, but relatively little progress had been made by the 1990s.

Overcoming years of complacency was an enormous task. Relatively few women applied for the positions at the professional rank; relatively few women were encouraged or seconded to ICAO by the member states; and relatively few women were appointed by the members as council representatives (although there were some notable exceptions, such as Betty C. Dillon, the U.S. council representative in the early 1970s). Fingers were also pointed at the educational systems in many contracting states where there were shortages of women in the technical and scientific areas and only a small number of graduates in aviation-related fields.[15] There were also the informal barriers to women throughout ICAO reflected in the working conditions and culture of the organization. These were difficult obstacles to overcome, and it was a slow process to change the way things had always been done.

In 1993 the council adopted an action plan with targets for the recruitment of women that were endorsed by the ICAO Assembly at the Thirty-First Session in 1995. The plan called for the increased representation of women by a minimum of 1 per cent per year for ten years, bringing the level of women in the professional ranks up from 20 per cent in 1993 to 30 per cent by 2003. It was an ambitious plan and was to be achieved through the specific targeting of potential female recruits and by making approaches to the member governments and regional offices to encourage qualified women to apply for the positions. Gender equality was also to be considered during the hiring process. 'In order to give greater priority to women,' one ICAO Council document explained, 'suitable female candidates are specifically drawn to the attention of the Secretary General when recommendations of the Appointment and Promotion Board are submitted to the Secretary General.'[16]

However well-intentioned the plan was, it fell far short of its targets over the following decade. In 2001 the percentage of women at the professional level reached only 22.8 per cent; by 2003 – the end of the ten year plan – the proportion rose to 23.8 per cent, although the actual number of women at the professional rank dropped from seventy-four to seventy-three.[17] In 2005 the council adopted an affirmative action plan that included further requests to the members to seek out and encourage women to apply for professional positions, the creation of committees within ICAO (and in the regional offices) to do the same, and the convening of training workshops on gender equality.[18]

Progress has been very slow. On 28 May 2004 A. McGinley, the Irish council representative, noted that at that time there were no female directors or principal officers at ICAO. The secretariat, she said, 'had failed miserably in achieving the objective which had been set in 1993.' Within the whole U.N. system, she continued, ICAO ranked twenty-sixth out of thirty organizations in the representation of women.[19] It was a dismal record, and it must not have gone unnoticed that, among all the council representatives, council president, and secretary general present at the meeting on that day in 2004, she was the only woman.

The first half of the 1990s were a busy few years for Kotaite, Rochat, and everyone in the head office, with the negotiation of a new Headquarters Agreement, the fiftieth anniversary celebrations, and the move to a new building. A Supplementary Headquarters Agreement had been signed in 1980 dealing with the headquarters building but within a few years negotiations began for a new agreement to supersede the 1951 agreement. Taxation problems remained, especially regarding ICAO employees who were Canadian citizens and whose salaries were not exempt from income tax. This was a lingering problem from the 1950s that was circumvented by the Canadian government through a system of reimbursements. Other problems had also arisen dealing with immigration, status, immunities, and privileges.[20] In ICAO's early years representatives tended to be aviation technicians and specialists, but gradually these professionals were replaced by civil servants, often from members' foreign ministries, and there was a growing feeling that these individuals were not granted the same diplomatic privileges accorded to other foreign government representatives and diplomats, and there was a desire for a new agreement to bring ICAO into similar arrangements with its host government as other U.N. organizations.[21]

A new Headquarters Agreement was signed with the Canadian government in 1990 and it came into force following the signing of an exchange of notes in 1992. The new arrangement essentially updated the 1951 agreement and left ICAO's relationship with the city and government largely as it was before. ICAO's premises were granted the 'same protection as is given to diplomatic missions in Canada' and permanent representatives were granted the status of diplomatic agents (not full diplomatic immunity but similar immunities and privileges to diplomats). In addition, Canadian citizens were finally exempted from paying income tax, although they would have only limited legal immunity, 'in respect of words spoken or written and of all acts performed by him in his official capacity.'[22] Problems in the relationship never completely disappeared,[23] but the new agreement settled the major lingering issues over the status of ICAO and its personnel.

Planning for the fiftieth anniversary began early in 1994 with support from the governments of Canada, Quebec, and Montreal.[24] Plans were made for exhibitions, symposiums, and conferences, and numerous other events were staged in Montreal, Chicago, and the regional offices over a six-month period beginning in November 1994. A special ICAO Council meeting was held at the Chicago Hilton (the former Stevens Hotel) to honour the signing of the Chicago Convention at that location fifty years earlier. A few weeks later, on 7 December, the Canadian government hosted a gala evening at the ICAO headquarters for eight hundred guests, including U.N. Secretary-General Boutros Boutros-Ghali.[25] An oversized coffee table book filled with short articles and advertisements was produced to note the occasion, and other magazines and journals acknowledged the moment in different ways.[26] Many of the activities were coordinated with IATA, which was also celebrating its fiftieth anniversary in 1995.[27]

Even more time consuming were the negotiations for a new building to house the organization. There were problems with the Sherbrooke Street building almost from the start, with complaints over air quality and poor elevator service, and with lease and rental negotiations and discussions with the Canadian government for financial aid to cover the rising costs.[28] And, with the rapidly increasing membership and staff, the need for more space increased with each year. To make matters worse, in 1988 the owner of the ICAO building took the adjacent piece of land – known as 'the ICAO Plaza' – and built a twenty-seven-storey office tower to serve as a Canadian bank's regional head office. Any hopes for expansion at this location were frustrated and the new construction created additional environmental and security headaches. Consequently, in 1991 the council initiated discussions with the Canadian authorities about ICAO's location and established a working group to examine alternatives.[29]

Several possibilities were researched, including renovating the existing location and a selection of new sites in the downtown core. Ultimately a site was chosen in conjunction with the Canadian government at 999 University Street, closer to the old part of the city but still only a few blocks from the previous location. There were numerous concerns about the new location, ranging from air quality and security to the shape of the proposed roof. Noting the flat roof in the original design, one British council representative called for 'something more imaginative … to reflect the harmonious conjunction between land and sky for which ICAO was itself a symbol.' The greatest fears, however, were raised over the auto expressway and ventilation tower which bordered the new proposed University Street building, and there were concerns that the expressway (the ICAO website refers to it as a 'prestigious gateway into Montreal') would cause noise and vibration problems for the organization.[30]

The go-ahead for construction was given in 1993, once the council's concerns over environmental issues, sound proofing, etc., were satisfied, and the building was ready for occupancy in late 1996. The new glass-covered building provided 40,000 square meters of office space and consisted of three sections: a fifteen-story tower and five-story conference block, connected by a six-storey atrium. As Secretary General Rochat noted during the opening ceremonies, this atrium emphasized 'the link between those two pillars of ICAO life – the work of the Secretariat and the many meetings of the governing bodies and panels of the organization.'[31] ICAO signed a long-term lease and it seemed as if ICAO's location was finally set, although by early in the new century there were more space problems and additional office space was rented in a nearby building.[32]

The conference block contained the assembly hall and meeting rooms for the different ICAO committees, including the council and Air Navigation Commission. In both latter cases more room was made necessary by expansion. On 26 October 1990 the assembly agreed to increase council membership from thirty-three to thirty-six (amending Article 50(a) of the Chicago Convention); one year earlier Article 56 had been amended to increase the ANC from fifteen to nineteen members. Both increases were a response to a growing membership; for example, several members were reportedly sending observers to ANC meetings on a regular basis, and there were the habitual calls for greater representation on the council, which remained the key decision making body of the organization. The American government was not opposed, as it had been regarding expansion of these two bodies in the past, and the amendments were passed, although it took several years for them to be ratified by a sufficient number of members to come into force. The council expansion entered into force near the end of 2002, and Chile, Singapore, and South Africa were elected new council members at the Thirty-FourthExtraordinary ICAO Assembly in Montreal in 2003; the expansion of the ANC came into force only in 2005. Complaints and concerns over the role and membership of the council remained, especially from African and Asian states that felt blocked and underrepresented on the council.[33]

Along with the growing unease in the 1980s and 1990s over aviation *security* (see Chapter 14) was a parallel and more general – and constant – concern for aviation *safety*. And, not for the first time, ICAO moved ahead in this regard in response to – or at least in concert with – international events. In 1990 an Avianca Boeing 707 crash landed at New York's JFK Airport (because of lack of fuel, not sabotage), and in its wake the Federal Aviation Administration launched a program of its own (International Aviation Safety Assessment) to verify the safety standards of foreign aircraft flying into U.S. territory to ensure that they conformed to ICAO standards. Those airlines that were found to be wanting could be restricted from landing at American airports. Of the aviation authorities assessed, somewhere near 70 per cent did not meet ICAO standards.[34] The Europeans were also looking at similar action, but there were complaints about the American plan from Europe and Latin America, which suggested that there were economic rather than safety motives behind the American program. In any event, the FAA action only sparked more calls – including from the FAA itself – for ICAO to take over this oversight role and to play a bigger role in ensuring the implementation of its safety standards and procedures.[35]

Late in 1994 the council agreed to a program for safety oversight and, following consultation with the members and the endorsement of the Thirty-First ICAO Assembly in 1995, the Safety Oversight Programme was launched. Its goal was to assess how members had implemented ICAO safety procedures and to examine problem areas, where states had not met ICAO standards, and to offer advice to members to help them implement or enhance their safety programs. There would be follow-up actions to ensure that progress was being made. In 1997, the ICAO Council approved the official establishment of the Universal Safety Oversight Audit Programme which called for regular, universal, and mandatory safety audits to assess the implementation of standards relating to Annex 1 (Personnel Licensing), 6 (Operation of Aircraft), and 8 (Airworthiness). The safety audits were more extensive than the 'evaluations' performed regarding aviation security, and these audits were mandatory. States were to sign a memorandum of agreement with ICAO giving their consent to the audits, thereby respecting state sovereignty.[36] The USOAP was endorsed at the Thirty-Second ICAO Assembly in 1998.

At roughly the same time, the ANC produced its own plan, the Global Aviation Safety Plan in 1997, and it was endorsed at the following assembly sessions in 1998 and 2001. The objective of the plan was simple: to reduce the number and seriousness of aircraft accidents regardless of the growth in international aviation. The ANC would study the reports from each year's accidents and use the material supplied by the ICAO safety audits, and the ANC would then examine the causes of air accidents, promote safety awareness among the membership, and make recommendations that would lead to improved safety. The first edition of the GASP appeared in 2001 and it was distributed to the contracting states; the second edition was published in 2004.[37]

By 2001 over 170 safety audits had been performed and the results were mixed. The large number of requests for assistance underlined the desire and need for the program; at the same time, it clearly revealed that many states had fallen well short of implementing ICAO's safety standards. It is difficult to accurately measure the state of affairs, given the tremendous variation between states and with members at different stages of implementation. And non-compliance was difficult to measure; 'In legal terms,' Secretary General Rochat told a reporter, 'silence from the state means that the standard has been implemented. But the reality is a bit different. Some states do not have the capacity of even notifying us of the differences. So we don't have a complete picture.'[38] The result, one analyst wrote, was a 'fragmented and inconsistent application of safety standards'[39] Some progress was being made nevertheless, by individual states and within regions, and by the end of the twentieth century virtually all members had action plans and were in the process of implementing them either by themselves or with ICAO's assistance.[40]

What had begun as a voluntary and rather informal matter had evolved into a permanent monitoring function. 'In a few short years,' the Australian council representative noted in 2001, 'the Universal Safety Oversight Audit Programme had become one of the most prominent features of ICAO's contemporary contribution to international civil aviation.' It also had brought the organization into new territory; ICAO 'had made a qualitative move from its traditional role as the paramount source of international aviation safety standards, into a new and fundamentally different role, as an assessor of national compliance with those standards.'[41] And once ICAO had assumed this role there was no turning back to the old ways.

The safety oversight program developed within the context of a general movement of reform and renewal in the organization. The goals of this renewal were encompassed in ICAO's Strategic Action Plan, a broad 'blueprint' for reform initiated and revised over the course of the decade. Early plans for renewal were discussed at the Twenty-Seventh ICAO

Assembly in 1989, and in the following months the council began organizing a kind of inventory of problems and challenges facing the organization. 'As aviation moves towards and into the 21st century,' the council reported in 1992, 'States and the civil aviation industry are facing unprecedented challenges posed by traffic which continues to grow but is at times difficult to predict, emerging new technology, a rapidly changing commercial and regulatory framework, a growing awareness of the need for protection of the human environment, and a requirement for substantial investment in infrastructure, equipment and human resources at a time of increasingly competitive pressures for financial resources.' As a result of these forces, it was agreed that the council and secretariat should initiate a broad and complete re-examination of ICAO's purpose, policies, and actions, all with an eye to helping the organization meet its existing challenges and to prepare it for the future.[42]

The ICAO Council sent the member governments a statement to this effect and requested their views; almost fifty governments responded with their ideas and proposals. Likewise, the views of other organizations with which ICAO was associated were sought, and input was received in various forms from IATA, IFALPA, the Airports Association Council International, and others, including the International Telecommunications Union, which was undergoing a somewhat similar review of its operations. Once the responses were received, the council established a ten-member working group, chaired by Frederick Neal, the veteran British council representative, and a multidisciplinary group from within the secretariat to oversee the development of the plan. By 1992 a fairly comprehensive strategic plan was in place and it was endorsed by the membership at the Twenty-Ninth ICAO Assembly in 1992.[43]

The Strategic Action Plan was a broadly based and systematic review of ICAO's policies, actions, and objectives. The 'major challenges' facing the organization were divided into four main groups: (1) technological/technical (airport congestion, the implementation of satellite navigational systems), (2) economic and financial (economic regulation, financial resources), (3) human and social (these included safety/security concerns, protection of the environment) and (4) legal (the need to ratify conventions and to speed up the process of development, etc.). Under these four broad headings a series of strategic objectives were determined, along with the method through which they would be attained.[44]

All of these activities were based on several premises – premises that reflected not only how the organization viewed itself but also revealed some of the problems and concerns that it faced. The organization needed to

ICAO: A History

address the fact that the process of formulating and amendment of the standards was too slow and cumbersome. Equally, there was an acknowledgement of the need to lessen the great disparity between members with respect to the implementation of the standards, and that more technical and financial assistance was necessary for those members who had fallen behind. There was also a tacit acknowledgement that all the work put into developing air law conventions was pointless unless the governments ratified them and, therefore, it was agreed that more emphasis was needed on prompting the members into action. Similarly, there was the recognition of a need for better communication between the organization and its members and between ICAO and other international organizations. Finally, there was a need for ICAO to examine its own operations in an effort to streamline its activities, control costs, and become more efficient and flexible.

There was an uneasy – and unwritten – sense in all this work that ICAO's place in the international community was slipping, and one additional premise emphasized the need for the organization 'to project a higher public profile and play a stronger and catalytic role in co-ordinating and representing international civil aviation.'[45] There were fears that ICAO was being sidelined in the rush to globalization. As Frederick Neal wrote, 'we have a new phenomenon of major developments of direct importance to the aviation industry increasingly arising in fields where aviation interests may be only a minor, if important, component in a wider context. Satellite technology, frequency spectrum management, environmental policies and international trade and services negotiations are all fields where aviation is not the predominant customer; where the primary commercial interests of governmental policies are not determined by aviation; and where the aviation community has to react to policies determined mainly by others, rather than plot its own course.' ICAO could not 'rest on the considerable laurels it has earned in the past,' Neal continued, and 'must adapt itself to this new reality if it is not to risk being overtaken either by technology or by the emerging roles of other global or regional bodies.'[46]

The goal of all this activity was to create a roadmap for ICAO to follow into the future and, after several years of discussion, consultation, and revision, the Strategic Action Plan was formally launched on 22 May 1997. It now contained eight primary objectives that were fairly general and essentially called for a more efficient organization that could continue to do the things it always had done but faster and more efficiently. ICAO must 'foster,' 'strengthen,' 'ensure,' 'assist,' and 'respond' to its members; standards must be created, amended, and implemented transparently, thoroughly, and rapidly; and ICAO's human, technical, and financial resources must be utilized effectively so that ICAO could maintain its central role in the development of international civil aviation. There were also forty-three 'related key activities which define the "core" programme of the organization,'[47] and these were more specific goals, often with clear target dates. Work had already begun on many of these activities. Under the direction of the secretary general, for example, administrative reforms to the secretariat were introduced and work begun to improve the coordination of activities with the regional offices. On the technical side, there was a specific goal to oversee the implementation of a new global navigational satellite system; under legal issues the SAP called for the updating of the Warsaw system of aircraft liability, which had languished at the committee level for decades.[48]

Perhaps the most interesting aspect of the plan and the one with the farthest reaching implications for the organization was the general shift of emphasis on ICAO's role. As in the case of the maintenance of safety standards, there was a gradual shift in emphasis in the plan 'from development to implementation.' As Chris Lyle, who was the leader of the secretariat team directly involved in the development of the plan, noted, ICAO's traditional role had been to develop Standards and Recommended Practices, legal conventions, and manuals, to collect and disseminate statistics, and so on, and then to leave it up to governments to implement the standards, apply the conventions, and use the manuals and information as they saw fit. In the Strategic Action Plan there is more emphasis on ICAO *overseeing* the compliance of governments in their implementation and maintenance of the standards.[49]

One of the key goals of the Strategic Action Plan was to develop an ICAO policy for satellite communication, navigation and surveillance and to oversee the introduction of new air traffic management techniques on a global level. The ICAO Council's working paper on the SAP noted that the 'basic communications, navigation, and surveillance (CNS) system for civil aviation in use today throughout the world is essentially the one implemented in the late 1940s, with periodic upgrades and enhancements over the years. It has, in many ways, reached its limit for expansion and has other inherent limitations. It has been accepted that a satellite-based CNS system, together with enhancements to ground-based systems, is essential to meet the growing requirements of civil aviation world-wide.'[50] The problem was that the technology was extremely complex and changing rapidly and new systems were in the process of development. The goal was to develop an 'ICAO-concept' and to oversee its global application.

Satellite communications were widely expected to transform air travel by the end of the century. As one ICAO official explained to a reporter in 1994, 'five years ago civil aviation used satellites for nothing. Five years from now they will be used for nearly everything.'[51] The new technology would enhance safety and make navigation, especially over the oceans, much more precise, and greater precision would enable aircraft to fly closer together and to take better advantage of prevailing wind patterns, thereby increasing speed and efficiency while reducing aircraft emissions. Few denied the improvements that the new technology would bring, or even the inevitability of its application, but for ICAO, and in particular its less developed member states, it was a matter of the cost and of not being left behind. It would be important to ensure universal application of the new technology; conversely, universal application would be very expensive. As one observer wrote, the planning and use of any new system with global coverage, 'will necessitate a regional or global level of understanding; enhancing the crucial need for worldwide cooperation between ICAO, governments and the aviation industry.'[52]

The transition to a global navigational satellite system was already under way and involved several international organizations and individual states. The Americans and the Russians were in the process of introducing their own satellite-based navigational systems; the American Global Positioning System and the Russian Glonass system. Both states offered the free use of their satellite technology to ICAO members, although ICAO's intention was ultimately to establish a multinational system.[53] Planning was also well under way for the implementation of a broader communications, navigation, surveillance, and air traffic management systems (CNS/ATM). The concept had two parts, the first to introduce a satellite-based system for communications, navigation, and surveillance; the second to introduce an automated and integrated system of air traffic management.[54]

Work began on the development of standards and recommended practices for the implementation of the new technology and involved many individuals and groups, including the Council, Air Navigation Commission, the Committee on Aviation Environmental Protection, and several smaller Planning and Implementation Regional Groups. In 1998 a large ICAO – CNS/ATM conference was held in Rio de Janeiro to discuss issues of financing and the problems arising from technical cooperation, and at the Thirty-Second ICAO Assembly in Montreal the assembly adopted a Charter on the Rights and Obligations of States Relating to Global Navigation Satellite Systems, which, among other things, guaranteed access for all states 'on a non-discriminatory basis under uniform conditions, to the use of GNSS services.' That same year, a Global Air Navigation Plan for CNS/ATM Systems was endorsed by the council. The first package of SARPs for GNSS (included in Annex 10) became applicable in 2001.[55]

Throughout the process the technology constantly evolved, and it was decided that rather than focusing on the type of equipment that was to be used it made more sense to specify what was called a 'required navigation performance.'[56] In other words, ICAO would establish the standard that needed to be met without specifying which equipment a state should use to achieve it. It was a logical way to keep up with technological change and to enhance compliance by states individually or on a regional basis. In any event, the implementation of a global CNS/ATM system was a long-term process and its development continued well into the twenty-first century. In the process, the International Civil Aviation Organization had ensured for itself a central planning and policy role in its progress.

Although called for in the Strategic Action Plan, it was outside developments that prompted ICAO into action regarding the revision of the Warsaw Convention. ICAO and its Legal Committee had made little progress on revising the convention since the mid-1970s, and during the 1980s the development of new conventions and protocols dealing with aviation security took priority over air carrier liability. 'ICAO does not deserve any credit for the new initiatives leading to the modernization of the Warsaw System,' wrote Michael Milde, former director of ICAO's Legal Bureau. 'After the adoption of the four protocols in 1975, ICAO assemblies only kept exhorting the contracting states to ratify Additional Protocol No. 3 and Montreal Protocol No. 4 and in hypocritically unanimous resolutions continued "flogging a dead horse" until 1995 when the industry's initiative started a new momentum and overtook the inertia of States.' It would be unjust, he continued, 'to blame ICAO as an institution for the lack of creative courage. ICAO is only an instrument of its 185 member States and reflects their political will.'[57]

The existing situation, however, was increasingly unacceptable to many nations, including several major aviation states. The Americans had never been happy with Warsaw and had worked to apply their own rules and could at any time threaten again to denounce the Warsaw Convention as they had in the 1960s. In addition, by the early 1990s the Japanese,

Australians, and Europeans were moving towards the formulation of their own liability regimes. Then in 1995, at a conference in Washington, D.C., IATA produced the 'IATA Intercarrier Agreement on Passenger Liability' which established a two-tier system of liability, and this agreement was widely embraced internationally.[58]

All of these developments occurred outside the ICAO framework, and for ICAO it was a question of taking action or being left behind by others who were creating their own patchwork replacement for the Warsaw System. It was unlikely that the council would step aside and allow the erosion of ICAO's international position; if anything, ICAO was the one organization that could produce a universal agreement that could be applied evenly across the board. Indeed, if the goal of the Strategic Action Plan was to renew the organization, to embrace the modern world, and enhance ICAO's place in it, then a leadership role in the revision of the Warsaw system was an absolute necessity.

At the Thirty-First ICAO Assembly in October 1995 – in the aftermath of the signing of the IATA agreement – the assembly invited the council to focus more of its attention on revising the Warsaw Convention. In the months that followed the Secretariat Study Group on the Warsaw System was created and this group produced a new draft convention for the council by October 1996. The ICAO Council appointed a *rapporteur* to study and report on the subject, and this report was discussed by the council and the Legal Committee from 28 April to 9 May 1997. In November that year the council established another group – the Special Group on the Modernization and Consolidation of the Warsaw System – which met 14–18 April 1998 and refined the draft text. In February 1999, briefing seminars were held at several regional offices, including Bangkok, Dakar, Mexico City, Nairobi, and Paris, to explain and discuss the details of the new proposals. Finally, the council announced the holding of a full international conference for May 1999. The goal was impressive: an international agreement on a single convention to replace the Warsaw system; one that would encompass the existing convention and protocols: the Warsaw Convention (1929), the Hague Protocol (1955), the Montreal Agreement (1966), the Guatemala City Protocol (1971) and the four Montreal protocols (1975) (see Chapter 9).[59]

The International Conference on Air Law was held in Montreal from 10 to 28 May 1999.[60] The major issues at the conference, and throughout the whole process, were concerned with liability and jurisdiction and with questions over what limits, if any, should be placed on air carrier liability; where the burden of proof should be placed; and to which courts could the victims appeal. The IATA agreement included a two-tier system (tier one: absolute liability up to 100,000 Special Drawing Rights; tier two: no limit, based on fault) and this was supported by most of the major airlines and governments in advance of the conference and favoured by the study group and Legal Committee. A large group of African nations and others from the developing world, however, advocated a three-tier system, where the second tier would place the burden of proof on the victim rather than the air carrier.

This almost traditional division in ICAO between the developed and the developing states that had appeared in previous discussions over the Warsaw System was apparent once more. It has also been pointed out that the study group that drafted the convention comprised mainly members from developed states, with little representation from Asia, Africa, or Latin America, and questions have been raised about the whole process, which unfolded somewhat differently from the usual way. As Michael Milde wrote, 'deep divisions in the basic concepts remain, in particular between the developed and developing countries, as they existed during the preparatory stages preceding the conference.'[61] What was also clear was that the members comprising the major airlines – most of whom had supported the IATA Agreement – were determined to achieve a new convention in Montreal.

On 28 May 1999 the Convention for the Unification of Certain Rules for International Carriage by Air was signed by fifty-two states, including the United States. The new Montreal Convention, as it came to be called, gave the prominent ICAO members who were responsible for most of the world's commercial aviation largely what they wanted. The new convention deals with the international carriage of people, cargo, and baggage, but it was the liability and jurisdiction articles that received the most attention. The Montreal Convention includes a two-tier system largely based on the IATA model: the first tier includes strict liability up to 100,000 SDRs, while the second tier has no predetermined liability limits and is based on fault, with the burden of proof falling on the air carrier. Specific reference to 'mental' injury was excluded from the convention, only the words 'bodily injury' remained. The air carrier was liable for damage 'upon condition only that the accident which caused the death or injury took place on board the aircraft or in the course of any of the operations of embarking or disembarking' up to 100,000 SDRs and above that amount unless it could prove 'such damage was not due to the negligence or other wrongful act or omission of the carrier or its servants or agents; or such damage was solely due to the negligence or other wrongful act or omission of a third party.'[62] In other words, there would be no limit to liability unless the air carrier could prove that it was not negligent or, in some cases, that the injury to a passenger was caused by the negligence of the person claiming the compensation. It also meant that in American courts, lawyers no longer had to prove that the air carrier was willfully negligent to be able to seek compensation above the limits set in the original Warsaw system.

In addition, a new category of jurisdiction was added to the Montreal Convention – known as the fifth jurisdiction. The existing four Warsaw jurisdictions included the state of destination of the air service, the state of domicile of the air carrier, its principle place of business, and the state where the contract had been made. The new one enables victims to claim jurisdiction in their state of principal or permanent residence (but not necessarily their citizenship) at the time of the accident, providing that the air carrier operates to and from that state with its own aircraft or an aircraft through an agreement with another airline. Moreover, under the terms of the new agreement airlines would be required to submit proof that they have acquired sufficient private insurance to cover their potential liability, and they were now required to make advance payments to those entitled passengers to help them meet immediate financial needs.

The two key innovations of the Montreal Convention – removal of liability limits and the fifth jurisdiction – were great victories for the United States, because it meant that American victims now would be able to seek compensation in American courts – where the settlements tended to be much higher than elsewhere – and the onus would be on the air carriers to prove that they were not at fault. Those in the smaller states expressed concerns that the high settlements in American courts would drive up the cost of insurance for everybody – leading to another situation of the 'peasants paying for the King' like the proposals discussed in the 1960s. On the other hand, it was argued that although this argument might have made sense in the 1940s and 1950s, or even later, by the end of the twentieth century air travel was so safe and accidents were so rare that even with the removal of liability limits the cost of insurance would be manageable for all air carriers.

Finally, in a situation somewhat similar to the convention on plastic explosives (discussed in Chapter 14), ICAO was given a permanent monitoring role overseeing the Montreal Convention. Under the agreement, ICAO was granted the right to review the liability limits established in the convention on a five-year basis and could adjust them based on changing inflation rates. Any revision ultimately required the approval of the members, but once ICAO made the decision to adjust the limits the new limit would come into effect within six months unless a majority of members registered their disapproval. In times of great inflation it was also possible for the members to force a review of the liability limits.

The Montreal Convention was to come into effect with its thirtieth ratification. Interestingly, no additional requirements were necessary, as in, for example, the Guatemala City Protocol, which needed the votes of a certain number of states responsible for a particular percentage of international air traffic to come into force (ensuring the need for American support). The Montreal Convention came into force in 2003 (including ratification by the United States); the question remains whether this new convention will be the final act in a decades-long process or merely another attempt – one among many – to solve an intractable problem that divided the developed and developing worlds.

The 1990s was a decade of resurgence for the International Civil Aviation Organization. When the decade began the Organization faced serious challenges from a number of sources, with other groups, organizations, and states and regional groupings intruding into areas that ICAO had always believed were its own. By the end of the decade it had largely reasserted its role in international civil aviation. ICAO had reassumed a leadership role as the machinery through which the discussion of the economic regulation of international civil aviation would unfold; in aviation safety it had responded to the challenges from the Americans and the Europeans with the introduction of ICAO's safety oversight program; and it had taken the initiative from IATA (and Japan and other states) to amend the Warsaw Convention on aviation liability. In the process, these accomplishments had produced a greater and more direct role for ICAO in the oversight and implementation of its conventions and standards. In the Montreal Convention and Convention on Plastic Explosives, ICAO maintained continuous involvement in their revision; and with respect to the latter convention it was a role that ICAO assumed not only for commercial aviation but for the international community as a whole.

ICAO ended the decade in a more stable and influential position in the international system and as the new century approached the council began to examine the possible negative implications for ICAO of the 'Y2K' problem. Within a few months these days were looked back on, almost nostalgically, as much simpler times.

17

Meeting the Twenty-First Century

The events of last September have tended to obscure the fact that civil aviation continues to be an inherently safe mode of transport.[1]

The events of 11 September 2001 had a profound impact on the International Civil Aviation Organization and civil aviation in general. 'It is an incontrovertible fact,' wrote one aviation specialist, 'that the sad and tragic consequences of the events of 11 September 2001 affected first and foremost the victims of those terrible attacks, and their families. It is equally unchallengeable that the second casualty in this horrendous series of events was aviation.'[2] It is unlikely that any of the terrorists had intended it this way, but their actions posed a direct challenge to ICAO and all of its efforts in aviation security. The Tokyo, Hague, and Montreal Conventions, the Montreal Protocol and Convention on Plastic Explosives, Annex 17, the *Security Manual,* and amendments such as Article 3 bis, were all brought into question.

So much of ICAO's work had been aimed at the detection of plastic explosives, bombs, and any kind of weapons that passengers might hide or carry onto an aircraft, but the 11 September terrorists brought none of these things on board and, instead, used the aircraft itself as the weapon. Rather than the aircraft being the *target* of sabotage – which was anticipated in the ICAO conventions and protocols – the aircraft became the *means* of attack. All the regulations on baggage reconciliation and the screening and searching of passengers and luggage were bypassed because the terrorists were unarmed and carried little luggage with them. The amendments to Annex 17 dealing with airport security, securing the airport perimeter, isolating checked passengers from visitors, the security of airport lounges, the tarmac and ramp, and securing access to the aircraft from all unauthorized personnel were ignored by the terrorists, who in all respects appeared normal and acted properly as they passed through all the checkpoints. Like every other passenger, the 9/11 terrorists did nothing wrong when they entered the airport, bought tickets, sat in the airport lounges, and, ultimately, boarded the aircraft.

In addition, decades of work on the issues of jurisdiction, extradition, and sanctions against those states that supported or harboured terrorists – as seen in the more traditional hijackings – were rendered meaningless that day by terrorists who were not interested in coming back or in seeking asylum in any state. There were no debates about 'aircraft in distress' or whether or not an ICAO member would be obliged to permit any of the hijacked aircraft to land in its territory, because the 9/11 terrorists had no intentions of 'landing' the hijacked aircraft. Traditional thinking before 11 September called for the crew not to attack hijackers but to cooperate to ensure the safe landing of the aircraft; and even if something could have been done to stop the terrorists, Article 3 bis committed ICAO members to refrain from armed attacks against civil aircraft. Clearly, traditional thinking did not apply that day.

Moreover, so much of ICAO's efforts before 9/11 had focused on state compliance and in bridging the gap between the developed and the developing world. Certainly, it was not lost on most observers that, despite years of efforts by – and pressure on – the developing states to implement and tighten security standards, it was in the United States (presumably the most technologically advanced, up to date, and secure of all ICAO members) that these breaches of security occurred. Years of American persuasion, complaints, and veiled threats of unilateral action if ICAO and its members failed to raise their safety standards to American levels made no difference on 11 September. Finally, there was even a degree of irony in that even though the 11 September attacks represented perhaps the greatest security challenge in ICAO's history, because the events occurred only in the United States, in American aircraft, and against American targets, it could be argued that they were technically attacks against American *domestic* rather than *international* aviation and, therefore, were outside the jurisdiction of the International Civil Aviation Organization.

The impact of the 9/11 attacks was felt immediately and dramatically in the world of commercial aviation. Commercial aviation was responsible for millions of jobs world wide, and millions more in the related travel and tourism industries; by early 2002 Council President Assad Kotaite reported the loss of 120,000 jobs in the airline business and another 170,000 layoffs in the aerospace industry as a whole. In 2001 the combined operating loss of the commercial airlines was estimated at over \$10 billion. Passenger and cargo traffic plummeted, with the corresponding drop in revenues for the airlines and airports. The airlines cut back routes, reduced in-flight services, deferred delivery on new aircraft, and turned to governments for financial support; others just went out of business. The Belgian airline Sabena suspended its flight services; the Swiss government stepped in with a loan to keep Swissair flying; Canada 3000 Airlines declared bankruptcy. In Africa, where most airlines were still wholly or in part state-owned, Air Afrique declared bankruptcy in 2002. The Brazilian government stepped in and provided a broad aid package for its airlines; in the United States, United Airlines and US Airways filed for bankruptcy protection, and the American government provided billions of dollars in compensation for its air carriers. Heightened fears, the loss of public confidence, and tighter security led to more passenger and baggage screening and, consequently, longer waiting times at airports. The cost of doing business rose, so did the cost of travelling, with the spreading of the misery into related industries.[3]

Within a week of 9/11, insurance underwriters gave seven days notice of the cancellation of air carrier war risk third-party liability insurance. It was a dramatic move by insurance companies that faced catastrophic losses from 9/11, and this action threatened to bring the industry to its knees. The contracting states – and their airlines – turned to ICAO to find a way to prevent the looming crisis. It was the kind of thing that ICAO could do best, when the members were motivated to find a solution. The ICAO Council immediately called on governments, urging them to step in to provide the necessary insurance protection for their airlines, but this was only a temporary stop-gap measure.[4]

On 22 October the council established a Special Group on Aviation War Risk Insurance to study the problem and come up with a durable solution. Meetings of the special group were held within weeks. By early 2002 a limited-term arrangement was put together, bringing together insurance companies, governments, and ICAO into a new agreement to provide war risk insurance for the airlines. Each state would contribute to the scheme and would have a cap on its maximum liability based on its level of ICAO assessments. The insurance would be paid for by the consumer, with each ticket purchased, and the member governments would act as guarantors to stabilize the whole affair. The new plan was dubbed 'Globaltime,' and the council gave the members until early 2003 to indicate their acceptance of the proposals. As was the case in other matters during that chaotic time, no one could be sure of how it would turn out, and the whole arrangement was to be reviewed after five years; by then its effectiveness would be clearer.[5]

The International Civil Aviation Organization was moving into a new – and difficult – period in its history. Assad Kotaite remained as ICAO's public face and was now a fixture of the organization as the membership demonstrated its confidence in his abilities every three years by re-electing him as council president. Overseeing the Secretariat were two men: Renato Cláudio Costa Pereira and Taïeb Chérif. The Brazilian Pereira had worked for the Brazilian government in aviation affairs and was president of the Latin American Civil Aviation Commission from 1992 to 1996, and headed the Brazilian delegations to ICAO assemblies in 1992 and 1995. He was appointed secretary general in 1997 and served until 2003. Chérif, a native of Algeria, completed a Ph.D. in air transport economics at the Cranfield Institute of Technology in the United Kingdom and acquired several decades of aviation experience as a civil servant in the Algerian government. He also served as Algeria's representative on the ICAO Council, from 1998 to 2003, and chaired the Air Transport Committee. He was appointed secretary general in 2003, and his term was renewed in 2006, lasting through to July 2009.[6]

On the day of the 9/11 attacks, preparations were already well under way in Montreal for the Thirty-Third Assembly scheduled to open two weeks later, on 25 September. From the moment when the council concluded its minute of silence in honour of the 9/11 victims at its meeting the morning of 12 September, the highest priority for the organization's upcoming triennial meeting became security. Kotaite gave instructions to ICAO's aviation security section to devise proposals and suggestions to improve aviation security and to bring together all the necessary documents for the assembly. Security at the ICAO building itself was heightened as well.[7]

The assembly that autumn opened in a rather somber mood, as delegation after delegation expressed its outrage, sadness, and condolences for the victims and the American people in general. Most of the 169 delegations at the assembly had citizens from their nations in the towers of the World Trade Center that day. 'The tragic events of 11 September in the United States' said Council President Kotaite, 'sharpened the resolve of Contracting States and other members of the international community present at the Assembly to ensure that air transport remains the safest and most efficient system of mass transportation ever created.'[8]

Several important resolutions were adopted. The first (A33-1) was the Declaration on Misuse of Civil Aircraft as Weapons of Destruction and

Other Terrorist Acts Involving Civil Aviation, which in addition to statements of principle and a call for a complete review of all of ICAO's security policies, directed the council to consider creating an ICAO Universal Security Audit Programme along similar lines to ICAO's Universal Safety Oversight Audit Programme (USOAP). The same resolution called on the council to convene a conference at the ministerial level as soon as possible with the 'objectives of preventing, combating and eradicating acts of terrorism involving civil aviation; of strengthening ICAO's role in the adoption of SARPs in the field of security and the audit of their implementation; and of ensuring the necessary financial means.' Other resolutions dealt with issues such as the insurance crisis (A33-20) and technical cooperation (A33-21) and a lengthy consolidated statement of all of ICAO's security policies (A33-2). In addition, Resolution A33-8 called for the expansion of the USOAP to include Annexes 11 (Air Traffic Services) and 14 (Aerodromes).

The conference called for by the Assembly opened in Montreal on 19 February 2002 and included over seven hundred participants from 154 contracting states and two dozen international organizations. At the end of the two days, the conference endorsed the council's broad range of proposals for a global strategy to enhance aviation security, in particular its 'ICAO Plan of Action.' This plan had evolved in light of the sssembly resolutions and called for the systematic review of ICAO's security policies (the conventions, protocols, and annexes, especially Annex 17) and for the 'identification and analysis of new, emerging and potential threats to civil aviation, strategy to deal with the threats, modular application ... and prioritization of actions.'[9] It recommended the review and formulation of policies dealing with subjects ranging from locking cockpit doors and aircraft design to biometric identification and machine-readable passports. At the heart of the plan was the proposal, endorsed earlier by the Assembly, for a universal security audit program that would be systematic and mandatory for all ICAO members.

These proposals were approved by the ministerial conference: the participants acknowledged that only through state action and international cooperation in the application of security standards could public confidence in air transport be restored. To that end, the conference endorsed the Council's Plan of Action which, in part, included the following:

- Identification, analysis and development of an effective global response to new and emerging threats, integrating timely measures to be taken in specific fields including airports, aircraft and air traffic control systems

- Strengthening of the security-related provisions in the Annexes to the *Convention on International Civil Aviation,* using expedited procedures where warranted and subject to overall safety considerations, notably in the first instance to provide for protection of the flight deck
- Regular, mandatory, systematic and harmonized aviation security audits to evaluate security in place in all Contracting States at national level and, on a sample basis, at airport level for each State, under the ICAO Aviation Security Mechanism
- Close coordination and coherence with audit programmes at the regional and subregional level
- Processing of the results by ICAO in a way which reconciles confidentiality and transparency; and
- A follow-up programme for assistance, with rectification of identified deficiencies.[10]

The cost of the plan was estimated to be at least U.S. $15.4 million for the first three years, with the funds to come from voluntary contributions, with a more permanent plan for funding either by including the cost in the general fund (and added to state assessments) or through long-term commitments to voluntary funding from individual members. All members were called upon to participate and support the plan, and to provide what funding they could. And all of this was to be in place by the middle of June 2002.

The next months were very busy. On 14 June the council approved the 'Plan of Action,' with its attached list of thirteen major projects, most of which fell under the responsibility of the Air Transport Bureau, although the Air Navigation and Legal Bureaus were also involved. New security training and guidance material was produced; existing courses and manuals were reviewed and updated; videos, DVDs, CD-ROMs were also completed; aviation security seminars and workshops were organized, including two held in collaboration with the European Civil Aviation Conference and the Arab Civil Aviation Commission. More aviation training centres were approved, and the regional offices were brought in to help coordinate the programs. Virtually every annex was amended in some way and a sixth edition of the *Security Manual* was produced. Amendments were introduced to Annex 17 dealing with the access to the cockpit and the mandatory locking of the cockpit doors, and, as of 1 July 2006, 100 per cent of baggage carried in an aircraft's cargo hold was to be screened. The council also approved a recommendation of the International Explosives Technical Commission to amend the technical annex to the Convention on the Marking of Plastic Explosives, removing one of the detection agents from the approved list; and changes were made to the list of prohibited items permitted to be carried on board aircraft.[11]

Perhaps the single most important project in the 'Plan of Action' was the Universal Security Audit Programme (USAP), which comprised 'regular, mandatory, systematic and harmonized audits to enable the evaluation of aviation security in place in all Contracting States.'[12] In July 2002, the Council established an Aviation Security Audit Bureau reporting to the director of the Air Transport Bureau. This unit was given the responsibility to develop and implement the USAP. Audits were to be undertaken at the national and airport levels to determine the state of security and, in particular, the level of application of the standards and recommended practices contained in Annex 17. The process was meant to be fair, transparent, consistent, and inclusive, and the sovereignty of each member was to be respected; furthermore, the results of the audits were to be controlled and open only to ICAO and the audited state.[13]

A training course and examination procedure was set up to train auditors; an audit manual and pre-audit questionnaire was developed to ensure consistency and to help members prepare for the audits. Preparations for an audit began months in advance and were undertaken by a team of four, with each audit lasting approximately eight days. The whole process included a briefing and confidential report which was to be followed by the State's 'corrective action plan.' Deficiencies were pin-pointed; the need for technical assistance discussed, and together a plan for improvements was to be drawn up and its implementation monitored by the audited-state and the organization.[14]

The first USAP audit was launched in November 2002; by July 2004 more than 125 individuals had been trained and certified as auditors, and approximately forty-five audits were in the process of completion. More members were audited each year and what was started as a triennial project became a permanent part of ICAO's activities. A second round of security audits was scheduled to begin in 2008. Voluntary contributions decreased with each year, and plans were introduced to have the financing for the 'Plan of Action,' including the USAP, to be integrated fully in the ICAO Regular Programme Budget by 2010, ensuring funding for the future.[15]

Running concurrently with the USAP was the USOAP – ICAO's Programme for Safety Audits. A new edition of the Global Aviation Safety Plan was published in 2004, and by the end of that year 181 safety audits had been performed and audit follow-ups had been conducted in 138 states.

The mass of information from the audits was in the process of review by the Air Navigation Commission for use in the preparation of further amendments of the annexes.[16] Only a few states remained unaudited, and these tended to be in areas of considerable turmoil. In 2006, audits were undertaken in Sierra Leone and Liberia, under very difficult circumstances; and audits remained uncompleted only in Iraq, Afghanistan, Somalia, and a very few other states.[17]

At the Thirty-Fifth Assembly in September–October 2004, the USOAP was expanded to include 'all safety-related ICAO standards' as of the beginning of January 2005. Audits within this more comprehensive plan were initiated, and by the end of July 2007 sixty-one audits had been completed. Nigeria's mandatory safety audit, for example, took place from 7 to 17 November 2006, and the ICAO audit team made sixty-nine findings which were then targeted for remedy in Nigeria's Corrective Action Plan.[18] Further expansion of the USOAP occurred in 2006 at a conference of directors general of civil aviation of 153 ICAO members where it was agreed to publish the USOAP results for all members on the organization's website by March 2008. This expanded and comprehensive USOAP was scheduled to complete its six-year cycle in 2010, and internal discussions began to extend the plan or possibly turn it into a continuous monitoring program.[19]

To help implement its goals the International Civil Aviation Organization produced a new mission statement setting out its strategic objectives for the period 2005 to 2010. The list included six objectives. Aviation safety had always been the organization's first objective and, since the 1960s, it had been coupled with security. The third objective of environmental protection was a product of more recent times, and the remaining three included efficiency, continuity, and the rule of law. These objectives were to be achieved through the traditional means of study and planning, information exchange, technical cooperation, training, and the preparation of international air law. But, in addition, much greater emphasis was now to be placed on ICAO's newer role in the monitoring of the implementation of its standards, its safety and security audits, the preparation of remedial plans, and the general oversight of safety and security in international civil aviation.[20]

To this end, in 2005 ICAO initiated the development of a Global Aviation Safety Roadmap. The Roadmap was prepared under the leadership of IATA and involved a diverse group of airlines, operators, manufacturers, and organizations, including the Airports Council International, International Federation of Airline Pilots' Associations, Airbus, and

Boeing, in an effort to enhance aviation safety through coordination and the elimination of the duplication of efforts, and to bring together both the regulators (states, governments, and organizations) and the regulated (airlines, airports, and industry) in a common global effort. The first stage of the Roadmap was endorsed in 2006.[21]

An example of this new strategy was the Comprehensive Regional Implementation Plan for Aviation Safety in Africa (Africa-Indian Ocean [AFI] Plan) developed by the ICAO secretariat and approved by the council in 2007. Starting with the commitment of the African Union to reduce air accidents in Africa to the global average, the AFI Plan (under the leadership of the African Civil Aviation Commission) built on existing initiatives in the Africa-Indian Ocean region and helped bring ICAO into a greater role in monitoring and assessing the efforts to improve flight safety in the region.[22]

Throughout all of these activities the emphasis was placed on the implementation of the existing standards rather their amendment or the creation of new ones. 'I am happy to say,' declared the incoming council president, 'that there is now within ICAO a clear shift in focus towards implementation of standards. Of course, existing standards will continue to be updated where necessary to keep pace with the evolving aviation industry and new standards will reflect high-level requirements, with a clear benefit for safety. Yet implementation will prevail as the privileged path to improved safety.'[23]

Life went on at ICAO in the early years of the twenty-first century much as it had in the century before. A few new members arrived, including Andorra, Saint Kitts, and Nevis, bringing the membership to 189 states. Demands for the organization to do more seemed to go hand-in-hand with the reality of having to get along with less; annual expenditures rose slowly, as did expenses, and there was a constant problem of members not paying their assessments. At the end of 2003 there was a small deficit in the General Fund; as of May 2004, Secretary General Chérif informed the council that thirty members had their voting power suspended for failure to pay their assessments; thirteen of these states had failed to pay for more than three years.[24]

Requests for technical assistance remained high; obtaining the necessary financial resources was more difficult, as there was never enough money to go around and competition within the United Nations Development Programme was 'intense,' the council reported in 2002. 'The situation becomes even more critical when recipient countries change priorities away from civil aviation to favour programmes considered to be more essential.'[25] Still, each year's annual report contained many pages filled with projects and recipient nations, from Afghanistan to Vietnam. In 2001 ICAO returned to the Democratic Republic of the Congo to survey its airport conditions as part of a peacekeeping mission in conjunction with the U.N. Department of Peacekeeping Operations. Moreover, the Technical Co-operation Programme was expanded in 2004. Its connection to the UNDP remained and its activities continued to include the provision of experts and training of personnel, aid in procuring equipment and in the drafting of aviation regulations and legislation, and the establishment of training schools, etc., but the program was broadened to include non-state bodies (public and/or private), so long as they were involved in projects meant to improve aviation safety and security.[26]

Some problems were familiar, almost as old as the organization itself. Problems involving language and translation never went away; for example, in June 2004, the French council member raised the issue of the delays in the official launch of the French-language version of the ICAO website.[27] More seriously, the problems in the Middle East were reflected in the council as they had been many times before, including following the Israeli bombing of the Gaza International Airport in December 2001 and January 2002. Neither the Israelis nor the Palestinians were council members but both were invited to send representatives to the meetings. The old divisions remained and much of the rhetoric was familiar; in the end the council passed a resolution condemning the attacks and called on Israel to 'comply' with the terms of the Chicago Convention.[28] Only a few months later the focus turned to a surface-to-air missile attack on an Israeli airliner taking off from Kenya's Mombassa International Airport.[29] ICAO had as little impact on the outcome of these disputes as it had had on previous occasions.

Some new issues appeared and others garnered increasing attention. Much more attention was paid to the issue of unruly passengers and 'air rage,' and dealing with refugees or inadmissible air travellers.[30] ICAO also found itself working in cooperation with the World Health Organization on health issues such as Venous Thromboembolism and, following the 2003 SARS crisis, containing the spread of diseases through airports.[31] Similarly, ICAO worked with ACI to announce, in early 2007, the creation of the Airport Management Professional Accreditation Programme aimed at improving the professional skills and knowledge of airport managers. Another major development was the introduction of a new standard (in Annex 9) requiring all members to issue ICAO-standard machine readable passports by 2010. It was an idea that ICAO had supported and studied since the 1970s (for security and facilitation reasons), and by 2005, when the new standard was introduced, more than 100 members had already embraced the new-style passports.[32]

New problems, like the increasing threat posed by cyberterrorism or the introduction of suborbital flights were approached in typical ICAO fashion – through the creation of panels and committees, discussion and study, and debate and resolution. The latter issue was especially import-ant, as suborbital flight seemed to be on the horizon and no longer a matter of conjecture. Space flight posed a direct challenge to state sover-eignty, and the question of how high up does a nation's airspace go – the 'vertical limit of airspace' – was no longer a theoretical one.[33] And, of course, the council and its main committees continued to study, refine, and amend the Annexes, bringing them up to date. For example, in 2001 Annex 14 (Aerodromes) was amended to provide specifications to accommodate the anticipated arrival of aircraft larger than 747s. In its 162nd session in February – March 2001, the council adopted amend-ments to Annexes 1–4, 6, 8, 10–15, and 18.[34]

The environment and, in particular, aircraft greenhouse gas emissions emerged as a major issue for the International Civil Aviation Organization. It could be argued that ICAO had always been involved in some way with environmentalism – its years of work on noise pollution, for example – but with the signing of the 1997 Kyoto Protocol and the rise of the new, stronger environmental movement at the turn of the century, much more public – and governmental – attention was brought to the problem in a way not seen before. ICAO was directly involved through the larger framework of the United Nations Environmental Programme and the Kyoto Protocol, which gave ICAO the responsibility for overseeing the task of reducing aircraft engine emissions.

Following the Thirty-Second Assembly in 1998 the council created the Committee on Aviation Environmental Protection (CAEP) to examine the question of greenhouse gas emissions and to recommend policies to help reduce or limit them. It was – and remains – a difficult problem, and, given the fairly steady increase over the previous decades in the numbers of aircraft in the air, it was a major challenge even to limit the rate of in-crease in the use of fuel. The new committee looked for action in areas ranging from technological advancements to help aircraft burn less fuel and operate more efficiently, to improvements in air traffic management, better airport planning, and other ways to minimize energy use on land and in the sky, to the use of taxes or charges such as a fuel tax, or a trading system for emissions between groups, to voluntary methods that states could implement on their own. In 2004 CAEP recommended a 12 per cent reduction from 1999 levels in oxides of nitrogen standards.[35]

Progress on the environment has been very slow. Introducing new more fuel-efficient aircraft is time-consuming and a very expensive process; revamping existing standards and procedures is equally deliberate, and nothing can be accomplished without the active support of the membership. In the event, by 2007 the aviation world found itself 'in the eye of an unusual climate-change storm,' wrote one journalist on the eve of an ICAO colloquium on aircraft emissions. 'Many travelers, rich and not-so-rich, have recently begun to feel that air travel is a guilty pleasure that needs some kind of environmental atonement.'[36]

Environmental protection was one of the main items on the agenda of the Thirty-Six Assembly in Montreal in September 2007. The assembly agreed to establish a new group of government officials, the Group on International Aviation and Climate Change, to make recommendations to reduce engine emissions. The group is to devise a strategy for future discussion, but there are no targets to be met, only an agreement to meet again at a later date. Even within this limited achievement there was a great deal of debate at the assembly over the setting of specific targets and the use of emissions trading systems.[37] Aircraft emissions contribute only a relatively small percentage of global greenhouse gases, but they are now imbedded in the public imagination as a major part of the problem[38] and dealing with them remains a work in progress at ICAO.

An older issue – and also one that remains unfinished on the ICAO agenda – is the economic regulation of the air transport industry. Even before 9/11 some consideration was being given to hosting another international conference to examine issues around the liberalization of air transport within a global framework. It took a couple of years to make the arrangements, but from 24 to 28 March 2003, ICAO hosted the World Wide Air Transport Conference, the fifth in a series of conferences dating back almost twenty years. It was a large, well-attended conference, with representatives from 145 contracting states and twenty-six observer delegations. There was general support for the 'gradual, progressive and safeguarded liberalization' of international air transport, and it was agreed that the goal of the conference would be to focus 'on "how to" rather than "whether to" liberalize international air transport.' Beyond that, however, the qualifying of goals, terms, and time frames started soon after the opening ceremonies, and divisions appeared, with some states supporting bilateral arrangements and others looking for multilateral or regional or subregional solutions. Some states called for an emphasis on 'fair competition' rather than 'free competition,' expressing their concerns that 'unfettered competition might lead to irreversible changes which could be detrimental to the international air transport network.' It was even conceded that 'it was up to each State to decide what would constitute "gradual and progressive liberalization."'[39]

The basic divisions from earlier conferences, between the developed and developing world, remained. As the conference report explained, 'a substantial number of developing States, citing the imbalance in their economies and airlines *vis-à-vis* those of developed States, saw a need for an aviation mechanism to ensure fair competition and safeguard their effective and sustained participation in international air transport.'[40] A working paper submitted by a group of fifty-three African states expressed some of their concerns about liberalization – in language reminiscent of 1947: the African states 'did not support liberalization of market access on a global basis that would include unrestricted granting of traffic rights beyond the Third and Fourth Freedoms of the air.' Instead, the paper continued, 'underlying traffic rights should be the basis for the authorization of operations within the framework of commercial agreements.'[41] As a result, the conference ended with many areas of agreement, but relatively little movement forward. As one conclusion stated, 'while multilateralism in commercial rights to the greatest extent possible continues to be an objective of ICAO, conditions are not ripe at this stage for a global multilateral agreement for the exchange of traffic rights.'[42]

The most positive outcome of the conference was the official Declaration of Global Principles for the Liberalization of International Air Transport, a five-page document aimed at a broader audience 'beyond the aviation community' undertaken in an effort to 'set out key principles designed to guide the future development of international civil aviation for many years to come.'[43] The declaration consisted of a series of statements committing ICAO and its members to the gradual liberalization of international air transport, all within the context of the principles of the Chicago Convention; it would be undertaken in a safe and orderly way, with each member deciding how fast and far to go, with respect to state sovereignty and the principles of fairness and equality. The declaration also guaranteed a role for ICAO calling on the organization to 'continue to exert the global leadership role in facilitating and coordinating the process of economic liberalization and ensuring the safety security and environmental protection of international air transport.'[44]

No one could disagree with these basic principles, but they could not mask the fact that the International Civil Aviation Organization had made relatively little progress overseeing the framing of a multilateral agreement on commercial rights. Nevertheless, there was nothing preventing those nations that wanted liberalization from achieving it on their own, *outside* ICAO. Indeed, in 2001 there were eighty bilateral air agreements signed, and most exhibited some aspects of liberalization. In addition, between 1995 and 2001 approximately eighty-five 'open skies' agreements were signed (with full market access, and no restrictions on routes, capacity, or frequencies).[45] And, given that in 2002 four countries – the United States, Japan, the United Kingdom, and Germany – accounted for 47 per cent of the total volume of scheduled passenger, freight, and mail traffic (31%, 6%, 5%, 5% respectively) and 37 per cent of all international traffic,[46] it was possible for a relatively few states to ensure the advent of liberalization in international air transport for most of the world. Perhaps the greatest movement to liberalization will come from the European Union and the United States. In 2003 negotiations were launched between the European Commission and the American government for an Open Aviation Area Agreement to replace all the existing bilateral agreements with a new arrangement to govern air services between Europe and the United States. A final agreement is to be achieved in stages and once complete it would create a single aviation market encompassing a majority of the world's international air traffic.[47] Similar negotiations were launched by the European Commission with the governments of Israel and New Zealand in 2007 and 2008.

'The liberalization with which we are dealing is an irreversible yet gradual process.' declared Council President Kotaite at the beginning of the 2003 conference.[48] He could have been speaking about the whole history of ICAO, but for the first time in almost fifty years that process would unfold without him. Following his re-election (for the eleventh time) in 2004, Kotaite announced that this would be his final term and that the transition to a new council president should begin. A council election was held in March 2006, with two contenders: former Secretary General Philippe Rochat and Roberto Kobeh González, from Mexico. Both men had significant experience in the field of aviation and both knew ICAO well; Rochat from his years as secretary general and Kobeh González as the Mexican council representative since 1998. Before that, Kobeh González had been a professor of aeronautical electronics and had worked in the Mexican government and served as director general of the Air Navigation Services of Mexico from 1978 to 1997. Kobeh

González defeated Rochat by a vote of twenty-four to twelve on 2 March, and the new president took office on 1 August 2006.[49]

For only the third time in its history the International Civil Aviation Organization underwent a change of leadership at the very top. Edward Warner oversaw the creation of the organization and the establishment of its goals and objectives; Walter Binaghi, who both as council president and earlier as the chair of the Air Navigation Commission, guided the development, approval, and application of the great majority of ICAO's Annexes, and directed the evolution of the organization into a multicultural and global organization; and Assad Kotaite, who brought to the job his own brand of aviation diplomacy and oversaw the expansion of ICAO's international role into a more public, diplomatic, and political one and led the organization through a series of difficult crises from the downing of the Korean Airliner and Iranian Airbus to the terrorist attacks of 9/11.[50] Now it fell to Kobeh González to lead the organization into the new era of globalization in international commercial aviation, in terms of economics, safety, security, and environmentalism. New demands on the organization for transparency and accountability will continue to influence its activities, but González's greatest task may well be to complete the transition of ICAO from its traditional role in preparing SARPS and Annexes into an organization that oversees and monitors the implementation of its standards and procedures.

ICAO's greatest strength is also, perhaps, its greatest weakness. The organization was founded on the principles of the recognition of the state's sovereignty over its territorial airspace and of state sovereignty within ICAO. The organization is welcoming to its membership; no state is forced to take action against its will; no government is threatened or coerced into action. Consequently, ICAO's greatest achievements have been made through negotiation and the formation of consensus, and its decisions have received almost universal acceptance, if not compliance. There have been many divisions and debates in tension-filled meetings, but the council has acted almost always with a nearly unanimous voice; and, despite all the differences of opinion and the multitude of voices at the table, rarely did the more political overtones affect the outcome of a council decision when it came to matters of the safety and security of international aviation. In the same sense that Fiorella LaGuardia could proclaim at the Chicago Conference in 1944 that 'everyone is against bad weather' it can be stated today that everyone is in favour of safer aircraft and airports and a more secure air transport industry. The fact that ICAO has as its focus aviation safety and security insulated it a little from outside debates – in the Cold War, for example – and made it different from many other organizations, in particular the United Nations, in that there was a basis for cooperation right from the start. As Assad Kotatie later reflected, throughout ICAO's history there was no room for compromise when it came to air safety.[51]

Conversely, that same state sovereignty puts serious limits on what ICAO can accomplish. ICAO can make standards and procedures but it cannot force states to comply or implement them, even in the case where the state in question was a strong supporter of the action in the first place. It can negotiate conventions and protocols but it cannot force states to ratify them, or punish them if they fail to live up to their terms. Time and again it was demonstrated that when the contracting states were motivated great strides were made in a spirit of cooperation and things were done very quickly. When the members were not motivated, however, action was postponed, committees bogged down, and progress was delayed. Consensus was often reached but more often than not only when accompanied by bargaining and concession, where one side accepted change only when it was rephrased to make it more palatable or its implementation was delayed to suit those less willing and or able to take action. And state sovereignty left it to the members to implement the standards created by ICAO; governments decided on the pace of implementation and on the degree of compliance. Only in recent years has ICAO moved in a major way into the oversight of the implementation of its standards and procedures through projects such as the Universal Security Audit and Universal Safety Oversight Audit Programmes.

Perhaps the best example demonstrating the limits of ICAO's power has been the decades-long effort towards achieving a multilateral method for the economic regulation and liberalization of international air travel. From Geneva in 1947 to Montreal in 2003, ICAO hosted the conferences and refereed the discussions, but it could not force a solution. As an organization, ICAO has no specific policy on liberalization and multilateralism, other than in a very general way. It can only reflect the views of the membership and on this question the organization remains divided. It is unlikely that a solution will be found, at least within ICAO, unless and until a greater international consensus can be reached.

The basic sovereignty of the states remains at the heart of ICAO today, although through more than sixty years a great body of air law has evolved under the auspices of ICAO, along with a host of regulations, commitments, and associations that bind the members in a cooperative venture.

As one aviation specialist wrote, 'the sovereignty principle has therefore evolved to become a cohesive system of coexistence in the air by states which respect the exclusive rights of each state to sovereignty over its airspace. Mutual obligations have sprung up between states bringing as their corollary a deep respect for the principles of international law and the rights of individual states.'[52] By accepting and adopting these ICAO principles, each member has tacitly accepted limits on its actions, and ICAO has evolved into an independent institution, with a real presence and a degree of influence in the international community.

It is not difficult to measure the value of ICAO's role in the development of international civil aviation: air flight is the safest mode of transportation in the world, and the safety standards introduced and maintained by ICAO have made a significant contribution to that success. ICAO has played that role within the context of its membership in the United Nations system and in cooperation with other organizations dealing with aviation safety including the International Air Transport Association, the International Federation of Airline Pilots' Associations, Airports Council International, the regional aviation groups, and individual states. In addition, through its annexes, conventions, amendments, and legal instruments ICAO has made a significant contribution to the safety of *all* commercial aviation, not just international aviation. In 1944 the line between international and domestic civil aviation was fairly clear, but that line has virtually disappeared today, with hundreds of airports and airlines participating in international air transport. In the process, ICAO's standards and procedures have increasingly come to be applied to both international and domestic aviation. The security conventions and the standards for aircraft and airports established rules that are followed everywhere by everyone, not just on the international side of things. And whereas in the 1940s and 1950s ICAO represented only a select group – largely the victors of the Second World War and their allies – by the turn of the twenty-first Century ICAO's membership included almost every nation on earth, and its standards were applied domestically and internationally all around the world.

The International Civil Aviation Organization began as a collection of wartime allies with the good idea that an international body was necessary to oversee the safe development of international air travel. There was little support for resurrecting the International Commission for Air Navigation, so a new organization was necessary. In its early years the organization was dominated by a handful of members, primarily from North America and Europe. In the 1960s and 1970s, ICAO evolved into a diverse and multicultural organization with global reach and all the problems associated with rapid growth. Fault lines appeared on the divisions of power, wealth, geography, and language. The organization acquired a political dimension, which began to interfere and mar aspects of the workings of ICAO. In the process of becoming a modern global organization at least a few questions were raised about the very survival of the organization, but at no time did politics trump the central goal of air safety.

In the modern era a new – and unanticipated – role for ICAO appeared with the rise of air hijacking, sabotage, and armed attacks against civil aviation. When it came to armed attacks by ICAO members, such the Soviet Union, the United States, or Israel, ICAO provided the machinery – and the diplomatic initiative – to help ease international tensions. In the search for solutions to international aviation terrorism, ICAO emerged as the prime vehicle for the establishment of international air law and the regulations for ensuring aviation security. ICAO embraced the task, and its role in aviation security is probably the single most distinguishable feature of its public profile today.

It is harder to measure success in aviation security. ICAO never freed a single hostage or captured a terrorist; it never conducted negotiations with terrorists or authorized military action against states that harboured or aided terrorists and hijackers. It is not a police force, intelligence service, court of justice, or state authority. Rarely did it ever take an overtly political stand beyond the position established by the United Nations, and more often than not in its own council it condemned the *act* of terrorism rather than the terrorists, their state, or their cause. ICAO also appeared at times to be in a constant state of catch-up to the latest terrorist action, from the first hijackings and acts of sabotage to the Air India and Lockerbie disasters of the 1980s to 9/11. It continues today: in August 2006, days after the failed terrorist plot against aircraft flying from the United Kingdom to North America the ICAO Council called on its AVSEC panel to begin an investigation into the threat to commercial aviation posed by liquid explosives, and the council issued security guidelines that were developed for screening liquids and aerosol products.[53] Likewise, several years after 9/11, preliminary studies are now under way to either amend an existing convention or develop a new one to deal with the use of civil aircraft as weapons.[54]

It is not the whole story, however. What is missing is the recognition of the constant effort in ICAO to build international consensus; frame conventions and protocols; amend the SARPS to reflect changing technology, consumer patterns, and the growth of global aviation; and oversee the implementation of all these standards and procedures by all of its members. ICAO's biggest challenge is to motivate governments to come to agreement on terms, ratify its conventions, implement its standards, and take concerted action against terrorism. And it is only one important component of a larger international effort to combat terrorism in all its forms.[55]

Ultimately it is impossible to be definitive about the level of success. Just as air safety is measured in the public mind by the number of air crashes (rather than by the more mundane millions of passenger-kilometres flown), security in the air is only as successful as the latest terrorist attack. What is clear is that complete victory against aviation terrorism is impossible to attain but, equally, the failure to act is unacceptable. ICAO, the contracting states, and their citizens have to be prepared to live with maintaining that struggle, knowing that it is never enough, and never knowing if there is something else that should be or could have been done.

It's all about safety – the safety of aircraft and airports and international air travel. In pursuing this goal of safety in aviation ICAO has acted as part legal and technical think-tank and research institute, part information collection agency, part international public forum and debating club, part foreign aid service, and as a global regulator, monitor, referee, and support group all rolled into one. Air transport has become 'a fundamental instrument in society, a catalyst of the economy and the development of different sectors,' said Assad Kotaite at one of his last council sessions, 'no-one could imagine a world without air transport.'[56] In the same breath he might have added that no one could imagine the world of international commercial aviation without the presence and contribution of the International Civil Aviation Organization.

Appendix:
Convention on International Civil Aviation (1944)

PREAMBLE

WHEREAS the future development of international civil aviation can greatly help to create and preserve friendship and understanding among the nations and peoples of the world, yet its abuse can become a threat to the general security, and

WHEREAS it is desirable to avoid friction and to promote that co-operation between nations and peoples upon which the peace of the world depends,

THEREFORE, the undersigned governments have agreed on certain principles and arrangements in order that international civil aviation may be developed in a safe and orderly manner and that international air transport services may be established on the basis of equality of opportunity and operated soundly and economically,

Have accordingly concluded this Convention to that end.

PART I – AIR NAVIGATION
CHAPTER I
GENERAL PRINCIPLES AND APPLICATION
OF THE CONVENTION

Article 1
Sovereignty

The contracting States recognize that every State has complete and exclusive sovereignty over the airspace above its territory.

Article 2
Territory

For the purposes of this Convention the territory of a State shall be deemed to be the land areas and territorial waters adjacent thereto under the sovereignty, suzerainty, protection or mandate of such States.

Article 3
Civil and state aircraft

a) This Convention shall be applicable only to civil aircraft, and shall not be applicable to state aircraft.

b) Aircraft used in military, customs and police services shall be deemed to be state aircraft.

c) No state aircraft of a contracting State shall fly over the territory of another State or land thereon without authorization by special agreement or otherwise, and in accordance with the terms thereof.

d) The contracting States undertake, when issuing regulations for their state aircraft, that they will have due regard for the safety of navigation of civil aircraft.

Article 4
Misuse of civil aviation

Each contracting State agrees not to use civil aviation for any purpose inconsistent with the aims of this Convention.

CHAPTER II
FLIGHT OVER TERRITORY OF CONTRACTING STATES

Article 5
Right of non-scheduled flight

Each contracting State agrees that all aircraft of the other contracting States, being aircraft not engaged in scheduled international air services shall have the right, subject to the observance of the terms of this Convention, to make flights into or in transit non-stop across its territory and to make stops for non-traffic purposes without the necessity of obtaining prior permission, and subject to the right of the State flown over to require landing. Each contracting State nevertheless reserves the right, for reasons of safety of flight, to require aircraft desiring to proceed over regions which are inaccessible or without adequate air navigation facilities to follow prescribed routes, or to obtain special permission for such flights.

Such aircraft, if engaged in the carriage of passengers, cargo, or mail for remuneration or hire on other than scheduled international air services, shall also, subject to the provisions of Article 7, have the privilege of taking on or discharging passengers, cargo, or mail, subject to the right of any State where such embarkation or discharge takes place to impose such regulations, conditions or limitations as it may consider desirable.

Article 6
Scheduled air services

No scheduled international air service may be operated over or into the territory of a contracting State, except with the special permission or other authorization of that State, and in accordance with the terms of such permission or authorization.

Article 7
Cabotage

Each contracting State shall have the right to refuse permission to the aircraft of other contracting States to take on in its territory passengers, mail and cargo carried for remuneration or hire and destined for another point within its territory. Each contracting State undertakes not to enter into any arrangements which specifically grant any such privilege on an exclusive basis to any other State or an airline of any other State, and not to obtain any such exclusive privilege from any other State.

Article 8
Pilotless aircraft

No aircraft capable of being flown without a pilot shall be flown without a pilot over the territory of a contracting State without special authorization by that State and in accordance with the terms of such authorization. Each contracting State undertakes to insure that the flight of such aircraft without a pilot in regions open to civil aircraft shall be so controlled as to obviate danger to civil aircraft.

Article 9
Prohibited areas

a) Each contracting State may, for reasons of military necessity or public safety, restrict or prohibit uniformly the aircraft of other States from flying over certain areas of its territory, provided that no distinction in this respect is made between the aircraft of the State whose territory is involved, engaged in international scheduled airline services, and the aircraft of other contracting States likewise engaged. Such prohibited areas shall be of reasonable extent and location so as not to interfere unnecessarily with air navigation. Descriptions of such prohibited areas in the territory of a contracting State, as well as any subsequent alterations therein, shall be communicated as soon as possible to the other contracting States and to the International Civil Aviation Organization.

b) Each contracting State reserves also the right, in exceptional circumstances or during a period or emergency, or in the interest of public safety, and with immediate effect, temporarily to restrict or prohibit flying over the whole or any part of its territory, on condition that such restriction or prohibition shall be applicable without distinction of nationality to aircraft of all other States.

c) Each contracting State, under such regulations as it may prescribe, may require any aircraft entering the areas contemplated in sub-paragraphs (a) or (b) above to effect a landing as soon as practicable thereafter at some designated airport within its territory.

Article 10
Landing at customs airport

Except in a case where, under the terms of this Convention or a special authorization, aircraft are permitted to cross the territory of a contracting State without landing, every aircraft which enters the territory of a contracting State shall, if the regulations of that State so require, land at an airport designated by that State for the purpose of customs and other examination. On departure from the territory of a contracting State, such aircraft shall depart from a similarly designated customs airport. Particulars of all designated customs airports shall be published by the State and transmitted to the International Civil Aviation Organization established under Part II of this Convention for communication to all other contracting States.

Article 11
Applicability of air regulations

Subject to the provisions of this Convention, the laws and regulations of a contracting State relating to the admission to or departure from its territory of aircraft engaged in international air navigation, or to the operation and navigation of such aircraft while within its territory, shall be applied to the aircraft of all contracting States without distinction as to nationality and shall be complied with by such aircraft upon entering or departing from or while within the territory of that State.

Article 12
Rules of the Air

Each contracting State undertakes to adopt measures to insure that every aircraft flying over or maneuvering within its territory and that every aircraft carrying its nationality mark, wherever such aircraft may be, shall comply with the rules and regulations relating to the flight and maneuver of aircraft there in force. Each contracting State undertakes to keep its own regulations in these respects uniform, to the greatest possible extent, with those established from time to time under this Convention. Over the high seas, the rules in force shall be those established under this Convention. Each contracting State undertakes to insure the prosecution of all persons violating the regulations applicable.

Article 13
Entry and clearance regulations

The laws and regulations of a contracting State as to the admission to or departure from its territory of passengers, crew, or cargo of aircraft, such as regulations relating to entry, clearance, immigration, passports, customs, and quarantine shall be complied with by or on behalf of such passengers, crew or cargo upon entrance into or departure from, or while within the territory of that State.

Article 14
Prevention of spread of disease

Each contracting State agrees to take effective measures to prevent the spread by means of air navigation of cholera, typhus (epidemic), smallpox, yellow fever, plague and such other communicable diseases as the contracting States shall from time to time decide to designate, and to that end contracting States will keep in close consultation with the agencies concerned with international regulations relating to sanitary measures applicable to aircraft. Such consultation shall be without prejudice to the application of any existing international convention on this subject to which the contracting States may be parties.

Article 15
Airport and similar charges

Every airport in a contracting State which is open to public use by its national aircraft shall likewise, subject to the provisions of Article 68, be open under uniform conditions to the aircraft of all the other contracting States. The like uniform conditions shall apply to the use, by aircraft of every contracting State, of all air navigation facilities, including radio and meteorological services, which may be provided for public use for the safety and expedition of air navigation.

Any charges that may be imposed or permitted to be imposed by a contracting State for the use of such airports and air navigation facilities by the aircraft of any other contracting State shall not be higher,

a) as to aircraft not engaged in scheduled international air services, than those that would be paid by its national aircraft of the same class engaged in similar operations, and

b) as to aircraft engaged in scheduled international air services, than those that would be paid by its national aircraft engaged in similar international air services.

All such charges shall be published and communicated to the International Civil Aviation Organization: provided that, upon representation by an interested contracting State, the charges imposed for the use of airports and other facilities shall be subject to review by the Council, which shall report and make recommendations thereon for the consideration of the State or States concerned. No fees, dues or other charges shall be imposed by any contracting State in respect solely of the right of transit over or entry into or exit from its territory of any aircraft of a contracting State or persons or property thereon.

Article 16
Search of aircraft

The appropriate authorities of each of the contracting States shall have the right, without unreasonable delay, to search aircraft of the other contracting States on landing or departure, and to inspect the certificates and other documents prescribed by this Convention.

CHAPTER III
NATIONALITY OF AIRCRAFT

Article 17
Nationality of aircraft

Aircraft have the nationality of the State in which they are registered.

Article 18
Dual registration

An aircraft cannot be validly registered in more than one State, but its registration may be changed from one State to another.

Article 19
National laws governing registration

The registration or transfer of registration of aircraft in any contracting State shall be made in accordance with its laws and regulations.

Article 20
Display of marks

Every aircraft engaged in international air navigation shall bear its appropriate nationality and registration marks.

Article 21
Report of registrations

Each contracting State undertakes to supply to any other contracting State or to the International Civil Aviation Organization, on demand, information concerning the registration and ownership of any particular aircraft registered in that State. In addition, each contracting State shall furnish reports to the International Civil Aviation Organization, under such regulations as the latter may prescribe, giving such pertinent data as can be made available concerning the ownership and control of aircraft registered in that State and habitually engaged in international air navigation. The data thus obtained by the International Civil Aviation Organization shall be made available by it on request to the other contracting States.

CHAPTER IV
MEASURES TO FACILITATE AIR NAVIGATION

Article 22
Facilitation of formalities

Each contracting State agrees to adopt all practicable measures, through the issuance of special regulations or otherwise, to facilitate and expedite navigation

by aircraft between the territories of contracting States, and to prevent
unnecessary delays to aircraft, crews, passengers and cargo, especially in the
administration of the laws relating to immigration, quarantine, customs
and clearance.

Article 23
Customs and immigration procedures

Each contracting State undertakes, so far as it may find practicable, to establish
customs and immigration procedures affecting international air navigation in
accordance with the practices which may be established or recommended from
time to time, pursuant to this Convention. Nothing in this Convention shall be
construed as preventing the establishment of customs-free airports.

Article 24
Customs duty

a) Aircraft on a flight to, from, or across the territory of another contracting
State shall be admitted temporarily free of duty, subject to the customs regulations of the State. Fuel, lubricating oils, spare parts, regular equipment and
aircraft stores on board an aircraft of a contracting State, on arrival on the
territory of another contracting State and retained on board on leaving the
territory of that State shall be exempt from customs duty, inspection fees or
similar national or local duties and charges. This exemption shall not apply to
any quantities or articles unloaded, except in accordance with the customs
regulations of the State, which may require that they shall be kept under
customs supervision.

b) Spare parts and equipment imported into the territory of a contracting
State for incorporation in or use on an aircraft of another contracting State
engaged in international air navigation shall be admitted free of customs duty,
subject to compliance with the regulations of the State concerned, which may
provide that the articles shall be kept under customs supervision and control.

Article 25
Aircraft in distress

Each contracting State undertakes to provide such measures of assistance to
aircraft in distress in its territory as it may find practicable, and to permit, subject
to control by its own authorities, the owners of the aircraft or authorities of the
State in which the aircraft is registered to provide such measures of assistance
as may be necessitated by the circumstances. Each contracting State, when

undertaking search for missing aircraft, will collaborate in co-ordinated measures which may be recommended from time to time pursuant to this Convention.

Article 26
Investigation of accidents

In the event of an accident to an aircraft of a contracting State occurring in the territory of another contracting State, and involving death or serious injury, or indicating serious technical defect in the aircraft or air navigation facilities, the State in which the accident occurs will institute an inquiry into the circumstances of the accident, in accordance, so far as its laws permit, with the procedure which may be recommended by the International Civil Aviation Organization. The State in which the aircraft is registered shall be given the opportunity to appoint observers to be present at the inquiry and the State holding the inquiry shall communicate the report and findings in the matter to that State.

Article 27
Exemption from seizure on patent claims

a) While engaged in international air navigation, any authorized entry of aircraft of a contracting State into the territory of another contracting State or authorized transit across the territory of such State with or without landings shall not entail any seizure or detention of the aircraft or any claim against the owner or operator thereof or any other interference therewith by or on behalf of such State or any person therein, on the ground that the construction, mechanism, parts, accessories or operation of the aircraft is an infringement of any patent, design, or model duly granted or registered in the State whose territory is entered by the aircraft, it being agreed that no deposit of security in connection with the forgoing exemption from seizure or detention of the aircraft shall in any case be required in the State entered by such aircraft.

b) The provisions of paragraph (a) of this Article shall also be applicable to the storage of spare parts and spare equipment for the aircraft and the right to use and install the same in the repair of an aircraft of a contracting State in the territory of another contracting State, provided that any patented part or equipment so stored shall not be sold or distributed internally in or exported commercially from the contracting State entered by the aircraft.

c) The benefits of this article shall apply only to such States, parties to this Convention, as either (1) are parties to the International Convention for the Protection of Industrial Property and to any amendments thereto; or (2) have enacted patent laws which recognize and give adequate protection to inventions made by the nationals of the other States parties to this Convention.

Article 28
Air navigation facilities and standard systems

Each contracting State undertakes, so far as it may find practicable to:

a) Provide, in its territory, airports, radio services, meteorological services and other air navigation facilities to facilitate international air navigation, in accordance with the standards and practices recommended or established from time to time, pursuant to this Convention.

b) Adopt and put into operation the appropriate standard systems of communications procedure, codes, markings, signals, lighting and other operational practices and rules which may be recommended or established from time to time, pursuant to this Convention.

c) Collaborate in international measures to secure the publication of aeronautical maps and charts in accordance with standards which may be recommended or established from time to time, pursuant to this Convention.

CHAPTER V
CONDITIONS TO BE FULFILLED WITH RESPECT TO AIRCRAFT

Article 29
Documents carried in aircraft

Every aircraft of a contracting State, engaged in international navigation, shall carry the following documents in conformity with the conditions prescribed in this Convention:

a) Its certificate of registration;

b) Its certificate of airworthiness;

c) The appropriate licenses for each member of the crew;

d) Its journey log book;

e) If it is equipped with radio apparatus, the aircraft radio station license;

f) If it carries passengers, a list of their names and places of embarkation and destination;

g) If it carries cargo, a manifest and detailed declarations of the cargo.

Article 30
Aircraft radio equipment

a) Aircraft of each contracting State may, in or over the territory of other contracting States, carry radio transmitting apparatus only if a license to install and operate such apparatus has been issued by the appropriate authorities of the State in which the aircraft is registered. The use of radio transmitting apparatus in the territory of the contracting State whose territory is flown over shall be in accordance with the regulations prescribed by that State.

b) Radio transmitting apparatus may be used only by members of the flight crew who are provided with a special license for the purpose, issued by the appropriate authorities of the State in which the aircraft is registered.

Article 31
Certificates of airworthiness

Every aircraft engaged in international navigation shall be provided with a certificate of airworthiness issued or rendered valid by the State in which it is registered.

Article 32
Licenses of personnel

a) The pilot of every aircraft and the other members of the operating crew of every aircraft engaged in international navigation shall be provided with certificates of competency and licenses issued or rendered valid by the State in which the aircraft is registered.

b) Each contracting State reserves the right to refuse to recognize, for the purpose of flight above its own territory, certificates of competency and licenses granted to any of its nationals by another contracting State.

Article 33
Recognition of certificates and licenses

Certificates of airworthiness and certificates of competency and licenses issued or rendered valid by the contracting State in which the aircraft is registered, shall be recognized as valid by the other contracting States, provided that the requirements under which such certificates or licenses were issued or rendered valid are equal to or above the minimum standards which may be established from time to time pursuant to this Convention.

Article 34
Journey log books

There shall be maintained in respect of every aircraft engaged in international navigation a journey log book in which shall be entered particulars of the aircraft, its crew and of each journey, in such form as may be prescribed from time to time pursuant to this Convention.

Article 35
Cargo restrictions

a) No munitions of war or implements of war may be carried in or above the territory of a State in aircraft engaged in international navigation, except by permission of such State. Each State shall determine by regulations what constitutes munitions of war or implements of war for the purposes of this Article, giving due consideration, for the purposes of uniformity, to such recommendations as the International Civil Aviation Organization may from time to time make.

b) each contracting State reserves the right, for reasons of public order and safety, to regulate or prohibit the carriage in or above its territory of articles other than those enumerated in paragraph (a): provided that no distinction is made in this respect between its national aircraft engaged in international navigation and the aircraft of the other States so engaged; and provided further that no restriction shall be imposed which may interfere with the carriage and use on aircraft of apparatus necessary for the operation or navigation of the aircraft or the safety of the personnel or passengers.

Article 36
Photographic apparatus

Each contracting State may prohibit or regulate the use of photographic apparatus in aircraft over its territory.

CHAPTER VI
INTERNATIONAL STANDARDS AND RECOMMENDED PRACTICES

Article 37
Adoption of international standards and procedures

Each contracting State undertakes to collaborate in securing the highest practicable degree of uniformity in regulations, standards, procedures, and organization in relation to aircraft, personnel, airways and auxiliary services in all matters in which such uniformity will facilitate and improve air navigation.

To this end the International Civil Aviation Organization shall adopt and amend from time to time, as may be necessary, international standards and recommended practices and procedures dealing with:

a) Communications systems and air navigation aids, including ground marking;

b) Characteristics of airports and landing areas;

c) Rules of the air and air traffic control practices;

d) Licensing of operating and mechanical personnel;

e) Airworthiness of aircraft;

f) Registration and identification of aircraft;

g) Collection and exchange of meteorological information;

h) Log Books;

i) Aeronautical maps and charts;

j) Customs and immigration procedures;

k) Aircraft in distress and investigation of accidents;

and such other matters concerned with the safety, regularity, and efficiency of air navigation as may from time to time appear appropriate.

Article 38
Departures from international standards and procedures

Any State which finds it impracticable to comply in all respects with any such international standard or procedure, or to bring its own regulations or practices into full accord with any international standard or procedure after amendment of the latter, or which deems it necessary to adopt regulations or practices differing in any particular respect from those established by an international standard, shall give immediate notification to the International Civil Aviation Organization of the differences between its own practice and that established by the international standard. In the case of amendments to international standards, any State which does not make the appropriate amendments to its own regulations or practices shall give notice to the Council within 60 days of the adoption of the amendment to the international standard, or indicate the action which it proposes to take. In any such case, the Council shall make immediate notification to all other states of the difference which exists between one or more features of an international standard and the corresponding national practice of that State.

Article 39
Endorsement of certificates and licenses

a) Any aircraft or part thereof with respect to which there exists an international standard of airworthiness or performance, and which failed in any respect to satisfy that standard at the time of its certification, shall have endorsed on or attached to its airworthiness certificate a complete enumeration of the details in respect of which it so failed.

b) Any person holding a license who does not satisfy in full the conditions laid down in the international standard relating to the class of license or certificate which he holds shall have endorsed on or attached to his license a complete enumeration of the particulars in which he does not satisfy such conditions.

Article 40
Validity of endorsed certificates and licenses

No aircraft or personnel having certificates or licenses so endorsed shall participate in international navigation, except with the permission of the State or States whose territory is entered. The registration or use of any such aircraft, or of any certificated aircraft part, in any State other than that in which it was originally certificated shall be at the discretion of the State into which the aircraft or part is imported.

Article 41
Recognition of existing standards of airworthiness

The provisions of this Chapter shall not apply to aircraft and aircraft equipment of types of which the prototype is submitted to the appropriate national authorities for certification prior to a date three years after the date of adoption of an international standard of airworthiness for such equipment.

Article 42
Recognition of existing standards of competency of personnel

The provisions of this Chapter shall not apply to personnel whose licenses are originally issued prior to a date one year after initial adoption of an international standard of qualification for such personnel; but they shall in any case apply to all personnel whose licenses remain valid five years after the date of adoption of such standard.

PART II
THE INTERNATIONAL CIVIL AVIATION ORGANIZATION
CHAPTER VII
THE ORGANIZATION

Article 43
Name and composition

An organization to be named the International Civil Aviation Organization is formed by the Convention. It is made up of an Assembly, a Council, and such other bodies as may be necessary.

Article 44
Objectives

The aims and objectives of the Organization are to develop the principles and techniques of international air navigation and to foster the planning and development of international air transport so as to:

a) Insure the safe and orderly growth of international civil aviation throughout the world;

b) Encourage the arts of aircraft design and operation for peaceful purposes;

c) Encourage the development of airways, airports, and air navigation facilities for international civil aviation;

d) Meet the needs of the peoples of the world for safe, regular, efficient and economical air transport;

e) Prevent economic waste caused by unreasonable competition;

f) Insure that the rights of contracting States are fully respected and that every contracting State has a fair opportunity to operate international airlines;

g) Avoid discrimination between contracting States;

h) Promote safety of flight in international air navigation;

i) Promote generally the development of all aspects of international civil aeronautics.

Article 45
Permanent seat

The permanent seat of the Organization shall be at such place as shall be determined at the final meeting of the Interim Assembly of the Provisional International Civil Aviation Organization set up by the Interim Agreement on International Civil Aviation signed at Chicago on December 7th, 1944. The seat may be temporarily transferred elsewhere by decision of the Council.

Article 46
First meeting of Assembly

The first meeting of the Assembly shall be summoned by the Interim Council of the above-mentioned Provisional Organization as soon as the Convention has come into force, to meet at a time and place to be decided by the Interim Council.

Article 47
Legal capacity

The organization shall enjoy in the territory of each contracting State such legal capacity as may be necessary for the performance of its functions. Full juridical personality shall be granted wherever compatible with the constitution and laws of the State concerned.

CHAPTER VIII
THE ASSEMBLY

Article 48
Meetings of Assembly and voting

a) The Assembly shall meet annually and shall be convened by the Council at a suitable time and place. Extraordinary meetings of the Assembly may be held at any time upon the call of the Council or at the request of any ten contracting States addressed to the Secretary General.

b) All contracting States shall have an equal right to be represented at the meetings of the Assembly and each contracting State shall be entitled to one vote. Delegates representing contracting States may be assisted by technical advisers who may participate in the meetings but shall have no vote.

c) A majority of the contracting States is required to constitute a quorum for the meetings of the Assembly. Unless otherwise provided in this Convention, decisions of the Assembly shall be taken by a majority of the votes cast.

Article 49
Powers and duties of Assembly

The powers and duties of the Assembly shall be to:

a) Elect at each meeting its President and other officers;

b) Elect the contracting States to be represented on the Council, in accordance with the provisions of Chapter IX;

c) Examine and take appropriate action on the reports of the Council and decide on any matter referred to it by the Council;

d) Determine its own rules of procedure and establish such subsidiary commissions as it may consider to be necessary or desirable;

e) Vote an annual budget and determine the financial arrangements of the Organization, in accordance with the provisions of Chapter XII;

f) Review expenditures and approve the accounts of the Organization;

g) Refer, at its discretion, to the Council, to subsidiary commissions, or to any other body any matter within its sphere of action;

h) Delegate to the Council the powers and authority necessary or desirable for the discharge of the duties of the Organization and revoke or modify the delegations of authority at any time;

i) Carry out the appropriate provisions of Chapter XIII;

j) Consider proposals for the modification or amendment of the provisions of this Convention and, if it approves of the proposals, recommend them to the contracting States in accordance with the provisions of Chapter XXI;

k) Deal with any matter within the sphere of action of the Organization not specifically assigned to the Council.

CHAPTER IX
THE COUNCIL

Article 50
Composition and election of Council

a) The Council shall be a permanent body responsible to the Assembly. It shall be composed of 21 contracting States elected by the Assembly. An election shall be held at the first meeting of the Assembly and thereafter every three years, and the members of the Council so elected shall hold office until the next following election.

b) In electing the members of the Council, the Assembly shall give adequate representation to (1) the States of chief importance in air transport; (2) the States not otherwise included which make the largest contribution to the provision of facilities for international civil air navigation; and (3) the States not otherwise included whose designation will insure that all the major geographic areas of the world are represented on the Council. Any vacancy on the Council shall be filled by the Assembly as soon as possible; any contracting States so elected to the Council shall hold office for the unexpired portion of its predecessor's term of office.

c) No representative of a contracting State on the Council shall be actively associated with the operation of an international air service or financially interested in such a service.

Article 51
President of Council

The Council shall elect its President for a term of three years. He may be re-elected. He shall have no vote. The Council shall elect from among its members one or more Vice Presidents who shall retain their right to vote when serving as acting President. The President need not be selected from among the representatives of the members of the Council but, if a representative is elected, his seat shall be deemed vacant and shall be filled by the State which he represented. The duties of the President shall be to:

a) Convene meetings of the Council, the Air Transport Committee, and the Air Navigation Commission;

b) Serve as representative of the Council; and

c) Carry out on behalf of Council the functions which the Council assigns to him.

Article 52
Voting in Council

Decisions by the Council shall require approval by a majority of its members. The Council may delegate authority with respect to any particular matter to a committee of its members. Decisions of any committee of the Council may be appealed to the Council by any interested contracting State.

Article 53
Participation without a vote

Any contracting State may participate, without a vote, in the consideration by the Council and by its committees and commissions of any question which especially affects its interests. No member of the Council shall vote in the consideration by the Council of a dispute to which it is a party.

Article 54
Mandatory functions of Council

The Council shall:

a) Submit annual reports to the Assembly;

b) Carry out the directions of the Assembly and discharge the duties and obligations which are laid on it by this Convention;

c) Determine its organization and rules of procedure;

d) Appoint and define the duties of an Air Transport Committee, which shall be chosen from among the representatives of the members of the Council, and which shall be responsible to it;

e) Establish an Air Navigation Commission in accordance with the provisions of Chapter X;

f) Administer the finances of the Organization in accordance with the provisions of Chapters XII and XV;

g) Determine the emoluments of the President of the Council;

h) Appoint a chief executive officer who shall be called the Secretary General, and make provision for the appointment of such other personnel as may be necessary, in accordance with the provisions of Chapter XI;

i) Request, collect, examine and publish information relating to the advancement of air navigation and the operation of international air services, including information about the costs of operation and particulars of subsidies paid to airlines from public funds;

j) Report to contracting States any infraction of this Convention, as well as any failure to carry out recommendations or determinations of the Council;

k) Report to the Assembly any infraction of this Convention where a contracting State has failed to take appropriate action within a reasonable time after notice of the infraction;

l) Adopt, in accordance with the provisions of Chapter VI of this Convention, international standards and recommended practices; for convenience designate them as Annexes to this Convention; and notify all contracting States of the action taken;

m) Consider recommendations of the Air Navigation Commission for amendment of the Annexes and take action in accordance with the provisions of Chapter XX;

n) Consider any matter relating to the Convention which any contracting State refers to it.

Article 55
Permissive functions of Council

The Council may:

a) Where appropriate and as experience may show to be desirable, create subordinate air transport commissions on a regional or other basis and define groups of states or airlines with or through which it may deal to facilitate the carrying out of the aims of this Convention;

b) Delegate to the Air Navigation Commission duties additional to those set forth in the Convention and revoke or modify such delegations of authority at any time;

c) Conduct research into all aspects of air transport and air navigation which are of international importance, communicate the results of its research to the contracting States, and facilitate the exchange of information between contracting States on air transport and air navigation matters;

d) Study any matters affecting the organization and operation of international air transport including the international ownership and operation of international air services on trunk routes, and submit to the Assembly plans in relation thereto;

e) Investigate, at the request of any contracting State, any situation which may appear to present avoidable obstacles to the development of international air navigation; and, after such investigation, issue such reports as may appear to it desirable.

CHAPTER X
THE AIR NAVIGATION COMMISSION

Article 56
Nomination and appointment of Commission

The Air Navigation Commission shall be composed of twelve members appointed by the Council from among persons nominated by contracting States. These persons shall have suitable qualifications and experience in the science and practice of aeronautics. The Council shall request all contracting States to submit nominations. The President of the Air Navigation Commission shall be appointed by the Council.

Article 57
Duties of Commission

The Air Navigation Commission shall:

a) Consider, and recommend to the Council for adoption, modifications of the Annexes to this Convention;

b) Establish technical sub-commissions on which any contracting State may be represented, if it so desires;

c) Advise the Council concerning the collection and communication to the contracting States of all information which it considers necessary and useful for the advancement of air navigation.

CHAPTER XI
PERSONNEL

Article 58
Appointment of personnel

Subject to any rules laid down by the Assembly and to the provisions of this Convention, the Council shall determine the method of appointment and of termination of appointment, the training, and the salaries, allowances and conditions of service of the Secretary General and other personnel of the Organization, and may employ or make use of the services of nationals of any contracting State.

Article 59
International character of personnel

The President of the Council, the Secretary General, and other personnel shall not seek or receive instructions in regard to the discharge of their responsibilities from any authority external to the Organization. Each contracting State undertakes fully to respect the international character of the responsibilities of the personnel and not to seek to influence any of its nationals in the discharge of their responsibilities.

Article 60
Immunities and privileges of personnel

Each contracting State undertakes, so far as possible under its constitutional procedure, to accord to the President of the Council, the Secretary General, and the other personnel of the Organization, the immunities and privileges which are accorded to corresponding personnel of other public international organizations. If a general international agreement on the immunities and privileges of international civil servants is arrived at, the immunities and privileges accorded to the President, the Secretary General, and the other personnel of the Organization shall be the immunities and privileges accorded under that general international agreement.

CHAPTER XII
FINANCE

Article 61
Budget and apportionment of expenses

The Council shall submit to the Assembly an annual budget, annual statements of accounts and estimates of all receipts and expenditures. The Assembly shall vote the budget with whatever modification it sees fit to prescribe, and, with the exception of assessments under Chapter XV to States consenting thereto, shall apportion the expenses of the Organization among the contracting States on the basis which it shall from time to time determine.

Article 62
Suspension of voting power

The Assembly may suspend the voting power in the Assembly and in the Council of any contracting State that fails to discharge its financial obligations to the Organization.

Article 63
Expenses of delegations and other representatives

Each contracting State shall bear the expenses of its own delegation to the Assembly and the remuneration, travel, and other expenses of any person whom it appoints to serve on the Council, and of its nominees or representatives on any subsidiary committees or commissions of the Organization.

CHAPTER XIII
OTHER INTERNATIONAL ARRANGEMENTS

Article 64
Security arrangements

The Organization may, with respect to air matters within its competence directly affecting world security, by vote of the Assembly enter into appropriate arrangements with any general organization set up by the nations of the world to preserve peace.

Article 65
Arrangements with other international national bodies

The Council, on behalf of the Organization, may enter into agreements with other international bodies for the maintenance of common services and for common arrangements concerning personnel, and with the approval of the Assembly, may enter into such other arrangements as may facilitate the work of the Organization.

Article 66
Functions relating to other agreements

a) The Organization shall also carry out the functions placed upon it by the International Air Services Transit Agreement and by the International Air

Transport Agreement drawn up at Chicago on December 7th, 1944 in accordance with the terms and conditions therein set forth.

b) Members of the Assembly and the Council who have not accepted the International Air Services Transit Agreement or the International Air Transport Agreement drawn up at Chicago on December 7th, 1944 shall not have the right to vote on any questions referred to the Assembly or Council under the provisions of the relevant Agreement.

PART III
INTERNATIONAL AIR TRANSPORT
CHAPTER XIV
INFORMATION AND REPORTS

Article 67
File reports with Council

Each contracting State undertakes that its international airlines shall, in accordance with requirements laid down by the Council file with the Council traffic reports, cost statistics and financial statements showing among other things all receipts and the sources thereof.

CHAPTER XV
AIRPORTS AND OTHER AIR NAVIGATION FACILITIES

Article 68
Designation of routes and airports

Each contracting State may, subject to the provisions of this Convention, designate the route to be followed within its territory by any international air service and the airports which any such service may use.

Article 69
Improvement of air navigation facilities

If the Council is of the opinion that the airports or other air navigation facilities, including radio and meteorological services, of a contracting State are not reasonably adequate for the safe, regular, efficient and economical operation of international air services, present or contemplated, the Council shall consult with the State directly concerned, and other States affected, with a view to finding means by which the situation may be remedied, and may make recommendations for that purpose. No contracting State shall be guilty of an infraction of this Convention if it fails to carry out these recommendations.

Article 70
Financing of air navigation facilities

A contracting State, in the circumstances arising under the provisions of Article 69, may conclude an arrangement with the Council for giving effect to such recommendations. The State may elect to bear all of the costs involved in any such arrangement. If the State does not so elect, the Council may agree, at the request of the State, to provide for all or a portion of the costs.

Article 71
Provision and maintenance of facilities by Council

If a contracting State so requests, the Council may agree to provide, man, maintain and administer any or all of the airports and other air navigation facilities, including radio and meteorological services, required in its territory for the safe, regular, efficient and economical operation of the international air services of the other contracting States, and may specify just and reasonable charges for the use of the facilities provided.

Article 72
Acquisition or use of land

Where land is needed for facilities financed in whole or in part by the Council at the request of a contracting State, that State shall either provide the land itself, retaining title if it wishes, or facilitate the use of the land by the Council on just and reasonable terms and in accordance with the laws of the State concerned.

Article 73
Expenditure and assessment of funds

Within the limit of the funds which may be made available to it by the Assembly under Chapter XII, the Council may make current expenditures for the purposes of this Article from the general funds of the Organization. The Council shall assess the capital funds required for the purposes of this Article in previously agreed proportions over a reasonable period of time to the contracting States consenting thereto whose airlines use the facilities. The Council may also assess the States that consent any working funds that are required.

Article 74
Technical assistance and utilization of revenues

When the Council, at the request of a contracting State, advances funds or provides airports or other facilities in whole or in part, the arrangement may provide, with the consent of that State, for technical assistance in the supervision and operation of the airports and other facilities, and for the payment, from the revenues derived from the operation of the airports and other facilities, of the operating expenses of the airports and the other facilities, and of interest and amortization charges.

Article 75
Taking over of facilities from Council

A contracting State may at any time discharge any obligation into which it has entered under Article 70, and take over airports and other facilities which the Council has provided in its territory pursuant to the provisions of Article 71 and 72, by paying to the Council an amount which in the opinion of the Council is reasonable in the circumstances. If the State considers that the amount fixed by the Council is unreasonable it may appeal to the Assembly against the decision of the Council and the Assembly may confirm or amend the decision of the Council.

Article 76
Return of funds

Funds obtained by the Council through reimbursement under Article 75 and from receipts of interest and amortization payments under Article 74 shall, in the case of advances originally financed by States under Article 73, be returned to the States which were originally assessed in the proportion of their assessments, as determined by the Council.

CHAPTER XVI
JOINT OPERATING ORGANIZATIONS AND POOLED SERVICES

Article 77
Joint operating organizations permitted

Nothing in this Convention shall prevent two or more contracting States from instituting joint air transport operating organizations or international operating agencies and from pooling their air services on any routes or in any regions, but such organizations or agencies and such pooled services shall be subject to all the provisions of this Convention, including those relating to the registration of agreements with the Council. The Council shall determine in what manner the provisions of this Convention relating to nationality of aircraft shall apply to aircraft operated by international operating agencies.

Article 78
Function of Council

The Council may suggest to contracting States concerned that they form joint organizations to operate air services on any routes or in any regions.

Article 79
Participation in operating organizations

A State may participate in joint operating organizations or in pooling arrangements, either through its government or through an airline company or companies designated by its government. The companies may, at the sole discretion of the State concerned, be state-owned or partly state-owned or privately owned.

PART IV
FINAL PROVISIONS
CHAPTER XVII
OTHER AERONAUTICAL AGREEMENTS AND ARRANGEMENTS

Article 80
Paris and Habana Conventions

Each contracting State undertakes, immediately upon the coming into force of this Convention, to give notice of denunciation of the Convention relating to the Regulation of Aerial Navigation signed at Paris on October 13th, 1919, or the Convention on Commercial Aviation signed at Habana on February 20th, 1928, if it is a party to either. As between contracting States, this Convention supersedes the Conventions of Paris and Habana previously referred to.

Article 81
Registration of existing agreements

All aeronautical agreements which are in existence on the coming into force of this Convention, and which are between a contracting State and any other

State or between an airline of a contracting State and any other State or the airline of any other State, shall be forthwith registered with the Council.

Article 82
Abrogation of inconsistent arrangements

The contracting States accept this Convention as abrogating all obligations and understandings between them which are inconsistent with its terms, and undertake not to enter into any such obligations and understandings. A contracting State which, before becoming a member of the Organization has undertaken any obligations toward a non-contracting State or a national of a contracting State or of a non-contracting State inconsistent with the terms of this Convention, shall take immediate steps to procure its release from the obligations. If an airline of any contracting State has entered into any such inconsistent obligations, the State of which it is a national shall use its best efforts to secure their termination forthwith and shall in any event cause them to be terminated as soon as such action can lawfully be taken after the coming into force of this Convention.

Article 83
Registration of new arrangements

Subject to the provisions of the preceding Article, any contracting State may make arrangements not inconsistent with the provisions of this Convention. Any such arrangements shall be forthwith registered with the Council, which shall make it public as soon as possible.

CHAPTER XVIII
DISPUTES AND DEFAULT

Article 84
Settlement of disputes

If any disagreement between two or more contracting States relating to the interpretation or application of this Convention and its annexes cannot be settled by negotiation, it shall, on the application of any State concerned in the disagreement, be decided by the Council. No member of the Council shall vote in the consideration by the Council of any dispute to which it is a party. Any contracting State may, subject to Article 85, appeal from the decision of the Council to an *ad hoc* arbitral tribunal agreed upon with the other parties to the dispute or to the Permanent Court of International Justice. Any such appeal shall be notified to the Council within sixty days of receipt of notification of the decision of the Council.

Article 85
Arbitration procedure

If any contracting State party to a dispute in which the decision of the Council is under appeal has not accepted the Statute of the Permanent Court of International Justice and the contracting States parties to the dispute cannot agree on the choice of the arbitral tribunal, each of the contracting States parties to the dispute shall name a single arbitrator who shall name an umpire. If either contracting State party to the dispute fails to name an arbitrator within a period of three months from the date of the appeal, an arbitrator shall be named on behalf of that State by the President of the Council from a list of qualified and available persons maintained by the Council. If, within 30 days, the arbitrators cannot agree on an umpire, the President of the Council shall designate an umpire from the list previously referred to. The arbitrators and the umpire shall then jointly constitute an arbitral tribunal. Any arbitral tribunal established under this or the preceding Article shall settle its own procedure and give its decisions by a majority vote, provided that the Council may determine procedural questions in the event of any delay which in the opinion of the Council is excessive.

Article 86
Appeals

Unless the Council decides otherwise, any decision by the Council on whether an international airline is operating in conformity with the provisions of this Convention shall remain in effect unless reversed on appeal. On any other matter, decisions of the Council shall, if appealed from, be suspended until the appeal is decided. The decisions of the Permanent Court of International Justice and of an arbitral tribunal shall be final and binding.

Article 87
Penalty for non-conformity by airline

Each contracting State undertakes not to allow the operation of an airline of a contracting State through the air space above its territory if the Council has decided that the airline concerned is not conforming to a final decision rendered in accordance with the previous Article.

Article 88
Penalty for non-conformity by State

The Assembly shall suspend the voting power in the Assembly and in the Council of any contracting State that is found in default under the provisions of this Chapter.

CHAPTER XIX
WAR

Article 89
War and emergency conditions

In the case of war, the provisions of this Convention shall not affect the freedom of action of any of the contracting States affected, whether as belligerents or as neutrals. The same principle shall apply in the case of any contracting State which declares a state of national emergency and notifies the fact to the Council.

CHAPTER XX
ANNEXES

Article 90
Adoption and Amendment of Annexes

a) The adoption by the Council of the Annexes described in Article 54, subparagraph (1), shall require the vote of two-thirds of the Council at a meeting called for that purpose and shall then be submitted by the Council to each contracting State. Any such Annex or any amendment of an Annex shall become effective within three months after its submission to the contracting States or at the end of such longer period of time as the Council may prescribe, unless in the meantime a majority of the contracting States register their disapproval with the Council.

b) The Council shall immediately notify all contracting States of the coming into force of any Annex or amendment thereto.

CHAPTER XXI
RATIFICATIONS, ADHERENCES, AMENDMENTS, AND DENUNCIATIONS

Article 91
Ratification of Convention

a) This Convention shall be subject to ratification by the signatory States. The instruments of ratification shall be deposited in the archives of the Government of the United States of America, which shall give notice of the date of the deposit to each of the signatory and adhering States.

b) As soon as this Convention has been ratified or adhered to by twenty-six States it shall come into force between them on the thirtieth day after deposit of the twenty-sixth instrument. It shall come into force for each state ratifying thereafter on the thirtieth day after the deposit of its instrument of ratification.

c) It shall be the duty of the Government of the United States of America to notify the government of each of the signatory and adhering States of the date on which this Convention comes into force.

Article 92
Adherence to Convention

a) This Convention shall, after the closing date for signature, be open for adherence by members of the United Nations and States associated with them, and States which remained neutral during the present world conflict.

b) Adherence shall be effected by a notification addressed to the Government of the United States of America and shall take effect as from the thirtieth day from the receipt of the notification by the Government of the United States of America, which shall notify all the contracting States.

Article 93
Admission of other States

States other than those provided for in Articles 91 and 92 (a) may, subject to approval by any general international organization set up by the nations of the world to preserve peace, be admitted to participation in this Convention by means of a four-fifths vote of the Assembly and on such conditions as the Assembly may prescribe: provided that in each case the assent of any State invaded or attacked during the present war by the State seeking admission shall be necessary.

Article 94
Amendment of Convention

a) Any proposed amendment to this Convention must be approved by a two-thirds vote of the Assembly and shall then come into force in respect of States which have ratified such amendment when ratified by the number of contracting States specified by the Assembly. The number so specified shall not be less than two-thirds of the total number of contracting States.

b) If in its opinion the amendment is of such a nature as to justify this course, the Assembly in its resolution recommending adoption may provide that any State which has not ratified within a specified period after the amendment has come into force shall thereupon cease to be a member of the Organization and a party to the Convention.

Article 95
Denunciation of Convention

a) Any contracting State may give notice of denunciation of this Convention three years after its coming into effect by notification addressed to the Government of the United States of America, which shall at once inform each of the contracting States.

b) Denunciation shall take effect one year from the date of the receipt of the notification and shall operate only as regards the State effecting the denunciation.

CHAPTER XXI
DEFINITIONS

Article 96
For the purpose of this Convention the expression:

a) "Air Service" means any scheduled air service performed by aircraft for the public transport of passengers, mail or cargo.

b) "International air service" means an air service which passes through the air space over the territory of more than one State.

c) "Airline" means any air transport enterprise offering or operating an international air service.

d) "Stop for non-traffic purposes" means a landing for any purpose other than taking on or discharging passengers, cargo or mail.

SIGNATURE OF CONVENTION

In witness whereof, the undersigned Plenipotentiaries, having been duly authorized sign this Convention on behalf of their respective governments on the dates appearing opposite their signatures. DONE at Chicago the 7th day of December, 1944, in the English language. A text drawn up in the English, French and Spanish languages, each of which shall be of equal authenticity, shall be opened for signature at Washington, D.C. Both texts shall be deposited in the archives of the Government of the United States of America, and certified copies shall be transmitted by that Government to the governments of all the States which may sign or adhere to this Convention.

* Source: United Nations Information Office, *Report of the Chicago Conference on International Civil Aviation* (London: 1944)

Notes

1 The Puritan and the Peer

1 Handley Page, 'The Future of the Skyways, A British View,' 404.
2 Berle and Jacobs, eds., *Navigating the Rapids 1918–1971*, 481.
3 Balfour, *Wings over Westminster*, 202.
4 Bender and Altschul, *The Chosen Instrument*, 372.
5 Schwarz, *Liberal: Adolf A. Berle and the Vision of an American Era*, 202–3.
6 Quoted in ibid., 208.
7 Ibid., 240.
8 Holmes, *The Shaping of Peace*, vol. 1, 67–8.
9 Bender and Altschul, *Chosen Instrument*, 365; Ray, 'The Takoradi Route: Roosevelt's Prewar Venture beyond the Western Hemisphere,' 340–58; for more on American pre-war commercial aviation policy, see Thayer, *Air Transport Policy and National Security*, 26–38.
10 See, e.g., U.S. National Archives and Records Administration (hereafter NARA), RG 59, FW800.796/458, W.A. Patterson, 'International Trans-Ocean Air Transport and the Domestic Airlines,' 30 Sept. 1943.
11 For the views of the CAB, see Franklin D. Roosevelt Presidential Library, Hyde Park, New York (hereafter Roosevelt Library), President's and Secretary's Files, box 93, file: Aviation: 1944, Special Report of CAB, 'International Air Transport Policy,' 12 April 1944.
12 Whitnah, *Safer Skyways*, chapters 6–7; Taneja, *U.S. International Aviation Policy*, 5–6; Corbett, *Politics and the Airlines*, 289–94.
13 See Lissitzyn, *International Air Transport and National Policy*; Wilson, 'The Shape of Things to Come: The Military Impact of World War II on Civil Aviation,' 262–7.

14 Department of State, *Proceedings of the International Civil Aviation Conference, Chicago, Illinois, Nov. 1 to Dec. 7, 1944* (Washington, 1948), vol. 1 (hereafter DOS, *Proceedings*), 464.

15 For instance, using an American airline as an example, third freedom rights meant that it could fly passengers from New York to London; fourth freedom meant that the American airline could pick up passengers in London and return them to New York; fifth freedom meant that the American airline could fly passengers from New York to London and then pick up additional passengers and fly them on to Paris.

16 In subsequent years additional freedoms were added, changing the definition of the sixth freedom.

17 Quoted in Berle and Jacobs, *Navigating the Rapids*, 482–3. See also NARA, RG 59, Records of the Office of European Affairs (hereafter ROEA), box 11, 'Proposals for Consideration by the Principal Committee,' 19 June 1943. The minutes from Berle's committee can be found in NARA RG 59, Records of Harley A. Notter, 1939–45, box 43.

18 DOS, *Foreign Relations of the United States* (hereafter *FRUS*), *1944,* vol. 2, 360–2, Adolf Berle, Memo of Conversation, 11 Nov. 1943.

19 See, e.g.,Warner, 'Airways for Peace,' 11–27; 'The Logic of the Air,' *Fortune* 27/4 (1943), 72–4; NARA, RG 59, ROEA, box 11, Matthews-Hickerson file, A.M. Buden memo, 5 June 1943; Miller, 'Air Diplomacy: The Chicago Aviation Conference of 1944 in Anglo-American Wartime Relations and Postwar Planning,' 103–5.

20 NARA, RG 59, ROEA, box 11, Matthews-Hickerson file, Livingston Satterthwaite memo, 2 March 1944.

21 See the views about British aviation in Roosevelt Library, Hopkins Papers, Container 336, file: Air Conference, Post War Aviation no. 2, W. Burden, 'Notes on Present British Opinion on Post-war Air Transport Policy,' 5 June 1943.

22 See, e.g., Hall, 'The British Commonwealth as a Great Power,' 594–608.

23 'Logic of the Air,' 73.

24 Fearon, 'The Growth of Aviation in Britain,' 35; Dobson, 'The Other Air Battle,' 433. See also Dobson, *Peaceful Air Warfare*, chapter 5.

25 Engel, *Cold War at 30,000 Feet*, 29–31.

26 Dobson, *Peaceful*, 128; see also, Dierikx, 'Shaping World Aviation,' 799–800.

27 See MacKenzie, *Inside the Atlantic Triangle*, 106–10.

28 See Brewin, 'British Plans for International Operating Agencies for Civil Aviation, 1941–1945,' 91–110; Handley Page, 'Future of the Skyways,' 404–12; Oxford University, Bodleian Library, Papers of Frederick James Marquis, 1st Earl of Woolton, box 8, file: Committee of Inquiry, Civil Aviation, 1937–41.

29 See McCormack, 'Missed Opportunities,' 205–28.

30 Sir Peter Masefield interview; Lord Balfour of Inchrye (Harold Balfour) interview. On Beaverbrook, see A.J.P. Taylor, *Beaverbrook*.

31 National Archives, Public Record Office, Kew Gardens (hereafter PRO), FO 371, 36444 W14948/2/802, Beaverbrook memo to Churchill, 14 Oct. 1943.

32 See the minutes and some verbatim accounts in House of Lords Record Office, Beaverbrook Papers, D/238; Berle's side can be found in Roosevelt Library, Berle Papers, box 63, file: London Air Conversations, April 1944, Berle, Report on Air Conversations, 19 April 1944.

33 A copy of the invitation can be found in U.N. Information Organization, *Report of the Chicago Conference on International Civil Aviation* (hereafter U.N., *Report*), 1–2.

34 Berle and Jacobs, *Navigating the Rapids*, 492–3.

35 Roosevelt Library, Berle Papers, box 59, file: ICAC, General Correspondence, Nov. 1944 to Jan. 1945, Berle to Beaverbrook, 30 Dec. 1944.

36 Harold Begbie, quoted in Cross, *Lord Swinton*, 62–3.

37 University of Durham, Malcolm MacDonald Papers, file: 14/6/53–4, Lord Cranborne to Malcolm MacDonald, 29 Dec. 1944.

38 Lord Bridgeman, quoted in Cross, *Lord Swinton*, 91.

39 Bender and Altschul, *Chosen Instrument*, 389.

40 Cross, *Lord Swinton*, 248.

41 Roosevelt Library, Berle Papers, box 216, file: Diary Nov.–Dec. 1944 (hereafter Berle Diary), Memo for the Under Secretary of State, 26 Nov. 44.

42 Quoted in Cross, *Lord Swinton*, 248.

43 Lord Swinton, *I Remember*, 250.

44 Library and Archives Canada (hereafter LAC), MG 27, III B20, C.D. Howe Papers, v. 97, file: 61-6(11), J.R. Baldwin memo, 13 Dec. 1944.

45 Schwarz, *Liberal*, 250; Berle makes reference to these cables in Berle Diary, Memo for the Secretary of State and interested Offices and Divisions, 2 Dec. 1944.

46 Lord Athlone, quoted in NARA, RG 59, 800.796/1-2045, Ray Atherton to John Hickerson, 20 Jan. 1945. Not everyone was sorry to see Beaverbrook go: Stokely Morgan wrote Hickerson, 'As a matter of fact, I believe that when we first heard that Beaverbrook was not coming we were somewhat relieved because he had not shown himself a very satisfactory person to negotiate with during the preliminary talks.' NARA, ibid.

47 See Taneja, *U.S. International Aviation Policy*, 1.

48 Cooper, 'Some Historic Phases,' 190–1. See also Jönsson, *International Aviation and the Politics of Regime Change*, 79–81.

49 Quote taken from Lissitzyn, *International Air Transport*, 366; Warner, 'International Air Transport,' 280; Cooper, 'Some Historic Phases,' 194.

50 Lissitzyn, *International Air Transport*, 368–9.
51 Warner, 'The International Convention for Air Navigation,' 234.
52 Lissitzyn, *International Air Transport*, 369–70; Warner, 'International Air Transport,' 280–8.
53 For a good overview of ICAN, see Tombs, *International Organization in European Air Transport*, 83–99; see also Freer, 'ICAO at 50 Years,' 19–31.
54 Lissitzyn, *International Air Transport*, 369; Cooper, 'Some Historic Phases,' 195–6.
55 Lissitzyn, *International Air Transport*, 370–3. For a comparison of the Paris and Havana conventions, see Warner, 'International Convention for Air Navigation,' 221–308, and Gates, 'International Control of Aviation in Time of Peace,' 439–53; Burchall, 'The Politics of International Air Routes,' 89–107.
56 Lissitzyn, *International Air Transport*, 14.
57 Ibid., 56.
58 Moore-Brabazon, quoted in ibid., 57. See also, Beaumont, 'A New Lease on Empire,' 84–90.
59 For a list and overview of the development of international aviation, see Gidwitz, *Politics of International Air Transport*, 37–43.
60 PRO, Cmd. 5414, Air Ministry and General Post Office, 'Empire Air Mail Scheme,' May 1937.
61 On Imperial Airways and British aviation in general, see Higham, *Britain's Imperial Air Routes*, and two articles by the same author: 'The British Government and Overseas Airlines,' and 'British Airways Ltd, 1935–40,' 113–23. See also Cooper, 'Some Historic Phases,' 189–201; Burchall, 'Politics of International Air Routes,' 89–107; Myerscough, 'Airport Provision in the Inter-War Years,' 41–70; and Fearon, 'Growth of Aviation in Britain,' 21–40.
62 For more on international rivalries in the period between the wars, see Dierikx, 'Struggle for Prominence: Clashing Dutch and British Interests on the Colonial Air Routes,' 333–51; Megaw, 'The Scramble for the Pacific,' 458–73; Stannard, 'Civil Aviation: An Historical Survey,' 497–511. For the rivalries in Latin America, see: Newton, 'International Aviation Rivalry in Latin America,' 345–56; Randall, 'Colombia, the United States, and Interamerican Aviation Rivalry,' 297–324; and Haglund, '"De-Lousing" Scadta,' 177–90. For Africa, see the following by McCormack: 'Man with a Mission: Oswald Pirow and South African Airways, 1933–1939,' 543–57; 'War and Change: Air Transport in British Africa,' 341–59; and 'Imperialism, Air Transport and Colonial Development: Kenya,' 374–95.

63 See, e.g., Warner, 'What Airplanes Can Do,' 339–57; Smith, 'The Intercontinental Airliner and the Essence of Airplane Performance,' 428–49;
and Vincenti, 'Technological Knowledge without Science,' 540–76.

64 MacDonald, quoted in Dobson, *Peaceful Air Warfare*, 79.

65 Dobson, *Peaceful*, 66; for more on the disarmament conference, see Tombs,
International Organization, 14–23.

66 Dobson, *Peaceful*, 70.

67 See, e.g., ibid., 69.

68 See Australian Archives (hereafter ACT), Department of Defence, Central
Office, Sir Frederick Sheddon Collection, A5954/1 1979/159, War Cabinet
(hereafter WC) Minute, No. 3097, 'Civil Aviation Policy and Organization
during the War and Post-War Period,' Dec. 1943.

69 See MacKenzie, *Canada and International Civil Aviation*, 123. See also
Bothwell and Granatstein, 'Canada and the Wartime Negotiations over Civil
Aviation,' 585–601.

70 PRO, WC Paper, Committee on Reconstruction Problems, R.P. (42) 5 (The
Shelmerdine Report), 5 Jan. 1942.

71 Ibid., R.P. (42) 48 (The Finlay Report), 18 Dec. 1942.

72 Wallace, quoted from the *Saturday Evening Post*, in LAC, MG 31, E46,
Escott Reid Papers, v. 10, file: 37, Future of International Air Transport,
8 April 1943.

73 Solberg, *Conquest of the Skies*, 284, 278, 280.

74 See, e.g., Herbert, *Independent Member*, 277–8, and Massey, *What's Past Is
Prologue*, 395. For Winston Churchill's wartime views, see Solberg,
Conquest of the Skies, 280. One British civil servant likened the shock of
arriving at the Goose Bay airport 'as great as if he found the Ritz Hotel in
the middle of the Kalahari Desert.' PRO, DO 35 /1375, Chadwick to Tait,
10 Aug. 1943.

75 For some comments on Wallace's proposals, see NARA, RG 59,
800.796/258, Berle to S. Welles, 3 March 1943.

76 Luce, quoted in 'Logic of the Air,' 72–4.

77 Brewin, 'British Plans,' 91–2.

78 For a draft multilateral convention based on the Paris Convention, see
PRO, FO 371, W12238/2/802, memo, n.d. (probably Aug. 1943).

79 Lissitzyn, *International Air Transport*, 415.

2 Chicago: The Ambitious Dream

1 Fiorello LaGuardia to conference delegates, Chicago, 22 Nov. 1944, DOS,
Proceedings, 12.

2 Soviet press release, quoted in U.N., *Report*, 2. See also *FRUS, 1944,* vol. 2, 562, Ambassador in the Soviet Union to Secretary of State, 19 Oct. 1944; 579, Soviet Ambassador to Acting Secretary of State, 30 Oct. 1944.

3 Roosevelt Library, Berle Diary, E.S. (Edward Stettinius) to Berle, 8 Nov. 1944.

4 Ibid., Berle to Stettinius, 11 Nov. 1944. For more on the Soviet refusal, see Gidwitz, *Politics of International Air Transport,* 47–8.

5 See Yoder, *The Evolution of the United Nations System,* 4–5.

6 See Mézière and Sauvage, *Les Ailes Française: L'Aviation Marchande de 1919 à nos Jours.*

7 A complete list of conference participants is printed in DOS, *Proceedings,* 29–41; for the breakdown of participants, see U.N., *Report,* 2.

8 LAC, MG 31, E46, Escott Reid Papers, v. 5, file: 6, Reid, 'Part II, Canada's Role at the Conference,' 14 Dec. 1944. See also Pogue, 'The International Civil Aviation Conference,' 4; and Reid, *Radical Mandarin,* 179.

9 LAC, MG 27, III B20, C.D. Howe Papers, v. 97, file: 61-6(11), J.R. Baldwin memo, 13 Dec. 1944.

10 Nicolas Cheetham interview.

11 DOS, *Proceedings,* 42–3.

12 Ibid., 44.

13 For a complete list of the committees and their membership, see U.N., *Report,* 3.

14 Nicolas Cheetham diary. I would like to thank Sir Nicolas Cheetham for allowing me to read and quote from his personal diary.

15 PRO, CAB 65, WC Conclusions, 123 (44) 18 Sept. 1944.

16 Nicolas Cheetham interview; for more on Irish aviation, see Share, *The Flight of the Iolar,* and MacKenzie, 'Ireland, Canada, and Atlantic Aviation,' 31–47.

17 They may have had cause for concern; one DOS official noted at the time: 'My impression is that when the chips were down Canada preferred our views to those of the British although neither was too well suited to Canadian requirements. At any rate, Canada has been of service to us during the conference.' NARA, RG 59, FW800.769/11-3044, Graham Parsons memo, 30 Nov. 1944.

18 PRO, FO 371, 42576 W15415/10/802, Swinton to A. Street, 25 Oct. 1944.

19 House of Lords Record Office, Beaverbrook Papers, D/234, Swinton to Street, 27 Oct. 1944.

20 University of Durham, Malcolm MacDonald Papers, file: 14/6/10-12, MacDonald to Cranborne, 12 Dec. 1944. For more on the Canadians at Chicago, see MacKenzie, *Canada and International Civil Aviation,* chapter 8.

21 J.R. Baldwin interview.

22 Berle Diary, Memo for the Under Secretary of State and interested Offices and Divisions (hereafter Memo to SOS etc.), 4 Nov. 1944.

23 Ibid., 15 Nov. 1944.

24 See Bender and Altschul, *Chosen Instrument*, 387.

25 Roosevelt Library, Berle Papers, box 59, file: ICAC, Chicago, Nov. 1944, Business Corres., Notes, Appointment Diaries, Berle to Stettinius, 18 Nov. 1944.

26 Berle and Jacobs, *Navigating the Rapids*, 500–1; PRO, CAB 66, WP (44) 621, Churchill memo, 4 Nov. 1944; Sir Nicolas Cheetham to author, 26 Feb. 1987.

27 LaGuardia, quoted in 'Verbatim minutes of Plenary Session of Committees I, III, IV, Dec. 1,' DOS, *Proceedings*, 496.

28 Berle Diary, Memo to SOS etc., 1 Nov. 1944.

29 Sir Peter Masefield interview.

30 French Foreign Ministry Archives, Paris, Nations Unies et organizations internationals Papers (hereafter FFMA), S.4.6.7, box 31, file: Chicago (aviation) 1945–46, 'La France et la Navigation Aérienne Internationale au Lendemain de la Guerre,' n.d.

31 Many of these views are set out in Roosevelt Library, Berle Papers, box 59, file: ICAC, unsigned DOS memo, 'Comparison of views of countries with whom exploratory talks have been held with respect to post-war civil air transport,' 26 Sept. 1944. See also, National Archives of Ireland, Dublin (hereafter NAI), Cabinet Memoranda and Papers, S13562A, Memo by Minister for Industry and Commerce, 4 Oct. 1944; and De Valera, 'Directives for the Delegation to the International Aviation Conference,' 13 Oct. 1944. For the French and Soviet views, see *FRUS, 1944,* vol. 2, 516–20, Berle memo, 2 Aug. 1944, and Morgan memo, 2 Aug. 1944; for the eagerness of the Canadians to start flying, see MacKenzie 'Sitting Pretty,' 253–61. For the Latin Americans, see the 'Cuba-Mexico Proposals on Interim Council,' in U.N., *Report,* 11.

32 See Department of Foreign Affairs and Trade (hereafter DOFAT), *Documents on Australian Foreign Policy 1937–49*, vol. 7, *1944* (hereafter *AFP,* vol. 7), doc. 26, Australian-New Zealand Agreement 1944, 21 Jan. 1944.

33 The text of the resolution can be found in U.N., *Report,* 7.

34 ACT, Cabinet Agenda A2700/xm1, v. 14, pt. 2, Arthur Drakeford, 'Report on the ICAC,' 23 Jan. 1945; U.N., *Report,* 9. 'Verbatim Minutes of Plenary Session' (hereafter VMPS), Nov. 8, DOS, *Proceedings,* 539–47. See also DOFAT, *AFP,* vol. 7, doc. 159, Curtin to Forde, 19 May 1944. For more on the Australians at Chicago, see MacKenzie, 'Wartime Planning for Postwar Commercial Aviation,' 50–70; and, more generally, 'Canada and Australia in the World of International Commercial Aviation,' 99–123.

35 *FRUS, 1944,* vol. 2, 603, Berle to Roosevelt, 7 Dec. 1944. This argument was repeated later, see Warner, 'The Chicago Conference: Accomplishments and Unfinished Business,' 414.

36 For the 'U.S. Proposal of a Convention on Air Navigation,' see DOS, *Proceedings,* 554–65; for a summary of the American proposals, see U.N., *Report,* 4.

37 Press conference reported in U.N., *Report,* 8. Some British officials thought that the idea of two Commonwealth seats was a good one. 'This proposal has certain advantages,' wrote one Foreign Office official. 'We have always tended to favour unitary representation of the Commonwealth.' PRO, FO 371, W16082/10/802, unsigned memo, 9 Nov. 1944.

38 Berle Diary, Memo to SOS etc., 11 Nov. 1944, and Berle to Stettinius, 11 Nov. 1944; Mexican-Cuban press conference, quoted in U.N., *Report,* 11–12. More generally, see Kaeckenbeeck, 'The Function of Great and Small Powers in the International Organization,' 306–12.

39 Berle Diary, 'Outline of the American Position,' n.d.; Berle explains the U.S. position more thoroughly in VMPS, Nov. 2, DOS, *Proceedings,* 54–63.

40 The text of the White Paper (Cmd. 6561) *International Air Transport, Text of a White Paper Presented by the Secretary of State for Air to Parliament, Oct. 1944,* can be found in DOS, *Proceedings,* 566–70, and in U.N., *Report,* 5–6.

41 PRO, CAB 65, WC Conclusions, 12 Oct. 1944; see also PRO, CAB 66, Cabinet Memo, WP (44) 564, 9 Oct. 1944.

42 Ibid., 26 Oct. 1944; PRO, FO 371, 42577/ W15523/10/802, Swinton to Sir Arthur Street, 27 Oct. 1944; ibid. / W15530/10/802, FO to Embassy in Washington, t.9403, 28 Oct. 1944.

43 The minutes of the April Berle-Beaverbrook meetings can be found in PRO, CAB 87/88.

44 *FRUS, 1944,* vol. 2, 576–79, Lewis Clark (for the U.S. ambassador in Canada) to Secretary of State, 28 Oct. 1944. For Berle's view, see his 7 Dec. 1944 report on the conference, in ibid., 601. Concern was often expressed over the effects of British persuasion on the Dominions as 'they are subjected to the smooth and expert type of pressure that many hundred years of experience have made the British masters of.' NARA, RG 59, ROEA, box 11, Matthews-Hickerson file, Livingston Satterthwaite to Joe Walstrom, 26 Jan. 1944.

45 PRO, FO 371, 42579 W15751/10/802, William Hildred to W.G. Hayter, 30 Oct. 1944.

46 Day, 'P.G. Taylor and the Alternative Pacific Air Route,' 6–19. On Pacific aviation, see, 'D,' 'Pacific Airways,' 60–9; and Kirk, 'Wings over the Pacific,' 293–302.

47 For the Canadian draft 'Canadian Revised Preliminary Draft of an International Air Convention,' see DOS, *Proceedings*, 570–90; for a summary of the Canadian proposals, see U.N., *Report*, 7.

48 'Minutes of Meeting of Subcommittee I of Committee I,' 7 Nov., DOS, *Proceedings*, 647.

49 Ibid., Appendix V.

50 *FRUS, 1944*, vol. 2, 583–4, Berle to Stettinius, 11 Nov. 1944.

51 See PRO, FO 371, 42577 W15445/10/802, Street to Swinton, 26 Oct. 1944.

52 Ibid., 42581 W16157/10/802, Swinton to Sir E. Bridges, t.44, 9 Nov. 1944.

53 Berle Diary, 'Memo to SOS etc.,' 11 Nov. 1944.

54 PRO, FO 371, 42582 W16327 /10/802, Swinton to Bridges, t.68, 12 Nov. 1944.

55 LAC, MG 31, E46, Escott Reid Papers, v.5, file: 6, Reid to Norman Robertson, 12 Nov. 1944.

56 PRO, FO 371, 42585 W16412/10/802, W.G. Hayter memo, 15 Nov. 1944.

57 Ibid.

58 Ibid., Ministerial Committee to Swinton, t.31, 16 Nov. 1944. The French government informed its delegation not to accept any agreement that included the fifth freedom. See NARA, RG 457, Records of the National Security Agency (hereafter RNSA), 'Magic' Diplomatic Summaries, March 20, 1942 to Aug. 15, 1945, box 14, file: 'Nov. 1944,' quotes from Foreign Minister Bidault to Max Hymans, 23 Nov. 1944.

59 PRO, FO 371, 42586 W16676, W.G. Hayter memo, 21 Nov. 1944. The next day he added: 'This is probably the most influential ciphering error in history; it may affect the whole future of civil aviation!' Another official noted: 'It may even save the Civil Aviation Conference!' 22 and 23 Nov. 1944, same file.

60 Ibid., Swinton to Bridges, t.100, 20 Nov. 1944. The original telegram no. 25 (15 Nov. 1944) can be found in FO 371, 42582 W/16327 /10/802.

61 Ibid., W16675/10/802, Swinton to Bridges, t.99, 19 Nov. 1944

62 Berle and Jacobs, *Navigating the Rapids*, 503.

63 LAC, MG 30, E336, J.R.K. Main Papers, v. 3, file: Diaries: 1942, 1943, 1944; diary, 21 Nov. 1944.

64 'Three-Power Draft on Air Convention,' U.N., *Report*, 19–22.

65 Quoted in ibid., 22–3.

66 *FRUS, 1944*, vol. 2, 589, Roosevelt to Churchill, 24 Nov. 1944. The correspondence between Roosevelt and Churchill on this matter can be found here, 584–99.

67 Ibid, 592. Churchill to Roosevelt, 28 Nov. 1944.

68 Taneja, *U.S. International Aviation Policy*, 10; see also Pogue, 'The International Civil Aviation Conference (1944),' 35.

69 PRO, FO 371, 42591 W17313/10/802, Swinton to Bridges, t.140, 30 Nov. 1944; on Berle's resignation, see Berle and Jacobs, *Navigating the Rapids*, 506–9.

70 Welch Pogue traces the origins of the five freedoms agreement back to the 10 November meeting of the American delegation. See Pogue, 'International Civil Aviation Conference,' 24–6. See also Pogue, 'Personal Recollections from the Chicago Conference,' 35–48. On the views of the Latin American states on the fifth freedom, see Morgan, 'The International Civil Aviation Conference at Chicago and What It Means to the Americas,' 35–6.

71 'French Draft of Amendments to Documents 433 and 435,' DOS, *Proceedings*, 1341.

72 Berle Diary, Memo to SOS etc., 2 Dec. 1944; for the motion by the Netherlands and the statement by Hymans, see U.N., *Report*, 39. See also PRO, FO 371, 42593 W17414/10/802, British Delegation to FO, t.154, 3 Dec. 1944.

73 PRO, FO 371, 42582, W16285/10/802, British Delegation to FO, t.61, 11 Nov. 1944.

74 Ibid., Ministerial Committee to Swinton, 14 Nov. 1944. One FO official supported Canada over Bermuda and Paris, see note in same file, W16311/10/802.

75 LAC, RG 70, Air Canada Papers, v. 23, file: TCA 3-3-4 (v. 2), J.R. Baldwin, 'Report of ICAC, Chicago 1944,' 29 Dec. 1944; see also PRO, FO 371, 42593 W17484/10/802, Swinton to Bridges, t.167, 5 Dec. 1944.

76 VMPS, Dec. 5, DOS, *Proceedings*, 93–4.

77 PRO, FO 371, 42585 W16448/10/802, Swinton to Bridges, t.82, 15 Nov. 1944.

78 Berle Diary, Memo to SOS etc., 18 Nov. 1944.

79 NARA, RG 457, RNSA, 'Magic' Diplomatic Summaries, box 14, file: Nov. 1944, 'French Report on American Handling of Civil Aviation Conference,' n.d.

80 The Latin American states, e.g., raised the problem of time delays in waiting for translation into Spanish, and the Mexican representative noted his regret that Spanish was not an official language of the Conference. See 'Verbatim Minutes of Joint Plenary Meeting of Committees I, III, and IV,' DOS, *Proceedings*, Nov. 22, 454, and Nov. 27, 475.

81 LAC, MG 31, E46, Escott Reid Papers, v. 12, file: 49, Reid to Norman Robertson, 26 Nov. 1944.

82 Ibid., MG 27, III B20, C.D. Howe Papers, v. 99, file: 61-6 (19), J.R. Baldwin to Howe, 1 Dec. 1944. For the language problems earlier in ICAN, see Warner, 'International Convention for Air Navigation,' 306–7.

83 *FRUS, 1944*, vol. 2, 610; Berle to Roosevelt, 7 Dec. 1944.

84 LAC, RG 25, Department of External Affairs (hereafter DEA) Records, A12, v. 2108, file: AR405/2 part VI, Escott Reid, 'Memo on the Election of the Interim Council, Dec. 6 and 7, 1944,' 11 Dec. 1944.

85 Berle Diary, 'Memo to SOS etc.,' 18 Nov. 1944. On the role of the neutral states at the conference, one Canadian wrote: 'The neutrals were on the whole careful about their participation in the conference. Spain said very little. Turkey said nothing. The Swiss representative spoke only once when he made a helpful attempt to keep the size of the Council down to reasonable proportions. Portugal had a little more to say. Ireland spoke quite frequently, both in committees and in drafting committees.' LAC, MG 27, III B20, C.D. Howe Papers, v. 97, file: 61-6(11), J.R. Baldwin, 'ICAC,' 13 Dec. 1944.

86 PRO, FO 371, 42582 W16265/10/802, Swinton to Bridges, t.56, 11 Nov. 1944.

87 Ibid., Cheetham note, 14 Dec. 1944 (emphasis in original).

88 VMPS, Dec. 7, DOS, *Proceedings*, 104–5.

89 For who signed what, see U.N., *Report*, 42.

90 VMPS, Dec. 7, DOS, *Proceedings*, 111.

91 A good explanation of the SARPs can be found in Cheng, *The Law of International Air Transport*, 70–1. For more on the Convention and the powers of the Council, see two articles by Abeyratne: 'The Legal Status of the Chicago Convention and Its Annexes,' 113–23, and 'Law Making and Decision Making Powers of the ICAO Council,' 387–94.

92 On the functions and operations of the ICAO Assembly, see Schenkman, *ICAO*, 145–54.

93 See, e.g., LAC, MG 31, E46, Escott Reid Papers, v. 12, file: 50, Reid memo, 'The President and the Secretary-General,' 28 Feb. 1945. It has been pointed out that it was a little unusual to have both a president and a secretary general. See Guldimann, 'The Chicago Convention Revisited,' 355.

94 See Schenkman, *ICAO*, 163–9.

95 Warner, 'Chicago Conference,' 406–21; Morgan, 'International Civil Aviation Conference at Chicago,' 33–8; 'After Chicago: Imperial Interests in Civil Aviation,' *Round Table* 35 (March 1945), 130–6; Cameron, 'The Chicago Air Conference,' 227–9; Gore-Booth, *With Great Truth and Respect*, 129–32. Gore-Booth wrote: 'This was not the worst conference I have ever attended ... But it was, from beginning to end, one of the oddest' (129).

96 Pogue, 'Personal Recollections,' 38. For more views on the conference and the convention, see Cooper, 'Air Power and the Coming Peace Treaties,' 441–52; Cooper, 'The Chicago Convention – After Twenty

Years,' 333–44; Milde, 'The Chicago Convention – After Forty Years,'
119–31; Freer, 'Chicago Conference (1944) – U.K.-U.S. Policy Split
Revealed,' 22–4; Freer, 'Chicago Conference (1944) – Despite Uncertainty, the Spirit of Internationalism Soars,' 42–4; Matte, 'Chicago
Convention,' 371–99.

3 PICAO: 'An International Conference Always at Work'

1 Lord Swinton, 'Verbatim Minutes of Joint Plenary Meeting of Committees I,
 III, and IV,' Nov. 22, DOS, *Proceedings*, 453.
2 Taneja, *U.S. International Aviation Policy*, 12. See also, Walstrom, 'Bilateral
 Air-Transport Agreements Concluded by the United States.'
3 See MacKenzie, 'The Rise and Fall of the Commonwealth Air Transport
 Council,' 105–25. See also Fysh, *Qantas at War*, 204–5.
4 See Dierikx, 'Shaping World Aviation,' 815.
5 See PRO, PREM 4, 5/13, Memo by the Minister of Civil Aviation (hereafter
 MCA), C.P. (45) 19, 7 June 1945; and NARA, RG 59, 711.0027/7-1745,
 Walstrom memo for CAB, 17 July 1945.
6 See the memo on Labour's aviation policy by Lord Winster, the new MCA,
 PRO, CAB 129, Cabinet Memo, CP (45) 222, 12 Oct. 1945; on the Aug.
 discussions, see ibid., CAB 134 57, Civil Aviation Committee Memo, C.A.C.
 (45) 4, 12 Sept. 1945, and NARA, RG 59, 841.796/9-445, t. 25188, Satterthwaite to Secretary of State, 4 Sept. 1945.
7 Taneja, *U.S. International Aviation Policy*, 12.
8 McKim, 'World Order in Air Transport,' 228.
9 PRO, PREM 4 5/13, Cabinet Memo, CP (45) 19, 7 June 1945; ibid., 8/16,
 Brief for the PM, no date. See also, ibid., 'Brief for PM on U.S.–U.K.
 Relations in Civil Aviation,' n.d. (probably Sept.–Oct. 1945).
10 Ibid. Taneja, *U.S. International Aviation Policy*, 12.
11 See Gidwitz, *Politics of International Air Transport*, 53–9. For the early postwar
 actions of the CAB and its dealing with applications for air services, see
 Carlson, 'The Origins and Development of the CAB,' chapter 8.
12 On the origins and role of IATA, see Chuang, *International Air Transport
 Association*; Brancker, *IATA and What It Does*, and Clark, 'IATA and ICAO,'
 125–31.
13 Quoted in 'Men of 46 Airlines Meet in Montreal,' 103; see also Hildred,
 'What Is IATA?' 54, 58.
14 'Men of 46 Airlines Meet in Montreal,' 103.
15 PICAO, doc. 1554, A/4, 'Report on the Work of the Organization for the
 Period 6 June 1945 to 30 April 1946, Presented by Interim Council to the
 First Interim Assembly,' 30 April 1946.

16 On the Preparatory Committee, see PICAO, doc. 1554, A/4, 'General Summary of PICAO Activities from 6 June 1945 to 30 April 1946.' Robert English, an American in the Ottawa embassy, wrote that this committee was 'made up of energetic young officers who are thoroughly familiar not only with the city of Montreal and who have business and social connections there, but men who are also well versed in the workings of the Canadian Government and who have had previous organizational experience.' NARA, RG 59, 800.796/7-5445, English to Secretary of State, t.2747, 5 July 1945.

17 LAC, RG 70, v. 24, file: TCA 3-7, Symington to Street, 19 Feb. 1945.

18 Ibid., v. 23, v. 2, file: TCA 3-3-4, Pogue to Symington, 2 March 1945; RG 25, v. 3375, file: 72-ADU-40c (pt. 1), Morgan to Escott Reid, 26 April 1945.

19 Ibid., MG 27, III B20, Howe Papers, v. 97, file: 61-6(11), John Baldwin memo, 'Establishment of International Aviation Organization,' 12 April 1945.

20 Hildred, quoted in Johnston, *To Organise the Air*, 154.

21 LAC, RG 25, A-12, v. 2114, file: AR 412/11, 'Report on the First Meeting of the Interim Assembly of the PICAO, Montreal, May 21st to June 7th, 1946.'

22 *PICAO Journal* 1/1 (1945), 7.

23 For Roper's view on his ICAO experience, see Roper, *Un homme et des ailes*, 321–6.

24 LAC, MG 31, E46, Escott Reid Papers, v. 12, file: 50, Reid memo, 'PICAO,' 11 Jan. 1945, and Lester Pearson to Secretary of State for External Affairs, t.511, 27 Feb. 1945; RG 70, Air Canada Papers, v. 24, file: TCA 3-7, J.J.S. Garner to John Baldwin, 26 May 1945.

25 Sir Peter Masefield, quoted in Johnston, *To Organise the Air*, x.

26 NARA, RG 59, Subject Files of Durward V. Sandifer, box 9, file: ICAO, Louis Hyde, 'Informal Comments on Trip to Montreal Headquarters of the PICAO, April 9–12, inclusive 1946.'

27 PICAO, doc. 3120, C/391, 'Decisions of the Interim Council, Aug. 15, 1945 to May 7, 1947.'

28 Ibid., doc. 1837, A/46, 'Consolidated List of Resolutions Adopted by the First Interim Assembly,' 7 June 1946; doc. 1554, A/4, 'General Summary of PICAO Activities.' For Warner's resignation from CAB, see Harry S Truman Presidential Library, Independence, Missouri (hereafter Truman Library), White House Central Files (hereafter WHCF), Official File, box 36, file: OF 3-I CAB (1945–46), Warner to Truman, 17 Aug. 1945.

29 PICAO, 'Decisions of the Interim Council.'

30 Ibid., 'Consolidated List of Resolutions.'

31 See Freer, 'The PICAO Years – 1945 to 1947,' 37–9. For the role and make-up of the ANC, see PICAO, 'Report on the Work,' chapter 2, 30 April 1946.

32 For an overview of the work of the PICAO technical divisions, see PICAO, 'Report on the Work,' 39–56.

33 NARA, RG 237, Records Relating to ACC Facilitation Subcommittees, Inspection Tours, and Gov. Surveys, 1946–51, box 1, file: PICAO: Facilitation Reports, etc., PICAO, News Release, 13 April 1946.

34 PICAO, doc. 1696, A/32, Interim Assembly, Minutes, 2nd Plenary Meeting, 24 May 1946.

35 Warner, 'Notes from PICAO Experience,' 30.

36 'Regional Structure Enhances Air Navigation Planning,' *ICAO Journal* 46/7 (1991), 49–50.

37 Hyde, 'Informal Comments on Trip to Montreal.'

38 NAI, SPO S13778, file: 'International Conference, Dublin, March 1946,' De Valera memo, 13 Dec. 1945.

39 See 'Regional Air Navigation Meetings in Dublin and Paris,' *PICAO Journal*, 1, 4(March/April 1946), 5–6.

40 NARA, RG 237, PICAO: Facilitation Reports, etc., PICAO, news releases, 25 and 26 April 1946.

41 PICAO, doc. 1686, A/29, 'Minutes of the First Plenary Meeting, Interim Assembly,' 21 May 1946.

42 See, e.g., Gilbert, 'PICAO Middle East Regional Air Navigation Meeting,' 1079–81, 1083.

43 'Status, Constitution and Functions of Regional Offices,' *PICAO Journal*, 1, 7 (July/August 1946), 19.

44 Johnston, *To Organise the Air*, 141.

45 Including organizations such as the Combined Air Traffic Advisory Committee – Europe, the International Telecommunications Union, the International Meteorological Organization, the International Chamber of Commerce, the ILO, the International Hydrographic Bureau, the International Geographical Union, the Pan-American Institute of Geography and History, the International Aeronautical Federation, and the Universal Postal Union.

46 PICAO, 'General Summary.'

47 Hyde, 'Informal Comments on Trip to Montreal.'

48 PICAO, 'General Summary.'

49 Hyde, 'Informal Comments on Trip to Montreal.'

50 *PICAO Journal* 1/1 (1945), 7.

51 LAC, 'Report on the First Meeting of the Interim Assembly.'

52 FFMA, S.4.6.7, box 31, file: Chicago (aviation) 1945–46, Hymans to Jules Moch, 27 May 1946.

53 PICAO, 'Minutes of the First Plenary Meeting.'

54 LAC, 'Report on the First Meeting of the Interim Assembly.'

55 PICAO, 'Consolidated List of Resolutions'; *PICAO Journal* 1/6 (1946), 43; LAC, RG 25, v. 3380, file: 72-ADU-15-40c, McKim to Pierce, 14 May 1946 and Wrong to Pierce, 21 May 1946. For more on Italian membership, see the file in PRO, FO 371, 54632. The British MCA wanted to be selective; he didn't want 'hangers-on,' only those states which would contribute to the organization. See the memo, 8 May 1946.

56 ACT, DEA Correspondence files (1946), A1067/1 UN46/ICA/2/2, Arthur Drakeford, 'Report on the First Assembly of the PICAO.'

57 PICAO, 'Minutes of the First Plenary Session.'

58 NARA, RG 237, PICAO: Facilitation Reports, etc., 'Report of Activities: First Interim Assembly (for week ended May 25, 1946); ACT, 'Report on the First Assembly'; LAC, 'Report on the First Meeting of the Interim Assembly.'

59 LAC, 'Report on the First Meeting of the Interim Assembly.'

60 NARA, RG 237, 'Report of Activities: First Interim Assembly (for five days ended June 7, 1946)'; ACT, 'Report on the First Assembly.'

61 PICAO, 'Minutes of the First Plenary Meeting.'

62 See *PICAO Journal* 1/ 6 (1946), 41–2. See also, NARA, RG 237, 'Report of Activities First Interim Assembly,' 1 June 1946.

63 One participant speculated on the Chinese move: 'As for the nomination of China by China, some accepted the Chinese statement that China was put forward merely as the opening of an offensive to be waged in international meetings designed to bring ultimately an international organization to China, either permanently or for meetings. Others observed that the nomination of China permitted that country to avoid making a decision.' LAC, 'Report on the First Meeting of the Interim Assembly.'

64 PICAO, doc. 1826, A/44, 'Minutes of the Fourth Plenary Meeting,' 6 June 1946. The value of having Montreal as the seat of ICAO was not lost on the Canadian government. Early estimates put the intake of foreign currency at around Can $2.5 million in 1946 and Can $3.5 million in 1947. In addition, having ICAO in Montreal would also bring IATA and more foreign currency. At the same time, the Canadian government would save Canadian dollars for travel expenses and, in a larger way, Montreal and the country as a whole would benefit from the arrival of foreign visitors and from the great prestige and free advertising of Canada throughout the world. See LAC, Howe Papers, v. 96, file: 61-6(8), Anson McKim to Lester Pearson, 16 April 1947.

65 PICAO, 'Minutes of the Fourth Plenary Meeting.' The only sour note came when the French delegate mentioned that Paris deserved some consideration

from the North Americans. The Canadian report on the Assembly noted: 'The French complaint that reaching a decision under existing conditions would show lack of consideration for war-shattered France was met by pointing out that the United States and Canada could not fairly be charged with want of sympathy for France and her problems of reconstruction.' LAC, 'Report on the First Meeting of the Interim Assembly.'

66 LAC, RG 25, v. 3380, file:72-ADU-14-40, Anson Mckim memo, 17 June 1946.
67 PICAO, 'Minutes of the Fourth Plenary Meeting.'
68 PRO, FO 371, 54632, unsigned memo, 8 May 1946.
69 Ibid., 54635 W8750, 'Brief for U.K. Representative in Negotiations for an Agreement between the United Nations & PICAO' (1946); same file, W9656, A Bottomley to Ernest Bevin, 30 Sept. 1946; LAC, MG 26, J, Mackenzie King Diary, 2 and 4 June 1946; FO 371 /54632 W6271/4551/802, N.J.A. Cheetham note, 18 July 1946. LAC, MG 27, III B20, Howe Papers, v. 96, file: 61-6(8), t.1050, Hume Wrong to Norman Robertson, 29 May 1946 and t.1305, Robertson to Wrong, 4 June 1946 in the same file.
70 PICAO, 'Minutes of the Fourth Plenary Meeting.' Although Montreal and Paris were nominated, the vote was actually for the host country; i.e., Canada won over France.
71 Drakeford, 'Report on the First Assembly.'
72 See PICAO, 'Consolidated Lists of Resolutions.' For a good review of the decisions and final reports of the assembly, see NARA, 'Report of Activities: First Interim Assembly (for five days ended June 7, 1946)'
73 PICAO, 'Report on the Work,' 30 April 1946. For more on the financial arrangements, see doc. 1624, A/23, 'Introduction and Outline of Financial Arrangements,' 13 May 1946.
74 PICAO, 'Decisions of the Interim Council.'
75 Drakeford, 'Report on the First Assembly.'

4 The First Assembly – and After

1 Edward Warner during the First Session of the First Assembly, ICAO, doc. 7325 C/852, 'Proceedings of the First Session of the Assembly, 6 May to 27 May 1947,' Dec. 1952 (hereafter ICAO, '1st Session').
2 ICAO, '1st Session.'
3 LAC, MG 27, III B20, vol. 95, file: 61-6(4), John Baldwin to Howe, 13 July 1946. See also, 'Work Commenced on Aviation Site,' Montreal *Gazette*, 29 May 1947.
4 Prentice, 'The First Assembly of the ICAO,' 1145.

5 ICAO, doc. 4023, A1-P/3, 'Review of the Activities of the PICAO June 8, 1946 to March 31, 1947.'
6 Schenkman, *ICAO*, 182–4.
7 On Montreal in the 1940s and 1950s, see Weintraub, *City Unique*, 61.
8 See ibid., 292.
9 Quoted in 'ICAO Ouster of Spain due Today as Vote Power Decision Reached,' Montreal *Gazette*, 13 May 1947.
10 Cambridge University Library, Royal Commonwealth Society, Sir Frederick Tymms Collection (hereafter Tymms Collection), box RCMS 20/1/2/1/8 – 20/1/2/2/2, J.H. Riddoch to Sir Frederick Tymms, 4 March 1957.
11 Truman Library, Russell B. Adams Papers, box 12, file: ICAO, 1944–53, file: Confidential Report on First Assembly, 'Confidential Report of the First Assembly of the ICAO, Montreal, Canada, May, 1947,' 1 Aug. 1947.
12 ICAO, '1st Session.'
13 Truman Library, WHCF, Official File, box 36, file: 3-I CAB (1945–46), 'Statement of James M. Landis, Chairman CAB before House Committee on Interstate and Foreign Commerce,' n.d.
14 See ibid., box 864, file: 249-C (folder 2), 'Survival in the Air Age: Report to the President by the President's Air Policy Commission, Jan. 1, 1948.'
15 PICAO, 'Decisions of the Interim Council,' meeting 4 March 1947.
16 ICAO, doc. 4428, C/529 and C/549, Council Minutes – First Session (hereafter lst Council Minutes).
17 See the correspondence in Tymms Collection, box RCMS 20/1/2/1/8 – 20/1/2/2/2, file: ICAO Council Member. See also, Johnston, *To Organise the Air*, 151–3.
18 Tymms Collection, file: ICAO Council Member, Ivor McClure to Tymms, 8 Aug. 1947. For the council discussion of the deputy secretary-general position, see ICAO, doc. 4428, c/552, 1st Council Minutes, 24 June 1947.
19 Truman Library, Adams Papers, 'Confidential Report.'
20 *PICAO Monthly Bulletin* (1 Nov. 1946), 1–2.
21 See Sochor, *The Politics of International Aviation*, 51. For a copy of the draft agreement see *PICAO Journal* 1/8 (1946–47), 32–6.
22 See ICAO, doc. 7970, 'Agreement between the United Nations and the International Civil Aviation Organization,' n.d.
23 NARA, RG 59, Subject Files of Durward V. Sandifer, box 9, file: ICAO, memo, 'Spanish Membership in the ICAO,' 6 Dec. 1946. See also Buergenthal, *Law-Making in the International Civil Aviation Organization*, 40.
24 Truman Library, Adams Papers, 'Confidential Report.'
25 Ibid.
26 ICAO, '1st Session.'

27 Irish Department of Foreign Affairs (DFA), Dublin, Departmental documents, file: 408/58, minute of meeting, 20 March 1947; and DFA to Spanish Legation, 23 April 1947.

28 PRO, CAB 134/58, Memo by MCA, 'First Meeting of the Assembly of the ICAO,' CAC (47) 12, 23 June 1947. For the Irish report, see NAI, Cabinet Memoranda and Papers, S13851A, 'Report of the Irish Delegation to the First Assembly of ICAO,' May 1947.

29 Truman Library, Adams Papers, 'Confidential Report.'

30 See ICAO, doc. A1-CP/32, Commission No.1, Constitutional and General Policy Questions, Minutes of Meetings, 8 May 1947.

31 Truman Library, Adams Papers, box 17, file: ICAO (Chicago, Nov. 1944) Multilateral Air Transport Agreement, Paris (Caffery) to Secretary of State, t.1744, 27 April 1947; see also PRO, CAB 134/58, memo by MCA.

32 PRO, CAB 134/58, memo by MCA.

33 The issue is explored in 'ICAO Ouster of Spain,' and 'Delegates from Peru in Disgrace for Backing Move to Oust Spain,' Montreal *Gazette*, 16 May 1947.

34 Truman Library, Adams Papers, 'Confidential Report.'

35 ICAO, '1st Session.'

36 The resolution is printed in ICAO, 'Agreement between U.N. and ICAO.'

37 ICAO, '1st Session.'

38 These events and the legal aspects of Spanish membership are covered fully in Buergenthal, *Law-Making in the ICAO*, 40–2.

39 The relationship is detailed in the agreement; see ICAO, 'Agreement between the U.N. and ICAO.'

40 For more on ICAO as a specialized agency, see Alexandrowicz, *The Law-Making Functions of the Specialized Agencies of the United Nations*, chapter 3; Luard, *International Agencies*, chapter 4; and Williams, *The Specialized Agencies and the United Nations: The System in Crisis*.

41 'Flying Ice Wagon Is Inspected Here,' Montreal *Gazette*, 10 May 1947.

42 For a review of the technical work of the organization in advance of the First Assembly, see PICAO, doc. 4023, 'Review of the Activities of the PICAO June 8, 1946 to March 31, 1947,' 17–32.

43 Truman Library, Official File, box 1520, file: 657 (Oct. 1946–47), 'Report of the ACC 1947,' 2 Feb. 1949. See also, Prentice, 'The First Assembly,'1149.

44 'I.C.A.O. Adjourns Wednesday – "But What Year"?' Montreal *Gazette*, 27 May 1947.

45 PRO, CAB 134 /58, Cabinet Civil Aviation Committee, CAC (47) 12, 'First Meeting of the Assembly of the ICAO,' 23 June 1947.

46 Government of Canada, Department of External Affairs and International
    Trade, *Documents on Canadian External Relations,* vol. 13, *1947* (hereafter
    DCER), doc. 305, 'Extract from Report on Meeting of First Assembly of the
    ICAO, Montreal, May 6 to May 27, 1947,' 573–75.
47 ICAO, '1st Session' (original emphasis).
48 Draper, 'Transition from CITEJA to the Legal Committee of ICAO,' 155.
    See also Warner, 'PICAO and the Development of Air Law,' 1–10.
49 See PICAO, 'Consolidated Lists of Resolutions Adopted by the First Interim
    Assembly,' 7 June 1946.
50 PICAO, 'Review of the Activities.'
51 FitzGerald, 'The ICAO and the Development of Conventions on Inter-
    national Law,' 51–64.
52 See Latchford, 'CITEJA and the Legal Committee of ICAO,' 487–97.
53 Truman Library, Adams Papers, 'Confidential Report.'
54 Ibid., 'Report of the Air Coordinating Committee 1947.' For a thorough
    examination of this issue, see Wilberforce, 'The International Recognition
    of Rights in Aircraft,' 421–58; Heiman, 'ICAO Gets Down to Business,' 421.
55 FitzGerald, 'Development of Conventions,' 69.
56 ICAO, '1st Session.'
57 *DCER,* 'Extract from Report on Meeting of First Assembly.'
58 PRO, CAB 134 /58, 'First Meeting of the Assembly.' See also ICAO, '1st
    Session.'
59 PRO, CAB 134 /58, 'First Meeting of the Assembly.'
60 *DCER,* 'Extract from Report on Meeting of First Assembly.'
61 See ICAO, doc. 5221, A2-P/5, 'Report of the Council to the Assembly on the
    Activities of the Organization June 1, 1947 to March 1, 1948,' 19 March 1948.
62 ICAO, doc. 5110, C/635, 'Council Minutes, 3rd Session,' 13 Jan. 1948
63 See, e.g., ICAO, doc. 4428, C/515 (28 May 1947) and C/551 (24 June
    1947), 'Council Minutes, 1st Session.'
64 Cheng, *Law of International Air Transport,* 70–1.
65 See ibid., 64–5; and Buergenthal, *Law-Making in the ICAO,* 80–5.
66 This wording is pointed out in FitzGerald, 'The ICAO – A Case Study in
    the Implementation of Decisions of a Functional International Organiza-
    tion,' 159.
67 Warner, 'Notes from PICAO Experience,' 32–3. In the more legalistic
    words of a former ICAO senior legal officer, this non-binding pressure was
    the 'sanction of reciprocity,' where 'non-compliance with the norm entails
    a disentitlement to enjoyment of the activity in the company of other
    States belonging to the norm-establishing organization.' FitzGerald, 'The
    ICAO,' 161.

68 Truman Library, Russell B. Adams Papers, box 12, file: ICAO, 1944–53: Confidential Report on Second Assembly, Sept. 1948, Adams memo, 'Air Navigation Committee vs Air Navigation Commission,' n.d.

69 Ibid.

70 Sheffy, 'The Air Navigation Commission of the ICAO, Part 1,' 295.

71 ICAO, Press Release, 29 June 1948.

72 Osieke, 'Unconstitutional Acts in International Organisations,' 5–8.

73 For a broad look at the ANC and its activities, see Sheffy, 'The Air Navigation Commission, Part 1,' and 'The Air Navigation Commission of the ICAO, Part II,' 428–43; Schenkman, *ICAO*, 170–5; Cheng, *Law of International Air Transport*, 53–4; Banes, 'Air Navigation,' 863–4; and Rhoades, *Evolution of International Aviation: Phoenix Rising*, 31–4. See also the ICAO website (ICAO.org) for how a SARP is created.

74 Schenkman, *ICAO*, 260–2. For more on each annex, including annexes 16–18, see Weber, *ICAO: An Introduction*, 55–68.

75 Warner, 'ICAO after Six Years,' 80.

76 Ibid. For more on some of the 'unresolved policy problems' in facilitation, see Dwight D. Eisenhower Presidential Library, Abilene, Kansas (hereafter Eisenhower Library) WHCF, Confidential Files, box 2, file: ACC (11), ACC, 'Review of National Aviation Policy – Facilitation of International Civil Aviation,' 23 Feb. 1954.

77 For one example, see Truman Library, Adams Papers, box 21, file: 'ICAO: Second Assembly, 1948, Book 1,' Statement by Chairman of U.S. delegation to 2nd Assembly, Geneva, 1 June 1948.

78 See, e.g., the discussion concerning the Technical Commission in ACT, DEA, Correspondence files, A1838 /1/717/31/7, 'Report on the 7th Session of the Assembly of the ICAO held at Brighton, England, 16th June to 6th July 1953,' n.d.

79 ICAO, '1st Session.'

80 Ibid.

5 Remembering the 'Forgotten Man'

1 ICAO, doc. 4510, AI-EC/72, Discussions of Commission No. 3, vol. 1, 'Development of a Multilateral Agreement on Commercial Rights in International Civil Air Transport,' Peruvian delegate to Commission 3 of the First Assembly, May 1947.

2 See Cooper, 'Air Transport and World Organization,' 1208–9.

3 PICAO, 'Minutes, 2nd Plenary Meeting.'

4 Ibid., doc. 1577, AT/116, 'Report of the Committee on Air Transport to the Assembly on the matters on which it was not possible to reach agreement

among the nations represented at the Chicago Conference,' 17 April 1946. The 'Agreement on Commercial Rights in International Civil Air Transport' is attached to this document as Annex A.

5　Ibid. One participant at the talks credited council president Edward Warner for the suggestion of the rate differential. See McKim, 'World Order in Air Transport,' 231.

6　PRO, CAB 129, Cabinet Memo, CP (46) 44, 6 Feb. 1946.

7　PICAO, 'Agreement on Commercial Rights.'

8　Ibid.

9　PRO, PREM 8/16, 'Brief for the PM.' On the discussions, see NARA, RG 59, 841.796/9-445, Satterthwaite to DOS, 4 Sept. 1945, and PRO, CAC (45) 4, 12 Sept. 1945, Winster memo.

10　PRO, PREM 8/16, Attlee note, 15 Nov. 1945.

11　Ibid., FO 371, 50272 W16612/24/802, Halifax to FO, t.8551, 24 Dec. 1945.

12　Ibid., FO to Washington embassy, t.44, 2 Jan. 1946. See also, Dalton's diary for 7 Dec. 1945, British Library of Economics and Political Science, Dalton Papers, vol. 33.

13　NARA, RG 59, 841.796/1-2746, Baker to Clayton, 27 Jan. 1946.

14　Quoted in Bullock, *Ernest Bevin: Foreign Secretary, 1945–1951*, 202.

15　*FRUS, 1946,* vol. 1, 1464–5, Byrnes to Winant, 31 Jan. 1946.

16　PRO, PREM 8 /138, Halifax to FO, t.663, 30 Jan. 1946.

17　Ibid., CAB 128, Cabinet Conclusions, 4 Feb. 1946.

18　Ibid. One last sticking point was the right of change of gauge. The British government was very reluctant to grant it but the Americans were equally insistent that it be included. On 9 February an understanding was reached. It was agreed that a change of gauge was to be permitted but on condition of 'there being an adequate volume of through traffic,' and a clause was added that seemed to offer sufficient protection to British interests by forcing the smaller aircraft to wait for the arrival of the larger aircraft before leaving, thereby preventing the operation of U.S. air lines in Britain as semi-regular services. See 'Bilateral Air Transport Agreement between the Government of the United Kingdom and the Government of the United States of America Relating to Air Services between Their Respective Territories,' Cmd. 6747.

19　'Bilateral Air Transport Agreement,' Cmd. 6747. There were no real surprises on the route selection. The British requested services from London and/or Prestwick to New York, Chicago, Washington, and several other U.S. cities; Bermuda to New York, Washington and Baltimore; from the West Indies to Miami, and from Singapore/Hong Kong to San Francisco. The Americans requested services from New York (and other major American cities) to London and on to points in Europe and Asia; through the

West Indies for services to South America, and for the use of Hong Kong and Singapore.

20 'Bilateral Air Transport Agreement,' Cmd. 6747.

21 See Truman Library, Official File, box 1556, file: 871, 'Statement by the President,' 26 Feb. 1946. Truman outlined the contents of the agreement and then added that because 'civil aviation involves not only problems of transportation but security, sovereignty and national prestige problems as well, the joint working out of air transport agreements between nations is a most difficult one.'

22 See, e.g., Taneja, *U.S. International Aviation Policy*, 13; Luard, *International Agencies*, 65.

23 Lowenfeld, 'A New Takeoff for International Air Transport,' 38.

24 The British were, however, somewhat reluctant converts to 'Bermuda principles,' and soon ran into conflict with the United States over agreements that BOAC negotiated with France and Argentina, both of which stipulated a strict division of capacity. Two months after the signing of the Bermuda Agreement Livingston Satterthwaite reported to Washington that there still were elements in British government circles that opposed Bermuda and were looking for ways to get around it. He had recently heard a speech by Ivor Bulmer-Thomas, parliamentary secretary in the Ministry of Civil Aviation, in which he described several recent aviation agreements negotiated by the United Kingdom, but made no reference to Bermuda. After the speech Satterthwaite approached Bulmer-Thomas and asked why he had omitted any reference to Bermuda. 'Thomas colored,' Satterthwaite noted, and 'said it was so important he forgot it. He would not say it was a good aviation agreement, but thought it was good for Anglo-American relations.' NARA, RG 59, 841.796/3-1346, Satterthwaite to Secretary of State, t.28775, 13 March 1946; Bulmer-Thomas interview.

25 Solberg, *Conquest of the Skies*, 291, 300; Gidwitz, *Politics of International Air Transport*, 51–5. For more on Bermuda, see Dobson, *Peaceful Air Warfare*, 173–210; Cooper, 'The Bermuda Plan: World Pattern for Air Transport,' 59–71; Dierikx, 'Shaping World Aviation: Anglo-American Civil Aviation Relations, 1944–1946,' 795–840; and MacKenzie, 'The Bermuda Conference,' 61–73.

26 NARA, RG 59, 800.796/ 8-1246, Acheson to Lord Inverchapel, 12 Aug. 1946. For some of the problems faced in trying to negotiate Bermuda-like bilaterals in India and the Middle East, see Truman Library, George A. Brownell Papers, box 1, file: ACC, file: Diary (Mission to India) Sept. 12 to Nov. 1, 1946. See also, Thomas, 'Civil Aviation: International Questions Outstanding,' 62–3.

27 *FRUS, 1946*, vol. 1, 1489, Acting Secretary of State to Certain Diplomatic Officers, 19 Sept. 1946. For the British views, see also ACT, DEA, Correspondence files, Series A1838/1, file: 890/36/5, E.C. Johnston to Director General of Civil Aviation, 3 Oct. 1946. For the complete report on the U.S. delegation see Truman Library, Russell B. Adams Papers, box 21, file: ICAO: PICAO, report of U.S. delegation, interim assembly meeting, 'Report of the U.S. Delegation to the PICAO First Assembly Meeting, Held in Montreal, Canada, May 21 to June 7, 1946;' for Ireland, see NAI, Cabinet Memoranda and Papers, S13851A, 'Report of Irish Delegation to First Assembly of PICAO, May–June 1946.'

28 ACT, DEA, Correspondence files (1946), A1067/1 UN46/ICA/2/2, Arthur Drakeford, 'Report on the First Assembly of the PICAO,' n.d.

29 NARA, RG 237, file: PICAO: Facilitation Reports, etc., 'Report of Activities First Interim Assembly,' 25 May 1946.

30 PICAO, 'Minutes, 2nd Plenary Meeting,' 24 May 1946 (original emphasis).

31 The report of the commission is 181 pages long. See ibid., doc. 2089-EC/57, 'Commission No. 3 of the First Interim Assembly: Discussion on the Development of a Multilateral Agreement on Commercial Rights in International Civil Air Transport,' Oct. 1946.

32 PICAO, doc. 1733, EC/21, 'Statement on Behalf of the U.S. by William A.M. Burden, Chairman of the U.S. Delegation, on the Report of the ATC of the Interim Assembly on the matters on which it was not possible to reach agreement among the Nations represented at the Chicago Conference,' 29 May 1946 (original emphasis).

33 PICAO, doc. 1837, A/46, 'Minutes, 5th Plenary Meeting, Appendix B,' 7 June 1946.

34 PICAO, 'Statement on Behalf of the U.S. by William A.M. Burden.'

35 LAC, RG 25, A-12, v. 2114, file: AR 412/11, 'Report on the First Meeting of the Interim Assembly of the PICAO, May 21 to June 7, 1946.'

36 FFMA, S.4.6.7, box 31, file: Chicago (aviation) 1945–46, Hymans to Moch, 27 May 1946.

37 PICAO, doc. 2866, AT/169, 'Multilateral Agreement on Commercial Rights in International Civil Air Transport, Proceedings of the ATC,' 26 Feb. 1947. See also Cooper, 'The Proposed Multilateral Agreement on Commercial Rights in International Civil Air Transport,' 125–49.

38 A copy of the draft agreement can be found in Truman Library, Adams Papers, box 18, file: ICAO Multilateral Air Transport Agreement, 'Draft Agreement on International Air Transport,' 12 Nov. 1946

39 See, e.g., the correspondence in ibid., box 17, file: ICAO (Chicago, Nov. 1944) Multilateral Air Transport Agreement, Douglas to Secretary of State,

t.2331, 21 April 1947, where it is noted the 'growing impression US did not want multilateral agreement'; and box 18, file: ICAO: Multilateral Air Transport Agreement, George Pendleton to Adams, 30 Jan. 1947.

40 Ibid., box 19, file: ICAO: Official Documents 3rd Assembly, Air Transport Division draft memo, 'Bargaining Advantages under Multilateral.'

41 Truman Library, WHCF, Official File, box 1395, file: 578-A, Oswald Ryan to Matthew Connelly, 15 Nov. 1947.

42 ICAO, doc. 4510, AI-EC/72, 'Development of a Multilateral Agreement.'

43 In a related way the British agreed, in that there were fears that the USSR, while on the one hand, remaining outside ICAO and excluding the West from its airspace, was, on the other, developing the air capabilities of its satellite states who *were* members of ICAO. Including the right to establish air routes in the multilateral agreement would effectively give the Soviets access to Britain (via a satellite nation) while withholding access to the Soviet Union itself. This issue is discussed in LAC, MG 27, III B20, v. 96, file: 61-6(7), 'Report on ICAO Conference on Multilateral Agreement on Commercial Rights in the Air,' Dec. 1947.

44 LAC, MG 27, III, B20, vol. 96, file: 61-6(7), McKim to Howe, 26 June 1947.

45 Truman Library, Adams Papers, box 17, file: ICAO (Chicago, Nov. 1944) Multilateral Air Transport Agreement, Paris (U.S. Embassy) to Secretary of State, t.1744, 27 April 1947. The telegram continues: 'it is indicative of the French conviction that they require protection, particularly against the Dutch and Swedes, which protection they do not feel the draft multilateral adequately provides.'

46 PRO, CO 937, 120 /1, 'Notes of a Meeting of the Committee on the Multilateral Convention Held in Mr Cribbett's Room in Ariel House at 10:30 a.m. on Wednesday 12th Feb. 1947,' 25 Feb. 1947.

47 Truman Library, Adams Papers, t.1744, 27 April 1947; LAC, MG 27, III, B20, v. 96, file: 61-6(7), Howe to McKim, 3 Feb. 1947; Irish DFA, Dublin, file: 408/58, memo by John Leydon, 18 April 1947.

48 ICAO, 'Development of a Multilateral Agreement.'

49 See MacKenzie, *Canada and International Civil Aviation*, 246–7.

50 For the debate on internationalization and British aviation policy in general, see the documents in Oxford University, Bodleian Library, Papers of 1st Viscount Boyd of Merton (Alan Lennox-Boyd), MS ENG c. 3388-89 and c. 3390-1; Bodleian Library, Papers of the Conservative Party, CRD 2/15/8. The Bodleian Library also contains the records of the U.N. Career Record Project, which elicits the written experiences of former participants in the U.N. and its agencies, like ICAO. Although it may change in the future, as of now, very few former ICAO employees have responded.

51 Truman Library, Adams Papers, box 12, file: ICAO, 1944–53: Confidential Report on First Assembly, Aug. 1947, 'Confidential Report on the First Assembly of the ICAO, Montreal, Canada, May, 1947,' 1 Aug. 1947.

52 ICAO, doc. 4521, A1-EC/73, 'Discussions of Commission No. 3 of the First Assembly,' vol. 2, 'International Ownership and Operation of Trunk Air Routes,' May 1947. For U.S. views see, Truman Library, Adams Papers, box 11, file: ICAO, 1944–53, CAB memo, 'ICAO matters – Air Transport – Multi-lateral Air Transport Agreement – Analysis of Discussion of Multilateral Agreement in Commission 3 of the First Assembly of ICAO,' 28 July 1947. For British views, see PRO, CAB 134 /58, Cabinet Civil Aviation Committee, CAC (47) 12, 'First Meeting of the Assembly of the ICAO,' 23 June 1947. For French views, see Institut Français du Transport Aérien, 'Aviation Contributions to the Development of International Cooperation – Inter-nationalization: Objectives and Methods,' 184–93. See also, Cooper, 'Internationalization of Air Transport,' 546–60.

53 Truman Library, Adams Papers, box 12, file: ICAO: Delegates & Positions, memo, 'Conversation between Cribbett, Satterthwaite, and Vass,' 25 June 1947.

54 Ibid., CAB memo, 'ICAO Matters.'

55 LAC, MG 27, III B20, v. 96, file: 61-6(7), Cribbett to John Baldwin, 10 Sept. 1947. For the discussions, see PRO, CO 937, 120/1, 'Notes of Informal Discussions on the Multilateral Agreement Held at the MCA on 1, 2 and 3 Sept., 1947.'

56 LAC, MG 27, III B20, v. 95, file: 61-6(6), 'Covering Note on a Multilateral Air Agreement; Canadian Proposals,' n.d. (probably Oct. 1947).

57 ACT, DEA, Correspondence files, A1838/1 890/36/5, 'Instructions to Delegations to Commission on Multilateral Agreement on Air Transport Rights,' 31 Oct. 1947.

58 E.A. He, 'Ink or Fuel? Two World Aviation Organisations: ICAO and IATA at Work,' 18. For the decision on location, see ICAO, doc. 4701 C/578, 'Council Minutes, 2nd Session,' 12 Sept. 1947.

59 LAC, MG 27, III B20, v. 95, file: 61-6(6), Howe to McKim, 14 Oct. 1947.

60 See *ICAO Monthly Bulletin* (Jan. 1948), 4–7. On the 1947 Geneva confer-ence, see McClurkin, 'The Geneva Commission on a Multilateral Air Transport Agreement,' 39–46.

61 Truman Library, Adams Papers, Ryan to Connelly, 15 Nov. 1947.

62 Ibid. The language issue is also discussed in LAC, 'Report on ICAO Conference.'

63 ICAO, doc. 5230 A2-EC/10, 'Records of the Commission on Multilateral Agreement on Commercial Rights in International Civil Air Transport,' April 1948.

64 LAC, MG 27, III B20, v. 96, file: 61-6(7), 'Report on ICAO Conference,' Dec.1947.

65 See, e.g., ACT, DEA, Correspondence files, A1838/1 890/36/5, Australian Delegation to Captain Johnston, 7 Nov. 1947, and LAC, MG 27, III B20, v. 95 file: 61-6(6), McKim to Howe, 5 Nov. 1947.

66 E.A. He, 'Mañana por la Mañana,' 53.

67 ICAO, 'Records of the Commission on Multilateral Agreement.' For the vote, see 'ICAO Fails to Draft Multilateral Pact,' *Aviation Week* 47/23 (1947), 56.

68 ICAO, doc. MAC-65, Rev. 1, 'Final Report,' 26 Nov. 1947. The Final Report can also be found in ICAO, doc. 5230 A2-EC/10, ibid.

69 ICAO, Rev. 1, 'Final Report.'

70 LAC, MG 27, 'Report on ICAO Conference,' Dec. 1947.

71 Truman Library, WHCF, Official File, box 1520, file: 657 (Oct. 1946–47), 'Report of the ACC,' 2 Feb. 1949.

72 On multilateralism, see Gunther, 'Multilateralism in International Air Transport,' 259–78, and Haanappel, 'Multilateralism and Economic Bloc Forming,' 279–320. On bilateralism see Lissitzyn, 'Bilateral Agreements on Air Transport,' 248–63, and Stoffel, 'American Bilateral Air Transport Agreements,' 119–36.

73 ICAO, doc. 6967, C/809, '24th Report to Council by the Chairman of the ATC,' 3 April 1950. For more on the early 1950s efforts for multilateralism, see Gunther, 'ICAO and the Multilateral Regulation of International Air Transport,' 131–53.

74 ICAO, doc. 6967, A4-WP/5, EC1, Appendix B, 'Further action to secure a Multilateral Agreement on Commercial Rights in International Air Transport,' 17 March 1950.

75 E.A. He, 'Sovereignty and Civil Aviation: Preparing for the ICAO Plenary Session,' 24 (original emphasis).

6 Headquarter Headaches

1 Canadian Prime Minister Pierre Elliott Trudeau at the opening of the new ICAO Headquarters, 3 Oct. 1975, quoted in 'ICAO Officially Inaugurates New Headquarters,' *ICAO Bulletin*, 30/10 (1975), 15.

2 ICAO, doc. 7310-C/846, 'Proceedings of the Council, 3rd Session, 13 Jan. to 20 April 1948,' Agenda Item 32. See also LAC, RG 25, v. 3379, file: 72ADU-3-40, 'Memo for the Minister of External Affairs and Treasury Board,' 18 March 1950.

3 'World Aviation Headquarters,' *Interavia* 5/8–9 (1950), 428; ICAO, doc. A3-P/4, 'Report of Council to the Assembly, Montreal, 11 April 1949.'

4　See ICAO, doc. 6968, A4-P/1, 'Report of the Council to the Assembly on the Activities of the Organization in 1949' (hereafter 'Report of [year] Activities'), 23 March 1950.

5　See, e.g., LAC, RG 26, v. 117, file: 3-24-36 vol. 1, Under-Secretary of State for External Affairs to Deputy Minister, Department of Mines and Resources, 1 June 1948. See also, 'ICAO Council Gets Diplomatic Status,' Montreal *Gazette*, 3 Sept. 1947.

6　LAC, RG 25, v. 3955, file: 9655-E-40, F.W. Bowhill to P.A. Cumyn, 30 July 1945.

7　Ibid., vol. 3954, file: 9655-E-2-40, W.H. Measures to Under-Secretary of State for External Affairs, 13 Jan. 1948.

8　Ibid., A.D.P. Heeney to Acting Secretary of State for External Affairs, 5 April 1949.

9　Ibid., v. 3380, file: 72-ADU-8-40, unsigned 'Note for File,' 27 May 1947.

10　Ibid., v. 6311, file: 72-ADU-30-40, Paul Martin to Lionel Chevrier, 21 Nov. 1952; for Warner's original letter of complaint, see RG 25 v. 33821, file: 72-ADU-30-40, Warner to C.S. Booth, 14 Oct. 1952.

11　The United States faced a similar 'source of great embarrassment' thanks to its policies of racial segregation, primarily at airports in the southern states, but including Washington's National Airport. See NARA, RG 237, Records Relating to ACC Facilitation Subcommittees, Inspection Tours, and Gov. Surveys, 1946–51, box 2, file: Racial Discrimination Letter, memo, 'Discriminatory Practices against U.S. Nationals and Certain Foreign Nationals at U.S. Ports of Entry,' 23 May 1947.

12　ICAO, doc. 7147, 'Agreement between the ICAO and the Government of Canada Regarding the Headquarters of the ICAO,' 27 April 1951.

13　LAC, RG 25, v. 6309, file: 72-ADU-40, pt. 6.2, L.D. Wilgress, 'Memo for the Minister,' 5 Feb. 1953.

14　Ibid. PRO, FO 371, 105662, file: GA 67/23, Tymms to Keel, 2 Feb. 1953.

15　See LAC, RG 25, v. 7208, file: 9655-E-2-40 (pt. 6.1), Memo to the Cabinet, 'Threatened transfer of ICAO Headquarters,' 25 Jan. 1956. For more on the taxation issue, see Milde, 'New Headquarters Agreement between ICAO and Canada,' 305–22.

16　LAC, RG 25, v. 7208, file: 9655-E-2-40 (pt. 6.1), Carl Ljungberg to L.B. Pearson, 9 April 1952. The rent was significantly higher than in several other organizations; see the comparative rental costs in Pearson, 'Memo to the Cabinet,' 14 May 1952, in the same file.

17　'Will Montreal's "Aviation Building" Lose Its Tenants?' *Interavia* 8/1 (1953), 43.

18　See the debate on the question in ICAO, doc. 7007, A4-EX/2, 'Final Report of the Executive Committee, 1950.'

19 For the American views, see NARA, RG 59, 1955 Central Decimal File (hereafter CDF), 399.72, box 1622, file: 399.72 – ICAO/6-1556, Dulles to U.S. Embassy, Caracas, 29 June 1956.

20 ICAO, doc. 7016, A4-P/2, 'Minutes of the Plenary Meetings,' 17 June 1950. For a good description of these events, see ACT, DEA, Correspondence files, A1838/1 717/31/4 Pt. 2, Australian MCA, 'Report on the 4th Assembly of the ICAO Held at Montreal during June, 1950,' n.d.

21 LAC, RG 25, v. 6313, file: 72-ADU-55-40 (pt.1.1), Irwin memo, 'Location of the Headquarters of ICAO,' 28 May 1952.

22 Ibid., (pt. 1.2), Secretary of State for External Affairs to Office of High Commissioner for Canada, London, 6 Aug. 1952.

23 Ibid.

24 ICAO, doc. 7297, A6-P/2, 'Minutes of 3rd Plenary Session,' 12 June 1952.

25 FFMA, S50-3-6, box 337, file: 6ième Assemblée Générale de l'OACI, Montréal, mai–juin 1952, Henri Bouché à le Ministre des Affaires Etrangères, 22 July 1952.

26 LAC, RG 25, v. 6313, file: 72-ADU-55-40 (pt. 2.1), Canadian Ambassador, Paris to Secretary of State for External Affairs, t.1548, 13 Sept. 1952. See the attached note from the French government. See also, FFMA, Bouché à le Ministre des Affaires Etrangères, 22 July 1952.

27 LAC, DEA to High Commissioner, London, 6 Aug. 1952. For an example of the Canadian efforts to persuade the French government, see the 'Aide-Memoire,' from the Canadian Embassy in Paris to the French government, 4 Sept. 1952, in FFMA, S50-3-6, box 336, file: Siege de l'OACI 1951–54 juillet.

28 LAC, RG 25, v. 7208, file: 9655-E-2-40 (pt. 6.1), DEA, Working Document, 'Brief History Statement,' 25 Jan. 1956.

29 PRO, FO 371, 165670, file: GA67 /180, 'Report on the 7th Session of the Assembly of ICAO,' 16 June 1953.

30 See, e.g., the view of the French delegation in FFMA, S50-3-6, box 337, file: 7ième session de l'Assemblé Générale de l'OACI, Brighton, juin–juillet 1953, French Delegation to Minister of Foreign Affairs, 21 Aug. 1953.

31 LAC, RG 25, v. 6526, file: 9655-E-2-40, C. Ljungberg to L.B. Pearson, 19 Feb. 1954. See also the analysis of the bill in D/Legal to Secretary General, 'Income Tax of the Province of Quebec,' 18 Feb. 1954; and Secretary General to Representatives on Council, 22 Feb. 1954.

32 Ibid., v. 7208, file: 9655-E-2-40 (pt. 6.1), Memo for Cabinet, 'The ICAO and the New Quebec Provincial Income Tax Law,' 13 April 1954.

33 See LAC, RG 2, v. 2654, Cabinet Conclusions, 14 April 1954. See also, Memo for Cabinet, 13 April 1954, and 'Memo to the Cabinet: Threatened Transfer of ICAO Headquarters,' 25 Jan. 1956.

34 These quotes were taken from ICAO, doc. C-Draft Min. XXI-12, 'Draft Minutes of the 12th Meeting of the Council,' 2 April 1954; a copy can be found in LAC, RG 25, v. 6313, file: 72-ADU-55-40 (pt. 3.1).

35 See ICAO, doc. C-Draft Min. XXI-14 (Closed), 'Draft Minutes of the 14th Session of the Council,' 7 April 1954, and ICAO, doc. A8-WP/16, EX/5, 'Question of Amending Article 45 of the Convention,' 12 April 1954.

36 See, e.g., ICAO, doc. 7505, A8-P/10, 'Minutes, 3rd Plenary Meeting,' 14 June 1954, and ICAO, doc. 7494, A8-EX/22, 'Final Report of the Executive Committee,' June 1954.

37 See LAC, RG 25, v. 6313, file: 72-ADU-55-40 (pt. 3.1), Under-Secretary of State for External Affairs to Canadian Embassy, Rio de Janeiro, Brazil, 28 July 1954.

38 The British position, e.g., was to oppose any move of the headquarters away from Montreal, but should the organization decide to move, then London should be put forward as a potential new headquarters location. See PRO, FO 371, 165670, file: GA67/180, 'Report on the 7th Session of the Assembly of ICAO,' 16 June 1953.

39 ACT, DEA, Correspondence files, A1838/1 717/31/8, 'Report of the Australian Delegation to the 8th Session of the ICAO Assembly,' June 1954. The New Zealand position before the start of the 1954 assembly had been to oppose any move of the headquarters but to support the amendment only if it included the 'proper safeguards.' See in the same file, Minister of External Affairs, Wellington to High Commissioner for New Zealand, Ottawa, t.29, 17 May 1954. For the French perspective, see FFMA, S-50-3-6, box 337, file: 8ème session de l'Assemblée Générale de l'OACI, Montréal juin 1954, 'Rapport à la 8ème session de l'Assemblée de l'Organisation,' 17 July 1954. For a good overview of the whole debate, see 'Amendment of Article 45 of the Convention on International Civil Aviation,' *ICAO Bulletin* 9/5 (1954), 15–18.

40 Resolutions A8-4 and A8-5.

41 LAC, RG 25, v. 6309, file: 72-ADU-40 (pt. 8.1), Booth to David Wilson, 8 July 1954.

42 ICAO, doc. 7621-C/855, 'Action of the Council, 25th Session, 17 May to 22 June 1955.'

43 LAC, RG 25, v. 7208, file: 9655-E-2-40 (pt. 6.1), DEA Working Document, 'Brief History Statement,' 25 Jan. 1956.

44 The move caused embarrassment for the Canadian government, the British High Commission in Ottawa, and even in the British government. See PRO, DO 35, 4869, U.K. High Commissioner in Canada to Commonwealth Relations Office, t.501, 29 June 1955, and the other correspondence in this file.

45 ICAO, Resolution A9-10. For a good overview of the debate on the resolution, see ACT, DEA, Correspondence files, A1838/2 717/31/9, 'Report on the 9th Session of the Assembly of the ICAO held at Montreal, Canada, May 30th to June 13th, 1955,' n.d.. See also FFMA, S50-3-6, box 337, file: 9ème session de l'Assemblée Générale de l'OACI, Montréal 1955, Henri Bouché to le Ministre des Affaires Etrangères, 3 Aug. 1955.

46 See ICAO, doc. C-WP/2070, Working Paper, President of the Council, 'Relations with the Province of Quebec,' 23 Nov. 1955.

47 E.g., see the document prepared in the Canadian Department of Finance in LAC, RG 25, v. 7208, file: 9655-E-2-40 (pt. 6.1), 'The Value to Canada of Having I.C.A.O. Headquarters remain in Canada,' 19 Sept. 1955.

48 LAC, RG 25, v. 7208, file: 9655-E-2-40 (pt. 6.2), Memo to the Cabinet, 'Headquarters of the ICAO,' 24 Feb. 1956, and attached documents. For the decision of the Canadian government to pursue these policies, see RG 2, v. 5775, Cabinet Conclusions, 1 March 1956.

49 See LAC, RG 25, v. 6314, file: 72-ADU-55-40 (pt. 3.2), 'Memo to Heads of Mission,' May 1956.

50 Ibid., v. 7208, file: 9655-E-2-40 (pt. 6.2), Memo, 'ICAO Headquarters,' 25 Jan. 1957.

51 ICAO, doc. A10-WP/150, Min. EX 1-17, 'Minutes of the Executive Committee, 13th Meeting,' 6 July 1956.

52 Resolution A10-10 (1956).

53 ACT, DEA, Correspondence files, A1838/1 717/31/10, 'Report on the 10th Session of the Assembly of the ICAO held at Caracas, Venezuela, June 19th to July 16th, 1956,' n.d.

54 LAC, RG 25, v. 4984, file: 72-ADU-16-40 (s), Macdonnell to Norman Robertson, 6 Sept. 1963. For ICAO's growing space problems, see v. 6714, file: 72-ADU-16-40 (pt. 3.1), and (pt. 3.2); and RG 2, v. 2745, Cabinet Conclusions, 31 July 1959.

55 See the preamble to Resolution A16-12 (1968).

56 'ICAO Officially Inaugurates New Headquarters,' *ICAO Bulletin* 30/10 (1975), 14.

7 Growing Pains

1 ICAO, doc. 5221, A2-P/5, 'Report of the Council to the Assembly on the Activities of the Organization June 1, 1947 to March 1, 1948,' 19 March 1948.

2 Buergenthal, *Law-Making*, 32–3. See also Mankiewicz, 'Air Law Conventions and the New States,' 52–64.

3 Buergenthal, *Law-Making*, 15–26. For more on Yugoslavia not joining ICAO, see LAC, RG 24, v. 17553, file: 004-4-ops vol.1, 'RCAF Intelligence Information Report,' 3 May 1956.

4 See ICAO, doc. 7007, A4-EX/2, 'Executive Committee Final Report,' 17 June 1950; on the Geneva assembly, see 'ICAO Concludes Geneva Meeting,' *Aviation Week* 49/1 (1948), 14.

5 Resolution A4-6. See also, NARA, RG 340, Office of the Administrative Assistant General File, box 90, file: ICAO Panel – General, DOS Confidential memo, 'Site of the 1953 Sessions of the ICAO Assembly,' 5 Sept. 1952. The U.S. opposed holding major assemblies away from the headquarters.

6 For an example of the competition between Venezuela and Mexico for holding the 1956 session, and the U.K. response, see the correspondence in PRO, FO 371, 115391.

7 ICAO, doc. A7-WP/18 EX/4, 'Executive Committee Working Paper,' 27 March 1953.

8 Ibid.

9 Ibid., doc. 7494, A8-EX/22, 'Executive Committee Final Report,' n.d.

10 For a review of these issues and a statement of U.S. policy, see NARA, RG 237, Interagency Group on International Aviation: Classified Correspondence and Reports, 1960–63, box 3, file: 14th Session of the ICAO Assembly, Section VI, 'Draft of U.S. Position for 14th Session,' 1 May 1962.

11 Resolution A12-2. See also ICAO, doc.7997, A12-EX/2, 'Executive Committee Final Report,' 1959, and NARA, RG 59, 1955–59 CDF, 399.72, box 1630, file: 399.72 – ICAO/7-259, 'Official Report of the U.S. Delegation to the 12th Session,' 6 Aug. 1959.

12 NARA, RG 237, Interagency Group on International Aviation, Classified Correspondence and Reports, 1960–63, box 6, file: 13th (Extraordinary) Session, Section 1, DOS, 'Proposed U.S. Position for the 13th – Extraordinary Session of the ICAO Assembly,' 15 May 1961.

13 Ibid.

14 FFMA, S50-3-6, box 839, file: 14ème Session de l'Assemblée, French Delegation to Minister of Foreign Affairs, 15 Nov. 1962.

15 ICAO, doc. 8167, A13-P/2, 'Executive Committee Final Report,' 17 July 1961.

16 Ibid.

17 See, e.g., PRO, FO 371, 158630, file: GA 13/7, Ministry of Aviation to R.J. Beveridge (of the FO), 21 March 1961.

18 Resolution A13 -1.

19 Resolution A13 -2.

20 There were suggestions, from unspecified sources, that 'someone may try to prevent States which have not ratified the amendment to the Convention from voting for more than 21 candidates or standing for any of the 6 extra seats,' noted one British official. 'This is a crack-brained idea, because, whatever the Convention may say about the binding effect of the amendment upon States which have or have not ratified it, there can only be one Council, and all States whose voting power is not suspended are entitled to participate fully in the election.' PRO, DO 160 /2, file: 31/127/2, Michael Custance (Ministry of Aviation) to J.R. Baldwin (and others), 3 July 1962.

21 ACT, DEA, Correspondence files, A1838/1 717/31/13, D.J. Medley memo for Director-General, Department of Civil Aviation, Melbourne, Australia, 28 June 1961. For more on the Australian position see ibid., 'Australian Brief, 13th Session (Extraordinary) – ICAO Assembly,' 1961. For a similar recommendation for swift ratification from the U.S. delegation, see NARA, RG 237, Interagency Group on International Aviation, Classified Correspondence and Reports, 1960–63, box 6, file: 13th (Extraordinary) Session, DOS, 'Report of the U.S. Delegation to the 13th (Extraordinary) Session of the Assembly, Montreal, Canada, June19–21, 1961,' 23 June 1961.

22 NARA, RG 237, International Program and Policy Div. Classified Subject Files, 1945–64,' box 7, file: 14th Assembly-General, memo on '14th Session of the ICAO Assembly,' n.d. (probably Dec. 1962).

23 PRO, DO 160 /2, file: 31/127/2, 'Note of 11th Meeting of European Directors-General of Civil Aviation at Dublin, June 1962,' n.d.. The British 'Brief for the U.K. Delegation' is also in this file.

24 ICAO, doc. 8270, A14-EX/31, 'Executive Committee Final Report'; PRO, FO 371, /165143, file: GA 13/84, Report of U.K. Delegation, '14th Session of the Assembly'; FFMA, S50-3-6, box 839, file: 14ème Session, Report of French Delegation, n.d.

25 See ACT, DEA, D.J. Medley memo, 28 June 1961; and PRO, FO 371, 158631, file: GA 13/13, '13th (Extraordinary) Assembly ... Report by the U.K. Delegation,' 26 June 1961.

26 PRO, FO 371, 127652, file: GA 12/61, Vandeleur Robinson to P.G.B. Giles, 23 Aug. 1957. He continued: 'Unhappy events during the last three years, including our advocacy of an unpopular policy and our unsuccessful candidature for the presidency, have caused us some loss of prestige and influence in ICAO. It may well be that if, at the next Assembly, we throw our weight behind Nicaragua's case (which is harmless in itself and from some points of view morally attractive) we might regain (as champion of the States of least importance!) some ground. Too much need not be made of this point however.'

27 See, e.g., PRO, DO 160 /2, file: 31/127/2, 'Brief for U.K. Delegation, Executive Commission,' n.d., but prepared for Aug. 1962 session in Rome.

28 Ibid. See the U.S. concerns expressed in NARA, 'Report of the U.S. Delegation to the 13th … Assembly,' 23 June 1961.

29 PRO, FO 371, 165143, file: GA 13/84, Report of U.K. Delegation, '14th … Assembly.'

30 FFMA, S50-3-6, box 838, file: Convention de Chicago (1944), Protocol d'amendement à l'article 50,' 'Rapport de la délégation française à la treizième Session Extraordinaire de l'Assemblée de l'Organisation de l'aviation Civile Internationale,' 3 July 1961.

31 ACT, DEA, D.J. Medley memo, 28 June 1961.

32 Boussard, 'After San Diego… ICAO Forges Ahead,' 1118.

33 LAC, RG 25, v. 3382, file: 72-ADU-34-40 pt.1, Memo for the Minister, 'Application of Italy for Election to the Council of ICAO,'15 April 1950.

34 A good example can be found in Australia's efforts before the 1959 council elections. See the documents in ACT, DEA, Correspondence Files, A1838/2 717/32/1 pt. 1.

35 LAC, RG 25, v. 3382, file: 72-ADU-34-40, Booth to C.G. Stoner, 13 March 1950.

36 Resolution A10-5.

37 Cheng, Law of International Air Transport, 56–62; see 'European Civil Aviation Conference Opens New Multilateral Agreement for Signature,' ICAO Bulletin 15/5 (1960), 81–3.

38 LAC, RG 25, v. 6715, file: 72-ADU-62-40 pt. 2, DEA memo, 8 Feb. 1956.

39 'Czechs Elected to ICAO Council,' Aviation Week and Space Technology 83/1 (1965), 26.

40 See PRO, FO 371, 165140, file: GA 13/37, R.S. Crawford memo, 1 Aug. 1962, and FO 371, 165142, file: GA 13/77, G. Ramage memo, 24 Aug. 1962.

41 NARA, RG 59, 1955–59 CDF, 399.72, box 1630, file: 399.72-ICAO /7-259, 'Confidential Report on the 12th Session of the Assembly of the ICAO,' 20 Aug. 1959.

42 See ACT, DEA, Correspondence files, A1838/1 717/31/4 pt. 2, 'Report on the 4th Assembly of the ICAO,' n.d.

43 FFMA, S50-3-6, box 337, file: 6ème Assemblée Générale de l'OACI, 22 July 1952.

44 Ibid., file: 7ème Session, R. Lemaire to Minister of Foreign Affairs, 21 Aug. 1953.

45 Truman Library, Adams Papers, box 12, file: ICAO, 1944–53: Confidential Report on Second Assembly, 'Confidential Report of Chairman, U.S. Delegation, 2nd ICAO Assembly,' Exhibit A, 27 Sept. 1948.

46 LAC, RG 25, v. 6309, file: 72-ADU-40 (pt. 7.2), Canadian ICAO Council Representative to J.R. Baldwin, 7 Feb. 1954.

47 See PRO, FO 371, 70156, Head of U.K. Delegation (Tymms) to MCA, 21 June 1948.

48 Ibid.

49 LAC, RG 25, vl. 6311, file: 72-ADU-36-40 (pt. 1.1), C.S. Booth to J.R. Baldwin, 11 April 1951.

50 Ibid., 14 April 1951.

51 Roper, *Un homme et des ailes*, 326.

52 ICAO, doc. 7270, A6 –P/1, 'Report of the Council, 1951.'

53 FFMA, S50-3-6, box 340, file: Nominations de Secretaire générale de l'OACI, M. MacDonnell – 1958, Bouché to Minister of Foreign Affairs, 22 Nov. 1958.

54 LAC, RG 25, v. 6714, file: 72-ADU-27-40 pt. 3.1, R.M. Macdonnell memo, 'Italian Candidacy for ICAO Council,' 20 May 1959.

55 FFMA, 'Nominations … MacDonnell – 1958,' Bouché to Minister of Foreign Affairs, 17 Dec. 1958. See also, 'Canadian Chosen ICAO Secretary,' Montreal *Star*, 17 Dec. 1958. For the Australian support of Tessyier, see ACT DEA Correspondence file, A1838 /2 717/32/2 pt.1, unsigned memo, 'ICAO Council Elections,' 5 May 1959. For more on Macdonnell, see the ICAO website.

56 Tymms Collection, box RCMS 20/1/2/1/8 – 20/1/2/2/2, Warner to Tymms, 20 Feb. 1957.

57 LAC, RG 25, v. 6309, file: 72-ADU-40 (pt. 7.2), letter to J.R. Baldwin, 7 Feb. 1954.

58 On Tymms' bid for the Presidency, see Johnston, *To Organise the Air*, 185–7.

59 For more on Binaghi, see 'The San Diego ICAO Assembly in Brief,' *Interavia* 14/8 (1959), 901, and the ICAO website.

60 PRO, FO 371, 127649, file: GA 12/3, FO to Mexico City, t.8, 21 Jan. 1957. See the correspondence in file GA 12/10 for the British approach to other nations in an effort to discover their views on Tymms' selection as council president.

61 LAC, RG 25, v. 3379, file: 72-ADU-4-40c, Economic Division memo to Under-Secretary, 27 Dec. 1956.

62 PRO, FO 371, 127649, file: GA 12/17, George Crombie (U.K. High Commissioner's Office, Ottawa) to Cyril Costley-White (Commonwealth Relations Office), 6 Feb. 1957.

63 Ibid., file: GA 12/10, British Embassy, Paris, to FO, 17 Jan. 1957.

64 FFMA, S50-3-6, box 336, file: Election President du Conseil de l'O.A.C.I., 1957, 'Rapport du Réprésentant de la France sur l'Election du Nouveau President du Conseil de l'O.A.C.I.,' 4 March 1957.

65 Ibid.
66 Ibid.
67 Quoted in Johnston, *To Organise the Air*, 186.
68 See Milde, 'New Headquarters Agreement between ICAO and Canada,'
   312.
69 Hargreaves, *Decolonization in Africa*, 190.
70 PRO, FO 371, 165143, file: GA 13/84, Report by U.K. Delegation, '14th …
   Assembly,' n.d.
71 FFMA, S50-3-6, box 839, file: 15ème Session de l'assemblée, Bouché to
   Minister of Foreign Affairs, 3 Nov. 1965.
72 PRO, FO 371, 176155, file: GA 13/45, FO memo, 'Note on Language
   Controversy in ICAO,' 11 Sept. 1964.
73 Ibid., unsigned FO memo, 'Note on Elections to the Council in 1965,' Sept.
   1964.
74 Ibid.
75 Resolution A3-6.
76 ICAO, doc. 7241, C/838 1951, 'Action of the Council, 14th Session, Sept.
   28 to 14 Dec. 1951.'
77 See Resolution A2-1; A3-6. See also Buergenthal, *Law-Making*, 35–8, and
   Cheng, *Law of International Air Transport*, 33.
78 See the debate in ICAO, doc. 7298, A6-EX/2, 'Executive Committee,
   Minutes of Plenary Sessions, 2nd meeting, 3 June 1952.' For more on
   American views, see NARA, RG 340, Office of the Administrative Assistant
   General File, box 90, file: ICAO Memorandums, memo on 'Action to be
   taken in the Case of Contracting States Failing to Discharge Their Financial
   Obligation to the Organization (ICAO Memo 58-53),' 12 May 1953.
79 See the correspondence in PRO, FO 371, 70156, file: W5417.
80 See Buergenthal, *Law-Making*, 47–8.
81 See, e.g., LAC, RG 25, v. 3379, file: 72-ADU-3-40, R.B. Bryce to J.R. Baldwin,
   2 June 1951.
82 NARA, RG 59, 1955–59 CDF, box 1627, file: 399.72-ICAO /7-358, 'Confidential Report on the 11th Session of the Assembly of the ICAO,' 4 July 1958.
83 ACT, DEA, Correspondence Files, A1838/1 717/31/11 pt. 2, 'ICAO – 11th
   General Assembly,' 18 June 1958. For the American view of the debate, see
   NARA, RG 59, 1955–59 CDF, box 1627, file: 399.72-ICAO /6-258, 'Official
   Report of the U.S. Delegation to the 11th … Assembly,' 19 June 1958
84 LAC, RG 24, v. 17548, file: 004-4, A.A.G. Corbet to Air Marshal R. Slemon,
   25 Feb. 1955.
85 NARA, RG 59, 1955–59 CDF 399.72, box 1620, file: 399.72 – ICAO /7-155,
   'Confidential Report of the 9th Assembly Session,' 12 July 1955. See the

attached clipping, Marie Grebenc, 'U.S. Delegate Blasts Canada for "Confusing" ICAO Issues,' Montreal *Herald,* 8 June 1955.

86 PRO, FO 371, 115390, 'Report by FO Representative, 9th Assembly of ICAO,' 13 June 1955.

87 See Gertler, 'Amendments to the Chicago Convention: Lessons from the Proposals that Failed,' 248.

8 Maintaining Standards

1 Binaghi, 'The Role of ICAO,' 29.

2 Hymans, 'Results of a Meeting,' 422.

3 Ibid.

4 Gidwitz, *Politics of International Air Transport,* 64–72. For a good review of early postwar development in international aviation, see ICAO, doc. 7636, A10–P/3, 'Annual Report of the Council to the Assembly for 1955' (hereafter 'Annual Report of the Council for [year]), n.d., and ICAO, doc. 7367, A7-P/1, 'Report of the Council to the Assembly on the Activities of the Organization in 1952' (hereafter 'Report of [year] Activities'), 31 March 1953; see also Taneja, *U.S. International Aviation Policy,* chapter 1.

5 ICAO, 'Annual Report of the Council for 1955,' and 'Report of 1952 Activities.'

6 Warner, 'ICAO after Four Years,' 281–2.

7 Buergenthal, *Law-Making,* 98–9.

8 See ibid., esp. 98–9 and 105–8. See also the early chapters in Cheng, *Law of International Air Transport*; Schenkman, *International Civil Aviation Organization,* chapter 10; FitzGerald, 'The International Civil Aviation Organization,' 156–205; 'ICAO Facilities Lag in Southern Europe, *Aviation Week* 66/4 (1957), 47; Ashlock, 'ICAO Seeks Improved Techniques for Testing Air Navigation Devices,' 26; and, more generally, Ellwood, 'Air Traffic Control, Then and Now,' 72–6.

9 FitzGerald, 'The ICAO,' 174, 181–4.

10 Some of these problems are discussed in LAC, RG 24, v. 17553, file: 004-4-MTG v. 2, 'World-Wide Air Navigation Meeting, Discussion Subjects,' 12 Sept. 1963. For more on the Comet, see Engel, *Cold War at 30,000 Feet,* 125–58, 173–5.

11 Sochor, 'From the DC-3 to Hypersonic Flight: ICAO in a Changing Environment,' 413.

12 ICAO, doc. 7997, A12–EX/2, 'Final Report of the Executive Committee,' 1959. For Walter Binaghi's views on the advent of new aircraft, see his 'The Role of ICAO,' 27–8.

13 See, e.g., ICAO, doc. 7894-C/907, 'The Economic Implications of the Introduction into Service of Long-Range Jet Aircraft,' June 1958; ICAO, doc. 8087-C/925, 'The Technical, Economic and Social Consequences of the Introduction into Commercial Service of Supersonic Aircraft: A Preliminary Study,' Aug. 1960.

14 Binaghi, 'Role of ICAO,' 27–8.

15 For some of these discussions, see Cambridge University, Churchill College Archives, Lord Duncan-Sandys Papers, file 7/2, memo, C (60) 111, 'Supersonic Airliner,' 12 July 1960, and the memo on meeting with the French Air Minister (n.d.), in file: 7/3/1.

16 John F. Kennedy Presidential Library, Boston, Massachusetts (hereafter Kennedy Library), President's Office Files, box 78, file: FAA Supersonic Transport FY64, Budget Message (A), N.E. Halaby Memo for the President, 15 Nov. 1962.

17 Ibid., Supersonic Transport Advisory Group, 'Report to the Chairman, Supersonic Transport Steering Group,' 11 Dec. 1962.

18 Ibid., U.S. FAA, microfilm, Roll 1, Statement by Halaby, 16 Oct. 1963.

19 ICAO, doc. 8775 A16-Min. P/1-9, 'Minutes of the Plenary Meetings, Assembly – 16th Session, Buenos Ares, 3–26 Sept. 1968,' 13.

20 See PRO, AVIA 120/6, file on aircraft noise, 1968–69.

21 ICAO, doc. 8869, A18-P/2, 'Annual Report of the Council for 1969,' June 1970, 61–2, 64, 80.

22 ICAO, doc. A21-Min. EX/1-14, 'Minutes of the Executive Committee,' 21st Session, 24 Sept. to 15 Oct. 1974, 18. See also, Sochor, 'International Civil Aviation and the Third World: How Fair Is the System?' 1312.

23 For a discussion of Annex 16, see *The Convention on International Civil Aviation ... the First 35 Years* (Montreal, ICAO, n.d.), 31–3.

24 See ICAO, doc. 9197, CAN/5, 'Report of Committee on Aircraft Noise,' 5th meeting, Montreal, 15–30 Nov. 1976.

25 ICAO, 'Annual Report of the Council for 1981,' 57.

26 W.A. Wilson, 'Decisive Step in Short Navigation? Bitter Anglo-American Dispute mars ICAO Choice of Navaids,' 364.

27 Freer, 'Maturity Brings New Challenges – 1957 to 1976,' 25.

28 See Schenkman, *ICAO*, 263; Jones, 'Amending the Chicago Convention and its Technical Standards,' 185–213; and for a general overview, Luard, *International Agencies*, 67–72.

29 ICAO, doc. 6968, A4–P/1, 'Report of 1949 Activities,' 23 March 1950.

30 See Warner, 'ICAO after Six Years,' 72.

31 See 'Regional Structure Enhances Air Navigation Planning,' *ICAO Journal* 46/7 (1991), 49–50.

32 ICAO, doc. 6433, A3–P/4, 'Report of the Council to the Assembly,' 11 April 1949.

33 'ICAO Special North Atlantic Meeting,' *Interavia* 20/5 (1965), 678.

34 Each year in its annual report the council lists ICAO's dealings with other international organizations. See, e.g., ICAO, 'Report of 1949 Activities.' See also Pepin, 'ICAO and Other Agencies Dealing with Air Regulation,' 152–65; and Clark, 'IATA and ICAO: The First Fifty Years,' 125–31.

35 Warner, 'International Financing of Air Navigation Facilities through ICAO,' 351.

36 Resolutions A1-64–66.

37 NARA, RG 237, Reports Relating to ACC Facilitation Subcommittees, Inspection Tours, and Government Surveys, 1946–51, box 1, file: PICAO: Facilitation Reports, etc., PICAO news release, 26 April 1946.

38 For the report on the 'Conference on Ocean Weather Observation Stations in the North Atlantic' (London, 17–25 Sept. 1946) and the U.S. acceptance of the agreement, see the material in Truman Library, WHCF, Official File, box 1395, file: 578-A.

39 For the U.S. position on the weather stations, including the military dimension, see Eisenhower Library, WHCF, Confidential File, box 1, file: ACC (1), 'Proposed U.S. Policy with respect to the North Atlantic Ocean Station Program,' 2 Oct. 1953, and, in the same box, file: ACC (2), 'Draft Minutes of the Meeting of the ACC Members on Oct. 6, 1953,' 6 Oct. 1953.

40 See Cheng, *Law of International Air Transport*, 81–94, and Schenkman, *ICAO*, 281–3.

41 ICAO, doc. 5221, A2-P/5, 'Report of June 1, 1947 to March 1, 1948 Activities,' 19 March 1948; Cheng, *Law of International Air Transport*, 79–81, and Schenkman, *ICAO*, 283–4.

42 ICAO, doc. 7564, A9 –P/2, 'Report of 1954 Activities,' 27 April 1955.

43 See Schenkman, *ICAO*, 269.

44 ICAO, 'Report of 1949 Activities.'

45 Ibid., 'Report of 1950 Activities.'

46 Eisenhower Library, WHCF, Confidential Files, box 2, file: ACC (12), ACC, 'Review of National Aviation Policy – International Aviation – Economic Aid and Technical Assistance,' 14 Jan. 1954.

47 Ibid., file: ACC (11), ACC, 'Review of National Aviation Policy – International Aviation – Provision of Aids to Air Navigation,' 12 Jan. 1954.

48 Kennedy Library, President's Official Files, box 78, file: FAA, International Air Transport Policy report, 1/63, Interagency Steering Committee, 'Report on the International Air Transport Policy of the United States,' Jan. 1963.

49 Ibid.

50 A good overview of the relationship can be found in ICAO, 'Report of June 1, 1947 to March 1, 1948 Activities'; see also Milde, 'The Chicago Convention – After Forty Years,'129–30.

51 ICAO, 'Report of 1949 Activities'; for a good overview of the administrative structure of the Technical Assistance Program, see ICAO, 'Report of 1959 Activities'; see also Schenkman, *ICAO*, 269–70.

52 ICAO, 'Report of 1949 Activities.'

53 For a full description of the program and its problems, see ICAO, 'Report of 1950 Activities'; and A5–WP/10. P/8, Working Paper, 'Supplementary Report of 1 Jan. to 31 May 1951 Activities' 1 June 1951.

54 E.R. Marlin, 'The ICAO Technical Assistance Programme,' 865; for the program in the early 1950s, see also Schenkman, *ICAO*, 272–6.

55 The direct quote is taken from Maloney, *Canada and U.N. Peacekeeping*, 111. On the crisis in the Congo, see also Hargreaves, *Decolonization in Africa*, 190–6, and Urquhart, *Hammarskjold* for the withdrawal of Belgian soldiers, 403–6; on the closing of the airports, 444–6.

56 See ICAO, doc. 8140 A14 –P/3, 'Annual Report of the Council for 1960,' 15 April 1961. The council's annual report for each of the following years describes the ICAO-related events in the Congo, and they are the major source for the following paragraphs.

57 ICAO, doc. 8219, A14–P/4, 'Annual Report of the Council for 1961,' April 1962.

58 See ICAO, doc. 8475, A15–P/3, 'Annual Report of the Council for 1964,' April 1965.

59 ICAO, doc. 8270, A14–EX/31, 'Report of the Executive Committee,' Agenda Item 15: ICAO's Activities and Policy on Technical Assistance, 1962.

60 'ICAO's 15th Assembly Reveals Serious Shortcomings,' *Interavia* 20/9 (1965), 1356.

61 See, e.g., ICAO, doc. 8522, A15–EX/43, 'Report of the Executive Committee,' Agenda Item 11: ICAO's Activities and Policy on Technical Assistance, 1965.

62 NARA, RG 59, Central Foreign Policy Files, 1967–69, Economic, box 532, file: AV3 ICAO, 10/1/68, 'Confidential Report of the U.S. Delegation to the 16th … Assembly,' 21 Oct. 1968.

63 ICAO, 'Annual Report of the Council for 1969.'

64 See ICAO, doc. 8792, A18 –P/1, 'Annual Report of the Council for 1968,' April 1969.

65 See ICAO, doc. 9046, 'Annual Report of the Council for 1972,' n.d.

66 ICAO, doc. 9266, 'Annual Report of the Council for 1978,' n.d.

67 Buergenthal, *Law-Making*, 121.

68 Ibid., 120.

9 Problem Solving in ICAO: The Unfinished Symphony

1 Milde, 'The Warsaw System of Liability in International Carriage by Air,' 162.
2 See MacKenzie, 'The Bermuda Conference,' 70.
3 For a thorough examination of this issue, see Buergenthal, *Law-Making in the ICAO*, 154–70.
4 Cheng, *Law of International Air Transport*, 104.
5 The rules were subsequently amended in 1975. ICAO, doc. 7782/2, *Rules for the Settlement of Disputes*, 2nd ed., 1975.
6 Schenkman, *ICAO*, 377.
7 Cheng, *Law of International Air Transport*, 100–1.
8 ICAO, doc. 7314- C/849, 'Action of the Council – 16th Session,' 1952.
9 Cheng, *Law of International Air Transport*, 102. See also Buergenthal, *Law-Making in the ICAO*, 137–40. For a complete account and a good map of the disputed area, see ICAO, doc. 7367, A7–P/1, 'Report of 1952 Activities,' 31 March 1953.
10 Warner, quoted in Schenkman, *ICAO*, 379–80.
11 Buergenthal, *Law-Making in the ICAO*, 162–4.
12 Ibid., 136 (emphasis in original).
13 Ibid., 195.
14 Schenkman, *ICAO*, 286–7.
15 Ibid., 288–9.
16 ICAO, doc. 7709, A10-EX/36, 'Executive Committee: Final Report,' 15 Aug. 1956.
17 ICAO, doc. 7788, A11–P/1, 'Annual Report of the Council for 1956,' 1958.
18 For the British side of things on the prohibited zone and its connection to the proposed referendum in Gibraltar, see the correspondence in PRO, FCO9 /600, /601, /602, and /603. See also, ICAO, doc. 8724, A16-P/3, 'Annual Report of the Council for 1967,' April 1968.
19 See ICAO, 'Annual Report of the Council for 1969.'
20 Ibid., 'Annual Report of the Council for 1971'; Agrawala, *Aircraft Hijacking and International Law*, 103–13. For a good review of the crisis, see Osieke, 'Unconstitutional Acts in International Organisations,' 8–14.
21 ICAO, 'Annual Report for 1971.'
22 See FitzGerald, 'The Judgment of the International Court of Justice in the Appeal Relating to the Jurisdiction of the ICAO Council,' 153. This article and others dealing with disputes and legal issues are reprinted in FitzGerald, *The International Civil Aviation Organization – A Case Study in the Law and Practice of International Organization*.
23 See Roy, 'Legal Work of ICAO,' 864–5.

24 For a good overview of the Legal Committee, its structure, and operations, see FitzGerald, 'The ICAO and the Development of Conventions on International Air Law (1947–1978),' 51–120.

25 PRO, FO 371, 105670, file: GA67 /180, 'Report on the 7th Session,' 16 June 1953.

26 Resoluton A7 -5 1953; see also FitzGerald, 'The ICAO and the Development of Conventions,' 57.

27 For the terms of the Rome Convention, see Schenkman, *ICAO*, 369.

28 FitzGerald, 'The ICAO and the Development of Conventions,' 68.

29 ACT, DEA, Correspondence Files, A1838 /1 717/31/10, 'Report on the 10th Session of the Assembly,' n.d.

30 NARA, RG 59, CFPF, 1964-66, Economic/Aviation (Civil), AV3, box 603, file: AV3 Organization and Conferences ICAO 5/1/65, 'Report of the U.S. Delegation to the 15th Session of the Legal Committee of the ICAO,' 28 May 1965.

31 FitzGerald, 'The ICAO and the Development of Conventions,' 83.

32 For a complete list, see ibid.

33 Beaumont, 'Notes on Some Aspects of the Legal Position of International Air Carriers,' 364. On the problems of Warsaw, see also, Mankiewicz, 'Charter and Interchange of Aircraft and the Warsaw Convention,' 707–25.

34 See ICAO, 'Review of June 8, 1946 to March 31, 1947 Activities,' 44–5.

35 For these early activities see Schenkman, *ICAO*, 371–3.

36 See ICAO, doc. 7686-LC/140, 'International Conference on Private Air Law,' The Hague, Sept. 1955, vol. 1, Minutes, vol. 2, Documents.

37 See FitzGerald, 'The ICAO and the Development of Conventions,' 70–1.

38 Sheinfeld, 'From Warsaw to Tenerife,' 662.

39 PRO, FO 371, 158631, file: GA 13/17, A. Kean (at Guadalajara Air Law Conference) to S.R. Walton, Ministry of Aviation, London, 30 Aug. 1961.

40 Lyndon B. Johnson Presidential Library, Austin, Texas (hereafter Johnson Library), White House Central Files, box 385, file: FG 675, Interagency Committee on International Aviation Policy, 'Memo on the Warsaw Convention, The Hague Protocol and the ICIA Recommendations from the NACCA Bar Association,' 2 Jan. 1963.

41 Quote taken from Johnson Library, National Security Files, Subject File, box 20, file: International Air-Travel Problem (Warsaw-Hague Convention), DOS telegram 86, 18 Oct. 1965.

42 NARA, RG 59, CFPF, 1964–66, Economic/Aviation (Civil), AV3, box 602, file: Organization and Conferences 1/1/66, Andreas Lowenfeld, 'Memorandum of Telephone Conversation with Senator A.S. Mike Monroney,' 26 Jan. 1966.

43 Johnson Library, Official Files of Harry McPherson, box 17, file: Warsaw Convention, Thomas Mann 'Memo for the President,' 14 Oct. 1965

44 See ibid., DOS memo, 'Protection for Passengers in International Aviation – Proposal to Withdraw The Hague Protocol and Denounce the Warsaw Convention,' n.d.

45 'ICAO May Resort to Diplomatic Conference to Save Warsaw Pact,' *Aviation Week and Space Technology* 84/8 (1966), 36.

46 See Mankiewicz, 'The 1971 Protocol of Guatemala City,' 521.

47 Milde, 'Warsaw System of Liability,' 161.

48 NARA, RG 59, CFPF, 1964–66, Economic, Aviation (Civil), AV3, ICAO, box 601, file: AV3, ICAO, 8/16/66, 'Report of the U.S. Delegation to the Special ICAO Meeting on Limits of Liability for Passengers under the Warsaw Convention and The Hague Protocol,' 15 July 1966.

49 Ibid. For the Montreal discussions, see ICAO, docs. 8584-LC/154-1 and /154-2, 'Special ICAO Meeting on Limits for Passengers under the Warsaw Convention and The Hague Protocol, Montreal, 1–15 Feb. 1966,' vol. 1, Minutes, vol. 2, Documents.

50 NARA, RG 59, 'Report of the U.S. Delegation.' The most thorough discussion of the Montreal conference, written by two participants, can be found in Lowenfeld and Mendelsohn, 'United States and the Warsaw Convention,' 497–602.

51 Johnson Library, Official Files of Harry McPherson, box 17, file: Warsaw Convention, DOS Press Release, 13 May 1966.

52 Some of these issues are discussed in Matte, 'Warsaw System and the Hesitations of the U.S. Senate,' 151–64.

53 Lowenfeld and Mendelsohn, 'U.S. and the Warsaw Convention,' 602.

54 NARA, RG 59, CFPF, 1967–69, Economic, box 532, file: AV3. ICAO, 11/1/68, 'Report of the U.S. Delegation to the Meeting of the Subcommittee on Revision of the Warsaw Convention as Amended by the Hague Protocol of the ICAO,' 13 Jan. 1969.

55 See Mankiewicz, 'The 1971 Protocol of Guatemala City,' 522–3. On the 17th Session of the Legal Committee, see ICAO, doc. 8878-LC/162, 'Legal Committee, 17th Session, Montreal, 9 Feb. to 11 March 1970, Minutes and Documents, Relating to the Questions of the Revision of the Warsaw Convention of 1929 as Amended by The Hague Protocol of 1955 and Other Matters.'

56 ICAO, doc. 8932/2.

57 The most thorough examination of the Guatemala City Protocol is Mankiewicz, 'The 1971 Protocol of Guatemala City'; see also Sheinfeld, 'From Warsaw to Tenerife,' 673–5. For the conference itself, see ICAO,

docs. 9040-LC/167-1 and /167-2, 'International Conference on Air Law, Guatemala City, Feb.–March 1971,' vol. 1, Minutes, vol. 2, Documents.

58 Sheinfeld, 'From Warsaw to Tenerife,'673.

59 Milde, 'Warsaw System of Liability,' 163.

60 Matte, 'Warsaw System,' 158.

61 The most thorough examination of the conference and the four Montreal protocols can be found in FitzGerald, 'The Four Montreal Protocols to Amend the Warsaw Convention Regime Governing International Carriage by Air,' 273–350. See also ICAO, docs. 9145 (Protocol no. 1), 9146 (no. 2), 9147 (no. 3), and 9148 (no. 4), all dated 1975.

62 Gerald R. Ford Presidential Library, Ann Arbor, Michigan (hereafter Ford Library), WHCF, Subject file CA, box 2, file: CA 9/9/76-1/20/77, Charles Robinson (DOS) to Ford, 23 Dec. 1976.

63 Ibid., Ford statement delivered to the Senate, 14 Jan. 1977.

64 Matte, 'Warsaw System,' 162–3.

65 See Milde, 'Warsaw System of Liability,' 165.

66 Appendix 1 of the council's annual report contains an up to date list of how many ratifications each document has received and contains the date when it came into force.

67 FitzGerald, 'ICAO,' 101.

68 Buergenthal, *Law-Making in the ICAO*, 123–4.

69 FitzGerald, 'ICAO,' 109.

70 Tobolewski, 'ICAO's Legal Syndrome Or: International Air Law in the Making,' 351–2.

71 Ibid., 354.

10 The Cold War Comes to ICAO

1 U.N. Secretary-General U Thant's written statement to ICAO, quoted in Allard, 'Keep Out Political Debate,' Montreal *Star*, 23 June 1965.

2 NARA, RG 59, Subject Files of Durward V. Sandifer, box 9, file: ICAO, 'Membership in ICAO,' 28 Jan. 1948.

3 Resolution A1-9.

4 NARA, RG 59, 'Membership in ICAO.' Some individuals were a little more selective, including Lord Winster, the British MCA in the early Attlee government; he didn't want 'hangers-on' and instead wanted only those nations that would contribute to the organization. See PRO, FO 371, 54632, MCA memo, 8 May 1946.

5 NARA, RG 59, 'Membership in ICAO.'

6 For some of the problems with aviation and the Chicago Convention arising
   from the Chinese Revolution, see Aristeides, 'Chinese Aircraft in Hong
   Kong,' 159–77; see also, Engel, *Cold War at 30,000 Feet*, 104–17.
7 Schenkman, *ICAO*, 131.
8 NARA, RG 59, 1955–59 CDF, box 1619, file: 399.72-ICAO/5-455, memo,
   'Chinese Representation,' n.d. (probably May 1955).
9 PRO, FO 371, 105662, file: GA67/26, 'Admission of Japan to ICAO,' 28
   March 1953.
10 Eisenhower Library, WHCF, Confidential File, box 1, file: ACC, DOS memo,
   'Relations with States and Other International Organizations, (b) China's
   Financial Proposals,' May 1953.
11 See PRO, FO 371, 165670, file: GA67/180, 'Report on the 7th Session,'
   16 June 1953; FFMA, box 337, S-50-3-6, file: 8ième Assemblée Générale de
   l'OACI, and Buergenthal, *Law-Making*, 35–8.
12 Resolutions A1-5 (Italy); A2-3 (Austria), and A2-4 (Finland) can be found in
   'Resolutions and Recommendations of the Assembly, 1st to 9th Sessions
   (1947–1955),' (Montreal, 1956). See also Buergenthal, *Law-Making*, 22–3;
   ICAO Monthly Bulletin, 'Relations with Other International Organizations:
   United Nations,' 2/12, 11; and PRO, FO 371, 70125 for files on the
   admission of Italy, Austria, and Finland.
13 See, e.g., 'Resumption of International Aviation by Japan and Germany,'
   ICAO Bulletin 9/4 (1954), 12–13; Heiman, 'German Hopes,' 71; 'Germans
   Get Allied Civil Air Proposals,' 51; Kroger, 'German Airline May Start
   in Year,' 21–2; 'State Signs German Bilateral Despite U.S. Carrier Objections,' 18; William Kroger, 'Treaty Spurs New German Air Industry,'
   13–15.
14 See 'A Japanese Come-back? "No" Says the Eastern Bloc – "Yes" Says the
   West,' *Interavia* 8/1 (1953), 36–9; ICAO, doc. 7564, A9–P2, 'Report of 1954
   Activities,' 27 April 1955. On the 1952 Japan-U.S. bilateral agreement, see
   Ide, 'Recent Developments in Air Transport Relations between Japan and
   the United States,' 119–41.
15 LAC, RG 25, v. 6309, file: 72-ADU-40 pt.6, 'Memo for Far Eastern Division,'
   3 Oct. 1952.
16 See FFMA, S50-3-6, box 337, file: 6ème Assemblée Générale de l'OACI, Le
   Chef de la Délégation de la France à le Ministre des Affaires Etrangères, 22
   July 1952.
17 PRO, FO 371, 'Admission of Japan to ICAO.'
18 NARA, RG 340, Office of the Administrative Assistant General Files, box 90,
   file: ICAO Memos, Air Force Liaison Officer – ACC, 'Memo for Mr Milton
   M. Turner,' 29 April 1953.

19 PRO, FO 371, 105667, file: GA67/125, 'Executive Committee, Brief for the U.K. Delegation,' June 1953.

20 Ibid.

21 NARA, RG 340, 'ICAO memo No. 51-53.'

22 PRO, FO 371, 105669, file: GA67/66, 'The Assembly of the ICAO Held at Brighton from June 16 to July 6,' 23 July 1953. See also ICAO Resolution A7-2, and FFMA, S50-3-6, box 337, file: 7ème Assemblée Generale de l'OACI, Le Président de la Délégation françaises à le Ministre des Affaires Etrangères, 21 Aug. 1953,

23 See ICAO, doc. 7594, A9-EX/25, 'Executive Committee, Final Report' (1955), and the several files in PRO, FO 371, /115388 and /115389.

24 PRO, FO 371, 115389, file: GA12/82, 'Brief for FO Representative on U.K. Delegation, Admission of Germany to the Organisation,' n.d. See also file: GA12/26, FO minutes on 'German Membership of the ICAO,' 25 March 1955, and NARA, RG 59, 1955–59 CDF, box 1620, file: 399.72-ICAO/7-155, 'Confidential Report of the 9th Session,' 12 July 1955.

25 PRO, FO371, 'Brief for FO Representative.'

26 Ibid.

27 NARA, RG 59, 1955–59 CDF, box 1619, file: 399.72-ICAO/5-455, 'Memo of Conversation,' 18 May 1955.

28 The British explained: 'It soon became obvious that if any such discussion arose, a number of countries would not accept the U.S. and United Kingdom position that only States with voting rights could exercise the right of assent. Moreover, Czechoslovakia sent a delegation to the Assembly and we had to reckon with the possibility that they might claim the right to intervene. On the other hand, we had to ensure that the resolution gave clear instructions to the Secretary-General of the Organisation to forward the resolution to the General Assembly of the United Nations without attempting to obtain the prior consent of Poland and Czechoslovakia.' PRO, FO 371, 115390, file: GA12/133, 'Report by FO Representative,' 13 June 1955.

29 A good review of this episode can be found in the report of the Australian delegation, ACT, DEA Correspondence files, A1838/2, 717/31/9, 'Report on the 9th Session,' n.d.

30 Resolution A9-1.

31 ICAO, 'Executive Committee, Final Report,' 1955.

32 NARA, RG 59, 'Confidential Report of the 9th Session of the Assembly of the ICAO.' There was considerable speculation why the Czechs remained silent. The French delegation believed that the Czechs did not want to disturb the international situation in advance of an anticipated meeting of

heads of states. See FFMA, S50-3-6, box 337, file: 9ème Assemblée Générale de l'OACI, Le Président de la Délégation françaises à le Ministre des Affaires Etrangères, 3 Aug. 1955. The American representative gave a few possible explanations: 'the Czechoslovakian Delegation took this action for any or all of several reasons. The Czechoslovak Government is anxious to regain its voting rights in the Organization by the payment of only a small percentage of the arrears accumulated since 1950. The Czechoslovak Government is believed to be anxious to maintain and even increase its civil air operations from Czechoslovakia to western Europe and therefore did not want to antagonize these states. Czechoslovak action adverse to the admission of Germany would have had a negating effect upon the Soviet invitation to Chancellor Adenauer to visit Moscow which was issued during the same week.' NARA, 'Confidential Report.'

33 www.hooverdigest.org
34 LAC, RG 25, v. 6716, file: 72-ADU-62-40 pt. 6.2, Main to Under-Secretary of State for External Affairs, 17 June 1960.
35 Buergenthal, *Law-Making in the ICAO*, 131–6.
36 See ibid., 17.
37 Quoted in LAC, RG 25, v. 6309, file: 72-ADU-40, pt. 6.2, Canadian Embassy, Washington to Under-Secretary of State for External Affairs, t.1329, 6 July 1953.
38 See the correspondence in PRO, FO 371, 115390, file: GA12/139.
39 Indian delegate quoted in ACT, DEA, Correspondence files, A1838/1 717/31/10, '10th ICAO Assembly – Political Developments,' 22 June 1956.
40 NARA, RG 59, 1955–59 CDF, box 1630, file: 399.72-ICAO, 'Confidential Report on the 12th Session,' 20 Aug. 1959.
41 Cronshaw, 'Tanzania Calls on ICAO Delegate to Support South African Expulsion,' Montreal *Gazette*, 24 June 1965.
42 See, e.g., PRO, FO 371, 158631, file: GA13/12, Edwin Jungfleisch to W.J.A. Wilberforce, 17 Aug. 1961, and 150730, file: GA13/32, unsigned minute, 'ICAO Diplomatic Conference to Agree on a Convention,' 3 Nov. 1960.
43 See the background papers for the American delegation to the 16th Assembly in Buenos Aires in NARA, RG 59, CFPF, 1967–69, Economic, box 531, file: AV3, ICAO, 8/23/68, 'Representation of China, Germany, Korea and Viet-Nam,' and 'Cuba.'
44 Ibid., file: 399.72-ICAO/7-358, 'Confidential Report on the 11th Session,' 4 July 1958.
45 Ibid., Subject Numerical File, 1970–73, Economic, box 595, file: AV3 ICAO, 6/18/71, 'Classified Report of the U.S. Delegation to the Eighteenth Session of the Assembly of the ICAO, Vienna, Austria, June 15 to July 7, 1971' (emphasis in original).

46 See Hargreaves, *Decolonization in Africa*, 219, and Northedge, *Descent from Power*, 322–5.

47 LAC, RG 25, v. 10457, file: 42-8-4-ICAO-12 (pt. 1.2), R. Duder to Under-Secretary of State for External Affairs, 31 March 1965. On South Africa's status in ICAO, see Sochor, *Politics of International Aviation*, 44–8.

48 See PRO, FO 371, 181220 file: GA13/33, R.S.S. Dickinson to P.G. Hudson (Ministry of Aviation), 23 March 1965.

49 NARA, RG 59, CFPF, 1967–69, Economic, box 531, file: AV3, ICAO, 8/23/68, 'ICAO 16th Session of the Assembly: Participation of South Africa and Portugal.' South Africa and Portugal were often linked in this matter, and the Portuguese were very concerned that they would be targeted for expulsion, but the real focus was almost always on South Africa. On Portuguese concerns, see PRO, FO 371, 181221, file: GA13/64, Portuguese Government Aide Memoire, 18 June 1965, and LAC, RG 12, v. 2832, file: 602-4-15 v. 2, J.R. McKinney memo 'Call by Portuguese Ambassador,' 24 June 1965.

50 LAC, RG 12, v. 2832, file: 602-4-15, t. 1192 to Canadian Embassies, 27 May 1965.

51 PRO, FO 371, 181220 file: GA13/33, Vandeleur Robinson to Hillier-Fry, 30 March 1965.

52 Ibid., Dickinson to Hudson, 23 March 1965.

53 Ibid., Robinson to Hillier-Fry, 30 March 1965.

54 Ibid., AVIA 109/1, E.L.J. Barton memo, 'ICAO Policy,' 5 April 1965.

55 Ibid., E.D.C. Cooper, memo, 'ICAO Policy,' 22 March 1965.

56 Ibid., 120/1, unsigned memo, 'Constitutional and Policy Factors Involved in Withdrawal Action from Assembly,' n.d. (c. April–May 1965).

57 ICAO, doc. 8522, A15-EX/43, 'Report of the Executive Committee – 15th Session of the Assembly, Montreal, 22 June to 16 July 1965.' See the resolution in Working Paper A15-WP/183, 8/7/65, agenda item 41.

58 Ibid., doc. 8516, A15-P/5, 'Minutes of the Plenary Meetings, Assembly – 15th Session,' 9 July 1965.

59 LAC, RG 12, v. 2832, file: 602-4-15 vol. 2, R Duder to Under-Secretary of State for External Affairs, 23 July 1965.

60 Ibid.

61 Resolution A15-7. See also NARA, RG 237, International Program and Policy Div. Classified Subject Files, 1945–64, box 7, file: 14th Assembly – U.S. Position, Delegation Paper & Chairman's Report, 'Report of the U.S. Delegation to the 15th Session of the Assembly of the ICAO,' 10 Aug. 1965. This report includes a list of how all the delegations voted (original emphasis).

62 ICAO, doc. A18-Min. EX/1-16, 'Minutes of the Executive Committee, 18th Assembly,' 67–106.

63 NARA, RG 59, 'Report of the U.S. Delegation to the 18th Session.'
64 See ICAO, doc. 9061, A19-Res., Min., 'Resolutions and Minutes,' 19th Session (Extraordinary) of the Assembly, New York, 27 Feb. to 2 March 1973.
65 NARA, RG 59, SNF, 1970–73, Economic, box 598, file: AV3, ICAO, 3/1/73, 'Confidential Report of the U.S. Delegation to the 19th Session.'
66 See, e.g., Resolution A18-4.
67 See Resolution A21-6. For some of the debate, see ICAO, doc. A21-Min. EX/1-14, 'Minutes of the Executive Committee, 21st Assembly Session,' 129–31.
68 Resolutions A26-5 and A27-5; see also 'Key Resolutions adopted by the 26th Session,' *ICAO Bulletin* 41/11 (1986), 23–6, and 'U.N. Air Body Votes for an End to Pretoria Links,' *Toronto Star*, 11 Oct. 1986.
69 See ICAO, doc., 9661, A31-Min. P/1-11, 'Minutes of the Plenary Meetings, Assembly – 31st Session, Montreal, 19 Sept. to 4 Oct. 1995,' 39–40; ICAO, doc. 9659, A31-EX, 'Assembly 31st Session, Executive Committee, Report and Minutes,' 36. See also, 'ICAO Council Lifts All Restrictions on South Africa's Membership,' *ICAO Journal* 49/7 (1994), 70.
70 NARA, RG 59, CFPF, 1967–69. Economic, box 531, file: AV3, ICAO, 6/B/68, DOS to various U.S. Embassies, 28 June 1968.
71 Ibid., 'Classified Report of the U.S. Delegation to the 16th Session,' 29 Oct. 1968.
72 For the whole story, see ibid.
73 PRO, AVIA 109/1, R.S.S. Dickinson memo, 'ICAO Organisation,' 2 Dec. 1969.
74 Ibid., J.F. Montgomerie memo, 'ICAO Organisation,' 21 Nov. 1969.
75 NARA, 'Classified Report of the U.S. Delegation to the 16th Session.'
76 NARA, Nixon Presidential Materials Project, WHCF, IT (International Organizations), box 6, file: ICAO 1/1/71 – [12/31/72], Secor Browne to Peter Flanigan (Assistant to the President), 20 July 1971.
77 Ibid., Flanigan to Browne, 20 Sept. 1971.
78 Northedge, *Descent from Power*, 313.

11 'Closer to the Heart than the Purse': ICAO and the Problem of Security

1 Kotaite, 'Security of International Civil Aviation – Role of ICAO,' 98.
2 Kennedy Library, WHCF, box 27, file: CA 4-1-63-6-30-63, 'Report on the International Air Transport Policy of the United States,' Jan. 1963. See also in the same file, N.E. Halaby (FAA Administrator) to Kennedy, 21 Jan. 1963

3 Bell, 'The U.S. Response to Terrorism against International Civil Aviation,'
   1327.
4 Evans, 'Aircraft Hijacking: Its Cause and Cure,' 698.
5 See Cooper, 'National Status of Aircraft,' 293, and more generally, Moss,
   'International Terrorism and Western Societies,' 418–30; and Richardson,
   What Terrorists Want.
6 See Faller, 'Aviation Security,' 370.
7 See the essays in Boulden and Weiss, eds., *Terrorism and the U.N.*
8 See Wallis, 'The Role of the International Aviation Organisations in
   Enhancing Security,' 83–100.
9 Ibid., 93–7.
10 For the early history of air piracy, see St John, *Air Piracy, Airport Security, and
   International Terrorism,* 1–7; for a list of acts of aircraft sabotage 1949–75, see
   Appendix 3.
11 Boyle and Pulsifer, 'Tokyo Convention,' 307–9. See also Abeyratne, 'Attempts at Ensuring Peace and Security in International Aviation,' 32–3.
12 Boyle and Pulsifer, 'Tokyo Convention,' 316–17.
13 Ibid., 318–22; Roy, 'Legal Work of ICAO,' 864–5. For the U.S. reaction, see
   NARA, RG 59, 1960–63 CDF, 399.72, box 848, file: 399.72-ICAO /1-261,
   Boyle to Dean Rusk, 9 Feb. 1961 and attached memo 'Proposed U.S.
   Comments to ICAO on Draft Convention on Offenses and Certain Other
   Acts Occurring on Board Aircraft,' n.d.
14 St John, *Air Piracy,* 1–3; Evans, 'Aircraft Hijacking,' 695.
15 For more on this Convention see Abeyratne, 'Attempts at Ensuring Peace
   and Security,' 29–31.
16 NARA, RG 59, CFPF, 1963, box 3337, file: Aviation (Civil) AV3 Organizations and Conferences, 'Report of the U.S. Delegation to the 14th Session
   of the Legal Committee of the ICAO, Rome, Italy, Aug. 28 to Sept. 15,
   1962,' 23 May 1963; Boyle and Pulsifer, 'Tokyo Convention,' 325.
17 NARA, 'Report of the U.S. Delegation to the 14th Session of the Legal
   Committee.' For the documents of the Rome Conference, see ICAO, docs.
   8302, LC/150-1 and /150-2, Legal Committee – 14th Session, vol. 1,
   Minutes, vol. 2, Documents.
18 See ICAO, docs. 8565, LC/152-1 and /152-2, International Conference on
   Air Law, Tokyo, Aug.–Sept. 1963, vol. 1, Minutes, vol. 2, Documents.
19 FFMA, S50-3-6, box 850, file: Conference Internationale de Droit aerien sur
   les infractions àbord des aèronefs, Tokyo, 1963, Report of French Delegation, 1 April 1964.
20 NARA, RG 237, Programs and Policy Division, International Planning and
   Policy Branch: Classified Country Files, Records Relating to International

Organizations, 1969, box 6, file: 'Tokyo Convention of 1963 "Crimes on Board Aircraft," Report of the U.S. Delegation to the Diplomatic Conference on Air Law Held under the Auspices of the ICAO,' 28 July 1964. In the same file see the FAA position paper for the U.S. delegation, which includes the U.S. response to the amendments suggested by the other ICAO members (31 July 1963).

21 Boyle and Pulsifer, 'Tokyo Convention,' 328–9.

22 ICAO, doc. 8364 (1963), 'Convention on Offences and Certain Other Acts Committed on Board Aircraft' (14 Sept. 1963). Following quotations are taken from this source.

23 For a clause-by-clause examination of the Tokyo Convention, see the 'Report of the U.S. Delegation,' and Boyle and Pulsifer, 'Tokyo Convention,' 328–52.

24 Abeyratne, 'Attempts at Ensuring Peace and Security,' 40–2.

25 Boyle, quoted in ibid., 42.

26 St John, *Air Piracy*, 9–10.

27 Hotz, 'Hijacking Get Worse,' 21.

28 On the American ratification see NARA, RG 59, CFPF, 1967–69, Economic, box 531, file: AV3, ICAO, 6/13/68, Allan Boyd to Dean Rusk, 18 June 1968; for the French ratification, see FFMA, box 850, S50-3-6, file: Convention de Tokyo (1963), G. de Chambrun 'Note Pour le Cabinet du Ministre,' 13 June 1969.

29 NARA, RG 59, CFPF, 'Report of the U.S. Delegation to the 16th Session,' 29 Oct. 1968.

30 See 'Legal Subcommittees Meet in Montreal,' *ICAO Bulletin* 24/11 (1969), 21–2.

31 ICAO, doc. AT-WP/1005, 28/4/69, Report, 'Aspects of Resolution A16-37 Falling within the Field of Interest of the Air Transport Committee,' 10–11.

32 Ibid., doc. 8827-C/987, 'Action of the Council,' 66th Session, Montreal, 24 Jan. to 10 April 1969.'

33 LAC, RG 25, v. 10461, file: 42-8-9-3-ICAO, pt. 1, L.S. Clark to DEA, 1 April 1969. (Emphasis in original.)

34 Ibid., 14 April 1969.

35 ICAO, 'Action of the Council,' 66th Session, 12–14; a copy of the council resolution can also be found in *ICAO Bulletin* 24/6 (1969), 9. See also ICAO, doc. 8798-26, C/983-26, C-Min. 66/26, Council – 66th Session, 'Minutes of the 26th Meeting,' 10 April 1969.

36 NARA, RG 59, CFPF, 1967–1969, Economic, box 532, file: AV3, ICAO, 5/1/69, Boyle to John Meadows (DOS), 14 May 1969.

37 Ibid., 6/1/69, 'Report of the U.S. Delegation to the Subcommittee on Unlawful Seizure of Aircraft, ICAO, Montreal Canada, Feb. 10 through 21,

1969,' 16 June 1969. The report noted: 'The United States received no support for its original proposal providing an unqualified obligation to extradite.' For more on the opposition of many members to the American proposals, see 'Britain Opposed to U.S. on Hijacks,' *Times* (U.K.), 12 Feb. 1969.

38 ICAO, doc. LC/SC SA – Report, 21/2/69, 'Report of the Subcommittee on Unlawful Seizure of Aircraft, 10–21 Feb. 1969.'

39 See ICAO, doc. 8849-C/990, 'Action by the Council and Other Decisions Taken and Work Done by ICAO on the Subject of Unlawful Interference with International Civil Aviation and Its Facilities,' Dec. 1969.

40 The unwillingness of the other members to change their views on this issue was noted earlier in the above U.S. report on the February subcommittee meetings

41 NARA, RG 59, CFPF, 1967–69, Economic, box 532, file: AV3, ICAO, 10/1/69, 'Report of the U.S. Delegation to the Subcommittee on Unlawful Seizure of Aircraft, ICAO, Montreal Canada, Sept. 23 through Oct. 3, 1969.' 'An atmosphere of urgency and accommodation in the Subcommittee existed at the beginning of the session,' the delegation reported, 'because of the major concession by the United States from its original position and the TWA hijacking in the Middle East. Efforts by the United States to strengthen the prosecution provisions, however, did not receive a sympathetic reaction ... The spirit of accommodation and urgency did not extend to major substantive points.'

42 ICAO, doc. LC/SC SA –Report II, 3/10/69, 'Report of the Subcommittee on Unlawful Seizure of Aircraft, 23 Sept. to 3 Oct. 1969.'

43 See PRO, FCO 14 /555, file: MUA1/39, Part E, telegram, FCO to Certain Missions, 16 Oct. 1969.

44 FFMA, S50-3-6, box 851, file: 24ème Session de l'Assemblé Générale, Réunion à Washington, 16 au 19. 12. 1969, 'Final Report of Chairman, Intergovernmental Meeting on Aircraft Hijacking,' 16–19 Dec. 1969.

45 Ibid.

46 Ibid., Gilbert Guillaume to le Ministre des Affaires Etrangères, 22 Dec. 1969.

47 Hotz, 'Murder on the Airlines,' 9. It was reported that things were getting so bad that CIA officials in the Nixon years supposedly took trains to Miami rather than flying for fear of being hijacked en route, see Campbell, 'Responses to Hijacking,' 287.

48 See, e.g., 'ICAO Actions May Reduce Aircraft Civil Violence Threat,' *Aviation Week and Space Technology* 93/2 (1970), 24.

49 See ICAO, doc. 8890 A17, Committee A, 'Report of Committee A,' (June 1970), and ICAO, doc. 8891 A17, Committee B, 'Report of Committee B,' June 1970.

50 PRO, FCO 14 /770, '17th (Extraordinary) Session of the ICAO Assembly: Report of the U.K. Delegation,' 1 July 1970. For the British proposals see PRO, PREM 13 /3090, 'Proposal for an International Convention on Violence against Aircraft' n.d.; for the Canadian proposals, see LAC, RG 25, v. 10462, file: 42-8-9-3-ICAO, 'Canadian Proposal for a Draft Resolution,' 13 May 1970.

51 For the report of the committee and its draft annex, see ICAO, doc. 9080, C/1014, C-Min. 80/22, Council Minutes, 12 Dec. 1973.

52 See Akweenda, 'Prevention of Unlawful Interference with Aircraft,' 436–6.

53 Kotaite, 'Security of International Civil Aviation,' 98; Sochor, *Politics of International Aviation*, 147. See also, 'Security in Air Transport – Achievements and Expectations,' *Interavia* 30/2 (1975), 176–8, and Marrett, 'An Overview of Civil Aviation Security Needs,' 12–14.

54 ICAO, doc. 8849-C/990/4 (4th ed.), *Aviation Security*, April 1987. For more on Annex 17 and the Manual, see 'ICAO Actively Pressing World-wide Aviation Security Programme,' *ICAO Bulletin* 37/7–8 (1982), 67–70; 'Unlawful Interference with Civil Aviation Has Decreased,' *ICAO Bulletin* 42/7 (1987), 68–9.

55 See ICAO, doc. 8892 A17-EX, 'Report of the Executive Committee,' June 1970, 4–6.

56 NARA, RG 59, SNF, 1970–73, Economic, box 593, file: AV3 ICAO, 6.22.70, 'Report of the U.S. Delegation to the 17th Session (Extraordinary) of the Assembly of the ICAO, Montreal, June 16–30, 1970,' 17 July 1970. For more on the Resolutions of the 17th Assembly, see ICAO News Release, Montreal, 3 July 1970, and 'Extraordinary Assembly Session on Unlawful Interference Recommends Strong Measures,' *ICAO Bulletin* 25/8 (1970), 12–13.

57 See St John, *Air Piracy*, 21–5, and Doty, 'Anti-Hijacking Proposals Proliferate,' 26–7.

58 See ICAO, doc. 8918 A18-P /3, 'Annual Report of the Council for 1970,' March 1971, 145–6. On the U.N. actions, see Abeyratne, 'International Responses Related to Aviation Security,' 119–44.

59 Kolcum, 'IATA Chief Spurs Anti-Hijack Program,' 32–3.

60 ICAO, doc. 8912, C/997, C-Min. 71/1, 'Council – 71st Session, Montreal, 18 Sept. – 16 Dec. 1970,' 18 Sept. 1970.

61 U.S. Information Service, press release, 22 Sept. 1970.

62 'Boycott Urged in Congress,' *Aviation Week and Space Technology* 93/12 (1970), 28; see also Doty, 'Anti-Hijacking Proposals Proliferate,' 26–7, and Woolsey, 'Prevention of Hijacking Switches from Passive to Active Measures,' in the same issue, 29–30.

63 ICAO, doc. 8920, Convention for the Suppression of Unlawful Seizure of Aircraft, Signed at The Hague on 16 Dec. 1970. The following quotations from the Hague Convention are taken from this source. See also, 'Strong Anti-Hijack Treaty Signed; May be Implemented by Mid-Year,' *Aviation Week and Space Technology* 94/1 (1971), 26; Hunnings, 'Current Legal Developments,' 348–9. For the documents on the conference, see ICAO, docs. 8979, LC/165-1 and /165-2, 'International Conference on Air Law, The Hague, Dec. 1970,' vol. 1, Minutes, vol. 2, Documents.

64 For the Montreal conference, see ICAO, docs. 9081, LC/170-1 and /170-2, 'International Conference on Air Law, Montreal, Sept. 1971,' vol. 1, Minutes, vol. 2, Documents.

65 ICAO, doc. 8966, 'Convention for the Suppression of Unlawful Acts against the Safety of Civil Aviation, signed at Montreal on 23 Sept. 1971.'

66 NARA, RG 59, SNF, 1970-73, Economic, box 595, file: AV3 ICAO, 9/1/71, 'Report of the U.S. Delegation to the International Conference on Air Law, Montreal, Canada, Sept. 8 through 23, 1971,' 20 July 1972.

67 PRO, CAB 164/992, 'International Conference on Air Law: The Hague 1 to 16 Dec. 1970, Brief for the U.K. Delegation,' n.d.

68 For an analysis of the Hague and Montreal conventions and some of the problems, see Shubber, 'Aircraft Hijacking under the Hague Convention 1970 – A New Regime?' 687–726, Pourcelet, 'Hijacking: The Limitations of the International Treaty Approach,' 55–8, and Abeyratne, 'Attempts at Ensuring Peace and Security,' 46–63. For a comparative review of all three conventions, see FitzGerald, 'Toward Legal Suppression of Acts against Civil Aviation,' 42–78. See also Dorey, 'Conventions Alone Will Not Ensure Civil-Aviation Security,' 18–20.

69 NARA, RG 59, SNF, 1970–73, Economic, box 593, file: AV3 ICAO, 10/16/70, DOS telegram to U.S. embassies, 16 Oct. 1970. For the Legal Committee meetings, see ICAO, docs. 8936, LC/164-1 and /164-2, 'Legal Committee, 18th Session, London, 29 Sept. to 22 Oct. 1970,' vol. 1, Minutes, vol. 2, Documents.

70 NARA, RG 59, SNF, 1970–73, Economic, box 593, file: AV3 ICAO, 9/23/70, DOS telegram to U.S. embassies, 25 Sept. 1970.

71 ICAO, doc. 8923-C/998, 'Action of the Council,' 71st Session, Montreal, 18 Sept. to 23 Dec. 1970, 52–7.

72 PRO, CAB 164/992, unsigned confidential memo, 'ICAO Resolutions on Joint Action,' n.d.

73 Ibid., unsigned memo for the prime minister, 'International Sanctions against Hi-jacking,' 29 Sept. 1970.

74 For the Canadian plan, see LAC, RG 25, v. 10462, file: 42-8-9-3-ICAO, 'Position Paper for use by Canadian Delegation at the 18th Session of the Legal Committee of ICAO,' 10 Sept. 1970.

75 See NARA, RG 59, SNF, 1970–73, Economic, box 593, file: AV3 ICAO, 7/1/73, Franklin Willis (DOS) to W. Cluverius, 13 Aug. 1973.

76 ICAO, 'Action of the Council,' 71st Session, 57; PRO, CAB 164/992, J.B. Russell to W.J. Coe, 9 Oct. 1970; ICAO, doc. 8912, C/997, C-Min. 81/6, 'Council Minutes, 1 Oct. 1970.'

77 NARA, RG 59, SNF, 1970–73, Economic, box 595, file: AV3 ICAO, 5/1/71, Franklin Willis (DOS) memo on ICAO Legal Subcommittee on Sanctions, 14 May 1971.

78 St John, *Air Piracy*, 25–6.

79 Quoted in ICAO, doc. LC/SC CR (1972), 'Report, Special Subcommittee of the Legal Committee, On the Council Resolution of 19 June 1972, Washington, 4–15 Sept. 1972.'

80 ICAO, doc. 9024, C/1007, C-Min 76/10, 'Council Minutes, 76th Session, Montreal, 19 June 1972.'

81 See Lindsey, 'Hijacking Accord Urged for Parley,' *New York Times*, 2 Sept. 1972.

82 See PRO, FCO 14/1073, file: MUA 20/30, K. J. Chamberlain memo on ICAO Legal Sub-Committee, 20 Sept. 1972, and LAC, RG 25, vol. 10462, file: 42-8-9-3 ICAO, A.E.R. 'Memo for the Minister,' 29 Sept. 1972.

83 'Sovereign Rights Position Snags Strong Anti-Hijacking Proposal,' *Aviation Week and Space Technology* 97/12 (1972), 25.

84 See FitzGerald, 'Recent Proposals for Concerted Action,' 161–224; Chamberlain, 'Collective Suspension of Air Services with States which Harbour Hijackers,' 616–32; Dempsey, *Law and Foreign Policy*, 359–66.

85 PRO, FCO 14/1073, file: MUA 20/32, 'Brief for Mr Earl Sohm's Call on Mr Kershaw on 26 Oct.,' 25 Oct. 1972.

86 See Brower, 'Aircraft Hijacking and Sabotage: Initiative or Inertia?' 872–75.

87 Sofaer, 'Terrorism and the Law,' 903–5.

88 PRO, FCO 14/1078, file: MUA 20/39, FCO, memo on 'Final Agenda Item 92,' 19 Oct. 1972.

89 Quoted in 'U.N. Rebuffs Resolution by U.S. for Firm Stand against Terrorism,' *Aviation Week and Space Technology* 97/25 (1972), 24.

90 PRO, FCO 14/1075, file: MUA 20/32, 'Brief: Civil Aviation – Proposed International Convention on Joint Action,' 2 Jan. 1973.

91 See Chamberlain, 'Collective Suspension of Air Services,' 625–30, and FitzGerald, 'Recent Proposals for Concerted Action,' 185–219.

92 PRO, FCO 76/816, Confidential unsigned memo for the Secretary of State, n.d.

93 Quoted in Sochor, *Politics of International Aviation*, 169.

94 PRO, FCO 76/816, Confidential unsigned memo for the Secretary of State, n.d.

95 Dempsey, *Law and Foreign Policy*, 366–7; Sochor, *Politics of International Aviation* 175–6.

96 See Dempsey, *Law and Foreign Policy*, 372–3. See also the correspondence and memo 'Civil Aviation Security,' in NARA, Nixon Presidential Materials Project, White House Special Files, Staff Member and Office files, Gil Krogh, 1969–73, box 35, file: Hijacking [1972].

97 Ford Library, National Security Adviser, NSC Latin American Affairs, Staff files: 1974–77, file: Cuba-Hijacking, 'Text of Note signed Today by Secretary of State William P. Rogers Containing Agreement with Cuba on Hijacking,' 15 Feb. 1973. The Cubans cancelled the agreement in 1976, taking effect in 1977. See, in the same file, 'Message to Swiss Embassy, Havana,' 11 Nov. 1976.

98 See Ford Library, WHCF, CA, box 1, file: CA 7/15/75-9/30/75, Department of Transport memo, 'Material for International Aviation Policy Review,' 15 July 1975; James M. Cannon Papers, box 20, file: 'La Guardia Airport Bombing,' William Coleman 'Memo for the President,' 12 Jan. 1976.

99 See Busuttil, 'The Bonn Declaration,' 474–87. See also, Chamberlain, 'Collective Suspension of Air Services,' 626–8, Dempsey, *Law and Foreign Policy*, 367–70, and Abeyratne, 'Attempts at Ensuring Peace and Security,' 63–72.

100 Jimmy Carter Presidential Library, Atlanta, Georgia (hereafter Carter Library), WHCF, Subject file: Civil Aviation, box CA-2, file: CA 1/1/80 – 1/20/81, 'Semiannual Report to Congress on the Effectiveness of the Civil Aviation Security Program,' 30 June 1980. For positive reaction to the Bonn Declaration, see the correspondence in ibid., Subject file: Foreign Affairs, box FO-44, file: FO 6-5.

101 For the 1981 G7 statement on Afghanistan, see Busuttil, 'The Bonn Declaration,' 474–5; see also Chamberlain, 'Collective Suspension of Air Services,' 627–8.

102 'Security in Air Transport,' *Interavia* 30/2 (1975), 176.

103 Dempsey, *Law and Foreign Policy*, 381.

104 St John, *Air Piracy*, 30–1.

12 Evolution Not Revolution: ICAO in a Changing World

1 See PRO, CAB 164 /992, memo on 'Soviet Union and ICAO,' 24 Nov. 1970. On the USSR entrance into ICAO see Massenkov et al., *Russia in ICAO*, 57–8.

2 NARA, Nixon Presidential Materials Project, WHCF, IT, box 6, file: 'ICAO 1/1/71 – [12/31/72],' Secor Browne to Peter Flanigan, 20 July 1971.

3 ICAO, doc. 8963, A18 Min. P/1-16, 'Minutes of the Plenary Meetings, Assembly – 18th Session, Vienna, 15 June to 7 July 1971,' 107–10; NARA, RG 59, SNF, 1970–73, Economic, box 595, file: AV3 ICAO, 8/1/71, 'Report of the U.S. Delegation to the 18th Session of the Assembly of the ICAO,' 6 Aug. 1971.

4 ICAO, doc. 9061, A19-Res., Min., 'Resolutions and Minutes,' 19th Session (Extraordinary) of the Assembly of the ICAO, New York, NY, 27 March 1973, 96.

5 For the whole debate, see ibid., 88–110.

6 NARA, RG 59, SNF, 1970–73, Economic, box 598, file: AV3 ICAO, 3/1/73, 'Confidential Report of the U.S. Delegation to the 19th Session,' 27 March 1973. The full American report can be found in box 599, File: AV3 ICAO, 6/16/73.

7 These events are surveyed in Schulzinger, *U.S. Diplomacy Since 1900*, 296–98.

8 ICAO, doc., 8982, A19-P/1, 'Annual Report of the Council for 1971.'

9 Ibid., doc. 9119, A21-Min. P/1-12, 'Minutes of the Plenary Meetings, Assembly – 21st Session, Montreal, 24 Sept. to 15 Oct. 1974.'

10 See Ducrest, 'L'Union Européenne: futur membre de l'Organisation de l'Aviation Civile Internationale?' 239–81.

11 Fink, 'Diplomatic Status Poses ICAO Dilemma,' 36.

12 See, e.g., ICAO, doc. 9216, A22-Min. P/1-3, 'Minutes of the Plenary Meetings, Assembly – 22nd Session, Montreal, 13 Sept. to 4 Oct. 1977,' 20–2, 84–7.

13 See Sochor, 'Conflicts in International Civil Aviation,' 144–50.

14 ICAO, doc. 8775, A16-Min. P/1-9, 'Minutes of the Plenary Meetings, Assembly – 16th Session, Buenos Aires, 3–26 Sept. 1968,' 81.

15 See ICAO, doc. 8931 A17-A P/7, 'Resolutions, Report and Minutes, 17th Assembly Session (Extraordinary), New York, 11–12 March 1971,' 29–64.

16 Sochor, *Politics of International Aviation*, 134.

17 See ICAO, doc. A21-Min. EX/1-14, 'Minutes of the Executive Committee, 21st Assembly Session,' 56–63.

18 ICAO, 'Minutes of the Plenary Meetings, Assembly – 22nd Session,' 147.

19 Ibid., 148, 150.

20 Resolution A22-6.

21 ICAO doc. 9317, A23-Min. P/1-13, 'Minutes of the Plenary Meetings, Assembly – 23rd Session, Montreal, 16 Sept. to 7 Oct. 1980,' 98.

22 Sochor, *Politics of International Aviation*, 129.

23 FFMA, S50-36, box 838, file: 'Convention de Chicago: amendment éventuel…,' 'Draft Report, Meeting of Directors-General of Civil Aviation in Europe, The Hague,' 6 Dec. 1967.

24 Ibid.

25 Tourtellot, 'Membership Criteria for the ICAO Council: A Proposal for Reform,' 61.

26 FFMA, S50-36, box 838, file: 'Convention de Chicago: amendment éventuel,' Embassy of the United States, 'Aide Mémoire' 13 Oct. 1969.

27 For the reports and minutes of this session, see ICAO, doc. 8931, A17-A P/7, 'Resolutions, Report and Minutes,' 17th Assembly Session, 11–12 March 1971.

28 NARA, RG 59, SNF, 1970–73, Economic, box 594, file: AV3 ICAO, 3/10/71, 'Report of the U.S. Delegation to Extraordinary Assembly 17A of the ICAO,' n.d.

29 See Osieke, 'Unconstitutional Acts in International Organisations,' 17–20.

30 ICAO, doc. A18-Min. EX/1-16, 'Minutes of the Executive Committee,' 18th Session, 35.

31 Ibid., 45.

32 FFMA, Embassy of the United States, 'Aide Mémoire' 13 Oct. 1969.

33 ICAO, 'Minutes of the Plenary Meetings, Assembly – 18th Session,' 125.

34 LAC, RG 12, ACC. 1984–85 / 219, box 41, file: 602-1-pt.3, W.M. McLeish memo, 'Interdepartmental Co-ordination Directed to ICAO Activities,' 5 Jan. 1978.

35 ICAO, doc., A22-Min. EX/1-16, 'Minutes of the Executive Committee,' 22nd Session, 100.

36 Ibid., 101.

37 Ibid., 103.

38 Freer, 'New Problems Arise, Old Ones Return – 1976 to 1986,' 32.

39 See the ICAO website, http://www.icao.int//icao/en/premises_history .htm. See also the documents in LAC, RG 12, Accession 1984–85/219, box 41, file 602-1, pt 4.

40 Freer, 'Maturity Brings New Challenges – 1957 to 1976,' 26.

41 'Interview with Dr Assad Kotaite,' http://www.icao.org//icao/en/pres/ pres_int.htm

42 ICAO, doc. 9163-C/1029, 'Action of the Council,' 86th Session, 17 Nov. 1975, 3–4.

43 Char, 'L'entrevue du Lundi – Assad Kotaite,' Le Devoir, 7 Dec. 1992.

44 See Sochor, 'Conflicts in International Civil Aviation,' 143–4.

45 For brief biographies of the secretary generals, see the ICAO website: http://www.icao.org/en/biog/

46 Quoted in Koring, 'Rare Election Challenge Causes Concern at ICAO,' *Globe and Mail*, 5 March 1988.

47 ICAO, doc. 9743, C/1128, C-Dec 123/7, Council Minutes, 8 March 1988.

48 Blackwell, 'Anti-terrorism Tops Agenda for World's Aviation Chief,' *Financial Post*, 5 May 1989.

49 ICAO, doc. A23-WP/14EX/2, 'Activities and Policy on Technical Assistance Provided under the UNDP and through Trust Fund (TF) Arrangements,' 2 April 1980, 2.

50 ICAO, 'Minutes of the Plenary Meetings, Assembly – 23rd Session,' n.d., 63.

51 ICAO, doc. 9415, A24-Min. P/1-15, 'Minutes of the Plenary Meetings, Assembly – 24th Session, Montreal, 20 Sept. to 7 Oct. 1983,' n.d., 91.

52 ICAO, 'Activities and Policy,' 2 April 1980, 8; see also Woolley, 'Aid to Third-World Airlines: ICAO and IATA Tackle Development Difficulties,' 1075.

53 Sochor, 'International Civil Aviation and the Third World: How Fair Is the System?' 1317.

54 Gupta, 'New Funds Crucial to ICAO Tech Support,' 60.

55 These changes are described in ICAO, doc. 9535, C-/1104, C-Min. 122/13, Council Minutes, 8 Dec. 1987.

56 See 'Regional Structure Enhances Air Navigation Planning,' *ICAO Journal* 46/7 (1991), 49–50.

57 ICAO, doc. 9568, 'Annual Report of the Council for 1990,' n.d., 64–5. For a good overview of the ICAO Technical Assistance Programme, see Challons, 'The ICAO Technical Assistance Programme – Today and Tomorrow,' 19–23.

58 For a survey of technological developments, see Mortimer, 'A Half Century of Technological Change and Progress,' 33–45.

59 See ICAO, 'Minutes of the Plenary Meetings, Assembly – 23rd Session,' 61.

60 Freer, 'ICAO at 50 Years: Riding the Flywheel of Technology,' 28.

61 See 'USA precipitates ICAO Financial Crisis,' *Interavia* 43/4 (1988), 291.

62 Jennison, 'Bilateral Transfers of Safety Oversight Will Prove Beneficial to All States,' 16.

63 ICAO, doc. 9188, 'Annual Report of the Council for 1976,' n.d., 70.

64 Freer, 'New Problems Arise, Old Ones Return,' 33.

65 ICAO, doc. 9347, C/1063, C-Min. 103/17, Council Minutes, 26 June 1981.

66 ICAO, doc. 9356, 'Annual Report of the Council for 1981,' n.d., 58; see also the ICAO publication, *The Convention on International Civil Aviation ... the First 35 Years*, 36.

67 See Weiss et al., *The United Nations and Changing World Politics*, 224–45.

68 Ford Library, Judith R. Hope Papers, box 20, file: Noise Control Policy, Jan. 1973 – Feb. 1975, Nixon to Pompidou, 19 Jan. 1973.

69 Ibid., George Humphreys Papers, box 20, file: Concorde, 'Issue Paper on Environmental Impacts of the Concorde,' 17 Dec. 1975.

70 Ibid., WHCF, Subject File CA, box 2, file: CA 9/8/76, 'International Air Transport Policy of the United States,' Sept. 1976, 31.

71 Ibid., Presidential Handwriting File, box 5, file: Civil Aviation – Noise Control (4), William Coleman, 'Statement of the President on Aircraft Noise,' 10 Oct. 1976.

72 Hughes, 'ICAO Members Set Noise Guidelines for Restricting Chapter 2 Aircraft,' 38–9; 'The Evolution of the World Air Transport Industry,' *ICAO Journal* 49/7 (1994), 57.

73 See Abeyratne, 'The Future of African Civil Aviation,' 36–7.

74 ICAO, doc. A23-WP/94, EX/19, 'Aircraft Noise and Engine Emissions,' 26 Sept. 1980.

75 See 'Key Resolutions Adopted by the 26th Session of the Assembly Concerned South Africa, Aircraft Noise Limits and Illicit-Drug Trafficking,' *ICAO Bulletin* 41/11 (1986), 23–6.

76 ICAO, doc. A28-WP/4, EX/2, 'Possible Noise Restrictions on Subsonic Jet Aircraft which Do Not Meet the Noise Certification Requirements in Annex 16,' 9 July 1990; see also ICAO, doc. 9564, A28-EX, 'Executive Committee – Report and Minutes, 28th Assembly Session (Extraordinary) Montreal, 22–26 Oct. 1990,' 8. The noise issue is debated at 21–6, 51–70.

77 Hughes, 'ICAO Members Set Noise Guidelines,' 38; see also, ICAO, 'Annual Report of the Council for 1990,' 107.

13 The Cold War Comes to ICAO – Again

1 Sochor, *Politics of International Aviation*, 132.

2 Ibid., 132; see also Choi, *Aviation Terrorism: Historical Survey, Perspectives and Response*, 155.

3 Choi, *Aviation Terrorism*, 155–7; Sochor, *Politics*, 133–5; 'Korean 747 Is Not the Only One,' *Flight International* 124/3880 (1983), 732; Augustin, 'ICAO and the Use of Force against Civil Aerial Intruders,' 49–64; along the same lines, see Sochor, 'ICAO and Armed Attacks against Civil Aviation,' 134–70.

4 ICAO, doc. C-WP/9781, 'Report of the Completion of the Fact-Finding Investigation Regarding the Shooting Down of Korean Air Lines Boeing 747 (Flight KE 007) on 31 Aug. 1983,' 28 May 1993, 6.

5 Pearson, *KAL 007: The Cover-Up*, 139–40.

6 Ibid. Kadell, *The KAL 007 Massacre*; Chubb, *KAL Flight 007: The Hidden Story*; Johnson, *Shootdown: Flight 007 and the American Connection*; and Hersh, 'The

Target Is Destroyed': What Really Happened to Flight 007 and What America Knew about It.

7 Public Papers of Ronald Reagan, 'Address to the Nation on the Soviet Attack on a Korean Civilian Airliner, Sept. 5, 1983,' accessed online: www.Reagan.utexas.edu/archives/speeches/1983/90583a.htm

8 Reagan quoted in Fischer, *The Reagan Reversal*, 114–15.

9 For the political connections, see Hersh, *Target Is Destroyed*, 105–78.

10 Ibid., 133.

11 Black, 'KAL Disaster and the Soviet Press,' 13.

12 Pearson, *Cover-Up*, 136.

13 See Kido, 'The Korean Airlines Incident on Sept. 1, 1983,' 1050–1102.

14 Pearson, *Cover-Up*, 191.

15 On this issue, see Tompkins and Harakas, 'ICAO and Aviation Accident Investigation,' 377–80.

16 ICAO, doc. 9428-C/1079, 'Action of the Council,' Extraordinary Session, Montreal, 15–16 Sept. 1983, 110th Session, Montreal, 14 Oct. to 16 Dec. 1983, 20–1. For the debate, see ICAO, doc. 9416, C/1077, C-Min. Extraordinary (1983) /1-4, Council Minutes, 15–16 Sept. 1983.

17 ICAO, 'Action of the Council,' 21–2.

18 See Bradbury, 'Interception of civil Aircraft,' 9–11.

19 ICAO, 'Action of the Council,' 23–5.

20 Ibid., 22–3. See also, Leich, 'Current Developments,' 244–5.

21 ICAO, doc. 9409, A24-EX, 'Executive Committee: Report and Minutes,' 24th Assembly Session, 20 Sept. to 7 Oct. 1983, 79.

22 ICAO, doc. 9415, A24-Min. P/1-15, 'Minutes of the Plenary Meetings, Assembly – 24th Session,' 25, 39, and 128.

23 Ibid., 52 and 54.

24 For details on the investigation, see Hersh, *Target Is Destroyed*, 186–9, and Pearson, *Cover-Up*, 270–1; 'ICAO Plans Meeting on Violence,' *Interavia* 38/12 (1983), 1255.

25 ICAO, 'Action of the Council,' 26; doc. 9427, C/1078, C-Min. 110/16, Council Minutes, 12 Dec. 1983.

26 Ibid., doc. C-WP/7764, 'Destruction of Korean Air Lines Boeing 747 over Sea of Japan, 31 Aug. 1983: Report of ICAO Fact-Finding Investigation, Dec. 1983,' 56.

27 Ibid., 56–7; see Kido, 'The Korean Airlines Incident,' 1053–5; Tompkins and Harakas, 'ICAO and Aviation Accident Investigation,' 380–4.

28 Tompkins and Harakas, 'ICAO and Aviation Accident Investigation,' 388.

29 Cheng, 'Destruction of KAL Flight KE 007,' 56.

30 Cox, 'Aftermath of the Korean Airline Incident,' 37.

31 Pearson, *Cover-Up*, 275.

32 ICAO, doc. 9427, C/1078, C-Min. 110/6, Council Minutes, 12 Dec. 1983.

33 Ibid., doc. C-WP/7809, 16/2/84, 'Final Report of Investigation as Required by Council Resolution of 16 Sept. 1983,' 14. See also, earlier ANC report, ICAO, doc. C-WP/7770, '1813th Report to Council by the President of the ANC, Interception of Civil Aircraft,' 6 Dec. 1983.

34 Ibid. doc. 9441, C/1081, C-Min. 111/6, Council Minutes, 6 March 1984; doc. 9442-C/1082, 'Action of the Council,' 111th Session, Montreal, 1 Feb. to 30 March 1984, 10–11.

35 Cheng, 'Destruction of KAL Flight KE 007,' 57.

36 See 'ICAO Assembly Bans Use of Weapons against Civil Aircraft,' *ICAO Bulletin* 39/6 (1984), 10–13.

37 ICAO, doc. 9437, A25-Res., P-Min., 'Plenary Meetings: Resolutions and Minutes,' 25th Session (Extraordinary) Assembly, Montreal, 24 April to 10 May 1984, 30.

38 Ibid., 57–8. For more on the assembly, see FitzGerald, 'The Use of Force against Civil Aircraft,' 291–311.

39 See ICAO, doc. 9438, A25-EX, 'Executive Committee, Report, Minutes and Documents,' 25th Session, 30, 37, 57–8.

40 Ott, 'Open Skies Haunts Chicago Convention,' 48.

41 Sochor, *Politics of International Aviation*, 137.

42 Cheng, 'Destruction of KAL Flight KE 007,' 61.

43 Ibid., 61–4; see also Richard, 'KAL 007: The Legal Fallout,' 147–61.

44 See Kido, 'Korean Airlines Incident,' 1067–8.

45 ICAO, doc. 9445-C/1084, 'Action of the Council,' 112th Session, Montreal, 11–29 June 1984, 9.

46 See Bradbury, 'Interception of civil aircraft,' 11.

47 Kido, 'Korean Airlines Incident,' 1062.

48 For the fullest discussion of this issue, see Milde, 'Interception of Civil Aircraft vs Misuse of Civil Aviation,' 105–29.

49 Quoted in ibid., 121.

50 Ibid., 129.

51 'Shootdown Law Ratified,' *Aviation Week and Space Technology* 15/10 (1998), 33; see also Augustin, 'Contracting States Urged to Ratify a Protocol Prohibiting Use of Weapons,' 11–13.

52 Sochor, 'Conflicts in International Civil Aviation,' 152–3; ICAO, doc. 9462-C/1088. 'Action of the Council,' 114th Session, Montreal, 24 Jan. to 29 March 1985, Extraordinary Session, Montreal, 22–3 April, 1985, 9–10. See also Abeyratne, 'Hijacking and the Teheran incident – A World in Crisis?' 120–8.

53 See 'A Tragedy Just Waiting to Happen,' Manchester *Guardian*; Koring, 'Experts Question U.S. Story.' See also Augustin, 'ICAO and the Use of Force,' 114–42.

54 McFadden, 'Aviation Experts Assess the Incident,' 'U.S. Pushes Inquiry on Downing of Jet; Questions Mount,' *New York Times*, 5 July 1988; 'For Iranians, Redress without Strings,' ibid., 13 July 1988.

55 'In Captain Rogers's Shoes,' ibid., 5 July 1988.

56 See Taubman, 'Soviets Urge U.S. Pullout from Gulf;' Erlanger, 'Similarities with KAL Flight Are Rejected by U.S. Admiral.'

57 Pelchat, 'L'Iran demande à l'OACI de tenir une réunion extraordinaire,' 'L'ONU et l'OACI se pencheront sur la tragédie'; see also, Gordon, 'Questions Persist on Airbus Disaster.'

58 Sochor, *Politics of International Aviation*, 139–40.

59 ICAO, doc. 9541, C/1106, C-Min. Extraordinary (1988) /1, Council Minutes, 13 July 1988, 7–9.

60 Ibid., 27.

61 Ibid., (1988) /2, Council Minutes, 14 July 1988, 47–8; see also, Burns, 'U.S. and Iran in Angry Exchange, But Agree to Help Airbus Inquiry'; Trudel, 'L'attaque américaine contre l'avion iranien: l'OACI fera enquête'; 'Aviation Body Inquiry into Downing of Airbus,' Manchester *Guardian*, 24 July 1988.

62 'Le débat à l'ONU sur l'Airbus abattu: Les États-Unis et l'Iran se renvoient la balle,' *Le Devoir*, 15 July 1988; Sochor, *Politics*, 140.

63 Barry and Charles, 'Sea of Lies,' (accessed online).

64 Moore, 'Human Error Blamed for Downing of Airbus.'

65 ICAO, doc. C-WP/8708, 'Destruction of Iran Air Airbus A300 in the Vicinity of Qeshm Island, Islamic Republic of Iran on 3 July 1988,' 7 Nov. 1988.

66 Ibid., 23–6.

67 ICAO, doc. 9743, C/1128, C-Min. 125/12, Council Minutes, 5 Dec. 1988.

68 For the council debate, see ibid., 5 and 7 Dec. 1988.

69 Ibid., 7 Dec. 1988.

70 A copy of the decision can be found attached to the minutes, ibid.

71 Ibid., doc. 9744-C/1129, C-Min 126/20, Council minutes, 17 March 1989.

72 Sanger, 'L'Iran persiste à blâmer les USA'; Pelchat, 'OACI: des voeux pieux en attendant un autre huis clos.'

73 ICAO, doc. 9744-C/1129, C-Dec 127/10, Council Decisions, 9 June 1989.

74 Sochor, *Politics*, 141.

75 Ibid., 142; Choi, *Aviation Terrorism*, 175; Barry and Charles, 'Sea of Lies.'

76 Sochor, *Politics*, 133.

77 On the 1976 bombing, see Bardach, 'Twilight of the Assassins,' 88–101.

78 See Simantirakis, 'The Cuban Shoot-Down of Two U.S.-Registered Civil Aircraft,' 30–2.

79 U.N. doc. S/PRST/1996/9, 'Statement by the President of the Security Council,' 27 Feb. 1996.

80 ICAO, doc. 9676 C/1118, C-Min. 147/9, Council Minutes, 6 March 1996;
    Mennie, 'U.S. Tightens Screws on Cuba: ICAO to probe Planes' Downing;'
    Brousseau, 'La guerre froide à Montréal;' see also Abeyratne, 'Aviation and
    Diplomacy,' 385–8.

81 'Shooting Verdict Angers Cuba, *Financial Times*; 'Cuba critique l'OACI,' *Le
    Devoir.*

82 ICAO, doc. 9681-C/1119, C-min 148/19 and 148/20, Council minutes,
    27 June 1996; Abeyratne, 'Aviation and Diplomacy,' 388; Augustin, 'ICAO
    and the Use of Force against Civil Aerial Intruders,' 158.

83 'ICAO Chides Both Sides in Cuba-U.S. Air Clash,' *U. N. Observer and
    International Report* 18/ 8 (1996), 14.

84 Simantirakis, 'Cuban Shoot-Down,' 92.

85 Witkin, 'Soviet Pilot Insists Downed Korean Jet Was Spy Plane.'

86 Tompkins and Harakas, 'ICAO and Aviation Accident Investigation,' 390;
    Bohlen, 'Russia Turns Over Data from KAL 007.'

87 For a good overview of ICAO's investigation, written by one participant, see
    Frostell, 'Completion of KE 007 Investigation Made Possible by Spirit of
    Cooperation,' 14–18.

88 ICAO, doc. C-WP/9781, 'Report of the Completion of the Fact-Finding
    Investigation Regarding the Shooting Down of Korean Air Lines Boeing
    747 (Flight KE 007) on 31 Aug. 1983,' 28 May 1993, 58–61.

89 ICAO, doc. 9615, C/1110, C-Min. 139/7, Council Minutes, 14 June 1993.
    See also 'ICAO Completes Fact-Finding Investigation of Flight KE 007,'
    ICAO Journal 48/5 (1993), 36–7.

90 See, e.g., Tompkins and Harakas, 'ICAO and Aviation Accident Investiga-
    tion,' 394; Slade, 'The Real Reason for the KAL Deaths.'

14 The Politics of Aviation Security

1 George Bush Presidential Library, College Station, Texas (hereafter
   Bush Library), CA 001, #108181, Paul Bremer, U.S. Ambassador-
   at-large for Counterterrorism, 'Testimony to the Committee on
   Foreign Affairs of the House of Representatives on Pan Am 103,'
   9 Feb. 1989.

2 For a fairly complete list of ICAO's security activities in these years see
   ICAO, doc. 8849, C/990/4, *Aviation Security: Digest of Current ICAO Policies
   and Actions on the Subject of Unlawful Interference with International Civil
   Aviation and Its Facilities,* 4th ed., April 1987.

3 See Wetmore, 'U.N. Spurs Antihijacking Drive,' 14–15; 'Unlawful Interference with Civil Aviation Has Decreased,' *ICAO Bulletin* 42/7 (1987), 68–9;

'While Unlawful Seizures of Aircraft Have Decreased, Associated Violence Is Increasing,' *ICAO Bulletin* 43/7 (1988), 58–9.

4 Luck, 'Another Reluctant Belligerent,' 95.

5 St John, *Air Piracy*, 32–7.

6 Abeyratne, 'International Responses Related to Aviation Security,' 122–3.

7 Dempsey, *Law and Foreign Policy in International Aviation*, 370.

8 Willis, *Combating Air Terrorism*, 16.

9 Oakley, 'International Terrorism,' 612–14; Dempsey, *Law and Foreign Policy in International Aviation*, 371–6; Bremer, 'Testimony to the Committee on Foreign Affairs,' 9 Feb. 1989.

10 ICAO, doc. 9486-C/1095, C-Min 118/17, Council minutes, 25 June 1986 (a copy of the Model Clause can be found here); Thaker, 'Model Clause on Aviation Security for Bilateral Air Transport Agreements,' 403–10.

11 Thaker, 'Model Clause on Aviation Security,' 410–34.

12 ICAO, doc. 9467 / C/1089, C-Min. 115/14, Council minutes, 27 June 1985.

13 ICAO, doc. C-WP/8079, 'Progress Report on the Plan of Action,' 2 Oct. 1985. See also Sochor, *Politics of International Aviation*, 148–9, for a critical review of the July 1985 meeting and the council's rather subdued response.

14 Sochor, *Politics*, 150; Willis, *Combating Air Terrorism*, 98–9; see also, 'Checked Baggage Screening,' *ACI: Airports Council International. The Voice of Airports*, 1–4.

15 Willis, *Combating Air Terrorism*, 22–3, 99.

16 ICAO, doc. A26-WP/41, 'Instrument for the Suppression of Unlawful Acts of Violence at Airports Serving International Air Transportation,' 14 July 1986; Hanlon, '30 Nations Back Canada's Plan on Airport Terrorism'; Milde, 'International Fight against Terrorism in the Air,' 150–1.

17 ICAO, doc. 9502, LC/186, Legal Committee, 26th Session, 'Report,' 28 April to 13 May 1987.

18 ICAO, doc. 9823-DC/5, International Conference on Air Law, 'Minutes and Documents,' Montreal, 9–24 Feb. 1988.

19 ICAO, doc. 9518, Protocol for the Suppression of Unlawful Acts of Violence at Airports Serving International Civil Aviation, 24 Feb. 1988.

20 Quoted in Wallis, *Combating Air Terrorism*, 33; Bush Library, CA 001, no. 059384, Executive Order, 'President's Commission on Aviation Security and Terrorism,' 4 Aug. 1989.

21 Trento, *Unsafe at Any Speed*, 67.

22 See, e.g., Mukai, 'The Use of Force against Civil Aircraft,' 581; Ramcharan, 'International Court of Justice,' 189.

23 Wallis, *Combating Air Terrorism* , 24–5.

24 Bush Library, Bremer, 'Testimony to the Committee on Foreign Affairs,' 9 Feb. 1989; see also 'La Grande-Bretagne propose un plan pour renforcer les mesures de sécurité des aéroports,' *Le Devoir.*

25 See, e.g., the statements by the representatives from Nigeria and Tanzania, ICAO doc., 9744-C/1129, C-min 126/7, Council minutes, 16 Feb. 1989; Sochor, *Politics*, 153–5.

26 ICAO, doc. 9744-C/1129, C-min 126/5, Council minutes, 15 Feb. 1989 (a copy of the Council Resolution can be found here); Bramham, 'ICAO Eight-Point Plan Adopted in 1989 Has Strengthened Aviation Security,' 29.

27 Quoted in ICAO, doc. 9801-DC/4, International Conference on Air Law, 12 Feb. to 1 March 1991, vol 1, Minutes.

28 Cartwright, 'Detection Specialists Continue to Play Vital Role in Fight to Protect Civil Aviation,' 11. On the definitions of explosives and marking agents, see Milde, 'Draft Convention on the Marking of Explosives,' 165–8.

29 See ICAO, International Conference on Air Law, Montreal, vol. 2, Sub-committee report, Jan. 1990, 7.

30 ICAO, International Conference on Air Law, Minutes, 15.

31 ICAO, doc. 9801-DC/4, International Conference on Air Law, 12 Feb. – 1 March 1991, vol 1., Minutes, 25-6.

32 ICAO, doc. 9571, Convention on the Marking of Plastic Explosives for the Purpose of Detection, 1 March 1991. For more on the Convention, see van Dam, 'A New Convention on the Marking of Plastic Explosives for the Purpose of Detection,' 167–77; Augustin, 'The Role of ICAO in Relation to the Convention on the Marking of Plastic Explosives,' 33–62; and Biernacki, 'Evolving Threat to Civil Aviation Is Countered by Legal Instruments as Well as New Technology,' 7–8.

33 ICAO, Council minutes, 15 Feb. 1989.

34 Coulon, 'Une note sale pour le tiers monde avec l'imposition des nouvelles mesures de l'OACI.'

35 ICAO, Council minutes, 15 Feb. 1989.

36 ICAO, 'Annual Report of the Council for 1990,' 96; Ali, 'Identify, implement, sustain,' 43; Coulon, 'Une note sale pour le tiers monde.'

37 ICAO, 'Annual Report of the Council for 1990,' 98; ICAO doc. 9700, 'Annual Report of the Council for 1997,' 57; Bhanot, 'Several Initiatives Are under way to Assist with Implementation of Security Standards,' 12–13; Bhanot, 'A Matter of the Highest Priority,' 5–6; Sutherland, 'ICAO Programme Offers Practical Means of Enhancing Security Training Performance,' 17–19, 29.

38 Gilchrist, 'ICAO Coordinates Multilateral Effort to Improve the Training of Aviation Security Personnel,' 7.

39 Wallis, 'Role of the International Aviation Organizations in Enhancing Security,' 87.

40 Durinckx, 'ICAO Workshops Encourage Development of National Aviation Security Programmes,'10; see also Knowles, 'Seminar in Asia/Pacific Region Focuses on Role of Human Factors in Aviation Security,' 16–18.

41 Ali, 'Identify, Implement, Sustain,' 43.

42 These figures were taken from ICAO doc. 9814, 'Annual Report of the Council for 2002,' A-54.

43 Karns and Mingst, *International Organizations*, 346–7.

44 ICAO, doc. C-WP/11065, 'International Convention for the Suppression of Terrorist Bombings,' 10 March 1999. A copy of the U.N. convention is attached to this document.

15 Back to the Future: The Return of Multilateralism

1 Naveau, *International Air Transport in a Changing World*, 168–9.

2 Ibid., 87 (emphasis in original).

3 Thayer, *Air Transport Policy and National Security*, 82–4.

4 ICAO, doc. 9233, 'Annual Report of the Council for 1977,' n.d., 9; ICAO, doc. 9327, 'Annual Report of the Council for 1980,' n.d., 13.

5 See 'The Evolution of the World Air Transport Industry,' *ICAO Journal* 49/7 (1994), 46.

6 Gidwitz, *Politics of International Air Transport*, 60–73; ICAO, 'Annual Report of the Council for 1977,' 9–11. More generally, see Bickley, 'World Air Transport Development,' 16–18, and the two special reports: 'Air Passenger and Freight Transport – Africa,' *ICAO Bulletin* 39/12 (1984), 10–48; and 'Special Report: Focus on Latin America and the Caribbean,' 5–17.

7 Gidwitz, *Politics*, 60–1.

8 Lowenfeld, 'New Takeoff for International Air Transport,' 44.

9 Jönsson, 'Sphere of Flying: The Politics of International Aviation,' 286. On U.S. airline losses in 1980, see Feazel, 'Trunk Profits Scarce in First Quarter,' 34.

10 ICAO, doc. 9216, A22-Min. P/1-13, 'Minutes of the Plenary Meetings, Assembly – 22nd Session,' 76.

11 Hammarskjold, 'One World or Fragmentation,' 84–5.

12 Ford Library, Judith R. Hope Papers, box 15, file: 'International Air Transport Association,' Knut Hammarskjöld, 'Address to the National Aviation Club,' Washington DC, 23 Sept. 1976.

13 Larsen, 'Status report on the Renegotiation of the U.S.-U.K. Bilateral Air Transport Agreement,' 85; Taneja, *U.S. International Aviation Policy*, 21.

14 Bridges, 'Bermuda II and after,' 11.

15 Carter Library, White House Central File, Subject file: Civil Aviation, box CA-1, file: CA 1/20/77 – 6/30/77, Special Ambassador Alan Boyd 'Memorandum for the President,' 18 March 1977.

16 For some of the differing views on Bermuda II, see 'Bermuda II Agreement (23 July 1977): Statements of Interpretation,' *Air Law*, 39–46.

17 Carter Library, White House Central File, Subject file: Civil Aviation, box CA-1, file: CA 9/1/78 – 12/31/78, 'Statement by the President,' 23 July 1977.

18 For the Bermuda Agreement, see Taneja, *U.S. International Aviation Policy*, 21–4; Lowenfeld, 'Future Determines the Past,' 2–10; Dobson, 'Aspects of Anglo-American Aviation Diplomacy,' 237–40; and Dobson, *Flying in the Face of Competition*, 119–40.

19 Dobson, 'Regulation or Competition?' 144.

20 See Gray, 'Impact of Bermuda II on Future Bilateral Agreements,' 17–22; Wessberge, 'Consequences of Bermuda II: Part One,' 873; and, more generally, Wessberge, 'Bilateral Clash between the United States and Japan,' 1–7. See also, Carter Library, White House Central File, Subject file: Civil Aviation, box CA-1, file: CA 3/1/78 – 1/20/81, Tim Deal to Zbigniew Brzezinski, 9 May 1978.

21 Jönsson, *International Aviation and the Politics of Regime Change*, 36–7.

22 Carter Library, White House Central File, Subject file: Civil Aviation, box CA-1, file: CA 9/1/78 – 12/31/78, White House Statement, 'U.S. Policy for the Conduct of International Air Transport Negotiations,' 21 Aug. 1978. For more on the aviation policies of the Ford and Carter administrations, see Dobson, *Flying in the Face of Competition*, 93–114, 147–73.

23 Dempsey, 'Role of the ICAO on Deregulation, Discrimination, and Dispute Resolution,' 535; Jönsson, 'Sphere of Flying,' 288. The campaign to have the Show Cause Order withdrawn is covered in Jönsson, *International Aviation*, 131–46.

24 Rhoades, *Evolution of International Aviation*, 39–40.

25 Ibid,, 37–9.

26 See, e.g., Gertler, 'Obsolescence of Bilateral Air Transport Agreements,' 39–63; Thomka-Gazdik, 'Multilateralism in Civil Aviation,' 130–6; Wessberge, 'What Are the Chances for Multilateralism,' 319–24.

27 ICAO, doc. A23-WP/25 EC/5, 'Consideration of Major Air Transport Problems on a World-Wide Basis,' 18 June 1980.

28 Dempsey, 'Role of the ICAO on Deregulation, Discrimination, and Dispute Resolution,' 538.

29 ICAO. doc. 9199, SATC (1997), Special Air Transport Conference Montreal, 13–26 April 1977, Report (1977), 11; see also Azzie, 'Second Special Air Transport Conference and Bilateral Air Transport Agreements,' 4; Feldman, 'Montreal: More Control Is the Message,' 1237; El-Hussainy, 'Bilateral Air Transport Agreements and their Economic Content with Special Reference to Africa.'

30 Hedlund, 'Toward Open Skies: Liberalizing Trade in International Airline Service,' 278.

31 Zacher, *Governing Global Networks*, 115.

32 Quoted in 'ICAO Moves toward Fare, Rate Policy,' *Aviation Week and Space Technology* 113/15 (1980), 35; on the problems facing the developing countries, see Abeyratne, 'Competition in the Air Transport Industry and Preferential Measures for Developing Countries,' 48–54.

33 Hussainy, 'Bilateral Air Transport Agreements,' 136.

34 Ibid., 142.

35 Quoted in 'ICAO Conference Rejects U.S. on Capacity Restriction Removal,' *Aviation Week and Space Technology* 112/8 (1980), 30. For the conference documents, see ICAO, doc. 9297, AT Conf/2, Second Air Transport Conference, Montreal, 12–28 Feb. 1980, Report (Montreal, 1980).

36 See Azzie, 'Second Special Air Transport Conference,' 8–9; Hammarskjold, 'One World or Fragmentation,' 100–1; ICAO, doc. 9245, C/1043, C-Min. 93/5, Council Minutes, 8 March 1978.

37 ICAO, doc. A26-WP/22 EC/4, 'Report by the Council on the Regulation of International Air Transport Services,' 9 July 1986.

38 Ibid. 9 May 1989.

39 Hedlund, 'Toward Open Skies,' 261.

40 See Dobson, *Globalization and Regional Integration*.

41 Hedlund, 'Toward Open Skies,' 260–4; on the EU, see Haanappel, 'Multilateralism and Economic Bloc Forming in International Air Transport,' 295–302.

42 Hedlund, 'Toward Open Skies,' 270–1.

43 Ott, 'Free Trade Advocates Foresee End of Bilaterals,' 30. More generally, see Wassenbergh, 'Regulatory Reform – a Challenge to Inter-governmental Civil Aviation Conferences,' 31–46; Wassenbergh, 'Regulatory Reform: National Jurisdiction (Domestic Law) vs International Jurisdiction (Bilateral Air Agreements),' 106–22; Petsikas, '"Open Skies" – North America,' 281–91; Ludwig Weber, 'The Chicago Convention and the Exchange of Traffic Rights in a Regional Context,' 123–33; Congdon, 'Bilateral Agreements – Who Wins?' 327–9. On the KLM-Northwest merger, see Phillips, 'Northwest Calls KLM Pact "Strategic Asset,"' 56–7.

44 See ICAO, doc. WATC (1992), Proceedings of the World-Wide Air Transport Colloquium: Exploring the Future of International Air Transport Regulation, Montreal, 6–10 April 1992. For the summation, see WATC 5.5.

45 Ott, 'Free Trade Advocates Foresee End of Bilaterals,' 30.

46 Hughes, 'ICAO Delegates Shun U.S. Free-Market Stance,' 37.

47 Gil, 'Liberalising Air Transport: Business as Usual?' 2.

48 Rivoal, 'Regulation of International Air Transport: Towards a New World Air Transport Order?' 4; Wassenbergh and Mendes de Leon, 'Impressions from the Fourth ICAO World-Wide Air Transport Conference,' 23. On the GATS and its impact on ICAO, see Haanappel, 'Multilateralism and Economic Bloc Forming,'305 –8; Abeyratne, 'Dispute Resolution in Trade in Civil Aircraft and Related Services,' 284–99; Abeyratne, 'Would Competition in Commercial Aviation ever Fit into the WTO?' 832–43; Abeyratne, 'Emergent Trends in Aviation Competition Laws in Europe and North America,' 155–64.

49 See ICAO, doc. 9470, AT Conf/3, Third Air Transport Conference, Montreal, 22 Oct. – 7 Nov. 1985, Report (Montreal 1985), 18–26.

50 ICAO, doc. 9644, AT Conf/4, Report of the World Wide Air Transport Conference on International Air Transport Regulation: Present and Future, Montreal, 23 Nov. to 6 Dec. 1994 (Montreal 1995), 5.

51 Lyle, 'Revisiting Regulation,' 34; Henaku. 'ICAO: Fourth Air Transport Conference,' 248. On the WATC, see Abeyratne, 'Would Competition in Commercial Aviation ever Fit into the WTO?' 819–29.

52 Chesen, 'Worldwide Air Transport Conference Plans for the Future,' 61–2.

53 See, e.g., Creedy, 'Bilateral Barriers Thwart Open Skies,' 22–4; Goldman, 'Multilateral Age Approaches,' 44–5; and, more generally, Jackman, 'Bilateral Issue Spurs Ongoing Debate,' 49–50; Young, 'Globalism vs Extraterritoriality, Consensus vs Unilateralism – Is There a Common Ground? A U.S. Perspective,' 140–50.

54 Lyle, 'Revisiting Regulation,' 32; see also Harvey, 'La conférence mondiale du transport aérien.' It was apparently only a coincidence that the conference coincided with the 50th anniversary; see Chartier, 'Sommet de l'aviation civile cet automne à Montréal.'

55 Rivoal, 'Regulation of International Air Transport,' 2.

56 ICAO, doc. 9644, AT Conf/4, WP/58, 13.

57 Ibid.

58 Rivoal, 'Regulation,' 2. For the reaction to multilateralism in Asia, see Harbison, 'Aviation Multilateralism in the Asia Pacific Region,' 138–45; Knibb, 'The Fifth Dimension,' 22–6.

59 ICAO, doc. 9644, AT Conf/4, Report of the WATC, 57–8. On the outcome of the WATC, see Wassenbergh and Mendes de Leon, 'Impressions from

the Fourth ICAO World-Wide Air Transport Conference,' 30–1; Lyle, 'Future of International Air Transport Regulation,' 2.

60 Hughes, 'ICAO Delegates Shun U.S. Free-Market Stance,' 38.

61 Ibid., 37.

62 Oum, 'Overview of Regulatory Changes in International Air Transport and Asian Strategies towards the U.S. Open Skies Initiatives,' 128; Humphreys, 'The Dangerous Repercussions for International Aviation,' 2–5; Dresner and Oum, 'Effect of Liberalised Air Transport Bilaterals on Foreign Traffic Diversion: The Case of Canada,' 317–30; Walker, 'Chicago Revisited,' 28–9.

63 Lyle, 'Future of International Air Transport Regulation,' 8; for reflection on the WATC, see Wassenbergh, 'Future Regulation to allow Multi-national Arrangements between Air Carriers,' 164–8; Gil, 'Liberalising Air Transport,' 1–6.

64 Oum, 'Overview of Regulatory Changes in International Air Transport,' 129.

65 Hiong, 'International Air Transport Regulation in The Future,' 15–16.

66 Kotaite, 'Liberalization of Air Transport,' 7.

16 From Development to Implementation: ICAO in the Modern World

1 See Hughes, 'ICAO Struggling to Keep Pace with Global Changes,' 42–3.

2 Lyle, 'Call for Reform,' 15.

3 See Ott, 'Russia Taking Over Soviet Commercial Aviation Authority,' 23; and, more generally, Zubkov, 'Major Challenges to Civil Aviation: Consequences for the East and the West,' 13–19.

4 See Milde, 'Aeronautical Consequences of the Iraqi Invasion of Kuwait,' 63–75; more generally, see Wassenbergh, 'Iraq/Kuwait and International Civil Aviation Relations,' 8–15.

5 See ICAO, doc. A28-WP/21, P/5. 'Report of the Executive Committee on Agenda Item 4,' 25 Oct. 1990. For the response of the U.N., its resolutions, condemnation of Iraq, authorization of force, and imposition of sanctions, see Taylor, *International Organization in the Modern World*, 209–49.

6 ICAO, doc. 9563, A28-Min. P/1, 'Plenary Meetings: Resolutions and Minutes,' 28th Session (Extraordinary), 40.

7 See 'ICAO Backs Kuwaiti Complaints over Seizure of Civilian Transports, Destruction of Facilities,' *Aviation Week and Space Technology* 133/19 (1990), 38.

8 Kotaite interview.

9 See 'U.N. and Its Agencies Heighten War against Illicit Drugs,' *ICAO Bulletin* 42/2 (1987), 9–10; 'Consensus Attained by U.N. Conference on Illicit Drugs,' *ICAO Bulletin* 42/9 (1987), 44–5.

10 ICAO, doc. A26-WP/28, 'Role of ICAO in the Suppression of Illicit Transport of Narcotic Drugs by Air,' 18 June 1986.

11 See Milde, 'Role of ICAO in the Suppression of Drug Abuse and Illicit Trafficking,' 139–41; see also Smith, 'Drugs, Testing and Flight Crew,' 19–26.

12 See Rigalt, 'Illegal Transport by Air of Drugs and Psychotropic Substances,' 17–35; Abeyratne, 'Recent Measures Taken by ICAO and the U.N. to Control the Illicit Transportation of Narcotic Drugs by Air,' 321–50.

13 Leconte, 'L'entrevue du lundi – Phillippe Rochat: Dépoussiérer l'OACI pour assurer sa survie.' See also http://www.icao.org//icao/en/biog/rochat.htm

14 ICAO, doc. 9595, A29-EX, Executive Committee, 'Report and Minutes, 29th Session, 22 Sept. to 8 Oct. 1992,' 56.

15 See, e.g., the discussion about the recruitment and status of women in ICAO at the 31st Assembly in 1995, in ICAO doc. 9659, A31-EX, Assembly 31st Session, Executive Committee, 'Report and Minutes,' 129–30.

16 ICAO doc. A35-WP/ P/, 'Report on the Recruitment and Status of Women in ICAO,' no date.

17 Ibid.

18 See ICAO, doc. 9874-C/1154, C-Min 178/13, Council minutes, 14 June 2006.

19 ICAO, doc. 9852-C/1148, C-Min 172/5, Council minutes, 28 May 2004.

20 There had long been rare but irritating problems for some ICAO representatives crossing the border into Canada. For one case, see, LAC, RG 12, Acc. 1984-85/219, box 41, file: 602-1, pt.4, Stuart Grant to J.R. Barker, 'Privileges and Immunities for ICAO Headquarters,' 4 Aug. 1978.

21 Milde, 'New Headquarters Agreement,' 309–11.

22 United Nations Treaty Series, vol. 1669, No. 28718, 'Headquarters Agreement,' 10. Feb. 1992; Milde, 'New Headquarters Agreement,' 315–17.

23 See, e.g., Freeman, 'Duty-Free Liquor Squabble Embroils U.N. Body.'

24 Chartier, 'Montréal, ville aérienne: D'importantes festivités marqueront l'hiver prochain dans la métropole le cinquantième anniversaire de l'OACI et de l'IATA.'

25 ICAO, doc. 9637, 'Annual Report of the Council for 1994,' 87–8.

26 See Blacklock, *ICAO: 50 Years Global Celebrations 1944–1994*; see also, the anniversary issues of the *ICAO Journal* 49/7 (1994), the *Annals of Air and Space Law* 19 (1994), conference anniversary issue; and '*Forces* consacre un numéro au 50e anniversaire de l'OACI,' *Le Devoir,* 9 Oct. 1994.

27 See Boyer, 'Un demi-siècle d'aviation civile à Montréal;' Harvey, 'Le cinquantième anniversaire de l'OACI.'

28 See LAC, RG 12, Acc. 1984-85/219, box 41, file: 602-1, pt.4, Memo to the Minister, re: 'Meeting with Secretary General of ICAO,' 28 Nov. 1979.

29 For the problems at Sherbrooke Street and the early discussions of moving, see ICAO doc. C-WP/9799, 'Proposal Received from the Government of Canada Regarding the Future ICAO Headquarters Premises,' 25 June 1993; see also Kucharsky, 'ICAO Plans Flight to New Building.'

30 ICAO, doc. 9615, C/1110, C-Min. 139/15, Council minutes, 30 June 1993; the quote from the British representative is here. See also http://www.icao.int//icao/en/premises_history.htm

31 Rochat, quoted in 'A Headquarters for a New Millennium,' *ICAO Journal* 51/10 (1996), 27.

32 ICAO, doc. 9827, C/1145, C-Min. 169/1, Council minutes, 16 April 2003.

33 See Bush Library, CA, ID no.117877 SS, James Baker to the President, 28 Feb. 1990; Fossungu, '999 University, Please Help the Third World (Africa) Help Itself: A Critique of Council Elections,' 339–75; see also, Sheng-ti Gau, 'Universal Territorial Representation within ICAO in the Age of Air Transport Globalization,' 105–25.

34 Jennison, 'Regional Safety Oversight Bodies Deliver Economies of Scale and Greater Uniformity,' 10.

35 McKenna, 'FAA Seeks Changes in ICAO Safety Efforts,' 58–9; McKenna, 'ICAO Backs Safety Plans,' 33; for another American view, see Carmody, 'ICAO Must Act on Member Compliance,' 59; see also, Jallow-sey, 'ICAO's Aviation Security Programme Post 9/11: A Legal Analysis,' 63–5.

36 'ICAO Moves Ahead with Safety Oversight Programme,' *ICAO Journal* 50/7 (1995), 24; Ducrest, 'Legislative and Quasi-Legislative Functions of ICAO,' 357–8; Weber and Jakob, 'Activities of the ICAO,' 323–4.

37 ICAO, doc. A35-WP/51, TE/2, 'Progress Report on the ICAO Global Aviation Safety Plan (GASP),' 23 June 2004.

38 Quoted in Ott, 'ICAO Faces Daunting Issues,' 56.

39 Ducrest, 'Legislative and Quasi-Legislative Functions,' 362. See two sides of the issue in Kalbfleisch, 'ICAO Lax in Enforcing Aircraft Safety Rules, Conference Told,' and Archer, 'International Aviation Body Is Not a Law-Enforcement Agency.'

40 ICAO, doc. 9785-C/1139, C-Min 163/10, Council Minutes, 15 June 2001, 112–13.

41 ICAO, Council Minutes, 15 June 2001, 113.

42 ICAO, doc. A29-WP/39, EX/8, 'Report by the Council,' 10 Aug. 1992.

43 Ibid.; ICAO, doc. 9595, A29-EX, Executive Committee, 'Report and Minutes, 29th Session, 22 Sept. – 8 Oct. 1992,' 56. The 31st Assembly in 1995 added a few more suggestions (Resolution A31-2), including more efficient voting procedures for council elections; a reduction in the duration of ICAO meetings and assemblies; better communication with the contracting states, and the maintenance of a direct link between the proposed plan and the program budget.

44 ICAO, 'Report by the Council,' 10 Aug. 1992.

45 Ibid.

46 Neal, 'ICAO's New Strategic Action Plan Is a Blueprint for Future Action,' 19 and 21.

47 'ICAO Strategic Action Plan Officially Launched,' *ICAO Journal* 52/4 (1997), 25.

48 For a good overview of the Strategic Action Plan, see Lyle, 'Plan for Guiding Civil Aviation in the 21st Century Represents a Renewed Commitment by ICAO,' 5–8; for more on the origins and progress of the Plan, see Abeyratne, 'Terror in the Skies: Approaches to Controlling Unlawful Interference with Civil Aviation,' 250–7; for material on re-organization within ICAO, see McMunn, 'Aviation security and facilitation programmes are distinct but closely intertwined,' 26–7.

49 Lyle, 'Plan for Guiding Civil Aviation,' 6.

50 ICAO, 'Report by the Council,' 10 Aug. 1992

51 Bill Fromme, director of ICAO's Air Navigation Bureau, quoted in Hughes, 'Air Navigation due for Dramatic Change,' 52.

52 Matte, 'The Chicago Convention – Where from and Where to, ICAO?' 385.

53 Lyle, 'Plan for Guiding Civil Aviation,' 7.

54 See ICAO, doc. 9661, A31-Min. P/1-11, 'Minutes of the Plenary Meetings, Assembly – 31st Session,' 87; van Dam, 'International Organizations,' 652–67.

55 ICAO, doc. 9786, 'Annual Report of the Council for 2001,' 7-8; Weber and Jakob, 'Activities of the International Civil Aviation Organization,' 321–6; ICAO press release, 'ICAO World-Wide Conference Produces Strong Recommendations for Financial and Managing CNS/ATM Systems Implementation,' 15 May 1998. The Rio Conference documents are found on the ICAO website http://www.icao.int/icao/en/ro/rio/press.htm.

56 Hughes, 'Air Navigation due for Dramatic Change,' 55.

57 Milde, 'The Warsaw System of Liability in International Carriage by Air,' 167–8.

58 Ibid., 164–6; see also Batra, 'Modernization of the Warsaw System – Montreal 1999,' 432–3.

59 For a review of these events, written by people who participated in them, see Weber and Jakob, 'The Modernization of the Warsaw System,' 333–53, and Poonoosamy, 'The Montreal Convention 1999,' 79–85.

60 ICAO, doc. 9975-DC/2, 'International Conference on Air Law,' Montreal, 10–28 May 1999, 3 volumes (minutes, documents, and report of Legal Committee).

61 Milde, 'Warsaw System,' 157–8; see also 168–70, and Batra, 'Modernization of the Warsaw System,' 65.

62 A copy of the convention can be found in Tompkins, 'The Montreal Convention of 1999: This Is the Answer,' 114–39; see also Mauritz, 'Current Legal Developments: The ICAO Conference on Air Law, Montreal, May 1999,' 153–7.

17 Meeting the Twenty-First Century

1 Assad Kotaite, quoted in ICAO doc. 9800, AVSEC-Conf/02, 'High-Level, Ministerial Conference on Aviation Security,' 19–20 Feb. 2002, Appendix A, A-1.

2 Abeyratne, *Aviation in Crisis*, 1.

3 ICAO doc. 9800, Appendix A, A-2; ICAO doc. 9786, 'Annual Report of the Council – 2001,' 7; ICAO doc. 9814, 'Annual Report of the Council – 2002,' 6; Rhoades, *Evolution of International Aviation*, 133–6, 172–3. See also '2001: Annual Civil Aviation Report,' *ICAO Journal*, 12–33, 45.

4 ICAO doc. 9786, 'Annual Report of the Council – 2001,' 7.

5 Abeyratne, *Aviation in Crisis*, 269–71; Weber and Jakob, 'Activities of the International Civil Aviation Organization (ICAO) in 2003/2003,' 398–400.

6 For more on these men, see the ICAO website: www.icao.int, and 'D. Taïeb Chérif reappointed ICAO Secretary General,' *ICAO Journal*, 30.

7 ICAO doc. 9779-C/1138, C-Min. 163/21, 'Council minutes,' 12 Sept. 2001.

8 ICAO doc. PIO 12/2001, Press Release, 5 Oct. 2001; see also 'United Nations Civil Aviation Authority Calls for Worldwide Audit of Security at Airports,' *National Post*. On the response of the U.N. to the 9/11 attacks see Fasulo, *An Insider's Guide to the U.N.*, 79–89.

9 ICAO doc. 9800, 2.

10 Ibid., 23; see also Abeyratne, *Aviation in Crisis*, 35–41.

11 See ICAO doc. A35-WP/49, EX/15, 'Developments Since the 33rd Session of the Assembly,' 6 Aug. 2004; ICAO doc. 9786, 'Annual Report of the Council – 2001,' 14, 88; and ICAO doc. PIO 13/06, Press Release, 6 Sept. 2006.

12 ICAO doc. A35-WP/49, EX/15, 'Developments since the 33rd Session of the Assembly,' 6 Aug. 2004.

13 ICAO doc. A35-WP/55, EX/18, 'Report on the ICAO Universal Security Audit Programme,' 26 July 2004.

14 Ibid.

15 See ICAO doc. 9874-C/1154, C-Min. 178/3, 'Council Minutes,' 29 May 2006.

16 ICAO doc. A35-WP/51, TE/2, 'Progress Report on the ICAO Global Aviation Safety Plan,' 23 June 2004, 3; a copy of the new edition of the GASP can be found here.

17 ICAO doc. 9874-C/1154, C-Min, 178/12, 'Council Minutes,' 14 June 2006.

18 Government of Nigeria, *The Changing Face of Aviation in Nigeria*, 14.

19 ICAO doc. A36-WP/64, EX/22, 'Progress Report on the Implementation of the ICAO Universal Safety Oversight Audit Programme (USOAP) under the Comprehensive Systems Approach,' 2 Aug. 2007; see also 'Comprehensive Safety Oversight Audits Are Well Under Way,' *ICAO Journal*, 61/2 (2006), 24, and, on the conference, see 'Global Safety Conference Heralds New Era of Openness,' *ICAO Journal*, 5–7, 32.

20 ICAO doc. CNS/SG/2-IP/07/A, Appendix, 'Strategic Objectives of ICAO for 2005–2010,' 22 April 2007.

21 ICAO doc. DGCA/06-IP/1, 'Directors General of Civil Aviation Conference on a Global Strategy for Aviation Safety,' revised, 13 March 2006. The full Roadmap document is attached.

22 ICAO doc. A36-WP/273, 'Report of the High-Level Meeting on a Comprehensive Regional Implementation Plan for Aviation Safety in Africa,' 20 Sept. 2007.

23 Address by Roberto Kobeh González to 3rd Annual Federal Aviation Administration International Safety Forum, Chantilly, Virginia, 2 Nov. 2006; see also ICAO doc. PIO 13/04, News Release, 8 Oct. 2004.

24 ICAO doc. 9852-C/1148, C-Min. 172/3, 'Council Minutes,' 25 May 2004.

25 ICAO doc. 9814, 'Annual Report of the Council – 2002,' 38.

26 ICAO doc. PIO 13/04, Press Release, 8 Oct. 2004.

27 ICAO doc. 9852-C/1148, C-Min. 172/9, 'Council Minutes,' 7 June 2004.

28 ICAO doc. 9802-C/1141, C-Min. 165/10, 'Council Minutes,' 13 March 2002.

29 ICAO doc. 9818-C/1143, C-Min. 167/12, 'Council Minutes,' 29 Nov. 2002.

30 See, e.g., Reiss, 'Air Rage: An Issue of Aviation Security and Safety,' 10–13, 47; and two articles by Abeyratne, 'Unruly Passengers – Legal, Regulatory and Jurisdictional Issues,' 46–61, and 'Air Carrier Liability and State Responsibility for the Carriage of Inadmissible Persons and Refugees,' 3–16.

31 ICAO doc. 9786, 'Annual Report of the Council – 2001,' 81; Weber, *ICAO: An Introduction*, 94.

32 ICAO Secretariat, 'ICAO Doctrine on Travel Documents,' *MRTD Report*, 1/1 (2006), 12–14.
33 ICAO doc. 9860-C/1151, C-Min. 175/15, 'Council Minutes,' 15 June 2005; Guill, 'Cyber-terrorism Poses Newest and Perhaps Most Elusive Threat to Civil Aviation,' 18–9, 26; see also Guicheney, 'Increased Cargo Security Becoming a Greater Priority for the Aviation Community,' 8–9, 24–5.
34 See ICAO doc. 9779-C/1138, C-Min. 162/1-13, 19 Feb. – 16 March 2001; ICAO doc. 9786, 'Annual Report of the Council – 2001,' 18.
35 Abeyratne, *Aviation in Crisis*, 306–9; ICAO doc. PIO 13/04, Press Release, 8 Oct. 2004.
36 Mittelstaedt, 'Aviation Industry in Eye of Climate-Change Storm.'
37 ICAO doc. PIO 10/07, Press Release, 'ICAO Commits to Aggressive Action on Aircraft Emissions, 28 Sept. 2007; personal observation, 36th Assembly, Executive Committee Meeting, 27 Sept. 2007.
38 Note the controversy surrounding the expansion of London's Heathrow airport in the summer of 2007; for one view, see Potter, 'Activists target Heathrow.'
39 ICAO doc. 9819, ATConf/5, 'Report of the Worldwide Air Transport Conference: Challenges and Opportunities of Liberalization,' Montreal, 24–8 March 2003, 6.
40 'Report of the Worldwide Air Transport Conference,' 35.
41 Ibid., 25.
42 Ibid., 28.
43 Ibid., 58.
44 For the *Declaration*, see 'Report of the Worldwide Air Transport Conference,' 59–63.
45 ICAO doc. 9786, 'Annual Report of the Council – 2001,' 5. On liberalization, see 'Icy Waters of Liberalization Prove Not so Cold in Reality,' *ICAO Journal*, 14–15, 34.
46 ICAO doc. 9814, 'Annual Report of the Council – 2002,' 3.
47 Dobson, *Globalization and Regional Integration*, 178–84.
48 'Report of the Worldwide Air Transport Conference,' 63.
49 ICAO doc. 9872-C/1153, C-Min. 177/6, 'Council Minutes,' 2 March 2006; for more on the new president, see the ICAO website: www.icao.int, and 'ICAO Council Elects Its Next President,' *ICAO Journal*, 29.
50 See the tribute supplement, 'ICAO Bids Farewell to Its Long Serving Council President,' *ICAO Journal*, S1–S8.
51 Assad Kotaite interview.
52 Abeyratne, *Aviation in Crisis*, 31.

53 ICAO doc. PIO 12/06, Press Release, 18 Aug. 2006; 'ICAO Addresses Security Concern Highlighted by Failed Terrorist Plot,' *ICAO Journal*, 31.

54 'Survey highlights need for new air law instrument,' *ICAO Journal*, 27–8.

55 For example, ICAO's recent collaboration with the U.N. on the threat of surface-to-air missiles; see ICAO doc. A36-WP/26, EX/4, 'Threat to Civil Aviation Posed by Man-Portable Air Defence Systems (MANPADS),' 3 July 2007.

56 ICAO doc. 9872-C/1153, C-Min. 177/6, 'Council Minutes,' 2 March 2006.

References

Primary Sources

Australia

Australian National Archives, Canberra:
    Department of External Affairs, Correspondence files
    Department of Defence, Central Office, Sir Frederick Sheddon Collection
    Cabinet Agenda
National Library of Australia, Canberra:
    Sir Robert Menzies Papers

Canada

ICAO Library, Montreal
    ICAO and PICAO documents
Library and Archives Canada, Ottawa:
    RG 2 Records of the Privy Council Office
    RG 12 Records of the Department of Transport
    RG 24 Records of the Department of National Defence
    RG 25 Records of the Departmental of External Affairs
    RG 26 Department of Citizenship and Immigration
    RG 70, Air Canada Papers
    MG 27 III B20, C. D. Howe Papers
    MG 31 E46, Escott Reid Papers
    MG 26 J, Mackenzie King Papers
    MG 30 E336, J.R.K. Main Papers

France

French Foreign Ministry Archives, Paris
  Nations Unies et organizations internationals Papers
  NUOI – Secrétariat des Conférences, 1945–1959

Ireland

National Archives of Ireland, Dublin:
  Cabinet Memoranda and Papers
Department of Foreign Affairs, Dublin:
  Departmental documents, file: 408/58

United Kingdom

British Library of Economics and Political Science, London:
  Hugh Dalton Papers
Cambridge University:
  Churchill College Archives
    Lord Swinton Papers
    Lord Duncan-Sandys Papers
  Royal Commonwealth Society
    Sir Frederick Tymms Collection
House of Lords Record Office, London:
  Beaverbrook Papers
Oxford University, Bodleian Library:
  1st Viscount Boyd of Merton (Alan Lennox-Boyd) Papers
  Papers of the Conservative Party
  Frederick James Marquis, 1st Earl of Woolton Papers
The National Archives, Kew:
  AVIA 109 Ministry of Aviation Records
  AVIA 120 Ministry of Aviation Records, Aviation Overseas Policy Division
  CAB 65 War Cabinet Minutes
  CAB 66 War Cabinet Memoranda
  CAB 128 Cabinet Minutes (from 1945)
  CAB 129 Cabinet Memoranda (from 1945)
  CAB 134 Cabinet – Civil Aviation Committees (1945–51)
  CAB 164 Cabinet Office: Subject (Themes Series)
  CO 937 Colonial Office: Communications Department: Original
    Correspondence
  DO 35 Dominions Office, Original Correspondence

DO160 Commonwealth Relations Office and Commonwealth Office:
    Communications Department
DR38 Civil Aviation Authority and Predecessors: ICAO Papers
FCO9 Foreign Office, Central Department and Foreign and Common-
    wealth Office, Southern European Department
FCO14 Foreign and Commonwealth Office: Aviation and Telecommunications
    Department
FCO 76 Foreign and Commonwealth Office: Marine and Transport Division
FO371 Foreign Office, Political Correspondence
PREM 4 Prime Minister's Office, Confidential Papers
PREM 8 Prime Minister's Office, Correspondence and Papers
PREM13 Cabinet Office digest
PREM 16 Prime Minister's Office, Correspondence and Papers
University of Durham Archives:
    Malcolm MacDonald Papers

United States

National Archives, Washington:
    RG59 Records of the Department of State
    RG237 Records of the Federal Aviation Administration
    RG340, Records of Secretary of the Air Force
    RG 457, Records of the National Security Agency
    Nixon Presidential Materials Project, White House Central Files
        White House Special Files, Staff Member and Office files
Franklin D. Roosevelt Presidential Library, Hyde Park, New York:
    President's and Secretary's Files
    Harry Hopkins Papers
    Adolf Berle Papers
Harry S Truman Presidential Library, Independence, Missouri:
    White House Central Files, Official File
    Dean Acheson Papers
    Russell B. Adams Papers
    George Brownell Papers
Dwight D. Eisenhower Presidential Library, Abilene, Kansas:
    White House Central Files, Confidential File
John F. Kennedy Presidential Library, Boston, Massachusetts:
    White House Central Subject Files
    President's Official Files
    President's Office Files
    U.S. Federal Aviation Agency Records

Lyndon B. Johnson Presidential Library, Austin, Texas:
  White House Central Files
  National Security File, Subject File
  Official Files of Harry McPherson
  Alan S. Boyd Papers
Gerald R. Ford Presidential Library, Ann Arbor, Michigan:
  White House Central Files
  National Security Adviser, NSC Latin American Affairs, Staff files
  Judith R. Hope Papers
  George Humphreys Papers
  Presidential Handwriting File
  James M. Cannon Papers
Jimmy Carter Presidential Library, Atlanta, Georgia:
  White House Central Files
    CA (civil aviation)
    Subject file: Foreign Affairs
George H. W. Bush Presidential Archives, College Station, Texas:
  White House Office of Records Management, Subject File
  Civil Aviation files (CA)

Interviews

Abeyratne, Dr Ruwantissa
Baldwin, J.R.
Lord Balfour of Inchrye (Harold Balfour)
Bulmer-Thomas, Ivor
Chagnon, Denis
Cheetham, Sir Nicolas
Kotaite, Dr Assad
Masefield, Sir Peter
Reid, Escott

Printed Sources

Abeyratne, Ruwantissa I.R., 'Air Carrier Liability and State Responsibility for the Carriage of Inadmissible Persons and Refugees,' *Air and Space Law*, 24, 1 (1999), 3–16
– 'Attempts at Ensuring Peace and Security in International Aviation,' *Transportation Law Journal*, 24, 1 (summer 1996), 27–72
– 'Aviation and Diplomacy – The ICAO Role,' *Annals of Air and Space Law*, 28 (2003), 367–95

– *Aviation in Crisis* (Aldershot, U.K.: Ashgate Publishing Ltd., 2004)
– 'Competition in the Air Transport Industry and Preferential Measures for Developing Countries,' *World Competition*, 20, 4 (June 1997), 48–54
– 'Dispute Resolution in Trade in Civil Aircraft and Related Services – A Comparative Study with Other Aviation Issues,' *Trading Law and Trading Law Reports*, 14, 4 (July-August 1995), 284–99
– 'Emergent Trends in Aviation Competition Laws in Europe and North America,' *World Competition*, 23, 1 (2000), 141–76
– 'The Future of African Civil Aviation,' *Journal of Air Transport World Wide*, 3, 2 (1998), 30–48
– 'Hijacking and the Teheran incident – A world in crisis?' *Air Law*, 10, 3 (1985), 120–28
– 'International Responses Related to Aviation Security: A Legal Analysis, Part I,' *ZLW: Zeitschrift für Luft-und Weltraumrecht*, 45, 2 (June 1996), 119–44
– 'Law Making and Decision Making Powers of the ICAO Council – A Critical Analysis,' *ZLW*, 41, 4 (1992), 387–94
– 'The Legal Status of the Chicago Convention and its Annexes,' *Air and Space Law*, 19, 3 (1994), 113–23
– 'Recent Measures Taken by ICAO and the United Nations to Control the Illicit Transportation of Narcotic Drugs by Air,' *Journal of Law and Economics*, 33, 3 (1998), 321–50
– 'Terror in the Skies: Approaches to Controlling Unlawful Interference with Civil Aviation,' *International Journal of Politics, Culture, and Society*, 2, 2 (Winter 1997), 245–82
– 'Unruly Passengers – Legal, Regulatory and Jurisdictional Issues,' *Air and Space Law*, 24, 2 (1999), 46–61
– 'Would Competition in Commercial Aviation ever fit into the World Trade Organization?' *Journal of Air Law and Commerce*, 61 (1996), 793–857
ACI: Airports Council International. The Voice of Airports, 'Checked Baggage Screening,' 1 (August 1994), 1–4
Agrawala, S. K., *Aircraft Hijacking and International Law* (New York: Oceana Publications, 1973)
Air Law, 'Bermuda II Agreement (23 July 1977): Statements of Interpretation,' 3, 1 (1978), 39–46
Akweenda, Sakeus, 'Prevention of Unlawful Interference with Aircraft: A Study of Standards and Recommended Practices,' *International and Comparative Law Quarterly*, 35 (April 1986), 436–46
Alexandrowicz, Charles Henry, *The Law-Making Functions of the Specialized Agencies of the United Nations* (Sydney: Angus & Robertson, 1973)
Ali, Shaukat, 'Identify, implement, sustain,' *Airlines International*, 5, 5 (September-October 1999), 42–4

Allard, Desmond, 'Keep out Political Debate,' Montreal *Star*, 23 June 1965

Archer, Hutton G., 'International aviation body is not a law-enforcement agency,' Montreal *Gazette*, 29 August 1995

Ashlock, James, 'ICAO Seeks Improved Techniques for Testing Air Navigation Devices,' *Aviation Week & Space Technology*, 83, 1 (5 July 1965), 26

Augustin, John V., 'Contracting States urged to ratify a protocol prohibiting use of weapons against civil aviation,' *ICAO Journal*, 52, 8 (October 1997), 11–13

– 'ICAO and the Use of Force against Civil Aerial Intruders,' Master of Laws thesis, McGill University, Institute of Air and Space Law, 1998

– 'The Role of ICAO in Relation to the Convention on the Marking of Plastic Explosives for the Purpose of Detection,' *Annals of Air and Space Law*, 17, 2 (1992), 33–62

Australia, Department of Foreign Affairs and Trade, *Documents on Australian Foreign Policy 1937–49 vol. VII, 1944*, W.J. Hudson ed., (Canberra: Australian Government Publishing Service, 1988)

Aviation Week, 'Germans Get Allied Civil Air Proposals,' 55, 25 (17 December 1951), 51

– 'ICAO Concludes Geneva Meeting,' 49, 1 (5 July 1948), 14

– 'ICAO Facilities Lag in Southern Europe,' 66, 4 (28 January 1957), 47

– 'ICAO Fails to Draft Multilateral Pact,' 47, 23 (8 December 1947), 56

– 'State Signs German Bilateral Despite U.S. Carrier Objections,' 63, 3 (18 July 1955), 18

Aviation Week & Space Technology, 'Boycott Urged in Congress,' 93, 12 (21 September 1970), 28–9

– 'Czechs Elected to ICAO Council,' 83, 1 (5 July 1965), 26

– 'ICAO Actions may reduce Aircraft Civil Violence Threat,' 93, 2 (13 July 1970), 24

– 'ICAO Backs Kuwaiti Complaints Over Seizure of Civilian Transports, Destruction of Facilities,' 133, 19 (5 November 1990), 38

– 'ICAO Conference Rejects U.S. On Capacity Restriction Removal,' 112, 8 (25 February 1980), 30

– 'ICAO May Resort to Diplomatic Conference to Save Warsaw Pact,' 84, 8 (21 February 1966), 36

– 'ICAO Moves Toward Fare, Rate Policy,' 113, 15 (13 October 1980), 34–5

– 'Shootdown Law Ratified,' 15, 10 (12 October 1998), 33

– 'Sovereign Rights Position Snags Strong Anti-Hijacking Proposal,' 97, 12 (18 September 1972), 25

– 'Strong Anti-Hijack Treaty Signed; May be Implemented by Mid-Year,' 94, 1 (4 January 1971), 26

– 'UN Rebuffs Resolution by U.S. for Firm Stand Against Terrorism,' 97, 25 (18 December 1972), 24

Azzie, Ralph, 'Second Special Air Transport Conference and Bilateral Air Transport Agreements,' *Annals of Air and Space Law*, 5 (1980), 3–15

Balfour, Harold, *Wings Over Westminster* (London: Hutchison & Co., 1973)

Banes, T. S., 'Air Navigation,' *Interavia*, 14, 7 (1959), 863–4

Bardach, Ann Louise, 'Twilight of the Assassins,' *The Atlantic Monthly*, (November 2006), 88–101

Barry, John, and Roger Charles, 'Sea of Lies,' *Newsweek*, 120, 2 (13 July 1992), 28–39

Batra, J. C., 'Modernization of the Warsaw System – Montreal 1999,' *Journal of Air Law and Commerce*, 65, 3 (summer 2000), 429–44

Beaumont, Roger, 'A New Lease on Empire: Air Policing, 1919–1939,' *Aerospace Historian*, 26, 2, (1979), 84–90

Beaumont, K.M., 'Notes on Some Aspects of the Legal Position of International Air Carriers,' *The International Law Quarterly*, 3, 3 (July 1950), 360–70

Bell, Robert G., 'The U.S. Response to Terrorism against International Civil Aviation,' *Orbis*, 19, 4 (Winter 1976), 1326–43

Bender, Marylin and Selig Altschul, *The Chosen Instrument* (New York: Simon and Schuster, 1982)

Berle, Beatrice B., and Travis Beal Jacobs, eds, *Navigating the Rapids 1918–1971: From the Papers of Adolf A. Berle* (New York: Harcourt Brace Jovanovich, Inc., 1973)

Bhanot, Manohar L., 'A matter of the highest priority,' *ICAO Journal*, 50, 10 (December 1995), 5–6

– 'Several initiatives are under way to assist with implementation of security standards,' *ICAO Journal*, 49, 5 (June 1994), 12–13

Bickley, Ronald A., 'World air transport development – 40 years of continuous growth,' *ICAO Bulletin*, 39, 11 (November 1984), 16–18

Biernacki, Halina M., 'Evolving threat to civil aviation is countered by legal instruments as well as new technology,' *ICAO Journal*, 52, 10 (December 1997), 7–8

Binaghi, Walter, 'The Role of ICAO,' in Edward McWhinney and Martin A. Bradley, eds., *The Freedom of the Air* (Leyden: A.W. Sijthoff, 1968), 17–29

Black, Larry, 'KAL disaster and the Soviet Press,' *International Perspectives*, (January / February 1984), 11–14

Blacklock, Mark, ed., *International Civil Aviation Organization: 50 Years Global Celebrations 1944–1994* (London: International Systems Communications Ltd., 1994)

Blackwell, Richard, 'Anti-terrorism tops agenda for world's aviation chief,' *The Financial Post*, 5 May 1989

Bohlen, Celestine, 'Russia Turns over Data from KAL 007,' *The New York Times*, 15 October 1992

Bothwell, Robert and J.L. Granatstein, 'Canada and the Wartime Negotiations over Civil Aviation: The Functional Principle in Operation,' *The International History Review,* 2, 4 (October 1980), 585–601

Boulden, Jane and Thomas G. Weiss, eds., *Terrorism and the UN: Before and After September 11* (Bloomington and Indianapolis: Indiana University Press, 2004)

Boussard, L. C. 'After San Diego... ICAO Forges Ahead,' *Interavia,* 14, 9 (1959), 1118

Boyer, Hélène, 'Un demi-siècle d'aviation civile à Montréal,' *Le Devoir,* 4 December 1994

Boyle, Robert P. and Roy Pulsifer, 'The Tokyo Convention on Offenses and Certain Other Acts Committed on Board Aircraft,' *Journal of Air Law and Commerce,* 30 (1964), 305–54

Bradbury, John N., 'Interception of civil aircraft,' ICAO *Bulletin,* 39, 8 (August 1984), 9–11

Bramham, Gill, 'ICAO eight-point plan adopted in 1989 has strengthened aviation security,' *ICAO Journal,* 53, 10 (December 1998), 4–6, 29

Brancker, J.W.S. *IATA and what it does* (Leyden: A. W. Sijthoff, 1977)

Brewin, Christopher, 'British Plans for International Operating Agencies for Civil Aviation, 1941–1945,' *The International History Review,* 4, 1, (1982), 91–110

Bridges, Lord Thomas E., 'Bermuda II and after,' *Air Law,* 3, 1 (1978), 11–16

Brousseau, François, 'La guerre froide à Montréal,' *Le Devoir,* 7 March 1996

Brower, Charles N., 'Aircraft Hijacking and Sabotage: Initiative or Inertia?' Department of State *Bulletin,* 18 June 1973, 872–75

Buergenthal, Thomas, *Law-Making in the International Civil Aviation Organization* (New York: Syracuse University Press, 1969)

Bullock, Alan, *Ernest Bevin: Foreign Secretary, 1945–1951,* (London: Heinemann, 1983)

Burchall, Lieut.-Colonel H., 'The Politics of International Air Routes,' *International Affairs,* 14, 1 (January 1935), 89–107

Burns, John F., 'U.S. and Iran in Angry Exchange, But Agree to Help Airbus Inquiry,' *The New York Times,* 19 July 1988

Busuttil, James J., 'The Bonn Declaration on International Terrorism: A Non-Binding International Agreement on Aircraft Hijacking,' *International and Comparative Law Quarterly,* 31, Part 3 (July 1982), 474–87

Campbell, Frank A., 'Responses to Hijacking,' in Mark Blacklock, cd., *International Civil Aviation Organization: 50 Years Global Celebrations 1944–1994,* (London: International Systems and Communications, Ltd., 1994), 287–91

Cameron, S.G., 'The Chicago Air Conference,' *Canadian Forum,* 24, 288 (January 1945), 227–29

Canada, Department of External Affairs and International Trade, *Documents on Canadian External Relations, Volume 13, 1947*, edited by Norman Hillmer and Donald Page, (Ottawa 1993)

Canadian Aviation, 'Men of 46 Airlines Meet in Montreal,' 18 (November 1945), 103

Carlson, Erik Dunton, 'The Origins and Development of the Civil Aeronautics Board and the Economic Regulation of Domestic Airlines, 1934–1953,' PhD thesis, Texas Tech University, 1996

Carmody, Carol, 'ICAO must act on member compliance,' *Aviation Week & Space Technology*, 141, 18 (31 October 1994), 59

Cartwright, Nick, 'Detection specialists continue to play vital role in fight to protect civil aviation,' *ICAO Journal*, 55, 5 (June 2000), 10–12, 25–6

Challons, Michael, 'The ICAO technical assistance programme – today and tomorrow,' *ICAO Bulletin*, 39, 11 (November 1984), 19–23

Chamberlain, Kevin, 'Collective Suspension of Air Services with States Which Harbour Hijackers,' *International and Comparative Law Quarterly*, 32, Part 3 (July 1983) 616–32

Char, Antoine, 'L'entrevue du Lundi – Assad Kotaite: Un avion pour le monde,' *Le Devoir*, 7 December 1992

Chartier, Jean, 'Montréal, ville aérienne: D'importantes festivités marqueront l'hiver prochain dans la métropole le cinquantième anniversaire de l'OACI et de l'IATA,' *Le Devoir*, 3 June 1994

– 'Sommet de l'aviation civile cet automne à Montréal,' *Le Devoir*, 15 July 1994

Cheng, Bin, 'The Destruction of KAL Flight KE007, and Article 3 *Bis* of the Chicago Convention,' in J.W.E. Storm van's Gravesande and A. van der Veen Vonk, eds., *Air Worthy* (Antwerp: Kluwer Law and Taxation Publishers, 1985), 47–74

– *The Law of International Air Transport* (London: Stevens & Son, 1962)

Chesen, Joseph R., 'Worldwide Air Transport Conference Plans for the Future,' *ICAO Journal*, 49, 7 (September 1994), 59–62

Choi, Jin-Tai, *Aviation Terrorism: Historical Survey, Perspectives and Response* (London: MacMillan, 1994)

Chuang, Richard, *The International Air Transport Association: A Case Study of a Quasi-Governmental Organization* (Leiden: A.W. Sijthoff, 1972)

Chubb, Oliver, *KAL Flight 007: The Hidden Story* (The Permanent Press, 1985)

Clark, Lorne S., 'IATA and ICAO: The First Fifty Years,' *Annals of Air and Space Law*, 19, part II (1994), 125–31

Congdon, Louise, 'Bilateral Agreements – Who Wins?' in Mark Blacklock, ed., *International Civil Aviation Organization* (London: International Systems and Communications, Ltd., 1994), 327–29

Cooper, John, 'Air Power and the Coming Peace Treaties,' *Foreign Affairs*, 24, 3 (April 1946), 441–452

– 'Air Transport and World Organization,' *The Yale Law Journal*, 55 (August 1946), 1208–09

– 'The Bermuda Plan: World Pattern for Air Transport', *Foreign Affairs*, 25, 1 (1946), 59–71

– 'The Chicago Convention – After Twenty Years,' *University of Miami Law Review*, 19, 3 (Spring 1965), 333–44

– 'Internationalization of Air Transport,' *Air Affairs*, 2, 4 (Winter 1949), 546–60

– 'National Status of Aircraft,' *Journal of Air Law and Commerce*, 17 (1950), 292–316

– 'The Proposed Multilateral Agreement on Commercial Rights in International Civil Air Transport', *Journal of Air Law and Commerce*, 14, 2, (1947), 125–49

– 'Some Historic Phases of British International Civil Aviation Policy', *International Affairs*, 23, 2 (1947), 189–201

Corbett, David, *Politics and the Airlines* (Toronto: University of Toronto Press, 1965)

Coulon, Jocelyn, 'Une note sale pour le tiers monde avec l'imposition des nouvelles mesures de l'OACI,' *Le Devoir*, 21 September 1989

Cox, David, 'The Aftermath of the Korean Airline Incident: Gathering Intelligence about Intelligence Gathering,' *Queen's Quarterly*, 92, 1 (spring 1985), 36–50

Creedy, Kathryn, 'Bilateral Barriers Thwart Open Skies,' *Interavia Aerospace Review*, 47 (January 1992), 22–4

Cronshaw, Keith, 'Tanzania Calls on ICAO Delegate to Support South African Expulsion,' Montreal *Gazette*, 24 June 1965

Cross, J.A., *Lord Swinton* (Oxford: Oxford University Press, 1982)

"D", 'Pacific Airways,' *Foreign Affairs*, 18, 1 (October 1939), 60–69

Day, David, 'P.G. Taylor and the Alternative Pacific Air Route, 1939–45', *The Australian Journal of Politics and History*, 32, 1 (1986) 6–19

Dempsey, Paul Stephen, *Law and Foreign Policy in International Aviation* (New York: Transnational Publishers, 1987)

– 'The Role of the International Civil Aviation Organization on Deregulation, Discrimination, and Dispute Resolution,' *Journal of Air Law and Commerce*, 52, 3 (spring 1987), 529–83

Dierikx, Marc, 'Shaping World Aviation: Anglo-American Civil Aviation Relations, 1944–1946,' *Journal of Air Law and Commerce*, 57, 4 (1992), 795–840

– 'Struggle for Prominence: Clashing Dutch and British Interests on the Colonial Air Routes, 1918–42,' *Journal of Contemporary History*, 26 (1991), 333–51

Dobson, Alan, P., 'Aspects of Anglo-American Aviation Diplomacy, 1976–93,' *Diplomacy & Statecraft*, 4, 2 (July 1993), 235–57

– *Flying in the Face of Competition: The Policies and Diplomacy of Airline Regulatory Reform in Britain, the USA and the European Community, 1968–94* (Aldershot, UK: Ashgate Publishing Co., 1995)

– *Globalization and Regional Integration: The Origins, Development and Impact of the Single European Aviation Market* (London: Routledge, 2007)

– 'The Other Air Battle: The American Pursuit of Post-War Civil Aviation Rights', *The Historical Journal*, 28, 2 (1985), 429–39

– *Peaceful Air Warfare: The United States, Britain, and the Politics of International Aviation* (Oxford: Oxford University Press, 1991)

– 'Regulation or competition? Negotiating the Anglo-American Air Service Agreement of 1977,' *Journal of Transport History*, ser. 3: 15, 2 (September 1994), 144–64

Dorey, F. C., 'Conventions alone will not ensure civil-aviation security,' *ICAO Bulletin*, 33, 1 (1978), 18–20

Doty, Laurence, 'Anti-Hijacking Proposals Proliferate,' *Aviation Week & Space Technology*, 93, 12 (21 September 1970), 26–7

Draper, R.A., 'Transition from CITEJA to the legal Committee of ICAO,' *The American Journal of International Law*, 42, 1, (January 1948), 155–7

Dresner, Martin and Tae Hoon Oum, 'The Effect of Liberalised Air Transport Bilaterals on Foreign Traffic Diversion: The Case of Canada,' *Journal of Transport Economics and Policy*, 32, 3 (September 1998), 317–30

Ducrest, Jacques, 'Legislative and Quasi-Legislative Functions of ICAO: Towards Improved Efficiency,' *Annals of Air and Space Law*, 20, 1 (1995), 343–65

– 'L'Union Européenne, future membre de l'Organisation de l'Aviation Civile Internationale?' *Annals of Air and Space Law*, 19, 2 (1994), 239–81

Durinckx, Frank, 'ICAO workshops encourage development of national aviation security programmes,' *ICAO Journal*, 49, 5 (June 1994), 10–11

El-Hussainy, Khairy, 'Bilateral Air Transport Agreements and their Economic Content with Special Reference to Africa,' *Annals of Air and Space Law*, 8 (1983), 117–44

Ellwood, William, 'Air Traffic Control, Then & Now,' *CAHS Journal*, 15, 3 (Fall 1977), 72–76

Engel, Jeffrey A., *Cold War at 30,000 Feet: The Anglo-American Fight for Aviation Supremacy* (Cambridge: Harvard University Press, 2007)

Erlanger, Steven, 'Similarities with KAL Flight Are Rejected by U.S. Admiral,' *The New York Times*, 4 July 1988

Evans, Alona, 'Aircraft Hijacking: Its Cause and Cure,' *The American Journal of International Law*, 63, 4 (October 1969), 695–710

Faller, Edmund, 'Aviation Security: The Role of ICAO in Safeguarding International Civil Aviation against Acts of Unlawful Interference,' *Annals of Air and Space Law,* 17, 1 (1992), 369–81

Fasulo, Linda, *An Insider's Guide to the UN* (New Haven: Yale University Press, 2004)

Fearon, Peter, 'The Growth of Aviation in Britain', *Journal of Contemporary History,* 20, 1 (1985), 21–40

Feazel, Michael, 'Trunk Profits Scarce in First Quarter,' *Aviation Week & Space Technology,* 112, 17 (28 April 1980), 34

Feldman, Joan, 'Montreal: more control is the message,' *Flight International,* 111, 3556 (7 May 1977), 1237

Financial Times, 'Shooting verdict angers Cuba,' June 1996

Fink, Donald E., 'Diplomatic Status Poses ICAO Dilemma,' *Aviation Week and Space Technology,* 109, 1 (3 July 1978), 35–6

Fischer, Beth A., *The Reagan Reversal: Foreign Policy and the End of the Cold War* (Columbia, Missouri: University of Missouri Press, 1997)

FitzGerald, Gerald, 'The Four Montreal Protocols to Amend the Warsaw Convention Regime Governing International Carriage by Air,' *Journal of Air Law and Commerce,* 42 (1976), 273–350

– 'The International Civil Aviation Organization – A Case Study in the Implementation of Decisions of a Functional International Organization,' in Stephen M. Schwebel, ed., *The Effectiveness of International Decisions: Papers of a Conference of the American Society of International Law, and the Proceedings of the Conference* (New York: A. W. Sijthof-Leyden Oceana Publications Ltd., 1971), 156–205

– *The International Civil Aviation Organization – A Case Study in the Law and Practice of International Organization* (Montreal: Institute of Air & Space Law, McGill University, 1986)

– 'The International Civil Aviation Organization and the Development of Conventions on International Law (1947–1978), *Annals of Air and Space Law,* 3 (1978), 51–120

– 'The Judgment of the International Court of Justice in the Appeal Relating to the Jurisdiction of the ICAO Council,' *The Canadian Yearbook of International Law,* 12, 1974 (Vancouver: University of British Columbia Press, 1975) 153–85

– 'Recent Proposals for Concerted Action Against States in Respect of Unlawful Interference with International Civil Aviation,' *Journal of Air Law and Commerce,* 40 (1974), 161–224

– 'Toward Legal Suppression of Acts Against Civil Aviation,' in Narinder Aggarwala, Michael J. Fenello, and Gerald Fitzgerald, *Air Hijacking: An International Perspective,* (*International Conciliation,* n. 585, November 1971) (New York: Carnegie Endowment for International Peace, 1971), 42–78

– 'The Use of Force against Civil Aircraft: The Aftermath of the KAL 007 Incident,' in *The Canadian Yearbook of International Law,* 22 (1984), (Vancouver: University of British Columbia Press, 1985), 291–311

Flight International, 'Korean 747 is not the only one,' 124, 3880 (17 September 1983), 732

Fortune Magazine, 'The Logic of the Air,' 27, 4 (1943), 72–74

Fossungu, Peter Ateh-Afac, '999 University, Please Help the Third World (Africa) Help Itself: A Critique of Council Elections,' *Journal of Air Law and Commerce,* 64, 2 (spring 1999), 339–75

Freer, Duane, 'Chicago Conference (1944) – U.K.-U.S. Policy Split Revealed,' *ICAO Bulletin,* 41, 8 (August 1986) 22–24

– 'Chicago Conference (1944) – Despite Uncertainty, the Spirit of Internationalism Soars,' *ICAO Bulletin,* 41, 9 (September 1986), 42–44

— 'ICAO at 50 Years: Riding the Flywheel of Technology,' *ICAO Journal,* 49, 7 (September 1994), 19–31

— 'Maturity brings new challenges – 1957 to 1976,' ICAO *Bulletin,* 41, 12 (December 1986), 24–6

– 'New problems arise, old ones return – 1976 to 1986,' *ICAO Bulletin,* 42, 1 (January 1987), 32–5

– 'The PICAO years – 1945 to 1947,' *ICAO Bulletin,* 41, 10 (October 1986), 36–39

Freeman, Alan, 'Duty-free liquor squabble embroils UN body,' *The Globe and Mail* (Toronto), 7 March 1996

Frostell, Caj, 'Completion of KE 007 investigation made possible by spirit of cooperation,' *ICAO Journal,* 48, 9 (November 1993), 14–18

Fysh, Hudson, *Qantas at War* (Sydney: Angus & Robertson, ltd., 1968)

Gates, Samuel E., 'International Control of Aviation in Time of Peace,' *The Journal of Air Law and Commerce,* 10, 4 (October 1939), 439–53

Gertler, Z. Joseph, 'Amendments to the Chicago Convention: Lessons from the Proposals that Failed,' *Journal of Air Law and Commerce,* 40 (1974), 225–58

– 'Obsolescence of Bilateral Air Transport Agreements: A Problem and a Challenge,' *Annals of Air and Space Law,* 13 (1988), 39–63

Gidwitz, Betsy, *The Politics of International Air Transport* (Lexington, Mass.: Lexington Books, 1980)

Gil, Avi, 'Liberalising Air Transport: Business as Usual?' *ACI Update,* 2 (January-March 1995), 1–6

Gilbert, Glen A., 'PICAO Middle East Regional Air Navigation Meeting,' US Department of State *Bulletin,* 15, 389 (15 December 1946), 1079–81, 1083

Gilchrist, I. G., 'ICAO coordinates multilateral effort to improve the training of aviation security personnel,' *ICAO Journal,* 50, 10 (December 1995), 7–8

Goldman, Michael, 'Multilateral Age Approaches,' *Airline Business,* (February 1994), 44–5

Gordon, Michael R., 'Questions Persist on Airbus Disaster,' *The New York Times,* 5 July 1988

Gore-Booth, Paul, *With Great Truth and Respect* (London: Constable, 1974)

Gray, Robert R., 'The impact of Bermuda II on future bilateral agreements,' *Air Law,* 3, 1 (1978), 17–22

Grebenc, Marie, 'US Delegate Blasts Canada for 'Confusing' ICAO Issues,' Montreal *Herald* (8 June 1955)

Guicheney, Gilbert, 'Increased cargo security becoming a greater priority for the aviation community,' *ICAO Journal,* 55, 5 (June 2000), 8–9, 24–5

Guill, Manuela, 'Cyber-terrorism poses newest and perhaps most elusive threat to civil aviation,' *ICAO Journal,* 55, 5 (June 2000), 18–9, 26

Guldimann, Werner, 'The Chicago Convention Revisited: Possible Improvements after 50 Years,' *Annals of Air and Space Law,* 19, 2 (1994, part 2), 347–62

Gunther, John, 'Multilateralism in International Air Transport – The Concept and the Quest,' *Annals of Air and Space Law,* 19, 1 (1994), 259–78

Gupta, Ravindra, 'New Funds Crucial to ICAO Tech Support,' *Aviation Week & Space Technology,* 141, 18 (31 October 1994), 59–60

Haanappel, P.P.C., 'Multilateralism and Economic Bloc Forming in International Air Transport,' *Annals of Air and Space Law,* 19, part I (1994), 279–320

Haglund, David G., '"De-Lousing" Scadta: The Role of Pan American Airways in U.S. Aviation Diplomacy in Colombia, 1939–1940,' *Aerospace Historian,* 30, 3 (September 1983), 177–190

Hall, H. Duncan, 'The British Commonwealth as a Great Power,' *Foreign Affairs,* 23 (1944–45), 594–608

Hammarskjöld, Knut, 'One World or Fragmentation: The Toll of Evolution in International Air Transport,' *Annals of Air and Space Law,* 9, (1984), 79–104

Handley Page, Sir Frederick, 'The Future of the Skyways, A British View,' *Foreign Affairs,* 22, 3 (April 1944), 404–12

Hanlon, Michael, '30 nations back Canada's plan on airport terrorism,' *Toronto Star,* 27 September 1986

Harbison, Peter, 'Aviation Multilateralism in the Asia Pacific Region: Regulatory and Industry Pressures,' *Air and Space Law,* 19, 3 (1994), 138–45

Hargreaves, John D., *Decolonization in Africa* (London: Longman, 2nd edition, 1996)

Harvey, Claire, 'La conférence mondiale du transport aérien, *Le Devoir,* 4 December 1994

– 'Le cinquantième anniversaire de l'OACI,' *Le Devoir,* 4 December 1994

He, E.A., 'Ink or Fuel? Two World Aviation Organisations: ICAO and IATA at Work,' *Interavia*, 2, 12 (December 1947), 18

– 'Mañana por la Mañana,' *InterAvia*, 3, 1 (January 1948), 53

– 'Sovereignty and Civil Aviation: Preparing for the ICAO Plenary Session,' *Interavia*, 2, 3 (March 1947), 24

Hedlund, Daniel C., 'Toward Open Skies: Liberalizing Trade in International Airline Service,' *Minnesota Journal of Global Trade*, 3, 2 (summer 1994), 259–99

Heiman, E.E., 'German Hopes,' *Interavia*, 3, 2 (February 1948), 71

– 'ICAO Gets Down to Business,' *Interavia*, 3, 8 (August 1948), 421

Henaku, B.D.K., 'ICAO: Fourth Air Transport Conference,' *ZLW*, 43, 3 (1994), 247–56

Hersh, Seymour M., *"The Target is Destroyed:" What Really Happened to Flight 007 and What America Knew About It* (New York: Random House, 1986)

Higham, Robin, *Britain's Imperial Air Routes, 1918 to 1939* (Hamden, CT: Shoe String Press, 1961)

– 'The British Government and Overseas Airlines, 1918–1939, A Failure of Laissez-Faire,' *The Journal of Air Law and Commerce*, 26, 1 (Winter 1959), 1–12

– 'British Airways Ltd, 1935–40,' *The Journal of Transport History*, 4, 2 (November 1959), 113–23

Hildred, Sir William, 'What is IATA?' *Canadian Aviation*, 19 (September 1946), 54, 58

Hiong, Ng Wee, 'International Air Transport Regulation In The Future: Business As Usual?' *Journal of Aviation Management*, (2000), 1–20

Holmes, John, *The Shaping of Peace: Canada and the Search for World Order, 1943–1957* vol. 1 (Toronto: University of Toronto Press, 1979)

Hotz, Robert, 'Hijacking Gets Worse,' *Aviation Week & Space Technology*, 91, 11 (15 September 1969), 21

– 'Murder on the Airlines, *Aviation Week & Space Technology*, 92, 12 (23 March 1970), 9

Hughes, David, 'Air Navigation due for Dramatic Change,' *Aviation Week & Space Technology*, 141, 18 (31 October 1994), 51–3

– 'ICAO Delegates Shun U.S. Free-Market Stance,' *Aviation Week & Space Technology*, 142, 1 (2 January 1995), 37–8

– 'ICAO Members Set Noise Guidelines for Restricting Chapter 2 Aircraft,' *Aviation Week & Space Technology*, 133, 19 (5 November 1990), 38–9

– 'ICAO struggling to keep pace with global changes,' *Aviation Week & Space Technology*, 137, 15 (12 October 1992), 42–3

Humphreys, Barry, 'The dangerous repercussions for international aviation,' *The Avmark Aviation Economist*, 14, 2 (February/March 1997), 2–5

Hunnings, N, 'Current Legal Developments,' *The International and Comparative Law Quarterly,* 20 (1971), 348–9

Hymans, Max, 'Results of a Meeting,' *Interavia,* 3, 8 (August 1948), 422–3

ICAO, *The Convention on International Civil Aviation ... the first 35 years* (Montreal: ICAO, n.d.)

ICAO Bulletin, 'Air Passenger and freight transport – Africa,' 39, 12 (December 1984), 10–48

– 'Amendment of Article 45 of the Convention on International Civil Aviation,' 9, 5 (June/July 1954), 15–18

– 'Consensus attained by UN Conference on illicit drugs,' 42, 9 (September 1987), 44–5

– 'European Civil Aviation Conference Opens New Multilateral Agreement for Signature,' 15, 5, (June 1960), 81–3

– 'Extraordinary Assembly Session on Unlawful Interference Recommends Strong Measures,' 25, 8 (August 1970), 12–13

– 'ICAO actively pressing world-wide aviation security programme,' 37, 7/8 (July/August 1982), 67–70

– 'ICAO Assembly bans use of weapons against civil aircraft,' 39, 6 (June 1984), 10–13

– 'ICAO officially inaugurates new Headquarters,' 30, 10 (October 1975), 15

– 'Key Resolutions adopted by the 26th Session of the Assembly concerned South Africa, aircraft noise limits and illicit-drug trafficking,' 41, 11 (November 1986), 23–6

– 'Legal Subcommittees Meet in Montreal,' 24, 11 (November 1969), 21–2

– 'Resumption of International Aviation by Japan and Germany,' 9, 4 (May 1954), 12–13

– 'United Nations and its Agencies heighten war against illicit drugs,' 42, 2 (February 1987), 9–10

– 'Unlawful interference with civil aviation has decreased,' 42, 7 (July 1987), 68–9

– 'While unlawful seizures of aircraft have decreased, associated violence is increasing,' 43, 7 (July 1988), 58–9

ICAO Journal, 'The Evolution of the World Air Transport Industry,' 49, 7 (September 1994), 46–58

– 'A headquarters for a new millennium,' 51, 10 (December 1996), 26–7

– 'Comprehensive safety oversight audits are well under way,' 61, 2 (March/April 2006), 24

– 'Dr. Taïeb Chérif reappointed ICAO Secretary General,' 61, 2 (March/April 2006), 30

– 'Global safety conference heralds new era of openness,' 61, 2 (March/April 2006), 5–7, 32

- 'ICAO addresses security concern highlighted by failed terrorist plot,' 61, 6 (November/December 2006), 31
- 'ICAO bids farewell to its long serving Council President,' 61, 4 (July/August 2006), S1–8
- 'ICAO completes fact-finding investigation of Flight KE 007,' 48, 5 (June 1993), 36–7
- 'ICAO Council elects its next President,' 61, 2 (March/April 2006), 29
- 'ICAO Council lifts all restrictions on South Africa's membership,' 49, 7 (September 1994), 70
- 'ICAO moves ahead with safety oversight programme,' 50, 7 (September 1995), 24
- 'ICAO strategic action plan officially launched,' 52, 4 (May 1997), 25
- 'Icy waters of liberalization prove not so cold in reality,' 61, 1 (January/February 2006), 14–15, 34
- 'Regional Structure Enhances Air Navigation Planning,' 46, 7 (July 1991), 49–50
- 'Special Report: Focus on Latin America and the Caribbean,' 51, 10 (December 1996), 5–17
- 'Survey highlights need for new air law instrument,' 61, 1 (January/February 2006), 27–8

ICAO Monthly Bulletin, 'Relations with Other International Organizations: United Nations,' 2, 12 (December 1947), 11

ICAO Secretariat, 'ICAO Doctrine on Travel Documents,' *MRTD Report,* 1, 1 (2006), 12–14

Ide, Yoshinori, 'Recent Developments in Air Transport Relations Between Japan and the United States,' *Annals of Air and Space Law,* 23 (1998), 119–41

Institut Francais Du Transport Aerien, 'Aviation Contributions to the Development of International Cooperation – Internationalization: Objectives and Methods,' *Journal of Air Law and Commerce,* 17 (1950) 184–93

Interavia, 'A Japanese come-back? "No" says the Eastern Bloc – "Yes" says the West,' 8, 1 (1953), 36–39
- 'ICAO's 15th Assembly Reveals Serious Shortcomings,' 20, 9 (September 1965), 1356
- 'ICAO plans meeting on violence,' 38, 12 (1983), 1255
- 'ICAO Special North Atlantic Meeting,' 20, 5 (1965), 678
- 'The San Diego ICAO Assembly in Brief,' 14, 8 (1959), 901
- 'Security in Air Transport – Achievements and Expectations,' 30, 2 (1975), 176–78
- 'USA precipitates ICAO financial crisis,' 43, 4 (1988), 291
- 'Will Montreal's "Aviation Building" Lose its Tenants?' 8, 1 (1953), 43

– 'World Aviation Headquarters,' 5, 8–9 (1950), 428

Jackman, Frank, 'Bilateral Issue Spurs Ongoing Debate,' *Aviation Week & Space Technology*, 141, 18 (31 October 1994), 49–51

Jallow-sey, Aisatou, 'ICAO's Aviation Security Programme Post 9/11: A Legal Analysis,' Master of Laws Thesis (McGill University: Institute of Air and Space Law, 2003)

Jennison, Michael B., 'Regional safety oversight bodies deliver economies of scale and greater uniformity,' *ICAO Journal*, 61, 1 (January/February 2006), 9–12, 34–5

– 'Bilateral transfers of safety oversight will prove beneficial to all States,' *ICAO Journal*, 48, 4 (May 1993), 16–7

Johnson, Julie, 'U.S. Pushes Inquiry on Downing of Jet; Questions Mount,' *The New York Times*, 5 July 1988

Johnson, R.W., *Shootdown: Flight 007 and the American Connection* (New York: Viking, 1986)

Johnston, E.A., *To Organise the Air: The Evolution of Civil Aviation and the Role of Sir Frederick Tymms, the Flying Civil Servant* (Cranfield University Press, 1995)

Jones, Helen Hart, 'Amending the Chicago Convention and its Technical Standards – Can Consent of all Member States Be Eliminated?' *Journal of Air Law and Commerce*, 16, 2, (1949), 185–213

Jönsson, Christer, *International Aviation and the Politics of Regime Change* (London: Frances Pinter, 1987)

– 'Sphere of flying: the politics of international aviation,' *International Organization*, 35, 2 (spring 1981), 273–302

Kadell, Franz A., *The KAL 007 Massacre* (Western Goals Foundation, 1985)

Kaeckenbeeck, Georges, 'The Function of Great and Small Powers in the International Organization,' *International Affairs*, 21 (1945), 306–12

Kalbfleisch, John, 'ICAO lax in enforcing aircraft safety rules, conference told,' Montreal *Gazette*, 19 August 1995

Karns, Margaret P., and Karen Mingst, *International Organizations: The Politics and Processes of Global Governance* (Boulder, Co.: Lynne Rienner, 2004)

Kido, Masahiko, 'The Korean Airlines Incident on September 1, 1983, and Some Measures Following it,' *Journal of Air Law and Commerce*, 62, 4 (April-May 1997), 1049–70

Kirk, Grayson, 'Wings Over the Pacific,' *Foreign Affairs*, 20, 2 (January 1942), 293–302

Knibb, David, 'The Fifth Dimension,' *Airline Business*, (December 1994), 22–6

Knowles, Alan, 'Seminar in Asia/Pacific region focuses on role of human factors in aviation security,' *ICAO Journal*, 49, 5 (June 1994), 16–18

Kolcum, Edward H., 'IATA Chief Spurs Anti-Hijack Program,' *Aviation Week & Space Technology*, 93, 23 (7 December 1970), 32–3

Koring, Paul, 'Experts question U.S. story,' *The Globe and Mail* (Toronto), 6 July 1988

– 'Rare election challenge causes concern at ICAO,' *The Globe and Mail* (Toronto), 5 March 1988

Kotaite, Assad, 'The Liberalization of Air Transport,' *ICAO Journal*, 55, 6 (July/August 2000), 7–9, 43

– 'Security of International Civil Aviation – Role of ICAO,' *Annals of Air and Space Law*, 7 (1982), 95–101

Kroger, William, 'German Airline May Start in Year,' *Aviation Week*, 56, 21 (26 May 1952), 21–22

– 'Treaty Spurs New German Air Industry,' *Aviation Week*, 56, 2 (2 June 1952), 13–15

Kucharsky, Daniel, 'ICAO plans flight to new building.' *The Globe and Mail* (Toronto), 9 April 1993

Larsen, Paul B., 'Status report on the Renegotiation of the U.S.-U.K. Bilateral Air Transport Agreement (Bermuda Agreement),' *Air Law*, 2, 2 (1977), 82–90

Latchford, Stephen, 'CITEJA and the Legal Committee of ICAO,' U.S. Department of State *Bulletin*, 17, (14 September 1947), 487–97

Leconte, Catherine, 'L'entrevue du lundi – Phillippe Rochat: Dépoussiérer l'OACI pour assurer sa survie,' *Le Devoir* (Montreal), 3 February 1992

Le Devoir (Montreal), 'Cuba critique l'OACI,' 21 June 1996

– '*Forces* consacre un numéro au 50e anniversaire de l'OACI,' 9 October 1994

– 'Le débat à l'ONU sur l'Airbus abattu: Les États-Unis et l'Iran se renvoient la balle,' 15 July 1988

– 'La Grande-Bretagne propose un plan pour renforcer les mesures de sécurité des aéroports,' 13 February 1989

– 'L'ONU et l'OACI se pencheront sur la tragédie,' 7 July 1988

Leich, Marian Nash, 'Current Developments,' *American Journal of International Law*, 78, 1 (January 1984), 244–5

Lindsey, Robert, 'Hijacking Accord Urged for Parley,' *New York Times*, 2 September 1972

Lissitzyn, O.J., 'Bilateral Agreements on Air Transport,' *The Journal of Air Law and Commerce*, 30 (1964), 248–63

– *International Air Transport and National Policy* (New York: Council on Foreign Relations, 1942)

Lowenfeld, Andreas, 'A New Takeoff for International Air Transport,' *Foreign Affairs*, 54, 1 (October 1975), 36–50

– 'The Future determines the past: Bermuda I in the light of Bermuda II,' *Air Law*, 3, 1 (1978), 2–10

– and Allan I. Mendelsohn, 'The United States and the Warsaw Convention,' *Harvard Law Review*, 80, 3 (January 1967), 497–602

Luard, Evan, *International Agencies: The Emerging Framework of Interdependence* (London: MacMillan, 1977)

Luck, Edward C., 'Another Reluctant Belligerent: The United Nations and the War on Terrorism,' in Richard M. Price and Mark W. Zacher, eds., *The United Nations and Global Security* (New York: Palgrave Macmillan, 2004), 95–108

Lyle, Chris, 'Call for Reform,' *ICAO Journal*, 50, 9 (November 1995), 15–17

– 'The future of international air transport regulation,' *Journal of Air Transport Management*, 2, 1 (1995), 3–10

– 'Plan for guiding civil aviation in the 21st century represents a renewed commitment by ICAO,' *ICAO Journal*, 52, 2 (March 1997), 5–8

– 'Revisiting regulation,' *Airline Business*, (April 1994), 32–5

MacKenzie, David. 'An "Ambitious Dream": The Chicago Conference and the Quest for Multilateralism in International Air Transport,' *Diplomacy and Statecraft*, 2, 2, (July 1991), 270–93

– 'The Bermuda Conference and Anglo-American Aviation Relations at the End of the Second World War,' *The Journal of Transport History*, 12, 1, (March 1991), 65–73

– 'Canada and Australia in the World of International Commercial Aviation,' in Margaret MacMillan and Francine McKenzie, eds., *Parties Long Estranged: Canada and Australia in the 20th Century* (Vancouver: UBC Press, 2003), 99–123

– *Canada and International Civil Aviation, 1932–1948* (Toronto: University of Toronto Press, 1989)

– *Inside the Atlantic Triangle: Canada and the Entrance of Newfoundland into Confederation, 1939–1949* (Toronto: University of Toronto Press, 1986)

– 'Ireland, Canada, and Atlantic Aviation, 1935–45,' *The Canadian Journal of Irish Studies*, 18, 1, (December 1992), 31–47

– 'The Rise and Fall of the Commonwealth Air Transport Council: A Canadian Perspective,' *The Journal of Imperial and Commonwealth History*, 21, 1, (January 1993), 105–25

– '"Sitting Pretty": The Creation of the First Canadian Transatlantic Air Service, 1935–1943,' *Aerospace Historian*, 34, 1 (December 1987), 253–61

– 'Wartime Planning for Postwar Commercial Aviation: Australia and Canada Compared,' *The Journal of Imperial and Commonwealth History*, 26, 3, (September 1998), 50–70

Maloney, Sean M., *Canada and UN Peacekeeping: Cold War by Other Means, 1945–1970* (St. Catherines, Ontario: Vanwell Publishing Limited, 2002)

Manchester Guardian, 'A tragedy just waiting to happen,' 10 July 1988

– 'Aviation body inquiry into downing of Airbus,' 24 July 1988

Mankiewicz, Reni H., 'Air Law Conventions and the New States,' *Journal of Air Law and Commerce*, 29 (1963), 52–64

— 'Charter and Interchange of Aircraft and the Warsaw Convention. A Study of Problems Arising from the National Application of Conventions for the Unification of Private Law,' *International and Comparative Law Quarterly*, 10, Part 4 (October 1961), 707–25

– 'The 1971 Protocol of Guatemala City to Further Amend the 1929 Warsaw Convention,' *Journal of Air Law and Commerce*, 38 (1972), 519–45

Marlin, E.R., 'The ICAO Technical Assistance Programme,' *Interavia*, 14, 7 (1959), 865

Marrett, John, 'An Overview of Civil Aviation Security Needs,' ICAO *Bulletin*, 27, 9 (September 1972), 12–14

Massenkov, V, B. Urinovsky, and V. Suvorov, *Russia in ICAO* (Moscow: Aeroflot, 1994)

Massey, Vincent, *What's Past is Prologue: The Memoirs of Vincent Massey* (Toronto: MacMillan, 1963)

Matte, Nicolas Mateesco, 'The Chicago Convention – Where from and where to go, ICAO?' *Annals of Air and Space Law*, 19, 1 (1994, Part 1), 371–99

— 'The Warsaw System and the Hesitations of the U.S. Senate,' *Annals of Air and Space Law*, 8 (1983), 151–64

Mauritz, Jeroen, 'Current Legal Developments: The ICAO Conference on Air Law, Montreal, May 1999,' *Air and Space Law*, 24, 3 (1999), 153–7

McClurkin, R.J.G., 'The Geneva Commission on a Multilateral Air Transport Agreement,' *Journal of Air Law and Commerce*, 15, 1 (1948), 39–46

McCormack, Robert L., 'Imperialism, Air Transport and Colonial Development: Kenya, 1920–46,' *The Journal of Imperial and Commonwealth History*, 17, 3 (1989), 374–95

– 'Man with a Mission: Oswald Pirow and South African Airways, 1933–1939,' *Journal of African History*, 20 (1979), 543–57

– 'Missed Opportunities: Winston Churchill, the Air Ministry, and Africa, 1919–1921,' *The International History Review*, 11, 2 (May 1989), 205–28

– 'War and Change: Air Transport in British Africa, 1939–1946, *Canadian Journal of History*, 24 (December 1989), 341–59

McFadden, Robert D., 'Aviation Experts Assess the Incident,' *The New York Times*, 4 July 1988

McKenna, James T., 'FAA Seeks Changes in ICAO Safety Efforts,' *Aviation Week & Space Technology*, 147, 19 (10 November 1997), 58–9

– 'ICAO Backs Safety Plans,' *Aviation Week & Space Technology*, 149, 15 (12 October 1998), 33

McKim, Anson, 'World Order in Air Transport,' *International Journal*, 2 (Summer 1947), 226–36

McMunn, Mary, 'Aviation security and facilitation programmes are distinct but closely intertwined,' *ICAO Journal*, 51, 9 (November 1996), 7–9, 26–7

Megaw, M. Ruth, 'The Scramble for the Pacific: Anglo-United States Rivalry in the 1930s,' *Historical Studies*, 17, 69 (October 1977), 458–73

Mennie, James, 'U.S. tightens screws on Cuba: ICAO to probe planes' downing,' Montreal *Gazette*, 7 March 1996

Mézière, Henri and Jean-Marie Sauvage, *Les Ailes Francaise: L'Aviation Marchande de 1919 à nos Jours* (Paris: Editions Rive Droite, 1999)

Milde, Michael, 'Aeronautical consequences of the Iraqi invasion of Kuwait,' *Air Law*, 16, 2 (1991), 63–75

– 'The Chicago Convention – After Forty Years,' *Annals of Air and Space Law*, 9 (1984), 119–31

– 'Draft Convention on the Marking of Explosives,' *Annals of Air and Space Law*, 15 (1990), 155–79

– 'Interception of Civil Aircraft vs. Misuse of Civil Aviation (Background of Amendment 27 to Annex 2),' *Annals of Air and Space Law*, 11 (1986), 105–29

– 'The International Fight Against Terrorism in the Air,' in Chia-Jui Cheng, ed., *The Use of Airspace and Outer Space for All Mankind in the 21st Century* (The Hague: Kluwer Law International, 1995), 141–58

– 'New Headquarters Agreement Between ICAO and Canada,' *Annals of Air and Space Law*, 17, 2 (1992), 305–22

– 'The Role of ICAO in the Suppression of Drug Abuse and Illicit Trafficking,' *Annals of Air and Space Law*, 13 (1988), 133–59

– 'The Warsaw System of Liability in International Carriage by Air: History, Merits and Flaws…and the New "non-Warsaw" Convention of 28 May 1999,' *Annals of Air and Space Law*, 24 (1999), 155–86

Miller, John Andrew, 'Air Diplomacy: The Chicago Aviation Conference of 1944 in Anglo-American Wartime Relations and Postwar Planning', (PhD thesis, Yale University, 1971)

Mittelstaedt, Martin, 'Aviation industry in eye of climate-change storm,' *The Globe and Mail* (Toronto), 14 May 2007

Moore, Molly, 'Human Error Blamed for Downing of Airbus,' *Washington Post*, 14 August 1988

Montreal *Gazette*, 'Delegates from Peru in Disgrace for Backing Move to Oust Spain,' 16 May 1947

– 'Flying Ice Wagon is Inspected Here,' 10 May 1947

– 'I.C.A.O. Adjourns Wednesday – "But What Year"?' 27 May 1947

– 'ICAO Council Gets Diplomatic Status,' 3 September 1947

– 'ICAO Ouster of Spain Due Today as Vote Power Decision Reached,' 13 May 1947

Morgan, Stokely, 'The International Civil Aviation Conference at Chicago and What It Means to the Americas', Department of State *Bulletin*, 12 (7 January 1945), 33–38

Mortimer, Les, 'A Half Century of Technological Change and Progress,' *ICAO Journal*, 49, 7 (September 1994), 33–45

Moss, Robert, 'International Terrorism and Western Societies,' *International Journal*, 28, 3 (summer 1973), 418–30

Mukai, Masukane, 'The Use of Force Against Civil Aircraft: The Legal Aspects of Joint International Actions,' *Annals of Air and Space Law*, 19, 2 (1994) 567–87

Myerscough, John, 'Airport Provision in the Inter-War Years,' *Journal of Contemporary History*, 20, 1 (January 1985), 41–70

National Post (Toronto), 'United Nations civil aviation authority calls for worldwide audit of security at airports,' 6 October 2001

Naveau, Jacques, *International Air Transport in a Changing World* (Brussels: Emile Bruylant, 1989)

Neal, Frederick, 'ICAO's new strategic action plan is a blueprint for future action,' *ICAO Journal*, 47, 11 (November 1992), 19 and 21

Newton, Wesley P., 'International Aviation Rivalry in Latin America, 1919–1927,' *Journal of Inter-American Studies*, 7, 3 (July 1965), 345–56

New York Times, 'For Iranians, Redress Without Strings,' 13 July 1988

– 'In Captain Rogers's Shoes,' 5 July 1988

Northedge, F.S., *Descent from Power: British Foreign Policy 1945–1973* (London: George Allen, 1974)

Oakley, Robert, 'International Terrorism,' *Foreign Affairs*, 63, 3 (1987), 611–29

Osieke, Ebere, 'Unconstitutional Acts in International Organisations: The Law and Practice of the ICAO,' *International and Comparative Law Quarterly*, 28, Part 1 (January 1979), 1–26

Ott, James, 'Free Trade Advocates Foresee End of Bilaterals,' *Aviation Week & Space Technology*, 136, 15 (13 April 1992), 30–1

– 'ICAO Faces Daunting Issues,' *Aviation Week & Space Technology*, 141, 18 (31 October 1994), 56

– 'Open Skies Haunts Chicago Convention,' *Aviation Week & Space Technology*, 141, 18 (31 October 1994), 46–8

– 'Russia Taking Over Soviet Commercial Aviation Authority,' *Aviation Week and Space Technology*, 136, 2 (13 January 1992), 23

Oum, Tae Hoon, 'Overview of regulatory changes in international air transport and Asian strategies towards the US open skies initiatives,' *Journal of Air Transport Management,* 4 (1998), 127–34

Pearson, David E., *KAL 007: The Cover-Up* (New York: Summit Books, 1987)

Pelchat, Martin, 'L'Iran demande à l'OACI de tenir une réunion extraordinaire,' *Le Devoir* (Montreal), 5 July 1988

– 'OACI: des voeux pieux en attendant un autre huis clos,' *Le Devoir* (Montreal), 6 December 1988

Pepin, Eugene, 'ICAO and Other Agencies Dealing with Air Regulation,' *Journal of Air Law and Commerce,* 19 (1952), 152–65

Petsikas, George, '"Open Skies" – North America,' *Annals of Air and Space Law,* 17, 1 (1992), 281–91

Phillips, Edward, 'Northwest Calls KLM Pact "Strategic Asset",' *Aviation Week & Space Technology,* 141, 18 (31 October 1994), 56–7

PICAO Journal, 'Regional Air Navigation Meetings in Dublin and Paris,' 1, 4 (March/April 1946), 5–6

– 'Status, Constitution and Functions of Regional Offices,' 1, 7 (July/August 1946), 19

Pogue, Welch, 'The International Civil Aviation Conference (1944) And its Sequel The Anglo-American Bermuda Air Transport Agreement (1946),' *Annals of Air and Space Law,* 19, 1 (1994), 1–47

– 'Personal Recollections from the Chicago Conference: ICAO, Then, Now, and in the Future,' *Annals of Air and Space Law,* 20, 1 (1995), 35–48

Poonoosamy, Vijay, 'The Montreal Convention 1999 – a question of balance,' *The Aviation Quarterly,* 4 (April 2000), 79–85

Potter, Mitch, 'Activists target Heathrow,' *Toronto Star,* 18 August 2007

Pourcelet, Michel, 'Hijacking: The Limitations of the International Treaty Approach,' in Edward McWhinney, ed., *Aerial Piracy and International Law* (New York: Oceana Publications, 1973), 55–8

Prentice, Edward S., 'The First Assembly of the International Civil Aviation Organization,' U.S. Department of State *Bulletin,* 16, (15 June 1947), 1145–51

Puchala, Donald J., Katie Verlin Laatikainen, and Roger A. Coate, *United Nations Politics: International Organization in a Divided World* (New Jersey: Pearson / Prentice Hall, 2003)

Ramcharan, B. G., 'The International Court of Justice,' in Paul Taylor and A. J. R. Groom, eds., *The United Nations at the Millennium: The Principal Organs* (London: Continuum, 2000), 177–95

Randall, Stephen James, 'Colombia, the United States, and Interamerican Aviation Rivalry, 1927–1940,' *Journal of Interamerican Studies and World Affairs,* 14, 3 (August 1972), 297–324

Ray, Deborah Wing, 'The Takoradi Route: Roosevelt's Prewar Venture beyond the Western Hemisphere,' *Journal of American History*, 62, 2 (1975), 340–58

Reid, Escott, *Radical Mandarin* (Toronto, University of Toronto Press, 1989)

Reiss, Peter T., 'Air Rage: An Issue of Aviation Security and Safety,' *Air Line Pilot*, 68, 6 (June / July 1999), 10–13, 47

Rhoades, Dawna L., *Evolution of International Aviation: Phoenix Rising* (Aldershot: Ashgate, 1988)

Richard, Ghislaine, 'KAL 007: The Legal Fallout,' *Annals of Air and Space Law*, 9 (1984), 147–61

Richardson, Louise, *What Terrorists Want* (New York: Random House, 2006)

Rigalt, Antonio Francoz, 'Illegal transport by air of drugs and psychotropic substances,' *Air Law*, 15, 1 (1990), 17–35

Rivoal, Colette, 'Regulation of international air transport: towards a new world air transport order?' *ITA Press*, 232 (1–15 February 1995), 1–4

Round Table, 'After Chicago: Imperial Interests in Civil Aviation,' 35 (March, 1945), 130–36

Roper, Albert, *La Convention Du 13 Octobre 1919*, (1930)

– *Un homme et des ailes: Albert Roper, Pionnier du Droit Aèrien International, 1891–1969* (Paris: Les éditions de l'Officine, 2004)

Roy, P.K., 'Legal Work of ICAO,' *Interavia*, 14, 7 (1959), 864–5

Sampson, Anthony, *Empires of the Sky* (London: Hodder and Stoughton, 1984)

Sanger, Daniel, 'L'Iran persiste à blâmer les USA,' *Le Devoir*, 3 December 1988

Schenkman, Jacob, *International Civil Aviation Organization* (Geneva: H. Studer, 1955)

Schulzinger, Robert D., *U.S. Diplomacy Since 1900* (New York: Oxford University Press, fifth edition, 2002)

Schwarz, Jordan A., *Liberal: Adolf A. Berle and the Vision of the American Era* (New York: The Free Press, 1987)

Share, Bernard, *The Flight of the Iolar: The Aer Lingus Experience, 1936–1986* (Dublin, 1986)

Sheffy, Menachem, 'The Air Navigation Commission of the International Civil Aviation Organization, Part 1,' *Journal of Air Law and Commerce*, 25 (1958), 281–327

– 'The Air Navigation Commission of the International Civil Aviation Organization, Part II, *Journal of Air Law and Commerce*, 25 (1958), 428–43

Sheinfeld, David, 'From Warsaw to Tenerife: A Chronological Analysis of the Liability Limitations Imposed Pursuant to the Warsaw Convention,' *Journal of Air Law and Commerce*, 45, 3 (Spring 1980), 653–83

Sheng-ti Gau, Michael, 'Universal Territorial Representation within ICAO in the Age of Air Transport Globalization,' *Air and Space Law*, 21, 3 (1996), 105–25

Shubber, Sami, 'Aircraft Hijacking Under the Hague Convention 1970 – A New Regime?' *International and Comparative Law Quarterly,* 22, Part 4 (October 1973) 687–726

Simantirakis, Christina, 'The Cuban shoot-down of two US-registered civil aircraft on 24 February 1996: study of a new case of use of weapons against civil aircraft,' Master of Laws thesis (McGill University: Institute of Air and Space Law, May 2000)

Slade, Robert, 'The Real Reason for the KAL deaths,' *The Globe and Mail* (Toronto), 28 August 1993

Smith, Peter, 'Drugs, Testing and Flight Crew,' *IFALPA International Quarterly Review,* (September 1997), 19–26

Smith, Richard K., 'The Intercontinental Airliner and the Essence of Airplane Performance, 1929–1939,' *Technology and Culture,* 24 (July 1983), 428–49

Soafer, Abraham D., 'Terrorism and the Law,' *Foreign Affairs,* 64, 5 (Summer 1986), 901–22

Sochor, Eugene, 'Conflicts in International Civil Aviation: Safeguarding the Air Routes,' in Robert N. Wells, (ed.), *Peace By Pieces – United Nations Agencies and their Roles: A Reader and Selective Bibliography* (Metuchen, N.J.: Scarecrow Press Inc., 1991), 144–50

– 'From the DC-3 to Hypersonic Flight: ICAO in a Changing Environment,' *Journal of Air Law and Commerce,* 55, 2 (Winter 1989), 407–40

– 'ICAO and armed attacks against civil aviation,' *International Journal,* 44, 1 (Winter 1988–9), 134–70

– 'International civil aviation and the Third World: how fair is the system?' *Third World Quarterly,* 10, 3 (July 1988), 1300–22

– *The Politics of International Aviation* (London: MacMillan, 1991)

Solberg, Carl, *Conquest of the Skies: A History of Commercial Aviation in America* (Boston: 1979)

St. John, Peter, *Air Piracy, Airport Security, and International Terrorism: Winning the War against Hijackers* (New York: Quorum Books, 1991)

Stannard, Harold, 'Civil Aviation: An Historical Survey,' *International Affairs,* 21, 4 (October 1945), 497–511

Stoffel, Albert, 'American Bilateral Air Transport Agreements on the Threshold of the Jet Transport Age,' *The Journal of Air Law and Commerce,* 26, 2 (spring 1959), 119–36

Sutherland, R. G., 'ICAO programme offers practical means of enhancing security training performance,' *ICAO Journal,* 53, 10 (December 1998), 17–9, 29

Swinton, Lord, *I Remember* (London: Hutchison & Co., 1948)

Taneja, Nawal. K., *U.S. International Aviation Policy* (Lexington, Mass.: Lexington Books, 1980)

Taubman, Philip, 'Soviets Urge U.S. Pullout from Gulf,' *The New York Times*, 5 July 1988

Taylor, A.J.P., *Beaverbrook* (New York: Simon & Schuster, 1972)

Taylor, Paul, *International Organization in the Modern World* (London: Pinter, 1993)

Thaker, Jitendra S., 'Model Clause on Aviation Security for Bilateral Air Transport Agreements,' *Annals of Air and Space Law*, 17, 2 (1992), 403–34

Thayer, Frederick C., *Air Transport Policy and National Security: A Political, Economic, and Military Analysis* (Chapel Hill: University of North Carolina Press, 1965)

The Changing Face of Aviation in Nigeria (Government of Nigeria, n.d.)

The Times (UK), 'Britain Opposed to US on Hijacks,' 12 February 1969

Thomas, Ivor, 'Civil Aviation: International Questions Outstanding,' *International Affairs*, 25, 1, (January 1949), 56–65

Thomka-Gazdik, J.G., 'Multilateralism in Civil Aviation,' *Air Law*, 4, 3 (1979), 130–36

Tobolewski, Aleksander, 'ICAO's Legal Syndrome Or: International Air Law in the Making,' *Annals of Air and Space Law*, 4 (1979), 349–57

Tombs, Laurence C., *International Organization in European Air Transport* (Rahway, New Jersey: Quinn & Boden Company, 1936)

Tompkins, George, 'The Montreal Convention of 1999: this is the answer,' *The Aviation Quarterly*, 3 (July 1999), 114–39

Tompkins, George N., Jr. and Andrew J. Harakas, 'ICAO and Aviation Accident Investigation – Lessons to be Learned for the Korean Air Lines 007 Investigation,' *Annals of Air and Space Law*, 19, Part II, (1994), 375–98

Toronto Star, 'U.N. air body votes for an end to Pretoria links,' 11 October 1986

Tourtellot, Christopher T., 'Membership Criteria for the ICAO Council: A Proposal for Reform,' *Denver Law Journal of International Law and Policy*, 11, 1 (Fall 1981), 51–80

Trento, Susan B. and Joseph J. Trento, *Unsafe at any Speed: Failed Terrorism Investigations, Scapegoating 9/11, and the Shocking Truth about Aviation Security Today* (Hanover, New Hampshire: Steerforth Press, 2006)

Trudel, Clément, 'L'attaque américaine contre l'avion iranien: l'OACI fera enquête,' *Le Devoir* (Montreal), 15 July 1988

United Nations Information Organization, *Report of the Chicago Conference on International Civil Aviation* (London, n.d.).

U. N. Observer & International Report, 'ICAO chides both sides in Cuba-U.S. air clash,' 18, 8 (August 1996), 14–5

United States, Department of State, *Proceedings of the International Civil Aviation Conference, Chicago, Illinois, November 1 -December 7, 1944*, 2 volumes (Washington, DC, 1948).

Urquhart, Brian, *Hammarskjöld* (New York: Alfred A. Knopf, 1972)

Van Dam, Roderick D., 'International Organizations,' *Annals of Air and Space Law*, 19, 2 (1994), 652–73

– 'A New Convention on the Marking of Plastic Explosives for the Purpose of Detection,' *Air Law*, 41, 4/5 (1991), 167–77

Vincenti, Walter G., 'Technological Knowledge Without Science: The Innovation of Flush Riveting in American Airplanes, ca. 1930–ca. 1950,' *Technology and Culture*, 25 (July 1984), 540–76

Walker, Karen, 'Chicago Revisited,' *Airline Business*, 16, 1 (January 2000), 28–9

Wallis, Rodney, *Combating Air Terrorism* (Washington: Brassey's (US), 1993)

– 'The Role of the International Aviation Organisations in Enhancing Security,' in Paul Wilkinson and Brian Jenkins, eds., *Aviation Terrorism and Security* (London: Frank Cass, 1999), 83–100

Walstrom, Joe, 'Bilateral Air-Transport Agreements Concluded by the United States,' Department of State *Bulletin*, 15, 390, (22 December 1946)

Warner, Edward, 'Airways for Peace,' *Foreign Affairs*, 22, 1 (1943), 11–27

– 'The Chicago Conference: Accomplishments and Unfinished Business,' *Foreign Affairs*, 23, 3 (1945), 406–21

– 'ICAO After Four Years,' *Air Affairs*, 3, 2, (1950), 281–97

– 'ICAO After Six Years,' *IATA Bulletin*, 15 (June 1952), 71–85

– 'International Air Transport,' *Foreign Affairs*, 4, 2 (January 1926), 278–93

– 'The International Convention for Air Navigation: And the Pan American Convention for Air Navigation: A Comparative and Critical Analysis,' *Air Law Review*, 3, 3 (July 1932), 221–308

– 'International Financing of Air Navigation Facilities Through ICAO,' *Air Affairs*, 2 (July 1948), 351–63

– 'Notes from PICAO Experience,' *Air Affairs*, 1, 1, (September 1946), 30–44

– 'PICAO and the Development of Air Law,' *The Journal of Air Law and Commerce*, 14, 1, (Winter 1947), 1–10

– 'What Airplanes can do,' *Foreign Affairs*, 20, 2 (January 1942), 339–57

Wassenbergh, Henri, 'Future Regulation to allow Multi-national Arrangements between Air Carriers (Cross-border Alliance), putting an End to Air Carrier Nationalism,' *Air and Space Law*, 20, 3 (1995), 164–8

– 'Iraq/Kuwait and International Civil Aviation Relations,' *ITA Magazine*, 63 (September/October 1990), 8–15

– 'Regulatory Reform – a challenge to inter-governmental Civil Aviation Conferences,' *Air Law*, 40, 1 (1986), 31–46

– 'Regulatory Reform: National jurisdiction (domestic law) versus international jurisdiction (bilateral air agreements),' *Air Law*, 40, 3 (1986), 106–22

– and Pablo Mendes de Leon, 'Impressions from the Fourth ICAO World-Wide Air Transport Conference, Montreal, 23 November – 6 December 1994,' *Air & Space Law*, 20, 1 (1995), 22–31

Weber, Ludwig, 'The Chicago Convention and the Exchange of Traffic Rights in a Regional Context,' *Annals of Air and Space Law*, 20, part 1 (1995), 123–33

– *International Civil Aviation Organization: An Introduction* (Netherlands: Kluwer Law International, 2007)

Weber, Ludwig and Arie Jakob, 'Activities of the International Civil Aviation Organization,' *Annals of Air and Space Law*, 23 (1998), 321–42

– 'Activities of the International Civil Aviation Organization (ICAO) in 2002/2003,' *Annals of Air and Space Law*, 28 (2003), 397–419

– 'The Modernization of the Warsaw System: The Montreal Convention of 1999,' *Annals of Air and Space Law*, 24 (1999), 333–53

Weintraub, William, *City Unique: Montreal Days and Nights in the 1940s and '50s* (Toronto: McClelland & Stewart, 1996)

Weiss, Thomas, David Forsythe, and Roger Coate, *The United Nations and Changing World Politics*, 2nd edition, (Boulder, Colorado: Westview Press, 1997)

Wessberge, Erik, 'The Bilateral Clash Between the United States and Japan,' *ITA Monthly Bulletin*, (April 1982), 1–7

– 'The Consequences of Bermuda II: Part One: Renegotiation of the United States-Japan Bilateral,' *ITA Weekly Bulletin*, 38 (14 November 1977), 873–77

– 'What are the Chances for Multilateralism in the Present International Air Transport System?' *ITA Weekly Bulletin*, 13, 6 (April 1981), 319–24

Wetmore, Warren C., 'UN Spurs Antihijacking Drive,' *Aviation Week & Space Technology*, 107, 20 (14 November 1977), 14–5

Whitnah, Donald, *Safer Skyways: Federal Control of Aviation, 1926–1966* (Ames, Iowa, 1966)

Wilberforce, R.O., 'The International Recognition of Rights in Aircraft,' *The International Law Quarterly*, 2, 3 (Autumn 1948), 421–58

Williams, Douglas, *The Specialized Agencies and the United Nations: The System in Crisis* (London: C. Hurst & Co., 1987)

Wilson, John M., 'The Shape of Things to Come: The Military Impact of World War II on Civil Aviation,' *Aerospace Historian*, 28, 4 (December 1981), 262–67

Wilson, W.A., 'Decisive Step in Short Navigation? Bitter Anglo-American Dispute mars ICAO choice of navaids,' *Interavia*, 14, 4 (1959), 364

Witkin, Richard, 'Soviet Pilot Insists Downed Korean Jet Was Spy Plane,' *The New York Times*, 19 May 1991

Woolley, David, 'Aid to Third-World airlines: ICAO and IATA tackle development difficulties,' *Interavia*, 39, 10 (1984), 1074–5

Woolsey, James P., 'Prevention of Hijacking Switches from Passive to Active Measures,' *Aviation Week & Space Technology*, 93, 12 (21 September 1970), 29–30

Yoder, Amos, *The Evolution of the United Nations System*, 2nd edition (Washington, D.C.: Taylor & Francis, 1993)

Young, Joanne W., 'Globalism versus extraterritoriality, consensus versus unilateralism – is there a common ground? A US perspective,' *The Aviation Quarterly*, 3 (July 1999), 140–50

Zacher, Mark W., with Brent A. Sutton, *Governing Global Networks: International Regimes for Transportation and Communications* (Cambridge: Cambridge University Press, 1996)

Zubkov, Vladimir, 'Major Challenges to Civil Aviation: Consequences for the East and the West,' *ITA Magazine*, 65 (January/March 1991), 13–19

Websites

www.hooverdigest.org
www.icao.org
www.Reagan.utexas.edu

Index

84–8; and internationalization,
21–2; Kennedy review of aviation
policy, 245–6; and loyalty screening, 133–4; and multilateral
agreement, 107–10, 113–23, 345–6,
349–52, 357–9; and NAOS, 182–3;
negotiates bilateral agreements,
60–2; and noise pollution, 296,
298; opposition to moving
headquarters, 135–6, 139; and Pan
Am flight 103, 334–5; postwar
international aviation policy, 7–10,
57–8; and questions over value of
ICAO, 238–41; relations with
Cubans, 230, 280, 324–5; and
sanctions, 266–72, 274; and
shooting down of Iranian Airbus,
317–23; and supersonic transport,
176; support for Binaghi, 161–2;
and technical assistance, 184–6,
189–92; and terrorism, 247, 329,
331, 339–40; and Tokyo
Convention, 249–55; and Warsaw
Convention, 205–13, 377, 380–1
Universal Postal Union, 180
Universal Safety Oversight Audit
Programme (USOAP), 386, 388–9,
397; created, 371–2
Universal Security Audit Programme
(USAP), 386, 388, 397
U.S. Airways, 384
USS Cole, 342
USS Stark, 317
USS Vincennes, 317–18
Uzbekistan, 364

van Hasselt, F.H. Copes, 99, 107
Vanuatu, 279
Velayati, Ali Akbar, 320
Venezuela, 88, 135, 141, 151, 152

Verhaegan, J., 68
Vietnam, 228, 308, 391; membership
disputes, 228–9, 279; membership
of South Vietnam, 228
Volpe, John, 264, 269

Wallace, Henry, 21
War on Drugs, 365–6
Warner, Edward, 26–7, 70, 72, 74, 81,
90, 100, 105, 141, 158, 173–4, 181,
197, 396; and Canadian immigra-
tion problems, 133; and draft
multilateral agreement, 114–15;
and resignation as Council
president, 158, 159–62; and
selection as Interim Council
president, 65–7; and selection as
Council president, 99
Warsaw Convention, 95, 195, 215,
229, 375; and the Montreal
Agreement, 209–10; negotiations
to amend, 205–13; and new
Montreal Convention, 377–81
West Indies, 4, 8
Western Samoa, 364
Willis, Rodney, 333
Willoch, Erik, 288
Winant, John, 111–12
Winster, Lord, 110, 112, 120–1
women, recruitment of, and ICAO,
366–8
World Health Organization, 180,
186, 231, 281; and SARS crisis, 391
World Trade Organization, 355, 359,
363
World Wide Air Transport
Colloquium (1992), 355–6
World Wide Air Transport Conference:
1994, 356–60; 2003, 393–4
Wright brothers, 13